Law of the Sea at the Crossroads: The Continuing Search for a Universally Accepted Régime

Veröffentlichungen des Instituts für Internationales Recht an der Universität Kiel

Herausgegeben von

Jost Delbrück und Rüdiger Wolfrum

Institut für Internationales Recht an der Universität Kiel

113

Law of the Sea at the Crossroads: The Continuing Search for a Universally Accepted Régime

Proceedings of an Interdisciplinary Symposium of the Kiel Institute of International Law July 10 to 14, 1990

Edited by

Rüdiger Wolfrum

Assistant Editors:
Ursula E. Heinz · Denise A. Bizzarro

Duncker & Humblot · Berlin

Die Deutsche Bibliothek – CIP-Einheitsaufnahme

Law of the sea at the crossroads : the continuing search for a universally accepted regime ; proceedings of an interdisciplinary symposium of the Institute of International Law, Kiel, July 10 to 14, 1990 / ed. by Rüdiger Wolfrum.
Assistant ed.: Ursula E. Heinz ; Denise A. Bizzarro. —
Berlin: Duncker und Humblot, 1991
(Veröffentlichungen des Instituts für Internationales Recht an der Universität Kiel ; Bd. 113)
ISBN 3-428-07240-5
NE: Wolfrum, Rüdiger [Hrsg.]; Institut für Internationales Recht ⟨Kiel⟩: Veröffentlichungen des Instituts . . .

Fremddatenübernahme: Berliner Buchdruckerei Union GmbH, Berlin 61
Druck: Color-Druck Dorfi GmbH, Berlin 49
Printed in Germany

ISSN 0720-7263
ISBN 3-428-07240-5

Foreword

Although the Convention on the Law of the Sea has not yet entered into force, it has already had a substantial impact upon the legislation of many States with regard to maritime issues. Such State practice has induced the view that parts of the Convention have already become customary international law. This view has been challenged on the grounds that the Convention on the Law of the Sea should be regarded as a "package" which excludes the entry into force of parts of it. In any case it must be noted that the ratification process has recently slowed down: a reluctance seems to exist on the part of the industrialized States to subscribe to the sea-bed régime as enshrined in Part XI and the relevant Annexes of the Convention on the Law of the Sea. Equally, there seems to exist at present a reluctance on the part of the developing countries to set the Convention on the Law of the Sea into force. The uncertainty over the future status of the Convention is unsatisfactory since the possibility cannot be ruled out that State practice may render some parts of the Convention obsolete. The Secretary-General of the United Nations has already indicated that State practice does not always reflect the delicate balance between the rights and duties of States embodied within the Convention. To preserve the achievements of the Convention, Ambassador *Mumba S. Kapumpa*, spokesman of the Group of 77, called for a dialogue between signatories and non-signatories of the Convention in 1988 with a view to overcome impediments for the universal acceptance of the Convention on the Law of the Sea. The intention behind this Symposium was to contribute to these efforts by providing an academic forum where new ideas may be voiced and discussed openly.

The Institute of International Law is greatly indebted to the Fritz Thyssen Foundation for funding this Symposium. The publication of the proceedings have been supported by the Federal Ministry of Foreign Affairs. Further assistance has been received by the Kieler Spar- und Leihkasse, Honeywell-Elac-Nautic Ltd., the Landesbank of Schleswig-Holstein, Salzgitter Ltd., Krupp MAK, DMT Marinetechnik, the Industrie- und Handelskammer in Kiel, the Bagge Foundation, Wintershall Ltd., Süverkrüp Automobile Ltd. and the Deutsche Bank, Kiel.

My personal thanks are extended to the staff of the Institute whose efforts have, as on many occasions before, made this Symposium possible. I am especially grateful to Mr *Enno Harders*, Dr. *Ursula Heinz*, Mrs *Denise Bizzarro* and Mrs *Rotraut Wolf* for their effective management of the symposium and its follow-up.

Rüdiger Wolfrum

Contents

Abbreviations

AALCC	= Asian-African Legal Consultative Committee
ACABQ	= Advisory Committee on Administrative and Budgetary Questions
ACP	= Africa-Caribbean-Pacific
AFDI	= Annuaire français de droit international
AJIL	= American Journal of International Law
BGBl.	= Bundesgesetzblatt
BYIL	= The British Year Book of International Law
CPC	= Committee for Programme and Co-ordination
CRAMRA	= Convention on the Regulation of Antarctic Mineral Resource Activities
CTC	= Centre on Transnational Corporations (United Nations)
doc.	= Document
ECLAC	= Economic Commission for Latin America and the Caribbean (United Nations)
EEC	= European Economic Community
EEZ	= Exclusive economic zone
EPIL	= Encyclopedia of Public International Law
FAO	= Food and Agriculture Organization
FRG	= Federal Republic of Germany
GA	= General Assembly (United Nations)
GATT	= General Agreement on Tariffs and Trade
GESAMP	= Group of Experts on the Scientific Aspects of Marine Pollution
GNP	= Gross national product
GYIL	= German Yearbook of International Law
IAEA	= International Atomic Energy Agency
ICAO	= International Civil Aviation Organization
ICES	= International Council for the Exploration of the Sea
ICJ	= International Court of Justice
ICNT	= Informal Composite Negotiating Text
IDA	= International Development Association
IFAD	= International Fund for Agricultural Development
ILC	= International Law Commission
ILM	= International Legal Materials
ILO	= International Labour Organization
IMF	= International Monetary Fund
IMO	= International Maritime Organization
IO	= International Organization
IOC	= Intergovernmental Oceanographic Commission

LOS	= Law of the Sea
MARPOL	= International Convention for the Prevention of Pollution from Ships
MSR	= Marine scientific research
nm	= Nautical miles
NYIL	= Netherlands Yearbook of International Law
ODILA	= Ocean Development and International Law
OTEC	= Ocean Thermal Energy Conversion
PrepCom	= Preparatory Commission for the International Sea-Bed Authority and for the International Tribunal for the Law of the Sea
res.	= Resolution
RV	= Research vessel
TRIMs	= Trade-related investment measures
TRIPs	= Trade-related aspects of intellectual property rights
TUSCH	= Tiefsee-Umweltschutz
UNCLOS III	= Third United Nations Conference on the Law of the Sea
UNCTAD	= United Nations Conference on Trade and Development
UNEP	= United Nations Environmental Programme
UNESCO	= United Nations Educational, Scientific and Cultural Organization
UNIDO	= United Nations Industrial Development Organization
UNITAR	= United Nations Institute for Training and Research
UNTS	= United Nations Treaty Series
UPU	= Universal Postal Union
WHO	= World Health Organization
WIPO	= World Intellectual Property Organization

Welcoming Address

Michael Müller-Wille*

Your Excellencies, Herr Bundestagsabgeordneter, Herr Minister, Spektabilität, Dear Colleagues, Ladies and Gentlemen:

On behalf of the Christian Albrecht University at Kiel, I have the great honour and pleasure to welcome you as participants of the symposium "Law of the Sea at the Crossroads: The Continuing Search for a Universally Accepted Régime."

We are thankful that so many of you have accepted our invitation. We consider this a vote of confidence in the capabilities of this university and its strong marine research facilities.

I wish to take advantage of welcoming the great number of eminent experts in the fields of law of the sea and related areas of research who have assembled here in Kiel as guests of this university and in particular of the Institute of International Law to briefly give you an overview of the many activities of the Christian Albrecht University at Kiel in the area of marine research. I further want to inform you of some of the initiatives that will be pursued at the University in the coming years. It would be impossible to offer you, in this short message, a comprehensive overview of all our endeavours. I will, therefore, limit myself to those projects which will likely interest most — if not all — participants from some 25 countries represented here.

The Christian Albrecht University at Kiel was founded in 1665. Today, about 18,500 students are enrolled in seven faculties and very soon another faculty will be added to the university. This will be a faculty of engineering and it is to be hoped that in the long run it will further strengthen the capabilities regarding the marine sciences.

Marine research as such at this University looks upon a tradition of 100 years. The international reputation of the University in this respect is manifested by the Institute of Marine Research, which constitutes an independent research and teaching department. The name of the Institute is carried all over the world by its four research vessels. Aside of traditional marine scientific research the *Institut für Meereskunde* is very active in the field of marine technology.

Apart from this Institute there exists a focal point of the University in marine geology and marine geophysics. Its emphasis is on the exploration of non-

* Prof. Dr. Dr. hc. *Michael Müller-Wille*, Rector of the Christian-Albrechts-Universität at Kiel.

renewable natural resources of the sea-bed as well as the exploitation of the sea-bed as a basis for stable offshore technology. The research in the areas of marine geology and marine geophysics mounted in 1986 in the decision for the establishment of GEOMAR at this university. GEOMAR is an abbreviation for *Forschungszentrum für marine Geowissenschaften*. GEOMAR is an independent body of the University which has — and that is quite a novelty — a commercial branch. It is this part of GEOMAR which has provided us with the exhibition in the hall. GEOMAR is active in four departments which are: marine environmental geology, marine geophysics, paleo-oceanography and petrology of the ocean crust. In combination with the marine-oriented institutes of the natural sciences faculty and the Institute for Marine Research with its long tradition, GEOMAR adds another focus in the area of marine research.

In the area of applied physics, special attention is given to the development of instruments for marine technology. Especially range-finders and plummets have been developed in co-operation with industry. These efforts are concentrated in the Research Center for Marine Technology. One of its current projects deals with "Gewinnung regenerativer Energien aus dem Meerwasser" (the exploration and use of the renewable energy resources of the sea-water). Such interests in the field of ocean technology are part of the co-operation between the University of Hawaii, Honolulu, and the Christian Albrechts University.

Finally, I would like to mention that marine issues are intensively dealt with in the faculty of economy and social sciences and the Institute on World Economy as well as in the Institute of International Law. The activities of the latter have resulted in numerous symposia as well as in the elaboration of studies concerning the European régime for offshore activities such as oil and gas.

All those working in the field of marine sciences, law or economy are integrated in a special working group which meets at least once a semester. In this group a vivid exchange of views takes place fostering the interdisciplinary approach to all sea related matters. I believe that this interdisciplinary approach is quite unique and an important feature of the Kiel University.

May I, in closing, express the hope that this symposium will lead to a lively exchange among the participants which leads to a better understanding and even an accomodation of the different positions taken so far.

I leave you with these broad prospects and offer you my best wishes for a pleasant and productive conference.

Opening Address

Franz Froschmaier*

Your Excellencies, Ladies and Gentlemen:

It is a great pleasure and honour for me to open this international symposium and to extend a very warm welcome to all participants on behalf of the Government of Schleswig-Holstein.

We are happy to host this conference in Kiel, organized by Professor *Wolfrum* and the Kiel Institute of International Law, at this particular moment in time when both Germanies are engaged in the process of unification with the help of our neighbours and friends and within the European and international framework. It should always be maintained that Germany is part of the international community of States, which in turn face problems and challenges of a global scale.

Thus, it is highly pertinent to take a fresh look at the law of the sea (LOS). It was *Satya Nandan*, the UN Under-Secretary-General for the law of the sea, who — speaking on "The 1982 UN Convention on the Law of the Sea at a Crossroad" in June 1989 — gave the "Leitmotiv" for this conference in Kiel when he stated that we are at a very important crossroad while time is running out for the Convention to enter into force. He also set the stage with his proposal that any changes can be incorporated in a "protocol," to come into force simultaneously with the LOS Convention.

With a view to the need for a new assessment of the LOS Convention let me make three short remarks:

First, the growing importance of marine environmental protection, including the problem of "global change," on the one hand and the somewhat reduced interest in deep sea-bed mining on the other, allows for different priorities. It is my view that this change of priorities calls for an early entry into force of the Convention, at least in its non-sea-bed subjects.

Second, there is a growing willingness among States to find an accomodation of the remaining "hard-core issues" for sea-bed mining. All partners of the European Community, the Soviet Union and a growing number of other countries share the view that realistic modifications are required. Moreoever, the chairman of the "Group of 77," Ambassador *Kapumpa* of Zambia, has reaffirmed the

---

* Dr. *Franz Froschmaier*, Minister for Economics, Technology and Transport of the Land Schleswig-Holstein.

group's readiness to hold serious and meaningful discussions to ensure the universality of the Convention. On the other hand, information presently available about sea-bed mining, its economics, technology and environmental risks is sparse and confusing. It is still unknown whether and when sea-bed mining will become a reliable and environmentally viable industry. This leaves us with a choice of alternatives ranging *inter alia* from a "Moratorium" to the "Protocol"-solution just mentioned. Whatever the choice, it will be more market-oriented than the old text was.

Third, it is vitally important to continue the dialogue between all States whether interested in sea-bed mining or not, because the whole system of the law of the sea with its institutions and procedures should be universally acceptable to all. The LOS Convention — as Ambassador *Jesus*, the chairman of the Preparatory Commission, put it recently — serves as a guide for the conduct of States in the peaceful use and the orderly sharing of marine resources. It is through such informal platforms like this symposium today that diplomats, lawyers and marine scientists have the chance to discuss controversial matters in a more relaxed and open way as compared to official negotiations.

It should be pointed out here that Schleswig-Holstein was among the first who advocated an active and innovative maritime policy in Germany for very obvious reasons. The law of the sea debate of the Seventies, its consequences and changes were among the reasons why this part of Germany was always represented within the German LOS delegation, where among others the candidature for the LOS Tribunal in Hamburg was born. Needless to say, all political circles of Northern Germany support this important institution in Hamburg.

As you may know Schleswig-Holstein — and in a wider context the whole area of Northern Germany — is the home of many public institutions and private firms specializing in marine affairs. Based on shipping, shipbuilding, fisheries, marine and offshore equipment industries, marine scientific research and more recently marine environmental protection we profit from a large concentration of scientific and technical expertise and some of our experts from institutes, industries and science will be with us during these days.

The marine industries and services of the Federal Republic of Germany roughly represent 40 scientific institutes, 400 enterprises in marine technology (excluding ship-building and ports) and 130,000 jobs in all marine industrial branches. Moreover, we do expect some re-inforcement from East Germany's competent industries and institutes, as it is common knowledge these days that both Germanies bring together their specific values.

In particular, the protection of the marine environment leads to rapid progress in the development of industrial components of marine environmental and research techniques as a necessary prerequisite for the exploration and exploitation of marine resources.

I am happy to say that the State government of Schleswig-Holstein is playing an active part in all marine affairs. The new Kiel-based centre for marine geosciences, GEOMAR, complemented by a privately operated company for marine technology and services as well as its future training centre, may serve as an example here.

To sum up, old and new instruments for co-operation with other States, institutes and companies are available and I want to stress that the Federal Republic of Germany is ready and willing to play her rôle in the enhancement of knowledge with regard to the sea as well as to the development of rational ocean uses. This includes the law of the sea as the one and only legal framework for all marine activities.

I do hope that the deliberations of this highly qualified international conference of leading LOS experts, representing so many different disciplines and interests, will be successful — and I am convinced of it — in producing some fresh ideas which we all need in these times of change.

Thank you very much.

Opening Address

Rüdiger Wolfrum*

Your Excellencies, Magnifizenz, Herr Abgeordneter, Dear Friends, Ladies and Gentlemen:

On behalf of the Institute of International Law at the Christian-Albrechts-University of Kiel I warmly welcome you to our Symposium "Law of the Sea at the Crossroads: The Continuing Search for a Universally Accepted Régime." I am particularly grateful that so many of you have responded positively to our invitation and I take it from your reaction that the search for a universally accepted régime on the law of the sea (despite having already been started by *Hugo Grotius*) has in fact not yet been completely finished.

Hopefully, by quickly glancing at the programme you will note that the Symposium will address various issues of interest to you. Some of these issues refer to the interpretation and application of Part XI as well as the implementation of resolution II of the the Third UN Law of the Sea Conference. Other presentations deal with the national implementation of the regulations on the exclusive economic zones, the archipelagic waters or new problems having emerged regarding the use of the high seas. The programme of the Symposium does not pretend to cover all issues which may be discussed controversially. Technical and economic changes evolve too fast for the resulting problems to be covered just by one meeting. Therefore, this Symposium should just be seen as the beginning of a sequence of further seminars and workshops.

As it is the practice of our Institute, we will approach the topics from different disciplines such as international law, political science, economics, and natural sciences. In having selected the topics of this Symposium, the Institute has proceeded from the premise that the Law of the Sea Convention, although it has not yet entered into force, has already had significant impact upon international law as well as upon the domestic law of States. It has been argued that parts of the Convention on the Law of the Sea represent a codification of already existing customary international law or have become customary international law. I hasten to say, however, that this view is not unchallenged.

I believe that everybody will agree that it is Part XI of the Law of the Sea Convention which still causes most of the discussion. This is certainly due to

---

* Prof. Dr. *Rüdiger Wolfrum,* Director of the Institute of International Law at the University of Kiel.

the fact that the deep sea-bed régime represents the most progressive part of the Law of the Sea Convention. Further, this Part does not provide for a complete régime on deep sea-bed mining activities since it was designed as a framework which needs further supplementation through the Preparatory Commission as well as the organs of the International Sea-Bed Authority. This approach pays tribute to the fact that when the Third UN Conference on the Law of the Sea concluded its negotiations the economic, technical and scientific implications were not quite clear and thus the Preparatory Commission as well as the organs of the International Sea-Bed Authority were endowed with the respective flexibility so as to cope successfully with the new situation which may be created by new technical, political and scientific developments. I hope that the Symposium will develop some results which are useful for the accomplishment of the difficult task imposed upon the Preparatory Commission.

I am sure that we are all united by the goal to finally reach a truly universally accepted régime on the law of the sea, although divergent approaches may exist as to how this goal is to be achieved. Whether or not we come to a better understanding will very much depend upon the openess of the discussion. In this respect, I plead that we make use of the academic forum here provided for and of the freedom of expression and opinion especially guaranteed within the academic world. Besides, I would like to assure you that, according to established practice, you will have the opportunity to review your contributions before the publication of the proceedings of this Symposium. Nothing will reach the publisher or leave this circle without your express consent.

Before coming to the end of my opening remarks, I would like to draw your attention to the exhibition on marine geophysical research prepared by GEOMAR. If you need further information about the activities of GEOMAR and its structure, please approach its members who are among us.

Finally, may I take the opportunity to thank all those who have made this Symposium possible, namely the *Thyssen* foundation and the donors mentioned in the programme. Equally, I would like to thank all those who were willing to prepare presentations and who have helped me in setting up this programme, namely Under-Secretary *Satya Nandan* and the members of the UN Office for Ocean Affairs and the Law of the Sea. Finally, I would like to thank the members of the Institute, whom you will recognize by the red dots on their name tags. They will do their best to solve any organizational problems which may arise during the meeting. Please address them, or myself, if you have any questions. Thank you.

Statement on the Issue of the Universality of the Convention

José Luis Jesus*

I. Introduction

Let me start by thanking Prof. *Rüdiger Wolfrum* and the Institut für Internationales Recht for having extended to me the invitation to be here. I am pleased to participate in this meeting and share with you some ideas on the very important issue of the universality of the Law of the Sea Convention. The topic of this symposium is a timely one, for, I believe, the time has come for us to find ways to promote the necessary accomodations to the existing problems of the international sea-bed régime with a view to securing the universal acceptance of and the legal adherence to the Law of the Sea Convention by all countries.

The historical significance of the Convention has been highlighted time and again, since its adoption in 1982 by almost everyone concerned with or related to the issue of Law of the Sea. Its important rôle in promoting peaceful co-operation among States has been portrayed as a model of international co-operation that should be emulated in other areas of international affairs.

The significance of the Convention is reflected on the positions expressed by almost all nations of the world that affixed to it their signature. I believe I will not be making a faux pas if I state that it commands, as a whole, the support of all countries. I know not of any country that today does not view the Convention as an important legal instrument that needs to be preserved and further strengthened. This does not mean, of course, that some countries do not have difficulties with some of its provisions.

In fact, the history of the Law of the Sea negotiations stands witness to the fact that almost every country that participated in them had, in one way or another, some reservations with respect to certain of its provisions. While some of these difficulties do not pose a threat to its integrity and widespread acceptance (for the Convention's achievements outweigh by far its shortcomings), the same cannot be said in respect to the serious difficulties posed by Part XI and related annexes to a number of important countries. It is on these difficulties of Part XI

* *José Luis Jesus,* Chairman of the Preparatory Commission, Ambassador of Cape Verde.

and possible ways and means to solve them that I'd like to take your time today to share some of my ideas, though still evolving.

Let me start by making an observation. And that is: the problems with the international sea-bed régime of the Convention, if not addressed in due time, have, in the long run, the potentials of becoming a destabilizing factor of its legal binding effect and its rôle as a point of reference for national legislations and policies. It would be a great loss if that was allowed to happen; for the Convention, as we all know, embodies major achievements in balancing the interests of nations in the peaceful use and exploitation of the sea resources. I for one do not believe that any future renegotiations would have a better chance to come up with consensual agreements on various ocean areas and issues than does the Convention of 1982.

It becomes, therefore, imperative that the problems of Part XI be addressed. The question that must be posed is thus how best the problems of the sea-bed régime can be addressed with a view to strengthening its integrity and achieving universal support. Part of the answer to this question will necessarily have to do with the framework, the issue, and the timing for the negotiations.

I came here especially interested in hearing from your discussions ideas that could help me to better understand the possible solutions. Meanwhile, let me share some of my own ideas with you in a first attempt to find myself an answer to the question. But before doing so, I would like to dwell for some time on the issue of States' unilateral activities under the high seas-freedoms versus an international régime.

II. Unilateral Activities of States

There is a line of thought, supported by some politicians and scholars, which advocates the total abandonment of the Convention's sea-bed régime. This line of thought believes that States should have the right to extend their activities unilaterally into what is the international Area under the Convention. They believe that since the sea-bed régime cannot be implemented the Area is to be governed by the rules and principles applicable to the high seas.

For this school of thought it is neither necessary nor advisable for States to become parties to the Convention because the "traditional uses" of the seas covered by the Convention are, in their view, considered today general international law. This approach, that fortunately seems to command no major support, is perhaps the one that, if followed by major industrialized countries, would militate against the integrity and the now much sought universal support for the Convention. Many arguments can be adduced to discourage the course proposed by this approach due to its nefarious consequences. Let me address at least two comments to it.

In my view it is not correct to argue that, apart from the international legal sea-bed régime, the remaining provisions of the Convention are to be considered customary international law. I think I do not need to dwell further on this issue to convince you, experts as you are in the field of international law, of the wrongfulness of such a characterization. While many legal concepts and legal institutions found in the 1982 Convention, such as the archipelagic State concept, the 12-mile territorial sea principle, and the two-hundred mile EEZ rule, amongst others, are considered by many of us as general international law today, the same cannot be said in respect of the detailed provisions in which these legal concepts and institutions are translated in the Convention. As you all know, it is a matter of record the discrepancies that exist amongst different national legislations and policy statements as to the interpretation of provisions dealing with fisheries conservation, marine scientific research, navigation and overflight rights, such as transit passage through straits, archipelagic sea-lanes passage and innocent passage.

This discrepancy in the interpretation of substantial provisions pertaining to the "traditional uses" of the seas is a clear indication that it takes more than wishful thinking, however well intentioned it might be in the instant case, to force States, all States, to abide by the spirit and the letter of the provisions of the Convention. It becomes therefore clear that *via* State practice alone it will be impossible to convince States to abide by the provisions of the Convention without them being parties to it. The uniformity of practice and interpretation of the provisions of the Convention that, I am sure, we all would like to see, can only be achieved when all States become parties to the Convention.

On the other hand — and this is my second comment to the approach — the erosive trends that one is already witnessing in some areas of State practice, would undoubtedly and dangerously increase if some States, however powerful they may be, were to undertake unilateral activities in and benefit from the resources of the area outside the *common heritage* framework. Such unilateral undertakings could invite the majority of the coastal State — which would not be in a financial or technological position that would allow them to also follow the path of unilateral activities — to take steps to extend their national claims of a continental shelf beyond the limits agreed in the Convention, as a compensatory measure. This possibility, which I hope will never be caused to occur, might be raised not only as a counter-measure for unilateral activities in the Area but also as a way of getting parity of treatment with those few States that under the Convention are entitled to an extended continental shelf of more than 200 miles. In effect, if the resources of the sea-bed were to be exploited unilaterally, on account of abandonment of the sea-bed international régime, the larger shelf States would benefit from larger continental shelf than the majority of the coastal States, without being obliged to share the resources of the extended shelf with the Authority, as mandated in art. 82.

I, therefore, think that this approach would seriously disrupt the delicate balance achieved in the Convention. It is because we are all interested in safeguarding that balance and working towards the creation of conditions to promote the universal acceptance of the Convention, that one should do whatever it takes to avoid that such an approach be considered as a valid alternative to the sea-bed régime.

In my view, the solutions for Part XI's problems lie in a different approach. It seems to me that, if we are to preserve the important achivements contained in the Convention, we should then concentrate our efforts on improving the existing provisions of the sea-bed régime with a view to finding a suitable accomodation for the problems that the United States and other industrialized countries have, for, I believe, there is no alternative to the international régime other than an improved international régime.

And this brings me to the issues related to the search for an improved international régime, namely the framework, the questions to be considered, and the timing.

III. The Framework of Negotiations

If on the one hand the approach of addressing specific provisions as a way of solving the sea-bed régime's problems seems, and rightly so, to command the overwhelming support, on the other hand there seems to be some misgivings and, to a certain extent, some confusion, as to what should be the proper framework to address the issues. In this regard, two main trends appear to have emerged:

a) one that would like to seek those changes outside and with the exclusion of the framework provided by the Preparatory Commission (PrepCom); and

b) another one that maintains that the proper framework would be negotiations inside the Preparatory Commission or undertaken with some form of connection with it.

Although my thinking on this issue is still evolving, I would like at this stage to share with you some of my perceptions as to the merits of these two different trends. Let us begin with the view in accordance with which change should be sought outside and with the exclusion of the framework provided by the Preparatory Commission. This trend appears to be predicated on the assumption that the PrepCom has no mandate to change the Convention and therefore if any meaningful accomodation is to be made, it should be done in a new and different setting.

My first observation to this argument is that there are many ways of achieving the same result. The forum in which this accomodation is to be made, seems not to be of much relevance. On the other hand, if the Preparatory Commission in whose work all the 159 States signatories of the Convention are entitled to participate as full members, lacks mandate to make those accomodations, which institutional body or framework would have a better mandate? In our view, that institutional body with a better mandate than the PrepCom could only be the Fourth United Nations Conference on the Law of the Sea. Such a possibility of convening the Fourth United Nations Conference on the Law of the Sea or an equivalent framework to deal with the issues of Part XI seems to raise the same risks and pose the same threats to the integrity of the Convention as does the approach of unilateral activities that I commented upon earlier.

I see in such a possibility two main areas of concern. One on political grounds and the other one of a legal nature. Politically, it seems that it would be next to impossible to have the whole international community agree on the convening of the Fourth United Nations Conference on the Law of the Sea or equivalent structure only to address problems pertaining to Part XI. We all know that many countries would welcome this opportunity to renegotiate provisions of the Convention related to navigational issues, maritime boundaries, jurisdiction allocation, etc. Such a disruptive possibility, obviously, is not supported by the overwhelming majority of nations including the United States that, apart from Part XI, would like to see the Convention untouched.

Even when, for a miraculous reason, the political concern was not to be raised, we would face a legal entanglement the effects of which would create further legal uncertainties, thus delaying the process of promoting the Convention's universal acceptance. I happen to share the feeling of those that are of the view that the best, less risky and more pragmatic way of tackling the sea-bed problems — at least before the entry into force of the Convention — would be to address them within the framework of the PrepCom or in an informal setting with links with it.

This feeling is based upon two main points:

1. To address the sea-bed régime difficulties within or in connection with the framework provided by the PrepCom would, in my view, eliminate any possibility of reopening consideration on any issue other than Part XI to the extent that the Commission is only concerned with that part and the Tribunal issues. In fact, apart from the ideological warfare of the North/South confrontation that made it impossible for the Conference to be willing to find, at its last stage, accomodation for the American concerns in the sea-bed régime, there was a strong factor that militated against the reopening of the negotiations on the sea-bed provisions. That factor was the fear that many delegations had that the renegotiations of some sea-bed provisions could, by sympathy, bring about a series of claims for renegotiations on other parts of the then draft convention. Such a possibility as I have previously stated, could not be accepted by the overwhelming majority of nations firmly against the reopening of negotiations in areas that represented major achievements.

This fear will surely not exist if negotiations were to be tackled in the context or within the framework of the Preparatory Commission.

2. As I stated on many occasions, it is my well-considered viewpoint that the Preparatory Commission does have a mandate to, constructively, take, as mentioned in resolution I that established it, any step or measure to bring the International Authority into effective functioning. Provided that the fundamental norms and principles (an example of which can be gathered in art. 155, para. 2) upon which lies the international sea-bed régime, are preserved, the PrepCom is mandated to make the necessary arrangements to revitalize provisions that were rendered obsolete by the changing circumstances, to ensure that the Authority will be in function upon the entry into force of the Convention. It is the same spirit and constructive approach that presided over the negotiations and adjustments which made the registration of the pioneer investors possible.

Would anyone today question the mandate of the PrepCom to have made the adjustments of 1986 to important provisions of resolution II rendered obsolete by the changing circumstances? I do not think so! Because the alternative would have been to render the pioneer system of resolution II totally unimplementable. The same can be said in respect to Part XI. The alternative to adjustment would be to render it unimplementable.

IV. Questions to Be Considered

Having expressed some ideas on the important issue of the framework for negotiations, allow me now to turn to the substantial issues to be reconsidered. I strongly believe that, if the difficulties of the sea-bed régime were to be circumscribed to the issues that have been identified in the past, the solution would not be out of our reach. Having dedicated some time myself to the analysis of these issues and possible areas of compromise, I think that, if the issues were to be considered, we could reach a compromise perhaps easier and faster than we think.

Our attitude of seeing the Convention as a document that should be preserved and cherished created a mythical aura around it that has prevented us from considering the merits of the difficulties posed in Part XI. I submit that we have to get away from that myth in order to be able to look objectively into the existing problems. It is on the basis of this objectivity that I dare to say that the difficulties that have been identified in Part XI are not really a North/South issue as it has been portrayed. I believe that industrialized countries, as well as developing nations, have the same interests in having all the institutions created by the Convention functioning on a cost-efficiency basis and operating on the basis of sound financial management.

I also believe that all nations would like to see an International Authority that could be a viable institution, viable in the sense of accomplishing the goals for which it was created and viable also in the sense of generating resources that could be shared amongst all nations. An International Authority whose operation is due to create, instead of resources for countries, heavy financial obligations for States, would not certainly command the support of any nation, especially those overburdened by financial and economic problems.

In the end, what matters the most is that the resources of the *common heritage of mankind* be exploited in such a way as to generate the highest income possible for the benefit of all States. This is what I think to be the ground rule governing the exploitation of the sea-bed resources by the future International Sea-Bed Authority.

It is in this framework that on a very preliminary way I will offer the following comments on some of the issues:

1. Entry into Force of Amendments to Part XI

On this issue, two main concerns were raised by the United States:

1. The agreed system of amendments to the sea-bed régime would run counter to the fundamental norms of the US Constitution, since it provides for the possibility of imposing amendments on the United States without them being accepted by the competent US constitutional body.

2. It would create uncertainty for the operators who would like to be assured that the terms of their contracts would not be left to the whims of the changes to the system.

As I believe the second point is already taken into consideration in Paragraph 5 of Article 155, the first one is a legitimate concern that I am sure all of us share, because, to the best of my knowledge, every nation's constitution upholds the principle in accordance with which no conventional obligation should be imposed on the State unless by means of an express act of the competent constitutional organ of the State concerned. Because it is a legal concern that we all share, I believe that we will find a way to circumvent it.

2. Decision-making

The issue of decision-making is perhaps the most difficult and intractable one, due to the political overtones it has and the spill-over effect it might have in setting precedents for all international organizations.

In addition to the US suggested change to the decision-making in the Council, proposals have been tabled in the PrepCom to introduce changes to the decision-making procedure of the Assembly, as well.

In the case of the Assembly, as I understand it, the suggested change in the decision-making procedure was prompted by the concern that the "automatic majority" would take decisions that might have financial implications the substantial percentage of which would be borne by major contributors to the budget of the Authority even if these major contributors were to be against those decisions.

In trying to find a solution to this concern, the PrepCom has concentrated its efforts on two areas:

1. As it has been already agreed, any decision which bears financial implications should be preceded by a statement of financial implications to be submitted by the Secretary-General, and the Assembly shall take into account the estimates before adopting any proposal involving expenditure from the Authority's funds.

2. The approval of the budget of the Authority is entrusted by the Convention to the Assembly. In accordance with our current consultations on the Finance Committee, this body would be entrusted with the important function of adivising the Council and the Assembly on the budget.

Although formal decisions on the approval of the budget are to be taken by the Assembly, the decision-building rôle in the budgeting process is going to be played first and foremost by the Finance Committee. Therefore it becomes more germaine to concentrate our efforts on the ongoing negotiations to address the issue of decision-making in the Finance Committee in such a way as to dilute that concern of the major contributors, thus rendering unnecessary any quest for change in the Assembly's existing decision-making procedure.

As far as the suggested change in the Council's decision-making procedure is concerned, I believe that most of its functions, at least the most important ones, are to be exercised upon recommendations to be made by the Legal and Technical Commission. One of these important functions is the approval of plans of work which will be decided on recommendation of the Legal and Technical Commission. Here again, the emphasis of decision-making should be shifted from the Council to the Legal and Technical Commission which might become the most important body in the process of approval of contracts.

Since the decision-making process in the Legal and Technical Commission was left to the PrepCom to resolve, I think we have an important opportunity here to address somewhat the concerns that led to the suggested change to the decision-making in the Council.

3. Representation and Seats in Permanence

It is my belief that there will not be major difficulties in accomodating the US position in granting them a seat in permanence at the Council. In fact in my view this issue is already addressed in art. 161 in accordance with which the US qualifies for membership on many grounds, including as one of the largest investors in the sea-bed and as a major consumer. The issue here seems to be more one of how to implement art. 161 rather than how to change it. I am sure that the Preparatory Commission would not have difficulties in making the recommendation that the US be granted a seat in the Council, due to its manifold qualifications as a candidate for membership in that body.

At the same time, to strengthen such a recommendation, efforts are being made in the ongoing consultations on the composition of the Legal and Technical Commission to ensure the membership of experts nominated by the largest investors and major consumers. Similar consideration is being given to the composition of the Finance Committee, where we have retained the "major contributors" as a criterion to be taken into account in that composition.

4. The Costs of Institutional Arrangements

The PrepCom has already indicated that it is for a lean and cost-efficient Authority. Such a decision becomes important because it gives assurance to all nations that the structure of the Authority will be developed as the needs require and in accordance with the financial capacity of member states. The industrialized countries should be aware that developing nations are the first ones interested in avoiding waste and unnecessary structures, for they are the ones that will bear the bulk of the financial burden resulting from the Authority's functioning, at least during the first years.

On the other hand, we might even explore the possibilities of decreasing the financial burden for States parties to finance the first mining operation of the Enterprise, since for many States the financial obligations with the funding of the Enterprise might become unbearable. This is more so if we consider the escalation of costs that have increased the projections for an integrated mining operation to the amount of two billion US dollars. It goes without saying that such a projection in ten years from now will probably be doubled. This leads me to believe that we might consider seriously the joint ventures arrangement with the Enterprise and other possibilities to relieve States parties from the heavy financial obligations that for many, I am sure, would become unbearable.

The financial health of the Tribunal should also concern us, especially in the first years of its existence where the overwhelming majority of States parties will be developing nations. The projections so far made for the annual costs of the Tribunal deserve our careful consideration. Even when the costs of that projection are streamlined, we run the risk of having a newly instituted Tribunal facing financial hardships for lack of payment of contributions on the part of States Parties.

Such a possibility, which I am afraid is almost certain to occur, would cripple the prestige of the Tribunal as a credible adjudicatory body, especially in the face of a strong competitor, a highly prestigious and well-financed International Court of Justice.

I believe that the International Tribunal for the Law of the Sea is an important body in the international judicial system that should be preserved. My country, for example, chose the International Tribunal for the Law of the Sea as the primary judicial body to deal with ocean conflicts. It is because I believe this Tribunal is such an important institutional development, that we might wish to explore the arrangements that would obviate the anticipated financial problems to be faced by the Tribunal. Surely, there are different arrangements that might be envisaged. One, however, seems to be especially appealing to me. And that is to explore the possibilities of funding the Tribunal's budget through the United Nations, at least until such time a minimum number of countries including potential major contributors become parties to the Convention. There is a good reason to do so. The Tribunal is an important mechanism that, if in operation, will help to implement major charter principles such as the peaceful solution of conflicts. It is in the interest of the United Nations, and totally within its purposes, to take steps to finance a major international judicial body concerned with the settlement of disputes arising out of activities undertaken in more than three fourths of the planet.

V. The Issue of Timing

We should take advantage of the remaining period before the entry into force of the Convention, to address, if not all, at least the issues the solution of which is fundamental to rally the overwhelming adherence to the Convention. In my view, the issues that have to be addressed before the Convention's entry into force, are more or less those that I have outlined. Other issues like the compulsory transfer of technology, production ceiling, and related matters of the mining code could be addressed after the entry into force of the Convention on the basis of a set of ground rules to be agreed upon, since exploitation seems to be postponed for many years, and the circumstances upon which those matters depend seem to change year after year.

In conclusion, I have tried to convey to you some of my ideas of what may be the issues to be tackled to secure the universality of the Convention. I think that today there is an ample acceptance of the idea that accomodation should be made to the sea-bed régime to secure the participation of the United States and other industrialized countries. It causes some concern, however, to see that those countries, like the United States, that in the past had sought accomodation on certain provisions seem today to have less enthusiasm to pursue their quest for change in Part XI. I hope that it is simply a question of time for them to indicate their position. Time, however, is running out while the risks to the integrity of the Convention increase. Let us hope for the best.

I thank you for your attention.

The Preparatory Commission for the International Sea-Bed Authority and for the International Tribunal for the Law of the Sea: An Evaluation

L. D. M. Nelson*

I. Introduction

Resolution I of the Third United Nations Conference on the Law of the Sea provided for a Preparatory Commission to prepare for the establishment of the International Sea-Bed Authority and for the International Tribunal for the Law of the Sea — thus giving effect to the provisions of the United Nations Convention on the Law of the Sea (referred to hereinafter as the Convention on the Law of the Sea) dealing with institution-building. The Preparatory Commission was also entrusted with the task of implementing the régime governing preparatory investment in pioneer activities relating to polymetallic nodules which has been provided for in resolution II of the Conference in order to protect the then existing investments in deep sea-bed mining. The Preparatory Commission which has been meeting twice a year since 1983 has recently established 1991 as the target date for the completion of its work.

II. Membership and Participation

The membership of the Commission consists of States[1] which have signed the Convention or have acceded to it. The representative of signatories of the Final Act may participate fully in the work of the Commission as observers but do not have the right to participate in the taking of decisions. There is a category of States — those who have ratified or have acceded to the Convention numbering now some 48 — which enjoy no formal status in the Commission but whose views on account of their relationship with the Convention must, in the opinion of this writer, be taken into account especially at this stage of the work of the Commission. In fact they form to a certain extent a category of players.

---

* *L. Dolliver M. Nelson*, Office for Ocean Affairs and the Law of the Sea, United Nations. The views expressed are personal and do not necessarily reflect the views of the Office for Ocean Affairs and the Law of the Sea or of the United Nations.

1 The Convention on the Law of the Sea was ratified by Namibia represented by the United Nations Council for Namibia on 18 April 1983. Namibia acceded to independence as an independent State on 21 March 1990.

III. Structure

The Preparatory Commission consists of the Plenary as the principal organ and four Special Commissions. Special Commission 1 is undertaking studies on the problems which would be encountered by developing land-based producer States from sea-bed minerals derived from the Area and will submit recommendations on this matter to the Authority. Special Commission 2 is preparing for the establishment of the Enterprise — the operating arm of the Authority. Special Commission 3 is drafting the regulations on prospecting, exploration and exploitation of the polymetallic nodules in the international sea-bed area (the so-called mining code). Special Commission 4 is dealing with the preparation of practical arrangements for the establishment of the International Tribunal for the Law of the Sea. The Informal Plenary is concerned with the preparation of the rules and procedure relating to the organs of the Authority — the Assembly, the Council, the Legal and Technical Commission and the Economic Planning Commission — and, *inter alia*, with the drafting of the Headquarters Agreement between the International Sea-Bed Authority and Jamaica, the Protocol on the Privileges and Immunities of the International Sea-Bed Authority, and the Agreement between the International Sea-Bed Authority and the United Nations. It also deals with the implementation of resolution II governing preparatory investment in pioneer activities relating to polymetallic nodules.

IV. The Progress of Work

1. The Implementation of Resolution II

During the last six or seven years it can fairly be said that the Preparatory Commission has focussed much of its attention on the implementation of resolution II. The registration of the first group of applicants — France, India, Japan and the Soviet Union — as pioneer investors was the first task of the Preparatory Commission. It was soon discovered that overlaps existed between the application areas of Japan and the Soviet Union and between those of France and the Soviet Union. These were all in the same region in the north-eastern part of the Pacific. India had no conflicts of overlaps with respect to its application area.

In 1984 the Chairman of the Preparatory Commission was requested to use his good offices to help the parties reach an agreement. After prolonged and difficult negotiations undertaken both outside and inside the Preparatory Commission, the first group of applicants was able to resolve their conflicts of overlaps and not long afterwards it was reported that the first group of applicants and the potential applicants had concluded a comprehensive settlement of practical problems.[2] The resolution of these conflicts paved the way for the registration of the

2 UN doc. LOS/PCN/90, reprinted in: *Renate Platzöder* (ed.), The Law of the Sea: Documents 1983-1989. The Preparatory Commission for the International Sea-Bed

pioneer investors and late in 1987 the General Committee, functioning as the executive body of the Preparatory Commission, approved the reports of the group of technical experts convened to review the applications, and registered France, India, Japan and the Soviet Union as pioneer investors under resolution II.[3]

It is of some significance that this process has resulted in some important *de facto* amendments to resolution II.[4] Here are some instances. Each of the first group of applicants was entitled to receive areas of its own choice. This method of self-selection was contrary to paragraph 3 (b) of resolution II, since under that paragraph it fell to the Preparatory Commission to select which part of the area is to be reserved for the Authority.[5]

Any developing country now has the right to apply as a pioneer investor under resolution II until the Convention enters into force. A group of socialist States of Eastern Europe or a group of their State Enterprises also has the right to apply as a pioneer investor under resolution II until the Convention enters into force.[6] This in effect amended the resolution since it had expressly identified the States and entities which would qualify as pioneer investors and had laid down certain specific requirements.[7]

Authority and for the International Tribunal for the Law of the Sea (referred to hereinafter as *Platzöder* (ed.)), Vol. I, 363.

3 The decisions by the General Committee concerning the applications can be found in UN docs. LOS/PCN/97 (France); LOS/PCN/94 (India); LOS/PCN/98 (Japan); and LOS/PCN/99 (USSR). For the Chairman's Report to the Preparatory Commission on the registration *see* UN doc. LOS/PCN/L. 55; Law of the Sea Bulletin, Special Issue II (1988). On 22 August 1990 the Preparatory Commission received an application from the People's Republic of China for registration as a pioneer investor (UN doc. LOS/PCN/113 of 24 August 1990; *Platzöder* (ed.), Vol. XI, 12). At the ninth session of the Commission the General Committee registered the China Ocean Mineral Resources Research and Development Association (application submitted by China) and also registered as a pioneer investor the Interoceanmetal Joint Organization (application submitted by Bulgaria, Cuba, Czechoslovakia, Poland and USSR (UN docs. LOS(PCN/L. 92 and LOS/PCN/L. 97).

4 *I. P. Blishchenko* (ed.), The International Law of the Sea, Moscow 1988, 104. Generally *see Philippe Kirsch / Douglas Fraser*, The Law of the Sea Preparatory Commission after six years: review and prospects, in: The Canadian Yearbook of International Law 26 (1988), 119-153; *Jean-Pierre Levy*, Un nouvel instrument de développement progressif du droit de la mer: La Commission préparatoire de l'autorité internationale des fonds marins et du tribunal international du droit de la mer, in: AFDI 34 (1988), 735-762; *Moritaka Hayashi*, Registration of the First Group of Pioneer Investors by the Preparatory Commission for the International Sea-Bed Authority and for the International Tribunal for the Law of the Sea, in: ODILA 18 (1987), 1-32.

5 *Cf.* art. 8 of Annex III of the Convention on the Law of the Sea. It may here be remarked that the procedures and mechanisms embodied in the Statement on the implementation of resolution II "shall not be construed as setting a precedent for the implementation of the régime for sea-bed mining under the Convention, nor do they purport to alter or amend that régime in any way" (UN doc. LOS/PCN/L. 41/Rev. 1, annex 1, para. 18; *Platzöder* (ed.), Vol. II, 84).

6 *Loc. cit.*, paras. 20-21. It was under this provision that the Interoceanmetal Joint Organization was registered as a pioneer investor (UN doc. LOS/PCN/L. 122).

The scheme embodied in resolution II for the relinquishment of areas[8] was in effect modified. An applicant who had practical problems in resolving its conflicts with respect to overlapping claims with potential applicants was entitled to make voluntary relinquishments of parts of the application areas simultaneously with its registration as a pioneer investor. This mechanism of prior relinquishment was designed to accommodate the interests of potential applicants. The relinquished areas were to be reserved to form part of the application areas of potential applicants qualified to apply as pioneer investors under resolution II.[9]

There are a few observations which can be made on the registration of pioneer investors. In the first place it may provide a model which can be profitably utilized by the International Sea-Bed Authority when deep sea-bed mining becomes a reality. For instance the processing of applications by the International Sea-Bed Authority can be based on the procedures and methodology adopted by the Group of Experts to determine whether the applications were in conformity with resolution II, "in particular with the principle of equal estimated commercial value."[10] The findings with regard to the difficult notion of "equal estimated commercial value" are of particular significance. It will be recalled that in the case of the applications of France, Japan and the USSR the Group of Experts had concluded that "based on the results of investigations and analysis of the data available at the present level of prospecting and exploration for polymetallic nodules, both areas offer similar potentials in terms of finding competitive mine sites in the respective areas. Accordingly, the estimated commercial value of the area proposed to be reserved for the Authority may thus be considered equal to the estimated commercial value of the areas proposed to be allocated to the applicant."[11] It may be noted that, in the case of the application of India, the Group of Experts had determined that the areas were of equal estimated commercial value.[12]

It has been justly noted that the registration of the first group of applicants constituted a "significant landmark in the implementation of the pioneer system, thus strengthening the régime for the international sea-bed as embodied in the Convention on the Law of the Sea."[13] In a sense it also gave strength to the Convention on the Law of the Sea taken as a whole.

---

7 In order to qualify as a pioneer investor the State or entity must have expended before 1 January 1983 an amount equivalent to at least $US 30 million in pioneer activities, no less than 10 per cent of which had to be expended in the location, survey and evaluation of the application area (para. 1 (a) of resolution II). Under para. 1 (a) (iii) a developing country which has signed the Convention must have met this requirement before 1 January 1985.

8 Paragraph 1 (e) of resolution II.

9 UN doc. LOS/PCN/L. 41/Rev. 1, annex, paras. 9-12; *Platzöder* (ed.), Vol. II, 82.

10 *Loc. cit.*, para. 4.

11 UN doc. LOS/PCN/L. 55; *Platzöder* (ed.), Vol. II, 154.

12 UN doc. LOS/PCN/BUR/R. 1; *Platzöder* (ed.), Vol. I, 92.

13 UN doc. LOS/PCN/L. 55; *Platzöder* (ed.), Vol. II, 157.

Following the registration of the pioneer investors in 1988 the Preparatory Commission turned its attention to the implementation of the obligations of the pioneer investors and their certifying States contained in resolution II.[14] The most important obligations of the pioneer investors, at least those that were perceived as such, are the obligations:

(i) to pay a fixed fee of $US 1 million commencing from the date of allocation of the pioneer area;[15]

(ii) to carry out exploration in the area reserved for activities by the Authority;[16] and

(iii) to train personnel designated by the Preparatory Commission.[17]

The consultations on the implementation of the obligations of pioneer investors proved difficult and time-consuming. It was not until the ninth session of the Preparatory Commission that this matter was resolved when on 30 August 1990 the General Committee, on behalf of the Preparatory Commission, adopted the Understanding on the Fulfilment of Obligations by the Registered Pioneer Investors and their Certifying States.[18]

It will be recalled that the Group of Experts had been convened to assist the Preparatory Commission in the search for an agreement on a plan for exploration of a mine site in the area reserved for the Authority in the central region of the North-East Pacific. The Group submitted a report containing an exploration plan from the first stage of exploration to the stage where a decision on exploitation could be taken.

It was this exploration plan which provided the key to the solution of the crucial question relating to the obligation of the pioneer investors to carry out exploration in the area reserved for activities by the Authority. The three registered pioneer investors (France, Japan and the Soviet Union) undertook to carry out free of cost the preparatory work and stage I of the plan for exploration embodied in the report of the Group of Experts.[19]

---

[14] At the meeting of the General Committee when the applications were approved, the Chairman of the Preparatory Commission read out the following statement: "The General Committee is of the view that, as a result of registration, certain rights accrue to the pioneer investors and, at the same time, certain obligations flow from registration for the pioneer investors and the certifying States, in particular under paragraphs 4, 5, 7 and 12 of resolution II and the Statement contained in LOS/PCN/L. 41/Rev. 1, annex" (UN doc. LOS/PCN/L. 55).

[15] Paragraph 7 (b) of resolution II.

[16] Paragraph 12 (a) (i) of resolution II and para. 14 of UN doc. LOS/PCN/L. 41/Rev. 1, annex.

[17] Paragraph 12 (a) (ii) of resolution II. The other obligations specified in resolution II concern the registration fee (para. 7 (a) of resolution II); transfer of technology (para. 12 (a) (iii) of resolution II); and periodic expenditures (para. 7 (c) of resolution II). The obligations of certifying States concerned funds for the Enterprise (para. 12 (b) (i) of resolution II) and periodic reports (para. 12 (b) (ii) of resolution II).

[18] UN doc. LOS/PCN/L. 87, annex, 30 August 1990; *Platzöder* (ed.), Vol. XI, 106.

[19] *See* UN doc. LOS/PCN/BUR/R. 5, 16 August 1989; *Platzöder* (ed.), Vol. I, 160.

With respect to stage II of the exploration plan it was understood that "this will be agreed upon following the completion of stage I and the review of the results obtained, and taking into account the decision of any pioneer investor to undertake stage II of the plan of exploration allocated to it. The terms and conditions for such further exploration shall be agreed upon in accordance with resolution II, paragraph 12 (a) (i)."[20]

It was agreed that the four registered pioneer investors shall provide training pursuant to para. 12 (a) (ii) of resolution II and in accordance with the Preparatory Commission Training Programme.[21] The cost of such training shall be borne by the registered pioneer investors.

Once the three pioneer investors, France, Japan and the Soviet Union, had "satisfactorily complied" with these obligations concerning training and exploration their duty "to pay $US 1 million per annum shall upon the completion of stage I of the exploration plan be waived as of the date of their registration." India's obligation to pay the annual fixed fee of $US 1 million was also waived.[22]

It is important to note that on the adoption of the Understanding the Chairman made this significant statement:

> (i) Should any agreement be made which would affect in any way this Understanding, such adjustments as may be necessary shall be made to it;
>
> (ii) The required date for the submission of a plan of work by each registered pioneer investor under resolution II, paragraph 8 (a), shall be reviewed in the light of the assessment of the Group of Technical Experts in accordance with paragraph 12 of the Understanding (LOS/PCN/L. 87).

The Understanding on the Fulfilment of Obligations by the Registered Pioneer Investors and their Certifying States produced its share of de facto amendments to resolution II. The long negotiations on the implementation of the obligations of the pioneer investors and their certifying States not surprisingly modified the pioneer investors régime as contained in resolution II. There are two such amendments which deserve particular comment. In the first place, in contradistinction to the Understanding resolution II provided no conditions for waiver of the annual fixed fee of $US 1 million to be paid by every registered pioneer investor from the date of the allocation of the pioneer area. In the second place, the statement by the Chairman on the adoption of the Understanding that the required date for the submission of a plan of work by each registered pioneer investor shall be reviewed in the light of the assessment by the Group of Experts at the time when commercial production may be expected to commence introduced an element which is not to be found in paragraph 8 of resolution II which quite simply stated that "within six months of the entry into force of the Convention and certification by the Commission ... of compliance with this resolution, the

---

20 *Loc. cit.* (note 18), para. 9.

21 *See below*, under section 4.

22 *Loc. cit.* (note 18), paras. 10 and 11.

pioneer investor so registered shall apply to the Authority for approval of a plan of work for exploration and exploitation in accordance with the Convention ..."

It may be argued that the Understanding even amended the Convention itself. Under the Convention the contractor's obligation to pay an annual fixed fee of $US 1 million from the date of the entry into force of the contract may only be waived for the period of postponement, "if the approved date of commencement of commercial production is postponed because of a delay in issuing the production authorization" (annex III, art. 13, para. 3). On the other hand the Understanding stipulates that "if, as a result of the review and the assessment, the Group of Technical Experts concludes that commercial production will not take place for an extended period of time, the Preparatory Commission shall recommend to the Authority that the annual fixed fee payable under annex III, art. 13, para. 3, be waived for a relevant period" (LOS/PCN/L. 87, annex, para. 12).

It is noteworthy that here again the Preparatory Commission evinced a considerable degree of flexibility and pragmatism in adjusting the pioneer investor régime to the changing economic and political conditions.

2. The Preparation of Draft Agreements, Regulations and Rules of Procedures for the Authority

The Informal Plenary has already provisionally adopted a large portion of the rules of procedure of the Assembly, of the Council, of the Legal and Technical Commission and of the Economic Planning Commission. In addition, the Plenary has already reviewed the draft Headquarters Agreement between the International Sea-Bed Authority and the Government of Jamaica and the draft Protocol on the Privileges and Immunities of the International Sea-Bed Authority. The main task left for the Plenary is to undertake informal negotiations on certain issues that were left pending during the consideration of the draft rules of procedure of the various organs such as: decision-making; majorities required for elections and financial and budgetary matters, and in this connection the Plenary is directing its attention to the establishment of a Finance Committee.

A Finance Committee is to be established to assist the Assembly and the Council in the financial administration of the Authority.[23] There is already general agreement on certain important aspects of the Committee, e. g. its status and composition. Informal consultations are still continuing on such matters as functions and decision-making. It is of some significance that a serious proposal was made during the debate in Special Commission 4 on the administrative arrangements, structure and financial implications of the International Tribunal for the Law of the Sea to give the Finance Committee for the Authority the responsibility to review the Tribunal's budget.

---

[23] UN doc. LOS/PCN/WP. 45; *Platzöder* (ed.), Vol. III, 443.

3. The Protection of the Interests of Developing Land-based Producer States (Special Commission 1)

The work of this Commission is hindered by certain important factors. The prevailing uncertainty as to when and under what circumstances commercial deep sea-bed mining will begin renders it difficult to recommend specific remedial measures to protect the economies of developing land-based producers from deep sea-bed mining. Moreover, it may also be difficult to identify the States which would be adversely affected simply because sea-bed production seems to be so far distant.[24]

This Commission, however, has now reached the stage when it was able to prepare a list of some 66 provisional conclusions which will form the basis of its final recommendations to the Authority. The topics dealt with include projection of production from the international sea-bed Area, relationship between production and determination of the problems or difficulties that would be encountered by the affected developing land-based producer States.[25]

4. The Enterprise (Special Commission 2)

The work of this Commission has also been affected by the unfavourable prospects for deep sea-bed mining, which render the choice of operational options for the Enterprise especially difficult.[26] In this connection the Commission has been focussing its attention on a 'nucleus' Enterprise. "There has been no agreement" it has been said "on the precise form and status of such an initial 'nucleus' since there are obvious uncertainties as to the prevailing situation at the time of entry into force of the Convention."[27] The changing perception with regard to the rôles of the public and private sector must inevitably have some effect on any thinking with regard to the Enterprise. It may be mentioned here that the prospect of the Enterprise entering into joint ventures is becoming increasingly attractive. It may be a mode of resolving the formidable problem of funding the first mine site of the Authority and may reduce the problems associated with the transfer of technology and, of course, will provide a secure mechanism for the training of personnel from developing countries.[28]

In 1989 the Preparatory Commission adopted a set of "principles, policies, guidelines and procedures for a Preparatory Commission Training Programme."[29] The training programme is to be found in document LOS/PCN/SCN. 2/L. 6/

---

24 UN doc. LOS/PCN/L. 9; *Platzöder* (ed.), Vol. I, 451.

25 UN doc. LOS/PCN/L. 78, 28 March 1990; *Platzöder* (ed.), Vol. XI, 23.

26 *See* UN docs. LOS/PCN/L. 40 and LOS/PCN/L. 60; *Platzöder* (ed.), Vol. II, 58 and 215.

27 UN doc. LOS/PCN/SCN. 2/WP. 16; *Platzöder* (ed.), Vol. VI, 199.

28 UN doc. LOS/PCN/L. 25; *Platzöder* (ed.), Vol. I, 519.

29 *See* UN doc. LOS/PCN/L. 77; *Platzöder* (ed.), Vol. II, 326.

Rev. 1. The Special Commission completed its work on the subject of training when the Preparatory Commission adopted at its last session a series of recommendations aimed at implementing the Preparatory Commission Training Programme.[30] The Training Panel held its first meeting at the 1991 New York session of the Commission (*see* UN doc. LOS/PCN/L. 97 of 29 August 1991).

The principal topic in the future programme of the Commission relates to the transitional arrangements for the Enterprise — the purpose and function of transitional arrangements and the type of structure which would be required to perform these functions.[31]

5. The Drafting of the Mining Code (Special Commission 3)

This Commission has made substantial progress in its preparation of the regulations on prospecting, exploration and exploitation of polymetallic nodules in the international sea-bed area (the so-called mining code). It has already examined the regulations concerning prospecting and application for approval of a plan of work; the financial terms of contract; the transfer of technology; and the regulations on production authorization.

The Commission has recently considered the draft regulations on the protection and preservation of the marine environment from activities in the Area.[32] These draft regulations generated a great deal of interest in the Preparatory Commission which was to be expected given the current importance of all matters relating to the protection of the environment. It was generally agreed that the lack of sufficient scientific knowledge of the effects on deep sea-bed mining made it very difficult at this stage to draft adequate regulations for the protection and preservation of the marine environment from activities in the Area.

Topics yet to be dealt with by the Commission include accounting principles and procedures, inspection and supervision of activities in the Area, labour standards, accommodation of activities in the Area and dispute settlement procedures.[33] Some observations on the work of this Commission will be made later.

6. The Tribunal (Special Commission 4)

This Commission has almost concluded its work. Widespread agreement has been reached on the rules of the International Tribunal for the Law of the Sea and it has completed its examination of the draft Headquarters Agreement between

---

30 UN doc. LOS/PCN/SCN. 2/L. 7, 30 March 1990; *Platzöder* (ed.), Vol. XI, 307.

31 Further *see* UN doc. LOS/PCN/L. 80, 30 March 1990; *Platzöder* (ed.), Vol. XI, 55.

32 UN doc. LOS/PCN/SCN. 3/WP. 6/Add. 5, 8 February 1990; *Platzöder* (ed.), Vol. XI, 352.

33 UN doc. LOS/PCN/L. 79, 28 March 1990; *Platzöder* (ed.), Vol. XI, 37. *See* also UN doc. LOS/PCN/L. 94, 28 August 1991.

the International Tribunal for the Law of the Sea and the Federal Republic of Germany and of the draft Protocol on the Privileges and Immunities of the International Tribunal for the Law of the Sea. The Commission is at present considering the draft agreement on co-operation and relationship between the Tribunal and the United Nations and the administrative arrangements, structure and financial implications of the Tribunal. The debate in the Commission on this document has thrown into relief the crucial importance the Preparatory Commission attaches to the financial implications of institution-building.

Some comments:

The question may well be posed as to why the Preparatory Commission has not yet finished its task. First of all, the fact that deep sea-bed mining may not occur before we are well into the 21st century has removed any urgency there might have been to produce a set of deep sea-bed mining regulations. Secondly, there is the slow pace of the ratification process which may itself reflect the concern of several States with the financial implications of establishing institutions from which little benefit would accrue at this stage. The second reason is evidently linked to the first. Thirdly, the Preparatory Commission is faced with the inherent difficulty of drafting rules and regulations for a part of the Convention which has not in fact received general acceptance.

V. The Preparatory Commission and the Convention on the Law of the Sea

To what extent can the Preparatory Commission in drafting the mining code or indeed other rules and regulations depart from the provisions of the Convention on the Law of the Sea? This is obviously a fundamental question. The United States took a clear position on this question in the Statement of the President on 30 December 1982. In refusing to fund the Preparatory Commission it was declared that "[t]he Preparatory Commission is called upon to develop rules and regulations for the sea-bed régime under the treaty. It has no authority to change the damaging provisions and precedents in that part of the treaty. For that reason the United States is not participating in the Commission."[34] According to that view the Preparatory Commission has no mandate to effect any changes in the provisions of the Convention.

This also accords with the view of the Chairman of the First Committee of the Third United Nations Conference on the Law of the Sea. He states "with regard to the functions of the Preparatory Commission, the utmost care should be taken to ensure that the results of its work conformed strictly to the provisions of the Convention and in no way upset the delicate balance of interests and concerns struck in the text of the Convention."[35] The Chairman of the Group of

34 Statement of President *Reagan*, 30 December 1982.

77 held that "it was important to avoid giving the impression that the Preparatory Commission was simply an extension of the Conference and to resist the temptation to pass on to the Commission any of the outstanding issues."[36] Truth to tell, there are those in the Preparatory Commission who to this day maintain the view that the Commission has no competence to make any changes in the Convention.

A somewhat different view was taken by France, in its declaration on signing the Convention. It noted that the "provisions of the Convention relating to the area of the sea-bed and ocean floor beyond the limits of national jurisdiction show considerable deficiencies and flaws with respect to the exploration and exploitation of the said area which will require rectification through the adoption by the Preparatory Commission of draft rules, regulations and procedures to ensure the establishment and effective functioning of the International Sea-Bed Authority."[37] Belgium, Italy, Luxembourg and the EEC also hoped that the shortcomings and defects of the deep sea-bed mining régime will be rectified by the rules, regulations and procedures adopted by the Preparatory Commission. This must also have been the view of the States which, in spite of their uneasiness with the Part XI régime, decided to participate in the work of the Commission.[38]

This matter is closely linked to what has been termed "the hard-core issues" facing the Preparatory Commission. Some of these "hard-core issues" crop up in the drafting of the rules of procedure of the various organs of the Authority, for instance financial and budgetary matters, the status of observers, decision-making on questions of substance, elections and the establishment of subsidiary organs. Several of these matters are either not dealt with in the Convention or have been dealt with quite inadequately, e. g. the Convention did not envisage the establishment of a Finance Committee as such.[39]

---

35 Official Records of the Third United Nations Conference on the Law of the Sea, Vol. XV, United Nations, New York 1983, 71, para. 7.

36 *Loc. cit.*, para. 9.

37 *See* Multilateral Treaties deposited with the Secretary-General: UN doc. ST/LEG/SER. E/8, 787.

38 In the course of a debate in the House of Lords on the United Nations Convention on the Law of the Sea, the Minister of State, Foreign and Commonwealth Office, Baroness *Young*, stated *inter alia*: "Our involvement with the Commission's work shows that the United Kingdom has not turned its back on the Convention but is seeking to improve the deep sea mining régime. The United Kingdom wishes to work with the international community to achieve a system for seabed mining which is generally acceptable and workable and to bring about generally agreed provisions for regulating marine matters.... Some solutions may be found through rules adopted in the Preparatory Commission which has been established to implement the seabed aspects of the Convention" (United Kingdom Materials on International Law 1984, in: BYIL 55 (1984), 559/560).

39 *See* UN doc. LOS/PCN/WP. 45. Article 162, para. 2 (y) provided, *inter alia*, that the Council shall establish a subsidiary organ for the elaboration of draft financial rules, regulations and procedures relating to: (i) financial management in accordance with articles 171 to 175; and (ii) financial arrangements in accordance with Annex III, article 13 and article 17, paragraph 1 (c).

The Convention has not provided any answers to the type of question being raised with respect to the status of observers in the Authority.[40] It does not contain a list of entities which should be granted observer status in the Authority and it is silent on the extent and nature of the participation of observers in the Assembly and the Council.

It should also be noted that the Convention expressly leaves the decision-making procedures of the Legal and Technical Commission and the Economic Planning Commission to be established by the rules, regulations and procedures of the Authority.[41]

In the view of this writer these issues may perhaps more readily lend themselves to general agreement since they are not viewed as attempts aimed at changing the provisions of the Convention. It is significant that the informal consultations now being conducted by the Chairman of the Preparatory Commission on some of these issues are progressing satisfactorily.[42]

There is another kind of "hard core issues" which are encountered for the most part in the drafting of the mining code. Chief among these are matters relating for example to production limitation, transfer of technology and the financial terms of contract, all of which are at the heart of the conflict between the industrialized world and the developing countries. It is important to note that all of these matters have been dealt with in great detail in the Convention on the Law of the Sea. On these matters it is difficult to produce a text which could command general acceptance without in fact amending provisions of the Convention and this brings us back to the question of the mandate of the Preparatory Commission.

It is noteworthy that during the consideration of the draft regulations on production authorizations,[43] which for the most part embodied the relevant provisions of the Convention, a number of States abstained from participation in the "detailed debate" since "the production policies as contained in the Convention were among the serious obstacles" to their acceptance of the Convention.[44]

Others held that, "as was the case with many other provisions of the Convention, articles 150 and 151, embodying the Convention's resource policies, were the result of a delicate compromise between the divergent interests of all States involved in its negotiations. The provisions of those articles therefore reflected the balance that had been struck on the matter, and which should not be upset."[45]

---

40 *See* art. 156, para. 3.

41 Article 163, para. 11.

42 *See* Statement by the Chairman of the Preparatory Commission, UN doc. LOS/PCN/L. 82/Rev. 1, 29 March 1990; *Platzöder* (ed.), Vol. XI, 71.

43 UN doc. LOS/PCN/SCN. 3/WP. 6/Add. 1; *Platzöder* (ed.), Vol. VI, 360.

44 *See* Statement to the Plenary by the Chairman of Special Commission 3 on the progress of work in that Commission: UN doc. LOS/PCN/L. 74, 30 August 1989; *Platzöder* (ed.), Vol. II, 308.

The same phenomenon occurred during the debates in Special Commission 3 on the draft regulations relating to the financial terms of contract.[46] On the one hand it was maintained that the provisions of the Convention could not be altered in the development of the rules and regulations for sea-bed mining. On the other it was held that "the Special Commission 3 could not merely repeat the letter of the Convention but be free to further build on the provisions of the Convention."[47]

Incidentally it may be mentioned here that certain members of the Group of 77 have themselves expressed reservations with respect to certain provisions in that part of the Convention dealing with deep sea-bed mining. The relationship of the Enterprise and the principal organs of the Authority, the Council and the Assembly,[48] is a case in point. The suggestion was that some of these rules in the Convention on this relationship were too restrictive. It was felt that "the Convention had given the Enterprise too many bosses and thus there may be a need for a liberal interpretation of these rules."[49]

The question of drafting regulations for minerals other than polymetallic nodules provides another illustration. It will be recalled that art. 162, para. 2 (o) (ii) had dealt with this issue. It stated, *inter alia*, that "[p]riority shall be given to the adoption of rules, regulations and procedures for the exploration for and exploitation of polymetallic nodules" and that "[r]ules, regulations and procedures for the exploration for and the exploitation of any resource other than polymetallic nodules shall be adopted within three years from the date of a request to the Authority by any of its members to adopt such rules, regulations and procedures in respect of such resource." Moreover, Special Commission 3 had decided to focus its work only on polymetallic nodules. Nevertheless, in the consideration of the draft regulations on the transfer of technology there were repeated attempts on the part of some members of the Group of 77 to expand the scope of the regulations to include other minerals in the deep sea-bed.[50] It was also contended that the regulations with respect to the transfer of technology should include processing technology since processing was an integral part of exploitation. The provisions of the Convention dealing with the transfer of technology, it can be argued, excluded processing technology.[51]

---

45 *Ibid.*

46 UN doc. LOS/PCN/SCN. 3/WP. 6/Add. 2; *Platzöder* (ed.), Vol. VI, 373.

47 UN doc. LOS/PCN/L. 46; *Platzöder* (ed.), Vol. II, 102.

48 Article 170, para. 2 and UN docs. LOS/PCN/L. 70, 22 March 1989; LOS/PCN/L. 75, 31 August 1989; *Platzöder* (ed.), Vol. II, 284 and 314.

49 *See* UN docs. LOS/PCN/L. 70 and LOS/PCN/L. 75 (note 48).

50 *See* UN doc. LOS/PCN/L. 59, 7 April 1988; *Platzöder* (ed.), Vol. II, 207.

51 *Ibid.*

VI. Conclusion

The need to produce a deep sea-bed mining régime which is generally acceptable and effective is being increasingly felt. During the 1989 summer meeting of the Preparatory Commission the Chairman of the Group of 77 stated that his Group was ready to hold discussions on any issue relating to the Convention and the work of the Commission and that any delegation or group of delegations be they currently involved in the work of the Preparatory Commission or not were welcome to an open dialogue with the Group of 77. The other important interest groups in the Commission supported the notion of universal participation in the Convention. The Secretary-General of the United Nations himself has taken the initiative of holding informal consultations aimed at achieving universal participation in the United Nations Convention on the Law of the Sea. He expressly noted that "eight years have elapsed since the Convention was adopted and that during that period a number of important political and economic changes have taken place, some directly affecting deep sea-bed mining, others affecting international relations in general."[52] These renewed efforts to facilitate universal participation in the Convention must surely indicate that there is a will to reopen negotiations in order to remedy what is viewed by some as defects on the Convention.[53] Given the difficulties, as we have seen, that the Preparatory Commission faces with any attempt to amend the Convention, difficulties associated with the very mandate of the Commission and the fact that the United States does not participate in the work of the Preparatory Commission, the forum for the negotiations and the form in which the results of such negotiations can be embodied are questions which merit some examination.

---

52 UN doc. A/45/721, para. 14. It may be notet that the Secretary-General has already held four of these informal consultations. All the outstanding issues, it is hoped, will be examined with a view to resolving them, and then a decision will be made on the *modus operandi* for dealing with those issues that remain unresolved.

53 *See* GA res. 44/26 of 20 November 1989. Generally *see Satya N. Nandan*, The 1982 United Nations Convention on the Law of the Sea: at a Cross-road, in: ODILA 20 (1989), 515-518.

Statement on the Implementation of Resolution II of the Third United Nations Conference on the Law of the Sea by the Preparatory Commission for the International Sea-Bed Authority

Cristian Maquieira*

The Preparatory Commission began its work at the conclusion of the Third Law of the Sea Conference with a dual mandate. On the one hand, it had to adopt rules, regulations and procedures in order to ensure the effective operation of the International Sea-Bed Authority and the régime for the exploration and exploitation of the sea-bed resources beyond national jurisdiction, as contained in the United Nations Convention on the Law of the Sea. Also, the Preparatory Commission was entrusted with the implementation of resolution II which contains the régime of pioneer investment protection.

The work done so far by the Preparatory Commission on all aspects of its mandate constitutes by far the most dynamic international activity in the domain of the law of the sea after the conclusion of UNCLOS III.

Nowhere has this dynamism been more clear and demanding than in the resolution of problems conducing to the implementation of resolution II. As we shall see, this has been a complex and very difficult negotiation, done within the context of the Preparatory Commission and outside of it, encompassing different groups of countries, developing, industrialized and socialist, constituting, in my view, both a North-South and an East-West negotiating exercise. The agreements reached were not quite foreseen in resolution II, and, I must add, the method of negotiations utilized was the consensus rule. Also, there are no detailed official records of the negotiations since it was conducted, be it on procedure or on substance, in informal meetings. The process, which has not been concluded since the question of obligations of pioneer investors has not yet reached a final solution, has been very long, starting immediately after the conclusion of the Third Law of the Sea Conference.

Resolution II foresees three categories of beneficiaries of the temporary régime it establishes. They must be signatories of the Convention and, which is a trigger mechanism, have invested at least 30 million dollars in pioneer activities and no less than 10 % of that amount in, as the resolution itself says, the "location, survey and evaluation of the area."

* *Cristian Maquieira,* Counsellor of the Foreign Ministry of the Republic of Chile.

These three categories are, on the one hand,

- France, India, Japan and the Soviet Union, operating through state enterprises of each of those countries;
- four entities, which are the Kennecott Group, the Ocean Management Incorporation (OMI), Ocean Mining Associates, the Ocean Mining Company, which are all controlled by private enterprises; and
- any developing country or group of developing countries, be it through a state or privately controlled enterprise that has carried out the expenditures cited above.

The object of resolution II is to grant exclusive rights over a certain area of the sea-bed to engage in pioneer mining activities before the entry into force of the Convention. Resolution II was drafted on the understanding that at least the first two categories of entities, which were conducting activities in the international Area at that time, would sign the Convention and submit applications for pioneer status. It also maintains that the applications should be devoid of any eventual overlaps and therefore potential applicants should ensure that the area of their application does not overlap with another before submitting their request for "pioneer status" to the Preparatory Commission. This being the case, resolution II does not contain procedures necessary for the determination of overlaps, exchange of co-ordinates, confidentiality of information, etc. It only provides for the resort to binding arbitration in the case that conflicts have not been resolved by a certain date, which is 1 March 1983, and establishes a calendar for the arbitration tribunal.

The fact that all the potential applicants did not submit applications and that resolution II made no provisions for the solving of overlapping claims was to be the wrench in the machinery that delayed the registration of pioneer investors for four years giving origin to a variety of negotiations in order to resolve the question of overlaps.

This question was considered initially before the conclusion of the Third Conference by an initiative taken up by Canada, which held consultations with a view to determining the existence of overlaps and to establishing procedures to resolve them. With the exception of India, which had carried out its activities in the Indian Ocean, all the other potential pioneer investors had conducted operations in the North Pacific, in the area known as the "Clarion-Clipperton" zone, which lies between Hawaii and the Baja California. These activities were realized in such a way that there was a potential for overlaps. Information is now being made available as to the details of the Canadian initiative, which was carried out between 1982 and 1983. All the potential pioneer investors began participating in these consultations and also some developing countries participated, as is the case of Brazil and Korea.

According to sources close to the negotiations, this effort to identify and resolve eventual overlaps ran into unforeseen problems when India and the Soviet Union decided that any procedure to resolve existing overlaps among potential pioneer investors could only be carried out between signatories of the Convention. Resolution II clearly states that in order to submit an application for pioneer status the certifying State must have signed the Convention, but signature is not a requirement for the resolution of eventual overlaps. It could not be a requirement since resolution II was drafted under the assumption that all benefiting States would eventually submit applications and therefore signature was needed in order to obtain the exclusive rights granted by the resolution.

According to one of the participants in this exercise, India's support of this position was due to its desire for early registration, since it had no problems of overlaps to solve. In the case of the Soviet Union, this country "wanted to take advantage of the fact that Western States designated as prospecting certifying States were not in a position to submit co-ordinates of sea-bed mining sites for the purpose of settling overlapping claims." Compounded with this, in the Canadian exercise, there also seems to have been some difficulties with these countries in settling a date for the exchange of co-ordinates in order to initiate the conflict resolution procedure. This problem could not be resolved and the effort headed by Canada ended in that format, but consultations continued between the Western States with a view to solving the problems of overlapping claims.

Parallel to this effort, the Preparatory Commission was beginning its functions with some difficulties in the election of officers and the organization of work. In the discussion of rules and procedures, there was made a proposal to include rules and regulations applicable to the implementation of resolution II, a proposal that did not gather the necessary consensus and was not supported by the Group of 77. At the resumed session in 1983, the Secretariat produced a separate working paper with draft rules governing the implementation of resolution II. Proposals were also submitted by the Western industrialized countries and the Socialist group. Although extensive discussions were carried out on the basis of these documents, no agreement was reached. There were four areas of controversy:

- procedures for resolution of conflicts of overlaps where the difference of opinions regarding the participation of non-signatories remained;
- the creation of a Group of Technical Experts;
- the confidentiality of the information contained in the applications; and
- the extension of which the obligations of pioneer investors had to be covered by the rules of procedure.

In the light of this debate, the PrepCom decided to request the Chairman to hold consultations with a view to arriving at a consensus. The result of those consultations, which were very extended, was a document entitled "Procedures and guidelines for registration of pioneer investors under resolution II," which was a proposal of the Chairman that did not constitute precise rules and regulations as some countries desired, but simply was a basis for the negotiation, which never took place given later developments.

In the meantime, after the failure of the Canadian initiative, two of the pioneer investors, the Soviet Union and India, took the problem of the resolution of overlapping claims to the Preparatory Commission. This was done by means of a letter in which the USSR stated its readiness to exchange co-ordinates with prospective certifying States, as is stated in para. 5 (a) of resolution II. It also pointed out that, should there be no response from certifying States by 1 May 1983, which is the date that triggered the arbitration procedure in the resolution, the USSR understood that it had complied with the requirements of resolution II with regard to resolution of conflicts and that it should be registered as the first pioneer investor. A similar letter was sent to the Commission by the delegation of India. Afterwards, these countries met in order to identify the possibility of overlapping claims between them, and since their activities were in different oceans, it was determined that there were no overlaps. 1 May 1983 is, as I have mentioned, the date set by resolution II that initiates the arbitration procedure for resolving problems of overlapping claims. What the Soviet Union and India were in fact saying was that, if there was no response by the indicated date, other interested parties would lose their rights.

This approach was soundly opposed by France, Japan, Belgium, the United Kingdom, and the Netherlands who argued with varying degrees of forcefulness that no registration of pioneer investors could take place without a prior procedure for settling problems of possible overlapping claims.

The Group of 77, the largest in the Preparatory Commission, was keen to protect the interests of the Enterprise and in their view, the Enterprise benefited from having the largest possible number of pioneer investors registered as such by the Preparatory Commission.

The problem here is that resolution II was overly optimistic regarding a calendar for conflict resolution and had set up dates which in the end proved to be unrealistic. Although the Canadian initiative had been concluded, the consultations between Western countries for the resolution of conflicts had continued and the efforts of France and Japan and others in PrepCom were to avoid the possibility of early registration until these and other possible overlaps were solved. Otherwise the Preparatory Commission would be granting exclusive rights over disputed sites.

These negotiations were concluded and the concerned governments adopted in August 1984 a "Provisional Understanding regarding Deep Sea-Bed Matters." Although presented as a simple agreement among States that have national legislation in order not to issue licenses regarding areas where other States Parties to this Understanding had also issued licenses, it had a very negative effect in the Preparatory Commission, where the Group of 77 took a very strong stand against this agreement declaring it "wholly illegal" and an effort to undermine the international sea-bed régime contained in the Convention. In the view of the Group of 77, there were elements in that agreement that clearly led to a treaty among the parties and this was totally unacceptable to them because it was seen as an effort by some to replace the régime in the Convention.

The conclusion of this Understanding permitted France and Japan, on the other hand, to formally submit their applications to PrepCom during that same month of August. The Soviet Union had already submitted its application in July 1983, and India had done the same in January 1984.

In the light of these submissions, it fell upon the Chairman of the Commission, the Honourable *Joseph Warioba*, to conduct consultations which concluded at the end of that session with two understandings relating to the resolution of conflicts among these countries that had submitted applications and setting up a procedure and a calendar for registration as pioneer investors. One of the problems created by these understandings was that a distinction was made between those countries in a position to apply for registration, such as France, Japan, the Soviet Union, and India, and those that would be potential applicants, which at that time were Canada and the Netherlands to be followed by Italy and Belgium, who became signatories at the end of that year. There was also the situation of Great Britain and the Federal Republic of Germany who had vested interests in the resolution of any conflicts of overlaps. What the understandings approved at that session and agreed by PrepCom established was the recognition of the right of other potential pioneer investors to submit applications, but these applications had to take into account the areas that had been allocated to the first group and those of the Authority. In fact, these agreements were granting a priority to the first group of applicants in turn to constitute the first major change to resolution II. These understandings, which allowed for the possiblity of breaking what seemed to be a clear impasse regarding conflict resolution, resulted in measures which were not foreseen in resolution II, particularly the priority allocated to the first group and limiting the conflict resolution to those four States and not to all potential pioneer investors.

By December 9 of that year, the final date to become a signatory of the Convention, which is 1984, no other applications were submitted although a serious but unsuccessful effort was carried out during the summer session of the Preparatory Commission in order to obtain the signature of the Federal Republic of Germany. The effort was stymied by the decision of the Socialist group to request an additional mine site for themselves and by the potential applicants who insisted that their rights should not be prejudiced by this initiative. The Group of 77 supported the possibility of obtaining the signature of the Federal Republic of Germany and a statement was drafted to this end. Unfortunately, the FRG was not entirely satisfied with its terms and decided not to sign the Convention when the date came up.

Since there were no other applications, the four countries of the first group began their meetings at the beginning of 1985 in order to exchange co-ordinates and identify possible overlaps. It was detected that these existed between Japan and the Soviet Union and between France and the Soviet Union. While the first overlap was resolved rather quickly, the second, between France and the USSR, required considerable work.

It has to be recalled here that France and Japan had already established what we would call "clean" sites ("clean" sites meaning those without overlaps) between themselves and the Consortia in the Provisional Understanding, and therefore it was extremely difficult for France to modify its co-ordinates in order to solve its overlap with the Soviet Union without impinging upon the site of another signatory of the Provisional Understanding. This was to have a considerable impact in the solution we will have to find later. The situation was made more complicated by the fact that resolution II requires that applications submitted for registration have to be of an area sufficiently large to allow mining operations. This seemed impossible in the case of the Soviet-French overlap. There was a risk, therefore, that the site allocated to the Authority could overlap with a site belonging to the Consortia which was a clearly undesired situation, particularly to the Group of 77.

In the meantime, the Preparatory Commission, in 1985, was faced with new situations arising from the national legislations of some of the non-signatory countries, particularly the United States, the United Kingdom, and the Federal Republic of Germany, other consequences of the issuance of licenses by these countries to the Consortia. Once again, these initiatives gathered negative reactions from the Preparatory Commission. The Group of 77 issued a Declaration reiterating that the only régime for the exploration and exploitation of the sea-bed beyond national jurisdiction was that contained in the Convention and that any activity regarding the sea-bed resources undertaken outside the PrepCom was incompatible with the Convention declaring once again that any such agreement was illegal.

After extensive negotiations on the draft declaration, it was agreed that the Preparatory Commission would adopt it without a vote, but at the same time registering the lack of support by a number of countries, particularly industrialized countries. This procedure was agreed upon due to the fact that while the majority of States in PrepCom felt the need to condemn these actions based on national legislation, there prevailed the desire to limit confrontation so that efforts conducted to the solutions of overlaps would not be seriously impaired.

Unfortunately, this was the case a year later when it was learnt that the governments of the United Kingdom and the FRG issued themselves licenses to the Consortia. The Group of 77 reiterated its earlier declaration but it had no impact on the behaviour of these countries and therefore, a stronger measure was required. The Draft Declaration presented on that occasion was adopted by a vote of 59 votes in favour, seven against, and 10 abstentions.

I move on now to the Arusha Understanding. As has been mentioned, the process of resolution of conflicts between the first applicants had come to a point where France and the Soviet Union had encountered severe difficulties in resolving their overlap. The use of the principle of a fair sharing of the overlapped area was not applicable due to the extension of their overlap. At the same time the other potential applicants became increasingly concerned by the turn of events which could lead to an early registration of the first applicants and the granting of exclusive rights over the sites which could have overlaps with their own. In August 1984, the Group called of potential applicants and on successive occasions later expressed the position that the question of overlapping claims demanded a comprehensive solution in order to achieve the objectives pursued in resolution II. They took the position that no pioneer investor should be registered as long as there was the possibility that overlaps could exist with entities that had rights recognized to them, as was the case with the potential applicants. There was a need then to solve the French-Soviet overlap in such a way that the requirement contained in resolution II regarding a viable site for the Authority be fulfilled and there had to be an adequate accommodation of the concerns of the potential applicants.

Chairman *Warioba* held extensive consultations in order to find a practical solution to these problems. Though no clear path emerged during the 1985 sessions on these questions, some ideas were floated and analyzed by the interested parties. One of these, which turned out to be fundamental in the final solution, was the possibility of early relinquishment of a part of the application area. Resolution II ascertains that pioneer investors, once registered as such, will initiate a process of relinquishment of parts of its area according to an eight year calendar. Early relinquishment meant that the applicant would reduce its area before registration, using this procedure as an instrument for solving problems of overlap.

Chairman *Warioba* then invited the delegations of the four countries that had submitted applications to Arusha, Tanzania, in February 1986 in order to discuss possible ways and means of solving pending problems. The result was the so-called Arusha Declaration which, although it set forth the elements of the final solution to the problems in question, considerably altered the terms of resolution II. In effect, the Arusha Declaration allowed France, Japan, and the Soviet Union to select their site, or a large part of it, instead of leaving this function in the hands of the Preparatory Commission as was stipulated by resolution II and, as a matter of fact, by the Convention itself.

Since activities will be carried out by the operators at the initial stage, leaving the selection of the site to the Preparatory Commission and the Authority was a means for ensuring that the Enterprise will receive a site of equal commercial value or one similar to that of the operator. By allowing the latter to select its site, as is contained in the Arusha Declaration, the commercial value comes into question. This is the fundamental change coming out of Arusha, while other elements in that agreement refer to the use of the relinquished formula to solve the overlaps; the areas relinquished will be deposited with the PrepCom for the potential applicants (instead of going back to the international Area as it is stated in resolution II) and create a commercially viable site of 52,300 square kilometres carved out of areas claimed by France, Japan, and the Soviet Union to be allocated to the Authority.

The Arusha Declaration was brought to the PrepCom during the spring session of 1986. The consultations were conducted under the helm of one of the Vice-Presidents, Mr *Jhingran* of India, since the responsibilities of the post of Prime Minister had kept Chairman *Warioba* from attending. Intense consultations were held on that document, and finally, all groups considered the Arusha Understanding a good basis for the resolution of conflicts of overlaps.

The Group of 77 had severe difficulties with the provision of the Arusha Understanding which allowed the pioneer investor to select its own site because it considered that the interests of the Authority were being jeopardized by the risk of the possiblity that it would receive a site of a doubtful commercial value in comparison with the value of the sites retained by the operators. They pursued this point with vigour, insisting that while retaining the amounts of square kilometres contained in the Arusha Understanding, since they refer to the extent of the overlaps, the final decision for the allocation of sites be taken by the Preparatory Commission, as is established in resolution II. Note must be taken of the fact that this decision, regarding allocation of sites for the pioneer investors, was the only provision of resolution II that came from the Convention itself which was applicable at this stage of the implementation of the resolution. Therefore, there was a concern in the Group of 77, regarding the possibilities that the Arusha Understanding becomes a precedent-setting agreement with regard to the régime contained in the Convention itself.

Regarding the commercial value of the site of the Enterprise, assurances were given by the pioneer investors, particularly France, Japan, and the Soviet Union, that — given the situation of overlaps — the site of the Authority would come from the area where all three had concentrated their overlaps, which, in their view, was an indication of the quality of the site. Apparently the pioneer investors had reluctantly agreed to allocating the site for the Enterprise in the area of their overlaps, since on the one hand it complicated conflict resolution among them and on the other, it clearly reduced the size of their site. Nevertheless, the Group of 77 remained somewhat unconvinced by this argument, but came to the conclusion that it could not detain the process which had encountered circumstances unforeseen by resolution II. There was a need to progress towards registration of pioneer investors under resolution II, which would allow for the implementation of the obligations of the pioneer investors that benefited the Authority.

Also, in accepting the Arusha Declaration, the Group of 77 proposed that the site selected for the Authority be explored free of cost by the pioneer investors in a manner of compensating for the selection of their own site. Resolution II foresees for the pioneer investors the exploration of a site for the Authority on a cost-reimbursable basis plus 10 per cent of interest. The proposal of the Group of 77 is separate from this obligation, constituting a new one, which was strongly resisted by the pioneer investors. In the end, consensus was obtained on the basis that the first group of applicants would assist the Authority and the PrepCom in the exploration of a mine site for the first operation of the Enterprise. The terms and conditions of that assistance were to be defined later and that would be the source of some controversy, since the pioneer investors understood the assistance to be as in resolution II, while the Group of 77 considered this a new obligation emanating from the particular conditions of the Arusha Understanding.

The Socialist group saw in the Arusha Understanding an opportunity to improve its relative position regarding mine sites since resolution II had only allocated one to the Soviet Union. It, therefore, agreed to the new document subject to the condition that they may apply for an additional mine site in the future. Also, the developing countries obtained, as part of the negotiations, an extension of the deadline to apply for pioneer status from 1 January 1985 until the entry into force of the Convention. On this basis, it was agreed that the Arusha Understanding constituted a good basis for negotiations.

These elements, which I have mentioned, were grouped into a new document which became to be called the "New York Understanding," to which was added a flexible calendar to achieve registration of the first group of applicants. This result is the consequence of three distinct negotiating exercises that were required in order to solve the problems of overlaps due to the political and technical circumstances relating to the implementation of resolution II. The first exercise among industrialized countries led to the Provisional Understanding whose terms and conditions limited the scope of possibilities of the exercise between France, Japan, and the Soviet Union, who had decided not to participate in the aforementioned negotiation and led to the changes that were brought about to resolution II. The objective realities at the start of the process of conflict resolution between France, Japan, and the USSR led to the Arusha Understanding which, while retaining the spirit of resolution II, considerably modified its text. Finally, the New York Agreement is an effort to solve the problems impeding registration where the Group of 77 managed to introduce a measure of balance with regard to the interests of the Authority and the Enterprise, which appeared diminished as a consequence of the resolutions of conflicts between the first group of applicants.

Nevertheless, registration could not go forward, until overlaps were solved between the USSR, which is referred to in the New York Understanding as "an applicant with practical problems," and the potential applicants. Based on the

New York Understanding, the Soviet Union proceeded to meet with the potential applicants which are signatories of the Convention first and with the United States, the Federal Republic of Germany and the United Kingdom later. It is clear that while these latter countries had severe reservations regarding Part XI of the Convention and the US does not participate in the work of the Preparatory Commission, they all had an interest in solving the problems of overlaps in such a way that would not hinder eventual development and exploitation activities.

Throughout 1987, intense negotations were conducted at the industrial and governmental levels between the USSR and the potential applicants, which included the United States. The Preparatory Commission assisted this negotations by extending the time limit for the first group of applicants to submit the new appliations which took into account the solutions reached. At the end of that session, the Soviet Union and the potential applicants announced to the acting Chairman of PreCom that all problems had been resolved and that a comprehensive settlement had been reached.

The agreement was formalized in two separate ceremonies: one held in New York, where the USSR subscribed an accord with Belgium, Canada, Italy, and the Netherlands; and one in Moscow, where an exchange of notes was carried out between the United States, the FRG and the United Kingdom. This has been called the "Midnight Agreement" since the New York part was signed shortly after midnight in order to coincide with the events in Moscow.

Once these overlaps have all been solved by the Preparatory Commission, we move on to registration of pioneer investors. It had been agreed by the Preparatory Commission that the General Committee would register the pioneer investors after a report by a Group of Technical Experts which would evaluate the applications to determine that they conform to the terms and conditions of resolution II, particularly regarding the equal commercial value of the sites of the Authority. Although it had been agreed that the first group of applicants would be registered together, it was decided that the Group of Technical Experts would meet in order to consider the application by India, which had been waiting for a long time to be registered. The Group of Technical Experts quickly came to the conclusion that the Indian application conformed to resolution II, reporting that the two sites it contained, classified as A and B, were of equal commercial value and suggested that B be reserved for the Authority. The General Committee approved the recommendation of the Group of Technical Experts and India was registered as a first pioneer investor on 17 August 1987.

The registration of France, Japan, and the Soviet Union was to be more complicated than that of India. These three countries submitted their revised applications, which were drawn up taking into account the solution of overlaps, in November 1987. The Group of Technical Experts had a difficult task before it, given the complicated solution discovered for the overlaps between these countries, and particularly attention had to be given to the questions concerning the equally estimated commercial value. The Group of Technical Experts met during two weeks and reached the conclusion that the site of the Authority may be considered to be of equally estimated commercial value to those of the pioneer investors. The Group of 77 reacted with considerable concern to this conclusion of the Group of Technical Experts, which in their view did not satisfy the requirements of resolution II. Informal consultations were held and explanations were offered regarding the procedure that was followed and the parameters to be employed to determine the equivalence of the sites and, most important, whether the information offered by the pioneer investors was sufficient in order to allow the Group of Technical Experts to do its work. The conclusions arrived at by the experts on the basis of the current level of perspecting were, in the view of the Group of 77, sufficient only to determine which sites were preferred by the pioneer investors.

Given this situation, the developing countries proposed that the pioneer investors pay a compensation, should the sites of the Authority be of an inferior commercial value once they were exploited in comparison with those of the registered pioneer investors. Finally, before registration could take place, the Group of 77 wanted to include the list of obligations in the decision of registration, in order to reinforce the fact that resolution II, while granting rights of an exclusive nature, also imposed some obligations which had to be fulfilled. This concern of the Group of 77 was a portent of future problems with regard to the question of obligations. Finally, on 17 December 1987, the registration of the first four applicants as pioneer investors took place and the corresponding certificates were issued.

At the start of the sixth session, in 1988, the Preparatory Commission was going to concentrate its work on the question of obligations. These obligations are contained in resolution II and the New York Understanding. When the moment arrived to discuss this question, the pioneer investors proposed the need to determine criteria, specific terms and conditions that should be established for the compliance of the obligations. In their view, changed economic and political conditions made this necessary. As an example, they pointed out, on the economic side, the depressed state of the price of metals and the prospect that they will remain so in the future. On the political side, it was argued that some major countries, which are potential operators, have not signed the Convention and did not appear to be in a position to adhere to it at this stage, which meant that their absence would make it practically impossible to create and efficiently operate the Enterprise.

Furthermore, it was also said by pioneer investors, who came at the surprise of the Group of 77, that their request for registration was not guided by the purposes of obtaining benefit in the short term. The main reason, in their view, for doing so was a desire to strengthen the Convention. Under this presentation, they proceeded to explain their interpretation of the obligations, which is essentially to waiver the obligation of the payment of the fixed fee of one million dollars and to fulfill the rest in accordance with the speed of their own work in their respective sites. In their proposal, they included a two stage plan for the exploration of the site of the Enterprise. The Group of 77 reacted in a negative way to this approach which had never been mentioned prior to registration, and did not agree to it. The developing countries insisted that the obligations be fulfilled as they were established in resolution II and the New York Agreement. This meant that the fixed fee of one million dollars had to be paid as of the date of registration and that there was some obligation such as training that had to be carried out as soon as registration had taken place.

In the light of these developments, the Chairman of the Commission took it upon himself to try to bridge the gap by making some informal proposals, and the Group of Technical Experts was convened again and requested to draw a comprehensive plan for the early stages of exploration of the mine site of the Enterprise and to take up the question of training. The Group of Technical Experts produced two reports on these questions, which assisted the Commission in its work towards an agreed solution. The report of the Group regarding the exploration of the site of the Authority divides the explorations into a preparatory phase, into two stages, the last one of which would include work at sea. It is estimated that the preparatory phase would take about six months and cost about 150,000 dollars. It would take two to three years to carry out Stage I at a cost of seven to nine million dollars, whereas Stage II would take some more years and its costs were estimated in the order of 35 - 40 million dollars. The total duration of Stages I and II is estimated to be seven to 10 years. With regard to training, the Preparatory Commission had agreed upon a set of principles, policies and procedures for the training program for personnel of the Enterprise to be carried out in the context of pioneer activities. It calls upon for the establishment of a 15 member panel to administer the programme.

While progress was being made on most of the obligations, the problem of the one million dollars remained outstanding, since the Group of 77 insisted that it was a clear, well known obligation contained in resolution II, that had to be fulfilled, while the registered pioneer investors argued that the reasons for establishing the obligation had changed considerably, ignoring the fact that the obligation remained and that it was part of the package that included the rights that were granted to them. They maintained that it was difficult to accept such a financial burden in the light of current sea-bed activity, which in their view was practically non-existent and without a clear deadline for the obligation to cease. The fact of the matter is that the registered pioneer investors did not want to fulfill this obligation which is contained in resolution II.

The issue was not resolved during the 1989 session, although some informal proposals were made that this fixed fee be used by the registered pioneer investors in the exploration of the mine site of the Authority. These proposals did not gather a sufficient basis for consensus. The spring session of 1990 proved to be slightly more successful in the sense that considerable progress was made regarding all outstanding issues of the obligations. It is to be hoped that during the summer session, this issue can be resolved in the context of all the obligations so that the implementation of resolution II can be concluded.

My final comments will be that, although many conclusions can be drawn from this long process, it is a major achievement which, nevertheless, changed resolution II. I will highlight only two of them:

— allowing the registered pioneer investors to select their own site constitutes a fundamental change to resolution II. This modification could bring into question whether the objectives pursued by resolution II have been attained, particularly with regard to the commitment of providing the Enterprise with an adequate site for its operations and its consequences for the *common heritage of mankind*;

— on the other side of the coin, the exercise of implementation of resolution II has demonstrated a unique capacity to look for solutions to practical problems that were encountered and not foreseen by the drafters of the resolution. This approach could be of use in the future as an instrument to solve the problems that are impairing the universal acceptance of the Convention.

Decision-making in the Council: An Assessment and Comparison

Rüdiger Wolfrum*

I. Introduction

Decision-making in international organizations is a complex process which is more than voting upon a given proposal in accordance with a prescribed voting system. A decision-making process obtains its particular characteristics through the rules on the composition of the respective organ, its voting procedure, the attribution of the right to initiate proposals and the relationship between the various organs participating in the making of a given decision. Any decision of an international organization has to balance the interests of the member States in respect of given issues or — in other words — is the result of an integration of different State oriented intentions or expectations to a common volition. Thus, the rules on decision-making have to reflect the character of the decisions to be taken and have to be modelled so as to allow the reception of the interests of all the States involved. A decision-making process resulting merely in the passing of recommendations, such as the resolutions of the General Assembly of the United Nations may, and even will have to be differently structured compared to that of an international organization having law-making or re-distributive (not rather distributive) functions. With respect to the latter, it is mandatory that the decision-making process is open for the reception of all interests involved and does not exclude the consideration of a particular one at the forefield. The differentiation between the various decision-making processes is legitimated through the principle of efficiency.[1] It is inevitable that within a decision-making organ with re-distributive functions, not only the receiving but also the donating States must be represented. Thus, any attempt to transfer the rules on decision-making of an organ with re-distributive powers such as the Board of Governors of the International Bank for Reconstruction and Development (World Bank) or of the Governing Council of the International Fund for Agricultural Development upon an organ with law-making or recommendatory functions and *vice versa* simply ignores the preconditions flowing from the interrelationship between the

---

* Prof. Dr. *Rüdiger Wolfrum*, Institute of International Law, University of Kiel.

1 *Robert E. Riggs/Jack C. Plano*, The United Nations: International Organization and World Politics, Chicago 1988.

structure of the decision-making process and the character of the decisions to be made.

As most international organizations must decide upon issues of a different character, various organs with different rules on decision-making have been set up. In the more recent treaties establishing an international organization, such as in the United Nations Industrial Development Organization, some issues can only be decided upon together by two or more organs each having a different decision-making structure.[2] This is especially true with respect to the International Sea-Bed Authority. Its functions have been divided between the Assembly and the Council as well as the Commissions of the Council, particularly the Legal and Technical Commission. There are, however, and this is a specific feature of the International Sea-Bed Authority, quite a number of questions which can only be decided upon by two organs, one having the right of initiative, the other one having the right of final decision.[3]

This presentation is limited to the decision-making process of the Council of the International Sea-Bed Authority. It will focus upon the following viewpoints: description of the respective rules of the United Nations Convention on the Law of the Sea; their evaluation as to which extent they seem appropriate to integrate the various interests involved with deep sea-bed activities[4] taking into account similar rules of other international organizations to the extent the functions of the respective organs can be compared with the ones entrusted to the Council. Upon this background, I shall try to fathom the various options offered by the provisions of the UN Law of the Sea Convention for a further structuring of the decision-making process of the Council with the view to accommodating some of the critiques voiced against the system established by art. 161.[5]

---

2 Articles 9, para. 4 (a) and (e),; 14 para. 2; 15; 18; Constitution of the United Nations Industrial Development Organization, United Nations Conference on the Establishment of the Industrial Development Organization as a specialized agency, UN doc. A/Conf. 90/19 of 8 April 1979.

3 For example, the establishment of a system of compensation of economic adjustment assistance involves the Economic Planning Commission, the Council and the Assembly (arts. 164, para. 2 (d); 162, para. 2 (n); 160, para. 2 (l); 151, para. 10); the adoption of the rules, regulations and procedures involves the Council and the Assembly (arts. 162, para. 2 (o) (ii); 160, para. 2 (f) (ii)).

4 Decisions having a budgetary implication are separately dealt with by *Klaus Dicke*'s presentation and the paper prepared by the UN Office for Ocean Affairs and the Law of the Sea (in this Vol.).

5 United States Delegation Report, Eleventh Session of the Third United Nations Conference on the Law of the Sea, New York, March 8 - April 30, 1982, app. H. It was argued that the International Sea-Bed Authority failed to give a proportionate voice to the nations most affected by decisions.

II. Composition and Decision-making in the Council according to Article 161

1. Composition

The Council shall consist of 36 members elected by the Assembly among the members of the Authority, according to the rules set out by art. 161[6] which are supplemented by rules of procedure of the Assembly of the International Sea-Bed Authority.[7] The composition of the Council is based upon two conflicting principles, namely the principle of equitable geographic representation and the principle of the representation of special interests. Both principles are used in international organizations for the composition of limited membership-organs. For example, the composition of the Economic and Social Council of the United Nations is governed by the principle of geographic representation. Representation on the basis of special interests has only recently become a frequent feature of executive organs of international organizations. The composition of the executive organs of the International Civil Aviation Organization (ICAO), the International Maritime Organization (IMO), the International Atomic Energy Agency (IAEA), the United Nations Industrial Development Organization and of the Common Fund of Commodities, among others, is based upon the representation of certain interests.[8] In the ICAO Council, States of chief importance in air transport and States which make the largest contribution to the provision of facilities for international civil air navigation are entitled to appropriate representation.[9] The Council of the IMO is composed of representatives of States with the largest interests in providing an international shipping service, or with the largest interests in maritime transport or navigation.[10] The members of the Governing Board of IAEA are representatives of the most advanced States in technology of atomic energy, and the members most advanced in nuclear technology in North America, Latin America, Western Europe, Eastern Europe, Africa, the Middle East and South Asia, South East Asia and the Pacific, and the Far East.[11] In the international

---

6 The legislative history of art. 161 is decribed by *Kathryn E. Yost*, The International Sea-Bed Authority Decision-Making Process: Does it give a Proportionate Voice to the Participant's Interests in Deep Sea Mining, in: San Diego Law Review 20 (1983), 659-678.

7 UN doc. LOS/PCN/WP. 20/Rev. 2 of 25 March 1988.

8 For a general evaluation of international organizations in this respect *see: Werner J. Feld/Peter S. Jordan*, International Organizations: A Comparative Approach, New York 1983, 133.

9 Article 50 of the Convention on International Civil Aviation, UNTS, Vol. 15, No. 102 as amended.

10 Article 17 of the IMO-Convention, UNTS, Vol. 289, No. 4214 as amended.

11 Article IV, para. A, No. 1 of the Statute of the IAEA as amended in 1984. The amendment has still not been ratified by the required two-thirds majority of the agency's membership, but in 1984 it was agreed that the board would start acting as if it had entered into force.

financial institutions such as the World Bank, the International Fund for Agricultural Development (IFAD) and the International Monetary Fund, members with the largest number of shares are assured representation in the executive organs. This is achieved through different techniques. Most interesting in this respect is the Governing Council and the Executive Board of the International Fund for Agricultural Development. Each member of the Fund is represented on the Governing Council, in which all the powers of the Fund are vested. The total number of votes in the council is 1800, distributed equally among the three categories of member States (category I: members belonging to OECD; category II: members belonging to OPEC; category III: other developing States). The distribution of the votes within the membership categories is left to the categories themselves. Category III allocates its 600 votes equally among its members, while categories I and II allocate only 17.5 per cent and 25 per cent, respectively of their votes on an equal basis. The remainder is shared in proportion to the members' contributions.

The procedure for the election of members of the Council of the International Sea-Bed Authority is quite complicated. It, together with the decision-making procedure, was among the most controversial issues of the Third UN Conference on the Law of the Sea. Article 161, para. 1 identifies four different interest groups which have to be represented in the Council. Four members must belong to those States Parties which have either consumed more than 2 per cent of total world consumption or have net imports of more than 2 per cent of total world imports of the commodities produced from categories of minerals to be derived from the Area. Among this consumer group one State from the Eastern European (Socialist) region as well as the largest consumer have a guaranteed seat. Four members which belong to the eight States Parties having made the largest investment in preparation for and in the conduct of activities in the Area form the second group. This investor group again has to contain at least one State from the Eastern European (Socialist) region. Another four members of the Council represent those States Parties which are major net exporters of the categories of minerals to be derived from the Area. The group has to include at least two developing States whose exports of such minerals have a substantial bearing upon their economies. The fourth interest group consists of six developing States Parties representing special interests.[12]

The other half of the members of the Council, however, are not elected so as to represent special interests, but according to the principle of equitable geographical representation. However, not the 18 seats under this category have to be distributed according to this principle, instead through the distribution of these seats an equitable geographical distribution of the seats in the Council *as a whole*

---

[12] These special interests include large populations, nations which are land-locked or have short coastlines, major importers of the minerals to be derived from the Area, potential producers of such minerals, and least developed States.

shall be reached. The application of such system has as a result that the overrepresentation of a given regional group under one or all special interest categories lowers the share of that very regional group under the principle of geographical distribution. Article 161, para. 1 (e), however, contains a safeguard clause in this respect. Each geographical region has at least one guaranteed seat under this rule.[13] Theoretically, this clause may lead to an overrepresentation of States Parties of one regional group.

According to art. 161, para. 2 (c) nominations are to be submitted to the Assembly by the group of States Parties to be represented in the Council. The Assembly proceeds to elect members for each category according to the order in which they are listed in art. 161, para. 1. The rôle of the Assembly, in this respect, is rather limited. It may only confirm the proposals made by the respective groups of the States Parties.[14] Contrary to the procedures concerning the appointment of the Secretary-General and the election of the members of the Governing Board, who are elected by the Assembly "from among the candidates proposed by the Council" or "upon the recommendation of the Council" (art. 160, para. 2 (b) and (c)), for the election of the members of the Council there is no list from which the Assembly could make a selection or a recommendation which the Assembly may or may not endorse. With respect to the election of the members of the Council, the Assembly merely has the power to rubberstamp the nominations made by the groups of States identified in art. 161.[15]

The term "group of States Parties" as used in art. 161, para. 2 (e) embraces the interest groups referred to in art. 161, para. 1 (a) to (d) as well as the regional groups listed in art. 161, para. 1 (e). Hence, for the determination of the electorate and the eligible States Parties the exact definition of the interest groups is of utmost importance. Unfortunately, the definition of the interest groups given in the Convention is all but precise. In respect of the consumer group (art. 161, para. 1 (a)) it is not clear whether the 2 per cent figure used in the above mentioned paragraph refers to any one commodity or an average of all commodities, whether the respective calculations should be made on the basis of the metal-value or on the basis of the amount of consumption. Further, the consumption of a metal can be measured at a number of points of its conversion. The

---

13 The geographical regions shall be Africa, Asia, Eastern European (Socialist), Latin America and Western European and Others.

14 *Felipe H. Paolillo*, The Institutional Arrangements for the International Sea-Bed and their Impact on the Evolution of International Organizations, in: Recueil des Cours 188 (1984/V), 135-338 (246); *Rüdiger Wolfrum*, Die Internationalisierung staatsfreier Räume, Berlin/Heidelberg/New York/Tokio 1984, 547.

15 This issue has been discussed contoversially in the Preparatory Commission for the International Sea-Bed Authority and for the International Tribunal for the Law of the Sea. The draft rules of procedure of the Assembly of the International Sea-Bed Authority (UN doc. LOS/PCN/WP. 20/Rev. 2) contain a bracket in draft rule 95 (97) which indicates that the elections of the Assembly should be made from among candidates proposed by the groups only.

mode of calculation is especially important for the identification of the major consumer. As to the exporter group art. 161, para. 1 (c) only speaks of the major net exporters and refrains from defining such term. It is questionable as to whether a share greater than 2 per cent of world exports already would qualify as a major net exporter. Here again, it still needs to be established whether the respective calculation should be based upon one mineral or an average thereof. All these points have to be clarified through the rules of procedure of the Assembly to be prepared by the Preparatory Commission. The present draft rules of procedure of the Assembly[16] restrict themselves to simply reiterating the words of the Convention.

Given the uncertainties explained, it is difficult to make a prognosis as to the future composition of the Council at present.[17] The estimates vary, mostly it has been assumed that the Western European States would get seven[18] or eight seats,[19] the Eastern European (Socialist) States two and the developing countries nine or eight seats distributed under the categories of art. 161, para. 1 (a) - (d). The number of seats each of these groups would receive under the principle of equitable geographical distrubution depends upon the formula used. Different formulas are used in this respect by the United Nations. Proceeding on the basis of the ratio enshrined in the resolution of the General Assembly 33/138 of 19 December 1978 for the distribution of the seats of the Vice-Presidents in the General Assembly, the Western European States may claim eight, the Eastern European (Socialist) three and the developing countries 25 out of the 36 seats of the Council. On the basis of the assumption that the Western European States will obtain seven and the Eastern European (Socialist) States two seats under the special interest principle both groups would, together with their assured one seat under art. 161 para. 1 (e), reach the appropriate number of seats. If, however, the Western European States would gain already eight seats under the special interest formula this group would then receive nine seats. For the composition of the Economic and Social Council a different formula was used.[20] According to this formula, the Western European States may claim nine, the Eastern European (Socialist) States four and the developing countries 23 seats in the Council.

---

16 UN doc. LOS/PCN/WP. 20/Rev. 2 of 25 March 1988.

17 The composition of the Council will equally depend upon which States have ratified the Convention on the Law of the Sea or have acceded thereto. It may happen that not all the seats for special interest groups may be filled properly. According to art. 161, para. 2 (c) these seats will not remain vacant.

18 *Wolfrum* (note 14), 551.

19 *Paolillo* (note 14), 241; *Bernard H. Oxman*, The Third United Nations Conference on the Law of the Sea: the Ninth Session (1980), in: AJIL 75 (1981), 211-256 (218/219); *Yost* (note 6), 673.

20 GA res. 2847 (XXVI) of 20 December 1971; the pattern for the geographical distribution of seats by this resolution for the 54-member council is as follows: 14 members from African States, 11 from Asian States, 10 from Latin American and Caribbean States, 13 from Western European States, 6 from Eastern European States.

Finally, one should mention in this context the formula used for the elections to the Industrial Development Board since art. 9 of the Constitution of the UNIDO expressly refers to the principle of equitable geographical distribution.[21] Using this formula for the Council would give the developing countries 23, the Western European States ten and the Eastern European (Socialist) States three seats in the Council.

In summarizing, it has to be stated that the notion of equitable geographical distribution is used differently in the United Nations.[22] Thus, this term used in the context of the composition of the Council needs further specification in the rules of procedure of the Assembly.

In spite of the uncertainties mentioned, it is to be expected that the Western European States will occupy between eight and ten, the Eastern European (Socialist) Countries between three and four and the developing countries between 25 and 21 seats of the Council. Thus, the group of developing countries will have at any case a two-thirds, but not a three-fourths majority. These figures are, however, no reliable indicator as to the future voting. It cannot be taken for granted that all members of the given geographical groups pursue the same objective. It is hard to say at present which States will endorse deep sea-bed mining and which States will object thereto. One may assume, however, that the States elected into the Council as consumers and investors will be in favour, whereas the members of the group of exporters are more likely to restrict deep sea-bed activities.

2. Voting System

The Council has no uniform voting system. Instead, the Convention distinguishes between different issues, each with a separate voting system. There are at least five different categories. For the adoption of decisions falling within the first category, namely questions of procedures, the rule of the simple majority of members present and voting will be applied (art. 161, para. 8 (a)).[23] However, there are some exceptions to this rule. The request for advisory opinions (art. 191) or the establishment of subsidiary organs (art. 162, para. 2 (d)), mostly qualified as mere procedural questions, are considered questions of substance in the Convention and require higher majorities, accordingly.

Decisions on all matters belonging to the second category of questions will have to be adopted by a two-thirds majority of members present and voting,

21 The Industrial Development Board consists of 53 members elected by the General Conference, of which 33 are to be from developing countries, 15 from the developed market economy countries and 5 from centrally-planned economy countries.

22 Another formula is used for the distribution of the non-permanent seats of the Security Council (GA res. 1991 (XVIII) of 17 December 1963).

23 Draft Rules of Procedure of the Council (UN doc. LOS/PCN/WP. 26/ Rev. 2, 30 June 1988, Rule 52 (52) just reiterates the wording of the Convention.

provided that such majority includes a majority of the members of the Council (art. 161, para. 8 (b)).[24] Due to the distribution of seats already described, these decisions can be made by the group of developing States alone. This second category embraces decisions pertaining to a small group of questions of substance, most of which are related to the reporting or controlling of functions of the Council or to its recommendatory powers. Apart from that, this category includes the entering into agreements with the United Nations or other international organizations; the review of the collection of payments to be made by or to the Authority; the recommendation of measures to be taken in the case of non-compliance; and the adoption of directives for the Enterprise. Other matters within this category are the formulation of recommendations with respect to the compensation system or other economic adjustments in favour of developing countries affected by production from the Area and requests for advisory opinions.

Most of the decisions on questions of substance belong to the third category for which a three-fourths majority of the members present and voting is required, including a majority of members of the Council. These questions may not be decided upon by the group of developing States alone. Instead, the co-operation of two groups is required. The respective questions include the formulation of recommendations concerning the general policies and the adoption of the specific policies of the Authority, the supervision and co-ordination of the application of Part XI; the proposal of candidates for the election of the Secretary-General of the Authority, the Members of the Governing Board and the Director-General of the Enterprise; the establishment of subsidiary organs; the submission of the annual budget of the Authority; the selection of applicants for production authorizations; the institution of proceedings before the Sea-Bed Dispute Chamber; the issuance of emergency orders; the disapproval of proposed areas for exploitation; the increase in the number of members of the commissions of the Council; functions related to the the financing of the Enterprise and loans to the Authority.

The fourth category embraces questions to be decided upon by consensus. The Convention is the first international agreement containing a definition of consensus (art. 161, para. 8 (e))[25] which is described as the "absence of any

---

[24] *Loc. cit.*, Rule 53 (53).

[25] *See also* Rules of Procedure of the Council (note 23), Rule 57 (57). Definitions of consensus may be found in other instruments such as the Final Declaration of the Preparatory Meeting for the Conference on International Co-operation where it is stated that consensus is the principle "according to which decisions and recommendations are adopted when the Chair has established that no member delegation has made any objections" (UN doc. A/C. 2/299 of 27 October 1975) or the recommendation annexed to the provisional rules of procedure of the World Population Conference, where it is stated that consensus is understood to mean "according to United Nations Practice, a general agreement without a vote, but not necessarily unanimity" (UN doc. E/CONF. 60/2). *See Erik Suy*, The Meaning of Consensus in Multilateral Diplomacy, in: *Robert J. Akkerman/Peter J. van Krieken/Charles O. Pannenborg* (eds.), Declarations on Principles — a Quest for Universal Peace, Leyden 1977, 259-274; *Paolillo* (note 14), 236.

formal objection." Generally speaking, the notion of consensus refers to two different procedures. Either the formal objection results in the rejection of the proposal to be decided upon or the formal objection only delays the decision which may be taken later by a majority vote. The consequences of the two procedures are quite different as far as the conduct of negotiations, the decision-making process and the protection of minority groups are concerned. The rules of procedure of the Third United Nations Conference on the Law of the Sea followed the latter,[26] the Convention the former approach.

According to art. 161, para. 8 (e) within fourteen days of the submission to the Council of a proposal the President of the Council has to determine whether there might be a formal objection and if so he has to establish and convene a conciliation committee. It is the purpose of such committee to reconcile the differences and to prepare a proposal which can be adopted by consensus. If the committee fails, the grounds upon which the proposal is opposed must be spelled out in a report to the Council, and then the proposed decision is rejected. There is no possibility to proceed now to majority voting. This procedure makes a co-operation between all members of the Council mandatory as each of them has the possibility to block the respective decisions of the Council. The consensus procedure is applied for the decision of the following questions: recommendation, adoption and provisional application of rules, regulations and procedures which will constitute the indispensable legal means to implement the provisions of the Convention and Annex III,[27] the adoption of measures for the protection of developing States against adverse economic effects resulting from the exploitation of the resources of the Area,[28] the adoption of amendments to Part XI,[29] the disapproval of a plan of work whose approval has been recommended by the Legal and Technical Commission and the determination of the majority required for the adoption of decisions on subjects not listed in art. 161, para. 2 which the Council is authorized to take.[30] The Council may also use consensus in some cases where it is doubtful which majority rule applies to a determined question.[31]

This list of questions to be decided by consensus looks quite impressive. However, account has to be taken of the following facts: The rules, regulations and procedures have to be prepared by the Preparatory Commission already and will be in place when the Law of the Sea Convention enters into force and the organs of the International Sea-Bed Authority assume their activities. Hence, the necessity to reach consensus in this respect protects the interests of each single State or group of States as much as it protects the respective rules from amendment

---

26 Articles 37 and 39.

27 Article 161, para. 8 (d) in connection with art. 162, para. 2 (o).

28 Article 161, para. 8 (d) in connection with art. 162, para. 2 (m) and art. 150 (h).

29 Article 161, para. 8 (d).

30 Article 161, para. 8 (d) and (f), art. 162, para. 2 (j) (i), last sentence.

31 Article 161, para. 8 (g).

afterwards. In any case, the restriction that such rules may only be amended by consensus is quite logical since the Preparatory Commission itself will have to pass such rules, regulations and procedures by consensus. The functions of the Council under art. 162, para. 2 (m) — protection from adverse economic effects of deep sea-bed activities — are limited. The establishment of an economic adjustment system according to art. 162, para. 2 (n), however, is decided upon by the Assembly upon the recommendation of the Council. Such recommendation as well as the decision in the Assembly only need a two-thirds majority, which means that the respective decisions may be taken by the developing States alone. The necessity that amendments to Part XI may only be taken by consensus loses some of its relevance through the fact that the Review Conference according to art. 155 may alter Part XI and the relevant Annexes by a three-fourths majority.[32]

The approval of plans of work constitute the fifth and last category of questions for which a special decisions-making procedure has been established. It ensures the automatic approval of such plans of work which fulfill certain requirements.[33] However, such approval does not contain a production authorization which needs a separate decision of the Council requiring a three-fourths majority.[34]

The plan of work is first examined by the Legal and Technical Commission which submits it to the Council together with its recommendations. These recommendations shall be solely based on the grounds stated in Annex III, art. 4 in connection with art. 6, para. 2 (b) which is meant to exclude considerations of a political or economic nature or concerning the general policy of the Authority or otherwise not directly related to the administrative, legal and technical matters referred to in Annex III.[35] It is recommendable to introduce a formulation into the rules of procedure of the Legal and Technical Commission which reiterates this important aspect.

The plan of work positively recommended to the Council by the Legal and Technical Commission shall be deemed to have been approved if no member of the Council has submitted in writing to the President of the Council within

32 In this respect *see Kiderlen*'s presentation in this Vol.

33 It is quite questionable as to whether the decision-making procedure of art. 162, para. 2 (j) are to be read as if the plans of work were elaborated unilaterally by the applicant and only needed to be rubber-stamped by the Authority. Article 153, para. 3 as well as Annex III, art. 3, para. 5 indicate that a plan of work shall be negotiated between the applicant and the Authority. A reference to such negotiations is equally contained in Annex III, art. 13, para. 1 dealing with the financial terms of contracts. Finally, art. 187 (d) refers to disputes between the Authority and an applicant concerning a legal issue arising in the negotiation of a contract. This again is a problem which needs to be solved through the rules of procedure.

34 Articles 151, para. 3, 162, para. 2 (q) in connection with art. 161, para. 8 (c); *Paolillo* (note 14), 237 rightly points out that the automatic approval was only accepted from the developing countries under the condition that it would not embrace a production authorization.

35 *Paolillo* (note 14), 239.

the 14 days a specific objection alleging non-compliance with the requirements of Annex III, art. 6. If such an objection is lodged, the conciliation procedure provided for to overcome an objection against a consensus decision must be applied. However, even if the attempt for conciliation fails and the objection persists, the plan of work will still be deemed to have been approved by the Council unless disapproved by consensus among the Council's members, excluding the State or States making the application or sponsoring the applicant.[36] If, finally, the Legal and Technical Commission recommends the proposed plan of work to be disapproved or if it makes no recommendation, the Council may still approve the plan by a three-fourths majority of the members present and voting, provided that such a majority includes the majority of the members participating in the session.[37]

It is obvious that in the context of this decision-making procedure the composition of the Legal and Technical Commission as well as the decision-making procedure for the adoption of its recommendations is quite crucial. Nevertheless, the Convention is not very explicit as far as these two issues are concerned. According to art. 163, para. 2 - 3 and art. 165, para. 1 the members of the Legal and Technical Commission shall have appropriate qualifications as to technical, scientific, ecological, legal or other relevant matters. Additionally, due account shall be taken of the need for equitable geographical distribution and the representation of special interests.[38] In respect of the voting procedure of the Legal and Technical Commission the Third United Nations Conference on the Law of the Sea was unable to reach an agreement. This question has to be dealt with by the rules, regulations and procedures to be issued by the Council and the Assembly.[39] From a methodical point of view it is quite surprising that the Third United Nations Conference on the Law of the Sea provided for detailed rules concerning the composition and the voting procedure of the Council whereas the same issues in respect of the Legal and Technical Commission, an organ which dominates one crucial type of decisions, namely the approval of plans of work, was left for the future.

The Draft Rules of Procedure of the Legal and Technical Commission[40] provide that decisions on questions of substance shall be taken by a two-thirds majority of the members present and voting. However, before a matter of substance is put to the vote, the Commission shall make every effort to reach agreement on such matters by way of consensus.

---

36 Article 162, para. 2 (j) (i), the same rules apply for the plans of work submitted by the Enterprise, art. 161, para. 2 (k).

37 Article 162, para. 2 (j) (ii); *Paolillo* (note 14), 239, note 121, points out that this provision is inconsistent with the fact that the Council has to be regarded as a permanently meeting organ.

38 Article 163, para. 4.

39 Article 163, para. 11.

40 UN doc. LOS/PCN/WP. 31/Rev. 2 of 30 June 1988, Rule 41 (40).

It is quite questionable, whether the introduction in this part of the decison-making process of the two-thirds majority principle and the demand to reach consensus is adequate given the nature of the decisions to be taken.

As to the last category of questions to be decided by the Council one has to summarize that the regulations of the Law of the Sea Convention are not yet complete. Above all, the composition of the Technical and Legal Commission as well as its rules on decision-making need further specification through the respective rules of procedure.

III. Assessment and Conclusion

1. Evaluation and Assessment

In evaluating the decision-making procedure of the Council it has to be stated that the respective rules are not yet complete. This provides the Preparatory Commission with a significant amount of flexibility which should be used to increase the acceptability of the Convention. The required supplementation of the Convention has to be achieved through the rules of procedure of the Assembly, the Council and the respective Commissions all to be prepared by the Preparatory Commission. In spite of being incomplete, the rules of the Convention concerning decision-making in the Council meet the criteria mentioned at the beginning. Above all, the rules on decision-making are differentiated enough to accommodate the requirements of the various types of decisions to be made. Especially, recommendations and decisions on general policies are decided on the basis of the well established two-thirds majority rule while no account has been taken of special interest groups. The principle of equitable geographical representation as well as the principle of a representation of special interests have been combined and thus both have been mitigated.

The system on the composition of the Council results in the establishment of a two level system. Whereas the geographical groups will be represented within the Council in more or less the same way as they are represented in the limited membership organs of the United Nations, the composition of each group of representatives will be based upon the special interests principle. This approach is quite innovative and an achievement to the established rules of decision-making in international organizations. It follows and further develops the principles set by the International Atomic Energy Agency, the United Nations Industrial Development Organization and, especially, the International Fund for Agricultural Development and the Common Fund for Commodities. This approach should not be seen under the point of view of a protection of special interests alone but rather as a means to secure the parity among the regional groups, too. The regional groups have to be seen as the first level where a clearance and integration of the States' intentions can be sought and achieved. In this respect regional groups play an important rôle in the preparation of the decision-making in the various organs of international organizations. Such integrational effect is achieved due to the existence of common interests and organizational ties developed outside of the international organizations.[41]

The representation of special interests, instead, is based upon a different line of thinking. It proceeds from the conviction that the entering into force and the enforceability of international law in general, which also includes acts of international organizations, largely depends upon the involvement and the endorsement of the respective act or rule by the State or States affected.[42] In the past, developing States have objected to the inclusion of special interest groups in the decision-making process of international organizations to the extent that this resulted in a privileged position for a small group of States. This objection was first voiced in the declaration of the Group of 77 at UNCTAD I[43] and was later articulated in the Declaration of the United Nations concerning the Establishment of a New International Economic Order.[44] The Charter of the Economic Rights and Duties of States[45] speaks of an equal participation of all States in the decision-making process, as the consequence of the equal sovereignty of States. This position, however, has been modified since the developing States accepted the principle of group parity which combines the representation of special interests with the principle of equitable geographical distribution for the composition of the Industrial Development Board and of the Governing Council as well as for the Executive Board of IFAD. After all the composition of the Council represents a compromise and thus should be, in general, acceptable to all groups of States.

The voting procedure of the Council seems to form, generally speaking, a viable basis for an integration of the various interests connected with deep seabed activities. It makes a co-operation between the groups necessary since most decisions on matters of substance need the approval of a three-fourths majority or are taken by consensus, although the need for co-operation could be further strengthened through the rules of procedure for the Council. Consensus decisions require the co-operation of all groups. Decisions to be taken by a three-fourths majority cannot be passed by the group of the developing countries alone, this group needs the co-operation of another group, or, according to the formula applied, even the co-operation from the members of two other groups. Neverthe-

---

41 *See Riggs/Plano* (note 1), 79.

42 *Rüdiger Wolfrum*, Neue Elemente im Willensbildungsprozeß internationaler Wirtschaftsorganisationen: Strukturelle Neuerungen in den Satzungen von IFAD, UNIDO and Gemeinsamer Rohstofffonds, in: Vereinte Nationen 29 (1981), 50-56 (52).

43 Proceedings, vol. I, Final Act and Report (UN-Doc. E/Conf. 46/141) para. 6, this plea was reiterated frequently, *see Wolfrum* (note 42), 52.

44 A/Res. 3201 (S-VI) of 1 May 1974, para. 4 c; A/Res./3202 (S-VI) sec. II 1 (d) and IX; for further details *see Marthinus G. Erasmus*, The New International Economic Order and International Organizations, Frankfurt am Main 1979, 143 *et seq.*

45 GA res. 3281 (XXIX) of 12 December 1974, art. 10.

less, the position of the group of developing States is, at least theoretically, quite dominant since the two other groups, even acting together, cannot pass any decision without the endorsement of the developing States. It is the result of the decison-making procedure of the Council that the group of Western European States and the group of Eastern European (Socialist) States acting together have a relevant negative voting power since they may block any decision on matters of substance to be decided by a three-fourths majority, however, they have no equivalent positive voting power. For the passing of decisions on matters of substance they are totally dependent upon the co-operation of the developing States.

This bi-polarization, developing States *versus* other States, however, may oversimplify the situation within the Council. Any question related to the production of minerals in the Area will align States according to certain economic, environmental and other interests disregarding regional or political groupings. It is more likely that new groups of States will join together — land-based producer States, sea-bed miners, potential producers, consumers, producers of technology, environmentally concerned States — and thus the traditional political and geographic alignments will be altered.[46] More attention should, hence, be paid to the question as to whether the decison-making process of the Council is properly balanced in this respect.

2. Suggestions

On this basis it seems to be possible to formulate some suggestions with the view to fill the already mentioned lacunae in the rules on decision-making in the Council. The existing lacunae are the following: The Convention does not define the method for an identification of special interest groups nor does it, despite the fact that different lists exist in this respect, define which States will belong to the group of developing States. Further, the rules of procedure of the Assembly have to specify the exact ratio on the basis of which seats shall be distributed in accordance with the principle of equitable geographical distribution. Finally, the decision-making procedure in the Legal and Technical Commission needs to be regulated. This is equally true in respect of the other Commissions.

As to the composition of the Council, the rules of procedure of the Assembly should provide for the setting up of a list identifying the consumer and importer States having consumed or imported more than 2 per cent of total world consumption of commodities produced from the categories of minerals to be derived from the Area. Such list should be revised in regular intervals. It is equally necessary to provide for lists identifying the eight main investor States, the main exporting States, the developing States and the States representing special interests among the group of developing States.[47] The establishment of such lists is not uncommon.

---

[46] *Paollilo* (note 14), 242.

Further, the rules of procedure of the Assembly will have to spell out the ratio according to which the equitable geographical distribution of the seats of the Council as a whole will be calculated. In this respect one should resort to the ratio used for the composition of the Industrial Development Board.

Finally, the rules of procedure of the Assembly should properly reflect that the electoral power of the Assembly concerning the composition of the Council is limited as the nomination is made by the members of the respective groups of States in the Council. Due to the delicate balance achieved among the special interest groups as well as the regional groups the proper implementation is crucial for the functioning of the decision-making process within the Council.

As to the Legal and Technical Commission the following suggestions can be made: Although the composition of the Legal and Technical Commission has not been exactly determined by art. 163, para. 2 - 3 and art. 165, para. 1, these rules, and especially the functions vested in this Commission in accordance with art. 165, para. 2 (b) and art. 4 and 6 of Annex III clearly indicate that the Legal and Technical Commission is meant to reflect competence rather than equitable geographical representation. Thus, the composition of this Commission should not mirror the composition of the Council. Such composition of the Legal and Technical Commission would run counter to the objectives pursued by the Convention with the establishment of these two organs. As such competence will mainly be found in the groups of investor and consumer States these should have a decisive influence upon the selection of the members of the Commission.[48] It would be one possibility to provide the investor and consumer group with a respective right to nominate candidates for that Commission.

Additionally, it seems to be necessary to strengthen the position of the members of the Legal and Technical Commission as experts. Its rules of procedure should contain a rule stating that the members of the Commission shall exercise their functions as independent experts, in the general interest of all States Parties to the Convention and that, in the exercise of their function, they shall neither seek nor accept instructions from any government or any other source.

Equally, it is necessary that the rules of procedure of the Legal and Technical Commission implement clearly how the Legal and Technical Commission is to perform its functions in accordance with art. 165, para. 2 (b), second sentence. It has to be spelled out that when considering a plan of work under art. 6, para. 2 (b) of Annex III, the Commission shall ascertain the requisite qualification of the applicant solely on criteria related to the financial and technical capabilities

---

[47] UN doc. LOS/PCN/SCN. 1/1989/CRP. 18 constitutes a first attempt in this respect. It tries to identify the land-based producer States possibly to be affected by sea-bed activities.

[48] The Draft Rules of Procedure of the Council (note 23) just reiterate the provisions of the Convention; respective suggestions have been made in UN doc. LOS/PCN/WP. 33 of 25 March 1986.

of the applicant as they have been defined by the Council, and, as the case may be, on his performance under a previous contract with the Authority.

Finally, it has already pointed out that the voting-procedure proposed for the Legal and Technical Commission seems to be inadequate. The two-thirds majority rule and the consensus principle are designed to protect certain interests within a given organ. Such protection of interests is meant to take place, according to the system elaborated by the Convention for the approval of plans of work, in the Council. Providing for the protection of interest groups, such as the exporter group, already in the Legal and Technical Commission would overemphasize their impact upon the decisions to be rendered and would make them dominate deep sea-bed activities. It should not be lost out of sight, that the same system applies to applications from States Parties or operators sponsored by States Parties and for applications of the Enterprise, too. It was the objective of the Third United Nations Conference on the Law of the Sea by providing for the special decision-making rules on the approval of plans of work to make sure that plans of work — and that applies equally to the plans of work of the Enterprise — are considered solely on the basis as to whether the applicant was sufficiently qualified. This objective is endangered if the required majority for recommending a proposed plan of work to the Council in accordance with art. 162, para. 2 (j) (i) is too high.

Apart from that, under the rules of procedure of the Legal and Technical Commission, as suggested at the moment, an abnormal situation may develop. The Commission may be unable to recommend the approval of a plan of work by a two-thirds majority, however, it may be equally unable to recommend its disapproval by the same majority. The fate of such application would be quite unclear as the lack of recommendation for approval according to art. 162, para. 2 (j) (i) cannot be regarded as recommendation for disapproval. Both decisions require a majority within the Legal and Technical Commission. One could only regard such applications as those for which no recommendation, neither a positive nor a negative one, has been made and apply art. 162, para. 2 (j) (ii) accordingly. Consequently, the rules concerning the recommendation of disapproval by the Commission would be applied which would clearly be inadequate. One cannot equate a plan of work which was perhaps endorsed by nearly two-thirds of the members of the Commission with a plan of work rejected by a two-thirds majority.

In spite of the lacunae mentioned, one may state that the decision-making process in the Council as provided for in art. 161 is adequate for the decisions to be made and the interests involved. It very much depends upon the Preparatory Commission as to whether the necessary supplementation of these rules will uphold and strengthen, or weaken the balance achieved.

Discussion

Treves:

I will limit myself to a few very short comments on Professor *Wolfrum*'s remarks and to a few slightly longer comments on other points of interest. As far as the subject considered by Prof. *Wolfrum* is concerned, I think that he addressed very ably questions where the Preparatory Commission can do something and areas where perhaps the Convention did not do enough. First, I agree that it is very important that something be done about the composition of the groups that compose the Council. The list of problems Prof. *Wolfrum* addressed is, I think, nearly perfect, although I would add the following: What about the way to deal with States that belong to more than one of these groups? How do we choose, or how do they choose, for which group they want to sit in the Council? Second, I would be slightly less optimistic than Prof. *Wolfrum* about the adequacy of the present system of the two-thirds/three-quarters majorities in order to make everybody satisfied. Whether this system is satisfactory or not will depend on the solution to the problem of how we compose the Council and how we compose its component groups. We will be able to pass judgment only after we know how the 36 members of the Council are elected.

I now move to Ambassador *Jesus*' presentation. This presentation is further proof of how thoughtfully the Chairman of the Preparatory Commission looks at the problems to be overcome in the long term. I was particularly struck by his idea to focus first on two areas on which the Convention left certain questions open, namely the decision-making of the Legal and Technical Commission and all aspects of the Finance Committee and that the more specific sea-bed mining issues could be left for a later time. I agree that the usefulness of negotiations on the substance of sea-bed mining, at this stage, may be doubtful; we would be discussing technical aspects of an activity that does not exist so far, we would be exchanging concessions we would not really know whether in our interest or in the opposite. So it might be a good idea that the so-called Sub-Commission 3 area is not regarded as urgent as the more political issues addressed. This is the positive side of Ambassador *Jesus*' intervention. Of course, there is no negative side, but there are some questions. First, whatever initiative is taken, it will aim at making the Convention universally acceptable, namely at making the Convention a document one can submit to parliaments and governments in the hope of getting approval and eventually ratification. So the improvements that may be produced must be "visible" in order for the Convention to be ratified: it is difficult to submit to a parliament the Convention including Part XI unchanged and then say that there is no need to worry, because it was understood that it would be applied in a flexible way. This is not the way to get ratification. There has to be a visible, legal way to do it. And following the ideas of Ambassador *Jesus*, then there may be a question also as to the continuation of negotiations on the Sub-Commission 3 questions after entry into force. On this I have a question, without having a solution in my pocket. Should there be a continuation of negotiations in the new Authority, or should they continue in a continued Preparatory Commission? If we were to continue them in the new Authority, we would have to realize that not everyone would be a member of the Authority, at least at the beginning. As the Authority will start when there will be sixty ratifications, the question of the observer States will arise. To have a continued PrepCom may be more attractive. Of course it would be against the Convention, so, if this solution were to be adopted, something will have to be done about that.

Koch:

I would like to make some remarks with regard to Prof. *Wolfrum*'s presentation. I am less convinced of the adequacy of the decision-making process of the Council. If we make an assessment of the adequacy we have to look whether all interests are represented in the Council. Certain interest groups are mentioned in the Convention but in my view two interest groups are ignored, namely the main contributors and those countries which may not be directly involved in deep sea-bed mining but which are producing and selling technology relevant to deep sea-bed mining. These two groups are not taken into account in the composition of the Council. With regard to the protection of the different interests involved we have to see whether they have a possibility to influence the decision-making process sufficiently. But as the Council is not only composed according to the different interest groups but also to the principle of equitable geographical distribution, the different interest groups may not have sufficient influence in the finding of decisions. It is not necessary that they can push through decisions which are in their interest but I think they must have a possibility to block decisions which affect their main interests. And if you look at the actual voting procedures it is very doubtful whether the interest groups really have a blocking minority. I am grateful for mentioning that the decision-making procedure may be influenced by the relationship between the Council and the subsidiary organs as the Legal and Technical Commission and the Finance Committee which may be established. But it is perhaps not sufficient that the main interest groups in these fields have a decisive say in the subsidiary organs but we also have to look at what happens later in the Council and perhaps in the Assembly with the decisions taken by these commissions, whether the Council and the Assembly can easily deviate from these decisions or whether they have to take them as recommendations which only can be agreed to or rejected and in the latter case if then the subsidiary organs have again to deal with these matters. These things have to be carefully considered when we talk about the decision-making procedure in the organs of the Authority.

Zegers Santa Cruz:

I would like to first make a comment. I regard the statement made by the chairman of the PrepCom, Ambassador *Jesus*, as a very important political statement. He stated the willingness and the urgency to hold negotations on Part XI without stopping at the legal difficulties which would be implied. I think this goes exactly in the direction of this seminar, the quest for universality: we are here for that.

Ambassador *Jesus* even mentioned some areas of concern, and he mentioned one, the Review Conference and the amendments on the Review Conference, which might require, let us say, a protocol? Because obviously I agree with him that has to be amended. And the amendment would have to have a legal form.

I believe the statement is of extraordinary importance, and I would like to make a comment in relation to what has been done with pioneer investors. We have heard three speakers very properly on the subject: *Cristian Maquieira*, *Dolliver Nelson* and Chairman *Jesus*. Well, resolution II was meant — in a stage in which we all thought that the submarine mining was there — to give guarantees to those who had made investments and who wanted to have an insured mine site. We seem to have lost sight of that. When I hear about the negotations I do not quite understand where they are going to, but I do see that some amendments have been made, but not only to resolution II but by implication to the Convention. We have been amending the Convention on the one hand, and on the other hand creating a *de facto* situation (because if we are disposing, let us say, of x number of mine sites, we, of course, are prejudging the Convention for a long time), I would think that emphasis or priority should be given to the renegotiation of Part XI, as contrasting with the negotiations which have taken place with a certain priority on this interim situation, which stands to become very definitive.

Ballah:

I have never disagreed with this, but the PrepCom is not seeking to amend the Convention. What it is in fact doing is interpreting creatively and innovatively some of those provisions of the Convention in the light of the doctrine of *rebus sic stantibus*, changing circumstances. Changing circumstances rather than changed circumstances, because they are changing still, they are not static. Hopefully, and following *Satya Nandan*, some of those creative interpretations and innovations of the Convention can find their way into a protocol of understanding that may come into force and effect at the same time as the Convention itself. We have had this morning some very fine presentations. In the course of time I will be able to address Chairman *Jesus*' presentation and the overall conspectus of the work of the PrepCom given by *Dolliver Nelson* and by my good friend *Cristian Maquieira*. So we have time.

I want to address one or two points that Professor *Wolfrum* made and that directly touch decision-making in the Council. I think that was a fine analysis of decision-making and he compared it to decision-making in other international bodies. Changing circumstances are in fact producing some new hard realities which are not being considered as realities by developed countries. It is felt that the only changed circumstance is the economic circumstance. This circumstance makes sea-bed mining a non-viable proposition possibly before 2015 A. D. But there are other hard realities when it comes to interest and decision-making in the Council. It has been largely assumed that the alignments which took place in the Conference of the Law of the Sea itself will continue in the Council. I do not think anybody needs to be reminded that some of those alignments were not quite developed when ranged against developing countries on the traditional issues. Not so at all! As you know, in the Group of Landlocked and Geographically Disadvantaged States in which Trinidad and Tobago falls you have Germany, you have Austria, you have Switzerland amongst others. But the new alignments within the Council that Professor *Wolfrum* talks about, which he did not go on to define with any precision at this time, are alignments that involve developing as well as developed countries. There can be no assumption that if Trinidad and Tobago becomes a member of the Council that it will vote alongside with Zambia or vote alongside with Chile on issues. There is no assumption that one can make that Trinidad and Tobago, in a joint venture with Venezuela and possibly Brazil, may not in fact be a major operator in the area. There is no assumption that can be made that some middle-eastern countries that have the capital to purchase technology would not also be major operators in the area. And as major operators in the area it means there is a kind of alignment in the decision-making in the Council that will not be structured on Group of 77 or UNCTAD divide-lines. In fact if that is realized some of the concerns that some of our industrial friends have about the Council and the parity of interests there would probably evaporate. They would indeed probably disappear. There was a kind of solidarity which existed in the Conference on Part XI issues, a developing country solidarity in situations where the majority of developing countries were not land-based producers of minerals. Some of them were consumers, albeit small consumers and the majority of them were States who were looking for benefits down the line as a result of sea-bed mining and therefore they could have no vested interest in restriction of sea-bed mining production.

I wanted to make this point at this point in time because I think it is important for Prof. *Wolfrum,* when he continues his analysis of these questions, to look at a parity of interests, and in fact the formation of the consensus may not work to the benefit of land-based producers or any group for that matter. The Council may in fact in reality be better balanced, and that is one of the hard realities that some developing countries will have to face and some of our friends that are land-based producers of minerals. Because a lot of developing countries, possibly Burkina Faso, would not want to see any possible benefit that it may obtain from sea-bed mining eaten up in the compensation packages to land-based producer countries even though they are all developing countries. And even in the course of the Conference itself, Canada, Chile — States with political and ideological differences — aligned themselves in support of the position of land-based mineral producers. Sometimes, I noticed *Zegers* of Chile in the course of the Conference embracing the Ambassador of Cuba. He always does that. He is one of the finest diplomats around.

Lee:

As has been said, this morning has provided a wealth of information and ideas. I would merely like to submit some minor points for your consideration. First, I would like to pursue Ambassador *Ballah*'s views regarding your paper. I thought your paper was a very fine analysis, I agree with the conclusions you have reached. One thing I would like to emphasize is that I think in practice if the present trend in decision-making continues we do not have to worry too much about voting. We have seen the patterns during the decade-long negotiations at the Law of the Sea Conference: there were plenty of negotiations, consultations. Only at the end, there was voting. And I think that kind of process will continue. We can follow the same trend in the PrepCom: on a great deal of important issues there were consultations and no voting was necessary. This practice may very well lead into the future Authority. If you also look at the practice in the international organizations: on all controversial issues, there are always extensive consultations and voting has been left aside. For example, in the implemantation of resolution II, voting was avoided through the adoption of understandings; there were continuous modifications in order to reach a consensus acceptable to everybody.

My second point relates to the themes which you have planted in the title of our symposium. I think you chose the title very well, for it addresses the present crisis in the law of the sea: that is, the Law of the Sea Convention is at the crossroads and secondly the need for continuing search for a universally accepted régime. In that context I would like to submit the following two points for your consideration. The first one is: How can we involve the non-signatories in the process of fixing the Part XI problems? Up to now, of course, we know that there are consultations and talks between the friends of the Convention and the non-signatories and I understand there has been progress. But this mechanism needs to be further developed to involve more active participation from the non-signatories in the process. Recently, I saw the May testimony in the US Congress. It appears that the Administration's view is still that the present attitude of the United States to remain outside the Convention is the best course of action. The other four witnesses stated that the Unites States could not continue to rely on customary international law and that it is highly desirable to have a universally accepted régime of the law of the sea. It appears that based on the result of the hearing, there is still a lack of enthusiasm on the part of the US Administration to be involved in a process to look for a universally accepted régime. Ways have to be found to attract and involve the non-signatories in the process.

My second point is the need to identify the problems of Part XI. I agree with Ambassador *Jesus* who has identified a number of problems in this regard. During the PrepCom many of the basic issues relating to Part XI have surfaced and some solutions have been found and additional ideas have been aired. But I think there is a need to identify particularly those problems that are of concern to the non-signatories. After all, the problems we knew are almost eight or ten years old and the situation may have changed, and other new problems may have come up. I think it is an important development that the American Bar Association has recently passed a resolution to call upon the United States to establish an internal group to conduct a review of the problems relating to Part XI. I do not know what the Administration's attitude towards this solution will be. It seems that some kind of mechanism of this nature would be helpful and that non-signatories should be encouraged to identify the problems of Part XI so as to adjust these problems and to find solutions.

Kapumpa:

My comments will be based upon what I can recollect from what has been said very brilliantly by the four gentlemen who spoke earlier. I will confine my comments to a statement that *Dolliver Nelson* made with regard to the assessment of the PrepCom. He was very modest by saying that perhaps he was not fully equipped to give an assessment and then went on to give us a very thorough assessment of what we have done so far. One point that came out very strongly from his assessment is the fact that perhaps the PrepCom is slowing down slightly because the urgency for sea-bed mining seems to have evaporated over time. Indeed, I recall that when we were in Montego Bay in December 1982 we believed, I for one at least believed, that by 1985 there would be sea-bed mining. In fact it seemed so urgent that people did think that certainly by the time we reached 1990, Zambia would have vanished from the surface of the earth because we would have lost all our copper sales because of sea-bed mining. But I think it is now very clear that we are talking about a régime that is certainly going to be still a long way off. Therefore, I think that some of the concerns, the fears that we had in 1982 can no longer be valid. Hence, I think it gives a much cooler atmosphere to discuss some of the issues we thought we would not be able to find solutions to. Indeed, I think the slowness of ratifications that *Dolliver Nelson* mentioned is a result of this. I think there was a time when everybody assumed that sea-bed mining was coming into effect and that the Convention must be operational right now. But things are a little bit slower now. The countries in the world which have a lot of money and technology to pursue sea-bed mining are now raising questions. I think it would not be too presumptious to say that the Soviet Union, for instance, in 1982, I think, had all the resources it required to undertake sea-bed mining the following year. But I think that the Soviet Union is now concerned with issues relating to bread and butter. They are now thinking of whether to pursue sea-bed mining or focussing upon the situation inside their country. So I think one could say that all those countries, including the United States, which had difficulties in joining hands with us can see now that we are no longer so scared of sea-bed mining as we once were. Therefore, we can now sit down a little bit more cooly and discuss whatever preoccupations and concerns they may have. That was the first comment.

My second comment relates to what Prof. *Wolfrum* referred to. I will only touch one small point and that is with regard to the composition of the Legal and Technical Commission of the Council. The point that I want to re-emphasize is the suggestion that perhaps there should be more emphasis on the composition of the experts who will form the Legal and Technical Commission of the Council to be selected, not so much with regard to which masters they will be listening to, when they make their comments and decisions. There should, however, be some provision which would say that these experts will give their comments, their opinions, their decisions purely basing them on their expertise without necessarily giving prominence to who they are and where they come from. In other words, there should be less and less political interference in their decision-making processes. I think that this is a thing that one sees already operating within the PrepCom. When we set up a group of fifteen experts from all over the world to look, firstly, at the applications of the four pioneer investors, and secondly at the request of the Group of 77 last year to look at an exploration plan which will be used to determine how sea-bed mining is going to be effected when it does come into operation, these experts coming from different political groupings, thoughts and aspirations, were able to work as experts. We have been told that whether there is an expert from Zambia or from Russia, Cameroon or whereever, they did not think in terms of whether they are developing countries or developed countries, they worked as experts. That is a point that one should re-emphasize. That is something that certainly would get our support whenever we were to talk in terms of rules and regulations pertaining to the selection and composition of the experts in the Legal and Technical Commission.

The last point relates to resolution II which my good friend Mr *Maquieira* referred to in his brilliant exposé and also to what Chairman *Jesus* talked about with regard to the possibility of creating and eventually arriving at a universally acceptable Convention. The process through which we, in the PrepCom, managed to resolve the overlapping claims and hopefully the process through which we are hoping to resolve the issue of obligations by the registered pioneer investors, is something that one would want to look back to at the time of the process through which the Convention itself was arrived at and this is what our good friend here has referred to. Throughout the negotiations for the Convention, issues were discussed, decisions were left at the very end. Indeed, I think this is what has been found, and I looked up some of the documents here, a declaration in a gentlemen's agreement which basically says that consensus must be found on all issues before coming to a vote. This is the process by which we have been talking and talking so that by the time we come to voting you will have virtually agreed on everything. And therefore, what one may want to say at this point in time is that the same procedure that was used in the Third Conference, the same procedure that we are now using in the PrepCom in resolving overlapping claims, in trying to resolve the issue of obligations by pioneer investors, can be applied to Part XI. Part XI is certainly causing a lot of difficulties and I am very positive in my own mind that if the United States or any other country which has refused to work within the PrepCom were to seriously come and say, look, let us begin talking, I am very sure that, using Ambassador *Lennox Ballah*'s words, creative and constructive interpretation can be effectively employed to find a solution to Part XI. Particularly now that we know that, firstly, sea-bed mining is not coming tomorrow, next month or next year and that, secondly, some of the concerns that countries like Zambia had at the time the Convention was being drafted are concerns that we no longer really see as problematic, because even with the formula in art. 151 relating to production limitation, which is based on nickel, we are now finding that the formula itself is not full proof. It is a "thing" that in fact can be easily worked upon. And I am very sure that if we all use the same process of discussion along with creative interpretation and constructive interpretation, we may be able to find a solution to Part XI, and, hence, create a Convention that may be universally acceptable.

Jesus:

I would like to address the two questions that have been posed to me by Prof. *Tullio Treves*. The first one was to know what, in my mind, the form would be through which the improvements, the accomodations would be made to the Convention, so as to make the improvements "visible" to facilitate the ratification (on the part of those States which have not ratified). As I mentioned in my statement, I made two points. One is that my ideas are still developing to leave the necessary flexibility to incorporate new aspects. Second, I said that what is fundamental is that we reach a compromise on the substance of the issues. Once we reach a compromise on substance, the form is not that important. People can compromise on the form if the form is to translate a compromise reached by consensus. But here again, I draw the following to your attention: it plays both ways. If it is important for those accomodations to be made in a kind of formal document, protocol-like, for the purpose of making those accomodations palatable for ratifications by those that have not ratified, it might also have a negative side for those that have ratified. If we require that the Protocol be ratified with the Convention by those that have not ratified, we might have to go back to those that have ratified, 43 countries, to ratify also the Protocol. And that could delay the process more than we think and even impede the entry into force of the Convention. Here again, we have to see the whole panorama of the situation. I am sure that constructively we might find a way that would take care of the problem posed by Prof. *Treves* and at the same time would obviate the difficulties of having to go back to ratify such a document by those many States that have ratified the Convention.

On the second question that he posed to me when I said that some of the issues might have to be postponed due to the fact that there are changing circumstances that are taking place and we do not know what will happen in 15 years or 25 years from now, and, therefore, so detailing a compromise now could end up being an embarrassment, as it is today, with respect to certain issues of Part XI — my idea is that we would in the PrepCom come up with agreed guidelines in what I call in my introduction "ground rules" as to what should be the areas of compromise on these various issues of the mining code and also guidelines as to the procedure of how to follow up the discussion in order to have a mining code ready to be implemented by the time the operators are ready to commence their activities in the Area. That is my idea. As to which kind of body would continue the development of those guidelines of ground rules agreed upon by the PrepCom, he mentioned two bodies. Whether the Authority should continue the negotiations after the entry into force of the Convention, on the assumption that PrepCom will cease to exist on the entry into force of the Convention, or whether we would have to extend the existence of the PrepCom. I believe that this second option should be eliminated. The first option would be the one that I think would be more adequate to take care of the development of the mining code on the basis of the ground rules and guidelines in the PrepCom.

Maquieira:

I pick up Mr *Kapumpa*'s point that he addressed to me regarding my presentation. The object of my presentation was to try to convey the impression that the negotiations of resolution II were prone to all sorts of difficulties, technical and political difficulties and that, nevertheless, in spite of those difficulties, solutions were found to the problems and a consensus was reached. Now, some of the solutions in my view were very hard to swallow. As probably is the case in any negotiating exercise. So, the idea simply to convey is that in an environment of extreme political and technical difficulties some solutions were found which seem to be satifactory to all parties. That is an image to look at regarding Part XI because it is unavoidable that there are some severe difficulties with Part XI. In the view of some people, the Law of the Sea Conference concluded without a final definite negotiation on Part XI and that is why it had to be adopted by a vote. Now, that negotiation may be pending or not, but the fact is that there is not a mirror image between Part XI of the Convention in terms of solutions to be sought compared with resolution II, and here I am deliberately avoiding the technicalities of comparing a resolution with a convention. It is simply an image that we had a situation of extreme difficulties, and at some times there was a clear possibility of a breakdown in the negotiations in resolution II and, nevertheless, we found solutions to the problem, some solutions were very difficult to be found and that should serve as a possibility to look at with regard to Part XI. Now, here is where the technical problems appear but in no way did I intend to say that we should continue using resolution II as an instrument for solving whatever problems some countries may have with regard to Part XI, because that is obviously not possible. It was simply just to image, to mirror, two possibilties which in my personal view have some similarities.

Wolfrum:

Several questions have been addressed to me and I shall try to address them in a logical manner.

I agree with Ambassador *Ballah* and Ambassador *Kapumpa* that within the future, new alignments unlike those of the Third UN Conference on the Law of the Sea will be formed. This mandates the rethinking of the composition of the Council as formulated by art. 161 LOS Convention and the various national positions taken in this respect. May I reiterate what I have argued in my presentation — actually nobody objected thereto — that the composition and the decision-making process in the Council has to be balanced by its composition and the decision-making process of the various commissions of the Council, e. g. the Legal and Technical Commission, the Finance Commission which has been mentioned by Ambassador *Jesus* and the Production Policy Commission. These suborgans play a very major rôle within the decision-making process of the Council. If one makes proper use of these suborgans, one can really have (and to that extent I come back to what has been said by *Tullio Treves*), an appropriate decision-making process in the Council.

Concerning the composition of the Council, I do not fully agree with *Jochen Koch* as far as he argues for special representation of the major contributors of the Council. Given the functions of the Council, this would be inappropriate. In taking into account the functions of the Finance Commission they should, however, play an important rôle in the decision-making of this Commission; it is, however, very important to properly structure the relationship between the Finance Commission on the one hand and the Council on the other. A special representation for a major financial contributor within the Finance Commission should be devised if and when the Sea-Bed Authority has become financially independent. The only reason why I did not further elaborate upon this point in my presentation is because Ambassador *Jesus* has already touched upon it and we shall have a presentation on this particular subject by Mr *Dicke*.

Let me now briefly comment upon the producers of technology as a group. I assume that they belong to the investors group and hence are already appropriately represented in the Council. Furthermore, I would like to associate myself with Mr *Ballah* who argued that in the long run or even within the next 10, 15 years we will experience a complete change with respect to deep sea-bed activities as far as the grouping of States is concerned. India has already become a major investor, which was never anticipated in 1972 when the negotiations started. The example of India is the best proof that the alignments of the Council will and must be altered as has been phrased by Mr *Ballah* under the principles of *rebus sic stantibus*.

In looking at the composition of and decision-making in the Council, one should not advocate an alteration of the Convention. Instead, use has to be made of the possibilities offered by the Convention itself for its modification, or maybe it is better to say "adjustment," of the rules of procedure of the Council; these are the proper mechanisms to use. These rules of procedure are in fact, as has been referred to, creative interpretations of the Law of the Sea Convention and thus the task of PrepCom. These means have not yet been exhausted and thus the task of PrepCom has not yet been fulfilled.

Environmental Impact Resulting from Deep-Sea Mining and Risk Assessment

Hjalmar Thiel*

I. The Precautionary Principle

Life is generally associated with disturbances and alterations. All organisms, from bacteria to whales, are open systems. Every single specimen alters its environment by input of energy or organic matter and subsequent output after alteration. Organisms are generally finely tuned to their environment which is composed of abiotic and biotic components arranged in multifaceted networks. Alterations occur within an individual's sphere of influence exhibiting time scales between seconds and eons.

People are also components in these systems, being both regularly altered by and altering their environment. This happens at every place on earth and throughout the atmosphere. No other species and no other assemblage of species has achieved such a far-reaching influence on the earth and its atmospheric envelope.

There is no problem in classifying all of mankind's actions within biology or under ecology, and we may contently lean back being convinced of the natural development of the overall ecosystem. Such manmade natural development, however, would soon guide us into worldwide suffering, which would not be restricted to mankind, but would affect many of the animal and plant species around us as well. Ecosystem alterations produced by man have grown to such an extent that species adaptation and evolution have fallen out of pace.

For his own sake and for that of all other living organisms the species *homo sapiens* has both the right and the responsibility to keep his ecosystem alterations in pace with evolution. This forces him to minimize ecosystem alterations. The only responsible behavior under these conditions is the application of the precautionary principle, the appropriate reaction to environmentally disquieting developments whenever the system is not fully understood or the effects of impacts cannot be properly assessed.

---

* Prof. Dr. *Hjalmar Thiel*, Institute for Hydrobiology and Fishery Science, University of Hamburg.

II. The General Problem: Mass Transport

This rather broad statement of environmental alteration applies to mining in general, and in the context of this symposium, to mining the deep sea-bed. Mining *per se* must be conducted on large scales for economic reasons. This implies large-scale impacts which are difficult to evaluate, since our knowledge of the oceans is limited. In such a situation we have to carefully consider and predict the potential impacts from deep-sea mining. Since mining technologies are not fully developed, and since economic calculations are not finalized, we cannot yet arrive at conclusive predictions.

However, we do know that for economic reasons, deep-sea mining will involve the transport of tremendous amounts of materials. This is true for all types of deep-sea mineral resources:

— manganese nodules

— manganese crusts

— metalliferous sediments

— massive sulfides

— phosphorite nodules.

Mining the metalliferous muds from the Atlantis II Deep in the Red Sea may serve as an example (*Thiel et al.* 1986). In former years it was planned to pump up 100,000 metric tons (mt) of mud to the mining ship on a daily basis. After a floatation process, the concentrated ore will amount to about 2% of this volume which would be shipped to a shore-based smelter. The remaining 98% are the tailings which would be disposed of at sea. At first, this material was expected to simply and happily splash down the ship's hull into the surface of the sea. No one is able to imagine the plume that would be created, and no one could imagine the volume represented by 98,000 mt of deep-sea muds. This mass of original sediment would fill a cargo train with a length of 46 km and such a discharge would occur for 10 months of the year over many years.

III. Mining Impacts

Mass transports associated with mining the other deep-sea mineral resources are considered to be less extensive, but the environment may be severely altered by all the various mining activities. Impacts will occur at different levels in the ocean. The figure illustrates the various impact sources for manganese nodule mining. The arrows indicate the different potential impacts and their location:

— on the bottom from collector system contact

— on the near bottom water layer from plume development

— on an intermediate water layer from tailings disposal
— on the surface layer from mining ship waste discharge
— on the surface layer from ore carrier waste discharge
— on the coastal ocean from processing plant tailings discharge.

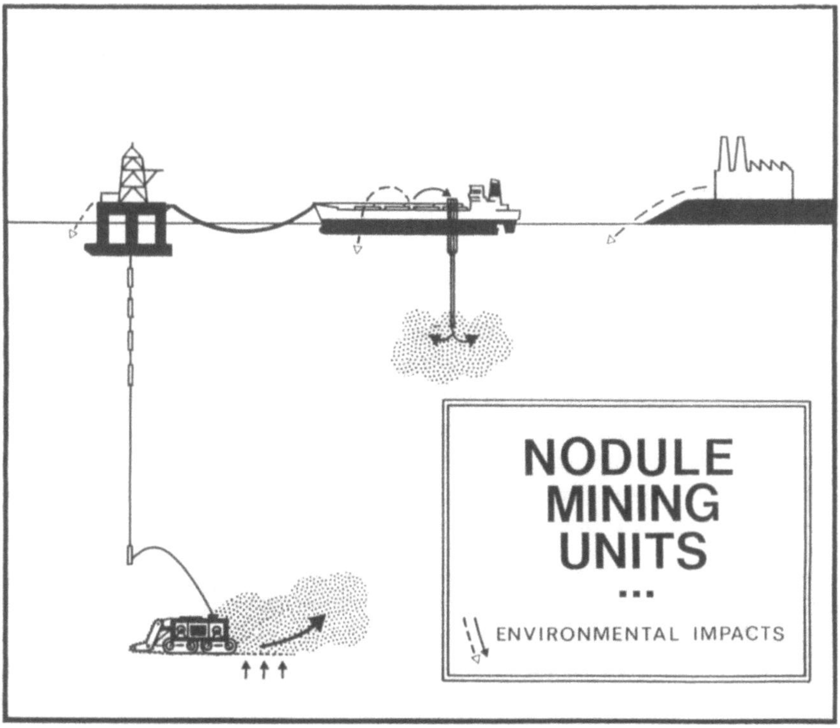

Avoidable (---▹) and unavoidable (⟶) impacts from mining manganese nodules.

1. Surface Water Impacts

Through responsible application of the precautionary principle, we can easily reduce the number of the listed impacts and impact sites. There is absolutely no need to impact the ocean surface. Tailings from the processing plant may be toxic from acids and mobilizable metal components. There is no need to discharge this material into the ocean. It should be stored in repositories on land, where it can be contained under regular and applicable control. Surface impacts from the ore carrier and the mining ship can already be averted during ship construction by the installation of large waste containers. All waste waters should be processed on the ships and particulate matter should be transferred from the mining ship to the shore by way of the ore carrier. These decisions would assist in keeping the ocean surface waters cleaner. There would then be no influence on primary production and no harm to plankton and fishes. Arguments in favor of positive effects through water fertilization do not consider the oligotrophic ocean régime that may be highly disturbed by increased plant production and alterations in food chains. However, this comment is not based on sound scientific results and investigations into the effects of surface discharge should be conducted.

2. Deep Water Impacts

Having rejected the need for surface impacts, the three deep water impacts remain to be discussed. They cannot be avoided, but every effort should be made to keep them as modest as possible.

a) Disturbance from Nodule Collection

During the course of mining, the first impact will be exerted on the sea-bed within the tracks of the collector system which consists of the actual nodule uptake device carried by a vehicle along the sea-bed. Although the collector may be mounted to the transport vehicle in such a way that its height above the sea-bed is adjusted automatically, the vehicle itself will penetrate deeply into the sediment. Along these tracks the fauna will be severely disturbed or destroyed, and the sediment will in part be squeezed sideways or compacted.

Although industry presently designs collector systems to minimize mud uptake and to blow out the sediments into the near-bottom water layer, a severe plume will be created. If one assumes the mining of 1 km^2 per day, an uptake depth of 25 mm, (with 20% of this layer corresponding to the volume of nodules), and all the ooze being separated from the nodules before they are lifted up to the mining ship, then a volume of 20,000 m^3 per day of the original watery upper sediment would be expelled into the near-bottom water layer. This sediment would create a plume from which many particles, especially those in aggregates, will resettle close to the collector track, but an unknown amount of finer particles will drift away with the near-bottom currents. The plume would, however, not only carry particulate matter, but also dissolved substances which will be released from the sediment with the interstitial water. These substances would not resediment with the coarser grains, but will drift away with the fine particles which may be kept in suspension for long periods of time.

The impact volume figures provided are certainly minimum assumptions. Industry will probably try to enlarge the collector capacity for economic reasons and the collector system may penetrate deeper into the sediment, at least where the nodules are larger. Before mining and monitoring on the scale of a pilot mining operations (PMO) are conducted, a true impact evaluation cannot be given. Engineers will strive for an optimum of economic gain. This will most likely tend to increase the uptake rate of nodules, to enlarge the collector system contact area, to increase the sediment plume, and to widen the area of resedimentation. Theoretical calculations may result in estimates for different impacts, but extrapolation to commercial mining and final risk evaluation demand large scale monitoring of a pilot mining operation.

b) Disturbance from Nodule Transport

Following the collection of nodules, they must be transported to the mining platform and from there to an ore carrier for shipment to the shore-based processing plant. For purposes of nodule transport from the collector system to the mining platform, hydraulic pumping or air-lift systems are under discussion. These would transport not only nodules, but in addition, some sediments as well. Although industry, in response to the demands of biologists and for purely economic reasons, will try to expel as much sediment as possible just above the sea-bed, some material will be sucked up with the nodules into the pipestring and will arrive at the sea surface. Some quantities of sticky sediments will be washed off the nodules during the turbulent upward transport. Mechanical interaction in the pipestring will abrade additional fine-grained materials from the nodule surfaces. On the mining platform, the nodules will be crushed and pumped in slurry form to an ore carrier. These processes add further fine-grained materials to the waste load in the mining system's water phase.

If we assume that no losses occur from the pipestring during the transport from the collector to the ore carrier, the transport water, together with the fine-grained materials including sediments and abraded nodule particles, must be pumped back into the sea. No accurate figures exist on the mass of these fine materials, but it may be on the order of 10% or more of the nodules collected. Therefore, some 500 mt to 1500 mt of particulate material may be discharged per day. Furthermore, the discharge water is derived from deep layers of the ocean and its chemical composition is different from that of intermediate water.

A primary environmental concern is the discharge depth. During the pre-pilot mining tests (PPMT) in 1978 and 1979, the tailings were discharged at the sea surface. This was acceptable for the small mining volume and the short test period. It will certainly not be acceptable in full-scale commercial mining. We need a decision on the discharge depth in order to study the behavior of the tailings and their influences on the environment and the biota during pilot mining operations. The large-scale monitoring of a pilot mining operation must allow extrapolation of commercial mining. This means that the pilot operation must closely simulate commercial mining in all its phases.

To my mind, the discharge must take place below the biologically active zone. How is this zone of biological activity to be defined since life is present in all depth horizons? Discharge below the euphotic zone was proposed to avoid alterations of the light and nutrient régimes for primary production. I believe, however, that this is not deep enough. The discharge must occur well below the zone of strong vertical migration which lies above 1000m depth. A discharge at or below 1000m will assure that upward transport of material within the zone of vertical migration can be excluded. Moreover, this will avoid the aggregation of particles with the loss of organic matter through scavenging from the upper water layers, and no accumulation of particulates at density interfaces will occur. This concept should be further discussed and the discharge depth should be adjusted to the oceanographic conditions at each locality.

A decision on the discharge depth based on oceanographic facts has to be made soon in order to enable industry to develop appropriate technology well before the start of a pilot mining operation. Of course, industry will argue against a deep discharge using costs and other economic reasons, but biologists or oceanographers have to establish limits for the sake of the environment. It will certainly raise the overall costs if a discharge system with a 1000m long pipe has to be installed, but already ten years ago, the extra construction costs for discharge at 200m were calculated to be negligible in comparison with the total investment (*Flipse* 1980).

In addition to the increase in costs, it will be time consuming to mount such a discharge pipe to an ore carrier each time it is to be loaded. This would, however, not be necessary if a buoyant and independent discharge unit, carrying the respective pumping system and the discharge pipe, is available at the mine site and is firmly connected with the ore carrier during the time of loading. Such a self-contained discharge system may minimize expenditures in time and costs. Detailed technical and economic considerations are not, however, a biologist's field of concern.

3. Precautionary Decisions

Most of the reasoning against surface discharge is not based on scientific results, but rather is founded on assumptions that cannot presently be substantiated with hard data. Such arguments were also brought forward against the objections to surface pollution and shallow water discharge. These are serious arguments or even criticisms for a scientist, but exactly this controversial situation should be the motivation for application of the precautionary principle if a decision has to be made now. Our knowledge of the oceanic ecosystem is limited to such an extent that, for example, we are not yet able to argue for or against surface or deep water discharge. Therefore, on a precautionary basis, we should move to the safer position to avoid harm to the environment and the organisms. We should favor the deep water discharge alternative unless convincing results demonstrate that no harmful effects occur through surface discharge.

IV. Precautionary Investigations

1. Research Demands

Marine research has been conducted intensively during the past 20 years and many important general and applied questions have been asked and answered. Yet our state of knowledge is far behind environmental demands, whether it is for shallow seas, like the North Sea, or for the deep sea. Therefore, risk assessments of mining impacts must be conducted at different levels.

Small-scale investigations:

This is the type of research generally done with probes and samplers of normal size, for example, collecting a few liters of water or O.25 m^2 of sediment.

Large-scale investigations:

This is defined as experimental work sufficiently large in extent to permit extrapolation of the results to large and massive environmental disturbances. The DISCOL project is an example (see below).

Small-scale monitoring:

In the present context, monitoring is used to refer to measurements and observations accompanying a Pre-Pilot Mining Test (PPMT). These are technical tests carried out by industry to demonstrate the technical feasibility of mining. Science must use these opportunities to acquire observations on the plumes and to gather experience for later, larger test mining activities.

Large-scale monitoring:

An example would be the monitoring of a large mining test, a Pilot Mining Operation (PMO), which is conducted at the scale of 1 : 10 or more of commercial mining and extends over several months. It may even represent the monitoring of an early commercial mining operation.

This scheme seems to be rather formalistic, but is designed to demonstrate the different levels at which oceanographic research in the context of deep seabed mining has to be dealt with. Additionally, it illustrates the high expenditure demands. Specifically, the monitoring of a PMO or of an early mining operation is certainly the most expensive part of the suggested research. However, to my mind this is also the most important research phase in risk assessment. The first three categories will rarely allow extrapolation to full-scale mining. Therefore, the major portion of risk assessment must be based on large-scale monitoring. This must include observations and measurements on sea-bed impact and on the plumes in the near-bottom water as well as in the midwater discharge layers. Such a monitoring program must include the time periods before and during the mining test, and will last for several months. It also has to be extended over a long period of time (possibly intermittently in its later phases) to study the fates of the two plumes. No consensus on resedimentation patterns of the plumes exists. Since they are composed of a high percentage of small particles, the plumes may drift through the ocean for long time periods and great distances. Research ships and personnel must be available for extended periods.

The costs for such large-scale monitoring will amount to enormous sums which cannot be charged to one nation's budget. This program has an absolute need for large-scale international collaboration to share in the responsibility for the environment, the high costs involved, and the knowledge to be gained.

2. The DISCOL Project

Small-scale research and the monitoring of PPMTs have been conducted, but the results from both large-scale experiments and large-scale monitoring are still missing.

DISCOL (the acronym stands for "Disturbance and Recolonization Experiment in a Manganese Nodule Area of the Deep South Pacific") is the first large-scale experiment in the deep sea. During commercial nodule mining, the sea-bed and the benthos will be disturbed by the collector systems. Nodules and sediment are scraped off in a thin layer and suspended sediment masses are transported by bottom currents, eventually resedimenting and blanketing areas outside the collector system tracks. DISCOL intends to examine the recolonization of a heavily disturbed area, a process that might last for decades.

The area chosen for the DISCOL experiment is situated at a depth of 4150m in the South Pacific Ocean close to a German mining claim. It is centered near 88° W and 7° S, about 400 miles south of the Galapagos Islands. The disturbance was created in an area of more than 10 km^2 employing a specially designed plow-harrow device. Twenty-four small plows were arranged in two rows so that 8m wide plow tracks were cut into the seabed. After plowing 78 transects across the circular area (diameter of 2 nautical miles), the sediment of about 20% of the area was turned over, whereas most of the remaining 80% received a more or less thick sediment cover through resettling of material in the plume.

Photographs from the bottom taken on DISCOL I expedition clearly documented the differences between the baseline assessment and the first assessment of conditions after the plowing phase (*Thiel* and *Schriever*, 1989, 1990; *Foell et al.* 1990). DISCOL II took place half a year later and the appearance of the plowing tracks, together with the diminished megafauna in the area, indicated a presumably long-lasting impact (*Schriever* 1990).

Plowing the deep sea-bed is certainly different from mining. This large-scale experiment will, however, inform us about the pace of life in the deep sea and will help in evaluation of mining impact upon the benthos. Extrapolation to the effects of mining should be more applicable than the results of *Wilson* and

Hessler (1987) who reported on studies of benthos densities near narrow tracks left by a test collector system five years after they were created during a PPMT carried out in 1978.

V. Precautionary Legislation

I am a scientist, not a lawyer or a politician. Legislation is not my business and I do not wish to penetrate this professional field. On the occasion of this symposium, I will, however, allow myself to comment on the Mining Code. This regulatory framework for deep-sea mining is under discussion in the Preparatory Commission for the Sea-Bed Authority of the United Nations and in various member countries. The document, in its present form, covers the environment in many of its articles. Few regulations therein, however, are based on factual oceanographic knowledge and much of the code is written in rather general terms. For the development of an effective mining code, further oceanographic data have to be obtained on specific questions. Therefore, the regulations should be kept open so that they can be modified and adapted as new knowledge is made available. Mining is not going to start in the immediate future, and there is still time to accomplish research and to make the results accessible for the purpose of modifying and improving regulations. Such a procedure I would like to describe with the term "precautionary legislation."

VI. Precautionary Articulation

As I have attempted to explain in the preceding sections, our knowledge of the abyssal ocean is limited. We have difficulties in clearly seeing through the fine meshes of the deep-sea ecosystem. Under these circumstances our capability for adequate impact evaluation and risk assessment of deep-sea mining are restricted. There also are other nets, and we must be careful not to get caught in social webs. Precautionary awareness may help us out of linguistic traps.

International and interdisciplinary co-operation are prerequisites for ecological research and for the inclusion of scientific results into legal frameworks. Difficulties emerge from the specific terminologies utilized in our respective disciplines, and misunderstandings may occasionally enter or consciously be included into the flow of words. One example may elucidate my precautionary warning: In the context of risk assessments, the expression "successful research" may be pleasing to the researcher, but it may transmit the impression to the decision-makers that environmental impacts are acceptable. One should habitually and carefully scrutinize the original description of the assessor and examine the true meaning behind the words "successful research." This is my personal experience and I urgently recommend that such articulations be evaluated with considerable precaution.

Literature

John E. Flipse, 1980: The potential cost of deep ocean mining environmental regulations. Report prepared by Texas A & M University, Sea Grant Program, for NOAA/OME.

Eric J. Foell/Hjalmar Thiel/Gerd Schriever, 1990: DISCOL: a long-term, large-scale, disturbance-recolonization experiment in the abyssal eastern tropical South Pacific Ocean, in: Proc. Offshore Techn. Confer., Houston, (OTC 6328), 497-503.

Gerd Schriever, 1990: Cruise Report DISCOL 2, Sonne — cruise 64, Callao/Peru — Valparaiso/Chile 02.09.-02.10.1989. Ber. Zentr. Meeres- u. Klimaforsch. Univ. Hamb.

Hjalmar Thiel/Horst Weikert/Ludwig Karbe, 1986: Risk assessment for mining metalliferous muds in the deep Red Sea, in: Ambio 15, 34-41.

Hjalmar Thiel/Gerd Schriever, 1989: Cruise Report DISCOL 1, Sonne — cruise 61, Balboa/Panama — Callao/Peru 02.02.-05.03.1989. Callao/Peru — Callao/Peru 07.03.-03.04.1989. Ber. Zentr. Meeres- u. Klimaforsch. Univ. Hamb.

Hjalmar Thiel/Gerd Schriever, 1990: Deep-sea mining, environmental impact and the DISCOL Project, in: Ambio 19, 245-252.

George D. F. Wilson/Robert R. Hessler, 1987: The effects of manganese nodule test mining on the benthic fauna in the North Equatorial Pacific, in: Environmental Effects of Deep-Sea Dredging, by *F. N. Spiess/R. R. Hessler/G. Wilson/M. Weydert*, Final Report to the National Oceanic and Atmospheric Administration on Contract NA83-SAC-00659, 24-86. Scripps Institution of Oceanography Reference 87-5, La Jolla.

Discussion

Lagoni:

As I am not a specialist in the field of biology at all, I would like to pose a question to Professor *Thiel*. I have learned that there exist some local places — I think you call them "hot spots" — with virtually unique biological systems. You have shown us only the general or normal situation of the environment in the deep sea. From an environmentalist point of view, do you think that one should also take into account those particular places in a mining code? Another point I would like to make does not refer to biology but to law: assuming that sediments, waste and residues of the nodules do not come under the London Dumping Convention, which is preserved under art. 311, para. 2 of the Law of the Sea Convention, there will be no problems concerning the dumping during the mining of the nodules at sea. On the other hand, however, there will be legal and practical problems with the large amounts of slag, the residues of the smelter process on land. There are, for example, in Hamburg serious environmental problems with the mud and silt dredged out of the port. Foreseeing large slag-heaps from the nodule smelters on land, I mean that one should not leave the serious environmental problems caused by the processing of the polymetallic nodules out of consideration.

Thiel:

To your first question: we certainly do have those places that you called hot spots or hot vents, but not in the areas where we have manganese nodules. Because of the short time available, I will confine myself now to the manganese nodules and to the experiment. These hot vents are found in the spreading centers between crustal plates along the ocean ridges. They are large distances away from the nodule mining areas and should not be impacted from nodule mining. If massive sulphides are going to be mined, then we would have to consider them as well.

Concerning your second question, I think you are partly right. I am not quite sure, other people may know this better, whether the London Dumping Convention really is effective in the Pacific Ocean. Somebody else may comment on this.

Koch:

Just a short question. You mentioned that there is a necessity for a large-scale pilot mining operation before you can really assess the effects of deep sea-bed mining. Does this mean that in every mining operation you need first a large-scale pilot mining operation or does this apply only to the first mining operations and that the knowledge you get by these first mining operations is sufficient for the evaluation of the effects of deep sea-bed mining on the marine environment in later operations?

Thiel:

I would say that we most certainly learn from every experiment we do. After we have completed a large-scale monitoring of one such test, we will have learned quite a bit and then we could possibly reduce our efforts for the next one. The first one should, however, be done very carefully and then we can determine what else has to be done. If the second test is based on similar techniques, and if the mining volume and transport are the same, then we do not need a second investigation; but if it is significantly different from the first one, we should certainly do more research.

Nelson:

How much research in terms of time will it take to produce the kind of scientific evidence on which adequate regulations for the protection of the marine environment from deep sea-bed mining can be based? Secondly, is it possible that the effects of deep sea-bed mining on the marine environment could be so harmful that it could either impede or even prevent deep sea-bed mining ever taking place?

Thiel:

Both are good questions. The first one is difficult to answer but if you think that we have another, let us say, 15 years before mining may begin, I think during this time we will be able to collect quite a bit of information. As I said, we intend to start further research within the next year. We are in the process of applying for money to do more research, so there is a good chance that after five or 10 years, we will have learned much more and will be able to carry out much better risk assessments. I also hope that other nations will do some further experiments. We more or less know everyone in the world studying potential mining effects. We are in contact and there will be no unnecessary repetitions of experiments either, so that we really can do this research rather effectively. I would not say that we will know everything after 10 years. But still, we have a good chance after 10 years to know much more.

As far as your second question is concerned, it is hard to explain and hard to answer because we do not know enough. If I had the answer that, yes, any mining is considered too harmful for the environment, then I would say without hesitation: no mining at all. I do not say this and I am convinced that mining can be done one day in a careful manner. I must say that many of my colleagues and other people have often asked me: Do you really think that your scientific activities and your personal engagement is successful at least in some way? Do you yourself think that you will be able to exert influence upon decision-makers? And I must say, yes, I hope so. And if some decision-makers are in this room, I hope we can influence them. There is another point. We have studied the potential impact from metalliferous mud mining in the Red Sea and we have discussed the results intensively, specifically with people from industry, and I think they do respond to what we say. So there is some response and we will be successful. I really hope that mining will be done with a maximum of prior and ongoing precaution.

Kimball:

I just want to ask you how comparable this area near the Galagapagos that you have been working in, how comparable that may be to the Clarion-Clipperton zone? I would have thought that there would be much more potential for species in the Galapagos area than in the deep sea-bed.

Thiel:

There are differences between the two areas. This is definite. The types of nodules are different. We have rather large nodules in the DISCOL area while there are many small nodules in the North Pacific. The type and thickness of sediment is also somewhat different. But if you compare the different localities, they are both deep sea areas with certain common characteristics. We are certainly able to extrapolate or to use the results we will obtain in the South Pacific as well for the Clarion Clipperton Fracture Zone, with some possible alterations or differences. And of course, the scientists working in the North Pacific are very careful and they observe us; we also discuss the results and so they should be applicable to this area as well.

Valle:

I am from Brazil and I am a diplomat. In 1992, my country will be hosting the United Nations Conference on the Environment, on a world-wide scale. Naturally, the agenda for this conference will be comprised of items on the environment which already have been affecting the world and are likely to affect it in the near future. All the problems are known to us all. Am I right in assuming by your remarks that to consider at this conference the possible impact of deep sea-bed mining on the environment would be premature or do you feel that there will be room in this conference to at least exchange ideas on this question?

Thiel:

I would say, it is always useful to discuss these things, wherever we go. And if it is a general conference on the environment, then, I think, we should not forget the deep sea. Of course, people before us forgot the deep sea because it is far away, it is very deep, it is cold, it is dark and inaccessible; but specifically since the industrialized nations have begun to penetrate this part of our world, we really have to consider it and I would say, yes, you should consider it.

Tytgat:

Prof. *Thiel*, I would like to ask you a series of small questions. One thing that you have not indicated, and I think it might be useful for people in the audience who are not specialists, is that in fact, the area which will be mined will be rather small, probably several small areas, and there will be, around those areas, some parts of the ocean where you will still have some species which could then be the source of re-colonization.

I just wonder also, if there has been any sort of assessment of what would be the most dangerous factor for the environment: Would it be the action of the bottom collector, or may it be the surface pollution, or may it be about equal terms? On the surface, I was struck by the fact that you reject the sediments from the transport ship. Would that be the rule or would it be more from the mining ship?

There is a point, which has also been raised on your experiment DISCOL, which I think was surely the best that could be done for the time being. It is a rather large disturbance; if you used the mining collector, would it really be going so deep in the sediment or would it just be the surface that is affected? We have seen on your photographs that you really have deep tracks which would may bring some difficulty for the organisms to move around, while maybe another type of collector may leave a flatter surface. Do you feel that it could have some importance or is it not relevant?

Thiel:

Let us start with the last question. We certainly have created an influence different from the collector system, but there is some discussion that a collector will pass above the surface of the sediment and very little sediment may be taken up, or very little impact may occur from the collector. And just by chance, not long ago, I had a discussion with engineers and I learned that the collectors are just those parts of the mining system which take up the nodules. Certainly the collector can then just go above the surface, but the vehicle carrying the collector will of course penetrate the bottom of the deep sea. It will sink into the sediment, leaving a deep track. The sediment will be displaced or compressed. The organism in this path will certainly be pressed into the sediment and I think there will not be much life left when the machine has passed this area.

The other question concerned the size of the area and the possibility of recolonization. When we compare it with the whole of the ocean or the whole of the

South Pacific, then of course the areas to be mined are relatively small. Specifically, the colleagues and engineers from France explained to us that they first of all will mine those places which have higher densities of nodules and high-grade nodules. This means that they will not mine in one large coherent area, but that they will mine an area of several square kilometres and then hop to another place to continue mining. So there are places which are more or less undisturbed, possibly having a thin cover of sediment from the plume. The organism there will survive and recolonization from these places is possible. Many species live in other areas where mining cannot take place because of rocky outcrops, for example; and the miners will, of course, avoid these areas. Although there are places which will not be mined, they may still be influenced by the plume settling to the bottom, but the influence is possibly not that strong.

The answer to your third question is that I do not mind whether the material will be disposed of from the mining ship or from the ore-carrier, but it was my idea that it should be technically easier to have just one disposal and not two disposal pipes. And if the ore-carrier has its own disposal pipe, I thought that the miner does not need another one. The other point is that industry may say that each ore-carrier having its own pipe is very expensive. There have been calculations of the expenses for disposing of the material at a depth of 200 m. This has been done some 10 years ago by *Flipse* in the US. The amount of money for such a deep disposal system, and that was calculated for 200 m, is a high amount. But if you compare this in relation to the total investment for mining, then it is really negligible. It does not make much difference as far as costs are concerned, whether you dispose at 200 or 1000 m, but I think one of the systems should be sufficient. I propose as well that all waste material from the ships, all the half-eaten steaks and rests of potatoes and everything else, should go down the same pipe into the deep ocean to avoid any surface impact.

Rao:

I am not a scientist. I am a lawyer by profession. I would just like to pose two questions. At the beginning of your introductory remarks you stated that we have little or less knowledge of the environment of the deep sea-bed. I agree. You know that the PrepCom has already started an exercise on a set of draft regulations concerning the deep sea-bed environment. In this context, I would like to ask two specific questions. What criteria, if any, do you think will be relevant for selecting a preservation or reference zone for purposes of assessing the environmental impact? That is one question. And the second one would be: What environmental parameters need to be specifically studied during the exploitation stage? Of course, you said that the exploitation stage has not been reached yet, we are still in the process of learning. Still from a theoretical point of view: What kind of environmental parameters need to be carefully looked into before you go into deep sea-bed mining?

Thiel:

What has to be studied is, well, as an oceanographer, I should say: everything. Of course we can't study everything, that would simply be too time-consuming. We really have to consider what happens when mining starts. Where are the impacts? As I explained, the impacts are on the bottom, in the near-bottom water-layer and then in and below the depth of disposal or discharge. If we take the discharge depth of 1000 m, we have to study the plankton around this depth, and we have to study the chemistry because the influence will be on the plankton and on the chemistry. We have to ask the question: What is the change by putting such a lot of material into this layer? The abraded nodule material, for example, is relatively coarse in relation to its sinking capacity. These particles will settle out relatively soon, I assume. The fine material from the sediment may drift through the oceans for long periods of time. They will, of course, spread out, they will dilute and then there is the question: Is such a plume really harmful or not? I cannot give you the answer, we have to study this. Within our project, we will certainly study these questions and we plan to go ahead as well with mathematical modelling. We will do this at two levels. The one would be at a small scale and near the place of impact while the other one would be a large-scale South Pacific Ocean modelling. Our oceangraphers are prepared to do this. So with the large-scale modelling we will know what the transport is in the different layers, and with the small-scale modelling how the particles will be distributed. If you ask me about the bottom, then we need to consult a specific branch of biology and we need geology. We have nutrients, we have dissolved metals in the deep-sea sediments and all this means that when we bring up this material, we will disturb the system. The bottom plume may alter the chemical balance. This has to be studied.

Your first question, I think, was on the Reference Areas. This is a concept which was brought up by American colleagues and has not been thoroughly discussed. The basic idea is to have test areas to see what the mining influence is (Impact Reference Area = IRA), as well as to see what the normal development is (Preservational Reference Area = PRA). If you mine a specific area, you have changed it and you do not know what would have been the normal development. Therefore, they want a Preservational Reference Area. This should be an area which is similar to the mining areas and it should be distant enough from the mining area so that it cannot be impacted from the sedimenting of mining plumes. There is the basic idea that several countries place separate reference areas along the sides of their different claims, so that they may be combined into one large area. That may be suitable, if this combined area is representative for all other areas. There should be discussions as well on the size of those reference areas and on their location. But I think that has to be done in the future.

Lee:

Prof. *Thiel*, in your presentation you recommended that the waste from the process by the smelter should not be sent back into the sea. I think, from an environmental point of view, that is certainly a very good recommendation. But I wonder if this is also acceptable from the economic point of view. It seems to be a generally accepted assumption by the industries that if you do not extract manganese, some 97% of the three million tons of waste would have to be disposed somewhere. (If you do extract manganese then still more than 70% would have to be disposed of.) This seems to me to have important implications in terms of the financial viability of mining. This would also narrow down significantly the choice of locations of the smelter. My question is: Do you think that there should be scientific studies (you have not recommended any scientific study) to find out the impact, if such waste were to be disposed back into the ocean.

Thiel:

There certainly needs to be an evaluation of this if some company pursues the idea of disposing the waste into the ocean. That has to be studied very carefully and then it has to be cost effective in scientific evaluation and finally there must be a decision. But I cannot tell you more on this. It has not yet been done to my mind and I think the processing of the material is not yet finally decided upon, so that the final type of waste disposal is not known, which means that these experiments cannot be done yet but they have to be done if the idea of ocean disposal is pursued.

Sherman:

You have indicated that up to now your research group has not determined as to what the nature of the tailings is from your activities. I am much more concerned because if you talk about dumping the tailings back into the ocean you must know about the chemical nature of the tailings as the dumping might have environmental implications. I would like to know what is the density of the polymetallic nodules in the particular area that you have studied? Further, I would like to know the composition of the nodules, because no two polymetallic nodules have the same mineral content. You might have more manganese than nickel etc. Hence, I would like to know the ratio of the minerals in the polymetallic nodules studied.

Thiel:

I think the question concerning the impact on the ocean is not relevant in this context because whenever we bring up the nodules (and we have the abraded nodules which will be discharged), we have no change in the chemical substance. I hope I am right, the people who know about this can correct me otherwise. In my opinion, the abraded material will not have been chemically changed, so there is no difference between what you take out of the ocean and what you put back into it as far as the chemical structure is concerned. So it does not matter what type of nodules you have.

Sherman:

The reason I ask is that art. 209 of the Convention declares that coastal States should take all measures necessary to prevent, reduce and control pollution from activities within the International Sea-Bed Area. So that if you are talking about mining in the deep sea areas, you have to take into consideration the environmental requirement(s) of art. 209 and of the other relevant provisions of the Convention dealing with the protection and preservation of the marine environment.

Thiel:

To my mind, the different chemical composition of nodules becomes a concern only in the final tailings from the smelter. And if you return this back to the sea, then you have to study the different types of tailings, but within the ocean you have only nodule particles which are not chemically active with seawater. In this way, it does not matter what type of particle or nodule type you have. Let us discuss it later with the help of some engineers, just in case I should be wrong on this.

Kollwentz:

I do not want to extend this discussion too long, but I just have one question for Professor *Thiel*. What kind of criteria would you foresee as making ocean mining impossible as a result of the environmental research? I understand it is difficult to say precisely, but what if you find, say, that the deep sea creatures will be extinguished or have to withdraw say two miles outside of this area, is this a criterion which would make mining impossible? What would such a criteria be in your opinion?

Thiel:

If you look into the literature as well as into the mining code, you always find the expression "harmful effects". Nobody knows really what a harmful effect is. Of course, if something is totally destroyed then we know it is a harmful effect and this is what we do not want. But we certainly will not totally destroy the deep-sea communities by mining. There is a good chance that we will influence organisms in surface waters if we discharge the material into the surface-waters. There we have fish-larvae, we have phytoplankton; there could be a very strong influence. And in this way I come back to the question that was posed to me earlier on, whether I thought that mining cannot take place at all. I think there is potential enough for the recolonization in the ocean and that the effects of mining activities can be reduced to an ecologically acceptable level. Would that answer your question?

Kollwentz:

I am thinking of natural events, too. In your opinion, how do they compare to mining in such an area which has been proposed for example in the Clarion-Clipperton zone, to disturbances through natural events? I am thinking of such events such as vulcanic action in deep sea flora, which we know is very active, and landslides through earthquakes and even the sediments brought in by the rivers and all that. How would this, as far as magnitude of impact is concerned, compare to ocean mining?

Thiel:

The magnitudes are difficult to compare. If you take, let us say, what you mentioned, the input from rivers. Where the input from rivers influences the ocean is in the water and on the bottom the communities have adapted, since the "event" takes place for a long time or even forever. There is some change in intensity over the years but you have this influence for thousands or millions of years and so the communities are adapted to this. And if you talk about landslides or about volcanic activity, then you have events which are relatively short when you compare them to mining. You cover a large area of the sea bottom and then the area will be regenerated after some time. We know that as a result of those slides, the fauna will be destroyed and then the same area will be recolonized after some time. This, I think, will happen the same way, that we do have recolonization in the area, but still, we do not know, how fast this will occur.

Archipelagic Waters: An Assessment of National Legislation

Barbara Kwiatkowska and Etty R. Agoes*

I. Introduction

A *sui generis* régime of archipelagic waters, as laid down in the 1982 Law of the Sea Convention (LOS Convention), is the most essential element of the archipelagic State régime. In a situation that the LOS Convention did not yet enter into force, a sound assessment of national legislation related to archipelagic waters has to be carried out keeping in mind legislative history of Part IV (Archipelagic States) which may highlight the reasons of the Convention's ambiguity.[1] This includes different justifications for positions taken during the Third United Nations Conference on the Law of the Sea (UNCLOS III) by archipelagic States and for that advocated by maritime powers, as well as for varying positions among archipelagic States themselves. Such justifications continuously play an important rôle in taking legislative and other measures by the archipelagic States, and in acquiescing or questioning such measures by the major powers and other States concerned. A pre-UNCLOS III evolution of the archipelagic State régime is equally important for any sound assessment of archipelagic States legislation.[2] This relates in particular to unsuccessful attempts of the two major archipelagic States, Indonesia and the Philippines, to gain recognition for the archipelagic State régime at the 1958 First and the 1960 Second United Nations Conferences on the Law of the Sea (UNCLOS I and II), as well as unprecedented legislative measures taken by these two States in the 1950s in order to legalize their claims.

* Prof. Dr. *Barbara Kwiatkowska*, Associate Director, Netherlands Institute for the Law of the Sea (NILOS), University of Utrecht, The Netherlands; Dr. *Etty R. Agoes*, Executive Director, Center for Law, Archipelago and Development Studies, and Indonesian Center for the Law of the Sea (ICLOS), Padjadjaran University, Bandung, Indonesia. Dr. *Agoes* contributed to "The Case of Indonesia" presented in this paper.

1 *See* United Nations Office for Ocean Affairs and the Law of the Sea (ed.), Archipelagic States, Legislative History of Part IV of the United Nations Convention on the Law of the Sea, United Nations, New York 1990.

2 Note that the new term "archipelagic waters" was first used by *Mochtar Kusumaatmadja*, The Legal Regime of Archipelagoes: Problems and Issues, in: *Lewis M. Alexander* (ed.), The Law of the Sea: Needs and Interests of Developing Countries, Kingston, Rhode Island 1973, 166-177 (171). For detailed examination, *see Hiran W. Jayewardene*, The Regime of Islands in International Law, Dordrecht/Boston/London 1990, 103-190; *D. P. O'Connell*, Mid Ocean Archipelagos in International Law, in: BYIL 45 (1971), 1-22 and 58-60.

This paper will assess various trends apparent in State practice[3] along several categories distinguishable in such practice. Practice of Indonesia and Philippines will be assessed separately, as the problems which this practice involves go into the heart of controversies surrounding the legal régime of archipelagic States. The navigational régime within the archipelagic waters will be considered, as far as possible, alongside with two other closely interrelated elements, namely the definition of the archipelagic State and the question of constructing archipelagic baselines. Prior authorization and/or notification required by States for passage of warships will not be regarded as a test of non-conformity to the LOS Convention. Subsequently, some problems of customary law formation in the context of trends apparent in the practice of States will be evaluated.

II. State Practice

1. Conforming Practice of Archipelagic States Not Using Archipelagic Baselines and Not Claiming Archipelagic Waters

Some States which qualify as archipelagic States under art. 46 of Part IV of the LOS Convention did not draw archipelagic straight baselines. This practice conforms to the LOS Convention, since under art. 47, para. 1 the archipelagic States are not obliged but authorized to draw archipelagic straight baselines. Examples of such States are Seychelles (comprising about 92 granit and coral islands) in the Indian Ocean, and Tonga (comprising over 150 islands) in the Southwest Pacific. Each of the two States is too widely scattered to produce acceptable water to land ratio to claim archipelagic status under the Convention as a single archipelago. According to art. 47, para. 1, this ratio must be between 1 : 1 and 9 : 1. This means that the water and land areas within archipelagic baselines must be of at least the same size (1 : 1) and that the water area cannot

[3] For the text of national legislation, *see Robert W. Smith*, Exclusive Economic Zone Claims. An Analysis and Primary Documents, Dordrecht/Boston/Lancaster 1986; and *id.*, Baselines: National Legislation with Illustrative Maps, United Nations, New York 1989. For summary lists of claims, *see* US Department of State, Limits in the Seas No. 36: National Claims to Maritime Jurisdictions, 6th Rev., Washington, D. C. 1990. For information on the US protests referred to in this paper, *see ibid.* and *Lee A. Kimball*, Problems in Implementation of the 1982 LOS Convention and Contrary State Practice, Memorandum to Panel of Experts on the Law of Ocean Uses of 13 April 1988, US Council on Ocean Law, Washington, D. C. For texts of declarations made by States upon signing and/or ratifying the LOS Convention, *see* the respective issues of the Law of the Sea Bulletin. For an overall review of State practice, *see Derek W. Bowett*, The Legal Regime of Islands in International Law, Dobbs Ferry, N. Y. 1979, 90-105; *Robin R. Churchill/Alan V. Lowe*, The Law of the Sea, new rev. ed., Manchester 1988, 106-108; *D. P. O'Connell*, The International Law of the Sea, Vol. I, Oxford 1982, 246-254, and also *id.* (note 2), 22-52; *Rüdiger Wolfrum*, The Emerging Customary Law of Marine Zones: State Practice and the Convention on the Law of the Sea, in: NYIL 18 (1987), 121-144 (123-127).

exceed the land area more than nine times (9 : 1). Tonga and Seychelles belong to those States which would encounter difficulty with not exceeding the maximum 9 : 1 ratio. At the same time, art. 47, para. 2 of the Convention specifies that the length of archipelagic baselines "shall not exceed 100 nautical miles, except that up to 3 per cent of the total number of baselines enclosing any archipelago may exceed that length, up to a maximum length of 125 nautical miles".

However, according to *Victor Prescott*, instead of a single set of archipelagic baselines, Tonga could produce baselines (as did Fiji) around some of its islands, in particular Tongatapu Islands, including the Nomuka Group, and 'Uta Vava'u Group.[4] Although *Prescott* does not mention a similar possibility for Seychelles, the latter could presumably also follow a similar approach. Seychelles — like a number of other States — requires prior notification on the innocent passage of warships through its territorial sea. This Seychellian practice was protested by the United States in 1982.

Another case of a scattered island State represents Mauritius (in the Indian Ocean) which has an archipelagic dependency and which in 1970 legislated for straight baselines, designating the enclosed waters as internal waters. As Mauritus' islands are located in long distances one from another, its 1970 legislation appears to rely on the separate baseline systems for each group, rather than on one archipelagic system of baselines which would result in extremely high water to land ratio.[5] Although Mauritius was — next to Indonesia, Philippines and Fiji — one of the main advocates of the archipelagic State régime during UNCLOS III, in its recent legislation, Mauritius drew ordinary straight baselines around its Chagos Archipelago. This legislation does not determine the legal status of waters enclosed by its straight baselines, but they are presumably, like waters enclosed under the 1970 legislation, the internal waters. Moreover, Mauritius (like Seychelles) requires a prior notification on the innocent passage of warships through its territorial sea, against which practice the United States protested in 1982. Seychelles, Tonga and Mauritius did not yet ratify the LOS Convention.

Other States with acceptable water to land ratio which did not claim archipelagic status are, among others, Jamaica in the Caribbean region and Bahrain in the Persian Gulf which both have already ratified the Convention. According to

---

4 *See J. R. V. Prescott*, The Maritime Political Boundaries of the World, London/New York 1985, 186. Note that *Alexander* lists both Tonga and Seychelles as having acceptable water to land ratio, *see Lewis M. Alexander*, Navigational Restrictions within the New Law of the Sea Context: Geographical Implications for the United States, Offshore Consultants, Inc., Peace Dale, Rhode Island, December 1986, Table 3 at 88.

5 According to *Alexander* (note 4), Table 10 A. at 91 and 285, only a few of Mauritius' islands could meet the definition of the physical requirements for an archipelagic State under the LOS Convention. Therefore, in his opinion, Mauritius — alongside with Western Samoa, Singapore, Saint Lucia, Japan, New Zealand and the United Kingdom — belongs to category of multi-island States which are not physically qualified for the archipelagic status.

Victor Prescott, Jamaica could employ a system of baselines which would have a longest segment of 102 miles and a water to land ratio of 1.2 : 1.[6] Bahrain would, in *Prescott*'s opinion, satisfy the water to land ratio of 1 : 1 assuming that the Howard Islands disputed by Bahrain with Qatar were part of Bahrain.[7]

A separate case in this category is provided for by the practice of the Bahamas (in the Caribbean region) which has already ratified the LOS Convention. The Bahamas comprises of some 700 islands of limestone and 2,000 cays of coral foundation. The islands stand upon a complex platform that extends beyond the land frontier to form what are referred to as the Great and Little Bahamas Banks. These features are permanently submerged, but the waters that cover them are so shallow that in most places they are nonnavigable except by vessels of the shallowest draught. Article 47, paras. 1 and 7 of the LOS Convention allow — for the express benefit of the Bahamas — the inclusion of waters lying within the fringing reefs of islands and atolls into the land territory of the archipelagic State for the purpose of determining a water to land ratio. Although the Bahamas did not legislate for an archipelagic régime, the Bahamas would, in *Prescott*'s opinion, meet all tests for archipelagic straight baselines and would have an acceptable water to land ratio for claiming the archipelagic status under the LOS Convention.[8] The Bahamas — which has a military alliance with the United States — recognizes the necessity to preserve the traditional freedom of transit through archipelagic waters. This is important because the Bahamian archipelagic baselines would enclose the Providence Channels, Crooked Island, Mayaguana, Caicos, and Turks Island Passages, of which the first two form parts of major navigation routes.

2. Conforming Practice Concerning Non-Self-Governing Archipelagic Territories

A separate category forms practice of those States which did not claim archipelagic status for their dependent territories that could qualify as archipelagos. This relates to claims of, among others,[9] the Netherlands with regard to the Netherlands Antilles, France with respect to New Caledonia,[10] the United States with respect to Micronesia,[11] and of New Zealand with respect of the Cook Islands and the Tokelau Islands. This practice conforms to the LOS Convention, as the non-

---

6 *Prescott* (note 4), 338.

7 Based on correspondence of *Barbara Kwiatkowska* with *J. R. V. Prescott* of April 1990.

8 Based on correspondence of *Barbara Kwiatkowska* with *J. R. V. Prescott* of March 1990. *Cf. O'Connell* (note 2), 56-57.

9 *Cf. Alexander* (note 4), Table 10 B. at 91.

10 *See Prescott* (note 4), 189-190.

11 Note that if enclosed by a single set of baselines, a water to land ratio of Micronesia would be of 40-50 : 1, while its baselines would measure one 600 miles and several 200 miles in length. *See Jayewardene* (note 2), 146 and note 346 at 186.

self-governing archipelagic territories do not qualify as archipelagic States under art. 46 of the Convention. Thus, until those archipelagos become independent States, they cannot under the Convention legitimately enjoy the archipelagic régime. Apart from this basic consideration, the United States and New Zealand may have preferred not to make use of the rules applicable to the archipelagic régime due to their vital interest in preserving freedom of navigation.

For the Netherlands, the main reason of not claiming archipelagic status for the Antilles (in the Caribbean region) appears to be the above-mentioned question of the Antilles' presently dependent status.[12] Otherwise the Leeward Islands of the Netherlands Antilles comprised of Aruba, Curaçao and Bonaire Islands would qualify as an archipelago under art. 46 of the LOS Convention, and the straight archipelagic baselines around those islands would meet the length criteria set forth in art. 47, para. 2 of the Convention.[13] The longest distances between those islands are less than 100 miles. The archipelagic baselines around the Leeward Islands would also conform to the water to land ratio which according to art. 47, para. 1 must be between 1 : 1 and 9 : 1. If Aruba would become fully independent, the archipelagic baselines around only Curaçao and Bonaire (together with the islets of Klein Curaçao and Klein Bonaire) would produce a water to land ratio 2 : 1, thus conforming to the Convention.

As regards the Windward Islands of the Netherlands Antilles comprised of the islands of Saba, Sint Eustatius, Sint Maarten and several smaller islands, the opinions of Dutch writers differ. In particular, *Monzón* maintains that the ratio of water to land (equal to 69 square kilometers in total) is in case of these islands 19 : 1, thus exceeding the permitted maximum ratio 9 : 1.[14] Another Dutch scholar, *Soons* agrees with *Monzón*'s opinion on condition that the Windward Islands are viewed as one archipelago.[15] However, according to *Soons* the Windward Islands could alternatively be regarded as consisting of several archipelagos. This approach seems to be supported by art. 46 specifying that archipelagic State means a state constituted wholly "by one or more archipelagos and may include other islands", while archipelago means "a group of islands, including parts of islands, interconnecting waters and other natural features ...." If two islands — as art. 46 appears to permit — could be regarded as "a group of islands", the water to land ratio of, for instance, Saba and Sint Eustatius islands would be of about 3-4 : 1, thus conforming to art. 47, para. 1.[16]

---

[12] *See Alfred H. A. Soons*, De Nederlandse Antillen en het recht van de zee, Commentaar (The Netherlands Antilles and the Law of the Sea, A Commentary), in: *H. Meijers* (ed.), Volkenrechtelijke Aspekten van Antilliaanse onafhankelijkheid, Alphen aan den Rijn 1980, 269-304 (273). Note that Aruba became a separate, autonomous part of the Kingdom of the Netherlands in 1986. Aruba's full independence was scheduled for 1996, but has recently been postponed.

[13] *See T. M. Monzón*, Een onafhankelijk Antillen: één groot zeegebied (The Independent Antilles: an extensive maritime area), in: *Meijers* (note 12), 223-267 (232).

[14] *Op. cit.*, 240.

[15] *Soons* (note 12), 274.

3. *Non-Conforming Practice Concerning Non-State Archipelagos*

The practice of States which do not fall within the definition of an archipelagic State laid down in art. 46 of the LOS Convention but, nevertheless, effected archipelagic enclosure around their outlying archipelagos, fits into the category of non-compliance with the Convention. This is due to the fact that, according to art. 49, para. 1 of the LOS Convention, archipelagic straight baselines can only be drawn by the archipelagic States. During UNCLOS III some eleven States, including Ecuador, India, Spain, Portugal, Canada, and France, have consistently advocated the extension of archipelagic State régime also to outlying archipelagos comprising a part of a State. However, UNCLOS III rejected such a wider scope of application of the régime, and limited the definition of an archipelagic State only to a State which is constituted wholly by one or more archipelagos and which may include other islands (art. 46). It was considered against the navigational interests of the international community if, as a result of a vague definition of an archipelago, there was to be a proliferation of archipelagic claims, especially in the enclosed and semi-enclosed seas.

The non-conforming claims falling into this category include those of, among others,[17] Denmark with respect to the Faeroes, Ecuador with respect to the Galapagos Islands (Colon Columbus Archipelago),[18] Norway with respect to Spitzbergen (Svalbard Archipelago), Spain with respect to the eastern group of Canary Islands (Islas Canarias), Australia with respect to the Houtman Abrolhos and Furneaux Islands, and India with respect to Andaman and Nicobar Islands.[19] The Ecuadorian claim, as originally made in 1951, was protested the same year by the United Kingdom and the United States.[20] The first three claims to Faeroes, Galapagos and Spitzbergen can, according to *Derek Bowett*, be typified in one category characterized by sufficient distance from, or other geographical relationship to, the mainland State which would justify separate baselines.[21] *Victor*

16 *Ibid.*

17 *Cf. supra* (note 9). Note a hypothetical possibility of drawing archipelagic baselines around the disputed Spratly and Paracel Islands in the South China Sea. If the Paracels (having total land area of 10 square kilometers) were enclosed by archipelagic baselines, they would have generated the 200 mile zone of 430 000 square kilometers. *See Kriangsak Kittichaisaree*, The Law of the Sea and Maritime Boundary Delimitation in South-East Asia, Oxford/New York 1987, 166.

18 Baselines around Galapagos are of 48, 62, 32, 124, 76, 47, and 147 miles. *See O'Connell* (note 2), 23-24; *Jayewardene* (note 2), 120, Figure 5.8 at 165 and 171; *Francisco Orrego Vicuña*, International Ocean Law Developments in the Southeast Pacific: The Case of Chile, in: *John P. Craven et. al.* (eds.), The International Implications of Extended Maritime Jurisdiction in the Pacific, Honolulu 1989, 217-229 (228-229).

19 *See Jayewardene* (note 2), 171-172, indicating that in the waters around Andaman and Nicobar Islands India, for many years, had limited navigational rights of foreign ships. Between those islands passes Ten Degree Channel. Note also that India requires a prior notification on the passage of warships through its territorial sea. In 1983 the USA protested against this latter India's practice.

20 *See O'Connell* (note 2), 61.

Prescott is of the opinion that generally, outlying (non-state) archipelagos can be surrounded by ordinary straight baselines if one main island is deemed to be fringed by the other islands in the group. This is the case with, for instance, Furneaux Group (in Bass Strait between Australian mainland and northeast Tasmania) but not with Houtman Abrolhos Islands (off western Australia).[22] It should also be noted that the claim of Hawaii which was rejected by the United States constitutes a separate case in this category. Moreover, Canada had for some time considered whether to apply the archipelagic régime to its Arctic islands, but refrained from doing so since the Arctic Archipelago does not meet the requirements laid down in art. 46 and other relevant provisions of the LOS Convention.[23] According to *Prescott*, archipelagic baselines could also be drawn by Japan around three of its archipelagos: Danjo Gunto, Sakishima Shoto, and the combined archipelagos called Okinawa Shoto and Amami Shoto.[24] However, Japan — which as a major maritime power attaches significant importance to the freedom of navigation — has shown no interest in drawing such archipelagic baselines. None of States belonging to this category ratified the Convention.

4. Archipelagic States Conforming to the Rules on Archipelagic Baselines and Archipelagic Waters

A number of States drew the archipelagic straight baselines and accorded the enclosed water status of archipelagic waters in a manner conforming to the LOS Convention. This relates to Fiji, Papua New Guinea, the Solomon Islands, Vanuatu, Sao Tome and Principe, Antigua and Barbuda, Grenada, and Saint Vincent and the Grenadines. All seven States meet the requirements laid down in art. 47 of the Convention with respect to the ratio of water to land (between 1 : 1 and 9 : 1) and the length of archipelagic baselines.[25] Fiji, Sao Tome and Principe, and Antigua and Barbuda already ratified the LOS Convention.

During UNCLOS III, Fiji was, next to Indonesia, the Philippines and Mauritius, one of the main sponsors of the archipelagic State régime. In fact it was a speech by Ambassador *Nandan* of Fiji to the UN Sea-Bed Committee on 22 July 1971 that initiated the proposals for a text on an archipelagic State régime to be

---

21 *Bowett* (note 3), 90.

22 Based on correspondence of *Barbara Kwiatkowska* with *J. R. V. Prescott* of March 1990.

23 *See Daniel Vignes*, La conformité au droit de la mer des lignes de base droites tracées par le Canada au nord du 70ème parallèle nord, in: *Yoram Dinstein / Mala Tabory* (eds.), International Law at a Time of Perplexity, Essays in Honour of *Shabtai Rosenne*, Dordrecht/Boston/London 1989, 1005-1019; *Wolfrum* (note 3), 123. The two Canadian baselines enclosing the M'Clure Strait and Amundsen Gulf are of some 100 miles in length.

24 *J. R. V. Prescott*, Maritime Jurisdiction in East Asian Seas, in: East-West Environment and Policy Institute Occasional Paper, No. 4 (1987), 26-30, including Figures 8 and 9.

25 *See Alexander* (note 4), Table 3 at 88.

considered at the UNCLOS III.[26] Since the enactment of the 1977 Fijian legislation, Ambassador *Nandan* emphasized conformity of this legislation to the negotiating texts and subsequently the final draft of the LOS Convention.[27] In a note to the United Nations Secretary-General of 21 April 1978 Fiji also announced that it had granted sea and air passage rights in and over its archipelagic waters. It should, however, be noted that for Fiji, geographical and economic unity are the essential elements of the régime. This makes Fiji's claim less controversial than claims of Indonesia and the Philippines for which the concept of archipelagic unity is construed in the broadest sense also comprising unity in political and security-oriented sense. The archipelagic waters of Fiji are important shipping routes for international navigation. The three straits enclosed by Fijian waters are Vatu-I-Ra Channel which is rather a difficult route bordered on both sides by extensive coral reefs, as well as Kandavu Passage and Nanuku Passage. But the distances between the main islands of Fiji (and likewise Mauritius) are — unlike is the case with Indonesia and the Philippines — rather long, sometimes exceeding 100 miles. Consequently, for Fiji it was easier to accept the free navigation and overflight through its archipelagic waters than it is for Indonesia and the Philippines, the main islands of which are separated by narrow passages.

Fiji drew, under its 1977 legislation, archipelagic straight baselines around the principal islands of the archipelago. The outlying Rotuma Island and Cerva-I-Ra (Conway Reef), which are located respectively 245 miles to the north and 270 miles to the southwest of the main group, were excluded from Fijian archipelagic baselines on account of their isolation. It is not clear whether an amendment, that was sought to allow an archipelagic régime for Rotuma, has been introduced. According to *Prescott*, the Rotuma's baselines, as established by Fiji in 1981, would satisfy art. 47 of the Convention, since the longest of these baselines measures 7.7 miles and the water to land ratio is of 1.1 : 1.[28] Fiji also drew inner baselines across gaps in reefs, thus enclosing lagoons within reefs as its internal waters. These and the enclosure of Conway Reef appear to have been established on the basis of art. 6 of the LOS Convention related to reefs. Article 50 of the Convention, which provides for the right of the archipelagic State to delimit internal waters within its archipelagic waters, does not make reference to art. 6. Therefore, it would seem that lagoons lying within reefs of an archipelagic State acquire the status of archipelagic waters rather than that of internal waters. However, an opposing interpretation seems also possible, especially that art. 47, paras. 1 and 7 allows inclusion of waters lying within the fringing reefs of islands and atolls into the land territory of an archipelagic State.

---

26 *See O'Connell* (note 2), 49-50.

27 UNCLOS III, Official Records, Vol. XIV, 67, para. 82, and Vol. XVII, 43-44, para. 83.

28 *Prescott* (note 4), 186.

The Solomon Islands — providing an instance of an archipelagic State consisting of a number of archipelagos — drew archipelagic straight baselines around each of its five archipelagos. In the vicinity of the main archipelagic unit of the Solomons (from south of Bougainville Island in the north to San Cristobol Island in the south) are at least 3 major navigation routes. They include the Bougainville Strait and Indispensable Strait which represent parts of a route between the Pacific and the Solomon and Coral Seas, as well as Manning Strait which provides access from the Pacific to The Slot (a narrow waterway separating two chains of the Solomons' Islands). The Indispensable Strait serves an ocean navigation route from Torres Strait to the Panama Canal.

The longest archipelagic baseline of Papua New Guinea measures 120 miles, and its ratio of water to land is 1.3 : 1.[29] Two island groups called Tauu and Nukumanu were left outside the baseline system, although — as *Prescott* reports — "they were defined as archipelagos, and it was noted that their internal waters might form part of the archipelagic waters of Papua New Guinea. The baselines around these two groups are defined as continuous lines between the outermost points of islands, shoals, rocks and reefs."[30] Nukumanu Island could not be included in the baseline system since it lies more than 125 miles from Tauu. In the case of Tauu the only reason against such inclusion appears to be the requirement laid down in art. 47, para. 3 of the LOS Convention that the baselines cannot depart to any appreciable extent from the general configuration of the archipelago.

Serious concern was apparent in the statement of Ambassador *Namaliu* of Papua New Guinea at the closing session of UNCLOS III in Montego Bay with respect to art. 53 of the Convention dealing with, in his opinion, the newly created right of navigation by submarines below the surface through territorial waters in areas designated as archipelagic sea lanes.[31] So far this is important that Papua New Guinea's archipelagic waters completely enclose the Bismarck Sea and are crossed by important north-south navigation routes. In the west, a coastal route through the Bismarck Sea utilizes the Isumrud Strait, and then passes through the Vitiaz Strait into the Solomon Sea.[32] An alternative to the Vitiaz Strait is the Dampier Strait. A third link between the Bismarck and Solomon Seas is provided by Saint George's Channel. The shortest route around southeastern New Guinea to Australia is through the Goschen Strait, with an alternative (60 miles longer) route passing to the east of the D'Entrecasteaux Islands. According to *Alexander*, the Dampier Strait handles some of the Japanese-Australian

---

29 *Op. cit.*, 185.

30 *Ibid.*

31 UNCLOS III, Official Records, Vol. XVII, 75, para. 125. *Cf. Camillus S. N. Narokobi*, The Regime of Archipelagoes in International Law, in: *Jon M. van Dyke et. al.* (eds.), International Navigation: Rocks and Shoals Ahead?, Honolulu 1988, 220-236 (230) and 261-262.

32 *See Alexander* (note 4), 170-171.

traffic, although a greater share travels *via* a broad, unnamed waterway between New Ireland and Bougainville.[33] All those straits and likewise the Torres Strait between Papua New Guinea and Australia lie partly both within the Papua New Guinea's archipelagic waters and its territorial sea.

The security aspects are also stressed in the Montego Bay statement of Ambassador *Regenvanu* of Vanuatu. While Vanuatu's legislation closely follows the Convention, Vanuatu — being like other South Pacific island States one of the sponsors of the South Pacific Nuclear Free Zone — is dissatisfied with art. 17 and other relevant provisions of the LOS Convention permitting the right of innocent passage of all foreign ships through the territorial sea.[34] Vanuatu's archipelagic waters do not cover any straits but are crossed (in the northern part) by a major navigation route which proceeds from Torres Strait to the Fijian port and capital, Suva. Vanuatu's archipelagic baseline system — which does not cover the disputed Matthew and Hunter Islands — consists of 21 segments connecting two sections of the low-water mark, with the longest section measuring 90 miles.[35] The water to land ratio of Vanuatu is 4.7 : 1.

Sao Tome and Principe (in the Southwest Atlantic) defined 12 archipelagic straight baselines, of which the longest measures 99 miles, while the ratio of water to land is 3 : 1.[36] The 1978 legislation of Sao Tome and Principe proclaiming its archipelagic régime (and 12 mile territorial sea) does not expressly provide — as does the legislation of the South Pacific States referred to above — for innocent passage and archipelagic sea lanes passage, but it specifies that Sao Tome and Principe, "in accordance with principles of international law", respects "freedom of navigation and overflight in straits or corridors ['des couloirs'] used for international navigation". Sao Tome and Principe, upon signing the Convention, made a Declaration under art. 310 thereof, specifying that the Convention's provisions on archipelagic waters are compatible with its national legislation. It reserved, however, the right to adopt laws and regulations relating to the innocent passage of foreign warships through its archipelagic waters and territorial sea, as well as to take any other measures aimed at safeguarding its security. But archipelagic waters of the Sao Tome and Principe are not traversed by important navigation routes.

Moreover, in the Caribbean region, Antigua and Barbuda, Grenada, as well as Saint Vincent and the Grenadines belong to those States which require a prior authorization for the passage of warships through the territorial sea. The United States protested against such practice of Grenada in 1982 and 1986, and against that of Antigua and Barbuda in 1987. The baselines of Antigua and Barbuda, the longest of which measures 54 miles, enclose areas (including Redonga Island)

[33] *Op. cit.*, 306.
[34] UNCLOS III, Official Records, Vol. XVII, 121-122, paras. 74 and 78.
[35] *See Prescott* (note 4), 185 and 198.
[36] *Op. cit.*, 318.

with a water to land ratio of 6.6 : 1, while those of Saint Vincent and the Grenadines devise a ratio of 1.3 : 1.[37] The longest segment of Saint Vincent and the Grenadines' baselines is of 17 miles. A single set of Grenada's archipelagic baselines, including the island of Carriacou, would require the longest segment of 20 miles and the system would provide a water to land ratio of 1.4 : 1.

Unlike the three States specified above, another archipelagic State in the Caribbean region which has already ratified the LOS Convention, Trinidad and Tobago, does not subject passage of warships to prior notification or authorization. The straight archipelagic baselines are drawn between 11 basepoints around the two main and 21 other islands of Trinidad and Tobago, while its water to land ratio amounts to 1.4 : 1 (2,027 square miles : 1,540 square miles), thus conforming to the LOS Convention. The Trinidad and Tobago's 1986 legislation specifically refers to the innocent passage, and adds that archipelagic sea lanes passage may be provided for by regulations. Although this legislation does not mention that until then the routes normally used for international navigation may be utilized, Trinidad and Tobago recognizes in practice the rights of other States to exercise archipelagic sea lanes passage through such routes. This is so far important that archipelagic baselines enclose the 19 mile wide Galleons Passage which is situated between Tobago and Trinidad and which is an important east-west navigation route between Venezuela and the South Atlantic. There is an alternate route north of Tobago, which would add about 30 miles to the passage of the South Atlantic.

Meaningly, the 1990 Delimitation Treaty (not yet in force) between Trinidad and Tobago and Venezuela explicitly grants Venezuelan vessels and aircraft "the right of transit passage" through "the existing strait between the island of Trinidad and the island of Tobago", while in the other straits in the Gulf of Paria the right of innocent passage applies (art. VI). In his Press Statement on the 1990 Treaty, Mr *Sahadeo Basdeo*, Trinidad and Tobago's Minister of External Affairs and International Trade, emphasizes that the Galleons Passage is a strait subject to the right of transit passage by ships and aircraft of all States. He also stresses that:

> Equally, the vessels and aircraft of all States enjoy the right of archipelagic sea lanes passage in sea lanes and air routes which the archipelagic State of Trinidad and Tobago may designate for their continuous and expeditious passage through or over its archipelagic waters and adjacent territorial sea. Even where such sea lanes are not designated, archipelagic sea lanes passage may be exercised through the routes normally used for international navigation. Trinidad and Tobago will in due course be defining its archipelagic sea lanes in the Galleons Passage (para. 25).[38]

---

[37] *See supra* (note 6).

[38] Text of Press Statement, as well as of the 1990 Treaty, and the Speaking Notes of 18 June 1990 for Minister of External Affairs and International Trade on the 1990 Trinidad and Tobago / Venezuela Treaty, were obtained by *Barbara Kwiatkowska* through kindness of the Permanent Secretary of Trinidad and Tobago's Ministry of External Affairs and International Trade.

The archipelagic status claimed by Fiji, Papua New Guinea, the Solomon Islands and Vanuatu — which have the best land/marine resource potential and the largest 200 mile zones amongst the South Pacific island States — may have important repercussions for international navigation. The Southwest Pacific is, on the one hand, an east-west transit area from Torres Strait to the United States, the Panama Canal, Fiji, and New Zealand. And on the other hand, it is important to north-south traffic between Japan and eastern Australia, as well as from eastern Australia to the Torres Strait. According to *Alexander*, the Southwest Pacific "is not yet a particularly significant strategic region, except to Australia and New Zealand, nor are most of the straits of real significance to international commerce. The principal navigational constraints that might develop here are, first, a perception of the danger of environmental damage leading possibly ... to the closing of certain maritime areas ...."[39] Such measures could affect international shipping if they were applied in the waters of the Solomon Islands and Papua New Guinea. This could also affect the interests of the United States for which the maintenance of access to the South Pacific's sea lanes is one of the major goals of providing development assistance to the 10 South Pacific island States, including the four archipelagic States.[40] The 1985 Rarotonga Treaty establishing the South Pacific Nuclear Free Zone referred to above does not introduce the general prohibition of passage of nuclear-powered ships and aircraft through the areas under State sovereignty, including archipelagic waters. Instead, it provides that:

> Each Party in the exercise of its sovereign rights remains free to decide for itself whether to allow visits by foreign ships and aircraft to its ports and airfields, transit of its airspace by foreign aircraft, and navigation by foreign ships in its territorial sea or archipelagic waters in a manner not covered by the rights of innocent passage, archipelagic sea-lane passage or transit passage of straits (art. 5, para. 2).

Meaningly, some South Pacific States, especially Vanuatu and the Solomon Islands, feel that the Rarotonga Treaty is too liberal in that it allows nuclear ships visits to continue at the discretion of the individual island States.

As *Alexander* anticipates, straits in this region could be of strategic significance both as a means to bypass Southeast Asia and to possibly exert influence on Australia and New Zealand.[41] Making use of these possibilities would, however, depend upon the practice of the South Pacific States concerned.

---

[39] *See Alexander* (note 4), 310.

[40] *See* statement of Mr *W. Clark*, Acting Assistant Secretary for East Asian and Pacific Affairs of 27 February 1989, in: Department of State Bulletin 49 (1989, No. 2146), 51-52.

[41] *Alexander* (note 4), 311.

5. Archipelagic States Conforming to the Rules on Archipelagic Waters but Not Determining Archipelagic Baselines

Some States proclaimed in their legislation the régime of archipelagic waters which conforms to Part IV of the LOS Convention, but they did not draw the archipelagic straight baselines. This relates to two other South Pacific States — Kiribati and Tuvalu, which (alongside with Niue, Tokelau and the Cook Islands) have the lowest level of economic growth in the region. They are both widely dispersed archipelagos consisting of small islands and have a water to land (including atolls) ratio higher than the maximum ratio 9 : 1 permitted by art. 47, para. 1 of the LOS Convention. Neither of the two States has ratified the Convention.

However, during UNCLOS III the water to land ratio, and likewise the criterion of the length of baselines, were subject to protracted debates between archipelagic States and the maritime powers. The 9 : 1 ratio now found in the Convention apparently prevents Kiribati and Tuvalu from drawing archipelagic straight baselines in accordance with art. 47. The 9 : 1 ratio is a matter of concern of the South Pacific Forum's member States which take the position that inability to participate in UNCLOS III deprived some of them of their opportunity to express their special needs in determining the archipelagic State régime.[42]

6. Archipelagic States Presumably Conforming to the Rules on Archipelagic Baselines and Archipelagic Waters

The legislation of Comoros (in the Indian Ocean), which did not yet ratify the LOS Convention, provides instance of a claim, the conformity of which to the rules related to both archipelagic straight baselines and archipelagic waters can only be presumed. Comoros is situated midway between Madagascar and the African continent, to the north of the Mozambique Channel, and consists of four main islands: Ngazidja (Greater Comoros), Ndzuani (Anjouan), Maore (Mayotte) and Mwali (Mohéli). It is not clear whether Comoros has yet drawn the archipelagic baselines for which its legislation provides. According to *Alexander*, Comoros (except for the French island of Mayotte) meets the requirements related both to the water to land ratio and to the length of baselines established in art. 47 of the Convention.[43] In *Prescott*'s opinion Comoros would have water to land ratio 3.9 : 1, while its archipelagic baselines could connect Grand Comore, Anjouan and Moheli.[44] The longest of those baselines would measure 76 miles.

---

[42] *Cf. J. Swan*, Highly Migratory Species. The South Pacific Forum Fisheries Agency, in: *Alfred H. A. Soons* (ed.), Implementation of the Law of the Sea Convention through International Institutions, Honolulu 1990, 239, 246.

[43] *See Alexander* (note 4), Table 3 at 88.

[44] Based on correspondence of *Barbara Kwiatkowska* with *J. R. V. Prescott* of March 1990.

As regards navigation in archipelagic waters, the Comoros' legislation provides merely for the right of innocent passage in accordance with art. 52 of the LOS Convention. The legislation does not mention archipelagic sea lanes passage. This does not need to imply non-conformity, since art. 53, para. 1 does not oblige but authorizes an archipelagic State to designate archipelagic sea lanes and air routes thereabove. However, art. 53, para. 12 states:

> If an archipelagic State does not designate sea lanes or air routes, the right of archipelagic sea lanes passage may be exercised through the routes normally used for international navigation.

National legislation discussed above which undoubtedly conforms to archipelagic waters' régime laid down in the LOS Convention, contains a special provision modelled upon art. 53, para. 12.[45]

Saint Kitts and Nevis in the Caribbean and Malta in the Mediterranean region would (similarly like Cuba or Haiti) encounter difficulty with meeting a minimum 1 : 1 ratio of water to land.[46] The water to land ratio of Saint Kitts and Nevis would be of about 0.8 : 1. For this reason Saint Kitts and Nevis, which did not yet ratify the LOS Convention, so far have not claimed archipelagic status. Should it decide to do so, the area of its potential archipelagic waters is not of importance for international navigation, due to an alternate route passing between Saint Kitts and Redonga Island. A water to land ratio of an area presently enclosed by straight baselines of Malta, which neither ratified the Convention, amounts to 0.64 : 1. The total area included within Maltese baselines amounts to 524 square kilometers, including 320 square kilometers of land area and 204 square kilometers of water area. For the purpose of those baselines the islands of Gozo, Comino and Fifla would have to be considered as fringing islands in the immediate vicinity of Malta, what seems questionable in the case of tiny Fifla Island.

7. Archipelagic States Presumably Conforming to the Rules on Archipelagic Waters but Not Conforming to those on Archipelagic Baselines

One archipelagic State, Cape Verde (in East Central Atlantic) which has already ratified the LOS Convention, drew in its legislation the archipelagic straight baselines which does not conform to art. 47, para. 2 of the Convention. In particular, 2 out of total 14 of Cape Verde's archipelagic baselines exceed 125 miles, while the longest one (linking Ponta Prainha and Ponta Preta) measures 137 miles.[47] These baselines — which were protested by the United States in

[45] *Cf. Wolfrum* (note 3), 125.

[46] Based on information obtained by *Barbara Kwiatkowska* on Saint Kitts and Nevis from *D. Freestone* in April 1990, and on Malta (including map) from *J. R. V. Prescott* in July 1990.

[47] *See Churchill/Lowe* (note 3), 106, and *Prescott* (note 4), 318. *See also Alexander* (note 4), Table 3 at 88. Note that in Limits in the Seas No. 36 (note 3), 29, it is incorrectly

1980 — would have to be adjusted to the criteria of art. 47, para. 2. According to *Victor Prescott*, such adjustment could easily be achieved by replacing the present longest segment by the one which would link the islands of Fogo and Sao Nicolau, and drawing additional segments which would link the islands of Santo Antao and Sao Nicolau on the one hand, and the islands of Brave and Fogo on the other hand.[48] The Cape Verde's ratio of water to land conforms to art. 47, para. 1 of the Convention, as it is 2 : 1. As regards the régime of archipelagic waters, the Cape Verde's legislation provides for a "freedom of innocent passage and overflight along established navigation routes" through its archipelagic waters. There is one important navigation route linking the English Channel with southern America which passes through the northwestern cluster of Cape Verde's islands to the west of Sao Nicolau.

In a Declaration made upon signing the LOS Convention and reaffirmed upon ratifying it, the Cape Verde declared that the Convention's provisions related to archipelagic waters are compatible with "the fundamental objectives and aims that inspire the legislation of the Republic of Cape Verde concerning its sovereignty and jurisdiction ...." It also added that this Convention recognizes the right of coastal States to adopt measures to safeguard their security interests, including those relating to the innocent passage of warships through archipelagic waters. However, the precise assessment of Cape Verde's legislative practice could again only be possible if the data on implementation of the navigational régime within its archipelagic waters were available.

The practice of the Maldives (in the Indian Ocean), comprised of some 1,800 various insular features which extend for almost 500 miles in an island chain, provides another instance of non-compliance with the LOS Convention's rules concerning archipelagic straight baselines. According to the Sri Lankan Ambassador, *Hiran Jayewardene*, in spite of the failure to qualify under the water to land ratio and the baseline length criteria as an archipelagic State, the Maldives has, in successive legal instruments, in effect established an archipelagic enclosure.[49] *Victor Prescott* is of the opinion that since the Maldivian constitutional rectangle does not touch land at any point, it cannot be considered as conforming to either ordinary or archipelagic straight baselines, although the Maldives would be able to draw archipelagic baselines and to satisfy the water to land ratio in accordance with art. 47, para. 1 of the LOS Convention which allows waters within fringing reefs of atolls to be counted as land.[50] But, in *Prescott*'s view, the use of

specified that the 1977 Decree of Cape Verde modified baselines established by the 1975 Law No. 14 which it superseded. According to *Prescott*, archipelagic baselines under the 1977 Decree follow the same course as those set out in 1975 Law.

[48] Based on correspondence of *Barbara Kwiatkowska* with *J. R. V. Prescott* of April 1990.

[49] *See Jayewardene* (note 2), 146, Figure 5.9 at 166, and note 448 at 190; *Victor L. Forbes*, The Maldives, in: Indian Ocean Review 1 (1988/4), 12-13, including map.

[50] Based on correspondence of *Barbara Kwiatkowska* with *J. R. V. Prescott* of March 1990; and *Prescott* (note 4), 161.

archipelagic baselines would give little advantage to the Maldives because of the linear arrangement of the islands. The exact status of the waters enclosed by Maldivian baselines is, according to Ambassador *Jayewardene*, "not determinable from the various instruments, but it is clear that some form of integration of these waters on the broad lines of the archipelago concept is intended".[51] The northern part of the Maldivian rectangle is crossed by a major navigation route proceeding from Port Said to Singapore. The Maldives, which did not yet ratify the LOS Convention, requires a prior authorization for the innocent passage of warships through its territorial sea, against which practice the United States protested in 1982. In its protest, the United States also contended non-conformity of the Maldivian Constitution to the existing rules of international law concerning baselines.

8. The Case of the Philippines

The legislation of the Philippines provides the most excessive instance of non-conformity to the LOS Convention's rules. This is due to the fact that this legislation regards the Philippine archipelagic waters as strictly internal waters in which — unlike the case of Indonesian legislation — no innocent passage of foreign ships is recognized. On the other hand, the fact that both the Philippines and Indonesia continue to rely on their pre-UNCLOS III legislation which they intend to modify, and the fact that both States already ratified the LOS Convention which they appear to follow in practice, are important elements to be taken into account in any assessment of practice of those two States.

The Philippines consists of some 7,104 islands arising from a common submarine platform and forming island chains on either side of a triangle composed of the islands of Luzon, Palawan, and Mindanao. The area occupied by the Philippine archipelago is at its greatest length and width 1,152 miles and 688 miles, while the water to land ratio of the Philippines is 1.8 : 1 and, thus, meets the criteria established in art. 47, para. 1 of the LOS Convention. The Philippines' 80 archipelagic baselines are delineated under the 1960/1968 legislation and have the total length of 8,174. 8974 miles.[52] While 3 out of these 80 baselines, thus 2.4 per cent, exceed 100 miles in length, one of them, in particular baseline to the southeast of Mindanao in the Gulf of Moro is of 140.05 miles in length. In both *Prescott*'s and *Jayewardene*'s opinion, this segment, at present drawn between Tongquil Island and a rock adjacent to the coast, could easily be brought into conformity with art. 47, para. 2 by reducing the single segment to shorter components linking other insular features closer to the shore.[53] The relevant adjustment to this effect is envisaged in the Bill No. 206 which is now pending

---

[51] *Jayewardene* (note 2), 172.

[52] *See Kittichaisaree* (note 17), 154; *Prescott* (note 4), 211.

[53] Based on correspondence of *Barbara Kwiatkowska* with *J. R. V. Prescott* of March 1990; and *Jayewardene* (note 2), 148-149.

in the Philippine Senate and which defines 79 archipelagic baselines, with the longest one measuring 120.8 miles in length.[54] The present baselines do not enclose the disputed Spratly Islands. Should the Philippines enclose Kalayaan by two archipelagic baselines, the latter would according to Prescott measure 117 and 102 miles, while the new water to land ratio would be 2.1 : 1.[55]

The Philippine Note Verbale of 7 March 1955 to the United Nations Secretary-General and another Note Verbale with virtually the same content sent to the International Law Commission on 20 January 1956 contain the first specific claim of the Philippines to a special archipelagic status. According to both notes, the right of innocent passage of foreign ships is allowed through Philippine archipelagic waters. These waters are regarded as internal waters subject to the exclusive sovereignty of the Philippines. All other water areas within the lines described in the 1898 Treaty of Paris between Spain and the USA and other related agreements are considered the territorial waters of the Philippines. The 1961 Philippine legislation (Act No. 3046), as amended in 1968 (Act No. 5446), confirms that the waters enclosed by archipelagic baselines are internal waters, but — unlike the previous Notes Verbale — contains no reference to foreign States' navigational rights in those waters. Moreover, in practice the Philippines — like some other States referred to above — requires prior authorization for passage of foreign warships and also the nuclear-powered ships, as well as insists upon prior authorization for overflight what resulted in several incidents with foreign aircraft. In 1961-1962 the protests were made against the Philippine claim by the United Kingdom, the United States, Japan and Australia. However, subsequently the United States agreed to the requirement of prior notification on the passage of its nuclear-powered ships which were not covered by the 1947 US Military Base Agreement with the Philippines, while Australia and the United Kingdom agreed to advance notification on the passage of their warships through the Philippine waters.[56] In 1968, the Philippines replaced the notification procedure by that of a prior authorization what was again protested in 1969 by the three States concerned.[57] The Philippines formally rejected these protests the same year.

The importance of position of the Philippines and likewise of Indonesia with respect to navigation through their archipelagic waters is due to their location

---

[54] *See* Congress of the Philippines, First Regular Session, Senate, S. No. 206, introduced by Senator *Leticia Shahani*, Explanatory Note and an Act to Define the Archipelagic Baselines of the Philippines, repealing Acts Nos. 3046 (1961) and 5446 (1968). The text of Bill No. 206 and a map were obtained by *Barbara Kwiatkowska* through kindness of *R. P. M. Lotilla* of the College of Law, University of the Philippines.

[55] *Prescott* (note 4), 230-231 and Figure 8.7. Note that *Shahani*'s Bill No. 206 (note 54) encloses the Kalayaan Islands by archipelagic baselines of the Philippines proposed therein.

[56] *See O'Connell* (note 2), 32-34.

[57] *Op. cit.*, 34-36 and 60-61.

in the Southeast Asian region, which is important as a transit route between the Pacific and Indian Oceans, between Japan and other countries of Northeast Asia and the Indian Ocean, and between Northeast Asia and Australia/New Zealand.[58] The region also is of considerable military concern to both the United States and the Soviet Union.

Out of some 45 straits used for international navigation in the Southeast Asia, 25 may be considered as major straits in terms of use and/or of strategic importance. They include Malacca-Singapore, Luzon (consisting of three Channels — Bashi, Balintang, and Babuyan), Formosa, Torres, and several of the straits of Indonesia and the Philippines. Balintang and Babuyan are two out of eight important straits lying wholly within Philippine archipelagic waters. The remaining six such straits are: Sibutu, Mindoro, Verde Island, San Bernardino, Surigao and Basilan.[59] Two other straits wholly enclosed by Philippine archipelagic waters are Maqueda and Polillo. Moreover, the Philippines also borders on Balut, Balabac and Bashi straits. The Philippine archipelagic waters are crossed by one major north-south and three important east-west navigation routes.

The Philippines and Indonesia are the only archipelagic States, some straits of which are qualified as the so-called "choke points" for the United States. According to *Lewis Alexander*, the choke points imply that there is the opportunity for a country to close off, or at least restrict, the flow of ocean-borne traffic critical, or of considerable importance, to a particular State or a number of States.[60] Among 17 waterways representing the choke points of critical importance to the US military and commercial traffic are: Surigao Strait lying wholly within Philippine archipelagic waters, and Luzon Strait, two (Balintang and Babuyan) of three Channels of which lie wholly within Philippine waters. Such critical choke points also include two straits — Lombok and Sunda — wholly enclosed by Indonesian archipelagic waters. Moreover, the 17 waterways cover two other straits — Balabac and Malacca-Singapore — which are bordered by the Philippines and Indonesia respectively. The Malacca-Singapore and Lombok (and/or Sunda) straits are included in the basic 9 of the 17 waterways.[61] Furthermore, according to *Alexander*, the United States shares responsibility for maintaining passage through additional choke points which are of primary concern to its allies and which include, among others, Mindoro Strait lying wholly within Philippine archipelagic waters, and Torres Strait lying partly within Papua New Guinea's archipelagic waters. The Philippines — unlike Indonesia and Papua New Guinea — has a military alliance with the United States.

58 *See Alexander* (note 4), 290, 296-297 and 361.

59 *Op. cit.*, 169 and note 51.

60 *Op. cit.*, 354-356.

61 Note that if these straits were closed, the transit passage from Japan to the Persian Gulf around Southern Australia would be about 14,000 miles, as opposed to 7,000 miles via Malacca/Singapore and 8,000 miles via Lombok, *see David L. Larson/Michael W. Roth*, The Law of the Sea and Maritime Strategy, in: Marine Policy 13 (1989), 193-217 (207).

During UNCLOS III the Philippines, which was one of the major sponsors of the archipelagic State régime, consistently emphasized that the right of innocent passage in archipelagic waters could not be the same as it was in the territorial sea. An archipelagic State should exercise more authority over its archipelagic waters than a coastal state exercises over its territorial sea. At the 1974 Caracas session, Minister *Arturo Tolentino* stressed the willingness of his delegation to consider any reasonable proposal for the régime of archipelagos as long as the essence of the archipelagic concept was maintained. That essence is "*the dominion and sovereignty of the archipelagic State within its baselines, which were so drawn as to preserve the territorial integrity of the archipelago by the inseparable unity of the land and water domain*" [emphasis added].[62] An acceptable solution from the Philippines' point of view, which in its opinion also accomodated the interests of international navigation, was to restrict the right of innocent passage of foreign ships through the archipelagic waters to the sea lanes designated by the archipelagic State. If the archipelagic State did not establish such sea lanes, then the entire archipelagic waters would only be open to innocent passage of ships. This approach was also shared by other major sponsors of the archipelagic State régime.

In the course of UNCLOS III, the Philippines (like other archipelagic States) compromised further this position up to an ultimate acceptance of the innocent passage alongside with archipelagic sea lanes passage.[63] The Joint Statement agreed by the Philippine President Marcos and the Indonesian President Suharto on 18 July 1979 in Puerto Azul, pointed out that the basic provisions on the archipelagic concept as proposed by UNCLOS III could be further improved and strengthened, and directed the delegations of the two states to consult and co-ordinate their efforts towards that end. However, the provisions in question did not undergo any further changes. This in the Philippines' opinion was due to the position taken by Indonesia that such changes would not be acceptable to the United States, what could affect final adoption of the Convention. On the other hand, Ambassador *Hasjim Djalal* of Indonesia generally characterized the Philippine position as much "stronger and inflexible" than that of Indonesia what, in his view, was due to "much more compact geographical set-up and historical factor" apparent in the case of the Philippines.[64]

Nevertheless, and since UNCLOS III also rejected the Philippine claim to its historic territorial sea beyond 12 miles, the recognition of the archipelagic State régime was in fact the determining factor in the Philippines' decision to sign

---

[62] UNCLOS III, Official Records, Vol. II, 264, para. 65, and also paras. 61-62 and 66.

[63] *Cf. Jose D. Ingles*, The United Nations Convention on the Law of the Sea: Implications of Philippine Ratification, in: Philippine Yearbook of International Law 9 (1983), 47-67 (50-58).

[64] *Hasjim Djalal*, The 1982 Law of the Sea Convention: A Southeast Asian Perspective, in: Indonesian Quarterly 13 (1985), 59-73 (64).

and subsequently ratify the Convention. At the closing session of UNCLOS III in Montego Bay, Minister *Arturo Tolentino* emphasized that one of the important reasons of the Philippines' satisfaction with the archipelagic State régime, as established in the Convention, is the fact that sovereignty of an archipelagic State is subject exclusively to Part IV of the Convention (art. 49, para. 3).[65] It follows therefrom that the archipelagic waters are subject only to two kinds of passage by foreign ships, namely innocent passage and archipelagic sea lanes passage. The transit passage available to foreign ships — under Part III of the Convention — in straits used for international navigation, does not apply in "national or domestic straits entirely within the archipelagic baselines." Minister *Tolentino* admits that such archipelagic straits could be subject to sea lanes passage if the archipelagic State so decided, and that the elements of sea lanes passage are practically the same as those of transit passage, but he re-emphasizes that:

> [w]hile transit passage is imposed by the Convention on the waters of the coastal States concerned, sea lanes passage can be exercised by foreign ships in archipelagic waters only in such sea lanes as the archipelagic State may designate and establish.[66]

The above position of Minister *Tolentino* that the archipelagic waters are governed by a *sui generis* régime of Part IV is correct. However, a complete omission in his statement of the two major elements comprised by this régime under the LOS Convention gives rise to a serious concern. One of those elements is the rule provided for in art. 53, para. 12 of the Convention that, if an archipelagic State does not designate sea lanes or air routes, "the right of archipelagic sea lanes passage may be exercised through the routes normally used for international navigation." And another element is that, unlike the innocent passage, the right of archipelagic passage also covers the right of overflight in the air routes "above" the archipelagic sea lanes.

The Philippine statement was expressly replied in the 1983 statement of the United States and also that of West Germany. The US statement reads as follows:

> One speaker also asserted that archipelagic sea lanes passage may be exercised only in sea lanes designated and established by the archipelagic State. This assertion fails to account for circumstances in which all normal sea lanes and air routes have not been designated by the archipelagic State in accordance with Part IV, including articles 53 and 54. In such circumstances, *archipelagic sea lanes passage may be exercised through all sea lanes and air routes normally used for international navigation. The United States regards these rights as essential components of the archipelagic régime if it is to find acceptance in international law* [emphasis added].[67]

65 UNCLOS III, Official Records, Vol. XVII, 69-70, paras. 56-57.

66 *Loc. cit.*, paras. 52 and 51.

67 *Loc. cit.*, 244.

The United States also responded to the Philippines' and some other States' assertion at the Montego Bay session that archipelagic sea lanes passage (and likewise transit passage) is a "new" right. In the US opinion:

> To the contrary, long-standing international practice bears out the right of all States to transit straits used for international navigation and waters which may be eligible for archipelagic status. Moreover, *these rights are well established in international law. Continued exercise of these freedoms of navigation and overflight cannot be denied a State without its consent* [emphasis added].[68]

When signing the LOS Convention on 10 December 1982, the Philippines made a Declaration under art. 310 thereof, subsequently reaffirmed when ratifying this Convention on 8 May 1984, that this shall not, among others, in any manner affect Philippine sovereign rights under the Constitution as well as the 1898 Treaty of Paris between Spain and the USA and the 1930 Treaty of Washington between the USA and Great Britain. Apart from equating archipelagic waters with internal waters already referred to above, the Philippine Constitution (Art. 1), basing on the Paris and Washington Treaties, also established the limits of the Philippine territorial sea, which from the points in Western and East Luzon extends to 140 and 290 miles respectively. During UNCLOS III, the Philippines failed to obtain recognition for this excessive territorial sea on historic grounds.[69] The Philippine Declaration specifically states that the 1951 Mutual Defense Treaty between the United States and the Philippines (regarded by the Philippines as acknowledging the excessive limit of its territorial sea) shall not be affected. Some other paragraphs of the Philippine Declaration specify that:

> 5. The Convention shall not be construed as amending in any manner any pertinent laws and Presidential Decrees of Proclamation of the Republic of the Philippines; *the Government ... maintains and reserves the right and authority to make any amendments* to such laws, decrees or proclamations *pursuant to the provisions of the Philippines' Constitution*;
>
> 6. The provisions of the Convention on archipelagic passage through sea lanes do not nullify or impair the sovereignty of the Philippines as an archipelagic State over the sea lanes and do not deprive it of authority to enact legislation to protect its sovereignty, independence and security;
>
> 7. *The concept of archipelagic waters is similar to the concept of internal waters under the Constitution of the Philippines, and removes straits connecting these waters with the economic zone or high seas from the rights of foreign vessels to transit passage for international navigation; ...* [emphasis added].

This Declaration has strongly been objected to by the Soviet Union, its two republics — Byelorussian SSR and Ukrainian SSR, as well as Bulgaria, Czechoslovakia and Australia. These States view the Philippine Declaration as incompatible with art. 310, and as constituting reservations which are prohibited under

---

[68] *Ibid.* For the F. R. G.'s statement, *see loc. cit.*, 240.

[69] *Cf. Ingles* (note 63), 48-49 and 61-62.

art. 309 of the Convention. The incompatibility with art. 310 is rightly asserted on the basis of a discrepancy between the Philippine legislative practice and the Convention. Therefore, the Philippine Declaration is deemed by the objecting States to have no legal effect. In 1986 the Philippine Declaration was, on the similar grounds, protested against by the United States in spite of the US access to all Philippine waters being secured under its 1951 Mutual Defense Treaty with the Philippines. The US protest emphasizes the customary nature of the archipelagic régime as reflected in the LOS Convention, and also formally questions the Philippine interpretation of the Paris (1898) and Washington (1930) Treaties referred to above.

It could be argued that the Philippine position expressed in paras. 5 and 6 of its Declaration quoted above does not necessarily imply a non-conforming conduct of the Philippines. Paragraph 6 reflects in fact the provision of art. 49, para. 4 of the Convention. And para. 5 could be construed as not going against the archipelagic régime laid down in the Convention, if the adequate amendment to Article 1 of the Constitution of the Philippines was effected. This was anticipated with respect to the 1973 Philippine Constitution. However, as is indicated in the protest of Australia, the concept of internal waters (and likewise of the territorial sea) held under the former Constitutions of the Philippines was recently reaffirmed in the new 1987 Philippine Constitution, except that the latter does not refer anymore to the Philippine historic title as the basis for its claims. The 1987 Constitution retains the former definition of internal waters restating in Art. 1: The waters around, between, and connecting the islands of the archipelago, regardless of their breadth and dimensions, form part of the *internal waters* of the Philippines [emphasis added].

The 1987 Constitution uses for the first time the term "archipelagic waters" providing in its Art. 12, para. 2 that: "The State shall protect the nation's marine wealth in its *archipelagic waters*, territorial sea, and exclusive economic zone, and reserve its use and enjoyment exclusively to Filipino citizens" [emphasis added]. But, notwithstanding this reference to "archipelagic waters", a basic lack of change of the Philippine Constitution seems to accentuate a non-conforming character of the Philippines' assertion made in para. 5 of its Declaration, and also that embodied in para. 7. Contrary to what the Philippines claims, the Convention's régime of archipelagic waters cannot be construed as similar to the régime of the Philippines' internal waters under its present Constitution. For the reasons which were already explained in connection with the 1982 Philippine statement in Montego Bay, and which were explicitly addressed in the 1983 US statement replying thereto and quoted above, also the assertion made by the Philippines with respect to straits within archipelagic waters, clearly contradicts the Convention.

In reply to objections raised against its Declaration made upon signing and ratifying the LOS Convention, the Philippines made another Declaration in 1988 reaffirming that its former Declaration is made in conformity with art. 310 and that it consists of "interpretative statements." The Philippines assures that it intends to harmonize its domestic legislation with the provisions of the Convention, and that: "The necessary steps are being undertaken to enact legislation dealing with archipelagic sea lanes passage and the exercise of Philippine sovereign rights over archipelagic waters, in accordance with the Convention." Thus, the Declaration evidences that the Philippines is willing to amend its legislation with a view to conform to the LOS Convention. This intention is to some extent reflected by the Senate Bill No. 206 already referred to above, which in its preamble explicitly refers to the necessity of delineating the Philippine "archipelagic baselines" in accordance with the LOS Convention. The Explanatory Note to this Bill specifies that the proposed legislation delineates archipelagic baselines in accordance with Part IV of the Convention and emphasizes that an archipelagic State exercises sovereignty over its archipelagic waters, sea-bed and air space. However, the Bill also repeats in its preamble the constitutional definition of national territory, as comprising the Philippine Archipelago, and the definition of its internal waters quoted above. The Bill's Explanatory Note indicates that the omission of any reference to historic title in the present constitutional definition of the Philippine Archipelago (national territory) reflects a formal recognition by the Philippines of the legal régime of mid-ocean archipelagos under the LOS Convention. But the repeated reliance on the constitutional concept of archipelagic waters as internal waters seems to evidence a major difficulty faced by the Philippines in introducing the relevant changes into its Constitution.[70] Consequently, the Act proposed by the Bill No. 206 does not provide for navigational rights of the third States within the Philippine archipelagic (internal) waters.

It should, however, be emphasized that, notwithstanding incompatibility of the existing and proposed Philippine legislation with the LOS Convention discussed above, the Philippines — like Indonesia — appears to conform in practice with the navigational régime set forth in the Convention by allowing foreign warships (submerged) and other ships to pass without notification or authorization through the routes used customarily for international navigation within its waters.[71] As regards the authorization and/or notification required for innocent passage outside those routes, due to diverse State practice it would not, as is discussed below, seem to be forbidden by customary international law. As is the case with Indonesia and other archipelagic States, a practical compliance by the Philippines with the Convention's rules indicated above can be regarded as

[70] Note also repeated emphasis in the Philippine academic writings that all waters within archipelagic baselines are internal waters forming part of the national territory of an archipelagic state; *see*, e. g., *Jorge R. Coquia / Miriam Defensor Santiago*, Public International Law, Quezon City 1985, 335.

[71] Based on consultations of *Barbara Kwiatkowska* with *J. R. Coquia*, Legal Adviser to the Philippine Foreign Office, and with *Mochtar Kusumaatmadja*, Director of the Center for Law, Archipelago and Development Studies, Jakarta, Indonesia, in May 1990.

resulting to important extent from the present lack of enforcement capacity. Therefore, and in view of the restrictive official position taken by the Philippines with respect to the navigational régime within its archipelagic waters discussed above, the adequate long-term guarantee of unimpeded navigation in accordance with the Convention would require an amendment of the Philippine Constitution and other relevant legislation.

However, in the present situation of political instability and the Presidential elections forthcoming in the Philippines in 1992, any measures to this effect seem unlikely. Moreover,the expiration of the US Military Base Agreement with the Philippines forthcoming in 1991, in combination with recent reduction in tensions between the United States and the Soviet Union, raised an anxiety in the Philippines and other Southeast Asian States that the United States (and likewise the European Economic Community) may rechannel their resources to help consolidate political and economic changes in the Eastern Europe. In order not to affect the negotiations on renewal of the US bases agreement in 1991, the Philippine President *Aquino* objected to a bill approved by the Senate in June 1988 which would ban nuclear weapons and passage of nuclear-powered ships and aircraft in the Philippines and, thus, affect the operations of two major US bases. For the same reason, the Philippines also reserved its position with respect to initiative of the Association of South-East Asian Nations (ASEAN) to conclude a treaty on the Southeast Asia Nuclear Weapon Free Zone (SEANWFZ) as a component of the Zone of Peace, Freedom and Neutrality (ZOPFAN) in Southeast Asia. Such a treaty, being especially promoted by Indonesia and Malaysia, was found totally unacceptable by the United States, as it would weaken the US nuclear deterrent but not place the Soviet Union under similar constraints. The United States relies more heavily than the Soviet Union on strategic nuclear missiles carried on submarines and, therefore, needs to keep the sea lanes of Southeast Asia open to passage of such weapons as a key link between the Pacific and Indian Oceans. The United States has repeatedly denied a possible reduction of its involvement in the region, emphasizing that the US aid programmes provide visible and highly welcome symbols of the US commitment to remain engaged in the region's affairs.[72]

9. The Case of Indonesia

Indonesia as an archipelagic State having unique geographical configuration and lying between two large continents and two major oceans, holds an important position in ocean affairs.[73] The word for "fatherland" is in Indonesian language

[72] *See Clark* (note 40), 50; on US Indonesian relations, *see op. cit.*, 52.

[73] For an excellent analysis, *see Mochtar Kusumaatmadja* (note 2), 174-177; and also *id.*, The Concept of the Indonesian Archipelago, in: Indonesian Quarterly 10 (1985), 12-26; *Michael Leifer*,International Straits of the World. Malacca, Singapore, and Indonesia, Alphen aan den Rijn 1978, 17-27.

(*Bahasa Indonesia*) "tanah air" meaning "land and water." It clearly shows that the Indonesian concept of archipelago is based on the unity: the interconnecting waters between the islands are regarded as a unifying rather than a separating element.

The former assessments indicated the total number of Indonesian islands equal to 13,667, while according to the presently updated data, this total number amounts to 17,508 islands. In particular, Indonesia consists of six main and 17,502 small islands, of which 5,707 islands are named.[74] The principal islands are: Sumatra, Java or Madura, Kalimantan or Borneo, Sulawesi or Celebes, and Irian Jaya (formerly West Irian) or West New Guinea. The total land area of the Indonesian archipelago is at present 5,193,250 square kilometers, including 2,027,080 of land and 3,166,080 square kilometers of archipelagic waters area.

Act No. 4 concerning Indonesian Waters of 1960 provides — in implementation of the 1957 Djuanda Declaration — for the use of straight baselines "connecting the outermost points on the low water mark of the outermost islands or part of such islands" of the Indonesian archipelago. Baselines are defined by 196 turning points and their total length amounts to 8,069.8 miles. According to *Prescott,* the baselines include five segments longer than 100 miles, two of which measure 124 miles, while the water to land ratio of Indonesia is 1.2 : 1.[75] These indicators are compatible with the criteria established in art. 47, paras. 1-3 of the LOS Convention with regard to the length of baselines, their conformity to the general configuration of the archipelago, and the water to land ratio what shows that the Indonesian model was of essential influence on the Convention's tests. It should, however, be noted that the baselines specified above have not been amended since the acquisition of East Timor as a province of Indonesia.

Similarly like the Philippines, Indonesia lies at the crossroads of busy international shipping and air routes between the Indian and Pacific Oceans, some of which routes connect both archipelagos. The major maritime traffic proceeds through the Malacca-Singapore Straits, the Straits of Lombok, Sunda, Makassar, and the Celebes Sea.[76] According to *Alexander,* apart from Lombok and Makassar Straits, eight other out of at least 10 major straits enclosed by Indonesian archipelagic baselines are: Gaspar, Karimata, Sunda, Ombai, Wetar, Manipa, Serasan, and Jailolo.[77] He also lists more than 14 other straits within the limits of Indonesian archipelagic waters that include: Berhala, Bangka Strait, Sapudi, Bali, Alas, Sape, Sumba, Roti, Boeton, Api, Koti, Bangka Passage, Greyhound, and Obi. In addition, Indonesia borders on Malacca and Singapore Straits, Great Channel, and Balut, what brings the total number of straits bordered by Indonesia to over 28.

---

74 This is an updated data based on inventory carried out by the Hydro-Oceanography Division of the Indonesian Navy up to 1986.

75 *Prescott* (note 4), 211.

76 *Cf. supra* (note 58).

77 *Alexander* (note 4), 165-169 and a map.

At the same time, as was noted above while discussing the case of the Philippines, Lombok and Sunda as well as Malacca-Singapore Straits are included into 17 waterways representing the choke points of critical importance to the military and commercial traffic of the United States. Lombok Strait is being developed as an alternative route to Malacca-Singapore Straits for ultra large crude carriers (ULCCs) passing from the Indian Ocean to the Japanese ports and to those on the west coast of North America. And the Strait of Sunda provides the most direct route between the US military base at Subic Bay in the Philippines and its communications facility at the British Island of Diego Garcia in the Indian Ocean. Indonesian archipelagic waters are crossed by five major and number of other navigational routes.

After gaining independence in 1945, a new policy concerning Indonesian waters was established in the Djuanda Declaration of 1957. A number of provisions of the 1939 colonial Ordinance on Territorial Sea and Maritime Districts (*Territoriale Zee en Maritime Kringen Ordonnantie*) were revoked, and the width of the territorial sea was extended from 3 to 12 miles. The Declaration, emphasizing that "for the purposes of territorial unity, and in order to protect the resources of Indonesia, *all islands and the seas in between must be regarded as one total unit*", states that:

> all waters, surrounding, between and connecting the islands constituting the Indonesian state, regardless of their extension or breadth, are integral parts of the territory of the Indonesian state and therefore, parts of the *internal or national waters which are under the exclusive sovereignty of the Indonesian state*. Innocent passage of foreign ships in these internal waters is granted as long as it is not prejudicial to or violates the sovereignty and security of Indonesia [emphasis added].

The Djuanda Declaration shows that security and defense concerns were important aspects justifying a new policy. A related factor of a political nature was the territorial integrity of Indonesia. Confronted with a critical situation of political disintegration, the government needed a concept that would act as a symbol of unity. The *Nusantara* or archipelagic concept formulated in the Djuanda Declaration provided a clear solution to this problem. However, as the Declaration enclosed within Indonesian internal waters and the 12 mile territorial sea the former areas ("pockets") of the high seas which were open to free navigation, it resulted in protests of Australia, France, the United Kingdom, Japan, New Zealand, the Netherlands, and the United States.[78] The only States that recognized an Indonesian claim as lawful were the Soviet Union and China, which at that time had limited maritime interests.

Having failed to obtain recognition of its new territorial concept at UNCLOS I in 1958, the Indonesian government decided to continue its policy outlined in the Djuanda Declaration by enacting the Act No. 4 of 1960 already referred to above. The Act reaffirms that all waters enclosed by these baselines are internal

---

[78] *See O'Connell* (note 2), 39; *cf. Leifer* (note 73), 22.

waters of Indonesia, in which innocent passage "is open" to all foreign ships. The elucidation to this Act specifies that, unlike is the case with innocent passage of foreign ships through the territorial waters which is a right recognized by international law, innocent passage through Indonesian internal waters is guaranteed by Indonesia as a "privilege" (or a "facility") rather than as a right, and can be withdrawn by Indonesia. Therefore, some Indonesian writers maintain that Indonesian legislation differs in this respect from the rules of the LOS Convention (art. 52) which provides for the right of innocent passage through archipelagic waters on the same conditions as through the territorial sea.[79] However, *Mochtar Kusumaatmadja* and some other authorities are of the opinion that foreign ships do enjoy "the right" (and not "privilege") of innocent passage through Indonesian internal (archipelagic) waters in accordance with the LOS Convention.[80] According to *Mochtar*, the inclusion of the right of innocent passage as an integral part of the *Nusantara* concept was done conciously in order to reduce the opposition of the major maritime powers to this concept. Nevertheless, in 1961 the United Kingdom, Japan, the USA and Australia have again protested against what they perceived as "reservation" made by Indonesia to the 1958 UN High Seas Convention.[81] Upon ratification of this Convention, Indonesia declared that the terms "territorial sea" and "internal waters" found therein were interpreted in accordance with its legislation.

In order to further emphasize the right of innocent passage for foreign ships in the waters of Indonesian archipelago, Indonesia has enacted on 28 July 1962 the Government Regulation No. 8 on Innocent Passage of Foreign Vessels Through Indonesian Waters. The Regulation affirms that the suspendable innocent passage of all ships is guaranteed, and specifies conditions thereof which conform to the basic rules of innocent passage now codified in Part II of the LOS Convention. This includes the requirement of submarines to navigate on the surface. For the purposes of innocent passage, the foreign ships are encouraged to use the shipping lanes as contained in pilots' logs that circulate in the shipping world. However, unlike what the LOS Convention does but some States do in practice, the Regulation requires foreign warships and noncommercial government ships to give a prior notification on their passage (art. 7).

The rules of the 1962 Regulation being of particular importance are those which concern the sea lanes, since these rules are precursory to the right of archipelagic sea lanes passage now found in the LOS Convention. According to the Regulation, whenever the Naval Commander-in-Chief has determined sea

---

[79] *See*, e. g., *Etty R. Agoes* on behalf of Indonesian National Study Team, Passage Through Waters Within National Jurisdiction: Indonesian Perspective, SEAPOL Studies No. 6 (a) (1987), 24.

[80] *Mochtar* (note 73), 15 *et seq.*; *Nugroho Wisnumurti*, Some Impacts of the 1982 Convention on the Law of the Sea on Maritime Jurisdiction: An Indonesian Perspective, in: *Craven et. al.* (note 18), 43-49 (46).

[81] *See O'Connell* (note 2), 40.

lanes, then foreign warships, noncommercial government ships, and fishing vessels must pass through these sea lanes. Such sea lanes passage is not subject to a prior notification, and the submarines are presumably allowed to submerged navigation. If the sea lanes are not established, the three categories of foreign ships specified above will, according to the Regulation, proceed in innocent passage (and submarines on the surface) subject to prior notification, and not — as the LOS Convention permits (art. 53, para. 12) — through the routes normally used for international navigation. Designation of air routes is not provided for by the Regulation. The sea lanes for ships would be determined by the Minister for Defense and Security of Indonesia, but so far this has not taken place, except sea lanes established for fishing vessels and those under the 1982 Jakarta Treaty with Malaysia referred to below. The rules specified above apply to all straits bordered by Indonesia, except the Malacca-Singapore Straits which are governed by the 1977 Tripartite Agreement between Indonesia, Malaysia and Singapore.

In practice — like is the case with the Philippine archipelagic waters — foreign ships, including warships apparently pass without notification through the routes customarily used for international navigation within the Indonesian waters.[82] However, due to complexity of the archipelagic waters régime under the LOS Convention and unclear status of the existing customary law addressed below, the passage through Indonesian waters may potentially give rise to controversies. This is exemplified by the temporary closure by Indonesia of Sunda and Lombok Straits in September 1988, which occurred after Indonesia ratified the Convention in December 1985 and the United States formally recognized Indonesian archipelagic status in exchange of letters which was initialed between the two States in May 1986 and attached to the 1988 Indonesian-US Income Tax Treaty. Although the United States has explicitly conditioned its recognition upon compatibility of Indonesia's practice with the LOS Convention, the 1988 closure of Sunda and Lombok was effected by Indonesia without designating alternative sea lanes as would conform to the Convention.

After ratification by Indonesia of the LOS Convention in 1985, Ambassador *Hasjim Djalal* of the Indonesian Foreign Office prepared an elaborated study on measures to be undertaken by Indonesia in implementation of this Convention.[83] As regards the archipelagic State régime, such measures include a re-examination and adjustment of Indonesian baselines delineated by the 1960 Act, as well as

[82] *See supra*, note 71. Note that in his 1971 article, *O'Connell* (note 2), 41-42, indicated that warships using the Sunda and Lombok Straits still gave a prior "low level" notification on their passage to the Indonesian Navy. In his work of 1982, *O'Connell* (note 3), 249, while discussing the 1962 and other Indonesian regulations, states that: "The regulations have been supplemented *to permit peaceful navigation of foreign vessels through those parts of the 'internal seas' which would be either high seas or territorial seas using normal baselines*" [emphasis added].

[83] *Hasjim Djalal*, The Law of the Sea Convention and Indonesia's Responses, Ministry of Foreign Affairs, Jakarta 1987 (obtained through kindness of the author).

a redefinition of the régime of passage and navigation through archipelagic waters and the territorial sea. At the same time, while the sovereignty claimed by Indonesia conforms to art. 49 of the Convention, the presently used term of "internal waters" should be replaced — in accordance with the Convention — by that of "archipelagic waters." This latter term is used in the 1982 Jakarta Treaty examined below which explicitly provides that: "'archipelagic waters of the Republic of Indonesia' means all the waters enclosed by archipelagic baselines drawn in accordance with the laws and regulations of the Republic of Indonesia and in conformity with international law" (Art. 1, para. 1). Some Indonesian authors recommend reconsideration of the prior notification presently required by Indonesia for innocent passage of warships and some other ships, but in view of non-uniform State practice in this respect such reconsideration would not seem feasible. The essential adjustment would have to occur with respect to the right of archipelagic sea lanes passage that should be defined along the detailed rules laid down in arts. 53-54 of the Convention. In accordance with the Convention's art. 51, Indonesia would also need to recognize the legitimate rights and interests of the immediately neighbouring States (especially Singapore), as it already did under its 1982 Jakarta Treaty with Malaysia.

A notable characteristic of Indonesian practice with respect to the *Nusantara* concept are the major efforts undertaken by Indonesia with a view towards securing an international recognition of its archipelagic concept. As *Mochtar* indicates, such recognition has on the one hand been sought directly through negotiations at UNCLOS III and in other multilateral fora, and on the other hand indirectly through concluding maritime boundary delimitation agreements, and inclusion of a special territorial clause in bilateral agreements on economic, finance, social, and other matters.[84] The bilateral 1982 Jakarta Treaty concluded between Indonesia and Malaysia is of particular significance from the viewpoint of recognition of the archipelagic State régime. The Treaty involves Malaysia's recognition of the *Nasuntara* concept on the one hand, and the recognition by Indonesia of Malaysia's rights in its archipelagic waters between East and West Malaysia on the other hand. A wide range of the recognized rights of Malaysia includes those concerning navigation and overflight, fisheries, submarine cables and pipelines, search and rescue, marine scientific research for the purposes directly connected with marine environmental protection, as well as the promotion and maintenance of law and order. Navigational rights of Malaysia, referred to by the Treaty as the rights of "access and communication" of ships and aircraft, conform to the right of archipelagic sea lanes passage as set forth in the LOS Convention. The right of innocent passage both in Indonesian archipelagic waters and the territorial sea and in accordance with international law is under the Jakarta Treaty applicable only to Malaysian traditional fishing vessels.

---

[84] *Mochtar Kusumaatmadja* (note 2), 19 and 21.

The Jakarta Treaty — similarly as does art. 53 of the Convention — provides for "the right" (and not "freedom") of access and communication of all ships (government and commercial) and aircraft (State and civil) of Malaysia, which right is non-suspendable. It also qualifies the right of access and communication in accordance with the Convention as the right of "continuous, expeditious and unobstructed" navigation and overflight. Passage of all ships, including warships, is confined to the two "corridors" (sea lanes) which are defined by a series of continuous axis lines and shown in the map annexed to the Jakarta Treaty. The specific tests somewhat differ from those set forth in art. 53, para. 5 of the LOS Convention for archipelagic sea lanes, since under the Treaty ships cannot deviate more than 10 (and not as Convention requires 25) miles to either sides of the axis lines in the corridors, provided that ships shall not navigate closer to the coasts than three miles. The Treaty does not specify whether the two corridors cover "normal passage routes" as is required under art. 53, para. 4 of the LOS Convention, but this appears to be implied by general applicability of the Treaty to the traditional rights of Malaysia. No notification for passage through the corridors is required.

As regards warships, there is no specification in the Jakarta Treaty that they should navigate in the "normal mode" which under art. 53, para. 3 of the Convention means submerged passage of submarines. However, such submerged passage in sea lanes appears to be permitted under the 1962 Indonesian Regulation which, like other relevant Indonesian regulations, applies to navigational rights under the Jakarta Treaty. While proceeding through the corridors, warships have, according to the Treaty, the right to conduct naval manoeuvres, provided that in the course of tactical exercise no firing of weapons is permitted. Naval manoeuvres are to be subject to appropriate arrangements between the two parties.

Unlike art. 53, para. 1 of the LOS Convention, the Jakarta Treaty does not confine the right of overflight to air space "above" the corridors designated for ships. Instead, the right of access and communication exercisable by both State (military) and civil aircraft applies to the "air space above the territorial sea, archipelagic waters and the territory of the Republic of Indonesia lying between East and West Malaysia." Military aircraft has the right of aerial manoeuvres on the same conditions as those applicable to naval manoeuvres referred to above. Civil aircraft is obliged to operate with due regard for the safety of overflight and for this purpose to "comply with the laws and regulations of the Republic of Indonesia in conformity with generally accepted international rules and regulations . . . ." This rule differs from that laid down in art. 39, para. 3 (a) of Part III of the LOS Convention obliging aircraft to observe the International Civil Aviation Organization (ICAO) Rules of the Air.

The Jakarta Treaty is an important achievement not only in terms of recognition of the archipelagic State régime of Indonesia, but also in terms of immediate implementation by a major archipelagic State of the régime of archipelagic sea lanes passage in accordance with the LOS Convention.

III. Evaluation

1. Definition of Archipelagic State and Construction of Archipelagic Baselines

The recognition of a concept of the archipelagic State, as defined in art. 46 of the LOS Convention with a view to preserve — basing on the unity between land and sea — the integrity of such State, could at present hardly be denied. From amongst variety of factors, including geographical, economic, political, security-oriented or historic ones, different factors are of, and are alternating in their, primary importance for particular archipelagic States. A continued importance of a security factor in the archipelagic concept seems to be a reflection of general sensitivity of the developing States with regard to security matters at the present stage of the North-South confrontation.

The elements of the definition of archipelagic State and archipelago are intrinsically linked with the rules established in art. 47 of the Convention with respect to constructing the straight archipelagic baselines. Accordingly, while drawing these baselines, States use in practice differently various insular elements so as to satisfy the geographical requirements set up in art. 47, in particular those laid down in its paras. 1 and 2 with regard to water to land ratio and the length of baselines. Most States claiming archipelagic status conform to geographic criteria or would be able to redraw their baselines so that the longest line would measure only 125 miles, no more than 3 per cent of baselines would be between 100 and 125 miles, and a water to land ratio would be between 1 : 1 and 9 : 1. Meaningly, some States, e. g. Papua New Guinea with respect to Tauu Islands, do not include islands lying more than 125 miles from the main group into their baselines system. States having baselines which exceed the permissible 125 miles are Cape Verde and the Philippines, as well as Ecuador with respect to its non-State Galapagos Archipelago. The Cape Verdian and Philippine baselines could easily be brought into conformity with the LOS Convention.

Generally, an adjustment to the Convention's rules would seem to be easier for widely scattered island States having a water to land ratio exceeding the permissible maximum of 9 : 1 (such as Kiribati, Tuvalu, Tonga, Seychelles, Mauritius, and the Maldives), than for States with a ratio below the minimum of 1 : 1. The assessment of conformity of actual or potential adjustments to the Convention's rules depends, however, on the interpretation of those rules. As was shown with repect to the individual cases above, for the purpose of adjusting their baselines and water to land ratio, States appear to be permitted, under art. 46, to draw baselines around two or more of their archipelagos (each consisting of at least 2 islands) and to include other islands into their baselines. They are also permitted under art. 47, paras. 1 and 7 to include waters lying within the fringing reefs of islands and atolls into their land territory. Potential claimants of archipelagic status having (like Cuba, Haiti, Madagascar, Malta, Saint Kitts and Nevis, Iceland, New Zealand, or the United Kingdom) a water to land ratio below the minimum of 1 : 1, would encounter more difficulty in adjusting their ratio, although even in this case some authors doubt why this is thought to be necessary.[85]

Generally, non-uniformity in the drawing of straight archipelagic baselines would not seem to be a major obstacle in the development of an archipelagic concept, as long as the uniformity of a navigational régime in archipelagic waters is ensured. This also relates to claims of a number of continental States with respect to their outlying archipelagos which, although not conforming to the Convention, may result in emergence of the new customary rules. In view of the impact of which possible proliferation of an archipelagic régime may have on international navigation, it would be desirable if the International Maritime Organization (IMO) considered — as it intended — its rôle with regard to publicity on charts and geographical coordinates of archipelagic baselines in accordance with art. 47, paras. 8 and 9 of the Convention.[86]

2. *The Nature of the Archipelagic State's Competence*

The paramount concern of an archipelagic State to safeguard and protect its political, geographical, economic and cultural unity as well as its territorial integrity and security, is given a legal basis in recognition of the sovereignty of this State over its archipelagic waters. This sovereignty, as expressly specified in art. 49, paras. 1 and 2 of the LOS Convention and claimed by States in practice, extends to the archipelagic waters enclosed by the straight archipelagic baselines regardless of depth of such waters or distance from the coast, as well as to the air space above archipelagic waters, their sea-bed and subsoil, and the resources contained therein. A significant confirmation of this sovereignty is also found in art. 2, para. 1 of the LOS Convention. These provisions clearly evidence that on the one hand, archipelagic waters — as do internal waters and the territorial sea — form part of the maritime territory which is subject to sovereignty of an archipelagic State. And on the other hand, although all other maritime spaces of an archipelagic State are measured from archipelagic baselines (art. 48), the legal status of archipelagic waters lying inward of those baselines differs from that of internal waters of a coastal State. The establishment by the archipelagic State of internal waters within its archipelagic waters is expressly envisaged in art. 50 of the Convention. Archipelagic waters do not have a status of the territorial sea, but a *sui generis* status which — as art. 49, para. 3 specifies — is governed by Part IV of the Convention. Indonesia and the Philippines, which claim an archipelagic status under the Convention in a manner conforming to its arts. 2, para. 1 and 49, would, therefore, have to amend their legislation

---

85 *See Churchill/Lowe* (note 3), 101.

86 *See* IMO doc. LEG/MISC/1 (1987), 56-57 and Annex, 4.

characterizing at present the waters enclosed by their baselines as internal waters. A similar amendment would be necessary in case of some potential claimants of archipelagic status, such as Mauritius, Tonga or Ecuador (Galapagos).

The conformity of State legislative practice to the Convention in this respect is so far essential that the nature of exclusive competence of an archipelagic State is strictly interrelated to the recognition of inclusive rights of the third States within archipelagic waters. In particular, unlike is the case with internal waters of be it an archipelagic or coastal State, the sovereignty of an archipelagic State over its archipelagic waters is, under Part IV of the Convention, subject to limitations resulting from:

— a suspendable right of innocent passage of all ships (art. 52),

— a non-suspendable right of archipelagic sea lanes passage of all ships and aircraft, which right may also apply to the territorial sea of an archipelagic State (arts. 53 and 54),

— existing rights and all other legitimate interests of "immediately adjacent neighbouring" States (art. 47, para. 6),

— existing agreements with other States on traditional fishing rights and other legitimate activities of "immediately adjacent neighbouring" States (art. 51, para. 1), as well as on existing submarine cables (art. 51, para. 2).

3. Right of Innocent Passage

The right of suspendable innocent passage of all foreign ships through archipelagic waters is, under art. 52 of Part IV, virtually the same as such right through the territorial sea of be it an archipelagic or coastal State under Part II of the LOS Convention. An aspect of this inclusive right which conflicts with an exclusive competence of an archipelagic State relates to the application of this right to warships and ships with special characteristics, such as nuclear-powered ships and ships carrying nuclear or other dangerous or noxious substances.[87] In particular, as was shown above, a number of actual (including Indonesia and the Philippines) or potential claimants of archipelagic status, contrary to the Convention, requires prior authorization for, and/or notification on, the innocent passage of warships. In addition, some conforming States, especially in the South Pacific, show a major concern with unauthorized passage of warships and ships with special characteristics. A tendency to restrict innocent passage may also result from the 1989 Basel Convention on the Control of Transboundary Movements of Hazardous Wastes and their Disposal, providing for a prior consent by the

87 While the latter ships are under art. 23 of Part II obliged to carry documents and observe special precautionary measures, the IMO recognized the need to consider the desirability of any such new or revised requirements, *see loc. cit.* (note 86), 27, 57 and Annex, 1-3.

States concerned (upon notification of the State of export) to transit of such waste through areas under their national jurisdiction.

The major maritime powers as, among others, a significant 1989 Joint Innocent Passage Statement of the United States and the Soviet Union evidences, take the position that the innocent passage of warships and ships with special characteristics is, under general international law, as reflected by Part II of the LOS Convention, not subject to a prior authorization or notification. Nevertheless, we share the opinion of *Rüdiger Wolfrum* that:

> As far as the passage of ships (including warships) through the territorial sea is concerned, ... no final definitive conclusion may as yet be drawn from State practice. Although there is no indication that the definition of innocent passage as enshrined in art. 19 CLOS will not, in long run, be accepted by State practice, *it seems to be rather unlikely that such a development will cover warships.* In so far as the lack of uniformity of national legislation is concerned, this will probably prevail despite the regulations of the Convention on the Law of the Sea [emphasis added].[88]

It seems therefore unlikely that archipelagic States would amend their legislation in this respect so as to conform to the Convention. The Philippines, however, would have to clearly stipulate — as it is not presently the case — the right of innocent passage in its legislation, while Indonesia would need to specify that innocent passage is the "right" enjoyed by foreign ships in its waters. The right of innocent passage would also have to be clearly established by the potential claimants of an archipelagic State régime which at present define the waters enclosed by their baselines as internal waters.

4. *Right of Archipelagic Sea Lanes Passage and Archipelagic Straits*

The right of non-suspendable archipelagic sea lanes passage of all ships and aircraft, as established in arts. 53 and 54 of Part IV of the LOS Convention and provided for in the legislation of a number of archipelagic States, is alongside with the innocent passage of warships the most controversial element of an archipelagic State régime. This is due to the fact that archipelagic sea lanes passage, which applies not only to archipelagic waters but also to the adjacent territorial sea of an archipelagic State (art. 53, para. 1), involves — like transit

---

[88] *Wolfrum* (note 3), 131-132. *Cf. William T. Burke*, in: *Jon M. van Dyke* (ed.), Consensus and Confrontation: The United States and the Law of the Sea Convention, Honolulu 1985, 294-296; *Alan V. Lowe*, Some Legal Problems Arising from the Use of the Seas for Military Purposes, in: Marine Policy 10 (1986), 171- 184 (173); *L. Dolliver M. Nelson*, The Delimitation of Maritime Boundaries in the Caribbean, in: *Douglas M. Johnston/Phillip M. Saunders* (eds.), Ocean Boundary Making, London/New York 1988, 142-203 (151-153); *Shao Jin*, The Question of Innocent Passage of Warships after UNCLOS III, in: Marine Policy 13 (1989), 56-67. The total number of states requiring prior notification and/or authorization for innocent passage of warships amounts to 45.

passage through straits used for international navigation under Part III — a submerged passage of submarines and an overflight above sea lanes. At the same time, although under art. 53, para. 1 an archipelagic State is not obliged but empowered ("may") to designate archipelagic sea lanes and air routes thereabove, this does not prevent applicability of the sea lanes passage. In particular, as follows from art. 53, para. 12, if an archipelagic State does not designate sea lanes and air routes, the right of archipelagic sea lanes passage may be exercised through "the routes normally used for international navigation."

The problem arises whether in case of those archipelagic States legislation of which, as was shown above, does not envisage the possibility of utilizing "the routes normally used for international navigation" or does not provide for the establishment of archipelagic sea lanes and air routes, the right to utilize the routes normally used for international navigation within their archipelagic baselines can be exercised under general international law.

A major question which has to be clarified is that the fundamental rules of archipelagic sea lanes passage through archipelagic waters are under Part IV of the Convention not wholly — as the maritime powers maintain — but only partly the same as those established in Part III of the Convention for transit passage through straits used for international navigation. Since archipelagic sea lanes passage has, as was already mentioned, its origin in the legislation of Indonesia, the Indonesian authors most consistently and extensively elaborate on actual differences between the régimes of archipelagic sea lanes passage and transit passage.[89] These differences are often underestimated due to three fundamental elements which both régimes have in common. The three elements as set forth in Parts III and IV include:

— the non-suspendability of both passages,

— the right of submarines to navigate submerged, and

— the right of overflight.

Meaningly, these elements are not applicable in case of the innocent passage, be it through archipelagic waters or the territorial sea, what clearly shows that military navigation and overflight was the reason for which the right of archipelagic sea lanes passage was established. It should also be noted that although both archipelagic sea lanes and transit passages are non-suspendable, the archipelagic and strait States are authorized to substitute sea lanes, what in restrictive interpretation of the Philippines is regarded as equal to suspension.[90]

The three elements specified above, in combination with a clause of the next art. 54 providing for applicability of several transit passage articles of Part III

---

[89] *See Hasjim Djalal*, Commentary, in: *Soons* (note 42), 201-202, and his reply to *Jean Pierre Queneudec*, 208-209; *Nugroho Wisnumurti*, Archipelagic Waters and Archipelagic Sea Lanes, in: *Van Dyke et. al.* (note 31), 198-209 (204-206).

[90] *See* Comments of the Philippines, ICAO doc. LC/26-WP/5-26 (1987), 1.

"*mutatis mutandis*" to archipelagic sea lanes passage, are often misinterpreted as implying virtual identity of both régimes. To avoid this confusion of the two separate régimes Indonesia attempted during UNCLOS III to write down exactly in art. 54 what is meant by using the term "*mutatis mutandis*" but the Chairman of Committee II, Ambassador *Aguilar* found that such specification would make this article too long. The use of the same term "transit" with respect both to straits used for international navigation and archipelagic sea lanes passage in the Convention and the State practice adds to confusion as to the two legal régimes.

Another provision which may result in confusing interpretations is art. 53, para. 3 stipulating that archipelagic sea lanes passage means the exercise of the rights of navigation and overflight for the purpose of transit "between one part of the high seas or an exclusive economic zone and another part of the high seas or an exclusive economic zone". Similarly, under arts. 37 and 38, para. 2 of Part III, transit passage applies to straits "between one part of the high seas or an exclusive economic zone and another part of the high seas or an exclusive economic zone." This may prompt interpretation that archipelagic straits could be regarded as connecting parts of the high seas and/or exclusive economic zone. Indonesia and the Philippines oppose such interpretation arguing that straits located within archipelagic waters connect *sensu stricto* either two parts of such waters or part of such waters with the territorial sea or economic zone of archipelagic States, and not parts of the high seas and/or economic zones. Accordingly, while the Straits of Malacca-Singapore or Bashi Channel qualify for transit passage under Part III, Indonesian Straits of Sunda and Lombok or the Philippine Strait of Surigao which lie wholly within archipelagic waters and are, as was already mentioned, the choke points for the US military and commercial traffic, do not qualify for transit passage but for archipelagic sea lanes passage under Part IV. For instance, the Strait of Lombok connects the Indonesian economic zone in the Indian Ocean to the Flores Sea within Indonesian archipelagic waters. To consider Indonesian and Philippine straits as falling under Part III would require to ignore a geographic notion of straits and to accept that, for instance, the Lombok Strait forms one unit with the Makassar Strait and then northeast with the Balut Channel between Indonesia and the Philippines where from this whole north-south route connects further to Northwest (Japan) and Northeast (USA) Pacific.

Perhaps in appreciation of peculiarity of such an argument, a statement by the US Assistant Legal Adviser for Oceans and International Environmental and Scientific Affairs made in 1989 in connection with a temporary closure by Indonesia of the Sunda and Lombok Straits in 1988, asserts duality of régimes applicable to archipelagic straits. According to the statement presented:

> Applying the objective criteria set forth in Parts III and IV of the LOS Convention, it is clear that *Lombok, Sunda and Malacca are unquestionably "straits used for international navigation" and, therefore, are subject to the straits transit régime, while Lombok and Sunda also qualify as "normal passage routes used for interna-*

tional navigation or overflight" and thus are subject to the régime of archipelagic sea lanes passage [emphasis added].[91]

Such duality of transit passage and archipelagic sea lanes passage régimes governing archipelagic straits of Indonesia and the Philippines is, however, untenable and appears also to be contradicted by the United States itself. In particular, the 1986 US protest against the Philippine Declaration referred to above, as well as the 1988 exchange of notes attached to the Indonesian/US Income Tax Treaty discussed below, expressly recognize archipelagic State principle and transit through archipelagic waters in accordance with Part IV, and not Parts III and IV, of the LOS Convention.

Apart from basic uncertainty discussed below as to whether archipelagic sea lanes passage is already applicable as a norm of customary international law, even when this will be the case, there remains an essential issue that in spite of similarities specified above the legal régime of archipelagic sea lanes passage is different than that of transit passage. Among a number of differences one could note the fact that unlike the case of transit passage, archipelagic sea lanes and air routes are required to include "all normal passage routes used as routes for international navigation or overflight through or over archipelagic waters" (art. 53, para. 4). However, if the archipelagic State does not designate sea lanes or air routes, it follows from art. 53, para. 12 that archipelagic sea lanes passage may be exercised not necessarily through "all" the routes normally used for international navigation. The Convention does not define what such "normal passage routes" or "routes normally used" for international navigation mean, what may be a source of a major difficulty. It could not with certainty be asserted that such routes would cover all archipelagic straits including those which, like the Philippine Surigao Strait and Balintang and Babuyan Channels or Indonesian Lombok and Sunda Straits, constitute choke points for the US military and commercial traffic. It is likely that archipelagic States will invoke restrictive interpretation limiting such routes to the shortest routes through archipelagic waters which are really essential for international navigation, while the user maritime States will claim to the contrary.[92]

Moreover, unlike is the case with the freedom of overflight under the régime of transit passage through straits, the right of overflight under the régime of archipelagic sea lanes passage is restricted to air routes "above" archipelagic sea lanes (art. 53, para. 1). A number of archipelagic States, in particular those situated in the South Pacific, do not specify in their legislation that the right of overflight must be confined to the air space above their archipelagic sea lanes.

91 Reprinted in: AJIL 83 (1989), 559, 560. *See also* 1983 US statement quoted in main text accompanying *supra* (note 68) and referring to "freedoms of navigation and overflight" in relation to both straits and archipelagic waters.

92 *See Wisnumurti* (note 89), 207; and also *id.*, Indonesia and the Law of the Sea, in: *Choon-ho Park/Jae Kyu Park* (eds.), The Law of the Sea: Problems from the East Asian Perspective, Honolulu 1987, 392-403 (398).

However, this results from the fact that, due to rather long distances between the main islands of those widely scattered States, the problem of overflight and likewise of navigation, including that for military purposes, is for these States, as was already mentioned, much easier to accomodate than it is for Indonesia and the Philippines. Therefore, the latter States objected during UNCLOS III to proposed substitution of the phrase "sea lanes and air routes thereabove" in art. 53, para. 1 by that of "air routes above the archipelago." The right of overflight only above the sea lanes clearly precludes applicability of this right to overflight above the land (island) territory of an archipelagic State.

Although not specified in the Convention, an understanding accompanying the phrase providing for air routes only "above" the sea lanes was that such air routes were most adequate for military aircraft. The requirement that air routes must be above archipelagic sea lanes was dictated not by the need of civil air navigation, but by the necessity to provide maneuvering possibilities for military aircraft while the naval forces of a particular fleet are passing through the sea lanes. Accordingly, art. 53, para. 9 obliges the archipelagic State to refer proposals on designating or substituting only sea lanes and traffic separation schemes — and not air routes — to the competent international organization. The latter word is used in a singular form implying, as is generally agreed, the involvement of IMO, and not in plural form which would imply involvement of also the ICAO. Moreover, in cases when the archipelagic State does not designate sea lanes and air routes, art. 53, para. 12 clearly provides for exercising the right of archipelagic sea lanes passage through the routes normally used for international "navigation", and not for "navigation and overflight." Thus, contrary to what is often maintained, a general right of free overflight above archipelagic waters can — due to its strict application to the air space above the archipelagic sea lanes — be implemented in practice only by military aircraft.[93] Civil aircraft could clearly not fulfill the condition of zigzagging above the archipelagic sea lanes and of overflying archipelagic waters without passing above archipelagic land (island) territory.

As the 1987 ICAO Secretariat Study indicates, art. 2 of the Chicago Convention has to be read now as meaning that the territory of a State includes the land areas, territorial sea and archipelagic waters, and any events such as aircraft accidents taking place in the archipelagic waters have to be considered as having occurred in the territory of the archipelagic State.[94] The *mutatis mutandis* clause of art. 54 in this context means that art. 39, para. 3 applies to archipelagic air routes as provided for by art. 53, that is practically to air routes for military aircraft strictly corresponding to the archipelagic sea lanes and only when such

---

93 *See* concordant views on this matter of former delegates to UNCLOS III, *Shigeru Oda* (Japan), *Komar Kantaatmadja* (Indonesia), *Nugroho Wisnumurti* (Indonesia) and *Thomas Clingan* (USA), in: *Van Dyke et. al.* (note 31), 268-269; *Hasjim Djalal* (Indonesia), in: *Soons* (note 42), 209; *Jayewardene* (note 2), 162.

94 ICAO doc. LC/26-WP/5-1 (1987), 16-17, para. 10.7.

sea lanes are established. Thus, the applicable rule is exclusively that which is formulated in art. 39, para. 3 (a), namely that state aircraft, i. e. aircraft used in military, customs and police services "will *normally* comply" with safety measures provided for by the ICAO Rules of the Air and will at all times operate with due regard for the safety of navigation [emphasis added]. Accordingly the only sound commentary which applies to archipelagic overflight is that made by ICAO Secretariat in the part of its Study related to straits used for international navigation, where it indicates that:

> The same "*rules of the air*" does not apply automatically to state aircraft . . .; such aircraft, nevertheless, should have due regard for the safety of navigation and the ultimate regard could best be secured by compliance with the Rules of the Air; . . . [emphasis added].[95]

The above interpretation of the right of archipelagic overflight is confirmed by the 1982 Jakarta Treaty between Indonesia and Malaysia which, although not restricting the right of overflight to air space "above" the sea lanes ("corridors") designated for ships between East and West Malaysia, bases on integration of the airspace above archipelagic waters into the Indonesian territory. These and other differences testify that in spite of similarities, navigational rights of third States are on the whole more limited under archipelagic sea lanes passage through archipelagic waters than under transit passage through straits used for international navigation.

In light of the foregoing, the contention of the maritime powers that transit passage through straits used for international navigation as established in the LOS Convention passed already into the corpus of general international law, apart from being questionable, does not — unlike these States believe — solve the question of passage through archipelagic waters, including archipelagic straits, which is governed by a different legal régime. The only exception thereto would form the waters of small archipelagic States which — as did Trinidad and Tobago — would expressly subject their waters to the transit passage régime. At the same time, as discussed below, the customary nature of archipelagic sea lanes passage could not be determined with all certainty. While not all archipelagic States provide for the establishment of archipelagic sea lanes, in the case of those States which envisage this possibility there is no evidence whether such sea lanes have actually been designated and, if they were, what specific rules have been followed to this effect. In addition, two archipelagic States especially affected by archipelagic sea lanes passage régime, i. e. Indonesia and the Philippines, continue to ascribe to its archipelagic waters status of internal waters, while Indonesia has only established sea lanes for fishery vessels and those under its bilateral Jakarta Treaty with Malaysia.

The 1989 US statement replying to Sunda's and Lombok's closure referred to above, based on the customary nature of rules found in art. 53, asserts that

[95] *Loc. cit.*, 14, para. 9.8.

Indonesia failed to fulfil its obligation under para. 7 thereof providing for designating or substituting archipelagic sea lanes through the procedure involving the competent international organization. However, apart from the disputable nature of such customary law contention, there is no procedure established within any competent organization, in particular the IMO for assisting archipelagic States in designating archipelagic sea lanes. IMO, which is the only global organization with the mandate to develop international regulations with regard to routing systems for ships, found it desirable to consider its rôle in publicity on dangers to navigation in archipelagic waters, as well as the need for special procedures related to State proposals on sea lanes and traffic separation schemes within archipelagic waters.[96] But while such procedures were not yet established, the IMO's rôle could be claimed as "somewhat dubious" due to the fact that the major issue relates to archipelagic sea lanes not for commercial navigation but for warships. Even more importantly, a question may be raised why, in a situation of the LOS Convention not being in force, archipelagic States should rely on the IMO — comprising major maritime States, all non-parties to the Convention — with respect to designation of archipelagic sea lanes under the Convention?[97] Similar doubts would also apply to the eventual involvement of ICAO.

5. Navigational Rights of Third States — The Essence of Controversy

An assessment of the "conflicting" navigational régime within archipelagic waters involves consideration of two issues which are already apparent from the above examination and which could be signalized by the key-words "warships" and "the US as a non-party". Both indicate that the problem is highly politicized which results in the confusion of various legal aspects related thereto.

A "warships" part of the problem is that the maintenance of traditional free military navigation and overflight was during UNCLOS III and remains at present the most crucial condition on which the United States and the Soviet Union as well as other maritime powers were and are willing to recognize the régime of the archipelagic State and its sovereignty over archipelagic waters under the new Convention. As Ambassador *Djalal* of Indonesia put it:

> [I]n fact, commercial navigation was used as hostage in order to gain concessions for the navigation of warships. In that context it was always projected that the interests of international community were tied up with the interests of warships, as if the coastal states were not part of the international community, and as if the coastal states were against international trade and communication.[98]

---

[96] *See supra* (note 86), 22-23, 52-53 and Annex, 4-5.

[97] *Loc. cit.*, 202-203; *Wisnumurti*, in: *Van Dyke et. al.* (note 31), 264-265, and in: *Craven et. al.* (note 18), 70-71 and 75-76. *See also* reluctant opinion of IMO's official, *Thomas S. Busha*, on the rôle of IMO and on the consultative nature of such rôle, in: *Van Dyke et. al.* (note 31), 262, 264 and 269.

A primarily military concern with respect to archipelagic waters régime is clearly illustrated by the opinion expressed by *Ashley Roach* of the US Department of State who, while discussing various categories of "excessive maritime claims" which are protested by the United States within its Freedom of Navigation Programme, distinguishes the category of: "archipelagic claims that do not permit archipelagic sea lanes passage in conformity with customary international law reflected in the LOS Convention, *including submerged passage of submarines, overflight of military aircraft, and surface transit of warships and naval auxiliaries, without prior notification or authorization, and including transit in a manner of deployment consistent with the security of the forces involved*" [emphasis added].[99] A general sensitivity of the developing archipelagic States with respect to security matters renders the issue even more complex. Such sensitivity, although justified at the present stage of the North-South confrontation, results perhaps in some underestimation on the side of archipelagic States of a crucial importance of the fact that until achievement of the ultimate objective of general and complete disarmament, military activities are the necessary means for the maintenance of international peace and security. There are therefore two kinds of conflicting concerns to be reconciled, that on the part of the major powers to ensure mobility of their warships as expeditiously and as safely as possible, and that on the part of archipelagic States to ensure that foreign warships and military aircraft do not threaten their national security.

The legal issues confused by the military side of the matter include the equating of transit passage through straits used for international navigation with archipelagic sea lanes passage what is incorrect in that, as was shown above, these passages involve two different legal régimes. Related thereto is a question of legal régime of archipelagic straits which — unless the archipelagic State chooses otherwise — are governed by archipelagic sea lanes passage and not, as is often maintained, by the transit passage régime. The problem of archipelagic air routes as well as that of the rôle of international organizations in establishing archipelagic sea lanes, as envisaged by the Convention, is also being confused. Such detailed questions enhance the confusion on the general issue of whether the archipelagic State régime, as laid down in the Convention, is a new or an old régime under international law. Part IV of the LOS Convention establishing the archipelagic State régime is neither totally old (declaratory) nor totally new (generating), but seems to belong to a medium category of treaty rules which crystallize customary law in process of formation. The maritime powers point out a binding nature of this part of the régime which protects inclusive navigational interests of third

---

98 *Djalal* (note 89), 200. *See also Coquia/Santiago* (note 70), 336; *Narokobi* (note 31), 232; Judge *Shigeru Oda*, The Passage of Warships Through Straits and Archipelagic Waters, in: *Van Dyke et. al.* (note 31), 155-157 and 260.

99 *J. A. Roach*, Excessive Maritime Claims (paper presented at the 84th Annual Meeting of ASIL, Washington, D. C., 28-31 March 1990), 7.

States, while archipelagic States accentuate another part thereof which aims to preserve exclusive interests of safeguarding the unity of the archipelagic State.

Even with its military connotation, the problem would perhaps not acquire a conflicting character if there was not another question involved, namely that of "the US as a non-party." The United States' position is that the Convention's provisions, except those on the deep sea-bed régime and the dispute settlement, are either declaratory of pre-UNCLOS III customary law or have become customary law in the course of their negotiation and adoption at the UNCLOS III.[100] This position was expressed in relation to specifically archipelagic waters in the 1983 US statement replying to the Philippine Montego Bay intervention, the 1986 US protest against the Philippine Declaration, and statement made by the US Assistant Legal Adviser for Oceans and International Environmental and Scientific Affairs in 1989 in connection with a temporary closure of the Indonesian Straits of Sunda and Lombok in 1988. The latter statement specifies that:

> Although the 1982 Law of the Sea Convention is not yet in force, *the archipelagic provisions reflect customary international law and codify the only rules by which a nation can now rightfully assert an archipelagic claim* [emphasis added].[101]

This position is also reflected in the exchange of notes initialed in 1986 and attached to the 1988 Indonesian/US Income Tax Treaty in which:

> The United States recognizes the archipelagic State principles as applied by Indonesia *on the understanding that they are applied in accordance with the provisions of Part IV of the 1982 United Nations Convention on the Law of the Sea and that Indonesia respects international rights and obligations pertaining to transit of the Indonesian archipelagic waters in accordance with international law as reflected in that Part.*
>
> *The confirmation of this understanding by the Government of the Republic of Indonesia will constitute the agreed interpretation of Article 3 (1) (a) of the Convention [emphasis added].*[102]

Thus, the United States and likewise other major powers maintain that, in accordance with consensus reached during UNCLOS III, without safeguarded navigation through archipelagic waters, the archipelagic State régime cannot be valid.

On the other hand, as the major maritime powers tend to underestimate, the agreement on the archipelagic State régime as embodied in the Convention required a tremendous compromise on the part of archipelagic States. Although maritime spaces of these States are now extended further seaward due to their

---

100 Note, however, that the US position is weakened by instances of non-conformity of the US legislation with the LOS Convention. *See* views of Ambassador *Tommy Koh, David Colson* and *Anthony D'Amato*, in: *Van Dyke* (note 88), 65-68, and of *Louis Sohn*, in: *Van Dyke* (note 31), 158.

101 *See supra* (note 91), 559.

102 *Loc. cit.*, 561.

measurement from the straight archipelagic baselines, compared with maritime spaces of a continental State, those of an archipelagic State are, as was already mentioned, governed by navigational régimes imposing much stricter limitations on the sovereignty of the archipelagic State. The most pronounced of those limitations, which do not apply to a continental State, result from the right of submarines to pass submerged through, and the right of military aircraft to overflight, archipelagic sea lanes not only in archipelagic waters but also in the territorial sea of an archipelagic State. The archipelagic States clearly agreed to such serious restrictions of their rights in a "package deal" comprising satisfactory solutions of other law of the sea issues as well. The United States, due to its objections to the deep sea-bed régime, did not sign the Convention and did not join the Preparatory Commission for the International Sea-Bed Authority (Prep-Com). Thus, in archipelagic States' perception, this US conduct may be viewed as an act of bad faith, as these States have compromised their position on the archipelagic (and likewise straits) régime with a view to meet the demands of the United States and furnish the progress in negotiations on the other elements of the "package", especially that of the deep sea-bed régime. Some US officials deny the existence of interrelationship between navigational issues and the deep sea-bed régime in the "package deal" negotiations during UNCLOS III,[103] but this view is not convincing.[104]

Therefore, Indonesia's position — as expressed in Montego Bay and also advocated in academic writings — is that, while the provisions of the Convention on the archipelagic State régime are gaining universal acceptance as new law, they should only be applicable to those who have accepted the "package" and should not benefit the non-parties to the Convention.[105] A temporary closure by Indonesia of the Sunda and Lombok Straits in 1988, and delaying by both Indonesia and the Philippines of amendments to their non-conforming legislation seem to illustrate the possible effects of this position.

It should be emphasized that, under existing international law, both the United States' and Indonesia's positions are questionable.[106] Nevertheless, the existence of those differences inclined a leading American authority, *Oscar Schachter*, to conclude in 1989 that it remains to be seen whether the archipelagic sea lanes

---

[103] *See David A. Colson*, in: *Van Dyke* (note 88), 48.

[104] *See*, e. g., *Djalal* (note 64), 69; *Phillippe Kirsch/Douglas Fraser*, The Law of the Sea Preparatory Commission after Six Years: Review and Prospects, in: The Canadian Yearbook of International Law 28 (1988), 119-131 (124); *Tommy Koh*, in: *Van Dyke* (note 88), 59-61.

[105] *See* statement of Minister *Mochtar Kusumaatmadja*, in: UNCLOS III, Official Records, Vol. XVII, 26, para. 23; *Agoes* (note 79), 21; *Djalal* (note 64), 68-69, and *id.*, The Effects of the Law of the Sea Convention on the Norms that Now Govern Ocean Activities, in: *Van Dyke* (note 88), 50-56 (52-56), 63-64 and 294; *Wisnumurti* (note 89), 207 and 211. *See also supra* (note 97) and main accompanying text.

[106] *See Francisco Orrego Vicuña*, The Exclusive Economic Zone, Cambridge 1989, 234, and his analysis, 228-234 and 252-257.

passage (and transit passage) will be generally accepted as customary law.[107] In his opinion, it is questionable that a series of bilateral agreements between maritime and archipelagic (coastal) States that include *quid pro quo* provisions will give rise to a finding of *opinio iuris* as to the general non-treaty right of passage. In fact, if such customary right of archipelagic passage was generally recognized, the bilateral assurances would not be needed.

A situation in which the United States and other major powers, that did not adhere to the Convention, maintain that there will be no archipelagic régime without safeguarded navigation, and in which the reply of Indonesia and the Philippines, that both ratified the Convention, seems to be that there may be no navigation safeguarded by a limitation of the sovereignty of the archipelagic State without the United States becoming a party to the Convention, seems not irreconcilable. In fact a recourse to the "package deal" theory might have been intended by the archipelagic States as a means of accelerating the US decision to rejoin the Convention. Such decision would certainly be desirable from the viewpoint of the progress in deep sea-bed works of PrepCom, on which it in turn depends whether the LOS Convention will be ratified by the major maritime and other States, and whether it will enter into force for the majority of the international community.

Otherwise, in spite of their major concern with preserving navigational and other communications freedoms, the maritime powers may find themselves in perhaps more vulnerable position than that of archipelagic (and likewise the straits) States. This is due to the fact that the development of the archipelagic régime is already irreversible. In the pre-UNCLOS III period the existence of a customary norm permitting an archipelagic State to close its waters by archipelagic straight baselines and to exercise sovereignty therein could be questioned. At present the issue seems to be not whether this sovereignty will be recognized, but rather what shape will it take in its further development. It should also be mentioned that in cases other than archipelagic State régime the United States practice since 1983 has been not withhold recognition of a coastal State claim to, for example, a 12 mile territorial sea, because it imposed a prior notification or authorization requirement for the innocent passage of warships.[108] Such practice weakens the US contention that the archipelagic State régime can only be

[107] *See Oscar Schachter*, Entangled Treaty and Custom, in: *Dinstein/Tabory* (note 23), 717-738 (737). For a similar view, *see* Ambassador *Tommy Koh*, in: *Van Dyke* (note 88), 298, and in: *Craven et. al.* (note 18), 436-437; *Luke T. Lee*, The Law of the Sea Convention and Third States, in: AJIL 77 (1983), 541-568 (557-564); *O'Connell* (note 3), 254; *Janusz Symonides*, Nowe Prawo Morza (The New Law of the Sea), Warsaw 1986, 134-135; Working Paper for Sub-Committee on the Law of the Sea, Asian-African Legal Consultative Committee, doc. AALCC/XXIX/90/4A 7-8 (1990). *Cf.* Council on Ocean Law, US Interests and the United Nations Convention on the Law of the Sea, Panel on the Law of Ocean Uses, June 1990; *William T. Burke*, Threats to the Public Order of the Oceans, in: *Van Dyke* (note 31), 384-391 (385-386).

[108] *Roach* (note 99), 2.

recognized on condition of archipelagic waters régime conforming to the Convention.

The United States and other major powers may achieve their objectives through bilateral concessions agreed within a framework of their broader political and economic relations with individual archipelagic States, especially with Indonesia and the Philippines, the archipelagic waters of which, as was discussed above, are of a considerable strategic importance. However, such conduct bears a risk that, as one author rightly indicates, "attempts by non-party States to rely upon supposed rights in customary law corresponding to rights included in the UNCLOS III 'package deal' could, in circumstances of political tension, be a further source of conflict."[109] The scope of such risk is illustrated by the fact that, since most of the major straits in the Southeast Asia pass through archipelagic waters of either Indonesia or the Philippines, these States could seek to close a series of alternative straits at the same time. Moreover, as was shown above, there is also a number of other actual or potential claimants of archipelagic status in the South Pacific, Indian Ocean and East Atlantic which may affect unimpeded navigation in archipelagic waters as well as restrict innocent passage of warships and ships with special characteristics. The probability of such measures will increase with the progressing development of enforcement capability on the side of archipelagic States.

It could, therefore, not be excluded that the development of the archipelagic State régime outside the Convention may gradually lead to the consolidation of the restrictive navigational régime within archipelagic waters in the form of the innocent passage through designated sea lanes subjected in case of warships and ships with special characteristics to authorization and/or notification as originally claimed by archipelagic States. This in conjunction with the possible proliferation of the archipelagic State régime through widening the criteria applicable to archipelagic straight baselines and inclusion of non-state archipelagos into the archipelagic concept, would mean a noticeable reduction of inclusive rights of third States to the detriment of their both commercial and military concerns. Such a perspective could not with certainty be excluded in at least the next one or two decades, since in the long run the basic transformation of the US/Soviet relations will nullify the military importance of the archipelagic waters régime and, thus, will deprive this régime of its controversial nature.

---

109 *See Lowe* (note 88), 181. This aspect is also stressed out by Ambassador *Tommy Koh*, in: *Van Dyke* (note 88), 299.

Discussion

Jesus:

I am grateful to Dr. *Barbara Kwiatkowska* for having made such a brilliant exposé on the archipelagic régime as contained in the Convention. I would like to make one comment. I participated last April in a symposium similar to this one but dealing with general issues of State practices and the UN Convention of the Law of the Sea and I was assigned to speak on the practices of African States with respect to the implementation of the 1982 Convention on the Law of the Sea. My conclusion with respect to the archipelagic régime as contained in the Convention, was that there was no problem whatsoever in accepting that régime today as customary international law. I believe that remains so. The only problem that might exist is not the régime itself. Nobody has questioned that. All States have accepted the régime as contained in the Convention. The only problem that remains is the implementation of certain provisions, in particular those that try to establish a balance for the navigational rights of any countries, especially the main maritime powers. There, we might have some differences of interpretation as to the application of those provisions as we have in all areas dealing with the so-called traditional uses.

But I believe that we will come to a position that will make the whole implementation of the régime possible, thus solving the difficulties. As far as, for example, my country is concerned, although during the conference we fought for prior notification of innocent passage, not only through archipelagic waters, but also through the territorial seas, as we believe that was a position that should not be taken to the limit in the context of international politics. We will try to accomodate and to interpret and apply the Convention to the best of our possibilities and try not to violate the spirit of the Convention. Right now our legislation might not be entirely in accordance with that régime as far as the baselines are concerned; but we are going to correct that because we believe that we have to comply, and that everybody has to comply with the Convention, even though we might have a special interest in interpreting this or that provision in order to maximize our interests. We have a paramount interest which is to have the Convention apply to everyone. If that is to be the result, we are prepared to sacrifice "certain interpretations." That would be more in our national interest.

Wolfrum:

I just have two brief questions. You mentioned that some States claim archipelagic waters, you have, however, refrained from naming them. Could you please do so? My second question relates to the first one. Do these States fulfil the qualification of art. 47, para. 1 LOS Convention? I refer to the ratio between land and water, an issue which was quite crucial when the archipelagic water-system was developed.

Kwiatkowska:

I do not have a list prepared because I must say, frankly, that I counted on our paper being distributed, where all this is indicated, but I can quickly list these countries now. That is: Indonesia, and the Philippines, there is no doubt that an archipelagic régime is claimed. Comoros, Fiji, Papua New Guinea, Kiribati, Solomon Islands, Tuvalu, Vanuatu; in the Caribbean — Antigua and Barbuda, Grenada, St. Vincent and the Grenadines, Trinidad and Tobago; in the East Atlantic — Cape Verde and Sao Tomé and Principe. These are States that have claimed archipelagic status. The Bahamas is a potential claimant. It meets the conditions laid down in the Law of the Sea Convention. I would say that the issues should be approached differently.

I appreciate the interesting statement of Ambassador *Jesus* that there is not really a problem regarding the implementation of the Convention, but our study shows that the practice is not uniform. We were giving the benefit of the doubt to the States whose practice is not clear — there is quite a number of States whose practice concerning the navigational régime could raise a certain amount of uncertainty. The water to land ratio and the length of baselines is really not a problem, because except Cape Verde (as Ambassador *Jesus* admitted) and the Philippines, all States meet the requirements of baselines. Even if they do not, as is the case with the two States I have mentioned, there is nothing easier than to adjust them. The problem lies, thus, not in adjusting the baselines. And the water to land ratio for most States potentially and actually claiming archipelagic status is also correct. There are some potential claimants like, for instance, Bahrain, the Maldives, Mauritius, the Seychelles, France (New-Caledonia), Tonga, Bahamas or Jamaica, as well as some depending territories, which I will omit at the moment. St. Kitts and Nevis is another potential claimant. The issue is rather how would these States implement the navigational régime. If there is no problem with navigation, but the ratios do not fit, nobody will really protest against that, as the issue is basically one of navigation. However, the detailed classifications of the nine groups of conforming and nonconforming States are to be found in our paper, including Indonesia and the Philippines which we treat as two separate cases.

Ballah:

First, I want to thank Prof. *Kwiatkowska* for a fine paper. Well, you know my sympathies are with archipelagic States. Unlike Indonesia and the Philippines, Trinidad and Tobago is not a historical archipelago, but it is part of what could be considered an ancient historical archipelago comprising all the islands in the Caribbean. And at one point in time it was thought that that kind of unity as a political entity would have produced a true historical archipelago. But there are a number of small archipelagos as political entities in the Caribbean. Trinidad and Tobago is a *locus classicus* of that kind of thing, but so are Grenada, Antigua and Barbuda, and St. Vincent and the Grenadines. As far as I know, the archipelagic status legislation for the islands in the Caribbean (and not only the Bahamas) fits the criteria enshrined in the Convention. In fact, I think basically they use that kind of criteria. Trinidad and Tobago for example satisfy it in every single way, particularly the land to water ratio between 1 : 1 to 9 : 1. Even though the United States did make certain protests, it was not because Trinidad and Tobago did not satisfy the criteria, but it was in order to clarify the status of what they considered to be a strait used for international navigation within archipelagic waters. It was not a protest; it was a letter seeking clarification. As far as I know that clarification has been given. I do not think there has been any formal protest as such. Trinidad and Tobago as a small archipelagic State has all the problems that some of the big archipelagos have. In the régime of passage I think its legislation is in conformity with the Convention.

Kwiatkowska:

I would then be interested to know: What was the explanation you mentioned given on the navigational régime of Trinidad and Tobago? I agree that what is written in the legislation is correct, but several important things are not included there and that could raise anxiety, because there is, as you know, this important route — the Galleon's Passage.

Ballah:

The Galleon's Passage has never been used as a strait in international navigation.

Kwiatkowska:

It has been used.

Ballah:

I do not know which one you mean. There may be an alternate route to the Galleon's Passage of similar convenience. The Galleon's Passage is the passage between Trinidad and Tobago. The Convention provides for transit passage in such a strait, where ships have traditionally passed. Some of our own people have argued that it would be difficult to re-route international navigation to the North of Tobago, because those ships that are coming up from the South American Atlantic coast, and even those tankers that are coming to collect oil tend to use the Galleon's Passage. That provision in the Convention relating to transit passage was not written clearly into the legislation, although the intent was that the legislation should follow faithfully the Convention. I do not work any longer in the Foreign Ministry. I do not know what answer has been given to the United States. But I know an answer has been given which seems to have satisfied our powerful neighbour.

Kwiatkowska:

That is the usual case, you see. The problem is that your legislation provides only for innocent passage and the whole issue is to get archipelagic sea lanes passage through the archipelagic waters.

Ballah:

There was no intention as far as I gather really to exclude it and therefore I do not know if the answer was perhaps a clarification or whether a later amendment would be made to the legislation to reflect it.

Kwiatkowska:

Therefore we qualified Trinidad and Tobago as presumably conforming.

Orrego Vicuña:

I have one question and one short suggestion. The question relates to the status of archipelagic régimes and waters in customary law. In my own paper, I have to discuss the issue of straits used for international navigation and I have come to the conclusion that such rules are not quite clearly becoming customary law except perhaps for a few elements here and there. I would gather from Dr. *Kwiatkowska*'s remarks that this is the case too with regard to archipelagic waters. But I would like to ask her if she could make the point more explicit so as to link it precisely with the case of straits and therefrom perhaps draw a parallel between the two. That is the question. The suggestion relates to one issue which is entirely different but it might be worth looking at from the point of view of some experts on the issue of archipelagic waters like Dr. *Kwiatkowska* and Dr. *Agoes*, which is the case of a very peculiar situation existing in the Antarctic peninsula. The Antarctic peninsula was for years thought to be a peninsula and ended up to be an archipelago, geographically speaking, linked up by the ice-shield. Legally speaking, it is a case where there are claimant States which probably would not qualify under the terms of the Convention, but there are also those that do not recognize claims. So you have a situation where geography says something and the law says something else, to the extent that the law is applicable to that particular situation. It might be worth looking at it in terms of some future development with regard to this subject.

Kwiatkowska:

I will answer briefly because the questions posed are a topic for a whole day session. We identified claims to off-lying archipelagos as a separate category clearly nonconforming to the Convention. There is quite a significant number of States advancing those claims. I learned during the break that Brazil would be interested in such status for some islands close to Brazil, but also many other States have similar interests. I see here a representative from India, maybe he could say something about it. He probably used a lot of energy to fight for it during UNCLOS III without achieving the expected result in the Convention. In the situation that the Convention is not in force and the time is not defined as to when it will enter into force and practice goes its own way, we indicate in the paper that this will become customary law and that the rule will permit claiming archipelagic baselines around non-State archipelagos as well. This will mean the proliferation of archipelagic régimes that will be one of the negative effects of non-entry into force of the Convention. Now, as I said, this would not really be such a problem as long as the navigational régime within those baselines would be provided in accordance with the Law of the Sea Convention.

But this brings us to another point Professor *Orrego Vicuña* made: What rules really govern in the case of those States which are not clearly specifying the navigational régime? Coming back to Trinidad and Tobago, its legislation does not clearly provide that if Trinidad and Tobago does not designate archipelagic sea lanes, foreign ships may use rules customarily used for international navigation. You will find provisions to this effect modelled upon the Convention in the legislation of Fiji and South Pacific States for which it is, as I said, a less pronounced problem due to the vast distances between their islands. If there is an omission in this respect in the case of any more narrowly set up archipelagos, the problem arises whether there is a rule of customary international law which permits archipelagic sea lanes passage through the routes customarily used for international navigations through those States. As I said, most archipelagic States, including Indonesia and the Philippines, in practice grant this right, but the right is not clearly involved under existing international law and the tension and the problem of conflicting situations is constantly in suspense.

Then we are coming to another aspect: Why is this right unclear? It is unclear because it is different from transit passage. Archipelagic sea lanes passage, archipelagic waters régime is not the transit passage, as it is often maintained by the major maritime powers because, of course, it suits their interests. But another, different argumentation may fit the interest of archipelagic States and there is no rule that has clearly evolved. There is not much written on this subject except of writings by Indonesian experts in international law. I assume you all know Ambassador *Hasjim Djalal* and you all know *Mochtar Kusumaatmadja*, former Foreign Minister of Indonesia, and a principal architect of the Indonesian claim, who both write on these differences. There is another excellent lawyer,

Nugroho Wisnumurti, who is at present the Deputy Head of the Indonesian Mission to the UN in New York, and the co-author of this paper, Dr. *Agoes*, wrote a whole Ph. D on that issue but in Indonesian, so I cannot recommend that you read it. Anyhow, there is a lot of good work done explaining in detail the differences between transit passage and archipelagic sea lanes passage régimes. There is no interest in the developed States to do this, because, as I said, it does not fit the interests of the developed States to underline the differences between the two régimes. But they are very clearly to be noticed in the Convention, in the legislation and in the implementation of these régimes. You can find the details concerning these problems in our paper.

Scully:

Since you described me as a proponent of the traditional usage of the ocean, I should say something with regard to your presentation, which I really enjoyed. I will put it in the form of questions. There were three points which I am not quite sure I understood. The first one relates to the distinction between transit passage in straits and archipelagic sea lanes passage. My question is: Did you wish to make the point that there are no straits used for international navigation in archipelagos? The point was made with regard to, I think, Indonesia. But is it your point that there can be no straits used in international navigation within the meaning of the Convention in archipelagos? May I stop here, to give you an opportunity to answer.

Kwiatkowska:

This is exactly my point. Because in order to qualify a strait used for international navigation under Part III subject to transit passage, this strait should connect a part of the exclusive economic zone and/or high seas with another part of the exclusive economic zone and/or high seas. All the straits we have in the archipelagic waters connect to archipelagic waters or to another strait within archipelagic waters. So, if we would like to regard, for instance, the Indonesian Lombok as a strait, then we would have to regard not Lombok as such, but the whole international route, of which Lombok is a strait. And then we would be changing the geographical notion of straits. Certainly we can do it, I mean States can do whatever they like to do, but that is not then the strait in the geographical notion as is now being understood. The only strait which is bordered by Indonesia and which is a strait used for international navigation is the Malacca Straits. The Malacca Straits are governed by the tripartite agreement between Indonesia, Malaysia and Singapore which raises no problems, all superpowers and other major powers accepted this régime. This is a very complicated issue, but the geographical point is that you would need to consider as a strait the whole route and not only the Lombok and Sunda Straits because they are not straits within the geographical sense and they do not fall under the provisions of Part III. And as far as this is concerned, the Philippines which very much stresses this point, is correct. Only, the issue remains: What régime of navigation applies there under the existing international law?

Agoes:

I would only like to add one point to what Dr. *Kwiatkowska* has been explaining to you with regard to the Malacca Strait: actually, if you look at the history of this strait, you will find that it consists of two straits — Malacca and Singapore. But as was said, they have been treated as one strait. So if you refer to the provision of art. 37, Malacca and Singapore do not fit to the definition contained therein. But since users of these straits and our tripartite agreement regard them as one strait, we considerd Malacca as falling under art. 37.

Scully:

That would confirm my view that since there is no definition on geographical limitation, placed upon the straits in the Convention, that it is in fact the route, the whole passage. Therefore, I would simply want to lodge this argument with respect to the interpretation that there can be no straits used for international navigations in an archipelago. However, let me make two other points. Was it your view, and I think you again referred to the United States, that in recognizing the validity of the 12 nautical mile territorial sea, the United States is thereby recognizing any assertion of jurisdiction within 12 nautical miles?

My final point was the distinction between military and civil aviation. Was that a legal point or a practical point, when you mentioned that military aircraft can zig-zag in a way civilian aircraft cannot and therefore you only apply it to military aircraft?

Kwiatkowska:

This is the practical illustration of a legal point. As is evident by the UNCLOS III negotiations, that is why the regulations about the sea lanes have been introduced.

Scully:

But that is an argument on negotiating history, and not in relation to the provisions of the Convention.

Kwiatkowska:

But we interpret those provisions in the light of the negotiations. As regards when it was decided, I would rather send you to Mr *Dolliver Nelson*, so that he can recall the history of negotiations on this point. I am absolutely sure that the idea was that "above" archipelagic sea lanes relate to overflight for military aircraft.

Murray:

My first point was similar but slightly differently angled concerning the point on archipelagic sea lanes passages in straits. I think it is perfectly plain, I must say I spend most of my time on Law of the Sea dealing with Part XI, so that coming onto Part IV, it is a wonderful feeling of relief to be able to say something in the Convention is completely unambiguous. I think art. 54 is completely unambiguous in that it applies art. 44 to archipelagic sea lanes passage. Article 44 says that States bordering straits shall not hamper transit passage, there should be no suspension of transit passage.

I think it is quite plain that almost all the shipping passing through Sunda and Lombok Straits is going from one part of the high seas to another part of the high seas and often to the Australian exclusive economic zone. There is no doubt at all in my mind that by any definition of what is normally understood by a strait, or by being in transit between one place and another, that those are straits used in international navigation. And there is no doubt in my mind that according to art. 54 applying art. 44 it is therefore completely against the Convention to close those straits. Whether that is the equivalent of being completely against customary international law is, of course, another point.

I come to my second point. I agree that this is an area where it is dangerous to rely on customary international law, because State practice can change. It is a fact that we believe strongly that the Convention does provide for transit passage through straits, giving an example of the way the Convention guarantees the freedom of navigation, which is why my country, the United Kingdom, is keen to solve the problems of the Convention so that we can accede to it. If people were to say that actually the Convention does not do much to guarantee the freedom of navigation, then our interest in the whole thing might wane further. So, I would agree with you on that point.

One final point, which is more a side issue: the question of the various States' national legislation. I am not sure to what extent you have to look to national legislation for a guarantee of the rights of passage through straits, provided it does not impede it. We were looking very recently at a copy given to us of the draft legislation before the Bahamas on their archipelagic sea lanes passage. And the point was made to us by various people that it did not include this, that or the other precise point that is in the Convention. On the other hand, it did not exclude them either. If I can give an example: in the United Kingdom we have several straits in our territorial waters which we acknowledge as being used in international navigation. This is transit passage for straits and not archipelagic sea lanes, but it is a parallel example, I think. We have absolutely nothing in our domestic legislation which says that we will keep those straits open to international shipping or that we accept it as a transit passage. We do accept it as a transit passage, we accept it as customary international law, so we do allow transit passage through all our straits within our territorial sea. But we have nothing in our domestic legislation that says we do. If people looked at our national legislation they might come to the conclusion that there were things lacking in it. What counts is the way States apply international law. Whether or not every last particle is in the national legislation is not necessarily important, and we can spend too much time poking about in each others legislation and interfering in each others affairs and telling each other what should or should not be in our legislation. I am not sure that this is particularly helpful.

Rebagliati:

I would just like to recall that this part relating to archipelagic States is of course a codification of progressive development of international law contained in the Convention. As it has been pointed out, an enhancement of this concept will be broadly accepted if the intention of the drafters would be preserved. We all recall that the whole Convention was a kind of package deal, including this very important part relating to archipelagic States. Within this package and within the concept of archipelagic States it was also a key element which is relating to the preservation of the freedom of navigation and overflights. At the time of drafting the Convention they called it as such, freedom of navigation and freedom of overflight, not freedom of transit or transit passage etc. In that respect, I would like to recall art. 34 in relation to the issue whether the straits régime applies or does not apply to archipelagic States. I quote: "The régime of passage for straits for international navigation established in this part, shall not in other respects affect the legal status of the waters forming such straits or their exercise . . .." *A contrario sensu*, it means that in this respect it could effect this part of the Convention. I think that this article along with art. 54 and those referred to by 54 back to Part III are quite eloquent about this prevalence from one part of the Convention upon the other part of the Convention.

As a final remark, I could recall that all parts of the Convention relating to national maritime jurisdiction would really apply to archipelagic States. Nobody would claim that the parts relating to the continental shelf or to the territorial sea or to the contiguous zone are not applicable to Part IV relating to archipelagic States. That is why I think a word of caution should be pertinent to consider this régime of navigation in the whole perspective of the general economy of the Convention in which the freedom of navigation and overflight was very clearly balanced. The régime relating to the exclusive economic zone, for instance, clearly balanced the economic and sovereignty rights of the coastal States, and the rights of third States or of the rest of the international community.

Treves:

I would just like to make a couple of remarks and pose a few questions. I was very interested in learning from your oral exposé that it is so far unlikely that the Philippines will abide by what it said in its note to the Secretary-General in answering in particular to the Australian objections to the declaration the Philippines made upon ratification. Perhaps it would be worth-while to think about the implications of what they said in their note on the Philippines' position at customary law. No State can invoke domestic law in order not to abide to international law, in particular treaty law but also customary law. So, I wonder whether the Philippines, after what they said, are justified in maintaining a régime of internal waters in their archipelagic waters. Considering that, after all, the archipelagic States are not many, and there is a kind of hierarchy between them, there being two big ones and a dozen or so smaller ones, does this position by one of the two big ones move somehow the balance of the whole picture?

My second question is completely different and purely out of curiosity. When there was the closure by Indonesia of the Sunda and Lombok Straits and the consequent protest by quite a few States, including the 12 member States of the European Community, one of the arguments that was reported as being raised by Indonesia was that, while there may be a right of transit in recognized routes, these routes have to be adopted by the IMO and this cannot be done because the Convention is not in force and the IMO has done nothing. Well, the IMO is doing many things which amount to an anticipated application of the Convention. I really wonder why on this particular subject, the IMO has been doing nothing. Has anybody asked the IMO? Has there been a resistance by the archipelagic States? Is that so that the IMO as an old-fashioned body considers archipelagic waters a new concept that it does not want to mix with?

Kwiatkowska:

Briefly, I will refer to some aspects which *Tuillo Treves* has just mentioned about the IMO, because this relates to another issue to which *Tucker Scully* referred to concerning the limitation of overflight to military aircraft. I think it is too difficult now to highlight all of these points. I believe the archipelagic régime is the question of the passage of warships and I agree with those Indonesian authorities who are emphasizing this side of it. It is also shown by the negotiations at UNCLOS III. The issue is about military navigation and the military overflight. And because the issue is there, the IMO is reluctant, simply because after all IMO does not have too much to do with it. That is my short answer but, as I have said, there is quite a lot written on the possible involvement of the IMO. The IMO is not keen on taking the initiative, although the question of archipelagic sea lines passage is mentioned in the major IMO report of 1987 on the tasks of the IMO under the Law of the Sea Convention. You will find there that the IMO feels qualified to talk about the issue. But, I think that the military side of the issue somehow does not suit the initiatives to this effect.

Now, I absolutely agree with everybody, and that was almost said by everybody, that the Convention represents a proper balance. It definitely does. The régime which is embodied in the Convention on the archipelagic régime and on the straits is definitely a very well done compromise. But the problem is, although you may take a political position that we follow the Convention and States do that, the problem is, that what is in the Convention is not exactly taken over already in the customary law. The customary law which at the moment exists is unclear. What are really the rules for passage, and we may talk the whole day about it, what are the differences and how should third States exercise the archipelagic sea lanes passage? The whole art. 53 is giving plenty of rules which are very ambiguous as to their scope and status. So the Convention is certainly balanced and it is an excellent solution, only this is not reflected in existing customary law. This somehow brings us to the main topic of this colloquium — the deep sea-bed, because I suppose that the reluctance of States with respect to the deep sea-bed and non-accession to the Convention is suspending many, not only the archipelagic sea lanes régime, but many very valuable parts of this Convention which represent a very well balanced compromise.

Agoes:

I would only like to add one comment, and in giving this comment I would like to quote an American, even though that may seem strange. In view of the discussion this morning with regard to deep-sea mining and now to the archipelagic States régime, I would like to support what *Ken Wood* said in his book, that we are now still at the brink of the ocean, rather than becoming part of it.

Ballah:

Mr Chairman, I never halt a glance against an opponent, particularly two so formidable as these young female professors. But, what I have to say probably has no relevance to whether some of these rules are rules of customary international law or not. What I want to ask Dr. *Kwiatkowska* to do is to look at the possibility of even Galleon's passage in a small archipelagic State like Trinidad and Tobago, qualifying both as a strait used for international navigation for a long time and so satisfying the definition for transit passage, and also satisfying the requirements for archipelagic sea lane passage. One other point I would like to make, and the Convention, though I do not recall all the *travaux préparatoires* of the Convention, one thing is clear: there is no form of positive obligation on any archipelagic State to designate sea lane passages. The language is quite clear in art. 53 of the Convention. And that language is: the State may designate sea lanes and air routes there above. In the absence of such designation (therefore

Trinidad is not obligated to write it in its law), the right of archipelagic sea lanes passage or transit passage may be exercised through the routes normally or traditionally used for international navigation. I am not seeking to confront you on this issue at this point in time, but hope that you look at it again to see if those possibilities do not in fact exist.

Joint Ventures for Sea-Bed Activities: A Viable Alternative

Günther Jaenicke*

My report does not advocate an immediately operable joint venture model for sea-bed activities irrespective of the entry into force of the Convention. The purpose of my report is rather to show that joint venture agreements between the mining industry and the Enterprise of the International Sea-Bed Authority — as they have been envisaged by the Convention as an alternative way of getting an authorization for mining on the international sea-bed — offer better prospects for an economically viable and more acceptable régime for deep sea mining under the Convention. There is still time to reconsider the rôle of the joint venture approach in the forum of the Preparatory Commission for the following reasons:

First: It is still uncertain when the Law of the Sea Convention will enter into force. At least this will be true for Part XI of the Convention which purports to establish a generally recognized legal basis for mining activities on the international sea-bed because this Part of the Convention needs amendments to become generally acceptable. It is very much desirable that the other parts of the Convention relating to the traditional uses of the sea should be put into force expeditiously either by making them provisionally applicable or by separating the entry into force procedure of Part XI from the entry into force of the other parts of the Convention. This would provide more time for reaching a consensus on the necessary amendments to Part XI and the supplementary rules and regulations for sea-bed mining.[1] In any case, no generally recognized legal basis for deep sea mining activities is presently in sight.

Second, the hopes that deep sea mining for manganese nodules will become economically attractive within the next future, have not materialized. The availability of sufficient terrestric deposits, the slackening demand for the respective metals due to modern methods of saving and recycling, and the unforeseen and comparatively higher costs of sea-bed mining have seriously damped, if not destroyed, the earlier enthusiasm of the international industry to undertake mining

---

* Prof. Dr. *Günther Jaenicke*, em., University of Frankfurt.

[1] This approach has been advocated by *Günther Jaenicke*, Vorläufige Anwendung der Seerechtskonvention von 1982?, in: Staat und Völkerrechtsordnung, Festschrift für *Karl Doehring*, Berlin/Heidelberg/New York 1989, 387-395.

ventures on the international sea-bed under present conditions and probably for quite a time to come.

Therefore, it is not the purpose of my report to propose an immediately operable joint venture model for sea-bed mining activities, but rather to advocate a model agreement which may be resorted to when market conditions will have developed to a point where the recourse to the mineral deposits of the deep sea-bed is needed and profitable. Opening an option for a joint venture agreement with the Enterprise of the International Sea-Bed Authority that is economically feasible and, at the same time, acceptable to the mining industry, might help to overcome some of the difficulties with Part XI of the Convention.

The essence of my proposition is to put the joint venture rather in the center than on the periphery of the terms under which deep sea mining activities may be undertaken once the international sea-bed régime of the Convention will have entered into force. *Joint venture agreements with the Enterprise of the International Sea-Bed Authority should then become the normal legal framework for deep sea mining under the Convention.* As the discussions in the Preparatory Commission have shown, the States which are interested in deep sea mining and have the industrial capacity to undertake such mining ventures, have ever since criticized the costly organizational structure of the International Sea-Bed Authority and its Enterprise for a small industrial sector, as well as the heavy financial burdens, the restrictive production control measures, and the technology transfer obligations imposed on deep sea miners. While the terms for sea-bed mining ventures as presently contained in Part XI and Annex III of the Convention are rather rigid and do not allow to take account of the uncertainties of deep sea mining, the special provisions of the Convention which apply to joint ventures with the Enterprise of the International Sea-Bed Authority are much more flexible. They allow for adjustments of the terms for deep sea-bed mining and, in particular, for incentives by lowering the fees and other financial charges imposed on deep sea mining.[2]

At the second part of the 2nd Session (August 1984) of the Preparatory Commission for the International Sea-Bed Authority, the *Delegation of the Federal Republic of Germany tabled a Model Joint Venture Agreement for Sea-Bed Mining,*[3] in response to the request of Special Commission 2 of the Commission for detailed studies on the joint venture option; other models have been proposed

2 Article 153, para. 3 of the Convention; art. 5, para. 6, art. 9, paras. 2 and 3, art. 11, art. 13, para. 1 (d) (f) and para. 14 of Annex III, and art. 6, para. 6 (g) of Annex IV of the Convention.

3 UN doc. LOS/PCN/SCN. 2/WP. 5 of 25 October 1984. This proposal was based on a study prepared by the Institute for Foreign and International Economic Law in Frankfurt/Main, published in: *Günther Jaenicke/Erich Schanze/Wolfgang Hauser*, A Joint Venture Agreement for Seabed Mining, Studies in Transnational Law of Natural Resources, Vol. 5, Deventer 1981.

by Austria,[4] Columbia,[5] and lately in a Joint Study of the Asian African Legal Consultative Committee and the International Ocean Institute.

The German proposal envisaged a model joint venture agreement of general application for the exploration as well as for the exploitation of the mineral resources of the international sea-bed under the terms of the Convention, while the other models concentrated rather on forming a joint venture between the present pioneer investors and the International Sea-Bed Authority for the limited purpose of fulfilling their initial obligations under resolution II of the Law of the Sea Conference relating to the exploration of a first mine site and the training of personnel of the Enterprise. The proposal for a joint venture agreement which I advocate today, follows to a large extent the Model Agreement which had been proposed by the German delegation in the Preparatory Commission.

Before I describe the salient features of a joint venture agreement with the Enterprise of the International Sea-Bed Authority, I would like to put forward some *basic assumptions which form the present scenario for such a joint venture*:

First, it is assumed that only a competent and financially strong multinational mining enterprise or consortium will be able to assemble the necessary technical and financial means for entering into a mining venture of such magnitude and to take the technical and financial risks involved in such a venture. This will be particularly true in view of the unforeseeable environmental risks that will have to be faced in the course of a deep sea mining venture.

Second, it will at present neither be recommendable nor necessary to build up the Enterprise of the International Sea-Bed Authority as a full-scale mining enterprise with the same managerial and operational capacity as its industrial joint venture partners have at their disposal. At any event, the limited number of mining ventures which will be started during the early period of deep sea mining does not justify to build up a large and fully-equipped international enterprise which specializes in deep sea mining only and will have no chance to diversify in other economic activities. This does not exclude that the Enterprise might later expand into an integrated mining enterprise capable of going alone, but during the initial phase of deep sea mining, the Enterprise should function as a purely administrative organ of the International Sea-Bed Authority representing the economic interests of the international community in the joint mining venture: It will administer the mining area and the funds at its disposal which it contributes to the joint venture, and it will exercise control over the mining operations through participation in the leading organs of the joint venture so that an appropriate share of the profits will be credited to the Enterprise for the benefit of the international community. For this task a small-sized institution (a "nucleus Enterprise") will suffice, with a very limited, but highly efficient admin-

[4] UN doc. LOS/PCN/SCN. 2/L. 2 of 28 February 1984.

[5] UN doc. LOS/PCN/SCN. 2/WP. 14 of 18 March 1987.

istrative staff. On the other hand, it will be incumbent on the industrial joint venture partner to provide the equipment and the technical and managerial staff for the mining operations and to act as the operator of the mining sector of the joint venture. Thus, the rôle of both joint venture partners will differ as to the means at their disposal and the form of their participation in the mining venture; but both will share the common interest in running a cost-effective and profitable venture.

Third, each deep sea mining venture will be a most singular activity. This is due to the specific topography of the individual mine site and to the multiple technological problems created thereby, and foremost due to the strict obligation of avoiding environmental damage. In particular, the environmental hazards connected with the disturbance of extensive areas of the deep sea-bed have increasingly become the object of widespread concern and will require cautious action and continuous scrutiny during the whole course of a mining venture on the deep sea-bed. It will be one of the main functions of the International Sea-Bed Authority to exercise tight control over the mining activities in this respect.

Under such conditions it is not possible to make a reliable assessment whether and when a particular mining venture will become cost-covering even under favorable market conditions. It cannot be expected that a deep sea mining venture will immediately yield a profit, nor can it be anticipated when it will eventually become profitable. Consequently, it would be counter-productive to impose from the outset heavy financial burdens on such a mining venture. Not before it turns out that the mining venture, after having recovered its research and development costs, will yield a net profit, this profit will then be available for distribution between the joint venture partners on the basis of an equitable cost and profit sharing formula. The share accruing to the Enterprise of the International Sea-Bed Authority will then directly become disposable for the benefit of the international community, and in particular for the benefit of the developing countries. Under these circumstances a joint venture agreement with the Enterprise of the International Sea-Bed Authority will be capable of taking account of the special cost and time factors of each particular mining venture and, thereby, best suited to induce the mining industry to start deep sea mining operations as soon as market conditions permit.

I shall now outline some of *the salient features of the proposed Model Joint Venture Agreement for Sea-Bed Mining* which I consider relevant within the scenario I have just described:

(1) The joint venture agreement should cover only the *mining stage*, that is the recovery of the minerals from the sea-bed; it should not cover the *processing of the minerals* nor the *marketing of the metals* produced therefrom which take place on land. The simple reason is that only the mining stage falls under the jurisdiction of the International Sea-Bed Authority;[6] the further stages (transport,

processing, and marketing) are beyond its jurisdiction and would require a different legal structuring of the joint venture agreement taking into account the jurisdiction of the country where the processing plant is located. This in no way excludes the possibility of extending the joint venture agreement to the subsequent stages of metal production and marketing at a later time, but it does not seem advisable, for the reasons already stated, to burden the Enterprise with the additional functions of processing and marketing. Thus, it is assumed that the recovered minerals are taken over by the industrial joint venture partner for processing and for marketing the metals derived therefrom as part of its own business operations outside the joint venture (the revenue splitting problem created thereby will be discussed later in paragraph 7).

(2) It will be immaterial whether the joint venture agreement covers a mine site which has been "*reserved*" for the Enterprise of the International Sea-Bed Authority under the so-called "parallel system" of Part XI of the Convention, or a "*non-reserved*" mine site which has been allocated to the industrial joint venture partner by the International Sea-Bed Authority.[7] The special provisions of the Convention and its Annexes relating to joint ventures with the Enterprise do not make a difference as to whether a mine site covered by the joint venture agreement is a "reserved" or a "non-reserved" area; what alone is relevant, is the partnership with the Enterprise of the International Sea-Bed Authority. It is recommended that the joint venture partners extend their mining operations to *both sites* under their joint venture agreement. This would allow them to start with the mining operations on the most promising parts of either site depending on the results of the exploration. This option has the further advantage that it would facilitate, if not render largely irrelevant the problem whether the two mine sites to be offered by an applicant for a mining permit will be of equal value and which of them will be selected by the International Sea-Bed Authority as the "reserved" site for its Enterprise.

(3) The partners of the joint venture agreement will for practical reasons establish an *operating company* for the mining sector, although it will probably not be necessary to invest it with legal personality by incorporating it under a national legal system because the processing of the recovered minerals and the marketing of the metal products derived therefrom will remain the sole business of the industrial joint venture partner. Moreover, the incorporation and the selection of a corporate seat may pose problems because the operating company will then be subject to the host State's national jurisdiction, including its tax jurisdiction. As the industrial joint venture partner will provide the equipment as well

---

6 Articles 153 and 157 of the Convention: the jurisdiction of the Authority covers only the "activities in the Area." These are defined in art. 1, paras. 1 and 3 of the Convention in the following terms: "Area means the sea-bed and ocean floor and subsoil thereof, beyond the limits of national jurisdiction" and "Activities in the area means all activities of exploration for, and exploitation of, the resources of the Area."

7 Article 8 of Annex III of the Convention.

as the technical staff for the mining operations, the management of the operating company will be nominated by the industrial joint venture partner, but this does not preclude that the Enterprise of the International Sea-Bed Authority will be represented in the leading organ of the operating company for the protection of its interests. Similarly, training facilities may be offered to personnel of the Authority and the Enterprise.

(4) The *decision-making mechanism* within the joint venture agreement is a very sensitive issue; it should at the same time protect the vital interests of each joint venture partner, but not prevent timely decisions when they are required by proper management. Where voting in the organs of the joint venture partnership or in the operating company will become necessary, the allocation of voting power should not depend primarily on the ratio of the capital contributed by the joint venture partners. The delicate problem of the valuation of the mine sites which are considered the common heritage of mankind and brought into the joint venture, may thereby lose its importance. It is assumed that the Enterprise would wish to exercise direct control over decisions with major financial or technical implications, but may be prepared to accept majority decisions of minor importance or of a routine character in the operating company if they are taken within a controllable institutional framework where the vital interests of all joint partners are adequately safeguarded. I cannot go into details here, but I may refer in this respect to the various precedents that may be found in the practice of modern land-based mining ventures. I may only mention here that it had proved to be useful to lay down the overall guidelines for the joint venture operations in a general investment plan which has to be established and, when necessary, amended by direct agreement between the joint venture partners. This investment plan may then serve as the normative framework for the decision-making within the operating company and for the protection of the interests of the joint venture partners.

(5) The *financial conditions* under which a joint venture agreement with the Enterprise of the International Sea-Bed Authority will have to operate, are of crucial importance to investors wishing to embark on a mining venture during the early period of mining operations on the deep sea-bed. Under the present terms of the Convention the Enterprise may claim exemption from the payments to the International Sea-Bed Authority which are otherwise imposed on deep sea miners, until it will become self-supporting, but no longer than 10 years from the commencement of its first commercial mining activity;[8] no similar exemption is accorded to an eventual national or multinational joint venture partner. More importantly, the Convention provides that financial incentives may be established by regulation of the International Sea-Bed Authority for deep sea miners if they enter into a joint venture agreement with the Enterprise;[9] there is no explicit

[8] Article 10, para. 3 of Annex IV of the Convention.

[9] Article 11, para. 2 and art. 13, paras. 1 (d), 14 of Annex III of the Convention.

authority for according similar incentives to the Enterprise after the expiration of the aforementioned 10 years, but as under article 170 (4), 171 (b), 173 (b) of the Convention the Authority is empowered to provide the Enterprise with the necessary funds out of its budget which itself is made up, *inter alia*, of payments received from deep sea miners under the financial terms of their mining licences, an implicit authority may be inferred therefrom to apply similar incentives to the Enterprise if it enters into a joint venture agreement. These incentives will have to be determined by a normative regulation of the International Sea-Bed Authority; they may, in principle, go so far as to waive the imposition of certain financial charges on sea-bed mining completely; in particular, they may exonerate the mining venture from the production charge which becomes due irrespective of whether it yields a profit.[10] However, in order to prevent artificial competitive advantages or distortions of the price level on the metal markets to the detriment of the land-based producers,[11] it may be advisable for the Authority to retain the power to suspend the exemption when a certain margin of profits has been reached or the processed metal is sold under the current price level on the international market. Under such a flexible financial system mining ventures in the initial period of their life-time would have the opportunity to develop safely, without being bound to the rigid time-tables and financial rules of article 13 of Annex III of the Convention, until they reach the zone of profitability.

(6) The rules on *obligatory transfer of technology* by deep sea miners to the Enterprise of the International Sea-Bed Authority which are contained in article 5 of Annex III of the Convention, are still considered problematic by some industrialized countries which are interested in deep sea mining. Article 5, para. 6, however, provides that in case of a joint venture with the Enterprise transfer of technology will be regulated by the terms of the joint venture agreement. Thus, this provision allows to dispense with the cumbersome and complicated procedure contained in article 5 for enforcing the technology transfer; it leaves the parties of a joint venture agreement wide discretion and flexibility how to arrange for the use of technology in the operation of the mining venture and for the enjoyment by the Enterprise of the benefits therefrom. In the situation of a joint venture the sharing of the best technology available will be the natural consequence of the parallel interests of the joint venture partners in the most effective and profitable exploitation of the mine site; it will lose its character as a one-way burden of the deep sea mining industry. It is clearly in the interest of each joint venture partner to provide the operating company with the best technology available (equipment, patents, licences, know-how). The joint venture partners may agree on supplementary provisions, e. g. on the valuation of the transferred technology or on the protection of the transferred technology against proliferation to competitors, where such additional agreements are considered useful or necessary.

---

10 Article 13, paras. 5 and 6 (a) of Annex III of the Convention.

11 Article 13, para. 1 (f) of Annex III of the Convention.

In this context the question may arise whether the industrial joint venture partner of the Enterprise should make his technology available not only to the operating company, and thereby to the Enterprise in its capacity as partner of the operating company, but also directly to the Enterprise for use elsewhere, thereby possibly benefiting industrial competitors. However, a claim of the Enterprise for using elsewhere the technology that has been transferred to the operating company, would go beyond the object and purpose of the joint venture and has no basis in article 5, para. 6 of Annex III of the Convention. On the other hand, the joint venture partner of the Enterprise may well have a commercial interest to make available or sell the technology which has been used or developed by the operating company to the Enterprise for use elsewhere provided that there is no cost-free proliferation to competitors.

(7) The distribution of *profits and losses* of the operating company between the joint venture partners will normally depend on the ratio of the investments put into the operating company. The parties may, however, also agree on a fixed ratio. The main problem, which may arise in this context, will be the necessary splitting of the proceeds from the sale of the metals on the market between the mining stage, which is covered by the joint venture agreement, and the further stages of the metal production and marketing of the metal products, which will be the sole business of the industrial joint venture partner. As the minerals recovered from the sea-bed are then taken over by the industrial joint venture partner for processing the minerals and marketing the metal, an equitable sharing formula of the proceeds, which result in total from the mining, processing and marketing of the metal value of the recovered minerals, must be devised. Otherwise, the processing sector might generate excess profits at the expense of the mining sector or *vice versa* because, in the absence of a market for the recovered minerals, their value cannot be objectively calculated in the transactions between the mining and the processing sector. It is, therefore, recommended that the joint venture agreement uses the equitable revenue splitting formula contained in article 13 of Annex III of the Convention which works as follows: The proceeds from the sale of the processed minerals are reduced by the total operating costs of both the mining and the processing/marketing sector; the so obtained net proceeds are then attributed to each sector in proportion to each sector's capital investment thus producing an equal rate of return for each sector's investment. By this calculation an equitable part of the net proceeds of the whole integrated chain of the metal production will be credited to the operating company for the recovery of the minerals.

(8) Specific attention should be paid to the problem of *conflict resolution*, and more particular to mechanisms of *conflict avoidance*. The joint venture agreement should provide for a set of institutionalized procedures for resolving differences which may arise between the joint venture partners about investment or operational policies before such differences might evolve into open legal conflict. Without going into details here, I would like to stress the importance of establishing an

institutionalized renegotiation procedure where the terms of the joint venture agreement or the general investment plan may have become impracticable or inequitable to one of the joint venture partners. Such procedures may consist in the formal establishment of permanent committees for consultation or renegotiation; if no settlement is reached, the matter may then be carried at the request of either party before a board of conciliators. For the resolution of *legal disputes relating to the interpretation of the joint venture agreement*, a compulsory arbitration procedure should be provided for.

The joint venture model which I have just outlined, will be advantageous to both sides: to the mining industry because it exonerates them from otherwise burdensome obligations, and to the Enterprise because it immediately participates in deep sea mining ventures with the prospect of an early share in the eventual profits. As the mining operations themselves are largely, if not totally left to the industrial joint venture partner, the Enterprise will be able to engage in several joint ventures simultaneously within the limits of the production ceiling if such ceiling will be maintained under the Convention.

On the other hand, two or more industrial consortia may join in a single joint venture with the Enterprise where each of them wants to restrict its financial engagement or where market conditions allow only a limited number of economically viable mining ventures. Although the Enterprise as well as the mining consortia are free whether or not to enter into a joint venture, the advantages connected with a joint venture agreement — if they are granted to their fullest extent — will most likely suffice to induce both sides to seek such a joint venture. Therefore, it does not seem necessary to establish a legal obligation of the Enterprise to enter into meaningful negotiations for the conclusion of a joint venture agreement; only with respect to a "reserved" mine site which has already been prospected by an applicant for a mining permit and then relinquished to the Enterprise under the parallel system of the Convention (article 8 of Annex III), this applicant should be accorded priority by the Enterprise in selecting a joint venture partner for this particular mine site.

It will be for the International Sea-Bed Authority or, as long as the Convention has not entered into effect, for the Preparatory Commission to enact appropriate regulations which will establish the special conditions and, in particular, the financial incentives that will apply to joint ventures with the Enterprise of the International Sea-Bed Authority. If the mining industry has an assured option for entering into a joint venture with the Enterprise under special terms and conditions on which the industrial joint venture partners can rely in their calculations, such an option would certainly make the international sea-bed régime more acceptable to the industry and might help to pave the way for the general acceptance of the Convention.

Discussion

Morrison:

Thank you, Professor *Jaenicke*. You have given us an interesting alternative which is not without some controversy. Now, in order to stimulate that controversy immediately, we will turn to Ambassador *Francisco Zegers de Santa Cruz* who will give us a slightly different view.

Zegers Santa Cruz:

I will only make a very general comment on the subject and especially on the very interesting statement which Prof. *Jaenicke* has just made on joint ventures as a sea-bed régime. Prof. *Jaenicke* has explored some possibilities within the context of the Convention today and thus limited the model he has proposed for joint ventures. Prof. *Jaenicke* had already suggested the idea of joint ventures during the course of the conference, and I would like to refer to this point. Clearly, what we have now in the Convention is a parallel system and, within the parallel system, the possibility of building in joint ventures, "joint arrangements," as stated in the Convention. It is a limited form of joint ventures which could be extended. Prof. *Jaenicke* has made a very interesting exploration in which he has gone into a number of details and possibilities of how a joint venture would function in fact.

I — in my comment — will limit myself to some very general problems. I will begin with the history of the setting of this régime. When we were at the early stages of the Sea-Bed Committee, before the Conference began, and also at the early stages of the Conference, it was suggested that joint ventures could be a general system for the exploration and exploitation of the sea-bed. Actually, 13 Latin American countries — and I remember that Ambassador *Ballah* sitting here introduced it — sent in a paper on joint ventures. The idea, I would say, was at that time favoured by a large number of developing countries and several representatives of developed countries, like Prof. *Jaenicke* has pointed out. At that moment, due to a number of circumstances, the so-called "parallel system" was preferred. There was a law in the United States for exploitation which created amongst other experiences this parallel system in which an operator explored an area and detected two sites, including one for the State, that chose between the two the one it wanted to have. The parallel system was preferred by many developed countries at that time, beginning with the United States, and was proposed by Secretary of State *Kissinger* at the Conference, because it was felt that the private operator would control his own site and his own process. It was coupled with something else: with the demand that we had full regulations of mining operations in the Conference, that is, that we had a kind of mining code. So the joint venture system as a whole was left aside, and instead we had the "parallel system" and what I would call the attempt of a "mining code," on which we worked for a number of years.

Through time the detailed system proved to be a burden, first for the negotiations and second during the negotiations. And then, afterwards, it raised most of the problems we have, which come probably through an excess of regulation; because of the fear of an excess of bureaucratic burdens or costs; and because, in general, the efficiency of the system has been put into doubt. Now, at that time, there was also the fear of what was called an automatic majority, and that is why it was attempted to include everything into the Convention or its Annexes. (Yesterday, we discussed something of this, and probably we will never have such an automatic majority. Besides, in the Conference we have always worked by consensus.) Finally, the interests are very diverse and we will not always have this division of developed and developing countries in the negotiations.

If one has to explore the viability of Part XI, perhaps it would be interesting to have a system of joint ventures as an alternative to the parallel system. The alternative would have to be an option, a system of joint ventures different from the parallel system. That is, the possibility to opt would have to exist. Perhaps, the operator or the contractor could opt when applying to a title for exploration and exploitation whether to follow the parallel system or whether to work in association with the international Authority. Moreover perhaps, such an association would be slightly more ambitious, than what Prof. *Jaenicke* has explained, that is open to every possibility.

In such an association, the Authority has the title over *common heritage*, and thus contributes to the resource of mankind, while the contractor or the operator would contribute the capital, the technology and the know-how. That is, we would have equivalent contributions, and we would have convergent interests in co-operation, in association, instead of the built in tension which is inherent to the parallel system. The joint venture approach would mean a simpler procedure, less regulation, less complication for both the operator and the Authority, diminished costs and, on the way, perhaps the solution of a number of problems which today arise, including the transfer of technology, which simply would not exist, because the technology would be used in common and would be known in common. If such an approach was taken, the *common heritage* system would of course have to be maintained, the principle of *common heritage* with all its implications — non-appropriations, peaceful use, distribution of benefits, etc. — as well the maintenance of the general powers of the Authority.

Now, how would this be done if we wanted something more general than what we have now in the Convention: If we wanted an option for somebody interested in exploring or exploiting the sea-bed? Perhaps it would be better to produce some authoritative agreement in the Preparatory Commission. But, if necessary, an Additional Protocol should not be discarded, although the way of the authority agreement would perhaps be simpler. If such an alternative was adopted, the Convention should remain intact, i. e. it should not be amended and/or changed. This could be negotiated through whatever channels, either informal arrangements, through the Preparatory Commission or other informal means. It would certainly solve many of the political problems, which we have, and not produce others, which a hypothesis of amendments would encourage.

As Prof. *Jaenicke* has mentioned, in the Preparatory Committee, several models or projects of joint ventures were explored, and some discussions took place during the course of the Conference on the Law of the Sea. There are many articles and publications on the matter, and this is a very appropriate forum for discussing it a little further. I think that the discussions we may have now may touch on both approaches: the more limited one within the Convention, of joint ventures contained within the parallel system; or a broader approach entailing an option, a system of joint ventures different to the parallel system, as I have tried to suggest.

Bouch:

May I just say how interesting I found both speakers on this subject. I have certainly read papers on this issue before but it is always useful to have an exposition from the front of the room. I very much applaud many of the things that Prof. *Jaenicke* has said. It is very interesting when talking to mining companies, to learn that they do see quite a great deal of merit in some of the proposals that he has outlined and, as he rightly pointed out, it is important that we continue to accord this matter, a central place in the overall debate, rather than one that may be construed as being a marginal. Indeed, it must be of central concern to us all if we are ever going to sell this particular régime to mining companies. Of course, mining companies have a great deal of experience in joint ventures of all sorts and therefore do not shy away from such matters, but the "devil is in the detail." The difficulty is how you actually make the leap between models, however theoretically good they may appear to be, and the actuality of the situation. The numbers are what matter to mining companies and they will simply say to you "Yes, of course, we can dream up all sorts of ideas" but until we actually know what the numbers look like, its extremely difficult to make the leap from theory to practice.

I would like again to emphasize that the relationship between joint ventures and other parts of the mining régime is extremely important. The transfer of technology point has often been cited in the context and we all know how difficult that is for many industrialized States. Indeed, I believe it is true to say that we could actually more or less take care of a number of those problems by joint venture arrangements. The relationship with production policy is interesting and that was touched on. This is a very difficult issue, I do not have any answers to it, but it is at least possible to conceive of a joint venture arrangement being, so to speak, a pilot scheme, which would at least obviate the problem for probably some considerable time of involving ourselves in the debate of production policy and production ceilings. In fact, more generally, we could use the first joint venture as a pilot operation from which we can draw all sorts of conclusions for the longer term.

My question really was concerned with the issue of distribution of profits. It seems to me that whilst one could conceive of a number of different schemes, many multinational companies would wish to assess the issue in terms of the entirety of a project: from the prospecting stage through processing and including marketing. They would wish to consider figures for each stage together in their balance sheets. The proposal is, as I understood it (but maybe I did not understand it very clearly), that in some way these operations could be divided. I would think it would be extremely difficult for multinational companies to separate these operations through operational companies. So I wonder quite what we can do with that part of the argument.

Jaenicke:

The division of profits is a very tricky question. At the Conference we had quite a lot of discussion about how to devise it for those cases where the mining sector is kept separate from the processing and marketing sector as it is suggested under the proposed joint venture model. But I think that the revenue splitting system as it has been devised for such a case in the Convention is an equitable one. It works the following way: the whole of the proceeds from the mining sector as well as from the processing and marketing sectors are counted together, then the operating costs of all sectors are deducted therefrom, and the resulting net proceeds are split up at a ratio corresponding to the investments made in either the mining sector or in the processing and marketing sector. This secures that each investment either in the mining or in the processing sector gets an equal rate of return. It prevents the shifting of profits from the mining to the processing sector or vice versa, which is, as you know, a frequently used accounting technique in international business. The revenue splitting formula of the Convention might be a suitable model for a joint venture restricted to the mining sector. We spent quite a lot of time at the Conference on this problem and we considered this formula as the most equitable system. But, of course, the parties are free to agree otherwise. If they think that what both sides are contributing to the joint venture is nearly equal, they may dispense with a revenue splitting formula and just divide the profits by 50:50. But that depends on the financial contributions and the circumstances of each case; it will, in particular, depend on how much the industrial joint venture partner wants to invest into the mining business and how much the Enterprise will be able to contribute by supplying capital and mine sites. It will, however, be difficult to evaluate the value of a mine site and the minerals therein. If some more simple formula could be found by the joint venture partners, they are free to agree on it.

Morrison:

One of the things one finds from other joint venture operations outside of mining is that once you have decided that you are going to do it, the accounting problem can be solved.

Golitsyn:

I found both presentations very interesting. It is an old subject but at the same time new; therefore, there are many questions that can be raised. When Prof. *Jaenicke* spoke about joint ventures he said that it is immaterial and even advantageous if both sites are included in the prospecting mining operations: the mining site allocated to the Enterprise and the mining site allocated, for example, to a pioneer investor. Do I understand him correctly that since it is advantageous to have both sites included a pioneer investor concerned will be given a preferential right for entering into a joint venture with the Enterprise? This is my first question. My second question is the following. If one has a joint venture where both sites are included but the rights to the activities are obtained under different conditions: How would it be possible to apply a single revenue sharing system to the profits derived from the activities on both sites?

Jaenicke:

I see no problem why pioneer investors as defined by resolution II should not have the first call on joint ventures with the Enterprise, because no one else will be there who is able and willing to mine at least in the initial stage. As to the second question, I do not understand what you mean by revenues which would have to be calculated differently in the mining and the processing sector. The first calculation is done under the joint venture agreement and the other is done by the industrial investor who processes the minerals and sells the metals. I cannot perceive why the rate of return of the respective investments should be different in both sectors.

Golitsyn:

No, what I actually meant is how the benefits will be divided then, because the rights were obtained under different conditions?

Jaenicke:

The division of profits between the Enterprise on the one hand representing the international community and the joint venture partner on the other concerns only the profits from the mining sector.

Morrison:

I believe, his question addresses the issue under the parallel system that half of the territory is the territory of the pioneer investor and the other half of the territory is the territory of the Enterprise. Is this correct, and how do you decide what profit derives from the development of the minerals?

Jaenicke:

It will be immaterial whether the joint venture agreement covers a reserved or a non-reserved site or both. The charges imposed on miners of a non-reserved site are, so to speak, the equivalent for getting the permit to mine this site, while in the case of a reserved site the Enterprise brings in that site as its contribution. In both cases the contributions of the respective mine site should not be valued differently, and with respect to the costs which the industrial joint venture partner has already spent in prospecting and exploring the site, they will be credited to his investment before the profits are divided.

Ballah:

We have been fortunate to have heard two noble exponents of the joint venture system, Prof. *Jaenicke* and Ambassador *Zegers*. In fact, I do not believe we have had a serious debate on this issue since the ,70s. Prof. *Jaenicke* has added to that debate by proposing the German proposal which was put — I think originally before the Sea-Bed Committee and then later in the course of the Conference. We have come a long way and I think it is time that the debate becomes serious again and I think this is probably the finest opportunity in a forum which is not controversial. I think people can express their ideas fairly well. I want to go back a little, although Ambassador *Zegers* hinted at it, but probably 19 years ago some young men including Ambassador *Zegers* himself used to meet alternately I think in the missions of Brazil and Argentina, sometimes in the Chilean Mission, where they were looking at what could be the best system for exploitation of the Area. In those days *Kissinger* and *Engo* had not done their worst in their luncheon by introducing the parallel system and one thing that Secretary of State *Kissinger* did then was to promise funding for the Enterprise. I think much of that is now forgotten in the United States and following that meeting *Engo* sold the parallel system to the first committee of UNCLOS III and it was sold easily to the developing countries because of the promise of funding for the first venture of the Enterprise in a parallel system. I think some of these things should be stated and I think some of these promises should be kept in good faith by successive administrations.

When that group of young Latin American men met 19 years ago, they looked at the Eco-petrol joint venture model of Colombia. The Eco-petrol joint venture model was in the *New York Times* at the time. It is a joint venture between Colombia and American private entities. In this model, Colombia's sovereignty over its natural resources, that is the oil and natural gas, represented its equity participation. Colombia did not have to put in any capital and it did not have to look for technology, too, because the company that was coming into the venture was bringing technology. Built into the joint venture model were provisions for training. That model seemed therefore to satisfy a number of the wishes of certain Latin American countries at the time in that they would not have had the problem of dealing with the transfer of technology, the question of training and the question of mobilizing the capital. Colombia's equity in that Eco-petrol model was its sovereignty, its permanent sovereignty over its natural resources. We were not quite sure whether you could equate Colombia then with the International Sea-Bed Authority. We were not quite sure that you could say that the Area was vested probably in the International Sea-Bed Authority and as such the International Sea-Bed Authority had sovereignty over the resources of the Area. We were not certain about that. But we felt that "notionally" there was that kind of sovereignty and therefore "notionally" the International Sea-Bed Authority could be placed in the very position of Colombia.

It was suggested then that there should be a unitary joint venture system and that there would be no other system operating in the Area but that system. The International Sea-Bed Authority through its operational and contractual arm, the Enterprise, would be a partner in each of those joint ventures whether it was with a public or private entity, national or international as the case may be. As Ambassador *Zegers* has said and my delegation had the honour presenting that position in 1978 in Geneva at a meeting of the Sea-Bed Committee, that position was sold to most developing countries which decided to support that system. And to put the record straight, Nigeria did introduce a proposal either in the Sea-Bed Committee or later in the Conference (the memory of an old man dims a little bit at this point in time) but we have some younger men here, like *James Kateka*, who probably would remember whether that Nigerian joint venture proposal was introduced in the Sea-Bed Committee.

Later on we had a Jeferad proposal which resembled in some way a joint venture proposal. It was a joint venture proposal for exploration and possibly for training. Unfortunately, the proposal was not adequately pursued, and therefore there were not any conclusions at that point and time. But at this point in time, I think it is right to put it back on the table. Colombia subsequently produced a proposal which was a refinement of the very Jeferad proposal. But they were all tending in the direction of joint ventures. Now, the issues once more arise and I agree that we have no problems as to how to share things because one thing the mining system is not short of is joint venture models; be it oil, natural gas, be it for copper, nickel or whatever. So it means we can find formulas with regard to sharing profits.

Philosophically, the question relates to what kind of joint venture we require, what kind of joint venture we want? What is the kind of joint venture that would be in keeping with the principle of the *common heritage*? I noticed that a new term is being used these days — sustainable exploitation. I think it connotes somewhat a little of the notion of *common heritage* whereby you take into account the environment in exploitation so as to ensure that the legacy goes on for generations and that no one generation is permitted to eat up the legacy to the detriment and peril of future generations. Maybe we have to forget the parallel system; the system then must be an integrated joint venture system. That is not a system which is a joint venture as proposed by Prof. *Jaenicke* just for mining, but a system which takes in down stream operations. It takes in transportation, it takes in processing, it takes in marketing. The joint venture itself need not do the transporting. It can contract that out. It also needs not process itself. It needs not market itself, but it remains an integrated joint venture between the partners in all the stages of the arrangement. That kind of arrangement in my view is more in keeping with the *common heritage* principle, the sustainable exploitation principle, a common legacy to be shared by all.

Another thing, which I noted, that the original *Jaenicke* proposal, if I can call it that, was a proposal where the beneficial equity was 51:49. I think that was in the original proposal and I am not certain now, if it was 50:50, well, in my view it has to be a 50:50 proposal and a beneficial equity must be in that kind of range. I think that is the only way to move on and that is the only we could possibly get full support for a joint venture arrangement.

Rao:

We have heard a very interesting exposition of the subject. Prof. *Jaenicke* has just outlined a model of joint venture which perhaps may open up possibilities for future development. But I am not sure whether the model suggested by him can constitute a viable alternative for the system of exploration and exploitation incorporated in the Convention. In fact, if you look back to the series of negotiations which have been recounted by Ambassador *Ballah* and Ambassador *Zegers* very succinctly, since several ideas including joint venture arrangements were articulated in the Conference and after having gone through the entire process, the joint venture as one of the modalities for implementing the system of exploration and exploitation was considered to be feasible and it was only in that context that art. 11 of Annex III incorporated certain specific provisions for facilitating the future joint arrangements. But now the proposal just put forward by Prof. *Jaenicke* confined the joint venture model to only one limited aspect of mining.

Mining constitutes a small segment and if you go by the information provided in several studies the deep sea-bed mining operation is likely to involve more than 60% costs in the processing and marketing sector. Unless we have an integrated system of joint venture arrangements the entire approach outlined in the Convention is likely to be defeated. As such, I fully share the views expressed by Ambassador *Ballah* and if we have to consider joint venture at all as an alternative model, we have to see it in an integrated fashion and not confine it to particular areas or segments. Otherwise, it may just happen that the resources are taken out from the deep sea-bed and transported by multinationals, or companies without corresponding benefit to the international community.

Kiderlen:

Just a rather brief remark. First, I would like to say that I am grateful for the reopening of the debate on joint ventures and I am very much in agreement with what *Lennox Ballah* just said about the seriousness of that debate and the timeliness of it. I just have one question in this regard. Prof. *Jaenicke*, you mentioned at the beginning of your statement a somewhat limited project for a joint venture which had been put forward, or which perhaps is still to be put forward by the AALCC, a joint venture limited to the purpose of a sort of preliminary régime which will cover the time until exploitation becomes viable. I have some doubts about the possibility of applying the joint ventures scheme to that limited purpose, because I cannot see the aim of this in terms of economic profit, which in my understanding is essential to a joint venture. But of course there is some activity to be envisaged in this interim period and I would be interested in hearing from you, if you think that the joint venture model may help solving the problem of time, that is bridging the time before deep sea-bed mining becomes viable. This interim period certainly presents problems for us which we have to solve much more urgently than perhaps the problems of the final régime. So my question would be, is the joint venture concept also applicable in your mind to solve the problem of an interim régime?

Jaenicke:

I wanted to distinguish my model from those other models which have a very limited purpose. As you have rightly remarked, these other joint venture models have been put forward for discharging the obligation of the pioneer investors to explore a mine site for the Enterprise before the entry into force of the Convention. This obligation cannot be well enforced against the mining industry alone as long as there is no prospect of profitable exploitation, and it will, therefore, become necessary that the money will primarily be provided by governments or other international sources. This is quite another scenario for having a joint venture and it is not comparable to that which I have in mind for the later exploitation stages. In response to Mr *Rao* I would say the following: The difficulty is that the processing will be done on land and not at sea. If the processing were to be done at sea on the spot, then, of course, mining and processing could be undertaken as an integrated venture. But if processing is done on land in the home country of the industrial joint venture partner or somewhere else in a third country, it will be very difficult to include the processing sector in the same joint venture agreement because the processing plant would probably not only produce the metals from the nodules recovered by the joint venture, but also from other sources in order to make the undertaking economically viable. So I have some doubts whether at least for the near future it will be feasible to extend the joint venture to the processing stage as well. At any event, the revenue-splitting formula will provide for an equitable sharing of the profits from the recovery of the nodules. So one might say that what is taken from the international sea-bed as the fruits of the *common heritage of mankind* will be equitably shared by the joint venture partners.

Orrego Vicuña:

I would say that this is a very timely debate particularly since it probably has not been undertaken since 1975, when there were a number of projects and thoughts introduced into the discussion including some by FAO, by Chile and a few other countries that participated formally and informally in the consideration of that first approach. After having heard the two presentations there would seem to be two angles to the discussion which I think would be worth underlining. The first is that from Prof. *Jaenicke*'s presentation one realizes that a number of technical details can be better dealt with through the negotiations that inevitably would have to be developed in order to get to a joint venture; that is the normal procedure for organizing a joint venture. I think that both Ambassador *Ballah* and Dr. *Rao* are right from the point of view that the question is not only whether the mining stage would be included, but if you look into the practice of joint ventures throughout the mining world you will find today that most usually the processing and marketing are included in any joint ventures scheme. But that is an aspect that will have to be discussed in the negotiations themselves. On the other hand this issue was raised during the negotiations about the profit sharing scheme to a very detailed extent.

The other issue is the one raised by Ambassador *Zegers* from the point of view that there is a much broader implication to the discussion, that is, to approach the issue of sea-bed mining from an entirely different perspective from that written in the Convention. In fact, in the approach that he has suggested I would venture to say that one can really think of doing away with the parallel system, or keeping it as an option which in any event would render it a dead option because no one would opt for it. Through that approach one can solve at least three other issues which are very important. Firstly, the transfer of technology within the joint venture. Secondly, production authorization, which would be enlarged to the extent that both sides, the Enterprise and the Authority and the operator would be combining their respective authorizations in the venture. Thirdly, of the participation in joint ventures of developing countries, which is another side of the whole picture that is built into the Convention. Those three issues, which are major issues of the deadlock, would be solved in the joint venture scheme, or could be solved.

And finally, there is one other thing which I think is also important to mention with due respect to Ambassador *Ballah*, which is that the Enterprise has been in the background of some concern from the point of view of being a kind of bureaucratic organization sponsored by international organizations which would not be very practical from the point of view of the operations to be undertaken. In a joint ventures scheme that concern is also taken care of because the Enterprise would be operating in the joint venture in accordance with what is the normal practice of such activities, including the approach to market economies and mining and metal markets and so on.

Kimball:

I think what *Francisco Orrego* said is very appropriate and I do not disagree at all with the advantages that he has just cited to this joint venture alternative that *Fernando Zegers* proposed. I do have a question in relation to the suggestion that you could either opt for a parallel system or opt for this other joint venture system, as Ambassador *Zegers* proposed. In that situation I would like to ask Ambassador *Zegers* what kind of incentives he would see for a private operator to choose the joint venture alternative to the parallel system. Presumably choosing the joint venture alternative would have to give more to that operator than the parallel system choice — for example, reduce the costs of providing a second site to the Authority as is now required by the Convention in the parallel system. In a parallel system, as *Francisco* said, the operator could get rid of the possibility of the mandatory transfer of technology, but are there other incentives which you think would have to be offered a private operator if he were to choose this joint venture alternative as opposed to the parallel system?

Zegers Santa Cruz:

Yes, I see several possibilities. First, you would have a simpler procedure, that is, you would enter directly into negotiations for the joint venture relating to the operation, while in the parallel system you have to follow a very lengthy and difficult procedure that is confusing. Second, I think that you can explore in a more relaxed fashion, because it was quite a problem to produce two equivalent mining sites; you would not have to do that. The third advantage has been mentioned: the transfer of technology. The fourth advantage is that you do not have the Enterprise as a competitor, it is not a competing factor, it is a partner. The private enterprise or private contractor, or potential contractors have looked at this Enterprise as a potential competitor and have therefore had a lot of misgivings. You have those four advantages. I would like to add that the whole system would be cheaper and, therefore, more profitable. I agree with *Francisco Orrego*, in the sense that everybody would opt, if one had the option, for the joint venture system.

Maquieira:

I do agree that we are at a point where it is timely to pick up the joint venture proposals and look at them seriously within the context of the Preparatory Commission. We have been unable to do that so far and it is of use that we take it up soon in order to explore some of the discussion which we have had here. I see in that discussion that the point to be taken into account is the fact that the Convention says basically nothing about joint ventures, it simply provides for them under certain circumstances. Therefore, it is another of those areas that we have discovered, where the Convention provides plenty of room for developing new mechanisms. And if an approach such as suggested by *Fernando Zegers*, for example, of developing a clear, alternative optional scheme could be done, it can be done within the context of the Convention since, as I have said, there are no precise provisions in it regarding joint ventures. I would like to put a question to Dr. *Jaenicke*. Could he perhaps elaborate on his decision-making scheme, that he included in his joint venture proposal as to how the volume would not depend on the ratio of the capital and how the Enterprise would be in direct control of certain decisions and also how the investment plan to be agreed upon may serve as a basis for this decision-making?

Jaenicke:

One has to distinguish between two planes of decision-making. The first and most important act is the determination of the general investment plan. This plan will have to be drawn up by agreement between the Enterprise on the one side and the industrial joint venture partner or consortium on the other side. There may be subsidiary committees which are charged with certain functions for the preparation and necessary adjustments of the general investment plan, and there a voting formula could be provided for, if voting becomes necessary. But on the plane of the operating company, where the responsibility for the operations rests mainly with the industrial joint venture partner, I do not regard it necessary to provide for an equal voting power of both sides. It has been the practice in modern land-based mining ventures to develop such a general investment plan, which has to be agreed between the joint venture partners and then forms the normative scheme or normative frame within which the operating company has to act. Under this system the operating company can act by the normal procedures of decision-making used by commercial companies without being hampered by a veto power held by one side. The main policy decisions relating to the joint venture have already been taken and, when necessary, adjusted by the general investment plan. The main interests of both partners are taken care of in this plan, how much money should be invested, how much should be produced, and where the operations should take place.

Kimball:

I just have one comment to follow up, and I do think this whole question of joint venture is very much worth pursuing. It is worth remarking, in relation what Mr *Maquieira* said, that there are no two sites if you have not got a parallel system. The question that bears further exploring is that there are no two production limits, no two production authorizations, and no two sites to deal with, that is the alternative that you are posing.

Imnadze:

I would like to raise a question of a more general nature. If my understanding is correct, both concepts presented by our distinguished speakers are based on the assumption that the International Sea-Bed Authority as a representative of mankind, has ownership rights with regard to the Area and its resources. I do not think that this is actually quite correct from a legal point of view, because in accordance with the *common heritage* principle the Area and its resources are reserved for common use of all nations and neither any nation nor mankind as such possesses that as a property. So I doubt whether the Authority acting on behalf of mankind has any rights to make a contribution to joint venture, by providing it with resources which do not belong to it. And consequently, I do not think that any revenue sharing system can be based on such grounds.

Zegers Santa Cruz:

On this point alone I would like to read out a part of the Convention. It says in art. 136 that "the area and its resources are the *common heritage* of mankind"; in Spanish and in French "common patrimony" ("patrimonio", "patrimoine"). Patrimony is a more precise word. And then we have to read art. 137, para. 2: "All rights in the resources of the Area are vested in mankind as a whole, on whose behalf the Authority shall act." It cannot be clearer.

Treves:

Two very quick remarks. One is that through the years the idea of joint venture has been raised and always been set aside for various reasons. In ,75 for instance it was the Socialist countries that felt that this idea was not compatible with their view of things. Later, when the Netherlands proposed again the same idea, it was turned aside on the ground that too much work had been done on the "parallel system" and that delegations should not be bothered with this "born again" idea.

The second, more general remark is that I have the feeling of discussing things that are not really there. We are talking about details of a situation in which deep sea-bed mining is assumed to be feasible in the short term such as whether it is preferable for the Enterprise to have 50% or 51% or 49% of the joint venture. This is really very abstract. There may, however, be a kind of joint venture that, without being so-called, is in the process of being developed in the PrepCom. This is, or could be, the co-operation which could be put together by the pioneer investors in order to explore the site of the Authority in accomplishing their obligations as pioneer investors. From what is emerging from the negotiations taking place, the three Pacific Ocean pioneer investors are moving towards some sort of collaboration for the exploration of the site of the Authority. This looks like a form of joint venture. Finally, I cannot resist making a comparison that may in fact be useful. The companies very often have been wary of going into joint ventures with the Enterprise. I think that their reaction is, or maybe was, that of a young man who is thinking about marrying the daughter of the boss. It can be useful for your career but you lose all prospects of making it on your own. So far, the companies have felt they do not want to marry the daugther of the boss.

Deciding upon the Budget of the United Nations: A Comparison

Klaus Dicke*

I. Introduction

As everyday life shows us, deciding upon a budget requires prudence, because a budget must be accepted at the very least by those who pay the bill. But as we learn from political experience, deciding upon budgetary decison-making procedures additionally requires wisdom. This is because the procedures by which a city, a State, or an international organization year-by-year decides upon its budget must be regarded as just and fair. Just and fair procedures only can ensure that every single budget finds acceptance by citizens or by States Members. Within nation States, it is the representative legislative organ which provides for prudence and fairness alike; political philosophers like *Plato, Machiavelli, Rousseau* or *Kant* therefore praised the *legislateur* who knows how people behave and who has deep insight into the principles of justice and fairness.[1]

In international relations, however, things are different. There is no representative legislative organ but governments representing sovereign States; there is no *legislateur* but rather a lot of diplomats. Without any doubt, governments and diplomats are prudent: they know their countries' interests and they have solid experience on how nations behave. Also wisdom is a widespread phenomenon in governments and among diplomats; how else would we find so many biographies on and memoirs by political leaders and diplomats? But no government and no diplomat in history grew old enough to reach the wisdom necessary for bringing up just and fair procedures to decide upon budgets of international organizations. Neither unanimity, consensus, "one State, one vote," nor weighted voting are recognized as just and fair procedures by all States Members of international organizations. What does that leave to governments and diplomats

---

* Dr. rer. soc. *Klaus Dicke*, Research Assistant and Senior Lecturer, Institute of International Law, University of Kiel.

1 For the combination of prudence and wisdom as attributes of the "*legislateur*," *cf. Reinhard Brandt*, Rousseaus Philosophie der Gesellschaft, Stuttgart-Bad Cannstatt 1973, 118 *et seq.*; *Karl Jaspers*, Kant's "Zum Ewigen Frieden", in: *K. Ziegler* (ed.), Wesen und Wirklichkeit. Fs. für *Helmuth Plessner*, Göttingen 1957, 131 - 152 (136 *et seq.*), and *J. G. A. Pocock*, The Machiavellian Moment. Florentine Political Thought and the Atlantic Republican Tradition, Princeton/London 1975.

to do, in particular to those who are concerned with negotiations on budgetary decision-making rules for the International Sea-Bed Authority? It was the German philosopher *Immanuel Kant*, who proposed a procedure to reach a sufficient amount of wisdom even in international relations. He simply took seriously the inclination of States to conclude secret agreements, but limited the right of governments and diplomats to secrecy to one single instance: they shall listen to wise men in secret.[2] This secrecy has a two-fold function: It saves governments the trouble of confessing in public that they had come to their wit's end; and it allows the public to identify scientists being responsible for any lack of wisdom in international relations. International conferences at the University of Kiel provide for secrecy in this very *Kantian* sense.

For three reasons, it is difficult if not discouraging to compare budgetary decision-making procedures of the UN system. First of all, it is the transparency and comparability of budgeting procedures of the UN system which time and again have been questioned by several UN organs.[3] The technical arrangements of budget preparation and presentation within the UN system vary greatly; there are annual and bi-annual budgets, objective-of-expenditure budgets and programme budgets, full budgeting and semi-full budgeting, etc.[4] Although the following comparison is not dealing with the technicalities it should bear in mind a warning which the Advisory Committee on Administrative and Budgetary Questions (ACABQ) in its first bi-annual report on the budgets of the specialized agencies and the International Atomic Energy Agency spelled out: the ACABQ regarded the budgetary arrangements of a given organization to be "a function of its programme and ... heavily influenced by its size and complexity." In this connection it cautioned "that harmonizing of the arrangements among agencies in respect of programme planning, budgeting and evaluation does not appear necessarily a desirable or feasible goal."[5] In other words, the budget of an international organization cannot be taken as an intervening variable; rather, it is conditioned by the size, the structure and the programmes of the organization in question.

A second difficulty derives from the so far published scholarly literature on the subject. There is a great amount of books or articles on decision-making in international organizations in general with the effect that *Cox* and *Jacobson* acknowledge the decision-making literature as representing an independent approach in studying international organizations.[6] This approach deals, if at all,

---

2 *Immanuel Kant*, Zum ewigen Frieden, in: Akademie-Ausgabe, Vol. VIII, Berlin 1968, 368 *et seq.*

3 For a most recent example, *see* Budgeting in Organizations of the United Nations System (prepared by *Siegfried Schumm*), UN doc. JIU/REP/89/9, Vol. I, Geneva 1989, 1.

4 *Loc. cit.*, (note 3), Vol. II, 3-7 shows a table comparing budgetary techniques of the UN and the specialized agencies.

5 UN doc. A/38/515, para. 36.

marginally with budgetary decision-making.[7] Its main focus is the pros and cons of "one State, one vote" versus "weighted voting." On the other hand, apart from a small number of older studies[8] there are very few books and articles on the specifics of budgetary decison-making and budgets of international organizations.[9] Against this background one could get the impression that a comparison of budgetary decision-making processes would boil down to the question of which procedure: unanimity, consensus, majority according to "one State, one vote," or majority according to weighted voting were preferable.[10] It is the task of my presentation to challenge this very impression.

It is not only a lack of detailed information on budgetary procedures or a lack of comparable empirical data which hinders a comparative analysis of budgetary

---

[6] *Robert W. Cox/Harold K. Jacobsen*, The decision-making approach in the study of international organizations, in: *Georges Abi-Saab* (ed.), The concept of international organizations, Paris 1981, 79 *et seq.*; for further details and a bibliography *see Rüdiger Wolfrum*'s presentation in this vol.

[7] *Johan Kaufmann*, United Nations Decision Making, Alphen aan den Rijn 1980, presents a lot of case studies, but ignores budgetary decision-making.

[8] *J. David Singer*, Financing International Organization, The Hague 1961; *John G. Stoessinger*, Financing the United Nations System, Washington 1964; *Richard Szawlowski*, Finanzen und Finanzrecht der internationalen zwischenstaatlichen Organisationen, in: Handbuch der Finanzwissenschaften, Tübingen 1965, 311-348.

[9] *Henry G. Schermers*, International Institutional Law, Alphen 1980, paras. 962 *et seq.*; *Alain Pellet*, Budgets et programmes aux Nations Unies. Quelques tendances récentes, in: AFDI 22 (1976), 242-282; *Rüdiger Wolfrum*, International Organizations, Financing and Budgeting, in: *Rudolf Bernhardt* (ed.), EPIL, Instalment 5, Heidelberg 1983, 115-119, with reference to the literature until 1980; *id.*, Haushalt, in: *id.* (ed.), Handbuch Vereinte Nationen, München 1991; *Rudolf Schmidt*, Art. 17, in: *Bruno Simma et. al.* (ed.), Charta der Vereinten Nationen. Kommentar, München 1991; *Jan Kolasa*, Financing, in: *René-Jean Dupuy* (ed.), A Handbook on International Organizations, Dordrecht/Boston/Lancaster 1988, 198-210; *Eckart Klein*, Beitragspflichten und Stimmrecht. Notwendigkeit und Möglichkeit, das Entscheidungsverfahren über Ausgaben der Vereinten Nationen neu zu strukturieren, in: *Rüdiger Wolfrum* (ed.), Die Reform der Vereinten Nationen. Möglichkeiten und Grenzen, Berlin 1989, 69-94. For detailed problems, *see Franz von Mutius*, Integrated Planning and Budgeting at the International Labour Office, in: *Joseph H. Kaiser* (ed.), Planung VI: Integrierte Systeme der Planung und Budgetierung, Baden-Baden 1972, 137-156; *Lothar Koch*, Die Erwartungen eines Mitgliedstaates an Haushalts- und Finanzpolitik der Sonderorganisationen im VN-System, in: *Klaus Dicke/Klaus Hüfner* (eds.), Die Leistungsfähigkeit des VN-Systems: Politische Kritik und wissenschaftliche Analyse, Bonn 1987, 82-90; *Margaret E. Galey*, Reforming the Regime for Financing the United Nations, in: Howard Law Journal 31 (1988), 543-574, with reference to articles on the UN financial crisis; *André Lewin*, Le group de Genève et les budgets de la famille des Nations Unies: vingt années d'efforts pour aboutir à la croissance zéro, in: AFDI 30 (1984), 637-648; *Jean-Pierre Masset*, Une non-institution: Le groupe de Genève, in: Société française pour le droit international (ed.), Les organisations internationales contemporaines, Paris 1988, 205-219. For empirical analysis, *see Francis W. Hoole*, Politics and Budgeting in the World Health Organization, Bloomington/London 1976; *id./Brian L. Job/Harvey J. Tucker*, Incremental Budgeting and International Organizations, in: American Journal of Political Science 20 (1976), 273-301, with further references.

[10] *Cf. Klein* (note 9), 80 *et seq.*, who argues in favour of a weighted voting system.

decision-making in international organizations. Additionally, there is no political theory of international organizations putting budgetary questions into perspective by relating them to the overall principles and objectives of international organizations.[11] Apart from *Inis L. Claude*'s writings[12] there is no theoretical effort comprehensive enough to bridge the gap between normative settings and the reality of life in international organizations or the gap between different — and partially conflicting — paradigms[13] determining the respective conception of international organizations which leads actors and/or analysts. By regarding budgetary questions as those of justice and fairness, it is the second task of my presentation to put into perspective the disputes on budgetary decision-making and to relate them to the overall aims and purposes of international organizations.

Methodologically, any comparison has to ask two questions before going into the details of comparing social phenomena: what are the phenomena to be compared, and what is the objective of the comparison, the *tertium comparationis*? Following this methodological principle, the first step has to be defining the variables "budget" (II.) and "deciding upon" (III.). As a second step, three rules of budgetary decision-making are proposed (IV.). The final chapter will apply the findings on questions of how to budget the International Seabed Authority (V.).

II. The Variable "Budget"

1. Objective-of-Expenditure Budgets

In search of a legal definition of "budget" the constitutive instruments of international organizations provide only little or no information. The articles relating to the budget, however, contain important elements determining the functions of a budget. In Art. 6, para. 5, the Covenant of the League of Nations provided: "The expenditures of the League shall be borne by the Members of the League in the proportion decided by the Assembly."[14] Article 17, para. 1 of

---

11 For a related criticism of reform efforts too narrowly concentrated on the technical aspects of budgetary questions, *see Jost Delbrück*, in: *Wolfrum* (ed.), Die Reform der Vereinten Nationen (note 9), 115-117.

12 *Inis L. Claude*, Swords into Plowshares. The Problems and Progress of International Organization, 4th ed., New York 1971; *id.*, The Political Framework of the United Nations' Financial Problems, in: IO 17 (1963), 831-859.

13 *Paul Taylor*, Prescribing for the reform of international organization: the logic of arguments for change, in: Review of International Studies 13 (1987), 19-38.

14 This provision replaced the original ruling which took over the Universal Postal Union's procedure to determine the contributions of State Members. On financing the League of Nations, *see Leland M. Goodrich/Edvard Hambro/Anne Patricia Simons*, Charter of the United Nations, 3rd ed., New York/London 1969, 149; *J. David Singer*, The Finances of the League of Nations, in: IO 13 (1959), 255-273; *Otto Göppert*, Der Völkerbund (Handbuch des Völkerrechts, Band 4, Abteilung 1 B.), Stuttgart 1938, 160 *et seq.*

the UN Charter simply states: "The General Assembly shall consider and approve the budget of the organization." *Mutatis mutandis*, the relevant provisions of the constitutions of the specialized agencies[15] follow this example. Four elements of these provisions are relevant here:

1. Their objective is the power to consider and to approve the budget. It is the plenary organ which is vested with that power, and, as a rule, the majority required to give effect to the approval is determined. In establishing the power to approve the budget by a separate article, constitutions of international organizations distinguish this power from other powers and functions of the plenary organ, in particular from the function to adopt resolutions with a recommendatory character. This constitutes a line of demarcation between decision-making in general and deciding upon the budget.

2. In exercising its power, the plenary organ estimates the income and expenditures of the organization in a legally binding manner. "It authorizes the organization to defray certain expenditures and it constitutes the legal basis for the payment of contributions if the organization has no independent sources of income at its disposal."[16]

3. The plenary organ is left free to decide upon financial regulations. Only a few instruments contain provisions regulating financial matters in some detail. Article XIV of the IAEA Constitution or arts. 55 to 58 of the WHO Constitution are cases in point. To get a complete picture of budgetary functions, the Financial Regulations and, for the specialized agencies, the Special Agreements between the agency and the UN must be included in the analysis.

4. There is no clear definition of the term "budget," but some provisions make clear that it is the paramount function of budgets as legal acts to authoritatively estimate the organization's income and expenditures in order to provide for its accountability to the governments and parliamentary organs of States Members. This accountability is made possible by balancing the income against isolated objectives of the organization's expenditures. For this understanding of an "objective-of-expenditure" budget, Art. 61 of the ICAO Constitution is a good example.[17]

---

15 *Inter alia*, art. 13, para. 2 (c) of the ILO Constitution; Art. IV, paras. 1 and 2 of the FAO Constitution; Art. IX of the UNESCO Constitution; Art. 18 (f) of the WHO Constitution; Art. 49 (e) of the ICAO Convention; Art. 16 (g) of the IMO Convention; Art. V, para. E (5) of the IAEA Statute. For a brief analysis of financing the specialized agencies, *see Douglas Williams*, The Specialized Agencies and the United Nations. The System in Crisis, New York 1987, 83-94.

16 *Wolfrum*, International Organizations, Financing and Budgeting (note 9), 115.

17 "The Council shall submit to the Assembly annual budgets, annual statements of accounts and estimates of all receipts and expenditures. The Assembly shall vote the budgets with whatever modification it sees fit to prescribe, and ... shall apportion the expenses of the Organization among the contracting States on the basis which it shall from time to time determine."

The understanding of an "objective-of-expenditure" budget is confirmed by the Financial Regulations as adopted by the General Assembly (GA) in 1946 and 1950. According to the relevant resolutions[18] the budgetary power of the GA implied the powers to regulate the manner in which estimates are presented, the procedures by which they are considered, the authorization of expenses, and the methods of accounting.[19] Although it appears to be out-dated if compared to modern budgeting in domestic administrations, this understanding of budgets is familiar to other international organizations including the European Economic Community, too.[20] It derives from or, at least, is embedded in a particular conception of international organizations. According to this conception, international organizations are collective instruments of governments to promote and execute common purposes as clearly defined by the organization's constitutive instrument. For the UN, this common purpose was to maintain international peace and security by means of collective security measures, peaceful settlement of disputes, and the promotion of human rights as well as economic and social well-being. The financing of this very organization had to be transparent, i. e. the expenditures had to be in accordance with the organization's purposes. This explains, *inter alia*, the inclination of States Members, particularly those in the minority position, to refuse their approval to the budget in cases where it was shaped along the lines of majority objectives rather than of common purposes or even to withhold payments for such activities they refused to recognize as legal according to the Charter provisions.[21] The most famous instance was the withholding of payments by the Soviet Union and other States for the Congo operation which led the UN into its first major financial crisis. Up to now, financing of peace-keeping operations is one of the most difficult budgetary questions of the organization.[22]

The understanding of "objective-of-expenditure" budgets and the conception of international organizations leading this understanding can explain a second

---

18 GA res. 68 (I) of 14 December 1949; res. 69 (I) of 14 December 1949; res. 74 (I) of 7 December 1949; res. 80 (I) of 11 December 1949; res. 456 (V) of 16 November 1950, Annex, Art. III. The updated Financial Regulations and Rules of the United Nations are published as UN doc. ST/SGB/Financial Rules/1/Rev. 3 (1985). For an analysis of the Financial Rules, *see Galey* (note 9), 549 *et seq.*

19 *Goodrich et al.* (note 14), 149 *et seq.*

20 *Cf. Thomas Läufer*, Haushalt und Finanzen als Konfliktfeld der EG-Organe und der EG-Mitgliedstaaten, in: GYIL 33 (1990), 184-213 (185 *et seq.*).

21 From 1947 on, the Soviet Union and other eastern countries in explaining their negative votes to the UN budget took the view that certain objectives were illegal. For the practice of withholding, *see Klein* (note 9), 73; UN doc. A/C. 5/35/13, annexes; *Elisabeth Zoller*, The "Corporate Will" of the United Nations and the Rights of the Minority, in: AJIL 81 (1987), 610 *et seq.*; *Christian Tomuschat*, Die Beitragsverweigerung in internationalen Organisationen, in: Internationales Recht und Wirtschaftsordnung, Festschrift *F. A. Mann*, München 1977, 439 *et seq.*

22 *Cf.* GA res. 44/192 of 21 December 1989 with the related report of the Secretary-General, UN doc. A/44/605.

development in UN budgeting as well. Starting in the late Forties[23] and culminating in the establishment of the United Nations Development Programme, State Members vested the UN System with a second type of budgets, the so-called voluntary budgets as distinguished from the proper or administrative budgets.[24] Volontary budgets were introduced because, *inter alia*, the US refused to establish a system of compulsory payments by UN members for the benefit of the Soviet Union and its allies. In other words, the UN budget should not be used to carry out operational activities or re-distributive policies appoved on by majority decisions. The voluntary budgets are administered by various funds within the UN system; they provide a means to bring up resources for special purposes and to develop operational activities. The funds are "voluntary" in so far as governments annually pledge their contributions and every fund's activities are to be "utilized and administered to the extent of its available resources."[25]

2. Programme Budgets

The *crescendo* of increasing membership, increasing tasks, increasing numbers of organizational units and increasing expenditures of the UN, however, changed the understanding of the budget's function. The introduction of programme budgets and their integration into a policy planning and evaluation process substantially extended the functions of the budget as well as it complicated budgetary procedures. One of the first organizations to introduce a programme budget was the International Labour Organization.[26] For the ILO, three arguments lead to the introduction of programme budgets: first, it enabled the organization to undertake a long-term planning of its activities; second, it would provide for an instrument of rationally setting priorities; third, it would allow a systematic evaluation of the policy planning and executing process and thus enhance the organization's overall effectiveness. The programme planning and control system was "intended to be a management tool that would help to allocate scarce resources in an effective manner for priority programmes."[27]

Budgets now possess a strategic meaning within the overall process of programme planning, execution and evaluation in so far as "the programme proposals

---

23 GA res. 58 (I) of 14 December 1946, establishing the International Children's Emergency Fund.

24 *Klaus Hüfner*, Die freiwilligen Finanzleistungen an das UN-System, in: GYIL 26 (1983), 299-342; *Hans Danelius*, United Nations Voluntary Funds, in: Nordic Journal of International Law 58 (1989), 185-187. Article 13 of the UNIDO Constitution distinguishes between "regular budgets" and "operational budgets."

25 GA res. 58 (I) (note 23); for operative spendings of the UN, *see* UN doc. A/44/324/Add. 1.

26 *Von Mutius* (note 9); *Victor-Yves Ghèbali*, The International Labour Organisation. A Case Study on the Evolution of UN Specialised Agencies, Dordrecht/Boston/Lancaster 1989, 166 *et seq.*

27 *Von Mutius* (note 9), 155.

in the budget shall aim at implementing the strategy in the plan and, therefore, shall be derived from its strategy statements."[28] Terms like "planning," "evaluation," "strategy," etc. indicate the language of the welfare state which in the late Sixties and Seventies raised in western industrialized countries and trickled down to the UN as well.[29] The new language expresses two major changes that the organization underwent after the developing countries challenged and eventually changed the US-dominated majority in the General Assembly. First of all the "common purpose" the organization is to serve changed in so far as the tasks of Art. 55 and accordingly operational activities for development became dominant on the UN's agenda. The aims of Art. 55, however, are determined in general language only and consequently need to be spelled out by detailed programmes as negotiated within the framework of the increasing number of UN organs.

The political significance of this observation is enhanced by a second observation: the General Assembly in its unanimously adopted res. 1219 (XII) of 14 December 1957, which eventually lead to the establishment of the Special Fund, emphasized that funds were "of proven effectiveness in promoting the economic development of the less developed countries." To legitimize the establishment of new funds, the General Assembly now refers to the "determination" of the UN "to promote social progress and better standards of life in larger freedom, and for these ends, *to employ international machinery for the promotion of the economic and social advancement of all peoples.*"[30] In view of the industrialized countries' reluctance to provide the increasing number of funds with the expected resources, the developing countries eventually attempted to increase the expenditures of UN regular budgets for technical assistance. Thus, the amount spent for related programmes more than doubled from 19 million US dollars in 1978 to 41 million US dollars in 1980. To pick up a typology of policies elaborated by *Theodore Lowi*[31] which proved to be valid for domestic policies and politics, the remarkable shift as indicated by these figures can be described as a shift from a budget concerning "regulatory" and "distributive" policies to a budget now covering "re-distributive" policies, too. To this shift the US reacted by efforts to withhold payments for technical assistance, as provided for by the *Helms* amendment.[32] Thus, the US adhered to the legal opinion according to

---

28 "Regulations Governing Programme Planning, the Programme Aspects of the Budget, the Monitoring of Implementation and the Methods of Evaluation," GA res. 37/234 of 21 November 1982, Annex, Art. 4.2.

29 *Charles William Maynes*, The United Nations: Out of Control or Out of Touch? in: Yearbook of World Affairs 31 (1977), 98-111 (105 *et seq.*).

30 GA res. 1215 (XII) of 14 December 1957 (emphasis added).

31 *Theodore Lowi*, Four Systems of Policy, Politics and Choice, in: Public Administration Review 32 (1972), 298-310.

32 *Robert F. Meagher*, United States Financing of the United Nations, in: *Toby Trister Gati* (ed.), The US, the UN, and the Management of Global Change, New York/London 1983, 101-128 (113 *et seq.*).

which technical assistance as a re-distributive policy is beyond the limits of the power to "promote" international co-operation as enshrined in Art. 1, para. 3 and Arts. 55 *et seq.* of the UN Charter.[33] The disputes, arising since 1980, on financing the UN thus prove to be constitutional in character.

Politically, the budget now serves as a focus for States Members to judge the overall efficiency and effectiveness of the organization concerned. This has an intra-organizational effect as well as it changes the relationship of States Members to the organization. The intra-organizational effect means that greater emphasis is given to the introduction and improvement of modern management methods and devices to control the budget processes. The establishment of the Joint Inspection Unit is only one point in case. More important are the changes which take place in the perception of international organizations by governments. As the establishment and evolution of the Geneva Group as well as the concern of the US public with financial matters of international organizations,[34] and as, above all, the 1982 initiative of Western countries towards a zero-growth of UN budgets[35] indicate, financing an international organization seems to enjoy more attention by governments and parliamentary bodies than the purposes of the organization do. This is as true for western industrialized countries as it is for developing countries, although their respective perceptions widely differ in substance. The perception taken by the US is shaped in terms of *economy and efficiency*. For this perception it is quite interesting to observe that in the list of criteria, by which former US Assistant Secretary for International Organization Affairs *Williamson* judges US support for international organizations, the first criterion reads: "The level of direct benefit or substantive importance of the agency's work to the United States in political, strategic, or economic terms," and only the seventh and last criterion reads "organization performance in fulfillment of its chartered mission."[36] On the other hand, the developing countries emphasize that it is by no means sufficient to judge international organizations in terms of economy and efficiency; instead they give paramount consideration to the fulfillment of the organizations' tasks and programmes, i. e. their *effectiveness.*[37] In their view, which is confirmed by the consensus of GA res. 1219 (XII),

[33] *B. Conforti*, Prolifération organique, prolifération normative et crise des nations unies: réflexions d'un juriste, in: *Daniel Bardonnet* (ed.), The Adaption of Structures and Methods at the United Nations (Hague Academy of International Law, Workshop 1985), Dordrecht/Boston/Lancaster 1986, 153-169. For a discussion of this legal opinion, *see Rüdiger Wolfrum*, Art. 55, in: *Simma et al.* (note 9); *id.*, Ursprüngliche Aufgabenzuweisung und jetzige Aktivitäten der Vereinten Nationen: Faktischer Wandel und normative Bewertung, in: *id.*, Die Reform der Vereinten Nationen (note 9), 129-156 (147).

[34] *Meagher* (note 32).

[35] *M. J. Peterson*, The General Assembly in World Politics, Boston 1986, 127.

[36] *Richard S. Williamson*, UN Agencies and the Budget, in: Department of State Bulletin 88, No. 2133, April 1988, 81-85 (84).

[37] In the general debate of the 42nd General Assembly, the representative of Mali in view of some reform proposals cautioned: "While supporting those recommendations,

the effectiveness of the UN depends upon the extension of agenda items and programmes spelling out the specifics of Art. 55 and increasing the organization's operational activities.

Against this background, programme budgets reveal two totally different conceptions of international organizations among States Members, the efficiency-oriented conception versus the effectiveness-oriented conception. No longer isolated objectives of expenditure are at stake when it comes to disagreement upon the organization's expenses. Rather, it is the perception of the organization as a whole which becomes a matter of controversy. The effectiveness-oriented perception which — due to the voting power of developing countries — became dominant is challenged by a minority of States Members which has the financial power to do so. This is what precisely happened when the US Congress adopted the *Kassebaum-Solomon* amendment[38] which called for the introduction of weighted voting to decide upon UN budgets.

III. The Variable "Deciding upon"

The approved budget of an international organization imposes legally binding obligations upon States Members and upon the organization concerned. The binding force of the approval on the budget qualifies approving procedure as the most important element of the overall process of "deciding upon" budgets. The following procedures of approval can be distinguished:

Since 1945, most international organizations decide to approve the budget by annual or bi-annual decisions of its plenary organ. In most cases, a qualified majority is required; for the General Assembly Art. 18 of the Charter requires a two-thirds majority, each of the States Members having one vote. The League of Nations followed the "one State, one vote" line, too. Instead of a qualified majority, however, it required unanimity. In view of the necessity to reach year-by-year the approval on the budget, League practice modified this rule to the effect that disapproval to the budget was excluded. Before voting upon the budget, the Assembly removed all estimates which were proposed for amendment from the draft budget and referred them back to the Finance Committee for further negotiations.[39] A third model of "one State, one vote" approval is represented by the consensus procedure. As a rule, majority according to the "one State, one vote" principle is preferred by smaller States because it provides for

we emphasize that criteria for choosing measures to implement them must take account of the universality of our organization and its objectives which can in no way be identified with those of a commercial enterprise," UN doc. A/42/PV. 22, para. 45.

[38] United States: Foreign Relations Authorization Act, Fiscal Years 1986 and 1987, Public Law 99-93-Aug. 16, 1985, sec. 143; 99 Stat. 405, reprinted in: ILM 25 (1986), 17-43 (27).

[39] *Cf. Göppert* (note 14), 161.

a "democratic" decision-making procedure. Consensus, on the other hand, is preferred by major contributors because it protects the special interests of all contributors alike by vesting them with a quasi-veto.[40]

As distinguished from these one State, one vote-based types of decision-making procedures, there is a second group of procedures to decide upon administrative budgets, namely, the "weighted voting" procedures. They are familiar to adminstrative unions like the Universal Postal Union or the Rhine-Commission, to the World Bank institutions, the development banks and the International Fund for Agricultural Development (IFAD) and to commodity agreements.[41] The well-known problem of weighted voting procedures is the establishment of criteria to measure the weight which is given to a single state.[42] The criteria are to balance the sovereign equality of States against various factual inequalities among States.[43] For budgetary decisions, the share of contributions which States are assessed for were proposed to function as a criterion. This criterion, however, is far from being just and fair. It is true: In absolute terms there are few "major contributors" against a majority of countries contributing a very small amount only.[44] If the contributions of several countries are related to their GNP, to their *per capita* income or to their population, however, things look different, as table 1 shows.[45]

Additionally, decisions organized by weighted voting are majority decisions, too. Consequently, the problems of overruled minorities and their demand to protect their special interests cannot be eliminated by weighted voting procedures. In conclusion, weighted voting protects dominating interests, but fails to protect all special interests alike.[46]

On the other hand, there is no doubt that the greater amount of money spent for an international organization establishes a special interest which calls for protection. To provide for such a protection, the constitutive instruments of some more recently established international organizations give one State or a group

---

[40] For related arguments, *see Klein* (note 9), 80 *et seq.*

[41] *Elizabeth McIntyre*, Weighted Voting in International Organizations, in: IO 8 (1954), 484-497; *Hanna Newcombe / Christopher Young / Elia Sinaiko*, Alternative pasts: a study of weighted voting at the United Nations, in: IO 31 (1977), 579-586; *Henry G. Schermers*, Weighted Voting, in: *Bernhardt* (note 9), 398 *et seq.*

[42] *See*, e. g., *Wolfrum*, in this vol.; *Williams* (note 15), 74 *et seq.*

[43] *Cf. Leonard Woolfe*, International Government, London 1916.

[44] For the assessment of contributions in the UN, see GA res. 43/223 of 21 December 1988 (scale of assessments for 1989, 1990 and 1991), and GA res. 44/197 of 21 December 1989.

[45] For further statistical information, *see Edward T. Rowe*, Financial Support for the United Nations: The Evolution of Member Contributions, 1946-1969, in: IO 26 (1972), 619-657; *Thomas M. Franck*, Nation against Nation. What Happened to the UN Dream and What the U. S. Can Do about It, New York/Oxford 1985, 254-264.

[46] *Cf. Stephen Lewis*, The United States, the United Nations, and the Budget Crisis, in: Proceedings of the 80th Annual Meeting, American Society of International Law, Washington 1986, 12-20, who confirms this line of argument.

of States a blocking minority, i. e. a *de facto*-veto. Organizations like UNIDO, the IFAD or commodity funds are cases in point. Here, weighted voting or "one State, one vote" is combined with a grouping or bunching of interests or with regional representation with the effect that coalitions of interest groups are necessary to reach an affirmative decision.[47] These rules stress the distinction between an affirmative and a negative voting power. They establish negative voting powers in order to produce negotiated decisions which avoid to overrule specific interests. It must be emphasized that negative voting powers do not enable major contributors to dominate all decisions of related bodies. States or groups of States vested with negative voting powers are compelled to negotiate and build coalitions in order to reach affirmative decisions.

Legally, there is no general rule of international law making one of the models referred to above mandatory. Politically, however, the one State, one vote decision was challenged from the very beginning of the UN for one reason: Under the special circumstances of international relations it fails effectively to protect the interests of the over-ruled minority. As annexed table 2 shows, from 1946 to 1986 this minority grew constantly. Between 1946 and 1963, the average of States disapproving was 8.1; between 1964 and 1977 the average grew to 14.7, and between 1978 and 1986 it amounted to 22.4. It was the so-called major contributors' growing disapprovals on UN budgets which were responsible for the increase of negative votes or abstentions after 1977.

Against this background, *Jeane Kirkpatrick* called to mind the slogans of "disproportion between power and responsibility" or of "disproportion between voting power and real power" and thus opened the discussion on amending the budgetary decision-making procedures within the UN.[48] In 1985, the *Kassebaum-Solomon* amendment called for the introduction of weighted voting to decide upon the UN budget. It is not necessary to go into the specific circumstances and into the details of related debates on the pros and cons of weighted voting. The discussions within the UN eventually lead to an interesting and revealing result. Between the *Kassebaum-Solomon* amendment and the adoption by the General Assembly of res. 41/213 the US slightly but decisively changed its view on decision-making upon budgets. The *Kassebaum-Solomon* amendment called for "the adoption by the UN and its specialized agencies of procedures which grant voting rights to each member state on matters of budgetary consequence. Such voting rights shall be *proportionate to the contribution* of each such member State *to the budget* of the UN and its specialized agencies."[49] The compromise

---

47 For a more elaborated analysis, *see Rüdiger Wolfrum*, Neue Elemente im Willensbildungsprozeß internationaler Wirtschaftsorganisationen. Strukturelle Neuerungen in den Satzungen von IFAD, UNIDO und Gemeinsamem Fond, in: Vereinte Nationen 29 (1981), 50-56; and *Wolfrum*'s presentation in this volume.

48 For the history of the US administration's concern with the UN budget, *see Galey* (note 9), 545 *et seq.*

49 *Supra* (note 38) (emphasis added).

as enshrined in GA res. 41/213[50] does not change the decision-making procedures of the General Assembly, rather it provides for participation of States Members in the preparation of the budget. Similar measures were taken by several specialized agencies.[51] These changes which established the filter of consensus at one point of the preparation and consultation of budgets met the approval of the US.[52] In his success report, *Williamson* dropped the above quoted call of the *Kassebaum-Solomon* amendment and referred only to the more general intention of the amendment that the UN and specialized agencies should make "substantial progress toward the adoption and implementation of decision-making procedures on budgetary matters in a manner that substantially achieves the goal of greater financial responsibility."[53]

This observation leads to a widened perspective in view of budgetary decision-making. As *Hoole* and others[54] showed, budgetary processes are circles starting some two years before the budget is approved and closing with the reports of auditors and the evaluation of programme performance two years or later after the approval. A second look into the constitutions of international organizations reveals that in addition to the rules establishing the budget power of plenary organs, there is another type of budgetary regulations establishing the budget procedure. One example is Art. 55 of the World Health Organization Convention: "The Director-General shall prepare and submit to the Board the ... budget estimates of the Organization. The Board shall consider and submit to the Health Assembly such budget estimates, together with any recommendations the Board may deem advisable."

As a rule there are three organs concerned with the establishment of a budget: the Director-General or Secretary-General who prepares the budget estimates and drafts a budget proposal; the Board or — for the UN — the Committee for Programme and Co-ordination as well as the 5th Committee in collaboration with the ACABQ,[55] which consider the proposal from both the point of view of governments and the point of view of financial expertise, and, finally, the Assem-

[50] For an analysis of res. 41/213 of 19 December 1986, *see Galey* (note 9), 564 *et seq.*; *Klaus Dicke/Klaus Hüfner*, Zur Einführung: Die Leistungsfähigkeit des VN-Systems. Fragen ihrer Messung, Bewertung und Verbesserung, in: *id.* (note 9), 5-10 (8 *et seq.*).

[51] *Williamson* (note 36); *Galey* (note 9), 554 *et seq.*

[52] For an analysis of the drafting history of res. 41/213 including the diplomatic efforts of, *inter alia* the Soviet Union to get US approval, *see Humayun Rasheed Choudhury*, United Nations Reform: Some Reflections, in: Ethics and International Affairs 2 (1988), 155-171.

[53] *Williamson* (note 36), 82.

[54] *Hoole* (note 9), 49 *et seq.*; Budgeting in Organizations of the United Nations System (note 3).

[55] The ACABQ was established according to Rule 156 of the Financial Rules by GA res. 14 (I). Predecessor of the ACABQ was the Supervisionary Commission (Comité de Contrôle) of the League of Nations. For similar bodies in other international organizations, *see Szawlowski* (note 8), 341.

bly which approves the budget according to one of the procedures mentioned above.[56] In such organizations which run a bi-annual budget there is an additional step in the preparation stage, namely, the establishment of an "outline" providing a framework and limitations for the Secretary-General's draft budget. On a second level, there are further considerations and decisions with regard to the budget: the General Assembly endorses or comments on the Reports of the Auditors, it receives reports by the Joint Inspection Unit and other organs and it undertakes or authorizes other organs to undertake an evaluation of programme performance. The information gathered on this control level is to assist and to influence governments and UN organs in the preparation process of the following budget.

IV. Just and Fair? A Comparative Assessment

The thus widened perspective of budgetary functions, budgetary decisions, and the various methods of deciding upon a budget provides a sufficient framework to catch at the questions of justice and fairness mentioned in the introduction. The main yardstick to judge justice and fairness is the legal framework in which the organization concerned is operating, i. e. the rules of general international law as well as the purposes and objectives of the organization as enshrined in its constitution. Under the sovereign equality of States, paramount consideration has to be given to decision-making procedures which provide for incentives rather than establish deterrent impediments for all States members alike to fully participate in carrying out the organization's objectives. Hence, to promote the full effectiveness of the organization by providing incentives to participate is Rule no. 1 to be observed in all policy and budgetary decisions. This rule covers, *inter alia*, the application and observance of regulations and decisions governing decision-making procedures. Rule observance by organs of international organizations and by States Members making use of international organizations has proved to be a very poor developed political virtue in the UN system.

A second, and perhaps more difficult yardstick to judge upon justice and fairness is the capacity of budgetary regulations to integrate different perceptions of international organizations. The introduction of programme budgets certainly could not eliminate tensions between the effectiveness-oriented and the efficiency-oriented approach as referred to above. However, the more sophisticated processes of budget preparation, consideration, approval and evaluation as established by programme budgets provide a means to moderate those tensions: The assistance of financial experts in preparing and considering the budget, effective auditing, evaluation procedures and an independent management control provide for efficiency and economy in the overall process of budgeting an international organization. On the other hand, the combination of budgetary planning with

[56] *Peterson* (note 35), 277, refers to this procedure as to a "three-side dialogue" and thus correctly emphasizes the co-operation of the organs involved.

the policy planning process of the organization takes account of the effectiveness-oriented perception. The integration of both elements into a single budgetary process calls upon States Members to consider efficiency in terms of effectiveness and effectiveness in terms of efficiency, accordingly. Integrating thinking in this institutional and political way is the second rule to be applied in budgetary decision-making.

A third call for justice and fairness is voiced by special interests. It is a call for negotiated decisions and not a call for weighted voting. In the more recent history of international organizations, this call met different answers. The first one is the establishment of blocking votes either in the consideration or in the approval procedures of the budget. It must be emphasized that related instruments met the approval of developing countries as, e. g., in the UNIDO or IFAD Constitution. A second means is the participation of States Members in the preparation or drafting of budgets. Related instruments, however, have not proved to be effective. The most recently established third means applies a consensus filter in the preparation and/or consideration stage of a budget. This means works under the condition that major contributors and other interests participate in the consensus-forming organ. If such an organ is composed according to the principle of regional representation, there should be no objection to replace consensus by a majority vote provided there is a negative voting power of smaller groups. For the time being, it is uncertain whether the consensus derived from GA res. 41/213 and from related provisions of specialized agencies will prove stable. The protection of special interests, however, by applying one of the instruments referred to above is the third rule in ensuring just and fair decision-making upon budgets.

In applying these rules we are prepared to answer the last question as to whether the International Sea-Bed Authority fits into the picture drawn so far.

V. Budgeting the International Sea-Bed Authority

This very question seems to produce a discouraging answer again. At a first glance, the Authority does not fit into the picture at all. The Authority will be the first international organization to take its Council decisions with majorities proportionate to the importance of the subject.[57] It will be innovative in conducting an operational organ, the Enterprise. At least in this regard its budget will have the function of allocating resources rather than distributing contributions to promote or carry out common purposes. Finally, the Authority is supposed to change its character when deep sea mining becomes operative. From that time

---

[57] *Fernando Zegers Santa Cruz*, Deep Sea-Bed Mining Beyond National Jurisdiction in the 1982 UN Convention on the Law of the Sea: Description and Prospects, in: GYIL 31 (1988), 107-119 (112); *Wolfrum*'s presentation in this volume.

on, the Authority will have sufficient income of its own to finance its administrative budget from its own resources.[58] But that is the future. For the time being, the contributions necessary for the Authority's administrative budget, although it may be rather small if compared to the UN budget, are far from being guaranteed. The 1982 Law of the Sea Convention (Convention) provides for "an agreed scale of assessment based upon the scale used for the regular budget of the United Nations" (art. 160, para. 2 (e)).[59] The Convention, however, envisaged universal membership, and up to now this expectation has proved to be too optimistic. This financial uncertainty calls for negotiations, but does not jeopardize the universality of the Convention. Article 310 of the Convention may invite one State or another when acceding to the Convention to declare that the references to the UN scale of assessment limit their contributions to the percentage spelled out by the UN scale of assessment in force. Another problem arises in respect of the financing of the Enterprise according to art. 11, para. 3 (c) of Annex IV. The respective funds come from five sources as identified in art. 11, para. 1 of Annex IV. Without going into details, here again uncertainties may arise if the Convention fails to reach universality.

Apart from that delicate issue, the question of budgetary decision-making has been one of the most controversial issues before the PrepCom.[60] The provisions as enshrined in the Convention are analysed elsewhere in this volume.[61] The negotiations within the PrepCom up to now completed the rules governing budgetary procedures by the Draft Rules of Procedure of the Assembly,[62] the Draft Rules of Procedure of the Council,[63] and the outline of the Finance Committee[64] which, *inter alia*, will have to elaborate the financial rules of the Authority according to art. 162, para. 2 (y) of the Convention.

58 Article 160, para. 2 (e) of the Convention.

59 The United States, the United Kingdom, and the Federal Republic of Germany are estimated to contribute approximately 40% of the Authority's budget. *Cf. Philippe Kirsch/Douglas Fraser*, The Law of the Sea Preparatory Commission after Six Years: Review and Prospects, in: The Canadian Yearbook of International Law 26 (1988), 119-154 (148).

60 *Cf.* Law of the Sea. Report of the Secretary-General, UN doc. A/44/650 of 1 November 1989, para. 125; *Kirsch/Fraser* (note 63), 148.

61 *Cf.* Budget of the International Sea-Bed Authority. The Provisions of the Convention on the Law of the Sea: An Assessment, prepared by the Office for Ocean Affairs and the Law of the Sea, in this volume. For general information on the financing of the Authority, *see Rüdiger Wolfrum*, Die Internationalisierung staatsfreier Räume, Heidelberg 1984, 603 *et seq.*; *Jens-Lienhard Gaster*, Der Meeresbodenbergbau unter der Hohen See. Neuland des Seevölkerrechts und der nationalen Gesetzgebung, Köln/Berlin/Bonn/München 1987, 188 *et seq.*; Potential financial implications for States Parties to the future Convention of the Law of the Sea. Report of the Secretary-General, UN doc. A/Conf. 62/L. 65 of 18 February 1981. Unfortunately, updated information on the costs of the Authority is not available.

62 UN doc. LOS/PCN/WP. 20/Rev. 1 of 2 April 1984. For proposed amendments, *see* UN doc. LOS/PCN/WP. 44 of 8 February 1988.

63 UN doc. LOS/PCN/WP. 26/Rev. 1; for proposed amendments *see* UN doc. LOS/PCN/WP. 44 of 8 February 1988.

There will be four main stages leading to the establishment of the Authority's budget: the proposal of the Secretary-General as to the scope of the budget and the estimates included therein; the decision of the Finance Committee as to which recommendations it should give to the Council and/or the Assembly, accordingly; the decision of the Council as to which final draft it should submit to the Assembly; and, finally, the decision of the Assembly to approve the budget. Each of these decisions must be analyzed in some detail.

The proposal of the *Secretary-General* is administrative in character: the Secretary-General has to collect all budget-related informations available, has to shape the budget's presentation and has to propose estimates according to the information at his/her hand. In carrying out these functions, the Secretary-General is bound by legal, political and administrative directives. *Legally*, he/she is to comply with the Financial Rules as well as with other internal law and rules of the Authority as decided upon by the Assembly. The latter include the general policies established by the Assembly[65] and the specific policies established by the Council[66]. *Politically*, the Secretary-General has to take into account priorities. With regard to the Authority's expenses, art. 173, para. 2 of the Convention establishes one such priority: "The Administrative expenses of the Authority shall be a first call upon the funds of the Authority." The same article leaves, however, a lot of further priorities to be established by every single budget. Is there any rank order and if so, which one, in the use of funds according to art. 173, para. 2 (a) to (c)? What should be the ratio of re-distributive expenses according to (a) and (c) against the expenses for investments in favour of the Enterprise according to (b)? Additionally, to take decisions with respect to the "benefit of mankind" (arts. 140 and 173, para. 2 (a)), to the funds to be provided for the Enterprise (art. 173, para. 2 (b)) and to the "compensation system" (art. 173, para. 2 (c) in accordance with arts. 151, para. 10 and 160, para. 2 (e)) the Assembly needs figures. The same is true for the Council in exercise of the Authority's borrowing power. The preparation of related figures and their balancing within the overall framework of annual budgets will be part of the Secretary-General's main responsibilities. It is up to the Assembly and to the Council to define criteria for such setting of priorities. In this respect, the Authority should learn from the General Assembly's failure to agree upon clearly defined guidelines on programme and budgetary matters. *Administratively*, the Secretary-General is responsible to economically and efficiently carry out the Authority's functions. Accordingly, the Assembly and/or Council should take no decision on policies without previously considering an estimate of expenditure as prepared by the Secretary-General and a related recommendation of the Finance Committee.[67]

---

[64] UN doc. LOS/PCN/WP. 45 of 11 August 1988; LOS/PCN/WP. 48 of 6 March 1989; LOS/PCN/1990/CRP. 38 of 15 March 1990 ("Preliminary List of Functions of the Finance Committee").

[65] Article 160, para. 1 of the Convention.

[66] Article 162, para. 1 of the Convention.

For this purpose, he/she needs the assistance of an at least small department of management.

In view of these directives, the Secretary-General in carrying out his/her responsibilities needs full authority. This authority can only derive from qualified and expert staff and from independence of external influence. To ensure this full authority, it must be the Secretary-General who according to art. 167, paras. 3 and 2 of the Convention decides as to whether the staff to be imployed meets the "highest standards of efficiency, competence, and integrity," and it must be the Secretary-General's responsibility to pay "due regard" to the staff's geographical distribution. Secondly, in drafting the budget the Secretary-General must be free of influence by governments. With regard to the efficiency and economy of budgetary procedures, the introduction of any kind of "administration by consensus" into the drafting process of the budget is like the introduction of an infectious virus into a computer system. Therefore, strong objections can be made to the proposal that the Finance Committee should "assist the Secretary-General in the preparation of the proposed annual budget."[68] The financial and management expertise necessary for the drafting of the Authority's budget must be borne by the secretariat. This is not to exclude the possibility to follow the UN example of bi-annual budgets and in off-budget years to establish an outline which, however, will be prepared by the Secretary-General, too. For annual budgets, the missing outline must be substituted by guidelines and priorities as established by the Assembly.

The second body to decide upon the budget will be the *Finance Committee*. According to the functions as proposed up to now, this Committee would combine functions which for the UN are carried out by the General Assembly's 5th Committee, by the ACABQ, by the Committee on Contributions, by the Joint Inspection Unit, and, in part, by the International Civil Service Commission. With regard to its composition, it would combine financial expertise with equitable geographical distribution and with the representation of special interests.[69] Apart from the drafting responsibilities resting upon the Committe its main responsibility will be to function as the Assembly's and the Council's financial conscience.

---

[67] *Cf.* proposed amendment by the delegations of Belgium, the FRG, Italy, Japan, the Netherlands and the United Kingdom to the Draft Rules of Procedure of the Assembly, Rules 107 and 108 (UN doc. LOS/PCN/WP. 27), in: UN doc. LOS/PCN/WP. 44 of 8 February 1988, at 5; "Preliminary List of Functions of the Finance Committee," UN doc. LOS/PCN/1990/CRP. 38 of 15 March 1990, Nos. 19 and 20.

[68] Proposal for an amendment by the delegations of Belgium, France, the FRG, Italy, Japan, the Netherlands and the United Kingdom (UN doc. LOS/PCN/WP. 21 and Corr. 1) to Rule 88 *bis* para. 2 (c) of the Draft Rules of Procedure of the Assembly, in: UN doc. LOS/PCN/WP. 44 of 8 February 1988, at 4. Assistance to the Secretary-General, however, is not mentioned in the "Preliminary List of Functions of the Finance Committee" of 15 March 1990 (note 68).

[69] For this crucial point, *cf. José Luis Jesus*' presentation in this volume.

It is not surprising that the squaring-of-the-circle exercise to negotiate such a committee's rules of procedure is one of the most controversial issues on the PrepCom's agenda. However, there seems to be consensus that the functions, the composition, and the decision-making rules of the Finance Committee are interrelated problems and call for an integrated solution.[70] With regard to the budget, the composition and decision-making are of main importance. The Committee is to discuss all financial matters of the Authority in an expert manner; therefore, all candidates nominated by States Members for membership in the Committee must have records of financial expertise. Additionally, the Committee should be authorized to ask for expert opinions on the financial, economic, and legal implications from within as well as from outside the UN.

On the other hand, the Finance Committee is the most important filter to provide for an approvable budget because its consideration of the budget represents the first stage of the overall budget process where governments have their say and the three rules elaborated above are to be applied. For this purpose, the composition of the Finance Committee has to combine equal geographical distribution with a blocking vote of major contributors. Given a membership of 15, the Committee could be composed by 9 members of the G 77, by two members of the — than perhaps: former — Eastern European Group, and by four members of the Western European and other States. With that composition, five members must be selected from the eight major contributors according to the scale of assessment in force. When it comes to decision-making, the procedure could be the following: By way of a legal fiction, the votes of the Committee could be run up by the number of main contributors not represented in the Committee thus making it a total of 18 votes. On the basis of 18 votes and 15 members voting, a two-thirds or a three-fourth majority were required to decide upon a recommendation, i. e. 12 or 14 votes, accordingly. In that case, two and more of the major contributors would have a blocking vote. To enhance the acceptability of this proposed ruling, it should be taken into account that the composition as well as the decision-making of the Financial Committee could be changed in case the Authority will be financed by its own resources. This is because from this time on there will be no major contributors to the Authority's administrative budget and only marginal major contributors' interests to be protected. The experience made up to that time will show whether it will be necessary to enlarge the Committee and whether, on the basis of equal regional distribution, a two-thirds or a three-fourths majority would have to be introduced.

For the third and fourth stages of the budget process, i. e. the consideration by the *Council* and the approval by the *Assembly*, it must be ensured that both organs pay due regard to the Finance Committee's recommendations. Related procedures could follow the EEC example and vest the Finance Committee with a veto on the budget. Another solution would introduce consensus in cases the

---

[70] UN doc. A/44/650 (note 64), para. 125.

Council or the Assembly would deviate from the Comittee's recommendations. A third solution, which has the advantage to be in conformity with the Convention, would introduce a blocking vote of the main contributors when decisions would overrule the Finance Committee's recommendation. As long as the Council and the Assembly follow the Finance Committee's recommendations they decide by three-fourths or by two-thirds majority, accordingly.[71]

The procedures to decide upon the Authority's budget as elaborated so far would establish a four-side dialogue which has three advantages:

1. It constitutes a linkage between the Authority's organs and, at the same time, leaves the organs free to fulfill their special functions;

2. it provides for sufficient protection of special interests, in particular of those of the main contributors, as long as such protection is called for;

3. it pays due regard to the political function of programme budgets as elaborated above in integrating policy planning and budgeting.

The procedure, however, must be completed by the establishment of at least two elements which are still missing. As provided for by art. 175 of the Convention, the Assembly will have to appoint independent external auditors. Given the economic implications of the Authority's activities the Assembly should not follow the UN example which appoints the General Auditors of three States Members for a three-years turn but should follow the practice of the World Tourism Organization and appoint commercial firms. A list of related firms should be prepared by the Secretariat. A second missing element is an evaluation process. In this regard it is feasible to establish a small evaluation unit following the example of UNCTAD or the UN Secretariat which is to serve a two-fold function: by a programme evaluation it is to provide for information necessary to economically and efficiently shape the policy planning and budgeting of the Authority. Related reports should be directed to the Assembly through the Finance Committee. The second function is to undertake year-by-year in-depth studies of one major programme with a view to enhance the Authority's overall effectiveness. For an additional control of the Authority's efficiency and effectiveness the Assembly should acknowledge the Joint Inspection Unit's mandate and thus authorize the Unit to prepare reports and notes on the Authority's working methods.

VI. Conclusion

In deciding upon the budget, both the UN and the Authority are to reconcile two different processes which determine the effectiveness of an international organization: the negotiation of compromises which integrate all interests involved and the fulfillment of normative aims and purposes of the organization

[71] Articles 161, para. 8 and 159, para. 8 of the Convention.

concerned. The picture drawn of UN budgeting revealed that the language of economy and efficiency gained momentum in the overall policy of the world organization. Economy and efficiency, however, are not goals in themselves. It is the function of budgetary decisions to strengthen the organization's effectiveness by providing economy and efficiency. In isolating the power to approve the budget from other decisions of the General Assembly the UN Charter pays regard to the legislative function of budgetary decisions. Negotiators on budgetary questions find themselves playing the rôle of *legislateur*. Therefore, it is of paramount importance that they are conscious of "how much the peace, security and economic well-being of the world rests on a procedure that is so unattractively entitled 'UN budget-making'."[72]

The same is true for the Authority. The process of establishing the Authority and of shaping its budgetary procedures is to prove that the negotiation of compromises, the protection of special interests, and providing for economy and efficiency is not only perfectly compatible with but is to give effect to the *Common Heritage of Mankind*.

[72] *D. J. Reeb*, Financing the United Nations, in: The Law of the United Nations (Thesaurus Acroasium II), Thessaloniki 1976, 61-79 (79).

Table 1

Contributions of a sample of States to a UN specialized agency (UNESCO) in 1984/85

State	Contributions 1984/85[73]		Population	GNP[74]	Contributions	
	%	US $	in Mill.[75]		per capita in US $	% of GNP
Afghanistan	0.01	17,235	16,28	168	0,001	0.0158
Algeria	0.13	224,055	20,33	1,920	0,01	0.0174
Bahrain	0.01	17,235	0,35	6,000	0.05	0.0121
Bolivia	0.01	17,235	6,8	570	0,002	0.0224
Chad	0.01	17,235	4,97	120	0,003	0.0034
Equat.-Guinea	0.01	17,235	0,38	330	0,004	0.0007
Fiji	0.01	17,235	0,46	1,850	0,02	0.0069
Germany, F.R.	8.44	4546,340	61,60	13,590	0,23	0.0057
Nepal	0.01	17,235	16,10	140	0,001	0.0130
Netherlands	1.76	3033,360	14,31	11,470	0,21	0.0005
Niger	0,01	17,235	6,04	330	0,002	0.0115
Senegal	0.01	17,235	6,18	450	0,002	0.0161
Thailand	0.08	137,880	48,80	670	0,002	0.0237
USSR	10.41	7941,635	273,80	—	0,06	—
US	25.00	3087,500	226,50	11,360	0,19	0.0005

73 Source: UN Yearbook 1983.

74 GNP *per capita* in US dollars, Source: The Stateman's Yearbook 1984/85.

75 Source: The Stateman's Yearbook 1984/85.

Table 2
Approval to the UN Budget

Budget	Resolution	as from	vote
1946/7	68 (I)	14.12.46	unanimous
1948	166 (II)	20.11.47	37-00-10
1949	252 A (III)	10.12.49	48-00-06
1950	356 (IV)	10.12.49	48-00-07
1951	471 (V)	15.12.50	50-00-05
1952	583 (VI)	21.12.51	47-05-00
1953	674 (VII)	21.12.52	50-05-00
1954	786 (VIII)	09.12.53	53-05-00
1955	890 (IX)	17.12.54	55-05-00
1956	979 (X)	16.12.55	56-07-01
1957	1083 (XI)	21.12.56	65-00-08
1958	1230 (XII)	14.12.57	68-09-02
1959	1338 (XIII)	13.12.58	66-00-11
1960	1443 (XIV)	05.12.59	71-00-09
1961	1584 A (XV)	20.12.60	81-09-01
1962	1734 A (XVI)	20.12.61	76-10-02
1963	1861 A (XVII)	20.12.62	88-11-02
1964	1984 A (XVIII)	17.12.63	96-10-03
1965	2124 A (XX)	21.12.65	92-09-07
1966	2125 A (XX)	21.12.65	97-01-16
1967	2242 A (XXI)	20.12.66	95-01-14
1968	2363 A (XXII)	19.12.67	102-01-14
1969	2482 A (XXIII)	21.12.68	101-01-13
1970	2613 A (XXIV)	17.12.69	103-06-09
1971	2738 A (XXV)	17.12.70	97-10-07
1972	2899 A (XXVI)	22.12.71	106-09-07
1973	3044 A (XXVII)	19.12.72	113-08-05
74/5	3195 A (XXVIII)	18.12.73	106-08-07
74/5	3359 A (XXIX)	18.12.74	109-09-07
76/7	3539 A (XXX) (Rev.)	17.12.75	113-09-05
76/7	31/207 A	22.12.76	119-10-01
76/7	32/202 A (Rev.)	21.12.77	122-09-04
78/9	33/205 A	29.01.79	98-15-09
78/9	34/223 A (Rev.)	20.12.79	116-09-11
80/1	35/226 A	17.12.80	111-20-05
80/1	36/234 A (Rev.)	18.12.81	120-16-04
82/3	38/226 A	20.12.83	120-14-09
84/5	39/237 A (Rev.)	18.12.84	124-17-06
84/5	40/239 A	18.12.85	125-12-10
86/7	41/211 A (Rev.)	11.12.86	122-13-10
86/7	42/213 A	21.12.87	adopted
88/9	43/218 A (Rev.)	21.12.88	adopted
88/9	44/193 A	21.12.89	adopted

Budget of the International Sea-Bed Authority — The Provisions of the Law of the Sea Convention: An Assessment*

I. Introduction

An examination of the provisions of the 1982 United Nations Convention on the Law of the Sea[1] shows that the Convention, upon its entry, sets out functions which are to be carried out by two new international organizations and by the United Nations. The International Sea-Bed Authority is one of the two new organizations, the other being the International Tribunal for the Law of the Sea.

It is relevant to note that the functions of the International Sea-Bed Authority within the context of the overall institutional arrangements provided for in the Convention, are to administer the resources of the Area, i. e., the sea-bed and ocean floor and subsoil thereof beyond the limits of national jurisdiction.[2] The powers and functions of the Authority are conferred upon it by the Convention in its Part XI and Annexes III and IV.

The International Tribunal for the Law of the Sea is the central judicial organ for the resolution of disputes under the Convention, and it will function in accordance with its Statute set forth in Annex VI of the Convention.

The Convention also entrusts a number of important responsibilities to the Secretary-General of the United Nations. One of these is to establish and service the new intergovernmental Commission on the Limits of the Continental Shelf.[3] This Commission will review scientific and technical data pertaining to the application of a complex formula for the demarcation of the legal limits between coastal State's continental shelf and the international sea-bed area. After a review of each case, the Commission will make recommendations to coastal States with regard to the limits of their continental shelf. The limits of the shelf established by coastal States on the basis of those recommendations will be final and binding and they, in turn, will establish the legal limits of the international sea-bed area.[4]

---

* Prepared by the United Nations Office for Ocean Affairs and the Law of the Sea.

1 The Law of the Sea. Official Text of the United Nations Convention on the Law of the Sea, United Nations, New York 1983 (hereinafter referred to as the Convention).

2 Article 157, para. 1 of the Convention.

3 Article 2, para. 5 of Annex II of the Convention.

4 Article 76, para. 8 of the Convention; *see also* Annex II of the Convention, in general.

The Secretariat of the United Nations will be called upon to provide substantive advisory services and support on the legal aspects, and also on specialized fields of marine geology, geophysics, geochemistry and hydrography, the elements of which are incorporated in the complex formula.

The Secretary-General of the United Nations will monitor and report on issues of a general nature that have arisen with respect to the Convention. He is also required to convene meetings of States Parties, as necessary, discharge specified responsibilities with regard to dispute settlement, and in addition to his normal depositary functions, carry out depositary functions with regard to a variety of formal instruments, including large-scale maps, charts, etc. establishing baselines, or delimiting maritime zones, and notify States of the submissions lodged with him.[5]

Thus, in the context of the overall institutional arrangements provided for in the Convention, the International Sea-Bed Authority deals with sea-bed mineral-related matters within one maritime zone, the international sea-bed area, with its mandate emanating from one of the 17 parts of the Convention. The International Tribunal for the Law of the Sea deals with the settlement of disputes concerning matters covered by the Convention. It is the United Nations that is entrusted with matters covering all maritime zones and all aspects of the implementation of the Convention, with its mandate emanating from the Convention as a whole.[6] Several specialized technical agencies and bodies within the United Nations system will continue to deal with certain specialized sectors of marine affairs within their respective areas of competence.

The United Nations is, at present, carrying out a number of functions, and will continue to carry out similar functions after entry into force of the Convention. These functions include facilitating uniform and consistent application of the Convention, promoting its widespread acceptance, and assisting States to formulate and execute national marine policies based on the integrated management framework provided by the Convention, and to realize the full benefits to be derived from the Convention through rational implementation of their rights and duties. The United Nations will also continue to support organizations within the United Nations System and harmonize marine affairs activities in the context of the Convention, with a view to ensuring consistency with the Convention and a more collective approach to the rational implementation of the Convention, providing co-ordination among the continuing sectoral and discipline-specific activities of the various organizations of the United Nations system.[7]

The following Chart I provides a summary of the responsibilities of the two new organizations and the United Nations.

---

[5] Articles 319, 16, para. 2, 47, para. 9, 75, para. 2, 76, para. 9 and 84, para. 2 of the Convention.

[6] *See, inter alia*, GA res. 44/26, 43/18, 42/20, 41/34, 40/63.

[7] UN doc. A/45/6 (Prog. 10) of 4 April 1990.

The present and future international organizations which are called upon to carry out functions upon entry into force of the Convention and their interrelationships.

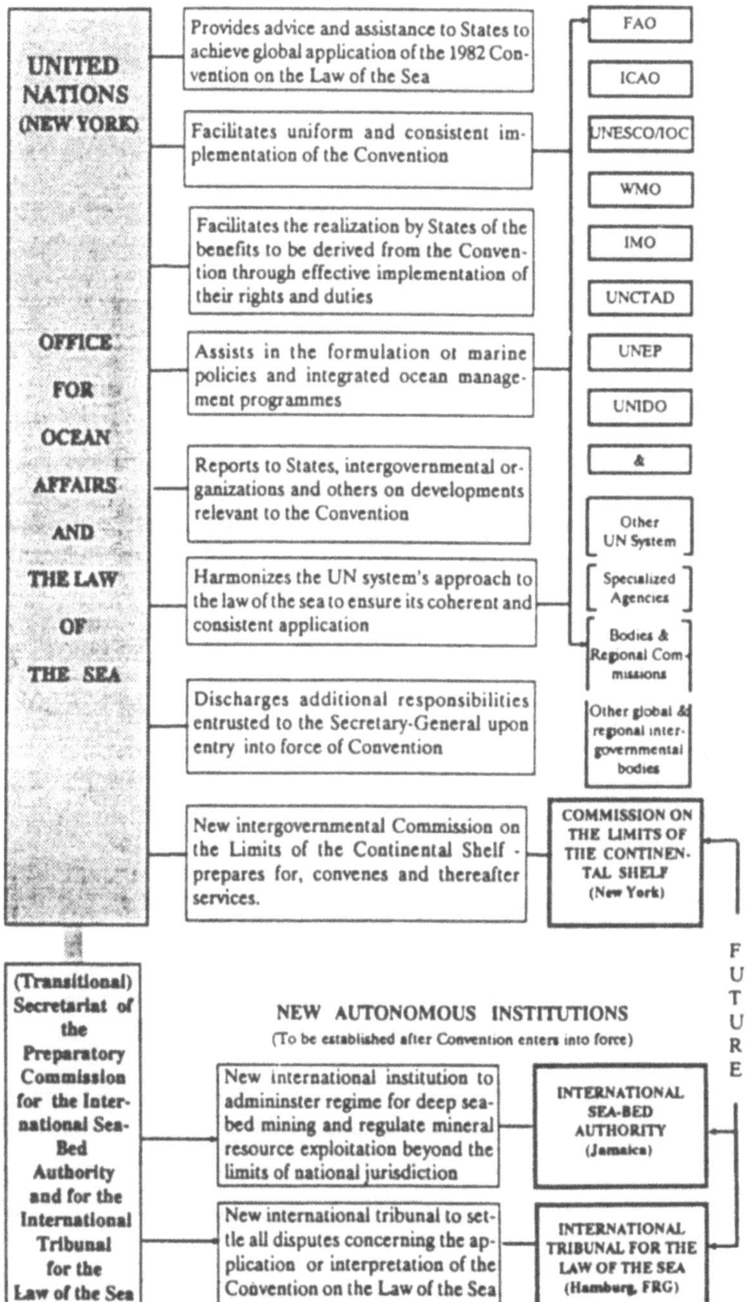

II. Budgetary Provisions of the Three Organizations

1. Budgetary Provisions of the United Nations

The financial requirements of the United Nations for the fulfilment of the responsibilities of the Secretary-General of the United Nations under the Convention will be met from the regular budget of the United Nations. These responsibilities were entrusted to the United Nations following the review of a study examining the requirements under the Convention.[8] As is well known, the funds for the regular budget of the United Nations are obtained from the assessed contributions of Member States of the United Nations in accordance with a scale of assessment.

2. Budgetary Provisions of the International Tribunal for the Law of the Sea

The expenses of the International Tribunal for the Law of the Sea (the Tribunal) are to be borne by States Parties to the Convention and by the International Sea-Bed Authority in accordance with the decisions taken at meetings of States Parties to the Convention. When an entity other than a State Party or the International Sea-Bed Authority is a party to a case submitted to the Tribunal, the Tribunal shall fix the amount which that party is to contribute towards the expenses of the Tribunal.[9] A preliminary assessment of the structure of the Tribunal and financial implications has been presented in a document of the Preparatory Commission for the International Sea-Bed Authority and for the International Tribunal for the Law of the Sea (UN doc. LOS/PCN/SCN.4/WP.8). Such assessment was facilitated by the experience of the most relevant existing institution with comparable functions, namely, the International Court of Justice; the assessment could also take into account, to a certain extent, other international tribunals.

3. Budgetary Provisions of the International Sea-Bed Authority

As for the International Sea-Bed Authority (the Authority), the Convention specifies that during the initial phase, the administrative expenses of the Authority shall be met by assessed contributions made by members of the Authority in accordance with an agreed scale of assessment. The scale will be based upon the scale used for the regular budget of the United Nations. This will apply until the Authority has sufficient income from other sources to meet its administrative expenses.[10]

---

[8] Third UN Conference on the Law of the Sea, Official Records, Vol. XV (UN doc. A/CONF. 62/L. 76).

[9] Article 19 of Annex VI of the Convention.

[10] Articles 173, para. 1 and 171 (a) of the Convention.

There is no relevant existing institution with comparable functions to the Authority and thus no existing basis for determining its institutional structure and the consequential financial implications. The examination of the budgetary requirements will be an extremely complex one. It first requires a study of the functions of the Authority, and of the factors that would influence the initial work-load of the Authority before appropriate approaches to the examination of the budgetary requirements can be determined. The following sections address these basic factors.

III. Functions of the Various Organs of the Authority

The principal organs of the Authority are the Assembly, the Council and the Secretariat.[11] The Assembly consists of all the members of the Authority.[12] The 36-member Council is the executive organ, and the Secretariat is the administrative arm of the Authority.[13] The organ through which the Authority shall directly carry out exploration for, and exploitation of, the resources of the Area, as well as transporting, processing and marketing of minerals recovered from the Area, is the Enterprise.[14] Two organs of the Council are specifically provided for in the Convention: the 15-member Economic Planning Commission and Legal and Technical Commission.[15] The Authority can also establish such other subsidiary organs as may be found necessary. The Preparatory Commission has under consideration the establishment of another subsidiary organ, a Finance Committee.[16]

According to the provisions of the United Nations Convention on the Law of the Sea, the first meeting of the Assembly of the Authority will be held one year after the 60th instrument of ratification or accession is deposited.[17] The first task of the Assembly will be to elect the Council.[18] The Secretary-General shall be elected by the Assembly from among the candidates proposed by the Council.[19] The staff of the Secretariat shall be appointed by the Secretary-General.[20]

The functions to be performed and the size of the initial set-up of the Secretariat will depend on the requirements of the Authority at that time and the nature and extent of the requisite tasks.

11 Article 158, para. 1 of the Convention.
12 Article 160, para. 1 of the Convention.
13 Articles 162, para. 1 and 166, para. 3 of the Convention.
14 Article 158, para. 2 of the Convention.
15 Articles 163, para. 1 and 163, para. 2 of the Convention.
16 UN doc. LOS/PCN/1990/CRP. 38 of 15 March 1990.
17 Article 308, para. 3 of the Convention.
18 *Ibid.*
19 Article 166, para. 2 of the Convention.
20 Article 167, para. 3 of the Convention.

1. The Assembly and the Council

The Convention sets out a detailed listing of the powers and functions of the Assembly and the Council.[21] An examination of these lists shows that, pursuant to the mandate of the Authority, the predominant functions of the Authority pertain to the organization and control of the resource-related activities in the Area; such activities include prospecting, exploration and exploitation of the resources.

Another important category of functions relate to organizational matters, such as: adoption and application of the rules, regulations and procedures relating to the financial management and internal administration of the Authority; preparation and adoption of the annual budget of the Authority; assessment of the contributions of the members of the Authority to its administrative budget; entering into relationship agreements with the United Nations and other international organizations; etc.

In addition to the above powers and functions, the Authority also has functions with respect to the promotion of marine scientific research and acquisition of technology and scientific knowledge relating to activities in the Area by developing countries.[22]

2. Organs of the Council

The functions of the two organs of the Council — the Economic Planning Commission and the Legal and Technical Commission — are also predominantly related to the mining of the resources of the Area.

The work of the Economic Planning Commission includes reviewing the trends of, and the factors affecting, supply, demand and prices of materials which may be derived from the international sea-bed area and examining any situation likely to lead to adverse effects on developing land-based producer States.[23]

The work of the Legal and Technical Commission includes reviewing formal written plans of work for activities in the international sea-bed area; supervising activities in the area; and performing certain duties with regard to protection and conservation of the marine environment. The Legal and Technical Commission is also to formulate and submit to the Council rules, regulations and procedures relating to prospecting, exploration and exploitation in the international sea-bed Area, and the financial management and internal administration of the Authority.[24]

---

21 Articles 160, para. 2 and 162, para. 2 of the Convention.

22 Articles 143-147 of the Convention.

23 Article 164, para. 2 of the Convention.

24 Article 165, para. 2 of the Convention.

3. The Proposed Finance Committee

The functions of the proposed Finance Committee include the elaboration of the draft financial rules, regulations and procedures of the Authority; provision of advice on various finance-related matters; and making recommendations regarding various aspects of the finances of the Authority and the Enterprise.[25]

4. The Enterprise

Finally, under the Convention, there is the Enterprise which is to carry out sea-bed mining directly and also the transporting, processing and marketing of minerals recovered from the Area. The Convention requires that, in carrying out these activities, the Enterprise shall operate in accordance with sound commercial principles.[26] The Enterprise will require approval from the Council for its projects, and like other operators will execute its projects on the basis of formal written plans of work.[27]

5. Tasks of the Secretariat Flowing from the Functions of the Organs of the Authority

The Secretariat of the Authority will be called upon to provide the appropriate administrative support to the various organs of the Authority, which will consist essentially of three categories of tasks:

(a) substantive backstopping for the work of the various organs, including collection and dissemination of relevant information and data, provision of analyses for the formulation of general and specific policies, and provision of advice as and when required;

(b) practical organization, administration and management of the institution; and

(c) conference servicing.

IV. Factors That Would Influence the Initial Set-up of the Secretariat of the Authority

Since the functions of the Authority are predominantly linked with the resource-related activities in the international sea-bed Area, it is obvious that the status of these activities will determine the nature and extent of the work-load of the Authority, and thereby the requirements for the Secretariat.

---

25 *See supra* (note 16).

26 Article 1, para. 3 of Annex IV of the Convention.

27 Articles 12, para. 1 and 12, para. 2 of Annex IV of the Convention.

1. Status of Resource-related Activities and Prospects for Commercial Exploitation[28]

The recent years have witnessed a slow-down of the rate of growth of demand for the metals contained in sea-bed minerals. Economic assessments of the experimental technologies that were developed and tested for mining and processing small amounts of sea-bed minerals, polymetallic nodules, demonstrated that they may not be cost-effective for large-scale mining operations. Furthermore, the distribution of nodules on the ocean floor appeared to be highly uneven with respect to abundance, metal content and microtopography (which determines mineability of the areas). The combined outcome of these three factors is that considerable extents of additional work and, consequently, funding are needed to delineate, in detail, mine sites composed of deep sea-bed areas with nodules of sufficient abundance and metal content and with acceptable microtopography, and to develop cost-effective mining and processing technologies.

The requirements for committing large amounts of funds (in the order of $ US 200-400 million) under the intrinsic uncertainties with regard to metal prices and development of cost-effective technology led to a virtual halt in the activities of a number of corporations; others that are continuing are proceeding at a low, cautious pace. By the late 1980's, only four entities respectively from France, India, Japan and the USSR registered themselves as pioneer investors with the Preparatory Commission, and were alloted pioneer areas where they have the exclusive right to carry out pioneer activities.[29]

Commercial exploitation of sea-bed minerals will occur only after its economic feasibility has been established. At present, the activities of the pioneer investors are focusing on detailed exploration of the pioneer areas allocated to them so that possible mine sites could be delineated, and on research and development with regard to modifying the existing experimental technologies or developing new technologies for mining and processing nodules so that they become cost-effective. As mentioned earlier, these activities involve large amount of funds, and there is no certainty that the outcomes would be satisfactory. It is estimated that under the most favourable conditions these activities would require 7-10 years to be completed.

---

[28] The following information on the status and prospects of sea-bed mineral development has been obtained from the proceedings of two expert group meetings: United Nations Office for Ocean Affairs and the Law of the Sea organized an Expert Group seminar on sea-bed mining technology in 1989; also, a Group of Technical Experts, established in accordance with the decision taken by the Preparatory Commission, met in 1989.

[29] Law of the Sea Bulletin, Special Issue II, April 1988, 9-13, 40-46, 64-69 and 95-104.

This R & D phase will be followed by a feasibility study with a view to verifying that the identified mine sites were mineable with the existing technologies and that the costs of mining and processing as compared with the revenues that could be expected from selling the final products would be such as to yield a reasonable rate of return on the huge investment necessary for a mining project (in the order of $US 1.5-2.5 billion). If the result of the investigation was positive, then a decision to start a mining project would be taken. The feasibility study phase is estimated to require 2-3 years. If the result was not positive, further work would be undertaken unless it was decided to await better economic conditions.

If it was decided to start a mining project, the construction of the mining system and the processing plant would follow. This phase is estimated to require 4-6 years. It is only after this phase was completed, commercial production of sea-bed minerals would commence.

2. *Impact of Projected Nodule-related Activities on the Work of the Authority*

It is evident from the above projections about the nodule mining related activities that after the establishment of the Authority, presumably during the first part of this decade, for a number of years it would be functioning in a "feasibility determination" period, followed by a "pre-production plant construction" period, if the outcomes of activities during the "feasibility determination" period were favourable. The Authority will deal with "production" period matters only after these two periods.

The nature and extent of the work of the Authority during these three periods are quite different, and more importantly, the Convention sets out the functions of the Authority in such a manner as to require a very limited extent of work with regard to governance and control of "feasibility determination" activities, moving on to a relatively increased level of work with regard to "pre-production" activities, and finally bringing into play the full set of functions required for the governance and control of "production" period activities.

It can be reasonably assumed that during the initial period, when the feasibility determining activities are being carried out by the pioneer investors and other potential investors, the tasks of the Authority would essentially comprise of monitoring and reviewing trends and developments relevant to sea-bed mining, especially technological development. It will also put in place the rules, regulations and procedures for prospecting, exploration and exploitation of sea-bed minerals (the sea-bed mining code). It is worth noting that the only portion of the sea-bed mining code the Authority may need to apply during the initial period is that dealing with the rules, regulations and procedures for prospecting and, possibly, exploration, if any plans of work for exploration are submitted by applicants. These constitute a relatively small part of the sea-bed mining code. During the initial period, the Authority may carry out certain preparatory work, such as preparation for entry into effective operation of the Enterprise, preparation for protection of developing countries from adverse effects resulting from sea-bed production, collecting baseline data for environmental monitoring, etc.

3. Impact of the Work of the Preparatory Commission on the Initial Work Load of the Authority

As evident from the previous section, the work of the Authority involves both the *formulation* and the *implementation* of general and specific policies and rules, regulations and procedures based on such policies with regard to resource-related activities as well as organizational matters. It is to be noted that the Preparatory Commission for the International Sea-Bed Authority and for the International Tribunal for the Law of the Sea (the Preparatory Commission) has been charged with the tasks of carrying out the preparatory work for the formulation of policies and, in many cases, the tasks of either making recommendations or drafting rules, regulations and procedures relating to most of the important policy areas, both with regard to resource-related activities and to organizational matters.[30] This work is being carried out by an intergovernmental conference which is virtually negotiating the requirements for the adoption and the implementation by the Authority of the rules, regulations and procedures. The work of the Preparatory Commission over the past eight years and in the future will significantly reduce the initial work-load of the Authority.

The Authority would have essentially been relieved of the task of formulating and drafting the rules, regulations and procedures for sea-bed mining (the sea-bed mining code), and for internal administration and financial management. The Preparatory Commission is already well advanced in carrying out these tasks and has also registered the pioneer investors and alloted them sites. These, for all practical purposes, may be the only ones the Authority has to deal with in the beginning. The Preparatory Commission will also have set up an initial programme of work for the Enterprise. It will also have made recommendations as to measures to protect developing countries from adverse effects resulting from sea-bed production. The Preparatory Commission will also have made recommendations on a number of other matters, such as relations between the Authority and the United Nations and other international organizations, and the first budget and the initial programme of work of the Authority. This reduction of the potential work load of the Authority has to be kept in mind in estimating the requirements for the initial secretariat set-up of the Authority.

30 Resolution I of the Convention.

V. Approaches to the Budget of the Authority

The nature of the work to be carried out by the Secretariat of the Authority, and the extent of its work-load is clearly dependent on the phases of development of the sea-bed mining industry.

1. Evolutionary Approach

The concept of "cost-effective, efficient and lean" international organizations has taken root generally and has led to stringent measures implemented by the United Nations itself and by organizations within the United Nations system. The best strategy to develop a cost-efficient and lean Authority would be to take an evolutionary approach whereby the Secretariat set-up will develop as the sea-bed mining industry moves from the "feasibility determination" stage to the "pre-production" stage and finally to the "production" stage.

a) The Initial Secretariat Set-up

It can be assumed that the initial Secretariat set-up would be relatively small matching the low level of requirements arising in the "feasibility determination" stage. The influence of the nature of the resource-related activities, the uncertainties associated with them as well as the cautious pace at which the pioneer investors are proceeding on the initial Secretariat set-up is recognized by all delegations of the Preparatory Commission. For example, in a statement made in the plenary session of the Preparatory Commission in September 1989, the Chairman of the Group of 77 stated, "[a] matter on which the Group of 77 would like to make its position clear is that regarding the initial size and cost of the Authority upon entry into force of the Convention. A false impression has been conveyed and perpetuated, despite repeated statements by Members of the Group of 77 to the contrary, that the Group of 77 contemplates the establishment of a large bureaucratic organization unrelated to the activities which the Authority is legitimately required to perform under the Convention from time to time. Nothing could be further from the truth. The Group of 77 is desirous of establishing an Authority which would be efficient and cost-effective, the size of which would be no larger or smaller than is required to enable the Authority to carry out its functions efficiently."[31]

Other regional and interest groups have concurred with the idea of an "efficient and cost-effective" Authority. In fact, this idea has permeated the work of the Preparatory Commission from the very outset. The first Chairman of the Preparatory Commission himself emphasized this idea in his report at the conclusion

---

31 Information about the Preparatory Commission: Statements made at the conclusion of the 1989 summer meeting, Law of the Sea Bulletin, No. 15, May 1990, 55.

of the third session of the Commission when he mentioned the "potential financial implication for States Parties to the United Nations Convention on the Law of the Sea taking into account, in particular, *the need for economy*, and minimizing the financial burden of States Parties[32] (emphasis added). The current Chairman reiterated the idea in his report at the conclusion of the eighth session of the Commission.[33]

Furthermore, the initial Secretariat set-up will certainly be influenced by the reduction of the initial work load of the Authority as a result of the work of the Preparatory Commission.

b) The Initial Enterprise Set-up

There has been a considerable extent of deliberation in the Preparatory Commission (in Special Commission 2 on the Enterprise) regarding the structure and organization of the Enterprise.[34] There is a consensus that, especially in view of the fact that the structure and organization of the Enterprise will largely be a reflection of the operational option it adopts for its first mining project, the Enterprise will evolve from an initial nucleus or core, which will deal with project planning and development, towards an organization implementing a mining project.[35]

It is clear that the project costs of the Enterprise can only be determined after the viability of sea-bed mining has been established (which may require a long period of time) and after operational strategies have been adopted. There is a large number of possible options for operations, including joint ventures and plant leasing, which have a significant bearing on the reduction of project costs.

Focusing on the pre-project (or pre-operational) period, it is evident from the discussion in the previous section that a long hiatus may occur between the time of entry into force of the Convention and the time when the viability of sea-bed mining is established with sufficient certainty to warrant the commencement of project planning and development. Special Commission 2 has also deliberated upon a special institutional arrangement for the Enterprise for this transitional period. The functions to be performed under the transitional arrangement are, basically, the monitoring of and reporting on all developments in, or affecting the sea-bed mining sector; studying available information and data related to sea-bed areas reserved for the Authority in order to determine which reserved area would call for priority attention for further exploration and project develop-

---

32 UN doc. LOS/PCN/L. 19 of 3 April 1985, 2.

33 UN doc. LOS/PCN/L. 82/Rev. 1 of 29 May 1990, 7.

34 *See* UN docs. LOS/PCN/SCN. 2/WP. 12, LOS/PCN/SCN. 2/WP. 15 and LOS/PCN/SCN. 2/1990/CRP. 5.

35 UN doc. LOS/PCN/SCN. 2/1990/CRP. 5.

ment for the Enterprise; elaboration of operational options available to the Enterprise; and elaboration of a managerial policy of the Enterprise.[36]

Who would perform these functions (staff of the Enterprise, staff of the Authority or an *ad hoc* group of experts), whether the 15-member Governing Board of the Enterprise would be formed or not, and if formed, partially or fully, whether or not an administrative budget should be clearly earmarked for the transitional arrangement or whether the costs would be subsumed under the Authority's budget — these matters are under further consideration in the Special Commission.[37] Nevertheless, what is clear is that the costs of the transitional arrangement would be minimal in view of the limited functions described above.

2. *Strategies for a Cost-Effective Initial Secretariat Set-up*

a) Staff Costs

Staff salaries and other costs directly related to the number and level of staff account for the major share of the budget of any international organization. At this time, it is extremely difficult to indicate an organizational chart and a staffing structure of the Secretariat of the Authority; these matters will be deliberated upon in the Preparatory Commission. However, a number of important observations of a general nature can be made.

The Secretariat of the Authority, basically, will have requirements for three groups of professional staff — one group will deal with conference servicing; the second group will deal with the administration and management of the organization; and the third group with substantive technical matters falling within the mandate of the Authority.

aa) Staff for Conference Servicing

The requirements for the conference servicing staff are directly dependent on the number and duration of meetings of each of the organs of the Authority, the number of official languages, and the documentation in the official languages. One important element of documentation which has a marked bearing on staffing requirements is the preparation of summary records of the meetings of the various organs of the Authority. Depending on the number of official languages and the need for summary records, the number of interpreters, precise writers, revisers, translators, and terminologists at the professional level, and of reference clerks and typists at the general service level, can be quite large indeed. For example, to give an order-of-magnitude estimate, 100 days of meetings in a year requiring summary records, with 6 official languages, would call for about 65 professional

---

36 *Ibid.*

37 *Ibid.*

staff and 50 general service staff. This large number of staff will account for a major share of the total staff salary and related costs.

It should be added that most of the important elements on which the staffing requirements for conference servicing depend, will be deliberated upon thoroughly in the Preparatory Commission.

bb) Administration and Management Staff

Administrative and management staff will be required to perform a variety of functions: planning of work programme, preparation of work programme, budgeting and financing (including receipts and payments, accounting, auditing, investment, procurement), monitoring and evaluation of the implementation of work programme, personnel administration, office secretarial services, general services, security services, medical services, printing and reproduction, supplies and materials, building management, etc. Some of these functions will require professional staff, and the others general service staff. Some of the related functions can be carried out by the same staff member depending on the work load.

cc) Substantive Technical Staff

These professional staff will provide the substantive support for the work of the various organs of the Authority. Staff will also be required for library services, computer services and public information services.

In order to estimate the initial staffing requirements for the substantive matters, it would be helpful to specify, as accurately as possible, the functions to be performed and the required expertise. The functions and the work load at the initial stage may be of such a nature as to permit the use of a single staff member with varied experience and expertise in related fields for the execution of several functions. An examination of the initial functions shows that the expertise required at the initial stage are in the fields of marine mining, mineral economics, and international law with emphasis on the law of the sea and knowledge of contract law.

It is worth noting that because of the interrelationships between the functions of the Authority and the areas of competence of existing international organizations, it may be possible to draw related expertise from various organizations, especially UN, IMO, UNIDO, UNEP, UNCTAD, IOC, and WMO, and thus permit the Secretariat of the Authority to maximize the services of the total expert capacity. In this context, it is very germane to note that under the Convention provisions, the Secretariat of the Authority is required to develop co-operative relationships with a number of United Nations agencies and organizations as well as other intergovernmental organizations, as the case may be, given the interrelationships that will exist between the work of the Authority and these organizations.[38] The Preparatory Commission is already considering how the UN can provide support to the future Authority and Tribunal in accordance with "relationship agreements" to be drawn up.[39]

Another source of expertise which can be utilized by the Authority is the members of the subsidiary organs, i. e., the Economic Planning Commission, the Legal and Technical Commission, and the proposed Finance Committee. According to the Convention, members of the Economic Planning Commission shall have appropriate qualifications in fields similar to those required by the substantive technical staff of the Authority. It should, therefore, be examined whether certain tasks of substantive backstopping, such as collection, processing, and dissemination of relevant information and data, review of trends and developments relating to sea-bed mining, provision of analyses for the formulation of general and specific policies, etc. could be performed directly by the members of the subsidiary organs themselves, thus reducing the work load of the Secretariat.

It is clear from the above discussion about the initial-phase work of the Enterprise that the technical staff and data resources needed by the Enterprise could equally serve the substantive needs of the other organs of the Authority. At its inception, the Enterprise would require a general manager to advise on the system management of sea-bed mining projects while the Authority would also need such a person to advise on general management aspects of the sea-bed mining industry; the Enterprise would require an engineering manager to advise on marine systems design and development while the Authority would need advice on the technological aspects of sea-bed mining industry; the Enterprise would require a financial manager to advise on economic and financial viability of sea-bed mining projects while the Authority's financial expert would advise on policy matters which would in turn relate to the economic and financial viability of the sea-bed industry; a manpower development manager would be required for the Enterprise to advise on training and development of staff and up-grading of skills while the Authority would need advice on human resources development for the sea-bed mining industry.

These similarities of expertise and functional areas provide an opportunity for the Authority and the Enterprise to pool their technical resources and make optimum use of their resources. Because of the community of interest, and the "group thinking" approach that would be necessary for the industry during the initial period before its technological and economical viability is tried, tested and established, there is a great opportunity for interface between the Authority and Enterprise for advisory and assistance arrangements. This interface can be developed to the extent that the Authority and the Enterprise are serviced by the same advisory group having various capabilities mentioned above. Thus, the

---

38 Articles 169 and 162 (f) of the Convention.

39 UN doc. LOS/PCN/WP. 50, forthcoming.

staff of the Authority and of the Enterprise could function interchangeably, at least in the fields of general industry and project management, technology assessment and acquisition strategies, economic assessment and financial management, and human resources development, thus optimizing the cross-fertilization between public sector and commercial endeavours; at the same time this interface and the interchangeability of personnel can lead to a considerable improvement in cost-efficiency.

dd) Use of Short-Term Staff/Consultants/Groups of Experts

The nature of some of the tasks to be performed by the Secretariat of the Authority is such as to permit utilization of substantive staff for a short-term, or of external consultants or *ad hoc* groups of experts for the purpose of, for example, collecting and analyzing information and data on specific items, or preparing studies on specific topics. An accurate listing of tasks and a comparative costing analysis is required before the optimal mix of long term staff/short term staff/consultants/groups of experts can be determined.

b) Other Items of Expenditure

In addition to staff salaries and related costs, attention should be paid to other items of expenditure. These fall under various categories. Temporary assistance for meetings may be required for language and secretarial services that cannot be performed by regular staff. General temporary assistance may be required to provide general service level support services such as those of additional secretaries, messengers, library assistants and telephone operators. Overtime requirements may arise to cover secretarial assistance to the organs of the Authority and for regular staff during peak work load periods. A provision may have to be made for staff travel for official purposes.

General operating expenses of the Secretariat of the Authority would have to be considered. These include rental and maintenance of office and conference premises, utilities, rental and maintenance of furniture, equipment and vehicles, communications, provision of miscellaneous services, supplies and materials (including stationery and office supplies, library books and supplies, data processing supplies, medical and health supplies, uniforms, etc.).

c) Non-Recurrent One-Time Expenditures

The seat of the Authority shall be in Jamaica.[40] It can be assumed that the Authority will rent office and conference premises and facilities in the initial period, until such time as is feasible for the Authority to build premises.

---

[40] Article 156, para. 4 of the Convention.

At the outset, consideration should be given whether office equipment, data processing equipment, transport, communications and reproduction equipment, etc. should be provided on a rental basis or as a capital outlay.

d) Cost-Sharing

aa) The Authority and Enterprise

Pooling of resources and sharing of costs between the Enterprise and the other organs of the Authority in relation to substantive staff has been discussed earlier. In view of the high costs of conference servicing, the conference services and facilities could also be utilized jointly by the Enterprise and the other organs of the Authority.

bb) The Authority and Other International Organizations

It is possible under relationship agreements specifically drawn up for the purpose, to share certain costs between a newly functioning organization and the already established organizations with headquarters in the same locality. In the absence of headquarters of any major international organization in Jamaica, the opportunities for cost-sharing may be minimal. Nevertheless, possibilities can be explored for sharing certain expenses with the local offices of the organizations of the UN system and other international organizations.

cc) The Authority and the UN

In spite of the distance between the United Nations Headquarters in New York and the seat of the Authority, it is possible, under a relationship agreement drawn up between the Authority and the UN, to make arrangements to share costs with regard to certain items. Careful analysis is required to identify such items.

3. Transitional Arrangements

As mentioned earlier, the staff of the Secretariat of the Authority will be appointed by the Secretary-General of the Authority, who will be elected by the Assembly of the Authority from among the candidates proposed by the Council. The Council itself will be elected by the Assembly which will meet on the date of entry into force of the Convention.

Under these circumstances, the most likely scenario is that the Secretary-General of the United Nations would convene the first meeting of the Assembly of the Authority, and the United Nations would service that meeting and perform the requisite tasks until the Secretary-General of the Authority has his own staff on board.

The costs to be incurred during the transition would have to be covered from the regular budget of the United Nations under supplementary authorization by the General Assembly, unless a special trust fund is established through the contribution of the members of the Authority or other entities during the transition period. In case the United Nations covers the transitional costs the usual practice is to make reimbursement to the United Nations at a later date when the funds are available at the disposal of the newly functioning organization.

VI. Financial Implications for the States Parties

In order to facilitate the examination of the potential financial implications for the States Parties to the Convention, some important information is presented below.

The assessed contributions to be made by members of the Authority would be in accordance with a scale of assessment based on the UN scale. The current scale of assessment used for the regular budget of the United Nations is presented in Table 1.

For the sake of illustration, it can be noted that the scale of assessment of 79 Member States is 0.01 per cent each, totalling 0.79 per cent of the regular budget of the United Nations; the scale of assessment falling between 0.02 to 0.09 per cent, between 0.10 to 0.99 per cent, between 1.00 and 9.99 per cent, and 10.00 per cent and above, apply to 28 (totalling 1.12 per cent of the regular budget of the United Nations, 35 (totalling 12.89 per cent), 15 (totalling 48.81 per cent) and 2 (totalling 36.38 per cent) Member States, respectively.

As of 30 June 1990, 43 ratifications of the Convention have been received; Table 2 presents the list of States and entities that ratified the Convention.

At the time of the preparation of the first administrative budget of the Authority, there may be a short-fall, as calculated according to the scale of assessment used for the regular budget of the United Nations. It is assumed that such a short-fall would be covered by the members of the Authority on a proportionate basis. For example, if there is a short-fall of 50 per cent, the scale of assessment of each of the members of the Authority for its administrative budget would be doubled.

Table 1

Current Scale of Assessment used for the Regular Budget of the United Nations

Member States	1989 Scale of assessments %
Afghanistan	0.01
Albania	0.01
Algeria	0.15
Angola	0.01
Antigua and Barbuda	0.01
Argentina	0.66
Australia	1.57
Austria	0.74
Bahamas	0.02
Bahrain	0.02
Bangladesh	0.01
Barbados	0.01
Belgium	1.17
Belize	0.01
Benin	0.01
Bhutan	0.01
Bolivia	0.01
Botswana	0.01
Brazil	1.45
Brunei Darussalam	0.04
Burkina Faso	0.01
Burundi	0.01
Byelorussian Soviet Socialist Republic	0.33
Bulgaria	0.15
Cameroon	0.01
Canada	3.09
Cape Verde	0.01
Central African Republic	0.01
Chad	0.01
Chile	0.08
China	0.79
Colombia	0.14
Comoros	0.01
Congo	0.01
Costa Rica	0.02
Côte d'Ivoire	0.02
Cuba	0.09
Cyprus	0.02
Czechoslovakia	0.66
Democratic Kampuchea	0.01
Denmark	0.01
Djibouti	0.69
Dominica	0.01
Dominican Republic	0.01

Table 1 (to be continued)

Member States	1989 Scale of assessments %
Ecuador	0.03
Egypt	0.07
El Savaldor	0.01
Equatorial Guinea	0.01
Ethiopia	0.01
Fiji	0.01
Finland	0.51
France	6.25
Gabon	0.03
Gambia	0.01
German Democratic Republic	1.28
Germany, Federal Republic of	8.08
Ghana	0.01
Greece	0.40
Grenada	0.01
Guatemala	0.02
Guinea	0.01
Guinea-Bissau	0.01
Guyana	0.01
Haiti	0.01
Honduras	0.01
Hungary	0.21
Iceland	0.03
India	0.37
Indonesia	0.15
Iran (Islamic Republic of)	0.69
Iraq	0.12
Ireland	0.18
Israel	0.21
Italy	3.99
Jamaica	0.01
Japan	11.38
Jordan	0.01
Kenya	0.01
Kuwait	0.29
Lao People's Democratic Republic	0.01
Lebanon	0.01
Lesotho	0.01
Liberia	0.01
Libyan Arab Jamahiriya	0.28
Luxembourg	0.06
Madagascar	0.01
Malawi	0.01
Malaysia	0.11
Maldives	0.01
Mali	0.01
Malta	0.01
Mauritania	0.01

Table 1 (to be continued)

Member States	1989 Scale of assessments %
Mauritius	0.01
Mexico	0.94
Mongolia	0.01
Morocco	0.04
Mozambique	0.01
Myanmar	0.01
Nepal	0.01
Netherlands	1.65
New Zealand	0.24
Nicaragua	0.01
Niger	0.01
Nigeria	0.20
Norway	0.55
Oman	0.02
Pakistan	0.06
Panama	0.02
Papua New Guinea	0.01
Paraguay	0.03
Peru	0.06
Philippines	0.09
Swaziland	0.01
Poland	0.56
Portugal	0.18
Qatar	0.05
Romania	0.19
Rwanda	0.01
Saint Kitts and Nevis	0.01
Saint Lucia	0.01
Saint Vincent and the Grenadines	0.01
Samoa	0.01
Sao Tome and Principe	0.01
Saudi Arabia	1.02
Senegal	0.01
Seychelles	0.01
Sierra Leone	0.01
Singapore	0.11
Solomon Islands	0.01
Somalia	0.01
South Africa	0.45
Spain	1.95
Sri Lanka	0.01
Sudan	0.01
Suriname	0.01
Sweden	1.21
Syrian Arab Republic	0.04
Thailand	0.10
Togo	0.01
Trinidad and Tobago	0.05

Table 1 (to be continued)

Member States	1989 Scale of assessments %
Tunisia	0.03
Turkey	0.32
Uganda	0.01
Ukrainian Soviet Socialist Republic	1.25
Union of Soviet Socialist Republics	9.99
United Arab Emirates	0.19
United Kingdom of Great Britain and Northern Ireland	4.86
United Republic of Tanzania	0.01
United States of America	25.00
Uruguay	0.04
Vanuatu	0.01
Venezuela	0.57
Viet Nam	0.01
Yemen	0.01
Yugoslavia	0.46
Zaire	0.01
Zambia	0.01
Zimbabwe	0.02
Total	100.00

Source: General Assembly, UN doc. A/43/981.

Table 2

List of States and Entities that ratified the Convention as of 30 June 1990

State / Entity
Antigua and Barbuda
Bahamas
Bahrain
Belize
Botswana
Brazil
Cameroon
Cape Verde
Côte d'Ivoire
Cuba
Cyprus
Demcratic Yemen
Egypt
Fiji
Gambia
Ghana
Guinea
Guinea-Bissau
Iceland
Indonesia
Iraq
Jamaica
Kenya
Kuwait
Mali
Mexico
Namibia
Nigeria
Oman
Paraguay
Philippines
Saint Lucia
Sao Tome and Principe
Senegal
Somalia
Sudan
Togo
Trinidad and Tobago
Tunisia
United Rep. of Tanzania
Yugoslavia
Zaire
Zambia

Discussion

Görner:

I would like to say a few words about the first discussion within the Special Commission 4 of the PrepCom concerning the administrative arrangements, the structure and financial implications of the International Tribunal for the Law of the Sea. The Special Commission discussed this important item on its agenda, on the basis of a working paper which was prepared by the Secretariat (UN doc. LOS/PCN/SCN. 4/WP8), Dr. *Nelson* referred to this document just a few minutes ago. This document was based on the organizational structure of the Tribunal as set out in the Convention on the Law of the Sea and the Secretariat had, as requested by the Special Commission, also taken into account the structure of existing international tribunals and courts and their experience, notably that of the International Court of Justice. In preparing the paper, the Secretariat took into account that, unlike the International Court of Justice, the Tribunal would not be an organ of the United Nations but rather an independent judicial body. It would not, therefore, have recourse to the support services and facilities that are available to the Court.

In discussing the paper, the Special Commission was in full agreement for the need for maximum economy, in the establishment and the functioning of the Tribunal while maintaining the highest possible level of efficiency. Several delegations pointed to the possibility that in the first few years after the entry into force of the Convention, there might not be more than 60 parties who would have ratified the Convention and therefore that is why it would be unlikely for the Tribunal to be faced with a large caseload in its initial stage. In the course of the discussion, many proposals were made to reduce the costs for the Tribunal. One of the proposals, which provoked a lively discussion, was that the general contributions of the Parties to the Convention to the budget of the tribunal should be minimized by providing that those who use the services of the Tribunal, whether States Parties or not, make a special contribution towards its costs, which would be applied in the reduction of the assessed contribution of States Parties. It was pointed out, that the application of the so-called "user pays" principle would also be useful in discouraging unnecessary applications to the Tribunal. With regard to any contribution towards costs required from States Parties generally, it was suggested that the Tribunal should be an operating expense of the Convention, so that, to the extent that the Authority would earn revenue, the costs of the Tribunal would be a charge against that revenue except to the extent that costs would be contributed by users. This suggestion was opposed by other delegations who pointed out that it ran counter to art. 19 of the Tribunal's Statute which provides that the States Parties to the Convention and the Authority contribute to the budget of the Tribunal, on such terms and in such a manner as shall be decided at meetings of the States Parties, while in cases where an entity other than a State Party or the Authority is a party to a case submitted to it, the Tribunal shall fix the amount which that party is to contribute towards the expenses of the Tribunal. The introduction of the principle of "users pay" would discourage the parties to a dispute from submitting it to the Tribunal. That principle would also encourage them to present their case to the International Court of Justice, which does not apply such a user principle.

In the discussion, many delegations pointed out that the proper functioning of the Tribunal must be assured and, for instance, they drew attention to the need that the remuneration of officials and other staff members of the Tribunal should not be below the level of other comparable institutions, in order to make employment with the Tribunal attractive to highly qualified specialists.

The Special Commission also discussed the question of an appropriate mechanism to control the budget of the Tribunal. One suggestion was that such control could be exercised by the Finance Committee proposed for the International Sea-Bed Authority on the grounds that both the Assembly of the Authority and the meetings of the States Parties (convened under art. 19 of the Statute of the Tribunal) would be composed of the States Parties to the Convention. Yesterday, Dr. *Nelson* referred to this interesting proposal. It was argued that the Authority's Finance Committee could very well be entrusted with control over the budget of the Tribunal without curtailing its independence. Another supportive argument was that since the Authority would in any case contribute to the budget of the Tribunal, the Finance Committee would have to review the Tribunal's budget as part of its review of the Authority's expenditures. This idea was supported by a few delegations on the grounds that it would make the establishment of a separate control mechanism superfluous and thus saves costs. Opposing this suggestion some delegations favoured the creation of a separate finance committee. Such a committee, they felt, should be appointed by the Meeting of the States Parties. Attention was drawn to the fact that in the interest of maintaining the independent status of the Tribunal, the Convention explicitly provides that it is for the Meeting of the States Parties and not for the Assembly of the Authority, even though both are constituted by the same States, to decide on the terms on which States Parties and the Authority would contribute to the Tribunal's budget and on the manner in which they would do so.

Allowance would also have to be made for the fact that there would be no mining activities on the sea-bed in the foreseeable future, which is why the time of commencement of future activities of the Authority and the Enterprise was somewhat uncertain. Consequently, a situation might be imaginable where the Tribunal assumes its functions without a finance committee of the Authority having been established. Besides, a finance committee of the Tribunal composed of a small number of experts would not impose a heavy financial burden on the States Parties. Other delegations proposed that the Tribunal should follow the practice of other international organizations and that the budget of the Tribunal be submitted to the United Nations for review by and recommendations of its budgetary bodies such as the Advisory Committee on Administrative and Budgetary Questions. Recourse to such a review mechanism of the United Nations would ensure that the independent status of the Tribunal would be maintained while the establishment of a cost-causing separate finance committee for the Tribunal would be avoided. There was agreement in the Special Commission on the need for an effective control mechanism for the budget of the Tribunal which should in no way affect its independence while ensuring that it would be as cost-effective as possible. The nature of such a mechanism is to be the subject of further discussions at the summer meetings of the 8th session when the Special Commission will continue the consideration of the institutional structure, the initial staffing needs and the financing of the Tribunal.

In preparation for the summer meeting the Secretariat was requested to present a document setting out a scenario for a tribunal, whereby it could begin its work on a reduced scale with a view to gradually increasing its size parallel to its increasing workload. We will also discuss the question of the number of the official languages to be employed by the Tribunal since that would have direct impact on costs. Yesterday, Ambassador *Jesus* spoke about the possibility that the Tribunal, in its initial stage, could be financed from the regular budget of the United Nations in order to ensure the proper functioning of the Tribunal from its very beginning. I think that the Special Commission should explore all these alternatives in preparing the appropriate recommendations concerning the financing of the Tribunal.

Morrison:

I have just a remark that relates to the Hamburg Tribunal. As I told you I am not a specialist in sea law, but a specialist in International Court of Justice law. One of the factors that I see looking at the Hamburg Tribunal is that for the foreseeable future that tribunal is going to be very underworked. It is going to be underworked both because of the number of ratifications and because of the absence of the deep sea-bed activity, which was supposed to be the core of its activity. It will also be underworked because it is for most matters only an optional tribunal in the first place and most of the ratifying countries are not going to choose to go before it rather than before other kinds of more regional tribunals, or arbitration, or using other dispute resolution procedures. It seems to me that one of the things that needs to be looked at in the budgeting process is the level of activity of the tribunal and how to make the expenditures consistent with that level of activity at least for perhaps the first decade. I do not have any solutions for that, but I know that Ambassador *Görner* made some comments in that direction. That may be one of the large avoidable expenditures.

Kateka:

Well, I would like to start by making a general comment and then ask a question. Generally, the current trend in the international community is towards fiscal responsibility. We are all concerned about costs and in the PrepCom even more so, especially for establishing an efficient and cost-effective Authority. That is why we do find it a bit of a perplexing affair at the moment to find some States, especially the friends of the Convention, still worried about the questions of costs and the financial burden which they will bear if they have to ratify the Convention. I would hope that this fear has been taken away by the statement of our chairman of September '89 and the general trend which is emerging and therefore this (the financial burden) should no longer be an excuse for not ratifying the Convention. People should talk of other reasons but not the financial burden emerging from an unwieldy Authority. Now, having said that, I wish to ask a question and I put this to Dr. *Dicke* who referred to the question of preferring independent commercial firms to audit the funds of the Authority, as opposed to the UN procedure, where we have a board of auditors composed of the representatives of States. Now, my question is: Does this proposal emerge from the experience from the UN board as not being satisfactory, or is it something which is being done in the hope that it will be a better way of auditing the funds of the UN and how would this commercial firm be chosen from which system and how would you come across it? Would it not be better to choose experts from different countries as long as they are qualified auditors, not politicians, or lawyers for that matter?

Dicke:

My proposal for the auditing procedure of the Deep Sea-Bed Authority was not founded on criticism of the related UN procedures although the UN procedures show some difficulties. The UN auditors serve for a three years' term; an auditor, however, needs at least two years to get familiar with the whole United Nations system to such a degree that he is enabled to submit proposals to enhance the organization's efficiency. My point was the economic impact of the activities of the Sea-Bed Authority seems to require auditors which are quite familiar with economic questions in general. And therefore, my proposal was to choose private firms. To prepare the appointment of auditors, the Secretary-General could prepare a list of adequate private firms and it would then be up to the Finance Committee to appoint an auditor for, let us say, five years. This suggestion is in accordance with the practice of other international organizations which perform operational activities; as an example the World Tourism Organization comes to mind.

Kapumpa:

I would like to make just a few quick comments. It looks like my good friend *James Kateka* has stolen the words out of my mouth. I had a similar problem on the budgetary issue with Dr. *Dicke* and I will pursue it slightly differently. The first comment is really to underline what has been quoted here. I presume the quote is referring to a statement that I was privileged to make on behalf of the Group of 77 last September, under page 60 of the delivery by *Dolliver Nelson*. What I really want to underline or re-emphasize is that this is a position as we see it in the G-77, that we do not at all envisage establishing some colossal bureaucratic Authority where all the retired civil servants of the international world will be sent to retire in peace in Jamaica! No, we are looking for a lean, mean, small but effective, efficiently-run system. We do not want 20 people to go there if two people can do the work. And in this new world of computers, we may need even less people to do the work, so the question of financial burdens arising out of the ratification of the Convention does not arise.

Secondly, I think it is important to re-emphasize this point because earlier in the day (and it is a pity that I never had a chance to talk about the joint venture issue) a comment came from among our colleagues on the floor, that one of the advantages of a joint venture is that the Enterprise is likely to be one colossal, inefficient operation and therefore if it were to go in joint operation with the private enterprise then it would be run more efficiently. I tend to disagree with that. There may be an advantage in the joint venture system between the Enterprise and some other, but I think we should not present it as a reason that the Enterprise may be inefficient because it is large and so on. I think generally everybody is in agreement that nobody wants to run an institution that carries passengers. People want to run an institution that has "doers," people who are actually there because they have a job to do. I cannot see (if we are talking about the Authority) how we would create an Enterprise that would be burdensome to anybody. So I think that is one point which ought to be emphasized.

As for the issue of the budget, I have two points. One has already been raised and the answer has been given, but to follow-up on that is that I tend to think that most organizations do not have auditors who are permanently doing the job. Five years looks like a long period of time in which to have anyone doing that job. Usually international organizations, at least those that I am familiar with, appoint auditors once every year, it may be the same one but there could also be a change. In other words, a properly qualified auditor does not need two years to get to know the system of an organization before he can audit, otherwise he becomes part of the system and then he cannot properly audit. One would expect, therefore, that unless we are talking about re-establishing an internal audit system within the Authority, then we might as well use the system in the UN that we have become accustomed to. However, if we are trying to move away from that system, then the system of appointing new auditors may perhaps be something to look at.

Secondly — I apologize in advance if I did not understand what Dr. *Dicke* said — but I have understood him as having said that the voting power system must somehow be related to the amount of contributions made to the Authority. If I understood him correctly, it looks like he was saying that the power-sharing system must be tilted towards those who contribute more. If that is so, and I did not misunderstand him, then I did not understand the justification for that arrangement and I would like him to comment on that.

Dicke:

I would like to comment on the last question. My presentation rested upon two premises: first, for a certain time the Authority will be financed by contributions; and second, the efforts in the process of establishing the Deep Sea-Bed Authority must be directed towards making the whole system universally acceptable and working efficiently and effectively. Therefore, it seems necessary that also possible main contributors, which is to say: main contributors according to the scale of assessment of the United Nations, will accede to the Convention. Given the universality of the Convention I would suggest a blocking vote for main contributors in financial matters. "Blocking vote" does not mean that these main contributors should have a majority in the Finance Committee, therefore I limited the number of main contributors to five. Under the decision-making procedures as proposed by my presentation, the special interest of main contributors are protected as long as the Authority is financed by contributions. On the other hand, an over-representation of main contributing countries in the Finance Committee can be avoided. That is quite important because the Finance Committee has, of course, other functions, too. It has not only the function to give recommendations on budgetary matters, but it has to negotiate on several issues. The extra-budgetary functions could be hindered by a majority of main contributors. I would not regard it to be fair, if the Finance Committee would have 15 members and 8 of these members were main contributors. I think a Finance Committee in that composition would not work. Therefore I tried to find some compromise which gives not a majority, but a blocking vote to main contributors in financial matters.

Maquieira:

Even at the risk of repeating what has been said by others, I think it is useful to hammer home again the trend of thought within in the Group of 77 in the Preparatory Commission about the size and volume of the Authority in the Enterprise. We are well aware of the level of activities which might be conducted on the sea-bed, once the Convention comes into force which may be just prospecting if that. We are also well aware that it may take some time before the Enterprise can get organized and the idea behind the Group of 77 is to establish a small Secretariat in proportion to the level of activity that has been conducted, something similar to what already exists. There is, for example, an office of the Secretariat in Kingston, Jamaica, which has, I think, three or four professionals and some supporting staff, which could be the basis for the initial Authority once the Convention enters into force. There is no need to organize a huge apparatus if you do not have the activity to justify it. From my perspective, I think that the basis of what will be the Authority once the Convention enters into force is already there, and it is, as I have mentioned, this office in Kingston which is headed by one person and has I think three or four, *Dolliver Nelson* can clarify this point, but it has two or three or maximum four professionals and some supporting staff which would be more than sufficient to deal with the mandate of the Authority once the Convention comes into force.

Also, as was said at some stage this morning and by *Dolliver Nelson* yesterday, the Preparatory Commission is also working towards a very small initial Enterprise with, of course, the built capacity to expand as activities and mine sites also expand. But it is not a question of the position of developing countries as it has been stated here by *James Kateka*, by *Mumba Kapumpa*, by myself, it is a general trend of thought within the group of countries of the Group of 77 regarding having a small enterprise and a very small secretariat to deal with the problems of the Convention once it is in force. So I think that even at the risk of repeating myself, this has to be hammered in, because it comes up again, and again, and again. Now, I am speaking in English and I have spoken in other official languages about the same thing with people who speak those languages, but nevertheless, they bring up the question again, and again, and again. So, as long as they continue to bring up the question we will continue to say "no", we think the following.

The other issue I would like to pick up is the question of weighted voting in the Finance Committee. I think that we have seen over the last few years a trend towards a more fiscal behaviour in international organizations, which has brought budgets down, has made them more manageable, has allowed for the concerns of donor countries to be accomodated. Now, I do not favour a blocking vote in the Finance Committee as such. I may consider the possibility of establishing a consensus at a prior stage, as is done, for example, in other international organizations. But I do not think that donor countries should have an instrument to direct the path the organization follows by having a blocking vote at a certain point. I do think that this trend toward a fiscal behaviour in the international organizations will increase and that will have to be trusted as such. Perhaps the possibility of some sub-committee may be considered, a sub-committee that prepares the budget to look at, into a form of approving it by consensus. But I would not be in favour of a blocking vote in the Financial Committee itself.

Lagoni:

I would like to refer to a point which Prof. *Morrison* made earlier. Talking about the International Tribunal for the Law of the Sea, which will be established in Hamburg, he mentioned that the LOS Tribunal will probably be the most unemployed court which has ever existed. I am not quite sure, whether I can share his skeptical prediction. We should not forget that besides the deep sea-bed issues, which we have discussed here for the last two days — a useful, but nevertheless future-oriented exercise, because there will be no deep sea-bed mining in the near future —, there are also important other parts of the Law of the Sea Convention from which the Tribunal soon may well be considerably employed. Let me give you two examples. One probable field of future litigation are delimitation issues. Remembering that the International Court of Justice has become particularly busy in this field of the law of the sea since the 1969 *North Sea Continental Shelf* cases, one can easily imagine that the parties of numerous maritime delimitation issues may find it particularly useful to submit their case to a Tribunal, which is especially established for law of the sea matters. Another field of activities of the Hamburg Tribunal is provided by art. 292 of the LOS Convention, which deals with the prompt release of detained vessels and crews upon posting a reasonable bond or financial security. The flag State may, as a last resort, apply to the Tribunal for prompt release of the ship and its crew. I can imagine that there may be quite a number of such cases, especially with regard to environmental laws and regulations in the exclusive economic zone. Therefore it seems unlikely that the International Tribunal for the Law of the Sea in Hamburg will be unemployed or underemployed at all.

Wolfrum:

I have only a brief remark which applies to all the speakers. It has been pointed out by Ambassador *Kapumpa*, Ambassador *Kateka* and by *Cristian Maquieira*, that the Authority is going to be lean, small and very efficient. However, even such an Authority will create administrative expenses and, hence, the question has to be answered: Who will have to pay for them? According to art. 160, para. 2 of the LOS Convention, these administrative expenses, whether they are substantial or not, will be distributed among the member States according to the scale of assessment of the UN. This reference causes some uncertainties as long as the membership to the Law of the Sea Convention has not yet reached universality. Which is your preference, if the Convention enters into force one year after the ratification or adherence of 60 members not including the major contributors in accordance with the UN scale of assessment?

Nelson:

The States who have ratified the Convention are not the most wealthy and it may be difficult for several developing States who will be parties to the Convention to increase the dues they are already paying to international organizations, especially where, as in the case of the International Sea-Bed Authority, there is no tangible benefit to be gained for some time. Given the difficult financial situation which would certainly face the Authority, the possibility of the Authority retaining the link which has been established between the Preparatory Commission and the UN needs to be examined. This link can be maintained until the Authority becomes financially self-supporting.

Dicke:

Theoretically, the Authority could apply the approach as taken by Specialized Agencies. The practice of international organizations within the UN family is to count the membership (say for example of the FAO which has a smaller membership than the UN has) up to 100% related to the UN membership and then increase the assessed percentage of each member's contributions, accordingly. In this case, however, one would have to introduce a regulation into the scale of assessment of the Authority which limits the highest contribution to 25%. It is doubtful, however, whether this solution could raise sufficient resources to run the Authority. My strong plea for the universality of the Convention was, *inter alia*, to overcome this very uncertainty.

Valle:

May I make an additional comment on the same issue and though speaking in a personal capacity, I will make a case for my own country. You have assessed the list of contributions, the percentages for the UN contributions and *Dolliver*'s document and you will note that Brazil pays 1.45% and at least until last year was the 12th biggest contributor, the first 11 obviously being developed countries. Therefore, the criteria established by the UN are questionable in my view. I will not go into the UN case, but if we think about the Authority, if the Convention comes into force with the limited number of 60 members and congregating the developing world, then of course the burden on my country, if the scale of assessment used in the UN is transposed to the Authority, would be obviously unbearable, both politically and economically. Moreover, we would go beyond the 25%, so this obviously would mean that we would have a legally impaired Convention and a financially unviable Convention. So the answer is obviously that we have to strive towards universality.

Kapumpa:

I am not really sure, whether I should make this comment, but I think the question Prof. *Wolfrum* asked is not only tricky, but it goes to the very heart of what we hope will happen on the question of the universality of the Convention, I have been looking at the paragraph he so kindly referred to, that is art. 160, para. 2 (e), which discusses, among other things, the functions of the Assembly and it says, among other things, that the Assembly is to assess the contribution of members to the administrative budget of the Authority, in accordance with an agreed scale over an assessment based upon the scale used for the regular budget of the UN. And further that the Authority shall have sufficient income from other sources to meet its administrative expenses.

Two things arise from this. Firstly, that whatever methodology is used to determine the contributions, it will be temporal, until such time as the Authority has to pay for itself. Number two is the question of who are the members? Now, I take that, as not referring to the members of the UN *per se*, but as referring to members of the Authority. The usage of the UN scale, which has now been questioned by our chairman, my brother and colleague from Brazil, is not absolute. I will venture and stick my neck out by saying that perhaps the paragraph is not stating that all members of the UN will have to pay contributions to the budget of the Authority. I think it is saying that all members of the Authority will contribute to the budget of the Authority. And how will they pay? We will use the UN scale. Obviously, the assumption, when this was drawn up, was that every member of the UN would be a member of the Authority. But now we know better. However, I think it will simply mean that there will be more burden imposed upon Brazil, on Zambia, (I am not sure whether we are 25th on the scaled list of UN contributions or whatever), but there will be more burden put on those of the UN members who are also members of the Authority. But I do not think it will require other members of the UN, who are not members of the Authority, to contribute.

Rao:

I would just like to make a brief comment on the presentation made by Dr. *Dicke* this morning, especially as regards the Finance Committee. The Finance Committee, which is not provided for in the Convention, is being conceived as a subsidiary organ. And this morning he rightly said, that the composition, functions and decision-making are interrelated and have to be considered together. But if you look at the rôle of the Finance Committee it will be mainly to advise and recommend on financial and technical matters. And I believe the Finance Committee will consist of technical and financial experts, who will be able to advise in a competent way the decision-making bodies. If this is so, where is the need to have a decision-making mechanism within the Finance Committee?

Jesus:

I have two points, I believe they are both comments. The first one is with respect to what Dr. *Dicke* said, the question of decision-making in the Finance Committee. He advises us to consider a blocking procedure for those that are considered major contributors. The Finance Committee in principle is supposed to be an expert body and experts are experts. You do not keep them by vesting them with a blocking vote capability. That is a political power that should be entrusted to member States. At the same time as an advisory body to recommend whatever issue to the political bodies, in the instant case to the Council and the Assembly, they are supposed to make their findings on the basis of technical aspects. So it would be really difficult to envisage that kind of possibility at that level. If your idea for a blocking vote is to be considered at the level of the Assembly or the Council then things would become even more complicated. Therefore, I would stop short of making any comment on that possibility. Now, I believe that you mentioned this morning in your intervention (you made a brilliant and detailed exposé) the experience of the United Nations system especially in the context of the 1986 budgetary reform. And you mentioned that the consensus procedure was reconfirmed as far as the CPC is concerned in dealing with the budgeting process of the United Nations. I believe that such a similar approach might prove to be more useful to give a guarantee to those major contributors than your proposal of "blocking capability."

Now, on the second comment, with respect to the funding of the Authority in the beginning, on the assumption that the body will not be universal in the sense of having, as it was intended to have, all States as members of the international organization which will be the Authority. And here in fact we might have some problems if that is to happen. I hope that we will be able to solve the problems of Part XI at least in political terms before the entry into force of the Convention, so that at least the majority of those industrialized countries that are potential major contributors, if not all of them, will be parties to the Convention a short while after its entry into force. But even when the internal processing of the ratification or the accession process takes some time that goes beyond the entering to force of the Convention, and on the assumption that there is a political compromise already achieved as regards the rest of the problems with Part XI, then I would not see any problem, politically speaking, for us to agree that perhaps the United Nations would fund the Authority until those countries join the Convention, on the assumption that they will be joining the Convention, since the political problems of Part XI have been addressed. And that should be seen favourably, if we take into account that the Authority was meant to be a universal body and the fact that while the expenses are to be borne only by those that will be members of the Authority in the beginning of its existence, the resources to be earned by the Authority out of the resources of the sea-bed, are supposed to be shared amongst mankind because they are the *common heritage of mankind*. If you do not see it as expenses for everybody and find a way of sharing the expenses amongst everybody, even if they are not parties formally speaking, then it becomes really difficult to think that those that are members of the Authority will pay for the expenses and then when it is producing resources everybody will have access to the resources. That will introduce necessarily a financial imbalance.

Perhaps, one of the ways, if there is no other way, to compensate those that paid for the expenses and to facilitate the existence of the Authority in the beginning, is when the Authority commences to produce resources, they will be compensated in a pro rata manner for the expenses that they paid, that in principle would have been shared by everybody, had the body been universal from the beginning. There are a lot of ways that can be envisaged. What is important right now is that we address the issues at hand, which are the problems of the system.

Platzöder:

I have a question for *Dolliver Nelson* and a few remarks concerning the paper prepared by the UN Office for Ocean Affairs and the Law of the Sea, which he has presented. I see that the paper is very general in nature and I must say, its a little bit disappointing in view of the fact that delegations to the Preparatory Commission have asked for years for a revision of the study done by the Secretariat in 1981. My question would be, is that paper the answer which so many delegations have asked for and are expecting?

Now, I have a few comments to make. The paper also addresses the expenses of the Tribunal and I do not see a phrase mentioning that one part of the problem is settled, namely the costs of housing the Tribunal. My government offered a long time ago to provide the premises and the building. The offer of the government is contained in many official documents, among them are two reports by the Secretary-General to the General Assembly in 1988 and 1989. I would have expected at least a small footnote explaining that because of the offer of the Federal Republic of Germany, which is contained in a letter dated 9 February 1987 from the Chairman of the Delegation of the Federal Republic of Germany addressed to the Special Representative of the Secretary-General for the Law of the Sea (UN doc. LOS/PCN/80, 12 March 1987), the costs for the Tribunal will be lowered to an appreciable extent.

In the paper you presented reference is made to a document of Special Commission 4, and here again I must say I am also a little bit disappointed about the wording. The wording in para. 2 refers to the existing institutions. But during the last session of PrepCom in Kingston we discussed this paper in the Special Commission 4 under the chairmanship of Ambassador *Görner* with quite satisfactory results. There was a very broad consensus among the delegates that we really have to do much more work on the question of financing the Tribunal. The document was not acceptable as presented, mainly because the document does not follow the structure of the ICJ or other international courts and tribunals. For instance, the registrar draws a very high salary from the very beginning, there is an unnecessary increase of professionals and an unacceptable decrease in the ranks of secretaries and interpreters. The proposal made by the Secretariat does not meet the generally agreed approach that the institutions established by the Convention shall be effective and also cost-effective.

Let me make a last remark. When we talk about the work for the future Tribunal, it is always forgotten that the Convention provides for compulsory dispute settlement procedures. Of course, the Tribunal in Hamburg will have to compete with the International Court of Justice and also with the arbitral tribunals to be set up by the Convention. Now, since these tribunals and courts will compete with each other, my government, which is going to be the host country for the Tribunal hopefully, has given a lot of thought to it. I think the host country is okay, the seat in Hamburg is okay, and also the site at the Elbchaussee. An international architectural competition was held, and we have now a design for the building, and I myself have tried to add as much as I can. I started collecting books for the library, because I think, the library is the heart of such an institution. I must say, that collecting books for a couple of months is very interesting and also revealing, you can see who is going to support the Tribunal. It might come as a surprise to most of you, or maybe not, that I got most of the books so far from American, Soviet and British colleagues. I just wanted to say that I have seen many encouraging signs that the Tribunal will be a success when it comes to dispute settlement and I think we should build on that.

Picht:

I understand that your interest is in funding and the contributions the governments have to make to get the Enterprise started. Let me take a long-term and, perhaps, an optimistic perspective. Suppose the Enterprise is generating revenues and suppose these revenues are larger than the costs. What are we doing with the profits? Are we distributing them according to the formula which is used for contributions right now? Well, this would not be sufficient, as you know, whenever profits are generated there is a large appetite to get more of these profits. I imagine that whatever the Enterprise is doing it has some market power in the respective markets and it could easily extract rents from these resources.

Zegers Santa Cruz:

Dr. *Dicke* referred or implied, but did not go back to the financing of the Authority. The ratifying States could perhaps pay the same percentage that they would pay at the UN, and the rest could be left to the budget of the UN, because the philosophy was that everybody should be a member and that those would be fair percentages.

Lilje-Jensen:

I have a very brief factual observation concerning the paper presented by Mr *Nelson*. In Table 1, the figure given for Denmark is .01. I am able to confirm that the correct figure is 0.69, so probably the figure .01 applies to Djibouti. It must be a typing error.

Dicke:

I can be very brief. I thank Ambassador *Jesus* very much for his comments and his observations; I am in full conformity with his view. My intention was to show, first of all, that one cannot concentrate on one single decision-making procedure at one single point of the overall process of budgetary decision-making, but that one has to take into account the decision-making process as a whole. Against this background, I referred to the UN procedures of budgetary decision-making as an agreed and overall accepted model of budgetary decision-making within international organizations. Perhaps I should have elaborated more on the CPC procedure as introduced by GA res. 41/213. In my opinion, this CPC procedure can be regarded as a compromise between those who stress weighted voting and those who insist upon the "one State, one vote" model without any limitations.

And this may be an answer to the question of Mr *Rao*, too. Mr *Rao*, I slightly disagree with your observation that expert bodies within the UN system are always bodies deciding on the basis of expertise. With regard to the UN, we know a lot of expert bodies, which due to their composition and due to their functions essentially are political bodies which actually fulfill functions beyond expert advice and consultation. The ACABQ is such a body. The ACABQ takes great influence on the UN budget. It was my intention to combine the ABACQ's functions with those of the CPC into one committee, the Finance Committee.

A last remark: in my view, our discussion has made a strong call for the universality of the Convention. As it was the underlying philosophy of my presentation to put emphasis on the desirability of a universally accepted régime of deep-sea mining. I thank all participants very much for their contributions.

Nelson:

I was going to remark that the financial implications for States, arising from their becoming parties to the Convention, have in fact prevented certain States from becoming parties to the Convention. We often get enquiries from States as regards the financial obligations of their becoming parties to the Convention. The Secretariat will produce a paper on financial implications for the next session of the Preparatory Commission. I may point out that it is not an easy task to produce such a paper. It is a case of relying on certain assumptions and it is always difficult to predict the future. Moreover, such an exercise will have political implications. I am grateful to Dr. *Platzöder* for her comments on the paper with respect to the Tribunal. I promise her that I will convey her concerns to those who wrote the paper and I am sure that these observations will be included in the printed version in the document. That also goes for the *Lilje-Jensen*'s remarks.

The Production Regulation of the Law of the Sea Convention: An Assessment and Alternatives

Klaus Brockhoff*

I. The Essence of the Law of the Sea Regulations

Article 151 of the United Nations Convention on the Law of the Sea attempts to establish production policies for deep sea mining operations within the so-called interim period. The exact intent of the article is not readily comprehensible. This is evident from the numerous papers prepared by the Secretariat[1] as well as by delegations for the sole purpose of explaining its content. Many sample calculations have been presented to demonstrate the consequences of the regulations. The difficulties related to problems in understanding have been aggravated by the adoption of a text that is different from the one suggested by statistics experts. The present formulation leads to unwanted consequences if taken at face value and without giving due consideration to its history.[2]

It is, however, possible to capture the main ideas of art. 151 in three diagrams. The determination of the production ceiling depends on the empirical development of nickel consumption and its reflection in a trend line which is a statistical artifact of the original nickel consumption data. If the growth rate of this trend line is greater or equal to 0.03, art. 151, para. 4 (a) and (b) (i) is to be applied (*see* Figure 1). It constrains future nickel consumption to the sum of 60% of the estimated growth of nickel consumption from the year prior to the year of the earliest commercial production to any year of the production period, and the total difference between the estimated nickel consumption for the year prior to the earliest year of commercial production and the year prior to the commencement of the interim period, which is usually assumed to occur six years before

* Prof. Dr. *Klaus Brockhoff*, Institute for Research in Innovation Management, University of Kiel.

1 For a very recent paper see: Preparatory Commission for the International Sea-Bed Authority and for the International Tribunal for the Law of the Sea, Special Commission 3, Production Authorizations — Explanatory Note Prepared by the Secretariat (UN doc LOS/PCN/SCN. 3/1989/CRP. 9, 16 August 1989).

2 *Klaus Brockhoff*, The Production Ceiling according to the United Nations Convention on the Law of the Sea, in: Weltwirtschaftliches Archiv 120 (1984), 541-557. This point could easily be corrected by substituting the following text into the last sentence of art. 151, para. 4 (i): "The linear regression of the logarithm of actual nickel consumption shall be referred to as the original trend line."

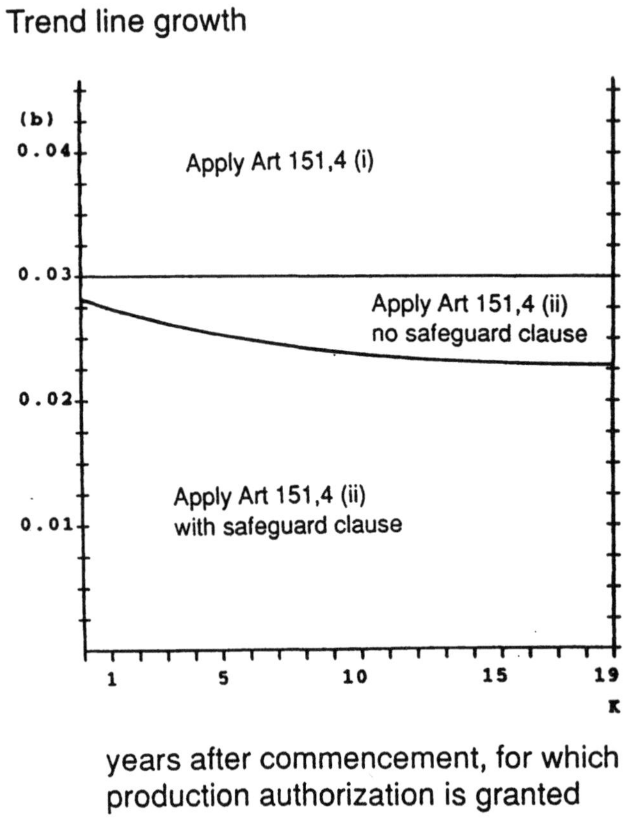

Figure 1: Growth rate, production period, and application of various calculation schemes

the earliest commercial production (*see* Figure 2). If this growth rate is smaller than 0.03, one has to apply art. 151, para. 4 (b) (ii), which establishes the so-called safeguard clause as well as the fictitious production ceiling calculated on an assumed 3% growth of the trend line where the smaller of the production ceiling values calculated from these two rules is the one to be applied. In Figure 1, it is shown that the range where either of the latter two conditions applies will depend on the year after the earliest commencement of the production. Presently the observed growth rate of the trend line of nickel consumption clearly falls into the region where the safeguard clause would have to be applied for all years during the interim period.[3]

[3] On the basis of the nickel consumption data from 1973 through 1987 we arrive at a growth rate of the trend line of approximately 1.37%.

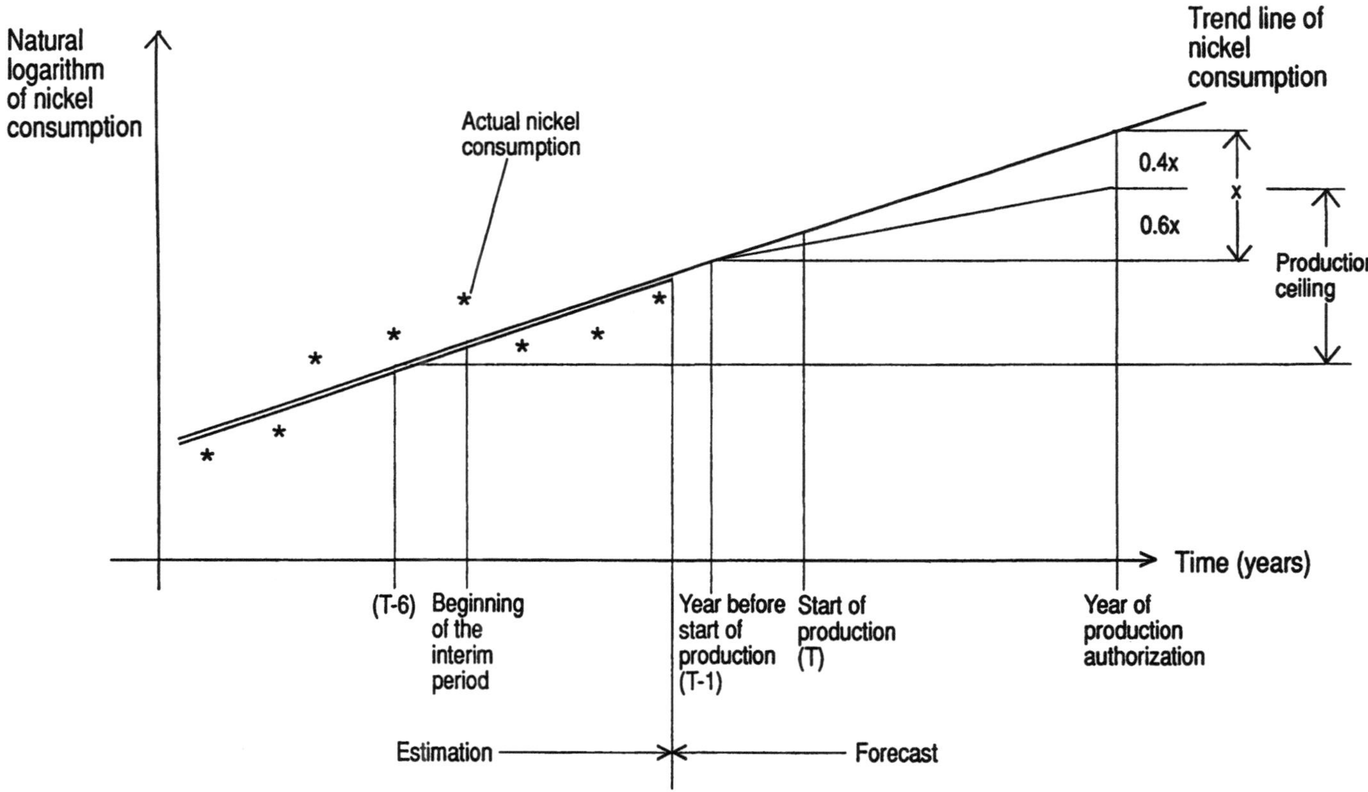

Figure 2: A schematic representation of the determination of a production ceiling for trend line growth larger than 3%

The production ceiling determines whether or not at least one operator will be granted access to an area. We assume that this operator should have the possibility to produce 38,000 metric tonnes of nickel as the Enterprise (art. 151, para. 5) and that no prior allocations have to be taken into account. We can then draw another figure which indicates under which combination of the growth rate of the trend line and the estimated trend line value for nickel consumption in the year prior to the earliest year of commercial production it would be possible to grant access to one operator beyond the activities of the Enterprise. This combination of points is shown in Figure 3. The "sawtooth-like" curve is due to the application of the three different rules referred to in Figure 1. The curve can be calculated for any greater number of areas. Also, the curve can be calculated for any other year after the commencement of the production; basically, it shifts to the left if one proceeds from year 1 to year 19 of the commercial production, which is due to the estimated or the assumed growth of nickel consumption.

From the figures, it can be noted that art. 151 is indeed a rather complicated regulation. However, once the trend of nickel consumption is known, it establishes a mechanistic procedure for determining production ceilings of polymetallic nodules.

II. An Assessment

The applicability of art. 151 can be limited by three types of problems. This article calls for the solution of a number of technical problems, it has political implications, and it has market implications. These will be dealt with accordingly.

1. Technical Problems

If the article should be applied as formulated, one would have to solve a number of technical problems.

Firstly, data collection on nickel consumption becomes a highly political problem, as the data determine the results of the calculations that are to be performed under art. 151. It is necessary to answer the questions which institution should be in charge of the data collection, what degree of accuracy should be achieved, and which legal instruments should be employed to enforce the international collection of data. The importance of these questions is highlighted by the observation that the growth of world nickel consumption from 1972 to 1986 appears to be 1.73%, while the growth of nickel production is 0.48% for the same period. It is difficult to assume that the difference is only due to stock depletion. The collection of data alone is not a small task. This task was described for instance in another context in the "International Agreement on Jute and Jute Products" of 13 November 1989. It says that the member States of the agreement "shall furnish statistics and information within a reasonable time to the fullest extent possible not inconsistent with their national legislation" (art. 31, para. 2).

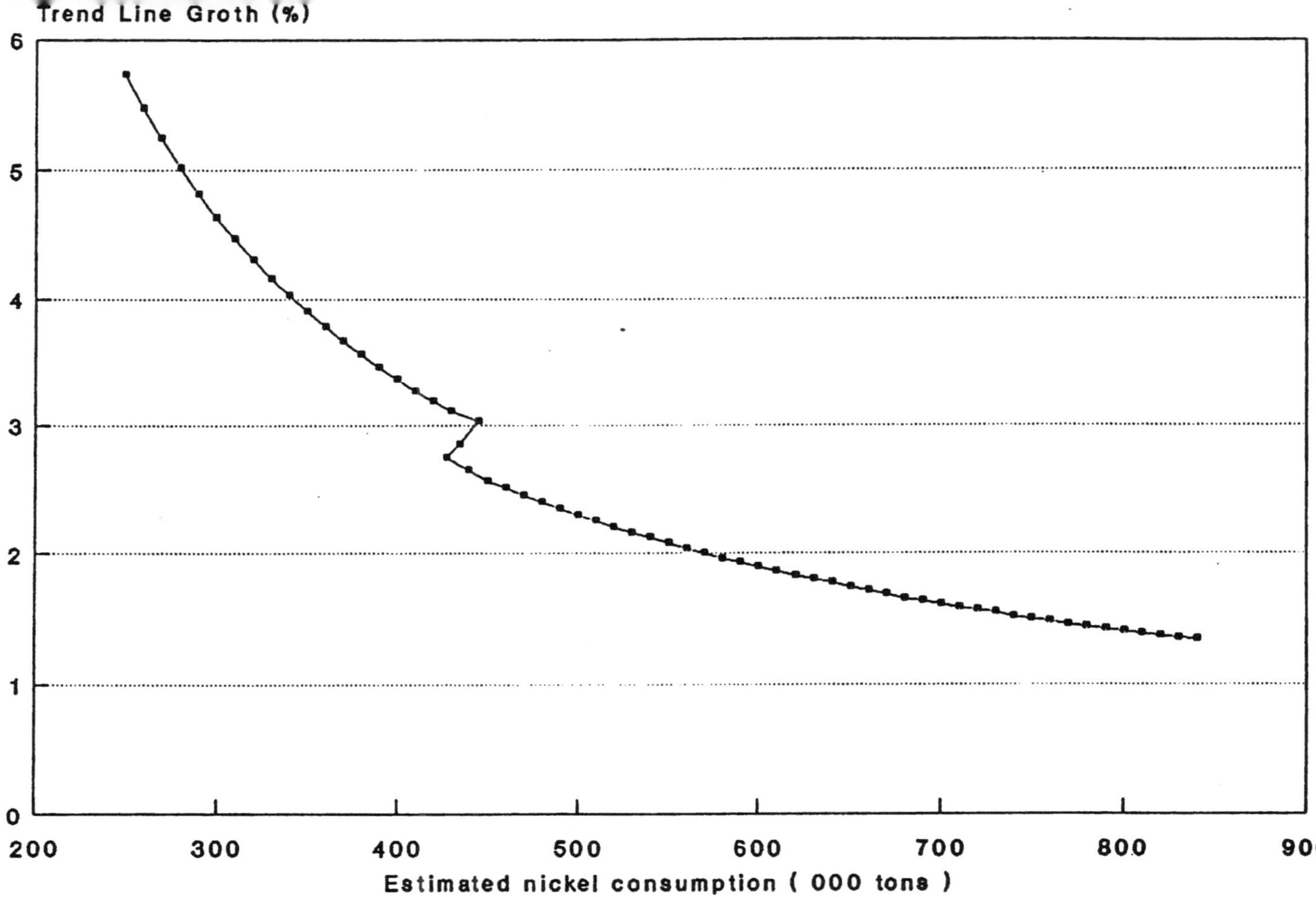

Figure 3: Conditions for production authorization in one area for the first year of production (after deduction of 38,000 tons for the Enterprise)

Here we can detect some of the problems that can arise: timeliness of data collection and transmission, degree of detail, restrictions by national legislation, and reference to the possibility rather than the necessity of a certain level of completeness and detail.

Secondly, data analysis has to be performed. This does not cause a major problem, since well tested standard software is available to perform the calculations that are needed to determine the trend line and to forecast it. However, the results of the estimation may not meet the statistical criteria for the so-called BLUE (best linear unbiased estimator) conditions. Thus, the estimate of the growth rate may not be unbiased, which leads to the question: What would be the correct growth rate? Also, the growth rate estimate may prove not to differ significantly from zero, even though its value is rather high, say beyond the 3% level. Furthermore, the assumption of a log-linear model for the representation of nickel consumption may prove to be incorrect, such that statistical criteria require the estimation of a different type of model. For those unfamiliar with statistical techniques, it has to be stressed that the possibility of calculating a growth rate does not imply that the result is reliable and valid. Reliability and validity can both be checked by statistical techniques which is a standard procedure in scientific publications, but which is rarely seen in any of the documents presented to the delegates who negotiated the Agreement. Thus, the assumption of an exponential growth of nickel consumption may have to be rejected, as other exponential growth assumptions have had to be rejected in the past. If any of the results would occur, the basis for determining the production ceiling would become meaningless.

2. *Political Implications*

Article 151 is explicitly mentioned within art. 150 which refers to various "policies relating to activities in the Area." Its subparagraph (h) decribes the specific objective of the "protection of developing countries from adverse effects on their economies or on their export earnings resulting from a reduction in the price of an affected mineral, or in the volume of exports of that mineral, to the extent that such reduction is caused by activites in the Area." Firstly, this leads again to a technical problem, namely to determine the causal link between the activities in the Area upon the economies or the export earnings of developing countries. Apart from the fact that causation is a very difficult concept both philosophically and statistically, one has to bear in mind that not only the production activities may affect some developing countries as described here. The mere announcement of activities may already create such effects. It will be difficult to discriminate between communicative effects and production related effects.

Secondly, this subparagraph uses unclear formulations in describing possible welfare losses. The term "their economies" is not operational unless better defined. Export earnings may be influenced much more by exchange rate fluctuations than by price fluctuations.[4]

Thirdly, art. 150 (h) leads to the problem of conflicting interests which has to be solved. While this article sets a rule to protect land based mining in developing countries, it does not at the same time consider the interests of the consumers of metals in all other developing or developed countries. This, however, is called for by art. 137, para. 2 which asks the Authority to act in the interest of "mankind as a whole," an idea that is repeated in art. 150 (i). It is well known that more developing countries are consumers than producers of the metals that could be produced by deep sea mining operations.[5]

Thus, establishing production policies and embedding them into a specific framework of policies leads to a considerable number of very delicate political problems due to possible conflicts of interests within the countries affected. These may be aggravated by certain implications of the production policies on the markets.

3. Market Implications

Among the policies to be considered is the "promotion of just and stable prices" (art. 150 (f)). It is only in passing in which we may note that this can hardly be achieved for two reasons. Firstly, the production authorization does not interest an operator in efficiency maximization, and might thus select one which produces at much higher prices than necessary. In fact, this would be in the interest of land based mining operators. Secondly, if demand increases, price stability could be maintained by increasing supply. This would be possible for the land based producers. For the deep sea mining operators it would be possible only within the restricted framework of art. 151, para. 6.[6] Thus, prices tend to be higher than without the constraints of the production authorizations. It remains to be shown that this is "fair to consumers" (art. 150 (f)). Tying production policies to past nickel consumption has important implications for market development.

"The promotion of long term equilibrium between supply and demand" (art. 150 (f)) should not be disturbed by the production policy. This implies that — whether or not such an equilibrium was achieved before the commencement of production in the Area — it should be achieved during the interim period. The scheme is based on the assumption that future demand grows as in a certain

---

4 This is shown with respect to the difficulties of buffer stock management by *Alexander J. Yeats*, A Note on the Functioning of International Commodity Price Stabilisation Agreements in Periods of Fluctuating Monetary Exchange Rates, in: Journal of Development Studies 23 (1986/87), 382-401 (389).

5 *Wilfried Prewo et al.*, Die Neuordnung der Meere. Eine ökonomische Kritik des neuen Seerechts, Tübingen 1982, 202.

6 *Op. cit.*, 201 at note 2.

fifteen-year period in the past, that the demand growth can be met partially by expanding land based mining operations, and that deep sea mining can and should provide for the difference between an assumed expansion of land based mining production and an assumed future nickel consumption. If actual consumption grows beyond the assumed level, this may lead to a further expansion of land-based mining activities that only in the long term broadens the basis for expanding deep sea mining. If the actual consumption falls short of the assumed level and production is not adjusted, it will lead to price cuts. Such price cuts are due to an erroneous prediction, or rather to the predictable failure in choosing an unappropriate forecasting model, and are not "caused" by deep sea mining.

Another problem of the mechanistic forecasting formula relates to the business cycle movements of demand for metals. The trend line averages consumption over the number of business cycles covered by the fifteen year period used for estimation of the growth rate. It is very likely that within fifteen years we will not observe a certain number of complete cycles. If one of these cycles enters the set of the observations only partially, this has important effects on the relationship of the forecasts to the actual developments. The inclusion of an upswing leads to a higher than average growth rate, the inclusion of a downswing produces a lower than average growth rate. These estimates cause an overshooting or an undershooting in the calculation of the production ceilings, which is in conflict with the aim of long-term equilibrium between supply and demand.

These problems become even more important if one takes into consideration that there are differences in the composition of metals contained in nodules harvested from different areas, that the grade of metal tends to vary, and that the recovery factors in the metallurgical processes differ.

Further problems are related to the choice of consuming a certain metal as the basis for determining future production of a multitude of metals as it occurs in the nodules harvested. The consumption of different metals does not grow at the same rate. In fact, taking the period from 1966 to 1981, one observes that growth of the trend line of nickel consumption was equal to 3%, the growth of copper consumption reached 2.8%, and the growth of cobalt consumption was 2.3%. Even if the production policy would achieve all its aims for nickel, this would not guarantee that the same aims could be achieved for other metals as well. This could lead to undersupply of some metals, and to oversupply of some other metals. The first case taxes the consumers, and the issue will again arise of whether this can be considered to be "fair" pricing (art. 150 (f)). The second case may lead to unnecessary waste (contrary to art. 150 (b)), and to different effects on land based producers (which would call for action according to art. 150 (h)). In fact, the Secretariat itself addresses this problem when it explains why nickel was chosen as the reference metal; however, it also mentions that the world demand for nickel, copper, cobalt, and manganese are in the proportions of 1 : 10 : 0.04 : 10.8.[7] This reinforces the necessity of discussing the aim of "just and stable prices remunerative to producers and fair to consumers" (art. 150 (f)).

4. Results

It becomes obvious that:

- art. 151 has to be seen in conjunction with art. 150 (and some other more general rules as well);
- production policies could only be applied after some technical problems have been solved;
- the multitude of aims that should be reached and that are all influenced by the production policies will lead to considerable debate, as they inevitably force political trade-off decisions;
- the mechanistic application of a retrospective scheme is not apt to stabilize markets;
- neither production efficiency nor allocative aims will be achieved by the kind of regulations suggested.[8]

Therefore, one should consider two issues: whether it is possible to simplify the structure of objectives and aims for the Authority and the Enterprise, a topic that will not be taken up here, and whether the mechanistic scheme of calculation of the production ceiling could be substituted by a more flexible and prospective approach. This line of thought does not attempt to merely cure symptoms of regulation, for instance by discussing alternatives to the numerical data that are used in the calculation of the production ceiling.

III. Alternatives

1. The Enterprise as the Only Producer

One could imagine that the Enterprise would be the only deep sea mining operator in all areas. Its operations would not be tied to the regulations previously discussed. This idea has to be ruled out as it would concentrate an enormous economic power at one point. Even if the operations of the Enterprise were controlled by an international body one could easily imagine the pressures placed upon this body or the Enterprise, and the temptations of their members. Also, the possible reduction of competition would tend to raise metal prices. The premise of the Enterprise as the sole producer is therefore dismissed.

---

7 Preparatory Commission (note 1), 3.

8 For this point *see again Prewo et al.* (note 5), 189 *et seq.*

2. *The Enterprise as a Buffer Stock Manager*

One could imagine that the Enterprise or the Authority would act as a buffer stock manager. Its task would not only be to achieve a maximum income, but also to stabilize prices. This does not seem to be a viable approach, either. Firstly, buffer stock operations are very risky and have occasionally led into severe problems[9]. They may help to stabilize prices[10] — if no systematic biases come into play — and to produce intertemporal shifts of welfare between producers and consumers[11]. However, art. 151 assumes a bias without the regulation. Also, the span between buying and selling prices of the buffer stock seems to be interdependent with the success of its operations.[12] Secondly, if the assumption of "overproduction" without the production policy regulations is correct, there will be a tendency for prices to fall. The buffer stock, acting in the interest of the land-based operators, would try to abrupt this by buying metal. If successful, this would invite continued overproduction at relatively high prices. This would not only cause problems as experienced through attempts to stabilize markets for agrarian products in the European Community, it would also be in conflict with the aims of avoidance of unnecessary waste production (because of the encouragement of overproduction) as well as fairness to consumers. The stock would require almost unlimited funds.[13] If, however, the assumption that led to the formulation of a production policy proves to be wrong, then the consumption of metals would be constrained by past production at levels lower than optimal in a welfare maximizing sense. Again, consumers would pay more than necessary, and thus constrain the development of their economies. Thirdly, "free rider" problems may occur as not all nations need become members of the buffer stock.[14]

---

9 The tin cartel is among the cases that come to mind. *Gramlich* argues that its failure was in part due to differences in the interests of producers and consumers, and the obligation of systematic intervention in the markets, again a mechanistic regulation, *see Ludwig Gramlich*, Intergouvernementale Rohstoffregimes im Zwielicht — Lehren aus dem Zinn-Debakel, in: Verfassung und Recht in Übersee 20 (1987), 486-514.

10 Econometric analyses shed doubt on the possibility of achieving the price stabilization goal at least for certain commodity agreements: *Roland Herrmann*, Internationale Agrarmarktabkommen. Analyse ihrer Wirkungen auf den Märkten für Kaffee und Kakao, Tübingen 1988; *Martin Hoffmeyer / Jörg-Volker Schrader / Torsten Tewes*, Internationale Rohstoffabkommen, Ziele, Ansatzpunkte, Wirkungen, Kiel (Institut für Weltwirtschaft) 1988.

11 *Kees Burger / Hidde P. Smit*, Long-term and short-term analysis of the natural rubber market, in: Weltwirtschaftliches Archiv 125 (1989), 718-747.

12 *Christopher L. Gilbert*, International Commodity Agreements: Design and Performance, in: World Development 15 (1987), 591-616 (594 *et seq.*).

13 UNCTAD, The role of international commodity agreements or arrangements in attaining the objectives of the integrated programme for commodities, UN Doc. TD/B/C. 1/270, Geneva 1985, 35.

14 *Loc. cit.*

Finally, intense negotiations would be necessary to determine formulae for a possible distribution of buffer stock income, the sources of funds for the operation of the stock, and the rules of procedure for the stock managements.

The most important argument, however, is that this suggestion would not solve the problem of an unrivaled use of the property rights in the areas. Therefore, the idea of the Enterprise as a buffer stock manager is also ruled out.

3. Auctions

The right to explore an area and to produce from it could be auctioned off. This suggestion has been made repeatedly.[15] It would assure maximum income to the Enterprise, given its policy of auctions, if the bidders are in competition. The bidders would take into consideration the future market developments without being tied to a mechanistic forecasting rule. Efficiency maximization would be in the interest of each bidder to increase his profits. Bidders would also use their full knowledge on the likely composition of the nodules harvested, the metallurgical processes available to them, and the likely developments of prices for various metals. If the parties participating in the auctions take into consideration their income from the sales of all the metals contained in the nodules, this will help to balance disequilibria.

The auctioning scheme could allow all interested parties to participate. This includes those who may want to protect the Area from mining activities, whether temporarily in the interest of present or future producers, or permanently in the interest of the protection of the environment, or for any other reason. The relative importance of all of these needs will be reflected in the price each bidder is willing to offer.

In order to provide for the constant flow of income for the Authority and to avoid additional financing problems for the bidders, the auction price should not be paid in a single lump sum. Rather, a stream of payments could be offered by each bidder. To facilitate matters, the Authority might announce the number of years for which it expects the payments to flow. This could be synchronized with the prospective proceeds from mining activities.

Foders[16] mentions a number of arguments that are raised against auctioning. These include the small number of participants that could lead to non-competitive prices, that might favour collusion, and a banding together of large firms to share information in order to decrease risks. The empirical evidence collected by *Hartung* on the US system of auctioning exploration and production rights in

15 *Prewo et al.* (note 4), 193; *Brockhoff* (note 2), 542; *Federico Foders et al.*, Meereswirtschaft in Europa. Rechtliche und ökonomische Rahmenbedingungen für deutsche Unternehmen, Tübingen 1989, 223 with respect to oil and gas exploration and production.

16 *Federico Foders*, Public Policy and Resource Use: The Case of Offshore Oil, in: Energy Exploration and Exploitation 5 (1987), 111-121.

offshore oil and gas fields shows that this has not occurred, which suggests that it can be avoided under proper arrangements and supervision.[17] Even the possible underinvestment of risk-avoiding bidders could be taken into account by risk-sharing arrangements, for instance by relating the auction price to future profits of the bidder. *Reece* has shown in a simulation study that such profit sharing bidding schemes lead to higher revenues from auction sales of leases than royalty or bonus bidding. However, it would "require the use of an economically rational definition of profits. Devising an appropriate accounting system may be no small task."[18]

The auction is an attractive alternative to the highly complicated and controversial regulations for the calculation of production charges according to Annex III of the Law of the Sea Convention.[19] Auctioning has been tried successfully not only in the United States for outer continental shelf hydrocarbon leases such that one can draw on these experiences. Auctioning is also considered to be superior to direct negotiations between a resource owner and potential private resource users, "which may be justified on non-economic grounds. From the point of view of economic efficiency, however, a discretionary mineral rights allocation policy can only be optimal under serious market imperfections."[20] Such imperfections can not easily be seen in the case of deep sea mining.

---

17 *Hans Hartung*, Verfahren zur Nutzung erschöpfbarer Ressourcen. Das Beispiel der Versteigerung von Offshore-Förderrechten in den USA, Tübingen 1986, 105 *et seq.*

18 *Douglas K. Reece*, An Analysis of Alternative Bidding Systems for Leasing Offshore Oil, in: Bell Journal of Economics 10 (1979), 659-669.

19 *See Klaus Brockhoff*, Gebührenregelung für den Tiefseebergbau nach der Seerechtskonvention, in: Zeitschrift für Betriebswirtschaft 54 (1984), 448-461.

20 *Federico Foders*, International Organizations and Ocean Use: The Case of Deep-Sea Mining, in: ODILA 20 (1989), 519-530 (521).

The Economic Adjustment System under Lomé, World Bank and Others: A Comparison

Denis Tytgat*

I. Introduction

1. Article 151, para. 10 of the Law of the Sea Convention indicates that "the Assembly shall establish a system of compensation *or* take other measures of economic adjustment assistance including co-operation with specialized agencies and other international organizations to assist developing countries which suffer serious adverse effects on their export earnings or economies resulting from a reduction in the price of an affected mineral or in the volume of exports of that mineral, to the extent that such reductions are caused by activities in the Area."

2. This paper will briefly present the characteristics of some economic adjustment systems presently in operation.

II. SYSMIN[1]

3. Established by the second ACP-EEC Convention (Lomé II), SYSMIN — a special financing facility for mining countries — was renewed in Lomé III and has been improved in Lomé IV signed by 68 ACP countries and the Community with its twelve Member States on 15 December 1989, to make it better suited to the ACP countries' economic restructuring requirements and provide a more flexible response to the problems of ACP mineral producers (budget 480 Mecus for 5 years).[2]

4. The purpose of the SYSMIN is to help the ACP States whose mining sectors occupy an important place in their economies and are facing difficulties that are already perceived or foreseeable in the near future. Its aims are to contribute towards a more solid and wider basis for the development of the ACP States while supporting their efforts:

* *Denis Tytgat*, Commission of the European Communities. The opinions expressed in this article are the personal views of the author only.

[1] This presentation is largely based on the text of Chapter 3 of Title II "Mining products: special financing facility (SYSMIN)" of the new Lomé IV Convention.

[2] The Lomé IV Convention is published in: The COURIER — African-Caribbean-Pacific — European Community No 120 (March-April 1990).

(a) to safeguard their mining production and export sectors by remedial or preventive action designed to alleviate the serious consequences for their economies of the loss of *viability* . . .;

(b) for States heavily dependent on exports of one mining product, to diversify and broaden the bases of their economic growth, notably by helping them complete development projects and programmes underway where these are seriously jeopardized owing to substantial falls in export earnings from that product.[3]

5. The special financing facility (which is now in the form of subsidies) shall be aimed at ACP States which export to the Community and which, during at least two of the four years preceding that of the request for aid, have derived either:

(a) 15% or more of their export earnings from one of the following products: copper (including cobalt), phosphates, manganese, bauxite and alumina, tin, iron ore whether or not in agglomerate form, uranium;

(b) 20% or more of their export earnings from all mining products (excluding precious minerals other than gold, oil and gas).[4]

Lomé IV has not changed the dependence thresholds of Lomé III, but has included two new products: uranium (on the list of products covered by the first window) and gold (in calculating overall dependence).

6. The main form of action by SYSMIN is therefore to contribute to the efforts made by the ACP countries concerned to restore the *viability* of the production capacity (even with reduced capacity, if necessary abandoning marginal activities) when that viability has been impaired,[5] as a result of the emergence of major technical, economic or political *difficulties*, whether temporary or unforeseeable, but beyond the control of the State or undertaking concerned. The damage to viability is assessed on the basis either of a drop in production or export capacities of the product in question of around 10% and/or a deterioration in its external trade balance.

7. Recourse to the special financing facility shall also be possible, if it is perceived in cases under paragraph 5 (a) above, that a *substantial fall of export earnings* from the mining product concerned, is seriously jeopardizing the completion of development projects and programmes underway. This is a new addition to the Lomé III concepts.

To be taken into consideration, such a fall in export earnings must:

(a) be caused by technical, economic or political *difficulties* and not artifically provoked, directly or indirectly, by policies and measures of the ACP State or the economic operators concerned;

---

[3] Article 214 of the Lomé IV Convention.

[4] Article 215 of the Lomé IV Convention. For the least-developed, land-locked or island ACP States, the figure given in (a) shall be 10% and the figure stipulated in (b) shall be 12%.

[5] *Loc. cit.*

(b) result in a corresponding fall in total export earnings of approximately 10% at least in the year before that of the request.

8. *The difficulties* mentioned above in 4 and 6 shall refer to disruptions such as accidents, serious technical incidents, serious internal or external political events, major technological and economic changes or major changes in trade relations with the Community.

9. The SYSMIN aid may therefore be used in different ways:

(a) when maintenance or return to *viability* of the mining enterprise affected seems possible for both the ACP State and the Community, the aid shall be used to finance projects or programmes, including the financial restructuring of the enterprise concerned, in order to maintain, re-establish or rationalize at a viable level the production and export capacity concerned;

(b) when the viability cannot be maintained or restored, the aid shall be used to broaden the bases of economic growth through the financing of viable horizontal or vertical conversion or diversification projects or programmes;

(c) when the economy is dependent on a mining product to a significant degree, diversification might be pursued even if viability can be re-established,

(d) in the case mentioned in 7 above, the objective of diversification shall be pursued through financial assistance to aid the completion of development projects and programmes under way outside the mining sector.[6]

10. Any decision to allocate funds to projects or programmes shall take due account of economic interests and the social implications of such aid in the ACP State concerned and in the Community and will be adapted to the economic restructuring needs of an ACP State.

11. The *request for aid* must include information:

(a) on the nature of the problems encountered;

(b) on the perceived or expected consequences of the disruption, both at national level and at the level of the mining enterprise;

(c) on the measures or actions undertaken or derived.[7]

12. A very detailed technical, economic and financial *analysis* shall then be made in order to assess both the eligibility of the request and the project or programme to be undertaken. This analysis shall take particular account of world market projects as well as the situation of the Community market for the products concerned. It shall also include an analysis of the possible implications of such an operation for the competing mining products of Member States and the possible implications of its non-implementation for the ACP State concerned.

13. A single decision shall be taken on eligibility and the financing proposal.

---

[6] Article 216 of the Lomé IV Convention.

[7] Article 217 (1) of the Lomé IV Convention.

III. Structural Adjustment Support in Lomé IV

14. One of the important innovations of Lomé IV is the new system of support for economic rationalisation (structural adjustment) policies of the ACP countries. The new mechanism has been endowed with a significant extra amount (1,150 Mecus) supplementing the existing instruments, which concentrate on the long-term development of the economies of the ACP countries. The financial assistance shall be given in the form of grants. This completely new chapter of the Convention should mean that the EC Commission can co-ordinate with other funders.

15. While the assistance shall support the ACP State's priority development objectives such as agricultural and rural development, food security, PMDT[8] and environmental protection, some principles contained in the Lomé IV are of interest:

(a) the ACP States shall bear primary responsibility for the analysis of the problems to be solved and the preparation of reform programmes;

(b) support programmes shall be adapted to the different situation in each ACP State and be sensitive to the social, culture and environment of these States;

(c) support shall be given in the context of a joint assessment between the Community and the ACP State concerned on the reform measures being undertaken or contemplated either at macro-economic or sectoral level.[9]

IV. World Bank[10]

16. The World Bank comprises two major organizations: the International Bank for Reconstruction and Development (IBRD) and the International Development Association (IDA). The World Bank comprising 151 Member countries, lends only to creditworthy governments of developing nations. The poorer the country, the more favourable the conditions under which it can borrow from the Bank (if per capital GNP is less than 790 US dollars, the IDA will intervene).

The World Bank exists to encourage the development of poor countries by providing technical assistance and funding for specific projects and policies that will realize the countries' economic potential. Although IBRD loans and IDA credits are made on different financial terms, the project criteria applied by the two institutions are identical.

17. Recent information indicates that the loan commitments for fiscal year 1990 (ending June 1990) reached 20.7 billion US dollars (IBRD 15.2; IDA 5.5),

---

[8] Processing, Marketing, Distribution and Transport.

[9] *See* Article 244 (a), (b) and (i) of the Lomé IV Convention.

[10] *See*: The World Bank and International Finance Corporation Documentation.

compared to 21.3 billion US dollars in 1988. For fiscal year 1991, the loans should reach 23 billion US dollars (17 for the Bank and 6 for IDA).

18. During its first two decades of existence (from 1944), two thirds of the assistance provided by the Bank went to electric power and transportation projects. Although such infrastructure projects remain important, the Bank has diversified its activities in recent years as it has gained experience and acquired new insights into the development process.

19. In 1980, the Bank has introduced the "Structural Adjustment loans" (SAL), as a way to help some developing countries to cope with a difficult economic environment by making policy and institutional changes made necessary by the rising cost of oil and falling terms of trade for some exports. They were formulated in conjunction with the stabilization programmes supported by the International Monetary Fund (IMF). The main objective of structural adjustment lending is to facilitate the restructuring of a developing country's economy so as to provide the best basis for economic growth on a sustainable level within 3 to 5 years. Loans support programmes that are intended to anticipate and avert economic crises through economic reforms and changes in investment priorities.[11]

These loans have represented up to 32% in 1989 of the total loan commitments of the Bank, but have diminished to 19% in 1990; they will lower slightly in the next years, as the Bank will concentrate its efforts on development projects.

V. Regional Development Banks[12]

20. These banks have been created in order to accelerate economic and social development in different regions of the world: the Asian Development Bank, the Inter-American Development Bank (IDB) and the African Development Bank. Requests from developing countries can be filed to the Bank of its region.

VI. Common Fund

In the future, the second Account of the Common Fund could receive the candidature of the International Sea-Bed Authority in order to be recognized as an International Commodity Body (ICB).

---

[11] *Loc. cit.*

[12] Preparatory Commission for the International Sea-Bed Authority. Information on existing international or multilateral economic measures which could be of relevance to the work of Special Commission 1 (UN doc. LOS/PCN/SCN. 1/WP. 5 of 29 August 1985).

VII. Conclusion

Mr *Satya N. Nandan*, in his speech made in Noordwijk aan Zee in the Netherlands on 12 June 1989,[13] indicated that:

> it will be necessary to address the problems of developing land-based producer States of the minerals affected by sea-bed mining. A possible solution for these States could be found by creating an economic assistance fund, rather than a compensation fund, from a percentage of the net proceeds of mining and by strengthening the anti-subsidy provisions for the commercial stage of sea-bed mining.

All anti-subsidy provisions are under negotiation in the GATT (General Agreement on Tariffs and Trade) within the Uruguay Round.

The proposal of Mr *Nandan* to ensure economic assistance to the developing countries instead of compensation is quite acceptable. But it should not be financed by imposing a further tax on the net proceeds from mining. The beginning of sea-bed mining has partly been delayed due to the heavy financial burden imposed on the operators for a commercial operation. When sea-bed mining has actually commenced, the Sea-bed Authority might financially participate in the economic adjustments, probably not in the first years of sea-bed mining when economic adjustment might be most necessary, but later when revenues are obtained from the operators.

In the experience of the Community and its Member States, economic adjustment assistance measures are so complex and so difficult to select, since they have to be seen in the framework of the world economy as a whole, that the detailed economic, financial and technical analysis and implementation of adjustment measures should be left to the competent organizations, such as the World Bank or the regional banks, in co-operation with the Authority.

---

[13] Speech by *Satya N. Nandan*, Under-Secretary-General for the Law of the Sea, Office for Ocean Affairs and the Law of the Sea, United Nations, at the 23rd Annual Conference of the Law of the Sea Institute and the Netherlands Institute for the Law of the Sea, Noordwijk aan Zee, The Netherlands, 12 June 1989.

Discussion

Zegers Santa Cruz:

The production policy is one of the issues which has been questioned of the sea-bed régime. Prof. *Brockhoff* said he would not refer to the history and philosophy of how arts. 150 and 151 came into being. It is important to have a word about that history and philosophy, only a word.

The considerations of the sea-bed at the United Nations and the Conference on the Law of the Sea began under the assumption that negative effects for land producers on the sea-bed would be prevented or minimized. This comes all the way from the very first report of the Sea-Bed Committee in 1968 up to the Convention itself, through several resolutions of the UN. Some of them approved, if I am not wrong, by a consensus.

Now, it is good to recall how the formula was achieved. Instead of limiting production on a case-by-case basis or any other — I would say socialistic formula — a market formula was devised; and the market formula was equivalent, in a way to an insurance policy for the land producers. The experts determined that the metal which was decisive in the production of manganese nodules was nickel. And the fundamental thing then was the demand on nickel. Therefore, a formula for an insurance policy could be that a percentage of the growth of the demand of nickel be authorized. It was calculated that more or less 60 per cent of that increase should be allowed.

Part of the understanding was that subsidies could not be mentioned. (Because, of course, prohibiting subsidies is extremely important to insure a correct operation of the market. But, some countries, including the EEC countries, opposed a direct reference to subsidies, because they were subsidizing their sea-bed mining industry. The matter could not be referred to, except on a reference to GATT negotiations. We have heard from Prof. *Tytgat* that GATT is still considering the matter.) Therefore, subsidies could not be mentioned; that is another asssumption.

Then we went into a negotiation of experts. One of the main consumers of nickel, the United States, at this time nominated several experts and one of the main producers, Canada, a number of other experts. These experts and delegates met, and they produced a formula which, like any formula, is open to discussion.

I could destroy any formula, because every formula has advantages and disadvantages. This one has been studied further, and I will come to that; the office on the Law of the Sea has a study on the formula. And the formula, according to that study seems to work to a point. The market has not evolved as it was previewed say 12 years ago, but the formula more or less, according to the experts who have worked for the UN, more or less could work.

In practice, the formula was aimed also at permitting that almost all or all the interested parties could exploit, when exploitation came. A number of 10 mine sites was thought of as a maximum possibility and that was covered.

Well, that is the philosophy of what was done. The consumers, of course, were very much taken into account, as art. 150 says. The idea was not to prevent any application at the time, which could be previewed, and the idea also was to permit a rational growth of the production. What was wanted was an insurance policy and no more. Of course, the interest of the land-based producers was not to be deleted, especially if subsidies were not going to be dealt with.

As to the calculations, Prof. *Brockhoff* has asserted that the formula does not function to protect copper. Well, there are plenty of UN studies and private experts studies, copper experts studies from our countries, which say otherwise, but I have a lot of respect for this assessment. But the experts have different and differing points of view. The effects of the formula, of course, again are a matter for review, the effects it has, may or must have. A study of the office on the law of the sea, if I recall correctly, seems to come to the conclusion that the formula, applied today, could permit six to eight mine sites, that touches on the practical problem which we have before us. Leave aside theologies, philosophies, calculations and experts. We need to know whether the mine sites will be sufficient or not. Now, if the formula should give, in the opinion of the UN Study (I am not an expert), six to eight mine sites, and we wanted for instance 10 mine sites, which is the apparently foreseen, there are two solutions. One is the so-called "grandfather clause", which has been spoken of, stating that the formula cannot produce less than 10 mine sites. Another possibility is to give a flexibility to the Authority or, in case of a depressed market (which is the case now), of course, to a certain point and with objective parameters and procedures. Those are practical possibilities and not theologies or philosophies.

One final word: Ambassador *Jesus* cautioned, when he made his very enlightened statement, against trying to resolve all the problems at the same time. And he divided those problems, which had been based on Part XI. He detected two or three which could be settled now (early), to put into motion and to acquire the universality of the Convention, and others, which could be left perhaps for a 10 year period. He put this problem into the second category.

Brockhoff:

Ambassador *Zegers*, first of all it is clear that we both seem to hold entirely different views as to what the objectives of an economic system are.

I am, as you are, aware of the history of this agreement and it was very interesting that you in your very first sentences referred again to the fact that at the very beginning of the negotiations, assumptions were made to minimize effects on producers. Contrary to this, I maintain that the study of economics is a set of institutional arrangements that are to serve consumers. And it is therefore its purpose to provide consumers with goods and at prices they can afford. An economy is not there to serve the well-being of producers. Your mentioning of consumers interestingly occurred almost at the end of your intervention. This might be the reason why we come to different conclusions.

Now, you called the formula adopted here a market formula. I do not quite see how one can come up with such an interpretation. A formula that necessitates allocation and that limits production could in my mind not be called a market formula. Because the market could demand something quite different from what is being laid down in the formula.

In passing, you related to subsidies, an item that I did not touch upon, however, I do not advocate subsidization of anyone who would for instance participate in the auction scheme that I have suggested. Then, you made mention of a number of studies that were performed by the Secretariat and various delegations. I have read quite a number of them. But I cannot see how one can conclude that, as you say, the formula "works". The formula has not been put into effect until now and the only thing one can say is that there are people who speculate that the formula might work but no one has proved that it would work. However, we have a lot of proof on how a market system of auctions could work. I have made reference to some of these cases and this could certainly be discussed in greater detail. In fact, the Secretariat in its statement from last year (LOS/PCN/SCN. 3/1989/CRP. 9) has mentioned a number of problems that would arise from the formula such as those that relate to tying the formula to just one type of metal.

You referred to the copper production problem. In fact, I do see difficulties here. Copper demand in the world is about 10 times the demand for nickel. And I do not quite see how if you would have achieved market equilibrium for nickel demand, this would at the same time mean that you would achieve an equilibrium in the copper markets which are ten times larger than the nickel market. I have no imagination for this suggestion.

Finally, you have been referring to the necessity, rather the assumed necessity of a division of problems. This in fact is a very questionable suggestion. Economics deals very much with inter-related issues. Everything seems to be related to everything else. Economists have come to think about economic systems in terms of optimizing the whole system and not dividing it into parts and sub-optimizing these. And in that respect I would advocate for not partitioning the problem areas but to look at them as being interrelated. I would like to add that as long as the calculations for the taxation of the companies according to Annex III remain unchanged, I do not believe that we are discussing the real problem. As an investor, I would not be interested in investing in a venture that promises such a low return after taxes at a relatively high risk.

Kapumpa:

Let me begin by immediately saying that I am neither an economist nor a mathematician, so I already have a disadvantage in looking at the issues. I am a lawyer and as we were told during lunch, lawyers tend to find problems where they do not exist. But in this particular case, I am a lawyer coming from a copper mining country. Zambia depends almost entirely on copper for its survival. But my being here rests to a great extent on the copper which enabled me to attend school. Both issues which have been so eloquently tackled by Prof. *Brockhoff* and my good friend from the Preparatory Commission, *Denis Tytgat*, are such that they are very close to my heart, in the sense that they touch on issues that we have been discussing for quite sometime.

Let me first begin by referring to the brilliant exposé by the Professor. Indeed, I think to look at the formula mentioned in the Convention without looking at its history poses some problems in the sense that the formula itself is very dry unless you are led to why it was introduced in the first place. I think, it has been already explained as to its history. But what I would just like to emphasize upon is the fact, I think, that the intention was to protect not just land-based producer States for the sake of protecting a producer. No, and this is not the economics that they teach in schools. We are not talking about the protection of a producer, we are talking about offering some protection to a developing, weak economy producer State. Now, even in economics, there has to be a difference between the United States of America as a producer and the Gabon as a producer. If economics does not show this difference, then economics is wrong. Now, having said that, it means that the philosophy behind the formula cannot be ignored. Once, it is ignored, then the whole premise is wrong.

Secondly, I am quick to admit that the formula is not 100% foolproof. Indeed, the fact that it was based on nickel consumption and production only rather than copper, cobalt and maganese and other possible minerals which may be extracted from the polymetallic nodules from the sea-bed area, suggest of course that it may not be 100% foolproof. But I believe the intention was that using that formula it may be possible then to use the same formula to make assumptions on possible consumption levels and production levels for the other minerals. Whether the assumption is quarrelsome is another matter. But then lawyers do not use the assumptions. It is economists. So I think we need to be told whether or not in fact whether in models used by mathematicians and economists, they do not use the word "assumption". I have always believed that they do, whereas in law we state what is there.

I believe that the formula is based upon an assumption that certain things are going to take place in the event of sea-bed mining actually taking place. That means that if sea-bed mining does not take place in 1995 in 20, 30, 40, or 50 years, then all we will see is that the formula has remained as cold as it is in the Convention and nobody will spend a sleepless night over it. But in the event that sea-bed mining were to occur then you utilize it to offer some protection not just to the producer, but also to the weak economy, land-based developing producer States. And why do you have to offer this protection? Go back to the very original principle of the Convention, the *common heritage of mankind*! As particular States which are developing, which have a weak economy, are also part of the world which owns the resources and as they are likely to be adversely affected by sea-bed mining, you offer such countries some protection. This again means that if Zambia is not adversely affected by sea-bed mining then Zambia will not be given any protection or any assistance, and that goes without saying. That means therefore, I believe, that if indeed the argument is that the formula in the Convention does not in fact offer any protection, then I think we should be now talking in terms of what else would offer protection, if we still believe that the *common heritage of mankind* philosophy and principle must apply.

Now, the Professor did indicate some possible alternatives, some of which he dismissed and, I think, there is no need to rehash those. There was, however, one particularly interesting alternative and this is the auction. I must confess that despite the many years that I have been privileged to work in the area of the law of the sea, this is the first time that this option is being presented and when the Professor was talking, I said to myself, "I wish he could be put on the next delegation to the Preparatory Commission in New York next month, so that other colleagues would be able to benefit from his comments and views, so that we could discuss it a little bit more." But what I seem to have heard him say is that the auction system will maximize the benefits that will go to the Enterprise, now either I got him wrong and if I got him wrong I apologize. If, however, I understood him correctly then this means again that the philosophy behind this is wrong. We were talking about maximizing benefits to the Enterprise (yes, indeed the Enterprise is the creature for all of us, who have signed or ratified the Convention and so on and so forth). But such a philosophy is moving away from that original philosophy and principle of offering some assistance to developing land-based producer States.

So, perhaps, my last comment there would be, to wonder whether Prof. *Brockhoff* sees that the auction system may assist a country like mine and if so how? Or is he maintaining, as he did a few moments ago in his response, that, economics tend to lean toward the protection of the consumer, rather than developing producer. Then obviously if that is the case, I will simply say that we are operating from two different philosophies.

A very quick comment, without taking too long, addressed to Mr *Tytgat*. He and I have always had interesting discussions during the Preparatory Commission as we both attend the Special Commission 1, which we all know has been set up by virtue of resolution I of the Third Conference, which, among other things, I have said, requires that the Preparatory Commission makes studies and discusses the possibilities of determining how to assist developing land-based producer States which are likely to be adversely affected by sea-bed mining. The literature on the law itself, the Convention, is very clear. It talks about the adverse effects on export earnings and also on economies and we have had interesting arguments (as to whether we should only talk about export earnings and not about economies) which we will not go into here, but suffice it to say that I think when we talk about possible adverse effects it has to be both on economies and export earnings of these particular States. The system that Mr *Tytgat* referred to under Lomé to me suggests a similar system for the Authority. In other words, he is talking about dependence levels, he is talking about trigger levels, that is exactly what we have been saying in the Preparatory Commission, that once you have been able to prove your dependence level under the trigger level of a certain percentage which can be agreed upon, then you make your request to the Authority. The assistance is not then automatic. The Authority will then undertake studies to determine whether indeed your calculation, i. e. your request is genuine and those studies, in my opinion, would not necessarily have to be done by the Authority itself. They could ask the EEC, they could say the EEC has been operating in Zaire every day, and knows how Zaire operates or the World Bank which operates in Cameroon every day, should find out without doing studies, whether what those two countries are applying for is actually correct and genuine. And then, it will be determined whether assistance can be provided.

Now, the philosophical problem in the EEC has apparently been that the word "compensation" itself is something that they do not want to hear about and hence, I noticed (I do not know whether I heard correctly), Mr *Tytgat* stated, the quotation from Mr *Satya Nandan*, the Under Secretary-General, that economic assistance fund may sound a little better than a compensation fund. Now, if that is correct, to us, I think, whether you call it the compensation fund, or whether you call it an economic assistance fund, or whether you do not call it a fund at all, what is important is that at the end of the day, you provide some assistance to a developing land-based producer State which has proved to have been adversely affected by sea-bed mining. That is really what we are saying.

Finally one word, which does not really fit in this category of discussion, but since Mr *Tytgat* mentioned it: I would say that, within the World Bank and now the EEC under Lomé IV, there is a new issue of structural adjustment for the economic rationalization for developing countries as a basis for economic development and so on. I have some personal experience with the so-called "structural adjustment" in my country, Zambia. This term, I am afraid, sounds very innocent on paper but structural adjustment to most developing countries, particularly the sub-Saharan Africa, simply means chaos. It means the destruction of the very fabric of those societies when they try to tighten their belts. Lives have been lost whenever this has happened. You name any country, whether Zambia or Ghana or Tanzania, in any of these countries there have arisen tremendous problems and I can only hope that it is not true what some people have said that the problem has been that the IMF is like a very bad doctor: You walk in with a toothache, he gives you a Panadol, you walk in with a cut on your leg, he gives you Panadol, you walk in with a lost finger and he still gives you Panadol! In other words, he has one prescription for every ailment. We are hoping now that, because the IMF has stocked its medicine chest that it will prescribe specific medication for specific use in developing countries, and that it shall be much better.

Brockhoff:

Thank you very much, Ambassador *Kapumpa*. First you referred to history. History shows that the auction scheme was introduced at the 98th meeting of the Preparatory Commission for the International Sea-Bed Authority last year. I would certainly be willing to go further on discussing this, so that the auctioning scheme may perhaps be better evaluated.

We can learn from history just how a present situation has arisen. This does not necessarily mean that we want to perpetuate a historically given situation for the future because what we have come up with might not be the "ideal" solution. So, even if we can explain something in historical terms there might come a point in time when we say: "Maybe we have been taken the wrong arguments, maybe we have evaluated the arguments wrongly and for that reason maybe we want to start to think about this certain issue anew". This is how I perceive of dealing with the historical perspective. Now, back to your arguments with respect to protecting specifically producers in developing States: Certainly, economics tells you that this is a different issue from the issue of protecting producers in a developed State, but as far as I can see in papers that were prepared for the Secretariat as well as some other papers, there seem to be more consumers in developing States than there are producers in developing States. You are certainly quite right in saying that chaos might prevail if you have to tighten your belts even further in Africa and I can easily subscribe to that. But this means also that if you raise prices for the producers, then the consumers would have to tighten their belts and this is the problem we would have to balance out. So, maybe one should look for a production rule that would help the consumers. If additional problems arise this would have to be dealt with something like a social policy in an individual nation. You referred to the assumption that underlies the formula. I see that there are two important, but questionable assumptions. First, that there could be exponential growth of consumption of metals. This is an assumption that if you really look at it in historical terms I would like to question. There is no guaranty for exponential growth in our future. Secondly, there is the assumption underlying the present, obtaining formulation that there is no shift in consumption patterns of the various metals. This again is contrary not only to our present day experiences but also to historical experiences. The proportions by which various metals have been used in the world have changed dramatically. Each and every new technology seems to influence this proportion. This would have to be reflected in the market prices for the different metals and consequently their production, and that could certainly not be reflected in a mechanistic type of formula.

Furthermore, it might very well be that land-based producers, be they located in developing or in developed countries, would be much less affected by an auction scheme than by the presently obtaining scheme. Why that? Because, if the market is in equilibrium in terms of supply equal to demand then there would be no demand for additional sea-bed mining. If, however, the land-based producers could not produce enough (that is: demand would be higher) then there would be demand for a producing from the deep sea. If, however, the situation were reversed, there would be nobody to bid for an Area and for that reason the land-based producers could continue producing without additional competition. Therefore, I do not quite necessarily see that they should be negatively affected by the suggestion that I have brought forward. And this also relates to the benefits to be achieved from the auction. If these go to the Authority, then consequently the Authority could use all or some of these proceeds to support, for instance, land-based producers in developing countries, although this again might need considerable economic evaluation because it in itself would disturb market relationships. Maybe one could come up with such an evaluation, namely that it might be better to support a land-based producer for the benefit of its whole economy, for the stabilization of its political system or for what other reasons, rather than to let it go down the drain. This assumes that you have proceeds to distribute. Under the present, obtaining system, as I stated before, I do not see where these proceeds would come from. Under the auction system, there is at least the chance that such proceeds could be collected.

Let me add one short remark. You used the term "to prove" that an economy is adversely affected by some kind of operation. Let me just say that it is awfully difficult to come up with such proof. Causation is an extremely difficult problem and while there might be some obvious cases where we could say this is caused by that, this is not at all clear in a lot of cases. For instance, if I were just to announce that I would open up another copper mine then prices might be driven down, even if later on it might turn out that I will never open up that mine and a copper producer could easily complain that you were adversely effected by my announcement, although I have never produced anything. You will see that it might be just a communicative effect that one has to deal with. So, this concept of causation or proof is very difficult, very few studies really come up with proof in this sense. This may be disappointing for somebody who has been educated in law and who is accustomed to dealing with "proof". For those who are educated in economics, it has become their daily business.

Tytgat:

I would like just briefly to react to what Ambassador *Zegers* said about subsidies. I do not think we should enter into a long discussion, but it is very clear that what is in the Convention is the wording which we could accept. We have always considered that the Law of the Sea Convention tackles problems which are outside national jurisdiction. Subsidies would be caused on land and if there was a problem, it had to be solved by the international organizations handling it, that is GATT. The wording used in the Convention for problems of subsidies which might arise in the national area was really the best approach. Now we are faced with requests by Australia, supported by Canada and others, to really have a detailed wording within the mining code. It is very difficult at this stage to consider that sea-bed mining is a particular problem apart from the whole question of subsidies world-wide; for that reason we refer back to the GATT negotiations. We hope very much that all nations will be much more sensitive to this particular sort of subsidies and that we are able to come up with a reasonable solution.

Referring to what Mr *Kapumpa* said, it is true that we mention mainly export earnings, as this is one criterion, while the Convention speaks about export earnings and economies. In the Sysmin system, its support will be adapted to the economic restructuring needs of the ACP State concerned. We understand very well at a certain moment you will have to look not just at the initial criterion but at the whole economy. You might have for structural adjustment a list of economic criteria or factors which have to be taken into account. We wanted to avoid a discussion in the Preparatoy Commission on the "economies" as a criterion, because it is so vague. At least you have the "export earnings" criterion, which is quite clear and can reasonably be calculated. We agree that there are difficulties with the statistics, but at least it gives you the best chance to arrive at a quick answer; later you have to examine all the economic factors. We recently had a problem with Papua New Guinea where its Bougainville mine was completely closed. A study was made just on the matter of economics as the government had to face the fact that Papua New Guinea was losing approximately 45% of its normal export revenues; it was a serious situation which the government and the Community had to tackle. Then the whole economy was certainly considered.

I note a very interesting point made by Mr *Kapumpa* that the study for evaluating the needs of developing countries should not necessarily be made by the Authority. I think to some extent he could even go further and agree that the resolution of the problems, might be done by somebody else than the Authority. This is really what we are considering, because we feel that this extremely complex matter should be solved by a group of people looking at the world economy as a whole and not by people who might have a more restrictive approach.

On the matter of structural adjustment in the Lomé Convention, I would say that there is as yet no extensive experience within the Community. This is a new approach. There is one advantage (I should not insist on it because everybody would like to come to the Community). The money is granted, so this might avoid some of the difficulties Zambia has been facing with IMF. I did not mention the IMF; I just mentioned the World Bank structure and I feel that the most important loans are really the project investment loans. But I just touched on the structural adjustment loans in order to give the whole picture. They are also mentioned in some Preparatory Commission documents, so I did not want to completely forget them. But I feel that in the Preparatory Commission, we should look again at the other project loans which are not mentioned in some documents and about which some information could be given.

Koch:

I would like to address two subjects mentioned by Ambassador *Kapumpa*. He argued that production limitation for deep sea-bed mining should protect developing land-based producer countries. I do not think that this argument holds true because if you look at the share of developing countries in the production of metals concerned then you discover that in three cases the major part of production comes from developed or Socialist countries. Only in the case of cobalt the main production comes from developing countries, that is to say around 75%. In the other cases, the main protection is for developed or Socialist countries, which are producing the larger share of these metals. The share of developing countries in the production of copper is around 46% and the share of developing countries in the production of nickel and manganese is around 26% and 28% respectively. So the production policy is mainly in favour of developed and Socialist countries and not in favour of developing countries and that is a feature which causes problems to other developed countries which are consumers and net importers of these metals. If we want to protect land-based producer countries which are developing countries, then we have to look for other means.

I think that the assistance for structural adjustment could be such a means. Ambassador *Kapumpa* said that structural adjustment normally creates difficulties in the affected countries. I do not think that this is true if you look at the intention. Structural adjustment means that a country should move away from a sector which is no longer economically viable and to move into other lines of production which are competitive on the world market. And I know there are difficulties in countries like Ghana, the Ivory Coast have actually difficulties, because of the fall in prices for cocoa and coffee. There is an overproduction of these commodities. In order to decrease the dependency on the export of these commodities the countries concerned should move to the production of other goods or commodities thereby strengthening the economic basis. If you look at structural adjustment in this sense then it should not create difficulties, but it should help to solve difficulties.

Kapumpa:

I am only speaking because it is really simply that my colleague who has just spoken, referred to the fact that the formula protects much more the developed producer countries. I think the Convention actually is very specific. It refers to the protection and assistance that has to be given to developing land-based producer States which means that if a developing land-based producer State is not adversely affected by sea-bed mining then it will not require protection or assistance. It is not every developing country which will go lining up for assistance, not only those who will be able to show, and I know the word "prove" is a little bit complicated, but who will have to show through studies, through analysis that their economies and/or their export earnings have been adversely affected by sea-bed mining.

My last comment is on structural adjustment. Structural adjustment (I am pleased that our distinguished colleague mentioned this) is okay, if you look at the intention. Real life is not intention. Real life is what is in practice. The intentions of structural adjustment, on paper or in theory, are excellent, but it is the means to achieve those particular intentions which have caused problems so far, in every State in sub-Saharan Africa. In other words, structural adjustment does not just require the question of shifting figures. It also involves massive withdrawal of subsidization, usually from the staple food of these particular developing countries. This is what has caused problems, because in an attempt to reduce the budget deficit of those countries, it has meant that you remove subsidization. The idea is that you then put your savings into developmental projects. But unfortunately in almost all these countries that money has not been put into development, it has been used to pay back debt, which is owed to the international community, to the IMF, and the various Paris-club countries and London-club commercial banks.

So that structural adjustment in Africa, therefore, has meant two things: Firstly, the withdrawal of subsidization, which has meant the immediate rising of prices for all the basic commodities that the locals have to pay for; and secondly, the money that is pumped into those countries is unfortunately not for the development of projects — the money has usually gone to pay off debt. So you borrow one debt to pay off another debt and in the meantime the locals are suffering because the prices have been going up and they cannot find the money to pay those sorts of prices, that is when strife comes into the country. I am not talking in terms of economic theories. I am talking in terms of the actual, practical, physical, real-life situations that has happened in Ghana, Zambia and several other countries.

Picht:

I like to make a brief comment on Ambassador *Kapumpa*'s remark on economics. I assume that there is only one science of economics so that it is applicable whether you in the developing world or in the modern, "developed" world. What I can see is that there are certain problems in the process of adjustment. However, if I look at the provisions we were talking about, for example, the production ceilings and the provisions Mr *Brockhoff* referred to, these are not temporary measures of protection for developing countries. Instead, they are formulated as something which is permanent. This is not in accordance with what I would consider as appropriate from an economic point of view.

There is another point I want to make with respect to Mr *Tytgat*'s paper, again with respect to economic adjustment. Yes, there is a need for assistance, occasionally. Yet this Convention is in place for quite some time already and we can easily conceive there will be another five to 10 years, or even more, until actual production takes place. So the developing countries have some time to adjust to new circumstances in the market. If you are offering or advocating structural help right now, my rational response as a recipient government would be to delay adjustment until I receive grants from the European Community. In other words, I am sceptical whether you are stepping in at the right time here.

Further, with respect to the *common heritage* and Mr *Brockhoff*'s comment on the revenues from the auction system, I would like to say that it is very much in accordance with the *common heritage* principle to get high profits from auctioning, and then use these proceeds for the benefit of developing countries. I assume that the rents from auctioning rights in natural resources are even higher than everything we have been discussing so far.

Orrego Vicuña:

First a comment about the remarks that have been made particularly by Prof. *Brockhoff*. I think that there are some points where one has to look beyond the ideological issue that is of course underlying some of this debate. It is true, as he said, that the formula of the Convention on production limitation has not proven to work thus far. But it is also true that it has not been proven that it does not work. I think that the criticism levied at it has been rather unconvincing, while admitting of course that there are a number of technical difficulties. But I think that most of those difficulties can be handled in one way or the other. There is one crucial aspect that Ambassador *Zegers* raised earlier and I would like to put it in a specific question to Prof. *Brockhoff*. If you were asked about how many mine sites under the present production policy would be allowed, what would be your answer?

The second major aspect that is worth reminding us of is that this formula originated in a compromise between Canada, France and the United States, and that the developing countries were basically lured into the scheme without having participated in its origins. So if anything went wrong as it might go wrong with a very complex approach one has to look for the blame elsewhere and I have the impression that the blame was being put on countries that are land-based producers. There are specific improvements that can be introduced and that will be the point to discuss. Finally, precisely because of all this comes from quarters that were looking, perhaps, into other interests, there is one suggestion that we have been discussing here and elsewhere and I suppose that it would be also quite relevant. It is that some of the major producers, particularly the copper producers, could undertake under the framework of CIPEC, for example, a study of what would be the specific measures that would eventually be suggested for a formula of this type. Without prejudging at all what the answer might be, because it might be that the present formula is sufficient or something else might be thought of, I think that the important question is that the perspective of those that are supposed to be benefitted by the formula has not been quite at hand since the whole thing was negotiated.

Zegers Santa Cruz:

What I would like to say about the debate is that what we have is probably not a limitation. What we have is a kind of an insurance policy. An insurance policy which is designed to protect land producers, especially developing land producers, and without impairing the production or the previewed production on sea-bed mining, that is, without affecting the consumers. So, everything that has been said about consumers *versus* producers is not pertinent.

Now, what I feel is that what has been disputed is the main philosophy on which we began, that is the common patrimony or *common heritage*. Starting from that notion, it is postulated: Let us have an insurance policy which does not prejudice a development. I understood Prof. *Brockhoff* to discuss not the economics of the matter, but its philosophy. I further do not understand how his proposal of auction relates to this problem and its solution. He is proposing an auction, but I do not see how it is meant to meet this problem, that is the problem of an insurance policy with this new production, which is the *common heritage of mankind*. That is the question, the philosophical question.

The practical problem, to which Prof. *Orrego* referred, is: Does anybody believe that there will not be enough mine sites under the present formula? And if so, how many are missing in the views of people? Because I have not heard anybody saying that there could be, for instance, need for more than 10 mine sites in the foreseeable future, provided, of course, that the market changed for the better and that there was an economic interest which does not exist at the time. That is the only practical problem we have to face.

And, of course, an insurance policy is or can be perfectly consistent with a market if you apply a market formula. That is the only thing I was saying.

What is not consistent is subsidy, because it is an unfair practice, which distorts the market. If we leave it to GATT, it leads to Doomsday, because, among other things, it is related to subsidies in farms. (I hope that subsidies in farming products disappear, but I am very sceptical to whether that would happen.) You see, the Convention on the Law of the Sea was negotiated in 1982 and we are still considering in GATT the problem of subsidies. It was a reality, because many countries considered that sea-bed mining had to be subsidized, based *inter alia* on security reasons. Yes, this does distort the market, the economy, and I would claim the philosophy.

I will end by saying that we have a practical problem here. We need to find a formula which satisfies everyone. That is one in which the industry can see that it can exploit anything it is interested in if possible at this moment, and land-producers can foresee that for an eventual situation they have an insurance policy, which is consistent with the common patrimony or heritage.

Brockhoff:

First of all, I would like to turn to the statements made by Professor *Orrego Vicuña*. I do not really want to have the argument that I had with Ambassador *Zegers* to be twisted by you. Let me just respond that I stated that there is no proof of the working of the formula. It has not been applied, consequently there is no proof for it having worked. And this is exactly what I wanted to say.

Now, you raised the question of how many mine sites should be allowed, and the same question was asked by Ambassador *Zegers*. First of all, if you have a profit maximizing Authority then the Authority can determine how many mine sites it will open or it wants to put on the auction block. There may be more or less demand for that (which affects the proceeds) and this will determine how many mine sites there should be. Certainly, if you do not want to accept such a scheme because you feel not equally insured, as you prefer to use the term, then you could put constraints on the number of blocks or areas to be auctioned. There could be policies by which you would constrain the number of areas to be auctioned off for every year, for instance. This could certainly be a matter of political negotiation. This would constrain the working of the market mechanism. The British and the American cases seem to show that there is a possibility to make this work so there is a proof for this type of regulation.

Ambassador *Zegers*' argument that the present regulation is an insurance policy for developing land-producers is the real reason why the two of us do not agree. I do not accept the idea that you should have an insurance for producers. You can make adjustments or corrections for adverse economic or social effects, but I do not see that economics is an institution where producers should get any kind of insurance (other than a legal framework for their operations). The idea of insured markets is a "guilt type" reasoning. If we had proceeded like that in the past we would still be at the level of the individual craftsman producing our daily goods and our standard of living would be much lower. So I do not want to have a regulated insurance policy for the producers whoever that may be. I think that the insurance problem in a market sense is probably taken care of in an auction scheme, because if the prices are too low then there is nobody to go into sea-bed mining and the production of the land-based producers will be assured.

To conclude, I do not see that there will be a formula that could satisfy everyone. My suggestion would not satisfy everyone, and the present formulation does not satisfy everyone, either.

Tytgat:

I will try to be very brief, but there were some questions raised by Dr. *Picht* about structural adjustment loans and even by Mr *Kapumpa.* At least I can say, working for EC Commission, that we are trying not to throw the money away, and we hope very much that we will learn by the previous mistakes of others, and we will be in a position to handle this instrument. I would agree with Mr *Kapumpa* that maybe for Zambia, it has presented some problems, maybe for some others also, but if you look at the amount of money which has been allocated by the World Bank for those structural loans, even if they present some difficulties that is still a lot of requests. If you look at the 1989 report, you have a list of the different requests, sometimes going into amounts as high as 150 million dollars. When it is IDA money with much better conditions, then the amount may be low, but that is still 20 to 25 million dollars. So, certainly, the world is not perfect but at least if the countries are still making those requests to the World Bank, there must be some equilibrium of advantages and disadvantages.

On the matter of subsidies, do not come back with the agricultural products otherwise we are lost. Certainly the matter of subsidies within industry, is a very important and permanent problem which even GATT may not be able to solve. I do not think you should always put the blame on the industrialized countries. As I have said, everybody is really giving some sort of subsidy at a certain point in time; at least for sea-bed mining, it must be clear that we cannot accept any new wording as long as the GATT text has not been agreed upon. And we hope very much that this wording will satisfy all the countries involved in the negotiation of the sea-bed mining régime. I think I have not convinced Ambassador *Zegers*, but maybe he cannot be convinced on this very delicate subject.

Technology Issues in the International Agenda: A Review of Two Decades of Multilateral Deliberations in the United Nations and GATT

Pedro Roffe*

I. Introduction

This paper attempts to review 20 years of the international agenda on technology. It addresses the growing concern over technology issues, chiefly the current efforts by industrialized countries to enhance the protection of technological assets. These new trends are compared with the aspirations of developing countries in the decade of the Seventies for better access to modern technology, particularly through attempts undertaken to revise international conventions (e. g. the Paris Convention for the Protection of Industrial Property) and to set up new principles and rules in this domain (e. g. the Convention on the Law of the Sea, and the draft international code of conduct on transfer of technology).

Firstly, a general background of the multilateral negotiations that have been carried out in the last twenty years is provided. Secondly, the aspirations and objectives of developing countries in the decade of the Seventies, focusing on the revision of the Paris Convention and the draft code of conduct on transfer of technology is examined. Then, the current technology policy issues and efforts, namely in GATT, to reinforce the protection of intellectual property rights is surveyed. The following section compares the two decades of deliberations on technology questions and, finally, the last section seeks to draw some general, tentative conclusions.

One of the conclusions drawn is that the nature of the changes that have taken place in recent years — including the new political realities of the 1990s and the manner technological assets are perceived by corporations and governments — will have a major influence on future relationships in this area. The prevailing conditions for the protection of intangible goods and for the transfer of technology will be drastically different from those of the decade of the Seventies, that made it possible for developing countries to venture some far-reaching initiatives in

* *Pedro Roffe*, staff member of the UNCTAD secretariat. The views expressed in this paper are personal and do not necessarily reflect those of the Organization. The author acknowledges the valuable comments and suggestions made by *C. Correa, G. V. Koch, L. Sise* and *A. Yusuf*.

this field. The trends of the 1980s will have a widespread influence and will set the tone in designing the blueprint of the 1990s.

In this presentation, positions of groups of countries are referred to, in broad terms, as corresponding, respectively, to developed or industrialized countries and to developing countries. This, no doubt, constitutes an oversimplification of the issues, of the nature of the problems and of the actual interests at stake of individual actors. However, in many respects, the positions attributed to one or the other group of countries do represent the formal negotiating position of countries in the processes described in this paper. It goes without saying that differences in emphasis, in some cases of significance, separate countries within these two broad groupings.

II. The General Background

The negotiations on the Law of the Sea[1] were held parallel to the discussions in the United Nations Conference on Trade and Development (UNCTAD) on the establishment of an international code of conduct for the transfer of technology[2] "corresponding to needs and conditions prevalent in developing countries."[3] These countries, also in the 1970s, promoted the revision of "international conventions on patents and trademarks ... to meet, in particular, the special needs of the developing countries, in order that these conventions may become more satisfactory instruments for aiding developing countries in the transfer and development of technology."[4] The main objective of the revision, in the case of the Paris Convention for the Protection of Industrial Property, has been to improve access by developing countries to proprietary technology through the introduction of new provisions in the Convention that would have proved, in general, less cumbersome to local authorities to license patented technology not adequately used in the country. The accomplishment of the revision of the Paris Convention and the successful completion of the negotiations on an international code of conduct have faced important obstacles. Both exercises are still inconclusive.[5]

1 *See* The Law of the Sea. Official Text of the United Nations Convention on the Law of the Sea, UN Publication, Sales No. E.83.V.5.

2 *See:* An International Code of Conduct on Transfer of Technology, UNCTAD, UN Publication, Sales No. E.75.II.D.15.

3 *See* GA res. 3202 (S-VI) of 1 May 1974 (Programme of Action on the Establishment of a New International Economic Order).

4 *See* GA res. 3362 (S-VII) on Development and International Economic Co-operation of 19 September 1975 (para. 3 of Section III).

5 On the revision process of the Paris Convention, *see:* Sixth Consultative Meeting of the Revision of the Paris Convention, Geneva September 18 to 22, 1989 (WIPO doc. PR/CM. VI/1); on the draft code of conduct, *see:* Negotiations on a draft International Code of Conduct on the Transfer of Technology, Reports by the Secretary-General of UNCTAD of 5 December 1986 (UN doc. TD/CODE TOT/51) and of 23 October 1989 (UN doc. A/44/554).

The character of the debate of the 1970s has dramatically shifted in recent years. As seen by the South "... the knowledge factor appears to be the most important element in the shaping of the new international economic order, as it alters radically the state of overall equilibrium created by the century-old industrial world and the associated comparative advantage that it has enjoyed."[6] Intellectual property at large, including all its elements (patents, trademarks, industrial designs, geographical indications, copyrights, trade secrets) has become a central topic of the current international trade agenda, not only between industrialized countries[7] but particularly between those nations and the developing ones. In the latter case, a number of developing nations, as a result of bilateral trade negotiations, have strengthened the protection of intellectual property rights. At the multilateral level the focus of attention has been on the General Agreement on Tariffs and Trade (GATT) and particularly the current Uruguay Round of Multilateral Trade Negotiations.[8]

1. The Decade of the Seventies

The initiatives of the 1970s received its inspiration in research work and in a number of case studies which emphasized the rôle of technology in the development process as well as the prevailing conditions in the flow of technology to developing countries.[9] They highlighted the technological dependence of developing countries from a limited number of technology suppliers. They also underscored the lack of appropriate technological capabilities in recipient countries, a factor that hindered an adequate absorption and adaptation of foreign technology. Furthermore, technology was being acquired under terms and conditions having important economic, social and financial costs for the recipient countries.[10] The legal environment for the acquisition, assimilation and development of technology in developing countries was inadequate or at a very incipient stage.

---

[6] *Ruben Ricupero*, Trade and Technology: Issues at Stake for Developing Countries, in: Technology, Trade Policy and the Uruguay Round, UNCTAD, UN publication (UN doc. UNCTAD/ITP/23).

[7] For illustration of the above point, *see* recent broad understanding between the United States and Japan under the Structural Impediments Initiative whereby Japan has pledged to reduce the time it takes to issue patents to 24 months from more than 37 months in: The New York Times, 29 June 1990, 1; *see also infra* (note 124).

[8] The Uruguay Round was launched in September 1986 in the Punta del Este Declaration. For the origins of the Round, *see A. Jane Bradley*, Intellectual Property Rights, Investment, and Trade in Services in the Uruguay Round: Laying the Foundations, in: Stanford Journal of International Law 23 (1987), 37-87.

[9] *See in particular* early work by the UNCTAD secretariat, e. g. study by *G. Oldham/C. Freeman/E. Turkman*, The Transfer of Technology to Developing Countries, with Special Reference to Licensing and Know-How Agreements (UN doc. TD/28/Suppl. 1 and Corr. 1 (1967)); Major Issues Arising from the Transfer of Technology to Developing Countries, UN Publication, Sales No. E.75.II.D.2.

[10] *See:* Major Issues Arising from the Transfer of Technology to Developing Countries (note 9).

In brief, according to this perspective, developing countries were not sharing the vast opportunities offered by new discoveries and developments in modern science and technology.[11]

The concern over the existing situation can be illustrated by a number of initiatives adopted by some developing countries in the late 1960s and early 1970s. One important area of attention was the restructuring of the existing institutional and legal framework governing the transfer and acquisition of foreign technology. Specific policies, enacted by developing countries and also by countries such as Portugal and Spain on the purchase and licensing of technology in foreign collaboration agreements,[12] have attempted to correct some imbalances in the functioning of the market. The kind of policies which were introduced had as their main objective the establishment of screening procedures for the acquisition of foreign technology by ascertaining, namely, its contribution to the acquiring country's economy, through *inter alia* the control of restrictive practices that could affect the further local development of the acquiring firm.[13] The introduction of these policies were, in general, accompanied with changes in the industrial property system.

From the point of view of developing countries, the industrial property system was considered unbalanced.[14] Supporting this thesis it was affirmed that eighty per cent of the patents granted world-wide were owned by developed countries' corporations and that of the patents granted in developing countries a small number was actually used in domestic production (five per cent to ten per cent would have been actually used in developing countries). According to one author:

> Five-sixths of the patents currently in force in developing countries are held by foreigners and have been registered on the basis of research conducted elsewhere. In other words, these patents bear no relation whatsoever to the flow of domestic inventive activity .... In short, the incentive to domestic inventive activity given by the grant of patents is marginal.[15]

A system, as originally conceived, to effectively reward the innovator and the efficient producer was considered beneficial to stimulate innovation and the acquisition of foreign technology,[16] but not one that in practice had only acknowledged privileges to foreign enterprises that through the system, as conceived, received exclusive rights over designated markets in support of global schemes

11 *See op. cit.* (note 2).

12 Common approaches to laws and regulations on the transfer and acquisition of technology (UN doc. TD/B/C. 6/91 of 7 October 1982).

13 As already mentioned in the paper, this type of initiative was inspired in Western principles of antitrust legislation, *see infra* (note 60), and in the Japanese experience on control of licensing arrangements (*see infra*, section V).

14 *See:* The Role of The Patent System in the Transfer of Technology to Developing Countries, UN Publication, Sales No. E.75 II.D.6.

15 *See Peter O'Brien*, Developing Countries and the Patent System: An Economic Appraisal, in: World Development 2 (1974), 27-36 (36).

16 *Op. cit.* (note 14).

for production and distribution.[17] The market, under this approach, was controlled by the corporation, by maintaining it captive, without exploitation, in the expectation of future investments or licensing arrangements that often would contain restrictions that under the patent system would be legitimate but which might entail significant limitations to recipient enterprises in their technological and managerial capabilities.[18] These criticisms to the system should be seen in the light of a broad suspicion prevailing in the 1970s towards the operation of transnational corporations in developing countries.

In line with the above and with the objective of facilitating the transfer of technology to developing countries and with the purpose of reinforcing national capabilities is that the process of revision of the Paris Convention was launched. The motion of reform was also accompanied by important initiatives taken at the national level, particularly in some Asian countries (India, the Philippines) and Latin America (Mexico, Brazil, the Andean Group countries)[19] in order to give new orientations to the traditional rules governing the grant of patents.[20]

At the same time, those attempts sought to reinforce the respective national systems by introducing a number of policy instruments aimed at a better local utilization of patents through improvements in the grant of compulsory licensing and in revocation procedures. Efforts were also made to introduce in industrial property laws, or as indicated above by the establishment of a special mechanism to deal in general with the transfer of technology transactions, of provisions aimed at controlling restrictive practices in licensing agreements.

In the area of trademarks, some countries instituted a system whereby all trademark licenses should include provisions for the development of a local mark. This system of "combined marks" was adopted with the intention of remedying the technological dependency to the foreign supplier by encouraging the development of a local new sign for the identification of the articles and services covered by the license agreement; the new sign would then replace the foreign trademark, once the arrangement has expired.[21]

17 *See Ulf Anderfelt*, International Patent-Legislation and Developing Countries, The Hague 1971; *Rajagopala S. Ayyangar*, Report on the Revision of the Patent Law, New Delhi 1959; *Edith Penrose*, International Patenting and the Less-Developed Countries, Economic Journal, September 1973; *Constantine Vaitsos*, Patents Revisited: Their Function in Developing Countries, in: The Journal of Development Studies 9 (1972), 71-96.

18 *See op. cit.* (note 14); *Bernard Remiche*, Le Role du Systeme des Brevets dans le Developpement. Le Cas des Pays Andins, Paris 1982.

19 *See:* The Implementation of Transfer of Technology Regulations: A Preliminary Analysis of the Experience of Latin America, India and the Philippines, Report by the UNCTAD Secretariat, August 1980 (UN doc. TD/B/C. 6/55) and Transfer of Technology Regulations in the Philippines, study prepared by *Lilia R. Bautista* at the request of the UNCTAD secretariat, October 1980 (UN Doc. UNCTAD/TT/32).

20 *See Remiche* (note 18).

21 *See:* The Role of Trade Marks in Developing Countries, UNCTAD, UN Publication, Sales No. E.79.II.D.5. The "combined mark" initiative elicited great opposition from transnational corporations.

2. The Eighties

a) Technology as a Major Factor in International Competitiveness

In contrast to the previous decade, the 1980s can be characterized as a period of re-evaluation, particularly in developed countries, of the strategic rôle of technology in modern society[22] and of the growing importance of intellectual property.[23] If technology has long been considered an important factor for national economic development, it has become in the 1980s an essential element in creating dynamic comparative advantages and for asserting competitiveness in international markets.[24] Intense international competition has eroded what had, at various stages of recent history, been considered the hegemony of technological leaders such as the United States in a number of individual industries.[25] Technological innovation and imitation in products and processes, "the exploitation of steep learning curves and the adoption of aggressive marketing strategies have enabled newcomers to challenge the position of established firms."[26]

Constant innovation and the technology/innovation component of exports (of tangibles as well as intangibles) have become a salient feature of industrialized countries.[27] However, these same countries are losing comparative advantages in some traditional sectors and are consciously shifting their attention and resources into areas of greater comparative advantage, "... activities that are creativity-, research-, and knowledge-intensive, and therefore intellectual property-intensive."[28] In this context, intellectual property becomes "the foundation of international competitiveness."[29]

---

22 *See:* Trade and Development Report, 1987, Part Two (Technology, Growth and Trade), UNCTAD, UN Publication, Sales No. E.87.II.D.7.

23 *See Kenneth W. Dam*, The Growing Importance of International Protection of Intellectual Property, in: The International Lawyer 21 (1987), 626-638.

24 *Ricupero* (note 6), 188.

25 *Inman* and *Burton* illustrate and analyze this relative decline of the United States. For example, in 1970, the US industry held a 90 per cent share of the American market for phonographs; today it holds 1 per cent. In the area of semiconductors, invented by two Americans in 1959, the Japanese by 1986 had taken 65 per cent of the world market against 30 per cent share to the United States. This against the background that by 1983, Japanese-based firms held a share of the world market equal to that of the American based firms, *see B. R. Inman/Daniel F. Burton, Jr.*, Technology and Competitiveness: The New Policy Frontier, in: Foreign Affairs 69 (1990), 117-134.

26 Impact of Technological Change on Patterns of International Trade, UNCTAD, in: Technology, Trade Policy (note 6), 97.

27 Foreign Protection of Intellectual Property Rights and the Effect on US Industry and Trade, US International Trade Commission (ITC), Pub. No. 2065 (1988).

28 *David Hartridge/Arwind Subramanian*, Intellectual Property Rights: The Issues in GATT, in: Vanderbilt Journal of Transnational Law 22 (1989), 893-910 (895).

29 Basic Framework of GATT Provisions on Intellectual Property, Statement of Views of the European, Japanese and the United States Business Communities, June 1988.

From a more technical point of view, the emergence of new technologies has blurred the more classical distinction between inventions (normally covered by patents) and artistic works (covered principally by copyright).[30] New technologies, such as biotechnology, computer technologies (including integrated circuits designs), and methods of medical treatment "challenge the world's intellectual property system because they do not fit within the historical dichotomy between 'inventions' and 'artistic works' on which it rests."[31]

Finally, new technologies are not necessarily the result of individual efforts but the fruit of teams involving great costs. It has been argued that it will take an average of 10 years and US$ 125-160 million to bring a pharmaceutical product based on a new chemical entity to the market.[32] As recently reported, *Thompson* and *Philips*, the French and Dutch electronics groups, have agreed upon a joint investment of US$ 3.6 billion to bring the first full high definition televisions (HDTVs) to European viewers by 1995.[33]

b) Immediate Antecedents to the Multilateral Agenda of the 1980s

In the light of the above observations, — namely of placing technology and technological assets, in particular, at the top of the international agenda —, the most immediate origins of the subject of trade-related aspects of intellectual property rights (TRIPs)[34] and its inclusion in the Uruguay Round of Multilateral Trade Negotiations is a series of studies and policy statements, including those of major corporations, on the current state of intellectual property protection in the world and on the disadvantageous position faced by private firms on the protection of their technological assets in third countries.

In the case of the United States this concern has been linked to the trade deficit that, according to advocates of the new agenda, would continue to deteriorate unless appropriate international intellectual property protection could be secured.[35] Within this line of thinking it has been argued that at a time when

30 *See:* Intellectual Property Rights in an Age of Electronics and Information, U. S. Congress, Office of Technological Assessment (OTA), OTA-CIT-302 US Government Printing Office, Washington D. C., April 1986.

31 *J. H. Reichman*, Computers Programs as Applied Scientific Know-How: Implications of Copyright Protection for Commercialized University Research, in: Vanderbilt Law Review 42 (1989), 639.

32 *Op. cit.* (note 29).

33 Financial Times, 16 May 1990, 1.

34 *See Bradley* (note 8).

35 The above argument does not necessarily meets consensus. According to *Barfield*: "Most economists would estimate that the bilateral trade flows between the US and Japan would change only 10 per cent to 15 per cent at the most if all the unfair trade practices on both sides were eliminated. Trade deficits stem from the fact countries are spending too much and not investing enough . . .", *Claude Barfield*, Services, Intellectual Property and the Major Issues of the Uruguay Round, in: Georgia Journal of International and Comparative Law 19 (1989), 307-312 (307).

the United States was liberal in its policies on access to markets and technology, third countries were restrictive and protectionist. Furthermore, the inadequate or inexistent protection of intellectual property, particularly in developing countries,[36] has been an important source of "international piracy"[37] causing not only effective losses to the trade balance of the United States but serious risks for consumers exposed to products that did not respect quality control normally associated with the protection of intellectual property.[38] Furthermore, according to the views of the business communities of the industrialized countries "[a] régime that adequately protects intellectual property can help improve and expand the industrial base and standard of living of developing countries . . .."[39]

The driving forces behind this important move have been private corporations heavily dependent on the protection of intellectual property in traditional sectors of high degree of international patenting (pharmaceuticals, chemicals) and in high-technological innovative sectors where new developments have introduced revolutionary changes in the industrial process and in international competitiveness (such as in information technologies and in general in the reprography sector). They expressed the urgent need to seek international arrangements to control "international piracy" due to inadequate intellectual property protection.[40]

It has also been argued that the inadequacy of protection has been compounded by technological changes that in many instances have made it much easier to copy products, i. e. the development of inexpensive technologies for the reproduction of audio, video tapes and TV and radio broadcasts.[41]

In support of the above claims, estimates have been given of actual losses suffered by firms in terms of market and job losses. In the exclusive area of copyright, the United States copyright industry has claimed that piracy in 12 developing countries has meant for the American industry actual losses in annual

---

36 Typical example of perceived inadequate intellectual property has been the total or partial exclusion of patentability of pharmaceutical and chemical products, *see Hartridge / Subramanian* (note 28).

37 The terms "piracy" and "counterfeiting" have been used in the debate in a loose way. Counterfeiting correspond to a more precise legal situation associated to the misuse of trademarks. Piracy is a vague term that has no settled legal definition, *see Levin*, What is the meaning of Counterfeiting, in: International Review of Industrial Property and Copyright Law 18 (1987), 435.

38 *See R. Benko*, Protecting Intellectual Property Rights, Washington, D. C. 1987.

39 *Op. cit.* (note 29).

40 *Carol J. Bilzi*, Towards an International Intellectual Property Agreement in the GATT: View from the Private Sector, in: Georgia Journal of International and Comparative Law 19 (1989), 343-351 (343).

41 From an economic point of view, unlike tangible wealth, intellectual property can be reproduced and used without depriving its owner of possession or use and almost without practical limit. "Once created, the marginal cost of reproduction is often near zero." *Frederick M. Abbot*, Protecting First World Assets in the Third World: Intellectual Property Negotiations in the GATT Multilateral Framework, in: Vanderbilt Journal of Transnational Law 22 (1989), 689-745 (697).

sales equal to 1.3 billion and 95 million (US dollars) for losses in access to markets.[42] One single country has been identified as responsible for losses due to market access for the equivalent of 63 million (US dollar).[43] World-wide losses to United States industries in 1986 were estimated to range from US$ 43 billion to US$ 61 billion.[44] According to European figures, counterfeiting alone has resulted in the loss of 100,000 jobs.[45] The estimates advanced on possible losses have been certainly biased but they have added an important and appealing reasoning for the case made by the intellectual property related-industry.[46]

In the instance of the United States, the main engine behind these new proposals,[47] the concern expressed by major corporations was translated in 1984 in the adoption of the Trade and Tariff Act that provided for a number of legislative measures including retaliatory trade sanctions for "unjustifiable" and "unreasonable" trade practices of other countries that restrict the trade of the United States, including inadequate protection of industrial property rights and barriers to import of American high-technology products.[48] The 1984 Generalized System of Preferences (GSP) Renewal Act has added industrial property protection as well as the reduction of barriers to investments and services to the eligibility criteria for GSP treatment of imports from developing countries. The same approach was followed in the Caribbean Basin Economy Recovery Act of 1983.[49]

The new Omnibus Trade and Competitiveness Act of 1988[50] has expanded the battery of legal instruments that the United States might utilize to strengthen the international protection of intellectual property. The Act has placed the protection of intellectual property as one of the principal priorities of the United States' trade policy.[51] It requires, *inter alia*, the United States Trade Representative (USTR) to identify countries that deny adequate and effective protection of intellectual property; to identify "priority countries" that are the most important

---

42 *Op. cit.* (note 29).

43 The country referred to is Brazil, *see* Financial Times, 25 April 1989, 6.

44 *Op. cit.* (note 27).

45 *Op. cit.* (note 29).

46 *See Abbot* (note 41), 692 and *Carlos M. Correa*, Propiedad Intelectual, Innovacion Tecnologica y Comercio Internacional, in: Comercio Exterior (Mexico) 39 (1989), 1059-1082.

47 *See Bradley* (note 8).

48 *See Kenneth J. Burchfield*, The Effect of U. S. Trade Legislation on Intellectual Property Rights, in: International Review of Industrial Property and Copyright Law 19 (1989), 295-302 and *Robert M. Feinberg*, Intellectual Property, Injury, and International Trade, in: Journal of World Trade 22 (1988), No. 2, 45-56.

49 Caribbean Basin Economic Recovery Act, Public Law 98-67, United States, 98th Congress, 5 August 1983, in: ILM 22 (1983), 1381-1388.

50 Public Law 100-418, United States, 100th Congress, 23 August 1988, in: ILM 28 (1989), 407-492.

51 *R. Michael Gadbaw*, Intellectual Property and International Trade: Merger or Marriage of Convenience?, in: Vanderbilt Journal of Transnational Law 22 (1989), 223-242 (223).

transgressors of intellectual property rights and that do not undertake or make progress in negotiations with the USTR; and to initiate accelerated investigations under section 301 of the Act, which may lead to the taking of remedial action, with regard to the practices of the identified priority countries.

A European analogue to the Trade Acts of the United States has been the European Communities' Council Regulation of 1984 on the strengthening of the common commercial policy with regard in particular to protection against illicit commercial practices.[52]

III. The Aspirations of the Developing Countries

As outlined above, during the decade of the Seventies, under the influence of the "new international economic order" (NIEO),[53] developing countries put forward a number of proposals that in the area of technology were perceived, particularly in industrialized countries, as a major re-writing of the existing "rules of the game." The Convention on the Law of the Sea, the draft international code of conduct on the transfer of technology and the revision of the Paris Convention fall under this broad but not necessarily orchestrated design of the developing countries.

The provisions of the Convention on the Law of the Sea relating to transfer of technology correspond, in general, to the endeavours voiced in the '70s towards promoting and encouraging the transfer of technology to the developing countries under fair and reasonable terms and conditions. Annex III of the Convention relating to the "Basic Conditions of Prospecting, Exploration and Exploitation" of the resources of the sea-bed deals specifically with some of these issues. It provides for an obligation to transfer to the Enterprise[54] any technology used by a contractor in carrying out activities in the Area under the contract.[55] These provisions of the Convention on the Law of the Sea, among a number of other outstanding questions, constituted for the United States a major stumbling block in the Law of the Sea process. It was viewed that:

> Under the Draft Convention, with certain restrictions, the Enterprise, through mandatory transfer, is guaranteed access on request to the sea-bed mining technology owned by private companies and also technology used by them but owned by others. The text further guarantees similar access to privately-owned technology by any developing country planning to go into sea-bed mining ....[56]

---

52 *See* Council Regulation (EEC) No. 2641/84 of 17 September 1984, in: ILM 23 (1984), 1419-1424.

53 *Supra* (note 3).

54 Under art. 170 of the Convention on the Law of the Sea, the Enterprise shall be the organ of the International Sea-Bed Authority which shall carry out activities in the Area.

55 *See* art. 5, para. 3 (c) of Annex III.

The Convention on the Law of the Sea, in the limited field of technology and particularly on the basic conditions of prospecting, exploration and exploitation of the resources of the sea-bed and ocean floor and subsoil area thereof,[57] was concerned with broad questions of access to technology for the Enterprise for the benefit of developing countries. The provisions of the Convention in this domain[58] go far beyond the mere aspirations for fair and reasonable terms and conditions on the transfer of technology. In a way, the objectives were analogous to those originally addressed by the developing countries in the process of reform of the Paris Convention for the Protection of Industrial Property aiming at better access to patented technology through the liberalization of the prevailing rules governing the grant of compulsory licensing.

On the other hand, the draft code of conduct, even if originally shadowed by concepts such as the *common heritage of mankind*,[59] was basically striving at setting general rules on the terms and conditions for transfer of technology arrangements. This latter undertaking had its roots in the traditional body of antitrust legislation prevailing in most industrialized countries.[60]

The above-mentioned manifestations found their origin in the concerns shown by developing countries on their technological gap and technological dependence *vis-à-vis* developed countries. This was clearly advanced in the Programme of Action of the New International Economic Order[61] and more specifically in the Charter on Economic Rights and Duties of States.[62] Article 13 of the Charter embodies the general tenets and the global aspirations of developing countries on transfer and development of technology. Under the Charter: "Every State has the right to benefit from the advances and developments in science and technology

---

56 Concerns as identified in the review made in the US Congress of the draft Convention, *see Bernard H. Oxman*, The Law of the Sea: The tenth session (1981), in: American Journal of International Law 76 (1982), 1-23.

57 *Loc. cit.* (note 55).

58 For other provisions of the Law of the Sea Convention on science and technology and transfer of technology, in general, *see* art. 144 (transfer of technology) and Part XIV on Development and Transfer of Marine Technology (arts. 266-278).

59 *See* original draft code of conduct submitted by the Group of 77 which proposed for the preamble of the code the following paragraph: "Convinced that technology is a part of universal human heritage and that all countries have the right of access to technology in order to improve the standards of living of their peoples." Report of the Intergovernmental Group of Experts on an International Code of Conduct on Transfer of Technology on its First Session (8 to 19 November 1976), UNCTAD (UN doc. TD/AC. 1/4).

60 *See D. Miller/J. Davidow*, Antitrust at the United Nations: A Tale of Two Codes, in: Stanford Journal of International Law 18 (1982), 347; *Wolfgang Fikentscher*, The Draft International Code of Conduct on the Transfer of Technology, Munich 1980; and *Guillermo Cabanellas Jr.*, Antitrust and Direct Regulation of International Transfer of Technology Transactions, ICC studies, vol. 7, Weinheim/New York 1984.

61 *Supra* (note 3).

62 *See* GA res. 3281 (XXIX) of 12 December 1974 (Charter of Economic Rights and Duties of States).

for the acceleration of its economic and social development." The Charter also provides that all States should co-operate with a view "to evolving internationally accepted guidelines or regulations for the transfer of technology, taking fully into account the interests of developing countries." The elaboration of such guidelines or regulations would have materialized in the conclusion of such instruments as the Convention on the Law of the Sea, the revision of the Paris Convention and the code of conduct on transfer of technology. The Paris Convention and the code of conduct were supposed to address those goals in more global terms. These two more general exercises are reviewed, with some detail, in the following sections.

1. The Revision of the Paris Convention

The Paris Convention for the Protection of Industrial Property of 20 March 1883[63] sets minimum standards to ensure appropriate protection to industrial property, namely through the principles of national treatment, independence of patents, priority rights, measures to correct abuses which might result from the exercise of the exclusive rights conferred by the patent, protection to well-known marks and rules governing unfair competition in the area of trademarks. The leading importance of the Convention has gone far beyond its present membership of almost 100 countries; it has influenced and shaped almost all national laws dealing with the protection of patents and trademarks.[64]

The Convention does not deal with all technical aspects of protection, a number of important questions are left to domestic laws to tackle, such as the subject-matter of patentability, the rights of the patent holder and the duration of the exclusive rights conferred to industrial property owners.[65] The Berne Convention for the Protection of Literary and Artistic Works as Revised at Paris in 1971,[66] contrary to the Paris Convention, contains more specific standards of protection, such as a minimum copyright term, establishment of moral rights of authors and the lack of formalities for obtaining copyright protection.

As already suggested, the national and some of the regional initiatives undertaken by developing countries were accompanied by efforts to revise the Paris Convention.[67] The broad objective of that process[68] was to revise the international

---

63 For the official text of the Paris Convention for the Protection of Industrial Property, *see* WIPO publication 201 (E).

64 *See:* Paris Convention Centenary 1883-1993, WIPO publication 875 (E).

65 *See G. H. C. Bodenhausen*, Guide to the Application of the Paris Convention for the Protection of Industrial Property, BIRPI, Geneva 1968.

66 Berne Convention for the Protection of Literary and Artistic Works, original text of the Paris Act (1971) as amended in 1979, WIPO publication 287 (E).

67 *See:* The International Patent System: The Revision of the Paris Convention for the Protection of Industrial Property, UNCTAD (UN doc. TD/B/C. 6/AC. 3/2).

68 *Supra* (note 4).

standards, taking into consideration the interests of developing countries.[69] The key aspects of the revision process, launched in 1975, were mainly placing on equal footing, in the Convention: the treatment of patents and inventors' certificates; the revision of art. 5A dealing with domestic legislative measures to control possible abuses of the patent monopoly; the establishment of preferential arrangements for developing countries; the revision of art. 5 *quater* (importation of products manufactured by a process patented in the importing country); and the revision of some of the provisions dealing with trademarks.

For the purposes of this presentation, the following sections will deal with the issue of inventors' certificates and the questions related to art. 5A of the Paris Convention.[70]

a) Inventors' Certificates

The issue of inventors' certificates in the revision of the Paris Convention is a valuable pointer to illustrate the changes that have taken place in the perception of problems in the area of technology in the last 20 years.

The subject of inventors' certificates was not a matter of general concern to the developing countries. Only a few of them (Algeria, Mexico), at the time of launching the revision process, recognized the certificates within their domestic legislation. The title was widely known in socialist countries of Eastern Europe and was primarily used by local inventors responding to the general prevailing economic philosophy of the system whereby the production was supposed to be undertaken by official State agencies. The certificate recognized an economic reward to the inventor but the actual use and exploitation of the invention was left to the State. As introduced into the revision process the equalization of patents and certificates was perceived, in general, as a political conflict led by the Soviet Union in order to obtain in the Paris Convention the recognition that this method of protection was as valid and important as patents. The full acceptance of certificates in the Paris Convention was in a way an unrealistic demand in view of the nature and features of this particular form of protection. The discussions on this item resulted in major difficulties at a conceptual level, such as the specific issue of freedom of choice between patents and certificates.

The current political realities in Eastern Europe as well as the nature of the present debate on technology — as discussed in section II above — makes the entire controversy over inventor's certificate completely *passé*.

---

69 Declaration of Objectives of the Revision of the Paris Convention, Industrial Property, Jan. 1976, 47.

70 For other issues *see:* Basic Proposals: Diplomatic Conference on the Revision of the Paris Convention, WIPO, WIPO doc. PR/DC/3 (1979).

b) Article 5A of the Paris Convention

Article 5A of the Convention provides that member countries have the right to adopt corrective measures to redress abuses which might result from the exercise of the exclusive rights conferred by the patent, for example, failure to work.

Most of the deliberations around the revision process has focused upon art. 5A of the Convention. It has been a key provision that has endured fundamental changes. For some scholars the history of the Convention has been identified with art. 5A.[71] As perceived by the developing countries, art. 5A was considered a disincentive for the local exploitation of patents. It was seen as a mechanism safeguarding, in extreme, the rights of the patent holder by providing that:

a) the importation by the patentee into the country where the patent has been granted of manufactured articles would not entail the forfeiture of the patent;

b) a patent may not be revoked before the expiration of two years from the grant of the first compulsory license;

c) the grant of a compulsory license for failure to work or insufficient working of a patent could not take place before the expiration of a period of three years from the grant of the patent or four years from the date of application, whichever period expires last; and

d) the patentee can oppose the granting of a compulsory license for legitimate reasons that could justify his inaction.[72]

Contrary to the above views and particularly under the current thinking on the need for adequate and effective protection of intellectual property rights, private firms in industrialized countries have discerned in art. 5A a major limitation to the patent holder. Article 5A of the Paris Convention would tacitly imply an obligation to exploit the patented invention in several markets. Under this view, the patent holder can be deprived of the right to trade in his invention.[73]

For developing countries art. 5A of the Convention, has not taken adequately into account the public interest. In this respect, developing countries sought the following amendments to art. 5A: That the importation of patented products

---

71 *See Casimir Akerman*, L'Obligation d'Exploiter et la Licence Obligatoire en Matiere de Brevets d'Invention, Paris 1936, at 51 and *E. Penrose*, The Economics of the International Patent System, Baltimore 1951, 78.

72 An important complement to Art. 5A is Art. 5 *quater*, added to the Paris Convention in the Lisbon revision of 1957. Article 5 *quater* deals with process patents. It recognizes rights to the inventor on imported products manufactured through a patented process. This provision is of particular significance to the pharmaceutical industry.

73 "The economic inefficiency of promoting manufacturing of every product in every country is apparent." *Richard A. Morford*, Intellectual Property Protection: a United States Priority, in: Georgia Journal of International and Comparative Law 19 (1989), 336-342 (340).

should not be equivalent to exploitation of the patent; that non-voluntary licenses, in some cases, should be exclusive; and that developing countries should enjoy a sort of preferential treatment to reduce the time-limits provided for in the Convention for the granting of non-voluntary licenses as well as of the power to de-link the possible revocation of the patent to the concession of a license.[74]

2. *An International Code of Conduct on the Transfer of Technology*

The driving forces towards the establishment of a code of conduct were those developing countries that had introduced new policies in the area of transfer of technology in the period 1969-1974.[75] In championing the formulation of a code of conduct, developing countries stressed the advantages to be gained for their economies as well as the opportunities that would be opened to small and medium-sized firms in industrialized countries to participate in the international market for technology. The code would thus amount to liberalizing trade in technology, with the consequent increase in trade flows.[76]

The substantive provisions of the draft code, which emerged from subsequent negotiating conferences, fall into two broad categories: those concerning the regulation of transfer of technology transactions and of the conduct of the parties to them, and those relating to steps to be taken by governments to meet their commitments to the code. The first category of provisions, establishing certain generally agreed and universally applicable standards, covers three areas:

(a) identification and clarification of responsibilities and obligations of parties (chapter 5);

(b) determination of practices and arrangements involving transfer of technology which are to be deemed undesirable, and under what conditions (chapter 4); and

(c) the law and forum to be selected for the settlement of disputes (chapter 9).

Provisions in the draft code under the second main category — steps to be taken by governments to meet their commitments to the code — can be classified into the following three main types:

(a) provisions related to the regulation of transfer of technology transactions by States (chapter 3);[77]

---

[74] *See op. cit.* (note 70).

[75] *See J. Jeffries Counters*, Regulation of Transfer of Technology: An Evaluation of the UNCTAD Code of Conduct, in: Harvard International Law Journal 18 (1977), 309 and *op. cit.* (note 19).

[76] *See* Report of the Intergovernmental Group on Transfer of Technology, UNCTAD (UN doc. TD/B/520, para. 103).

[77] Chapter 3 of the draft code, on the basis of some broad general principles therein enunciated, recognizes States the right to adopt measures with respect to transfer of technology transactions. It is interesting to note that under the negotiations in the area

(b) provisions relating to international collaboration, on a bilateral, multilateral, regional or inter-regional basis, to facilitate the flow of technology and the growth of the technological capabilities of developing countries (chapter 7) and special treatment to developing countries (chapter 6); and

(c) provisions concerning the establishment of an international institutional machinery responsible for the application and implementation of the code (chapter 8).

Negotiations on the draft code, under the auspices of UNCTAD,[78] began in 1976 and continued for almost 10 years. The negotiations encountered numerous obstacles originated in completely divergent views and philosophies on how to deal with the transfer of technology process. Hostile to the purposes of developing countries, developed countries, particularly major technology producing countries, perceived the code as an interventionist instrument which aim was to endorse bureaucratic structures in developing countries that would hinder the transfer process instead of facilitating it. However, it is relevant to note that notwithstanding the major obstacles faced during the negotiations, the process presented an opportunity to sort out a number of problems and to produce a large degree of agreement on significant portions of the draft code.[79] Its influence as a guide in the adoption of national policies, particularly in developing countries, has been immense.[80]

IV. The New Agenda of the Decade of the Eighties

In response to the new concerns of the decade, as outlined above, the agenda of the 1980s has been permeated mainly by the objective set forth by industrialized countries of reinforcing, nationally and internationally, technological assets. This overall strategy included the targeting of some selected countries for bilateral action aimed at improving domestic intellectual property protection. The targeting was not only centered on developing countries. Japan was also the focus of attention in the area of software protection when that country was considering the enacting of a *sui generis* protection that deviated from the conventional system of copyright already adopted by the United States. In the case of developing countries, a number of countries in Asia (Korea, Indonesia, Thailand, Singa-

---

of TRIMs in the current Uruguay Round, measures regulating technology transfers are to be considered as TRIMs, primarily because they tend to reduce imports, *see A. A. Fatouros*, Possible Standards for Trade-Related Investment Measures, in: Technology, Trade Policy and the Uruguay Round (note 6), 201-222 (205).

78 *See P. Roffe*, Transfer of Technology: UNCTAD's Draft International Code of Conduct, in: International Lawyer 19 (1985), 689-707.

79 *See:* Draft International code of conduct on the transfer of technology, as of 5 June 1985, UNCTAD (UN doc. TD/CODE TOT/47) and Report and notes by experts on the outstanding issues (UN doc. TD/CODE TOT/52).

80 *See op. cit.* (note 12).

pore) and in Latin-America (Argentina, Brazil, Chile, Mexico and the Andean Group countries) has been the center of bilateral action that in some specific cases has resulted in fundamental changes in their domestic legal systems.[81] It should be noted, that the targeted countries of the 1980s coincide, in general, with those countries active in the design of the 1970s strategy described above.

At the multilateral level, an important development was the instantaneous reaction of the international community to one specific area of concern to industrialized countries, derived from the trends in the United States[82] and Japan of protecting semiconductors chip designs through statutes based on reciprocity principles and not under the traditional national treatment philosophy prevailing in most intellectual property arrangements. Under the aegis of the World Intellectual Property Organization (WIPO), a diplomatic conference adopted on 26 May 1989 in Washington D. C. a Treaty on Intellectual Property in respect of Integrated Circuits. Overcoming the initial resistance of developing countries, the Treaty was finally accepted but with the opposition of the United States and Japan.[83] The objections of the United States to the Treaty were mainly on the following grounds: the proposed minimum duration of eight years of protection; the liberal rules with respect to compulsory licensing; the insufficient dispute settlement mechanisms; and the absence of compensation for innocent infringement.[84]

1. Intellectual Property and the Multilateral Trade Negotiations

The bilateral drive, forcefully pursued by the United States as important as it could have been, had limitations. The trade leverage was important for countries dependent on exports to the United States. Therefore, it was considered essential to follow a broader but complementary multilateral approach. The American multilateral initiatives found, in general, broad support in industrialized countries, particularly in industry circles and intellectual property lawyers.[85] These initiatives focused on GATT, regardless of the fact that the international law on intellectual property has been one important area of multilateral legislative action in established specialized fora. As described above, already in 1883, the commu-

81 *See:* Technology-related policies and legislation in a changing economic and technological environment, UNCTAD (UN doc. TD/B/C. 6/146) and International Trade: Strengthening Worldwide Protection of Intellectual Property Rights, US General Accounting Office, 9GAO/NSIAD-87-65.

82 *See K. A. Ammer*, The Semi-conductor Chip Protection Act of 1984, in: Law and Policy in International Business 17 (1985), 395.

83 For the history of the treaty, *see Carlos M. Correa*, Integrated Circuits: Trends in Intellectual Property, UNIDO, P. C. T., Nov. 1989, Vienna.

84 *See Abbot* (note 41) and *J. H. Reichman*, Intellectual Property in International Trade: Opportunities and Risks of a GATT Connection, in: Vanderbilt Journal of Transnational Law 22 (1989), 747-891.

85 *See op. cit.* (note 29) and *Hans Peter Hallstein*, The United States Proposal for a GATT Agreement on Intellectual Property and the Paris Convention for the Protection of Industrial Property, in: Vanderbilt Journal of Transnational Law 22 (1989), 265-284.

nity of nations perceived the need to internationally protect industrial inventions[86] and in 1974, the WIPO became a specialized agency of the United Nations. The Paris Convention of 1883 was followed by international instruments dealing with copyrights and related rights as well as by institutional arrangements to monitor the international régimes.

A number of justifications have been suggested by industrialized countries and particularly by private corporations to address intellectual property issues in a trade forum such as GATT and not in WIPO. First, existing agreements have inadequate rules, they have not provided for satisfactory minimum standards of protection. Second, the existing arrangements do not afford efficient means to enforce adequate protection in order to avoid trade in counterfeit products. These agreements do not contemplate mechanisms for dispute settlement. Third, the coverage of the agreements has been narrow, they have not encompassed new technological developments and more specifically they do not clearly protect software programmes and integrated circuits. Fourth, the national treatment principle provided for in these agreements does not secure suitable international protection; it becomes meaningless when the national laws, particularly of developing countries, are inadequate or not enforced.[87]

2. The Issues

The General Agreement on Tariffs and Trade (GATT)[88] contains only brief references to intellectual property rights insofar as they do not become barriers to legitimate trade.[89] The preceding multilateral trade rounds have not included intellectual property *per se* as a topic of negotiation. The subject was raised for the first time during the Tokyo Round with respect to trade in counterfeit goods but limited to the subject of trademarks. At that time, developing countries expressed no interest in dealing in GATT with the subject.[90] During the preparatory process for the launching of the Uruguay Round, developing countries objected, in general, to the inclusion in the multilateral trade negotiations of the so-called "new issues."[91] This resistance was led mainly by Brazil and India.[92]

---

[86] *See Henrich Kronstein/Irene Till*, A Re-evaluation of the International Patent Convention, in: Law and Contemporary Problems 12 (1947), 765-781.

[87] *See Michael Gadbaw/Timothy Richards*, Intellectual Property Rights, Global Consensus, Global Conflict?, Colorado 1988, and *op. cit.* (note 29).

[88] *See* General Agreement on Tariffs and Trade, Basic Instruments and Selected Documents.

[89] The references in the GATT to intellectual property are limited to a provision permitting the adoption of domestic legislation necessary to protect intellectual property (Art. XX d) and to a provision aimed at preventing the use of trademarks to misrepresent origin (Art. IX (6)).

[90] *See Bradley* (note 8) and Uruguay Round: Papers on Selected Issues, UNCTAD, UN Publication (UN doc. UNCTAD/ITP/10).

[91] It should be noted that in the 1982 Ministerial Declaration "the trade aspects of commercial counterfeiting" was identified as a matter for joint action. Contracting Parties of GATT, accordingly, established in 1984 a Group of Experts to study this question.

The Punta del Este Declaration of September 1986 incorporated, finally, after complex and protracted negotiations, a section dealing with "trade-related aspects of intellectual property rights, including trade in counterfeit goods" (TRIPs).[93]

The negotiating process within the Uruguay Round has been characterized, particularly in its initial phases, by an active and assertive attitude of developed countries and a defensive and formalistic approach followed by the developing countries. The latter have argued that, on the basis of the mandate originated in the Punta del Este Declaration, the areas of action in GATT should be limited and that universal international substantive standards of protection should only be negotiated in WIPO. The industrialized countries, less concerned about semantics, put forward, from the outset, comprehensive proposals on the premise that inadequate, excessive and discriminatory protection of intellectual property rights constituted a major distortion of and impediment to trade and should as such be dealt with in the framework of GATT.[94]

In general terms, the proposals have addressed three major issues. First, substantive standards or norms of intellectual property protection; second, procedures under national laws for the enforcement of intellectual property protection; and third, dispute settlement procedures between parties to any eventual agreement on TRIPs. The subsequent sections describe the proposals and positions, respectively, of industrialized countries and developing countries.

3. Main Proposals by Industrialized Countries

The European Economic Communities,[95] Japan, Switzerland and the United States[96] have made comprehensive proposals covering all of the three issues mentioned above.[97]

---

92 *See Bradley* (note 8) and Uruguay Round, Papers on Selected Issues (note 90).

93 The text of the Punta del Este Declaration of 20 September 1986 on trade-related aspects of intellectual property rights, including trade in counterfeit goods (TRIPs) reads as follows: "In order to reduce the distortions and impediments to international trade, and taking into account the need to promote effective and adequate protection of intellectual property rights, and to ensure that measures and procedures to enforce intellectual property rights do not themselves become barriers to legitimate trade, the negotiations shall aim to clarify GATT provisions and elaborate as appropriate new rules and disciplines."

"Negotiations shall aim to develop a multilateral framework of principles, rules and disciplines dealing with international trade in counterfeit goods, taking into account work already undertaken in the GATT."

"These negotiations shall be without prejudice to other complementary initiatives that may be taken in the World Intellectual Property Organization and elsewhere to deal with these matters."

94 *A. Yusuf*, Developing Countries and Trade-Related Aspects of Intellectual Property Rights, in: Uruguay Round, Papers on Selected Issues (note 92).

95 *See* proposal on a draft agreement on Trade-Related Aspects of Intellectual Property Rights of 29 March 1990 (GATT doc. MTN. GNG/NG11/W/68), as reported in: FOCUS, GATT Newsletter, 70 (April 1990).

With respect to the substantive standards to be embodied in a future agreement on TRIPs, the proposals have covered various aspects of intellectual property rights. In general, it is proposed that the principles of national treatment, most favoured nation treatment and non-discrimination and transparency should govern international rules and disciplines on the protection and enforcement of intellectual property rights.

In the domain of patents, they should be granted for all products and processes, which are new, useful, and not obvious and should cover all inventions in any technological field; no exceptions, in general, should be admitted on specific sectors. Under the proposals the proprietor should have exclusive rights to prevent third parties, not having his consent, from making, offering, putting on the market or using a product or process which is the subject matter of the patent, or importing or stocking the product for these purposes. A patent may not be revoked on grounds of non-working. The duration of the patent should be adequate. Twenty years from the patent application has been suggested. Compulsory licensing, one critical issue in the revision of the Paris Convention, as outlined above, should only be granted in exceptional cases and under conditions clearly specified.[98]

With respect to copyrights, the main proposals addressed the following main questions:

a) copyrights should encompass all forms of expressions, including new modalities such as software programmes and databases;

b) the grant of rights should be automatic from the creation of the work; no formality should condition the exercise of such rights;

c) the term of protection, including computer software, should be the life of the author plus fifty years and in the case of legal entities, the term of protection should be no less than fifty years from authorized publication;[99]

96 The proposals of the United States, Switzerland and Japan were made, respectively, on 11, 14 and 15 May 1990.

97 The proposals in general suggest to introduce a new article into the GATT. Under the EEC proposal the following article IX *bis* is suggested: "The contracting parties agree to provide effective and adequate protection of intellectual property rights in order to ensure the reduction of distortions and impediments to international trade. The protection of intellectual property rights shall not itself create barriers to legitimate trade. They therefore agree that they will provide for protection of intellectual property rights under their domestic laws and practices in conformity with the rules and disciplines set out in Annex II." Annex II contains the detailed rules and disciplines on the protection of intellectual property rights. Under the proposal made by Switzerland, a new Part V would be added to the GATT on "Trade and Intellectual Property."

98 Under the EEC proposal, compulsory licences may not be issued for non-working or insufficiency of working on the territory of the granting authority if the right holder can show that the lack or insufficiency of local working is justified by the existence of legal, technical or commercial reasons.

99 The EEC proposes that contracting parties may provide for a period of less than 50 years provided that the period of protection lasts at least for 25 years.

d) compulsory licenses should not be granted in general and particularly when local needs could be legitimately satisfied through voluntary licensing.

In the area of layout-designs of integrated circuits, in line with recent legislative trends in developed countries, it has been proposed that contracting parties shall make provisions for special protection. In this respect, exclusive rights should be granted for the reproduction, importation and distribution of integrated circuits.[100]

The proposals deal also with standards of protection in such other areas as trade secret, trademarks, industrial designs and models, geographical indications and appellations of origin.

On the second category of issues described above — procedures under national law for the enforcement of intellectual property rights —, the proposals, in general, include civil and administrative procedures and remedies that would enable to control at the importing border the export and transit of infringing goods. Countries would be required to establish effective and adequate enforcement measures through the provision at the domestic level of administrative and judicial procedures which owners of intellectual property rights can use to enforce the rights granted to them under the minimum standards and norms. Criminal procedures will also be provided for to be applied in cases of willful infringements of trademarks and copyrights on a commercial scale.

Finally, provisions are made on dispute settlement procedures between signatories on the basis of Article XXII (consultation) and Article XXIII (nullification or impairment) of GATT, which would be resorted to whenever the conformity of national legislation with the obligation under the agreement was at issue, or where there is an allegation that it had been applied in a manner inconsistent with the agreement.

The comprehensive proposals made by industrialized countries also include supplementary provisions dealing with technical assistance to developing contracting parties on the preparation and implementation of domestic legislation on the protection and enforcement of intellectual property as well as with the establishment of a Committee on Trade Related Intellectual Property Rights to monitor the compliance with the obligations to be embodied in the new arrangements. Transitional periods are recognized to developing countries and least developed countries to adjust to the new obligations to be assumed under the TRIPs arrangements.[101]

---

100 An important difference in this area between industrialized countries is that the EEC refers specifically to the substantive provisions of the Treaty on Intellectual Property in Respect of Integrated Circuits of May 26, 1989. No reference is made to the Treaty in Japan's, the United States' and Switzerland's proposals.

101 *See* proposal of the EEC (note 95).

4. Proposals by Developing Countries

As insinuated above, developing countries' attitude has been of great reserve and prudence concerning the negotiating mandate in GATT *vis-à-vis* the responsibilities of WIPO in the area of intellectual property. Bearing this in mind, a group of developing countries has recently submitted a proposal, within the Uruguay Round, on intellectual property and international trade containing the various elements that, in their view, should connote the final outcome of the negotiations in GATT.[102] The developing countries' contribution is built upon the need to take into consideration the public policy objectives underlying national systems for the protection of intellectual property, including developmental and technological objectives. Its coverage and content should be seen in the light of the deliberate resistance of developing countries to deal with intellectual property issues in GATT and of their traditional positions in the revision process of the Paris Convention. From this point of view, the mere presentation of a proposal in the negotiations on TRIPs is in a way a mayor strategical shift in the developing countries' stance.

The proposal covers trade in counterfeit and pirated goods and standards and principles concerning the availability, scope and use of intellectual property rights. It does not cover in detail all the areas addressed by the industrialized countries in their respective proposals but deals with each of the subject-matters of the present agenda.

The differences between the two groups of countries' contributions are still significant. Developing countries, for example, maintain that parties may exclude from patentability, on grounds of public interest, national security, public health or nutrition, certain kinds of products or processes for the manufacture of those products. Opposite to the views of the industrialized countries, developing countries propose that the duration of protection is a matter for national legislation to determine. In the case of patents, the owner has not only rights but also obligations such as to work the patented invention and to refrain from engaging in abusive or anti-competitive practices adversely affecting the transfer of technology. Developing countries also contemplate compulsory licenses as a remedy for non-working or insufficient working of patents. Finally, in the area of integrated circuits, it is proposed that parties should provide protection in accordance with the Washington, D. C. Treaty of May 1989.[103]

---

102 *See* communication from Argentina, Brazil, Chile, China, Colombia, Cuba, Egypt, India, Nigeria, Peru, Tanzania, Uruguay and Pakistan of 14 May 1990 (GATT doc. MTN. GNG/NG11/W/71).

103 *See supra* (note 83).

V. The Seventies and the Eighties: Two Agendas in Perspective

At the time of writing (June 1990), the negotiations on the various issues reviewed in this paper are under intensive discussions. The final outcome of the Uruguay Round[104] is difficult to predict. The negotiations in WIPO, on the revision of the Paris Convention, are to be resumed formally in November/ December 1991[105] and those on the draft code of conduct on the transfer of technology are in abeyance.[106] Notwithstanding these constraints, some general observations could be made specially from the historical perspective of comparing the current trends with those initiatives that dominated the 1970s.

In view of the changing nature of the issues and of the major developments that have taken place in recent years, the nature of the debate and the rôle of the respective actors have been severely altered in the 1980s agenda. The initiatives during the decade of the 1980s have been basically dominated by the new issues and by the perception of the industrialized countries, and particularly by those of private corporations, on how to deal with the new realities. The 1970s agenda focused chiefly on the aspirations of the developing countries towards improving their standing in the prevailing system. Some of the issues of the decade of the 1970s, e. g. the equalization of patents and inventors' certificates, are past history. Others continue to be sound proposals, but probably under entirely distinct assumptions.

1. The Different Settings: the 1970s and the 1980s

The 1970s were still dominated by the preoccupations of a number of developed countries in the future of developing countries and of their insertion in the international economic system. Development was an important theme of the international community and access to technology was a rather loose concept that could be shared intellectually with developing countries. Developing countries, on the other hand, particularly on the eve of the energy crisis, had some leverage, at least to formulate proposals and demands. From this perspective, the situation has drastically changed in the 1980s.

---

[104] A full understanding of the Uruguay Round implications in technology matters would also need to consider the discussions under TRIMs and those concerning the liberalization of services. The latter sector represents one of the principal beneficiaries of major technological changes. It also accounts for some 40-45 per cent of the total stock of foreign direct investments by the major countries. *Constantine V. Vaitsos*, Radical Technological Change and the New "Order" in the World Economy, in: Technology, Trade Policy and the Uruguay Round (note 6).

[105] *See:* International Union for the Protection of Industrial Property (Paris Union), Sixth Consultative Meeting on the Revision of the Paris Convention (Geneva, Sept. 18-22, 1989) (WIPO doc. PR/CM/VI/1).

[106] *See op. cit.* (note 6).

From a more parochial angle, the traditional patent issues in the world of the 1970s have moved to an era where living microorganisms may qualify as patentable subject matters[107] and where patentability may extend to "everything under the sun that is made by man."[108] Also some competition law premises have changed from a more restrictive approach in industrialized countries towards the conflict between intellectual property and competition in the preceding decade[109] to a situation where unrestricted use of intellectual property rights are being seen as necessary for the functioning of a competitive, market-based economy.[110]

From a more critical approach to the operation of transnational corporations in the 1970s[111] we are witnessing a reassessment of their rôle and of their contribution to growth and development.[112] Equally, from a period dominated by a major chasm between the West and the East which has been manifested by the Coordinating Committee for Multilateral Export Controls (CoCom) dictating what technology could be legally exported to countries from Eastern Europe, the world is observing a gradual dismantling of a system established after the Second World War.

Technology in the decade of the 1980s has become a key factor in competitiveness among firms and among nations. Access to new markets and economic power, in general, have been linked to technological knowledge and to innovation. It has been claimed that by 1986, over 27 per cent of the United States exports contained an intellectual property component, compared to 10 per cent when GATT was negotiated in the post Second World War period.[113] American products with high intellectual property content (chemicals, books, movies, records, electrical equipment and computers) have more than doubled to more than 25 per cent of all United States exports.[114] In this sense and contrary to the prevailing views in the decade of the 1970s, the appropriation of knowledge has become critical and of a universal character, not confined, as in the traditional intellectual property system, to national geographical boundaries.

---

107 *See Diamond* v. *Chakrabarty*, Supreme Court of the United States, No. 79-138 (June 16, 1980), reprinted in: ILM 19 (1980), 983-991.

108 *See Dam* (note 23), quoting a Patent and Trademark Office administrative tribunal decision of 1985.

109 *See* the 1974 OECD Council Recommendation on Patents and Licensing.

110 *See:* Technology-related policies and legislation in a changing economic and technological environment (note 81).

111 *See* GA res. 3202 (S-VI) of 1 May 1974.

112 *See* GA res. S-18/3 of 1 May 1990 (Declaration on International Economic Co-operation, in particular the Revitalization of Economic Growth and Development of the Developing Countries); Changing Production Patterns with Social Equity, ECLAC, UN Publication, UN doc. LC/G. 1001 (SES. 23/4) of 19 March 1990, and *Sidney Dell*, The United Nations and International Business, UNITAR 1990.

113 *See Gadbaw* (note 51).

114 *Robert W. Kastenmeier / David Beier*, International Trade and Intellectual Property: Promise, Risks, and Reality, in: Vanderbilt Journal of Transnational Law 22 (1989), 285-307 (286).

At a more conceptual level, some scholars have suggested that the historical distinction between tangible and intangible property (intellectual property) "becomes increasingly anachronistic the more that economics everywhere are driven by the need to innovate."[115] Others insinuate that the world of the future will be dominated by goods of a "nomade" character where the information component would be the key factor.[116] This incipient but major trend is useful to retain in order to understand and perceive the ramifications of the ongoing debate.

2. The Basic Premises of the Intellectual Property System and Its Evolution

Intellectual property rights has been by its nature of a territorial character. The prevailing international conventions, conceived in the latter part of the 19th century, were built upon the principle of "independence" in the sense that the protection in one country should be autonomous of the protection granted for the same invention in a third country.[117] This principle was based on the theory that the protection for intangible assets should correspond to the criteria and conditions prevailing in the granting state.

From a historical perspective, intellectual property rights were founded on the principle of rewarding and stimulating the innovative activity of individuals with the objective of improving the competitive position of local industries and thereby encourage industrialization. Those objectives were clearly advanced, respectively, in the adoption in the United States and in France of two of the most modern and influential statutes on patents.[118] The same premises prevailed in the formulation of the major international conventions on intellectual property. The founders of these conventions abandoned a uniform law approach in favour of the principle of national treatment, "... a principle that implied a commitment to developing minimum standards from the bottom up rather than from the top down."[119]

The protection of intellectual property was always based upon the need to strike a proper balance between the encouragement of creativity, innovation, and the optimization of social welfare arising from the fruits of that creativity and its contribution to the scientific and technological development of the local environment. The main objective was to reward the individual but on the basis of a social goal.

---

115 *Reichman* (note 84), 806. *See also* OTA (note 30).

116 *Jacques Attali*, Lignes d'horizon, Paris 1990.

117 *See* Art. 4 *bis* of the Paris Convention (note 63) on independence of patents obtained for the same invention in different countries.

118 The French law of 1791 gave the following justifications for the enactment of the new statute: The backwardness of French industry, the threats posed to the French economy by the penetration of English products, and the desire of the French Government to ameliorate the situation of the French industrial workers, *see Anderfelt* (note 17), 15-16.

119 *Reichman* (note 84), 779.

Even if the aspirations of the decade of the 1970s appear in distinct contradiction with the initiatives of the 1980s, they are consonant with the evolution of the intellectual property system. In spite of that fact, the policies and motivations of developing countries have been depicted by the advocates of the new design as protective and equivalent to disincentives to investment and technology flows particularly of new technologies. According to this line of thinking, technology would naturally flow to more liberal markets. The latter, no doubt, constitutes an important factor but not a sufficient one. Investment and technology flows would tend to be determined by a combination of factors which would include a receptive environment that offers the necessary conditions and incentives for profitability and growth.[120]

The history of developed countries in their early phase of development, including more recent cases such as Japan, suggests that technology was transferred and subsequently absorbed and developed not necessarily in a liberal environment. In the case of Japan, copying imported products, whether protected by patents or not, was tolerated by the government.[121] Japan also applied strict controls on technology agreements and related imports during the take-off period. Technology was acquired from abroad only through strict government-controlled licensing agreements.[122] The same country recognized patents to foreigners only in 1899.[123] The United States was during the 19th century a leading publisher of English works without extending copyright protection to these works.[124] The United States, again, only acceded to the Berne Convention in 1988. In the disputed area of pharmaceuticals, effective and adequate protection has been recognized by Japan and most of the European countries only in the recent last 25 years.[125]

---

120 "Such flows would tend to be determined by different combinations of factors over and above the level of intellectual property protection, such as the investment climate of the particular country, the size of its market, the global investment strategies of the particular investors, the type of technology involved and the feasibility of protecting it by other means, and the country's scientific and industrial infrastructure." *I. K. Minta*, Intellectual Property Rights and Investment Issues in the Uruguay Round, in: The CTC Reporter 29 (1990), 43-46 (46).

121 This policy "... benefitted their economy in the early period of development without producing long-term negative effects." *Carter Mackley*, The Role of the Patent System in Technology Transfer: The Japanese Experience, in: Columbia Journal of Transnational Law 26 (1987), 131-166 (165).

122 *Vaitsos* (note 104), 77.

123 *Mackley* (note 121), 135.

124 *See Kastenmeier / Beier* (note 114), 290. The well-known "manufacturing clause" in the US copyright law was declared illicit under a GATT Panel in 1984 (United States Manufacturing Clause), GATT Panel, Report of 15/16 May 1984, Basic Instruments and Selected Documents, 31st Supp. 74 (1985). The manufacturing clause was subsequently abolished.

125 *See Alberto Bercovitz*, Historical Trends in Protection of Technology in Developed Countries and their Relationship to Protection in Developing Countries, UNCTAD 1989 (mimeographed).

The flexible policies on protection, followed in the past by almost all present industrialized countries,[126] are considered unacceptable in the current prevailing environment on the basis that "free riders" would have no place, or a very limited space, in an interdependent and global economic system. But, as has been rightly observed, "free riders", as was the case of presently industrialized countries, have not violated existing international legal norms.[127] In this respect, it could be noticed that the new emerging standards, as advocated by the "maximalists," are intended to limit the potential for newcomers to emulate the technological path followed previously by European countries, the United States, Japan and the newly industrialized countries.[128]

Compared to the initiatives of the decade of the 1970s and the wishes of the less technologically advanced countries of bridging the technological gap with the industrialized world, under the current movement the rules of the game, the standards to be applied and the so-called "social balance"[129] of the intellectual property system, would be set by the needs and existing conditions in more technologically advanced countries. Probably, in political terms and observing the evolution of international law, the latter would be a logical consequence led by the industrial powers as the main actors in the international economic arena. Developing countries with different levels of development and different national priorities, are not in a position of bargaining for a deal that might take into account their past aspirations. The 1970s agenda, even if formally reiterated during the current debate, has little likelihood of acceptance under the prevailing scenario. Though one qualified observer has noted that the negotiations on the draft code of conduct on transfer of technology and on a code of conduct on transnational corporations "appear to have lost the impetus they once had, yet their relevance to current trade negotiations, with respect both to TRIMs and to trade in services, is so evident and so immediate that the prospect of their revival seems less unlikely than it looked a short while ago."[130]

---

126 *See E. Schiff*, Industrialization without National Patents: The Netherlands, 1869-1918; Switzerland, 1850-1907, Princeton 1971, and *R. Gerster*, Switzerland and the Revision of the Paris Convention, in: Journal of World Trade Law 15 (1981), 111.

127 *Reichman* (note 84), 770.

128 *Correa* (note 46), 1080.

129 The "social balance" is still a prevailing concept in the United States. In *Bonito Boats, Inc., Petitioner* v. *Thunder Craft Boats, Inc.*, the Supreme Court of the United States held: "... From the outset federal patent law has been about the difficult business, of drawing a line between the things which are worth to the public the embarrassment of an exclusive patent, and those which are not .... The federal patent system thus embodies a carefully crafted bargain for encouraging the creation and disclosure of new, useful, and non-obvious advances in technology and design in return for the exclusive right to practice the invention for a period of years." Supreme Court, 57 L. W. 4205 (decision of 21 February 1989).

130 *See Fatouros* (note 77), 220.

VI. Conclusions

This paper has attempted to compare two major agendas in the area of technology: the agenda proposed by developing countries in the decade of the '70s and the current one formulated by the industrialized countries. It has reviewed recent technology-related developments and trends that have radically shifted the nature and the tone of the debate.

A general observation to be made relates to the sometimes ideologized tone of the controversy on technology protection between a "maximalist" and a "free-rider" school. These two extreme schools of thought are not based on the historical features of the intellectual property system, neither on the broader considerations underpinning the system. A more detached approach, in line with the historical evolution of intellectual property, might help to overcome some of the present obstacles and find the necessary adjustments.

An obvious implication of the current debate is that the scheme of the Seventies, proposed by the developing countries, need to be re-evaluated and fine-tuned. It is not any longer entirely valid. The measures and policies promoted domestically and at the international level, including the provisions in the Convention on the Law of the Sea, would not have found today the relative receptivity that they have met in the decade of the 1970s. The motivations of this decade assumed a permissive international environment governed mainly by the tenet of national treatment and not by the concept of reciprocity which is firmly embedded in GATT,[131] which might guide future international intellectual property relationships. At the same time, the full respect of intellectual property rights in developed countries was traditionally counter-balanced by the strict enforcement of competition policies to control possible abuses of market power. Furthermore, the 1970s was not permeated by the pervasive influence of new and emerging technologies and the crucial rôle now being attributed to technology in international competitiveness.

It has been argued in this respect that developing countries need to revise their position as regards intellectual property and respond to the demands of the North in a gradual manner.[132] In a way, this is the offer being made in GATT to the developing countries by recognizing that they should adapt gradually their domestic systems to the new emerging standards. This approach is partially correct. Developing countries, and probably not only developing countries,[133]

---

131 *See Abbot* (note 41), 733; *Reichman* (note 84), 851; and *Karl M. Meessen*, Intellectual Property Rights in International Trade, in: Journal of World Trade Law 21 (1987), No. 1, 67-74.

132 *See Carlos Alberto Primo Braga*, The Economics of Intellectual Property Rights and the GATT: A View from the South, in: Vanderbilt Journal of Transnational Law 22 (1989), 243-264.

133 According to the United States Trade Representative (USTR), "... no foreign country currently meets every standard for adequate and effective intellectual property

need to review and re-adapt their intellectual property policies. However, a revised system that would not recognize the different realities of development and that would not incorporate appropriate rules to maintain an efficient competitive market regulating abuses, would probably be doomed to maintain present tensions and isolate from the system technologically less advanced countries.

It needs to be emphasized that tensions would necessarily prevail between the industrialized countries and the technologically less advanced countries, unless corrective measures are designed to rectify imbalances and avoid the perpetuation of the existing international division of labour.[134] The new emerging standards, at least in the industrialized countries, respond to new requirements in the current stage of trade in goods and services with a high technological content and to developments in the world economy as well as to the challenges posed by new technological discoveries. Unfortunately, for the less technologically advanced countries, these new standards will put them in a different and more difficult position. In this respect, *Abbot* has argued that

> ... industrialized countries should provide trade concessions to the extent necessary to ameliorate short-term economic dislocations in the developing countries resulting from the adoption of new intellectual property rules. This is because the developing countries reasonably relied on previously agreed norms in the development of their internal policies.[135]

A striking feature of some of the new proposals in GATT is the lack of a link between the granting of intellectual property rights and the promotion of domestic technological development.[136] From the perspective of the South, viewing intellectual property exclusively from the angle of trade is tantamount to ignoring their paramount rôle in technological innovation and in access to and transfer of technology.[137] As already suggested, one important implication of the new tendency is the eventual consolidation of an international framework consisting

---

protection as set forth in the United States proposal [to GATT] on intellectual property tabled in the Uruguay Round". USTR Fact Sheets, reprinted in: *Abbot* (note 41), 709.

134 "The present process of technological change poses challenges to developing countries. ... The increasing monopolization of technological progress by the developed countries and the relatively small technology base and capability of developing countries to bridge the gap is aggravated by barriers placed on access to high technology ... it is critical that regimes on intellectual property effectively promote technological development in developing countries and their access to high technologies ..." Joint Communique by Fifteen Heads of States or Governments of Developing Countries in Meeting of the Summit Level Group for South-South Consultation and Cooperation (para. 18), Kuala Lumpur, 3 June 1990.

135 *Abbot* (note 41), 695.

136 It should be noted that this concern was present in the Punta del Este Declaration and in the Geneva Mid-Term Review of April 1989. In the Mid-Term Review it is stated: "Ministers agree that in the negotiations consideration will be given to concerns raised by participants related to the underlying public policy objectives of their national systems for the protection of intellectual property, including developmental and technological objectives." Mid-Term Review, in: FOCUS, GATT Newsletter 61 (May 1989), 8.

137 *See Yusuf* (note 94), 190.

of legal standards conforming to those of countries of an advanced degree of development.[138]

As a result of recent initiatives to universalize intellectual property standards, the classical "social balance" which has prevailed in intellectual property legal systems and that has been always demarcated within national boundaries would need to be redefined. It should also be admitted that this might be a logical effect of a growing economic interdependence and of the globalization of markets as well as of the increasing irrelevance of limited national boundaries in the case of some new technologies, particularly those related to information technologies.[139]

An open, improved and strengthened trading system, as proclaimed in the Declaration of Punta del Este, will be more meaningful if it provides opportunities to developing countries to enlarge their share of world trade. In a recent UNCTAD's secretariat paper it has been stated: "This would call for more secure and improve access to markets, and particularly for a reduction in the scope for imposing discriminatory measures and trade harassment to new entrants."[140] Precisely, the initiatives of the decade of the '70s were designed to address some of these issues but as suggested in this paper the present international environment is not propitious to their endorsement and acceptance. The new prevailing conditions call for a different type of arrangements and probably for new alliances among different group of countries — not necessarily circumscribed to the North-South dichotomy — which would need to reassess the existing situation and adapt some of the legitimate aspirations of the Seventies to the current changes in the world economy with the view of achieving a more balanced framework that could accommodate the interests of producers and consumers.

---

138 *Vaitsos* (note 104), 71, argues that "[a] main aim pursued consists in obtaining, within specific national and corporate economic spheres, control over the productive activities through which the diffusion of technical change takes." According to *Paolo Bifani*: "The purpose is to create comparative advantage and international competitiveness and to control global markets in order to reap the benefits of all the economies of scale and scope associated with the new emerging high technology sectors." *See:* The New Mercantilism and the International Appropriation of Technology, in: Technology, Trade Policy and the Uruguay Round (note 6), 196.

139 This applies particularly to transborder data flows where the actual transfer to parallel recipients, in different geographical sites, takes place simultaneously, regardless of geographical confines.

140 *Op. cit.* (note 26), 108.

Discussion

Craven:

We all owe a debt of gratitude to Prof. *Roffe* for a very informative and excellent presentation with respect to intellectual property perspectives. In the oceanic area I have observed a very interesting development by the Japanese. For the past 10 years, they have been developing a concept called the International Ocean Communications City. Their concept involves the construction of a floating city, which would have as its primary function the locale and locus of development of information technologies. One of the primary motivations for an oceanic floating city was security, with respect to the intellectual property associated with these technological developments. Now, a countervailing factor with respect to this motivation is the fact that the sea is notorious as an environment in which this kind of security cannot be maintained. Once one gets a large industrial plant floating in the ocean in a ship or something of that kind, it is only a matter of time before it moves around the world and becomes the template, so to speak, for various forms of intellectual property piracy.

It is this observation that leads to the question that I would like to ask the speaker. Does he concur with the opinion of many of the intellectual property experts, that intellectual piracy (and by piracy I do not mean counterfeiting) in a rapidly expanding technological world, in fact, increases the total market and that the possessors of the organized intellectual property product will discover that their market has increased, as a result of the increased number of consumers that the piracy market has developed? In answering this question I would call your attention particularly to such corporations as the *Borland Corporation*, a manufacturer of computer software. The *Borland Corporation* deliberately sells all of their software material without copy protection; and in addition to that, the *Borland Company* sells excellent software which allows you to copy protected software. The *Borland Company*, of course, has a message which flashes on the screen, that says this programme shall not be used to do the only thing it is capable of doing. So I would like to pose the following question: Do you feel as many of us feel, that enforcement in a modern technological world will not be effective? To use the term that *Harlan Cleveland* uses, is that intellectual information leaks, it is porous, and that in coming up with any future régime we must face the fact that some legalized form of piracy must be developed. If we do not, the pirates may well succeed in any event.

Roffe:

You are perfectly correct. In my view, I think it would be very difficult to enforce an international system, a system that could correct all the imbalances which might be produced by the so-called piracy, or counterfeiting. However, if you look into the proposals now being made in GATT, they might entail closing all possible gaps. The type of enforcement procedures being envisaged in GATT will demand, especially from developing countries, a major effort toward securing the protection of intellectual property rights. I do not know how many countries would really be in a position to carry out the spirit of those proposals. What you said about the importance of both the market, and the possibilities opened up by counterfeiting is already evident. I did not really have the opportunity to go into details in this area, which I would have liked to have done, in order to really give you the full picture of the historical evolution of the system. However, in the case of most of the industrialized countries today, countries like the United States or like Japan, copying or what you could call "counterfeiting" was a major strategic policy. It was an official policy in the case of Japan and has been, until very recently, the attitude of the United States in the case of copyright. When the United States considered that it was being challenged by the United Kingdom they then prevented the importation of copyright works and only protected those works that were manufactured in the United States; the so-called "manufacturing clause" of the copyright system of the United States was only abolished in 1986, when it was questioned by GATT.

Mathanjuki:

I would like to make a comment and possibily ask a question. Your presentation has been quite informative. Particularly in light of the comparative approach you have taken as regards the developing countries, and the approach they adopted during the '70s, in their relations with developed countries on transfer of technology as well as the current situation. I notice that today there is a very major change of attitude in the approach of the developed countries on this question and whereas the main emphasis in the early '70s was in favour of a permissive approach, such transfer of technology is now more on a restrictive practice basis. It is noticeable, that at that time the thinking was orientated more towards developing an a economic order, creating a fair economic environment between the developed and developing countries. This is no longer there. Now, my question is, what chance do you see of these traditional notions suceeding, with specific reference to the Law of the Sea Convention, in particular art. 144 which mentions the Authority as a multilateral organ being a source of transfer of technology today than the willing buyer/willing seller market situation. Particularly, since you mentioned that the developed countries are now more or less adopting a reciprocal and restrictive rather than permissive attitude? What chances then do you see of these notions enshrined in the Convention succeeding, particularly in the current negotiations of the Law of the Sea and for future operations between the North and South?

Roffe:

In my written paper, I have tried to develop and have attempted to speculate in that respect. As I mentioned before, I am not an expert on the law of the sea and as such, I would hesitate before such an audience to make any assessment in this area. My general impression, however, with reference to the historical perspectives to which you refer, is that those efforts of the '70s, compared to the present trends of the '80s, particularly the Law of the Sea Convention in the area of transfer of technology (especially on sea-bed prospecting) represented a major attempt and probably one of the most important one of the '70s and with the risk of exaggerating, perhaps even one of the most radical attempts to try to facilitate the transfer of technology, especially in favour of developing countries. That initiative comes very close to the purpose of the revision of the Paris Convention, in trying to liberalize the rules on compulsory licencing. Compulsory licencing in the Paris Convention is one of the measures that could be adopted at the national level to secure the local production of technology protected by the patent. In that respect the attempt of the Law of the Sea Convention was similar to the Paris Convention. If I can compare that effort to what was the code of conduct on the transfer of technology, the code was actually a more general appeal for more fair and reasonable terms and conditions in the area of technology, but was not a radical reform to transform the rules prevailing in the transfer of technology process. The contrast with what is going on now is striking. At the national level, in industrialized countries, the rules on competition have been completely liberalized. In the Uruguay Round, that I tried to describe briefly, compulsory licencing, according to the views of most industrial countries, should not be permitted, they should only be resorted to exceptionally. My conclusion, a very tentative conclusion, is that it would be very difficult to really implement those concepts and designs of the '70s! I do not think that the views of countries like the United States, that were very critical especially of the transfer of technology provisions of the Law of the Sea, would have changed. On the contrary, their position, would have to be consequential. They will have to be much more critical than they were in the '70s.

The Review Provisions of the UN Law of the Sea Convention and the Powers of the Review Conference

Hans-Joachim Kiderlen*

Not much has been said or written about the review provisions of the United Nations Convention on the Law of the Sea. However, these provisions form an important part of the Convention.

The more complicated a convention is, the more it has to deal with the unforeseeable, to catch the dynamics of evolutions in a specific field, the more there is a need for revision, for continous adaption to the changing reality. Otherwise the convention would become obstructive where it should be promotive, and eventually obsolete.

There are two principal ways of dealing in the framework of a conventional régime with changing realities. Decision-making institutions are the one basic instrument. If these are well designed and function to perfection, the other instrument — revision clauses — may not be necessary or of lesser importance. In the normal course of events review provisions are more like emergency brakes, red handles to be pulled, if the normal decision-making mechanism no longer is able to secure the good work of a conventional régime.

Let us briefly have a look now at the review provisions of the Law of the Sea Convention. Already a first glance tells us, that practically there are two sets of revision clauses, one set concerning the deep sea-bed mining régime, the other the rest of the Convention. That may not be surprising since the Law of the Sea Convention indeed is two conventions in one.

For the provisions other than those concerning the deep sea-bed mining régime the Convention again envisages two ways of proceeding.

Following art. 312, ten years after the entry into force of the Convention a conference of States Parties may be convened to consider amendment proposals. The Secretary-General of the United Nations shall convene such an amendment conference on the proposition of specific amendments by a State Party, if at least half of the States Parties support the convening of the conference. The conference shall work on the basis of making every effort towards reaching consensus; i. e. the rather successful patterns for decision-making of the Third UN Conference on the Law of the Sea shall apply, pushing back the eventuality

* *Hans-Joachim Kiderlen*, Foreign Office of the Federal Republic of Germany.

of voting as much as possible. Nothing is said about the nature of amendments to be submitted to such a conference, but it is to be assumed that the endeavour of a conference of States Parties only makes sense for proposals of rather important changes, interrelated with basic question of the law of the sea. The choice of procedure is for the proposing State Party.

The other way, provided for in art. 313, is called "amendment by simplified procedure." Amendment proposals under this provision are circulated by the Secretary-General; they are adopted within 12 months if no State Party objects to it.

In both cases, in accordance with art. 316, an amendment enters into force after ratification or accession by two-thirds of the States Parties or by sixty States Parties, whichever number is greater. The amendment enters into force only for those States Parties which have approved it; for the other States Parties the unamended Convention continous to be valid.

For the deep sea-bed mining régime things are different, not only procedurally, but also with respect to the system itself. Here a clear distinction is made between amendments in a more technical sense, and changes affecting the "system of exploration for and exploitation of the resources of the Area." In this framework three lines of action are foreseen.

First, art. 154 stipulates an automatic review to be undertaken regularly every five years by the Assembly of the International Sea-Bed Authority as to the "manner in which the international régime of the Area established in this Convention has operated in practice." The result of these reviews would be recommendations of measures within the framework of Part XI and the related Annexes. Although this procedure is situated at the periphery of actual review provisions, it is nevertheless an expression of the awareness on the side of the Law of the Sea Conference of a dynamic and to a large extent unknown process to be expected when deep sea-bed mining gets under way.

The second line are the "ordinary" amendment provisions of the Convention, which in arts. 312 ff contain special references to the deep sea-bed régime. Article 314, parallel to the "amendment by simplified procedure" under art. 313, deals specifically with "amendments to the provisions of this Convention relating exclusively to activities in the Area," but not "prejudging the system of exploration and exploitation" as such. In comparison with art. 313, which relates to the other parts of the Convention, art. 314 contains two important pecularities. First, the distinction between changes, affecting "the system of exploration and exploitation," and other changes is decisive for the use of the amendment procedure under art. 314. Second, it obviously was the view of the Law of the Sea Conference that the sea-bed régime should for practical reasons remain unsplit. The solution therefore was not, as for the other parts of the Convention and as foreseen under art. 40 of the Vienna Convention on the Law of Treaties, to allow "dissenters" to be bound only by the unamended Convention. A choice then had to be made, either to make amendments of the deep sea-bed mining régime dependent upon adherence by all States Parties, or to impose eventually the will of a — qualified — majority on a dissenting minority. For amendments under art. 314 the decision was, as stipulated in art. 161, para. 8 (d) of the Convention, that the approval of the Council of the Authority by consensus of its members present and voting will be necessary for their adoption, whereas their entry into force for all States Parties will depend on ratification or accession by three-fourths of them.

The "Review Conference" under art. 155, the third and most controversial line of action with respect to the revision of Part XI, can only to a certain extent be seen in parallel to the amendment conference of art. 312. It is not dealt with in Part XVII on final provisions, but in Part XI itself, so that it is in fact part of the very system which it is bound to review. Only one Review Conference is envisaged by the Convention, not a periodicity of Review Conferences. The purpose of this conference of States Parties is "the review of these provisions . . . which govern the system of exploration and exploitation of the resources of the Area."

Certain core elements and principles of the deep sea-bed régime are, in accordance with a list contained in para. 2 of art. 155, exempt from changes, i. e. in particular the principle of the *common heritage of mankind*, the principle of an international régime for the exploitation of the Area, and also the principle of the participation of States in activities in the Area. As for the amendment conference under art. 312, the procedural regulations require every effort to reach agreement by way of consensus. If five years after the beginning of the Conference agreement could not be reached, amendments may then during one additional year be adopted by a majority of three-fourths of the States Parties. Amendments enter into force for all States Parties 12 months after ratification or accession by three-fourths of them. Partly compensating for this majority rule of the Review Conference, art. 317 of the Convention allows for the denunciation of membership, without clarifying, which rights with respect to sea-bed mining a State leaving the Convention would retain.

What would be the critique of this rather complicated system? The history of the development of the review provisions of the Convention went in some ways contrary to a systematic approach, insofar as the provisions on the Review Conference have been worked out first, and then only the general amendment provisions, which form part of the final clauses of the Convention, were negotiated. This again points at the very special rôle the Review Conference plays in the framework of deep sea-bed régime.

The concept of a Review Conference was from the outset an integral part of the search for compromise between the different approaches under discussion for an international deep sea-bed régime. The decisive inter-sessional consultations of the UN Law of the Sea Conference, held in Geneva from 28 February to 11 March 1977 under the chairmanship of the head of the Norwegian delegation, Mr *Evensen*, defined the main opposing positions as, one, demanding "a clear right for States and private entities to carry out production in the Area" and, two, to give the International Authority the prerogative to decide on "the extent to which activities of States and private entities should occur."[1] The two basic elements of compromise were a parallel system of exploitation, including the requirement to equip the Enterprise of the Authority with sufficient financial and technological means for its operations, and the transitional character of this system. The paper produced by Mr *Castaneda*, the head of the Mexican delegation, which was particularly important for the formulation of the compromise, explained in this respect that "one essential condition for agreement is the common understanding that the régime now being established is completely new and therefore needs to be tested."[2] The head of the United States' Delegation, Mr *Richardson*, acknowledged before the Law of the Sea Conference that "practicable means to assure, after 20 to 25 years a systematic and unprejudiced review of the system of exploitation, in order to allow such modifications in the light of experience as might be indicated" was a "basic element" of a necessary compromise.[3] When examining the genesis of the Review Conference, a possible difference in perception between an instrument securing the transitional character of the parallel system and an instrument allowing for necessary modifications in the light of experience, should not be overlooked. The text of art. 155, as it finally resulted rather rapidly from the negotiations, in any case does not exclude maintaining the parallel system or its main elements after the review.

The Review Conference is also linked to the concept of an interim period of special production limitation for deep sea-bed mining, as contained in art. 151 of the Convention. In accordance with art. 151, para. 3 this interim period may, as one foreseen alternative, come to an end together with the Review Conference. It is thus assumed that the Review Conference should take up the subject of production policy.

The problem is not the existence in the provisions of the Convention of the Review Conference, but how it will work and what it might decide. Originally, in accordance with the idea of a transitory régime, the concept of what the Review conference could decide was very broad, with the aim of eventually coming back to a unitarian régime as advocated in particular by developing countries. There was also an element of taking up issues not resolved by the Law of the Sea Conference. In the course of negotiations the area of what the Review Conference could change was then narrowed down. If in the first draft the Conference was only obliged to respect the principles of the *common heritage*

---

[1] Note by the Secretariat of the Conference of 28 April 1977.

[2] Informal working paper by the Mexican delegation enclosed into the Note of the Secretariat of 28 April 1977.

[3] Statement by Ambassador *Elliot L. Richardson* of 10 June 1977.

of mankind and of an international régime directed by an authority, later a long list of aims and principles to be respected was introduced into art. 155, para 2. Among those principles is the rather enigmatic reference to the "rights of States and their general conduct in relation to the Area, and their participation in activities in the Area in conformity with this Convention." It could be argued, therefore, although perhaps not without some difficulties, that the Conference will not be in a position to abolish the direct access of States to exploration and exploitation of the deep sea-bed. However, it cannot be taken for granted that such access must be assured in the framework of the existing parallel régime.

The other problematic element of art. 155 is decision-making of the Review Conference and the entry into force of amendments. The first drafts proposed to leave the issue in the hands of the Conference, in accordance with the original concept of an as much as possible autonomous review.[4] In the Informal Composite Negotiating Text of the Convention (ICNT) of July 1977 it was then added that the Conference should follow the practice of the Law of the Sea Conference to resort to voting only after all efforts to reach consensus had failed. To make sure that the Conference would actually result in amendments, but also in a way prejudicing those results, another provision was introduced, which said that if the Conference failed to amend the Convention or to reach agreement within five years, activity in the Area would then be carried out by the Authority only, either through the Enterprise or through joint ventures under the control of the Authority. This was not a solution suitable for a compromise, nor was the idea, introduced in the ICNT of 1979, of a moratorium for contracts and plans of work, if five years after its beginning the Conference would not have come to satisfactory results, generally acceptable. The negotiations finally resorted to prescribing majority rule for the decision-making of the Conference as well as with respect to entry into force of amendments. The battle came to a standstill in the very last phase of the Law of the Sea Conference at the marker of a three-fourths majority, stopping somewhat short of granting the industrialized countries, if united and taken altogether, the possibility of a veto.

A conventional régime providing for amendments to enter into force for all States Parties without the consent of all, is nothing new as such. The best known example is the UN Charter, which in its Art. 108 allows for amendments to enter into force for all States Parties after adoption and ratification by two-thirds of them, including, and this of course is an important distinction, the permanent members of the Security Council. It is also well known that such a régime may create serious constitutional difficulties for some States with respect to the prerogatives of parliaments. If under the Basic Law of the Federal Republic of Germany for instance, as well as under the constitutions of other States, parliament has to approve treaties of a certain importance, this normally means that also changes of such treaties are to be approved by parliament before they enter into force.

[4] *Cf.* the Mexican proposal contained in the informal working paper of 28 April 1977.

Besides this constitutional problem, however, it is mainly a question of interests at stake, whether or not a majority rule approach may be considered an acceptable solution.

Let us now turn to the rest of the review provisions of the Convention. In a note generally on the issue of amendments dated 1 August 1979 the President of the UN Law of the Sea Conference made reference to the "overriding principle of the package deal" between all elements and parts of the Convention, and he mentioned the dilemma between safeguarding this principle and the necessity to provide for the possibility of amendments, which by nature affect only parts of the Convention, thus creating a "paradoxical" situation.[5]

The package deal concept, fundamentally important for the negotiating process of the Law of the Sea Conference, could for some time hinder the inclusion into art. 155 of special provisions on the entry into force of amendments adopted by the Review Conference. But a separate solution for Part XI had in fact been accepted since the negotiations of the parallel régime for sea-bed mining. The special rôle of the Review Conference for Part XI excluded its merger with the general amendment provisions of the Convention.

Still the first approach to the question of amendments to the Convention in general was that of a conference of States Parties to review "the implementation of the Convention" as a whole. In the course of negotiations the idea of a comprehensive review of the Convention could not be maintained. The conference approach stayed in the text of art. 312 of the Convention, but it was curtailed in two respects. The conference is now conceived only as an amendment conference, not as a periodic and comprehensive review conference. It will also deal only with amendments "other than those relating to activities in the Area," paralleling in a more modest way and with more limited purposes the Review Conference of Part XI.

The retention of the conference concept also for the other parts of the Convention made it necessary to look for simpler solutions for lesser amendments. The result is art. 313. In order to complete the review system of the Convention and because of the parallelism between Review Conference of art. 155 and amendment conference of art. 312, it then seemed necessary to introduce a simplified procedure also for amendments of Part XI. This was done outside Part XI, by way of art. 314, concerning changes not affecting "the system of explorations for and exploitation of the resources of the Area, pending the Review Conference in according with art. 155." A little loophole, however, still exists: Should the Review Conference not provide for an instrument succeeding it, changes of Part XI, after the Review Conference took place, will only be possible in the limited framework of art. 314.

---

[5] President's note, informal plenary on final clauses, doc. FS/4 of 1 August 1979.

With respect to amendments of Part XI under art. 314 a split system, as a result of amendments not agreeable for all States Parties, for practical and reasons on principle again did not seem acceptable. The solution, however, was different from that, found for the Review Conference: The not so important amendments under art. 314, will have to meet consent by all interested groups of States Parties in the Council of the Authority.

As we have seen, the review provisions of the Law of the Sea Convention are intensely linked to the negotiating history of the Convention as a whole and in particular to the history of the crucial points of the sea-bed mining régime. Initial concepts and perceptions related to the review and amendment instruments of the Convention have not, or at least not fully, been maintained in the course of negotiations.

It can be noted that, generally speaking, the emphasis — to a lesser extent in the case of the Review Conference for Part XI, quite largely in the case of the conference foreseen for the rest of the Convention — evolved, shifting from a comprehensive review to an amendment approach. Although this certainly was the result of a compromise between differing interests, it should not be seen simply as a defeat of originally consistent and pure concepts. Altogether the more modest amendment approach, leaving the main principles of the conventional régime untouched, offers positive aspects for a rational and secure management of the régime. The demand for a comprehensive review of a conventional régime is always of a very exceptional character. The enormous negotiating efforts which were necessary to bring about the parallel system for deep sea-bed mining and to tie up the whole package of the Convention are unlikely to be repeated in the foreseeable future.

The relative loss of importance of one of the two elements of the compromise found for Part XI, namely the transitional character of the régime, corresponds to a general trend in the negotiating process, not only of the Law of the Sea Conference but also of the on-going Preparatory Commission for the International Sea-Bed Authority and for the International Tribunal for the Law of the Sea. This development, going beyond Part XI, points into the direction of a perception of the main elements of the conventional régime as permanent and not liable to fundamental formal changes in the future. If it is true that the still unforeseeable future practice of deep sea-bed mining will demand great flexibility in the application of the régime, this will rather become a challenge for the proper work of the institutions of the Authority, in particular of the decision-making procedures, than a matter for fundamental review of the provisions of the Convention. In a way, the Review Conference approach is a child of the early times of negotiations of the environment régime.

The question what to do with the Review Conference of art. 155 in the framework of efforts to be deployed in order to make the law of the Convention universally acceptable has to be answered before this background. Basically two ways have been thought of to make it fit with such efforts, either making use of it, or reducing its rôle. Indeed, if the negotiations in or aside the Preparatory Commission will not prove able to solve the still pending issues of the sea-bed régime, the solution of those questions might be postponed until the time of commercial viability of deep sea-bed mining, and it might be thought of making advance use of the instrument of the Review Conference to adapt the mining régime to the then prevailing situation. The character of the conference as a review instrument might then find itself even enhanced. But it would be all the more difficult under such circumstances to think of majority rule, as foreseen in art. 155 of the Convention, as a suitable and successful method of decision-making.

Independent of this possibility, the normal trend would rather be to continue on the way of perceiving the Review Conference more and more as an amendment conference in the ordinary sense. This would presuppose on the one side a narrow interpretation of the mandate of the Conference in particular with respect to the "rights of States ... and their participation in activities in the Area," i. e. with respect to their access to deep sea-bed mining. On the other side this would mean to renounce prejudging in any way the outcome of the Conference. To satisfy the latter requirement would imply either the return to the principle contained in art. 40 of the Vienna Convention on the Law of Treaties, namely that amendments to multilateral conventions are binding only on those States Parties adhering to them, or, which might be more in accordance with the particular needs of the deep sea-bed mining régime, to make amendments to Part XI in one way or the other dependent on the consent of all the main interest groups, as it is already foreseen for the amendment procedure under art. 314 of the Convention.

Discussion

Jesus:

I am grateful to Mr *Kiderlen* for having spoken on one of the important issues of the Convention. I believe that at the very end of his statement, he hinted at, or even suggested a way of circumventing the difficulties. The legal difficulty, that I believe we all share, is the entering into force of the amendments which apply to all parties to the Convention. Amendments will be introduced, once adopted by the Review Conference, and ratified by two-thirds of the parties to the Convention even though some parties to the Convention have not themselves ratified the amendments. As was mentioned, such an attitude is not only in contravention to the general law of treaties, as contained in the Vienna Convention, but is also, as I see it, a violation of a fundamental rule of constitutions of nations as I made clear in my statement during this symposium. There is a major principle of constitutional law of any nation in accordance with which States only are bound internationally through conventional international law, only when the constitutional bodies have so signified through the normal legal channels. The Convention on the Law of the Sea, especially the amendment procedure of the Review Conference, seems to be at least at odds with this main principle of constitutional law of any nation and also of the Vienna Convention on the Law of Treaties.

I believe that we could have lived with that legal problem, had there not also been a major political problem with the Convention, as regards the sea-bed régime. To the extent we all have a problem that has to be dealt with, I anticipate that we will not have major difficulties in finding a solution to that political problem that raises equally legal difficulty. As such, I am accustomed to saying in my private conversations with people on this issue of Part XI that this is in fact a non-issue. We only have to seek a way of circumventing this problem that is a problem for all of us, at least, for many of us a legal problem, for others a legal and a political problem as well. You seem to suggest in the last part of your speech a way of circumventing the technical problem raised by this provision of the Convention. And that is perhaps not only two-thirds majority ratification as is at present required for an amendment to enter into force in relation to all parties of that Convention, but to qualify it with the idea that provided that the two-thirds majority of ratification of amendments includes the ratifications of all interest groups. I believe that is an important idea to be explored, in the context of any consultation to be undertaken to address this legal and political difficulty of entering into force of amendments approved in the Review Conference.

Kiderlen:

It is not really a reply I have to give, but first of all an expression of gratefulness for some clarification of what I thought about the matter myself. My thesis was that there were anyway two approaches to be distinguished with respect to the review clauses: in an initial phase fundamental changes were envisaged because of some uncertainty about the whole concept of the sea-bed mining, then, later a more — let us say — stabilized view prevailed, which now envisages these review clauses more under the view points of just normal amendment procedures. So, I think what you just suggested, Mr *Jesus*, made this trend clear and brought the idea to the conclusion, where I can see possibilities for a solution for the problem of the review clause which might not be radical, but more of the character, of an interpretation.

Maquieira:

I would like to ask Dr. *Kiderlen* if he sees any value in using the provisions in art. 154 (the 5-year periodic review) to trigger the possiblity of an amendment procedure, in the sense that the Convention says that every five years it will review the system. Now, should at the first review the conclusion be reached that the system requires major modifications, can it in his opinion provoke (from that 5-year review) a process of amendment, or must it wait until the period of time foreseen in art. 154 will be fulfilled? I ask this question because I see that there are some difficulties in getting into the Convention itself, without the Convention being in force in order to bring about a process of amendments. If we assume that we will amend the Convention, for example once this is in force, the first opportunity to do that is provided by art. 154. Otherwise you have to wait for the 20 years or 25 years in order to bring about the contents of art. 155. Now, the problem there is as to whether art. 154 in advancing the Review Conference, can go beyond of the terms and conditions established in art. 155. But I do think that art. 154 may become a very important article in terms of provoking, or advancing a review process on substantive aspects of the régime.

Kiderlen:

Thank you for that question. In fact, art. 154 in my mind is not so very much part of the review clauses. It is situated somewhat in between the decision-making procedures and the review clauses. So, I see this article more in the line of avoidance of a fundamental review by introducing an intermediate stage of periodic review within the system, not challenging the system itself. I think there is a positive rôle of that article in this direction. To address the other aspect of your question, as to whether art. 154 might play a rôle in this specific situation where the deep sea-bed régime is not yet operative and will probably not become operative for some time, I can see also in this respect a positive rôle for art. 154. Article 154 makes a critical review of the rules of deep sea-bed mining possible, even perhaps before the conventional régime enters into operation, without the necessity of — let us say — full-scale conferences, full-scale renegotiations, remaining in the existing rather modest frameworks of the Authority's mechanisms. So I would give this whole area perhaps a slightly different emphasis than your question indicated. I do not see art. 154 triggering off any big review process, rather I see art. 154 preventing big processes in this direction.

Treves:

Considering the revised assessment on when commercial production will start, I do not think art. 155 will have practical relevance at least within the lifetime of the youngest of us all. But it creates problems for those, or some of those, who may be called to ratify the Convention. The problem is how to eliminate this problem of principle and not that of whether and in which ways we could amend the Convention once it is in force. To solve the latter problem there are many mechanisms already in the Convention and many others that could be developed outside the Convention. The real problem is that the piece of paper that parliaments will have to approve has somehow to exclude art. 155. In order to do so there may be various mechanisms. Probably a side agreement excluding it in one way or another is the only way. I agree with Ambassador *Jesus* that politically this is a non-issue, because I do not see any strong constituency for retaining art. 155. It belongs to a package whose time has come and gone. However, it is still present in the Convention. We simply have to do something about it.

Kiderlen:

I can only agree with what *Tullio Treves* just said.

Deep Sea-Bed Mining: The Practice of the Pioneer Investors

Tullio Treves*

I. The Pioneer Investors: a Multi-Faceted Group

The term "pioneer investor" is defined in para. 1 (a) of resolution II of the Third United Nations Law of the Sea Conference.[1] Amongst them are four States (France, India, Japan and the Soviet Union) or state enterprises and four multinational consortia, whose component enterprises are nationals of or controlled by, one or more of the following States: Belgium, Canada, the Federal Republic of Germany, Italy, Japan, the Netherlands, the United Kingdom and the United States. These eight entities had already made considerable investments in sea-bed mining at the time the resolution was adopted. The Conference considered it useful to create a provisional régime to be applied before the Convention entered into force, in order to protect this investment and encourage its continuation. The resolution includes also a third category of an open-ended nature consisting of developing States or enterprises belonging to such States provided they make a substantial investment before 1 January 1985. This date has been postponed to the entry into force of the Convention by a decision taken by the Preparatory Commission of the International Sea-Bed Authority and the International Tribunal for the Law of the Sea (the PrepCom), which in 1986 has also added to this list a group of socialist States of Eastern Europe or a group of state enterprises of such States. The pioneer investors whose "practice" is of interest are, however, so far only the eight included in the two first categories mentioned in resolution II.

* Prof. *Tullio Treves*, University of Milano, Faculty of Law, currently Legal Adviser of the Italian Permanent Mission to the UN, New York. The views expressed in this paper are personal and do not necessarily reflect those of the Italian Government.

[1] On resolution II, *see Tullio Treves*, La protection des investissements préparatoires et la résolution n. 2 de la Conférence sur le droit de la mer, in: Annuaire français de droit international 28 (1982), 851 - 872; *Peter Brückner*, Preparatory Investment Protection and the PIP Resolution, in: *Albert W. Koers/Bernard H. Oxman* (eds.), The 1982 Convention on the Law of the Sea (Law of the Sea Institute Conference, Oslo 1983), Honolulu 1984, 181 - 193; *Felipe H. Paolillo*, The Institutional Arrangements for the International Sea-Bed and their Impact on the Evolution of International Organizations in: Recueil des Cours 188 (1984-IV), 137 - 337 (305 - 316); *Said Mahmoudi*, The Law of Deep Sea-Bed Mining, Stockholm 1987, 313 - 321.

Resolution II makes it very clear that pioneer investors are industrial entities, whether they are constituted by States or by state enterprises or by private enterprises. They are not "States" according to the international law interpretation. Such "States" are mentioned in the resolution as those whose nationality the pioneer investors have, or as "certifying States", which sponsor the pioneer investors in their application for acquiring "registered" status and thus enabling them to enjoy the rights and undertake the duties provided by the resolution. As the subject given to the present paper by the organizers is the "practice of pioneer investors", it seems necessary for our purposes to consider the practice of the States to which — by nationality or control — the pioneer investors belong. Indeed, in international law it makes sense to speak of "practice" only in connection with the subjects of international law. We shall concern ourselves with "pioneer investor States."

The category of pioneer investors is notable for the great variety of groupings in which its components — notwithstanding their small number — can be classified. We have already seen the distinctions emerging directly from resolution II: States, state enterprises, multinational consortia, developing countries and their enterprises. Looking at the "pioneer investor States", one can make further distinctions in alliance with their attitude towards the UN Law of the Sea Convention; in accordance with their attitude towards the PrepCom and resolution II; with respect to the adoption or non-adoption of domestic laws on deep sea-bed mining; regarding the participation or non-participation in agreements with other pioneer investor States.

Three of these States, the Federal Republic of Germany, the United Kingdom and the United States, have not signed the Convention, while all the others have, even though their positions on the sea-bed part of it range from the rather negative (Belgium, France, Italy, Japan, and more recently, the USSR) to the moderately negative (Canada and, apparently, the Netherlands), to quite positive (India). With regard to the attitude toward the PrepCom, all the signatories participate actively in its work, and, amongst the non-signatories, the Federal Republic of Germany and the United Kingdom utilize fully their status of "privileged" observers[2], while the United States remains completely absent. However only four States, namely France, India, Japan and the USSR, have taken advantage of the provisions of resolution II in order to apply for, and to obtain, the registration of their enterprises as pioneer investors.[3]

Looking at domestic legislation, Belgium, Canada, India and the Netherlands have not adopted any, whereas the other States considered have more or less extensive laws and regulations on sea-bed mining. With the exception of Italy and the Soviet Union, they have used such legislation in order to grant exploration

---

2 *See Tullio Treves*, "Observers Signatory of the Final Act" in the International Seabed Authority's Preparatory Commission, in: GYIL 27 (1984), 303-314.

3 *Infra*, chapter VII.

licenses to their enterprises. As for the agreements between these States, all the western pioneer investor States, with the exception, however, of Canada, are parties to a "Provisional Understanding" concluded in 1984, while Belgium, Canada, Italy, the Netherlands, the USSR and, as we will discover, indirectly the Federal Republic of Germany, the United Kingdom and the United States belong to the so-called "Midnight Agreement" concluded in 1987.[4]

In approaching the "practice" of the pioneer investor States, it seems important to bear in mind that the very concept of pioneer investors is derived from resolution II. Consequently, we consider it appropriate to focus upon the aspects of the practice of these States which are most directly connected with the resolution and, of course, with the long term prospects of the Law of the Sea Convention. We shall not dwell on the purely domestic aspects of the practice of these States. In particular, we shall not insist upon an analysis — which other scholars have conducted in great detail during the last decade[5] — of the various national laws on deep sea-bed mining.

II. The Background: the Different Positions on the Lawfulness of Unilateral Exploitation of the Deep Sea-Bed

Recent practice must be appreciated in the light of a question of principle which separates most pioneer investor States from the majority of States. This is the question of the lawfulness of exploitation of deep sea-bed resources outside the framework of the United Nations Law of the Sea Convention. Different views were expressed on this point when the first national laws on deep sea-bed mining were announced and then adopted in the late Seventies. The controversy — to which legal writers have devoted considerable attention[6] — arose once again in the mid-'80s when, on the basis of some of these laws, licenses were awarded for the exploration of certain portions of the sea-bed beyond the limits of national jurisdiction.

On the one hand, it was held that unilateral exploitation was incompatible with the principle, enshrined in the UN General Assembly's Declaration of Principles Governing the Sea-Bed and Ocean Floor,[7] according to which the

---

[4] *Infra*, chapters IV and VI.

[5] For a collection of these laws, *E. D. Brown*, Sea-Bed Energy and Mineral Resources and the Law of the Sea, Vol. 3, London 1986, para. III. 3. 1-228. They have been examined in detail in *op. cit.*, Vol. 2, para. II. 8. 1 to 51; and in *V. Game De Fontebrune*, L'exploitation des ressources minérales des fonds marins: législations nationales et droit international, Paris 1985; for a valuable shorter treatment *see Said Mahmoudi* (note 1).

[6] The literature on this point is very extensive. The present author has considerd it in *Tullio Treves*, Seabed Mining and the United Nations Law of the Sea Convention, in: Italian Yearbook of International Law 5 (1980-81), 22-51 (25-30), with references. For recent discussions *see Game de Fontbrune* (note 5), 133-185 and *Mahmoudi* (note 1), 244-253.

international sea-bed and its resources are the *common heritage of mankind.* It was argued that this principle corresponds to customary international law and renders all forms of unilateral exploitation unlawful.[8]

On the other hand, it was argued that the resolution was not a binding instrument and that the only limits existing to activities by States on the floor of the high seas were those which apply in general to the exercise of the freedoms of the high seas, namely that these areas are not subject to appropriation and that activities must not be conducted with reasonable regard for other free activities.[9]

When the United States, followed by the Federal Republic of Germany and the United Kingdom, granted licenses for the exploration of certain parts of the international sea-bed, the PrepCom issued two declarations of condemnation. Therein it was stated that the only régime for exploration and exploitation of the Area and its resources is that established by the United Nations Convention on the Law of the Sea and related resolutions . . . and that "any claim, agreement or action regarding the Area or its resources" undertaken outside the Preparatory Commission was wholly illegal.[10]

Although the first declaration was adopted without a vote, dissents were registered.[11] The second was voted upon and obtained 59 votes in favour, seven against and 10 abstentions. Of the pioneer investor States, the USSR and India voted in favour, while the others voted against.[12] The issue was discussed at the UN General Assembly in 1985 and 1986, as well as in some of the documents circulated at the PrepCom. The pioneer investor States in disputing the declarations underscored, among other things, that *only* when a vast majority of States, including all major groups and shades of interest in deep sea-bed mining, will have become party to the Convention, will it become the "treaty of a universal character, generally agreed upon" mentioned in the 1970 declaration of the General Assembly. Then, and only then will it become meaningful to talk of the régime "established" by the Convention for sea-bed mining as the "only régime".[13]

---

7 GA res. 2749 (XXV) of 17 December 1970.

8 Intervention by the representative of Fiji *S. Nandan* on behalf of the Group of 77 at the 109th plenary meeting of the Third UN Conference on the Law of the Sea on 15 September 1978, in: Third UN Conference on the Law of the Sea, Official Records, Vol. 9, 103; *see also* UN doc. A/CONF. 62/77 of 25 April 1979, *ibid.*, Vol. 11, 80.

9 Interventions by the representatives of the United States, *Richardson*, of France, *de Lacharrière*, of the Federal Republic of Germany, *Wolff*, of Italy, *Varvesi*, of Belgium, *Nolard*, of the Netherlands, *Bos*, at the 109th plenary meeting of the Third UN Law of the Sea Conference on 15 September 1978, in: Third UN Conference on the Law of the Sea, Official Records, Vol. 9, 104-107.

10 The first declaration was adopted on 30 August 1985, UN doc. LOS/PCN/33; the second on 11 April 1986, UN doc. LOS/PCN/78.

11 *Cf.* UN doc. A/40/923, para. 112.

12 UN doc. A/41/742, para. 123 and Press Release SEA/725 of 11 April 1986.

Moreover, two new aspects began to emerge in this debate. The first is that the critics of unilateral activities on the sea-bed started to distinguish between signatories and non-signatories of the UN Law of the Sea Convention as only the former were bound by the principle of the law of treaties not to defeat the object and purpose of the treaty before it enters into force.[14] The second aspect is that although the above-mentioned declarations lumped "exploration" and "exploitation" of the deep sea-bed together in their condemnation, these two activities were separated by one of the pioneer investor States, in replying to the argument drawn from the aforementioned principle of the law of treaties. The Government of the Netherlands stated the following:

> The obligation to refrain from acts which might defeat the object and purpose of the convention means in our view that a State which signs the Convention must refrain from acts which might make it impossible to apply the Convention in the future, after it has entered into force. As regards the application of Part XI [of the Law of the Sea Convention], this implies that there is an obligation to refrain from actually exploiting the sea-bed. Preparations for such exploitation, for instance the development of technology, the carrying out of marine research and the settlement of disputes about overlapping, continue to be permissible.[15]

III. Resolution II and the Need to Eliminate Overlapping between Pioneer Mining Sites

The provisional system for the exploration of the deep sea-bed contained in resolution II requires that pioneer investors, in order to submit to the PrepCom an application for registration, ensure that the sites for which they apply are not subject to overlapping with the sites for which other prospective certifying States are applying for registration of their pioneer investors. The resolution indicates a certain procedure for the elimination of overlapping including precise time limits and recourse to arbitration (para. 5).

Two interesting consequences emerged from the difficulty of following these prescriptions and from the need to implement those provisions of resolution II which had the most political visibility, namely those concerning the registration of pioneer investors. The first was that States were confronted with the need to modify resolution II. The second was that it became clear that the premise upon

---

13 Intervention by the representative of Italy on 10 December 1985, UN doc. A/40/PV. 110, 26. *See also* the interventions of the representatives of Belgium, the Netherlands, Canada and Japan, *loc. cit.*, 42, 52, 62, 73; and that of the United States at the following meeting of the General Assembly, UN doc. A/40/PV. 111, 6. For the positions of the Federal Republic of Germany and the United Kingdom *see* UN docs. LOS/PCN/33 and LOS/PCN/34.

14 Intervention of the representative of Cape Verde at the 40th session of the UN General Assembly on 10 December 1985 (UN doc. A/40/PV. 110, 67).

15 Statement of 3 August 1986, in: NYIL 18 (1987), 291 f.

which resolution II was built — namely, that all pioneer investors would file applications for registration — was incorrect, as certain pioneer investors did not file their applications while pursuing activities under national licences. As it was more than likely that overlapping existed not only amongst pioneer investors having applied for registration but also in respect of sites upon which the non-applying pioneer investors claimed exclusive rights under national legislation, the following question emerged: Was such overlapping to be deemed as irrelevant because the non-applying pioneer investors did not intend to submit (or to submit immediately) to resolution II, or were they, on the contrary, to be taken into consideration for the sake of avoiding conflicts?

IV. The Elimination of Overlapping amongst Western Consortia and Enterprises Belonging to States Applying for Registered Pioneer Status

In the beginning, the clash between opposing views on this last question blocked all progress. An attempt made by Canada to promote a "Memorandum of Understanding" for the elimination of overlapping between all the pioneer investors named in resolution II was stopped by the Soviet Union which declared that claims by States not partaking in the mechanism of resolution II should not be considered.[16]

In the meantime, at the end of 1983, the four multinational consortia, and the French and Japanese enterprises succeeded, through agreements within the industry, to eliminate the overlapping in existence between the sites for which they had applied for licenses under national laws.[17] An agreement concluded in Washington on 2 September 1982 between the United States, France, the Federal Republic of Germany and the United Kingdom had encouraged industry to follow this path.[18] The "Provisional Arrangement" signed in Geneva on 3 August 1984 between the same States, joined by Belgium, Japan, Italy and the Netherlands, provided the sanction of an inter-State agreement to the elimination of overlapping agreed by the industry.[19]

---

16 *See in particular* the Canadian letter of 8 April 1983 in: UN doc. LOS/PCN/24 and further explanations in UN doc. LOS/PCN/40; the Soviet letter of 3 April 1984 in UN doc. LOS/PCN/36*; the letter by Belgium, France, the Federal Republic of Germany, Italy, Japan, the Netherlands and United Kingdom in UN doc. LOS/PCN/41.

17 On these agreements, which have not been made public, *see J. M. Broadus/Porter Hoagland III*, Conflict Resolution in the Assignment of Area Entitlements for Seabed Mining, in: San Diego Law Review 21 (1984), 541-576 (533-534); *Marne Dubs*, Minerals of the Deep Sea: Myth and Realiy, in: *G. Pontecorvo* (ed.), The New Order of the Oceans — the Advent of a Managed Marine Environment, New York 1986, 85-121 (86, 117-120).

18 Reprinted in: ILM 21 (1982), 950.

19 Reprinted in: ILM 23 (1984), 1354.

Consequently, at the end of 1983, the probable remaining overlapping could only concern the Soviet Union, as it was well known that the Indian site was in the Indian Ocean while all the others were in the Clarion-Clipperton fracture in the middle of the Pacific Ocean. As at that time the Soviet Union was not ready to consider the claims of the non-applicants as relevant, and as France and Japan had settled their overlapping with the other western enterprises, the stage was set for the elimination of overlapping between the Soviet Union, France and Japan.[20]

The process began with an "Understanding on Resolution of Conflicts among Applicants for Registration as Pioneer Investors" and an "Understanding on the Procedures for Conflict Resolution among the First Group of Applicants" read to the PrepCom by its chairman.[21] Negotiations quickly permitted the obtainment of a provisional solution of the overlapping between the Soviet and the Japanese sites. On 28 February 1985, France, Japan and the USSR was required to communicate to the chairman of the PrepCom that France and the USSR

> were not able to settle their conflict on the basis of a fair sharing of the overlapping area due to the magnitude of the overlapping ascertained. It appears that the implementation of this principle could not allow the parties to fulfill the other condition set out in resolution II, para. 3, which provides that "every application shall cover a total area which need not be a single continuous area, sufficiently large and of sufficient estimated commercial value to allow two mining operations", a part of which being reserved for the International Sea-Bed Authority.[22]

This was in effect an announcement of the need for changes to resolution II, to be added to the tacit abrogation of the provisions of the resolution on time limits and upon recourse to arbitration for the elimination of overlapping areas.

Indeed, such changes were contained in the agreement between the four applicants for registration concluded with the good offices of the chairman of the PrepCom, Mr *Warioba*, at Arusha on 5 February 1986[23] and repeated with various modifications in the "Declaration on the Implementation of resolution II" adopted by the PrepCom at New York on 5 September 1986.[24] Leaving aside, for the time being, those concerning the position of the "potential applicants", the

---

20 On the questions considered in this chapter as well as in chapters V-VII, *cf. Philippe Kirsch/Douglas Fraser*, The Law of the Sea Preparatory Commission after Six Years: Review and Prospects, in: Canadian Yearbook of International Law 26 (1988), 119-154; *Elie Jarmache*, La Résolution II de l'Acte final de la 3ème Conférence des Nations Unies sur le droit de la mer, in: Collection "Espaces et ressources maritimes" 3 (1988), 19-41; *Moritaka Hayashi*, Registration of Pioneer Investors by the Preparatory Commission for the International Sea-Bed Authority and the International Tribunal for the Law of the Sea, in: Ocean Development and International Law 20 (1989), 1-33.

21 UN doc. LOS/PCN/L. 8 of 31 August 1984.

22 UN doc. LOS/PCN/56 of 12 March 1985.

23 The Arusha Understanding was never officially made public. However, it circulated widely among the delegations active at the PrepCom.

24 Annex of UN doc. LOS/PCN/L. 41/ Rev. 1.

changes, first of all, brought substantial modifications to the "parallel system" adopted by resolution II. France, Japan and USSR obtained the right to select a major part of their pioneer site (53,000 square kilometres out of 75,000), whereas according to the resolution, the PrepCom is entitled to select the part to be granted to the applicant. The principle according to which for each site granted to an applicant there must be a site of "equal estimated commercial value" reserved for the Authority is maintained. However, in the "central area" where nodule density is highest, the Authority obtains only one area of 53,000 square kilometres to be carved out of those the applicants had applied for, while the rest of the Authority's three sites is found in less desirable areas. Moreover, the registered pioneer investors accepted the condition to assist the PrepCom and the Authority "in the exploration of a mine site for the first operation of the Enterprise", "notwithstanding" the provision of resolution II on this subject, according to which, *inter alia*, such assistance shall be on a cost-reimbursement basis. Apart from these, further changes introduced are those previously mentioned concerning the extension of the time limit for the applications by pioneer investors from developing countries and the new pioneer investors from Eastern Europe.

V. The Interests of the "Potential Applicants"

The pioneer investor States participating in the PrepCom which did not apply for registration, the "potential applicants", namely Belgium, Canada, Italy, the Netherlands and — in their position of non-signatories — the Federal Republic of Germany and the United Kingdom insisted from the beginning of the process for the solution of overlapping amongst applicants that their interest was to be protected and that the Understandings of 1984 as well as the one concluded at Arusha were, as far as they were concerned, *res inter alios acta*. It was also clear that, unless their interests were satisfactorily taken into account, they were ready to create difficulties to the registration of the applicants through their representatives in the PrepCom's General Committee.

The Arusha Understanding contained an initial move towards meeting the requests of the "potential applicants." It provided that the "relinquishment" of portions of the pioneer area to be performed, according to resolution II, by registered pioneer investors over a certain number of years after registration, could be performed immediately and completely at the moment of registration, particularly by the applicants (i. e. the Soviet Union) having "practical problems", the code word for "overlapping", with non-applicants. The areas so relinquished remained deposited with the PrepCom in order to be utilized, if need be, for the future applications by potential applicants. This could not satisfy the potential applicants. They considered that the applicants "of the first group" were trying to solve unilaterally, without the potential applicants' participation, the overlapping between the four western consortia and the Soviet Union.

The New York Declaration of 1986, although it adopts by and large the same mechanism,[25] was accepted by the potential applicants because they had obtained sufficient guarantees both within the parameters of Declaration and outside of it. In the Declaration, they had obtained a paragraph according to which

> [t]he treatment to be accorded to potential applicants in respect of their applications shall be similar to the treatment given to the first group of applicants provided that potential applicants assume similar obligations to those of the first group of applicants before the entry into force of the United Nations Convention on the Law of the Sea.[26]

Potential applicants thus obtained, in particular, the right to select a substantial part of their sites which the Declaration had recognized to the first group of applicants.[27] Moreover, the modification of the "relinquishment" principle envisaged in the Declaration was indicated

> as an equitable approach to resolving any practical problems that might be anticipated between any of the first group of applicants and any potential applicants.[28]

The unilateralism still pervading the Arusha understanding as regards the solution of overlapping was extinguished.

VI. The Elimination of Overlapping between the Soviet Enterprise and the Four Western Consortia: the "Midnight Agreement"

The guarantees obtained by the "potential applicants" outside the New York Declaration were of even more importance. Two days before the New York Declaration was adopted, on 3 September 1986, the four potential applicants being signatories of the Convention had agreed with the Soviet Union on a procedure for negotiating the elimination of overlapping between the four western multinational consortia and the Soviet enterprise.[29] The United States, the Federal Republic of Germany and the United Kingdom were associated with this agreement. In order to take into account the residual Soviet reluctance to be perceived as negotiating with non-signatories, it was agreed that the political framework of the negotiation would be limited to the Soviet Union and the four potential applicants having signed the Convention. The "geographical solution" to overlapping was, however, to be worked out in a technical working group, to which preferably the officials of the entities directly affected by the overlapping should

---

25 *See especially loc. cit.*, para. 9.

26 *Loc. cit.*, para. 15.

27 This conclusion, drawn by the representative of Italy in intervening at the 41st session of the UN General Assembly (58th meeting on 5 November 1985, UN doc. A/41/PV. 58, 28) was not challenged.

28 Annex of UN doc. LOS/PCN/L. 41/Rev. 1, para. 19 (d).

29 This agreement has not been made public.

participate. The participation of the consortia, even when represented by citizens of the non-signatory States, was thus accepted and encouraged. Moreover, a side letter of the same date provided that "arrangements" would be made in order to ensure that the United States, the Federal Republic of Germany and the United Kingdom would respect the results of the negotiations.

This procedure was followed in the Agreement on Confidentiality of Data concluded in Moscow on 5 December 1986[30] and confirmed and made public with the "Midnight Agreement" concluded in New York on 14 August 1987. This agreement eliminated all overlapping between the mining sites claimed by the Soviet Union and those claimed by the four multinational consortia.[31]

The "Midnight Agreement", concluded between the USSR and the four signatories to the Convention, was completed by exchanges of notes between, on the one side, the Soviet Union and the United States, the Federal Republic of Germany and the United Kingdom and, on the other side, these three last States and each of the other four western participants. The effect of this network of notes is that all of the eight States are bound to each other by the rules set forth in the principal agreement.

VII. The Registration of the Indian, French, Japanese and Soviet Enterprises

With all "overlaps" being eliminated, the door was open in the PrepCom for the registration of the enterprises of India, France, Japan and the Soviet Union as pioneer investors under resolution II. Registration was made on 17 August 1987 for the Indian enterprise, and on 17 December 1987, after the relevant applications were corrected in order to take into account the results of the "Midnight Agreement," for the French, Japanese and Soviet enterprises.[32]

In conferring upon the registration, the PrepCom applied the principles contained in the 1986 New York Declaration with regard to the interests of the potential applicants. The Report on the Deliberations on Registration notes that certain areas had been "voluntarily relinquished" in accordance with the New York Declaration, and that

> [t]hese will be reserved to form part of the application areas of potential applicants qualified to apply as pioneer investors under resolution II, para. 1 (a) (ii), until the Convention enters into force.[33]

30 ILM 26 (1987), 1045 (the text of the exchanges of notes with the three States not being signatories of the 1982 Convention has not been published).

31 For the text, *see* Law of the Sea Bulletin, no. 11, July 1988, 28 *et seq.*; ILM 26 (1987), 1502 *et seq.*

32 The principal documents concerning the registration of the four pioneer investors are reproduced in: Law of the Sea Bulletin, Special Issue II, April 1988. To these one most add UN docs. LOS/PCN/54/Rev. 1 and 55, with the reports of the Chairman of the PrepCom.

VIII. The Importance of Certain Obligations in the "Midnight Agreement" for Future Developments

The "Midnight Agreement" contains obligations which bind parties beyond the time of registration of pioneer investors and even beyond the time of entry into force of the Convention. Not only do parties agree to respect the solution to the overlapping contained in the annex (art. 2) and not to prevent registration by the PrepCom of applications consistent with such solution (art. 3), but they agree that

> [t]he Parties shall not act, themselves or in association with third parties, in a manner which could lead to the creation of additional practical problems with respect to the deep sea-bed mining areas referred to in the Annexes to this Agreement

and that

> [a]ccordingly, the Parties shall not engage in or support deep sea-bed mining in, or seek to support registration in the Preparatory Commission of, a deep sea-bed mining area in a manner incompatible with respect for the areas specified in the Annexes to this Agreement (art. 4).

These provisions seem to imply that parties are bound not to grant licenses encroaching upon sites attributed to other parties, and not to participate in multinational consortia (such as the new East European one) which were to conduct activities on these sites. With the obligation not to support activities from which new overlapping can derive, the parties seem not only to disengage themselves from the co-operation in such activities but they also must refrain from supporting them with their vote, be it in the PrepCom or in the Authority.

Moreover, and also this obligation is not limited by time,

> Parties shall take all measures in conformity with international law and existing legislation to ensure that there is no physical interference with the activities of each other related to exploration and exploitation of hard mineral resources in the deep sea-bed mining areas referred to in the Annexes to this Agreement (art. 5).

Even though this provision does not state that sea-bed mining activities are the exercise of the freedom of the high seas, it implements the principle according to which lawful activities on the high seas must be conducted "with reasonable regard" for other lawful activities.

The importance of these obligations should not be underrated. The four multinational consortia have amongst them a guarantee by only one State, namely the Soviet Union, which is not party to the 1984 Provisional Understanding which, at least in the present situation, has the capability to conduct activities in their mine sites. The Soviet Union in turn has a guarantee that the States with the necessary capabilities, and which are not bound by the rules of resolution II, will not conduct activities within its mine site.

[33] UN doc. LOS/PCN/L. 55, para. 26.

IX. Trends of Practice after the Registration of Pioneer Investors

After the registration of the four pioneer investors, practice seems to take into consideration the peculiar characteristics of the present situation regarding deep sea-bed mining. These characteristics may be summarized as follows: First, the reasons of the industrialized States which are dissatisfied with the definitive régime of sea-bed mining set forth in Part XI of the Convention (amongst which the Soviet Union must now be counted) still exist and, apparently, have not been attenuated by the modest results so far attained by the PrepCom. Second, the industrial and economic interest for pursuing deep sea-bed mining in the foreseeable future is shrinking, while the projected costs are growing. Third, entry into force of the Convention, with the setting up of the International Sea-Bed Authority and the winding up of the PrepCom, does not seem to be too far away in time.

The most recent developments of practice seem to be projected towards the future in looking at the present-day realities mentioned above. Some of them are the immediate consequences of the registration of the four pioneer investors, others are more directly linked to the idea that it is time to seek ways for reconciling divergent positions on sea-bed mining.

X. The Obligations of Registered Pioneer Investors under the Test of the Realities of the Present Situation

According to resolution II, registration entails certain obligations for pioneer investors. They include the obligation to pay an "annual fixed fee" of one million dollars. Although due from the day of registration, the amount is payable from the moment the pioneer obtains a contract from the Authority.[34] Among the other obligations of registered pioneer investors, one must mention those concerning periodic expenditures to be incurred, the training of personnel of the Enterprise, and, as we have seen, under the 1986 New York Declaration, the exploration of the first mine site for the Enterprise.[35]

Even though the obligations are mentioned in the certificates of registration and were explicitly evoked at the moment of registration,[36] the pioneer investors soon made it known that they were not in the position to fulfill them. This was especially true for the annual fixed fee of one million dollars and for the exploration of the mining site for the Enterprise. The reason put forward by the registered pioneer investors was simply that the economic circumstances had changed. This justified the conclusion that

> at present one may say that the Area's resources may be exploited cost-effectively only in a distant future.[37]

---

34 Resolution II, para. 7 (b).

35 UN doc. LOS/PCN/41 Rev. 1, para. 14.

36 UN doc. LOS/PCN/L. 55, para. 25.

The Group of 77 rejected this claim stating that the obligations were legally binding and that the difficulties should have been announced before and not after registration. Negotiations on this matter have been going on since 1988. They are difficult because of the apparently strong legal position of the Group of 77, which is opposed to the political strength of the four registered pioneers. The "four" may argue that the functioning of the mechanism of resolution II would be frustrated without their pioneer activities, and that, consequently, they possess the necessary tools in which to transform the principle of the *common heritage of mankind* into reality.

Since the spring meeting of the PrepCom in 1990, a solution seems to be taking shape. According to it, the registered pioneer investors would accept the fulfillment of certain obligations, in particular on the training of personnel, as well as, although in a limited form and partially under the condition that they conduct the same activities on their sites, that of exploring the first mine site for the Enterprise. In exchange, the obligation to pay the annual fixed fee would be waived up to the time of the beginning of commercial production or, in any case, up to a moment to be determined taking into account such beginning.

Whatever the exact formulation in whichever agreement will be, what seems important is that the solution envisaged entails changes not only to resolution II but also to the 1982 Convention. The provision of the Convention that would be changed is that according to which a fixed annual fee of one million dollars is to be paid from the moment the contract for exploration and exploitation has been awarded to the applicant (art. 13, para. 3, of Annex III).

Thus the flexibility of resolution II, many examples of which emerged in the practice concerning the solution of conflicts on overlapping, seems to be extending, under the pressure of unforeseen circumstances, to the sea-bed provisions of the 1982 Convention. The changes considered come, so to say, from within the system: they originate with the necessity to ensure the functioning of the provisional régime of resolution II and its smooth transition into the definitive system. The solution now under consideration concerning the obligations of registered pioneer investors could, however, serve as a precedent for solving also the problems concerning States which stay outside of the provisional system of resolution II and which have major difficulties in accepting the Convention's definitive régime. This possibility seems strengthened because, with the possible exception of India, the registered pioneer investors seem to share the difficulties of the non-registered pioneer investor States with regard to the sea-bed provisions of the Convention. Thus, it cannot be ruled out that those changes which the registered pioneer States may find sufficient in order to accept the Convention

---

[37] "Aide-mémoire on the position of the registered pioneer investors on their obligations under resolution II" of 17 August 1988, summarizing the oral presentation made at the "Group of 33" created by the PrepCom to consider the question of the registered pioneer investors' obligations.

may one day appear sufficient also to the United States and to other similarly oriented governments.

XI. The Universality of the 1982 Convention as a Commonly Shared Objective

The need for a universal deep sea-bed mining régime has been underscored since the beginnings of the United Nations activities on the subject. The General Assembly's principles declaration of 1970[38] already announced that such régime should be established by "an international treaty of a universal character, generally agreed upon." Indeed, it would be difficult for a régime and an institutional mechanism accepted only by a part of the international community to efficiently manage the whole sea-bed beyond national jurisdiction. States remaining outside would resist being bound by the network of rules creating such a régime and mechanism.

However, only recently in 1989, the need for universality as a necessary character for an efficient régime for sea-bed mining has started to be publicly recognized beyond the circle of developed States. At the final session of the 1989 summer meeting of the PrepCom, on 1 September, the representative of Zambia, speaking on behalf of the Group of 77, stated that the Group was ready to discuss with any delegation or group of delegations any issues relating to the Convention and the work of the Preparatory Commission. The willingness to discuss — he stated — is borne out of a genuine desire to ensure the universality of the Convention, because the universality of the Convention has always been the objective of the Group of 77.

This statement was immediately met with positive reactions by other groups active in the PrepCom: the Eastern European Group, the members of the European Community, the eleven "Friends of the Convention," the Potential Applicants, the Group of Six industrialized countries.[39] It was echoed in the resolution adopted on the "Law of the Sea" item at the 44th session of the UN General Assembly on 20 November 1989. The resolution welcomes the expressions of willingness to explore all possibilities of addressing issues, as referred to in the statements made at the end of the meeting of the Preparatory Commission for the International Sea-Bed Authority and for the International Tribunal for the Law of the Sea, held in New York from 14 August to 1 September 1989, in order to secure universal participation in the Convention and invites all States to make renewed efforts to facilitate universal participation in the Convention.[40]

---

38 *See supra*, note 7.

39 These interventions, together with that of Zambia on behalf of the Group of 77, are published in: Law of the Sea Bulletin, no. 15, May 1990, 54 *et seq*.

40 GA res. 44/26 of 20 November 1989.

There is no doubt that these efforts will meet with difficulties. A forewarning can be seen, on the one hand, in the statement made at the UN General Assembly by the United States' representative. While sharing the desire for a universally acceptable Convention, he stated the United States' concern that,

> notwithstanding what appears to be a genuine desire for dialogue, many countries do not understand that from the United States perspective the sea-bed régime remains seriously flawed. We do not believe that a dialogue can succeed unless it is based on an understanding of this point. We therefore believe it would be premature now to consider negotiations.[41]

From the opposing side, Brazil, while stating that universal accession to the Convention is indeed desirable, insisted that universal participation in the Convention must be pursued within the scope of the Convention itself and the legal framework provided by the Preparatory Commission, as Part XI of the Convention was not "open for discussion".[42]

Notwithstanding the difficulties to be anticipated, the General Assembly resolution and the statements at the PrepCom seem very significant. Although with different emphasis, the importance of universality for the régime for deep sea-bed mining has been recognized. Even though varying degrees of optimism and enthusiasm have been expressed, it has been recognized that the way to obtain such universality is that of a dialogue, in other terms, of negotiation.

XII. Conclusions Drawn from Practice

The traditional legal problems envisaged under general international law when considering deep sea-bed mining — namely answering the question as to whether unilateral exploitation is lawful — seem less urgent in the light of recent practice. The likelihood that this question could arise in a specific case appears to be diminishing.

It must be emphasized that so far no exploitation activities have been conducted in the deep sea-bed. The activities carried out belong to the category of prospecting and, quite possibly, to the first phases of exploration. It would seem to us that these activities, the only ones that have been conducted in reality, are regarded as lawful by the international community, as it was remarked by the Government of the Netherlands in a statement previously quoted. It is true that the exploration licenses given by the United States, the Federal Republic of Germany and the United Kingdom have been condemned by the PrepCom. Even though couched in legal terms, these condemnations, which in any case, as we have seen, were not unanimous, seem to be predominantly of a political nature. What counts,

[41] UN doc. A/44/PV. 61, 41.

[42] UN doc. A/44/PV. 62, 31 *et seq.*

however, is, that the States meeting in the PrepCom have accepted that the applicants for registration as pioneer investors may negotiate for the settling of overlapping with multinational consortia and that certain zones of the sea-bed (upon which it is well known that national license have been given) remain reserved for possible future applications on behalf of the consortia.

As far as unilateral exploitation of the Area is concerned, it seems difficult to question that, if it were started in the legal and political situation of today, it would be met with condemnation by the PrepCom and possibly the General Assembly. Such condemnations, however, in the light of the precedents and of the engagements among industrialized States, would very probably not be unanimous, which would diminish their political impact.

However, no exploitation activity is currently undertaken or envisaged. Discussions at the PrepCom on the obligations of registered pioneer investors have made it clear that even exploration has not really commenced. The economic and industrial conditions for exploitation to start in a foreseeable future do not seem to be met, nor are they likely to be met for the next decades. What seems important, as a consequence, is how the legal situation existing at the opening for signature of the 1982 Convention has been modified by the practice under our present consideration.

Amongst the parties to the Provisional Arrangement of 1984 and the Midnight Agreement of 1987, the obligations of recognition, support and non-interference contained therein ensure that whatever unilateral exploitation activity is undertaken by those States that at present have the technical and financial capacity to engage in deep sea-bed mining will be protected as against the other States having such capacity. As we remarked before, these obligations have no time limits. They are limited, however, as they concern only activities to be conducted on specific areas of the sea-bed identified in the above-mentioned agreements.

Amongst all States, the current situation can be summarized as follows:

— States recognize that universality is a necessary requirement for a functioning sea-bed régime with an appropriate institutional mechanism;

— States fully realize that the 1982 Convention, as it is now formulated and as it could enter into force for a part of the international community, would not meet this requirement of universality;

— States recognize that in order to make the Convention universal it is necessary to engage in negotiations;

— States have proven that the process of negotiations within the PrepCom may be utilized in order to bring changes to resolution II and — up to a certain limit — to the Convention, taking advantage of the rule according to which the Authority shall conform to decisions taken by the PrepCom in implementing resolution II;[43]

— States are starting to envisage the possibility of agreements which might bring changes to the Convention.

XIII. Prospects for the Future

The results of recent practice just summarized seem to indicate that States, in order to avoid confrontations, which might even involve international judicial pronouncements on questions of principle, are ready to consider engaging in the path of negotiations. Such negotiations may occur within two possible formats.

The first format has already been subjected to experimentation within the framework of the PrepCom. The second kind of negotiations is the one alluded to and encompassed within the idea of a "dialogue," with the purpose of obtaining the universality of the Convention. It would consist in negotiations — probably, at least in part, outside the PrepCom — aiming at creating the conditions desired to obtain the ratification by the industrialized States.

The first kind of negotiations can still yield important results in terms of changes to resolution II and, perhaps, even limited changes to the Convention, aimed at adapting it to the economic realities of today. It seems, however, difficult to imagine negotiations in this framework attracting States that have so far kept their consortia outside the provisional régime of resolution II and, in particular, to bring about the desired agreement upon important changes to the régime. In this framework, provided they continue to endorse the main ideas contained under the label of the *common heritage of mankind*, the registered pioneer investors will be in a position strong enough for obtaining the changes necessary to permit them to conduct sea-bed activities of the form, quality and quantity compatible with the present economic conditions. The States of the Third World will have to accept the fact that these changes are a condition necessary in order for the principle of the *common heritage* to realize its implementation. Pressure by the registered pioneers will probably be reinforced by the argument that they cannot engage in the definitive system of the Convention unless they can be assured that they will not be in a disadvantageous position in the competition with other industrialized nations remaining outside the system. As for the "potential applicants," in order to keep open the possibility of their eventual entry into the system, they might request the recognition of their rights on the already identified mine sites also for the time after the Convention enters into force.

With regard to the second kind of negotiations, it would seem that, the exploitation of the deep sea-bed not being imminent, the international community has the time to negotiate on how to make the Convention universally acceptable. Entry into force of the Convention before these negotiations are engaged or concluded would certainly add further difficulties that should be avoided.

---

43 1982 Convention, art. 308, para. 5.

Which could be the modalities and the results of these negotiations? It must be admitted that at the present stage, the most difficult problem to be overcome is the preliminary one of gathering around the table all the participants required for the exercise to be meaningful. The questions to be considered, and from which it also depends upon whether it will be possible to launch the negotiations, regard the following aspects.[44] As far as the framework is concerned: Would negotiations be within or along the side of the PrepCom or completely outside it, or in part within and in part outside? As regards the participants: Should they be all States, or representatives of groups, or States having a particular rôle, or a mixture of these possibilities? As for the timing: Should negotiations take place before or after the entry into force of the Convention? With regard to the subject matter: Should the negotiations focus on changes to Part XI and the relevant Annexes of the Convention, or on mechanisms for postponing the entry into force or the implementation of this part and annexes? If the first alternative is preferred, which provisions should be changed? If the second alternative is adopted, should resolution II be maintained and with which changes?

These problems are currently discussed in diplomatic circles and also in fora like the present one. We shall limit ourselves to the observation that, for different reasons, the various groups of interest have good reason to engage in the negotiations. This appears to be true for the registered pioneers, who should be anxious to create a system which, by involving also the industrialized States that have so far remained outside, would avoid differences in position in the competition between enterprises. The States of the Third World should also be interested in obtaining a Convention that receives the universal acceptance necessary for ensuring that in some form at least the *common heritage* principle will be implemented. As regards the non-registered pioneer investors, they seem to be under less pressure than the other groups, at least as far as activities on the identified mining sites are concerned. Their interest seems however difficult to question in the light of long-term policy objectives. Indeed, while it is conceivable that good faith negotiations obtain the result of making the Convention's system universal, it seems hardly conceivable that the lawfulness of unilateral exploitation could find universal recognition.

Making the Convention universal would have an effect much more important than that of making the régime for sea-bed mining universal. This effect would be to transform the Convention as a whole into international conventional law

---

44 For discussions of these problems, *see Edward L. Miles*, Preparation for UNCLOS IV?, in: Ocean Development and International Law 19 (1988), 421-430; *Satya N. Nandan*, The 1982 UN Convention at a Crossroads, *ibid.*, 20 (1989), 515-518; *Francisco Orrego Vicuña*, The Deep Seabed Mining Regime: Conditions for its Renegotiation, *ibid.*, 20 (1989), 531-539; *Jean-Pierre Lévy*, Un nouvel instrument de développement progressif du Droit de la Mer: La Commission préparatoire de l'Autorité international des fonds marins et du Tribunal international du Droit de la Mer, in: Annuaire français de droit international 34 (1988), 735-763 (761-763).

applicable to all States. The vagueness presented by practice and the tensions to which practice exposes many compromise solutions set forth in the Convention on various important aspects of the law of the sea, make it clear that this is an objective of primary importance for the world community, and against which the importance of the deep sea-bed mining régime should be weighed.

State Practice and National Legislation Relating to the Exclusive Economic Zone, the Continental Shelf and Straits Used for International Navigation: Basic Trends

Francisco Orrego Vicuña*

Since the Law of the Sea Convention was signed in 1982 State practice and national legislation relating to its implementation or relying on its clauses has developed at a rapid pace. A part of this legislation antedates this Convention but was also generally influenced by the progress of negotiations on the Law of the Sea. The result of this process is that there is today over a decade of legislative activity and practice available as to determine its compatibility or incompatibility with the Convention and derive therefrom the basic trends emerging in the field. This article purports to undertake this examination in relation to three specific subjects and matters related thereto: the exclusive economic zone, the continental shelf and straits used for international navigation.

I. Trends Relating to the Exclusive Economic Zone

A recent compilation of national claims to maritime jurisdiction[1] shows that 80 States claim a 200 mile exclusive economic zone, a figure which has notably increased from the 69 States mentioned in another compilation published only a few years earlier.[2] Another 20 countries claim a 200 mile fishery zone, while four claim fisheries zones ranging from 12 miles to 25 miles and 50 miles. These figures confirm the trend that could already be observed from the negotiations of the Law of the Sea Conference, insofar as the modality that began to prevail was the exclusive economic zone, proportionally reducing to that extent the modality of the fishing zone that had predominated previously. The preferential fishing rights approach that had characterized the negotiations at the first two United Nations Law of the Sea Conferences gave way for the concept of sovereign rights and jurisdiction of the coastal State over the resources of its adjacent maritime areas, a process that was corroborated by State practice.

---

* Prof. Dr. *Francisco Orrego Vicuña*, Institute of International Studies and Law School, University of Chile.

1 US Department of State, Limits in the Seas No. 36: National Claims to Maritime Jurisdiction, 6th Rev., Washington, D. C., 3 January 1990, 5.

2 Law of the Sea Bulletin, No. 8, November 1986, 25-28; No. 11, July 1988, 46-56.

Although these general figures would be significant by themselves, it is also necessary to see them in conjunction with the parallel phenomenon that has occurred with regard to the territorial sea. The prevalent trend in this other field has been the 12 mile territorial sea claims, thus coinciding with the maximum distance presently authorized by international law. 107 coastal States claim a territorial sea of this breadth and only 16 claim smaller distances.

It is especially interesting to note that only 13 countries have made 200 mile territorial sea claims and another six have claimed distances fluctuating between 15 and 50 miles. Eleven other countries have reduced their claims in excess of 12 miles to meet the latter distance: Cape Verde, Gabon, Ghana, Guinea, Guinea-Bissau, Haiti, Madagascar, Maldives, Mauritania, Senegal and Tanzania.[3] Still a number of other countries are expected to reduce their claims in excess of 12 miles by means of their legislation implementing the Law of the Sea Convention, this being most notably the case of Brazil.

The conclusion emerging from the territorial sea trend is that in general a criterion complying with international law prevails with only very limited exceptions. State practice proves in this manner that the maritime zones claimed beyond the territorial sea cannot be assimilated into the latter because the nature and extent of such zones are different, with a manifest predominance of the functional elements. The evident conclusion arising from the negotiations of the Law of the Sea Conference was in this way confirmed.

1. Conceptual Content of the Claims

When the different national claims are analyzed in relation to their substantive content,[4] an important distinction stands out immediately. On the one hand, there is a significant concordance with the concept of the exclusive economic zone contained in art. 56, para. 1 of the Law of the Sea Convention, or occasionally with some of the drafts that led to this last formulation. But, on the other hand, there are significant differences in terms of the specific régimes that are applied to each of these conceptual categories.[5]

With respect to the claiming of sovereign rights for the purposes of exploration and exploitation of the natural resources of the exclusive economic zone, both

[3] *J. Ashley Roach*, Excessive Maritime Claims, in: American Society of International Law. Panel on the Law of the Sea: Evolving National Policies, Washington, D. C., 30 March 1990, 8.

[4] For the texts of national legislation *see generally Robert W. Smith*, Exclusive Economic Zone Claims, 1986; and: National Legislation on the Exclusive Economic Zone, the Economic Zone and the Exclusive Fishery Zone, United Nations, New York 1986.

[5] For detailed references to national legislation *see Francisco Orrego Vicuña*, The Exclusive Economic Zone, Regime and Legal Nature under International Law, Cambridge 1989, Chapter 6. Some conclusions of that chapter are used in this article.

living and non-living, as defined in art. 56, para. 1 (a) of the 1982 Convention, there is at the level of national legislations a consensus that can be qualified, without fear of exaggeration, as absolute. All the legislations on the exclusive economic zone, without exception, contain this fundamental concept.[6]

A significant number of States claim in this context other economic activities related to the exclusive economic zone, with particular reference to the production of energy from the waters, currents, and winds in the terms that art. 56, para. 1 (a) of the Convention specifies, occasionally with slight alterations also. However, this type of claim is less frequent than that on natural resources just examined. Of the 87 claims on the exclusive economic zone that are included in Smith's compilation, 57 claim these other economic activities, which amounts to 66 per cent.

An important number of national legislations also contain a specific claim concerning the jurisdiction of the coastal State over artificial islands, installations and structures within the exclusive economic zone, again following the basic conceptual elements of art. 56 of the 1982 Convention. 62 legislations of those included in the compilation mentioned have made this type of claim, representing 71 per cent. However, unlike the previously mentioned matters, in this other type of claim a certain discrepancy between some national legislations and the Convention's régime can be observed, with the first tending to adopt a broader interpretation.

The analysis of national legislation with regard to marine scientific research within the exclusive economic zone has led to different conclusions amongst the authors concerned with this subject. Also in this case, a significant number of claims specifically include scientific research, this being the situation of 63 countries. While one author finds that national legislations in this field are generally harmonious with the 1982 Convention,[7] another author is rather skeptical because of the restrictive policies that seem to derive from this legislative body, especially since it seeks to encompass all the scientific research activities that take place in that zone.[8] The difference in assessment seems to originate from the fact that while the former author discusses the conceptual content of the claim to a larger extent, the latter writer focuses on the terms of the specific régime that governs the matter, where again discrepancies with the extent of the Convention are observed.

The most complex type of claim is the one that refers to the protection of the marine environment as one of the component elements of the concept of the

---

[6] *See generally* the discussion by *Lawrence Juda*, The Exclusive Economic Zone: Compatibility of National Claims and the U. N. Convention on the Law of the Sea, in: ODILA 16 (1986), 1-58 (7-11).

[7] *Smith* (note 4), 38.

[8] *David Attard*, The Exclusive Economic Zone in International Law, Oxford 1987, 119-121.

exclusive economic zone. This complexity that is observed in the sphere of national legislations is undoubtedly related to the complexity of the subject in international law and the 1982 Convention. An overwhelming majority of the countries that claim an exclusive economic zone demand this protection in particular, with only ten exceptions in which this type of claim is not made. However, the extent of the jurisdiction claimed in this matter is not always clear, not even at the conceptual level. The majority of the States claim "jurisdiction", thus coinciding in principle with the extent of the Convention and other treaties. But there are also some countries that claim "exclusive jurisdiction." Furthermore, in relation to given aspects of the régime applicable in this matter, other countries claim actual or potential powers that have a considerably broader extent and its compatibility with the 1982 Convention is precarious or non-existent. Some of these powers have an impact on issues regarding navigation and other rights of third States in the exclusive economic zone.

If the aggregate of national legislations is examined within an overall perspective, it can be observed, as *Carroz* concludes, that although the type of jurisdiction claimed can vary considerably from one case to another this does not mean necessarily that there are major differences in terms of rights and duties of the coastal State and other basic characteristics of the exclusive economic zone.[9] It is certainly true that there are always exceptions, but they, more than anything, confirm the general rule indicated.

Notwithstanding the foregoing, it can also be observed that in most legislations the emphasis is placed on the coastal State's rights and only exceptionally is reference made to the obligations that fall upon this State. Similarly, there is a tendency to keep silent on the rights that could correspond to other States, as will be examined next.

2. *Trends Regarding the Rights and Duties of Third States*

If the legislative panorama is examined from the standpoint of the rights and duties corresponding to other States in the exclusive economic zone, it can be noted that the general trend is coincident with that discussed previously. As a general rule, the freedoms of navigation, overflight, and the laying of submarine cables and pipelines, as well as other associated freedoms, are recognized at the conceptual level, but the details and modalities of the respective régimes are not spelled out, barring some exceptional cases.[10]

A group of national legislations explicitly recognizes these freedoms of other States. Another group of legislations has kept silent on the freedoms mentioned.

---

9 *Jean Carroz*, Les problemes de la pêche à la Conférence sur le droit de la mer et dans la pratique des Etats, in: Revue Générale de Droit International Public LXXXIV (1980), 705-751 (728).

10 *See generally Jonathan I. Charney*, The Exclusive Economic Zone and Public International Law, in: ODILA 15 (1985), 233-288.

This silence, however, has not been interpreted as synonymous with a necessarily negative implication, for it should be considered in most cases as a simple omission that does not alter the conceptual extent of the exclusive economic zone.

Different is the case of other legislations that provide for the establishment of "designated areas" in the exclusive economic zone, in which the coastal State, in addition to the rights conferred by art. 56 of the Convention, claims the exercise of other types of jurisdiction. Among these types mention has been made of custom and fiscal matters, regulation of entry and passage of other States' ships, and the establishment of sea lanes, schemes of traffic separation or other arrangements related to the freedom of navigation that do not prejudice the interest of the coastal State.

Another general difficulty associated with the freedom of navigation derives from some national legislations that claim jurisdiction related to security in the contiguous zone, a concept that is not contemplated within the régime of the 1982 Convention. Thirteen cases of this type of claim have been reported, all of them having been protested by the United States government in view of being considered incompatible with the 1982 Convention.[11]

Besides the general trends that evolve from national legislations, there are many specific and particular aspects that have been posed within the framework of this extensive practice of States. An interesting study of the practice related to the use of the exclusive economic zone by third States carried out by *Scovazzi*[12] reveals that this type of particular problem is frequent. Issues such as military areas, laying of submarine cables and pipelines, the definition of international lawful uses of the sea, provisions on archeological objects, tourism and recreation, aquaculture, and others form a part of this broad inventory of particular questions brought up by national legislations.

Notwithstanding the complexity of many of these provisions, they do not reach the point of forming general trends and, consequently, neither do they affect the nature of the exclusive economic zone nor its basic conceptual elements. In this sense, despite the abundance of particular and problematic provisions, the same spirit of balance that characterizes the concept of that zone in the 1982 Convention prevails in the legislative practice of States.

3. Régime of Fishing and Conservation of Living Resources

Given the emphasis that the exclusive economic zone has in the régime of living resources, it is only natural that the provisions concerning fishing are the most abundant in national legislations.[13] But it is precisely at this level that there

---

[11] *Roach* (note 3), 11.

[12] *Tullio Scovazzi*, Coastal State Practice in the Exclusive Economic Zone: the Right of Foreign States to Use this Zone, in: Law of the Sea Institute Proceedings 20 (1988), 310-328.

are considerable discrepancies with the specific régime provided for in the 1982 Convention.

The general objectives of management of fisheries, on which the Convention puts considerable emphasis, are barely mentioned in national legislations, and if so it is mainly done at the level of general references that do not correspond to the precise wording of arts. 61 and 62 of the Convention. Some countries follow more closely the concepts of the Convention in this field, including those of maximum allowable catch and optimum yield, although with great variations among them.

The legal conclusions that can be extracted from this situation are not easy to determine. On the one hand, the point of view that national practice on this matter is in general in harmony with the basic objectives of management and conservation of the Convention has been advanced.[14] From the standpoint that there is no manifest contradiction, that conclusion is certainly pertinent. But, on the other hand, the fact that these specific objectives are not reflected in the legislation generally also indicates the eventual existence of different criteria in this respect, which are equally evident in relation to other provisions of the Convention.[15] In any event, for the identification of a rule of customary law the absence of contradiction does not suffice; what is needed is a positive concordance.

The spectrum of national legislations concerning the access to the fishing surplus of the exclusive economic zone is also of ample variety.[16] The complexity of this régime in the 1982 Convention itself explains to some extent this variety of orientations. Among other aspects, the régime includes the mechanism of allowable catch, conservation measures, maximum sustainable yield, optimum utilization, determination of surplus, general conditions of access, the situation of land-locked or geographically disadvantaged countries, the régime of species, and other matters.

Most national legislations keep silent over the access of third States to the surplus, although almost all of them provide for rules on fishing licenses and other general aspects. On the other hand, if what is taken into account is not

13 *See generally Barbara Kwiatkowska*, Conservation and Optimum Utilization of Living Resources, in: Law of the Sea Institute Proceedings 20 (1988), 245-275; *id.*, The 200 Mile Exclusive Economic Zone in the New Law of the Sea, Dordrecht/Boston/London 1989.

14 *Kwiatkowska* (note 13, 1988), 248.

15 For other evaluations of national practice and legislation *see generally Gerald Moore*, National Legislation for the Management of Fisheries under Extended Coastal States Jurisdiction, in: Journal of Maritime Law and Commerce 11 (1980), 153-182; *William T. Burke*, National Legislation on Ocean Authority Zones and the Contemporary Law of the Sea, in: ODILA 9 (1981), 289-322.

16 *William T. Burke*, The Law of the Sea Convention Provisions on Conditions of Access to Fisheries Subject to National Jurisdiction, in: Oregon Law Review 63 (1984), 73-119.

access to the surplus in a strict sense, but the possibility of access in general by third parties to fishing in the exclusive economic zone, with no relation to a single régime, the legislative panorama is much broader. In fact it has been observed that most countries allow access of third States under varying conditions in each legislation, and that although there are several that keep silent on this point, no country prohibits this access by third States. In this way, the controversial point does not lie in access by third States, but in the specific régime under which this access must take place. Again, it can be noted that the concept of rights and duties in the exclusive economic zone is reaffirmed, but not some of the detailed régimes contained in the Convention.

These same legislative trends can be perceived in relation to other mechanisms that are closely linked to that of the surplus, such as the criteria for its allocation and the determination of allowable catch, among other aspects.

With respect to the conditions for access to fishing, unlike the matters previously examined, national legislations coincide generally in the trend to contain detailed provisions that are either established in the laws that refer strictly to the exclusive economic zone or in specialized fishing legislation. Practically all of the legislations contain rules on these conditions. The aspects that generally are subject to regulation are related to fishing licenses and rights, management measures, supplying of information, observation, research, landing of catch, joint ventures, and technical measures. The problems related to the nationality of fishing boats and the conditions that are applied to nationals or foreigners also tend to form part of this type of legislation.

Although the specific conditions will naturally vary from one legislation to another, in this aspect there do not appear to be major deviations with regard to the general criterion established in the 1982 Convention, particularly in view that the latter does not establish detailed conditions, leaving their determination to the legislation and regulation of States. On the other hand, there is a tendency toward the harmonization of the conditions at the level of regions, either through agreements of the countries that participate in given regions or through fishing agreements with other countries interested in fishing.

A situation that has prompted expressions of concern entails those legislations that, in contradiction with art. 73, para. 3 of the Law of the Sea Convention, provide for imprisonment as a penalty for the violation of fishing legislation. Twenty countries have established penalties of this type in their legislations on the exclusive economic zone, and at least another 12 have done so in their specialized fishing legislations.

The aggregate of provisions of national legislation that has been examined in this section reveals that the coastal States that have established an exclusive economic zone, without necessarily ignoring the obligations that fall upon them in terms of optimum utilization and other concepts of the 1982 Convention, naturally tend to take maximum advantage of the sphere of discretion that the

Convention grants them. This is particularly evident with regard to the determination of catch, the establishment of the surplus and the granting of eventual access to the surplus, as well as its respective conditions, all of which have been correctly understood as part of that discretionary sphere.

4. Declarations of States and Other Functions of Interpretation

The examination of national legislation and practice also reveals that there is a systematic effort at interpretation of the 1982 Convention provisions in the light of the interest of a particular country. Most notably in this regard is the United States proclamation on the exclusive economic zone when dealing with issues such as jurisdiction over artificial islands, installations and structures, marine scientific research or highly migratory species.[17] Also the USSR decree on the "Economic Zone" puts special emphasis on the fishing provisions as interpreted by this country, and in other matters such as the continental shelf or scientific research.[18] Many other countries have undertaken this effort at interpretation, which can also be observed in bilateral fisheries agreements or broader schemes of regional co-operation.[19] Among the latter, special reference ought to be made to the EEC Common Fisheries Policy, the Forum Fisheries Agency arrangements and corresponding treaties, and the Convention on the Conservation of Antarctic Marine Living Resources.

In addition to national legislations and practice and the agreements signed by States, the declarations made at the time of signing, ratifying, or adhering to the 1982 Convention constitute another important source for understanding the interpretations that have been made of its provisions or other modalities regarding its application.[20]

A group of declarations has referred to the question of the legal nature of the exclusive economic zone, reaffirming the *sui generis* character of this concept and its differences from both the territorial sea and the high seas régime. The declarations by Cape Verde, Chile, and Uruguay can be classified in this group. It is interesting to observe that on this point no State has made declarations attempting to alter the sense of balance that characterizes the régime of the exclusive economic zone in the 1982 Convention, thus preserving the consensus reached on this concept.

---

17 *Orrego Vicuña* (note 5), 164-166.

18 *Op. cit.*, 166-167.

19 *Op. cit.*, 167-179.

20 For the texts of Declarations *see* Law of the Sea Bulletin, No. 5, July 1985, and Special Issue No. 1, March 1987. *See also Daniel Vignes*, Les déclarations faites par les États signataires de la Convention des Nations Unies sur le Droit de la Mer sur le base de l'article 310 de cette Convention, in: AFDI 24 (1983), 715-748.

Different is the situation of some of the specific régimes that are applied in the exclusive economic zone with respect to which discrepancies in interpretation are expressed. Military uses of the exclusive economic zone represent one of the cases of discrepant interpretations. The question of residual rights has also been the subject of conflicting declarations.

The situation of artificial islands, installations and structures has also been subject to conflicting opinions. In a manner similar to what has happened with national legislation, the orientation of some States has been to claim a type of broad jurisdiction in this matter, while for others the distinctions contained in the régime of the 1982 Convention limit the extent of that jurisdiction.

The extent of the régime applicable to fishing in the exclusive economic zone is another aspect in which some declarations have sought to establish special interpretations, with particular reference to the question of reciprocity. The régimes that are applied to the different species also have been the object of declarations of this nature. The application of arts. 69 and 70 of the Convention has also led to interpretations by some States, mostly with regard to the implication for fisheries.

One aspect of this series of governmental opinions and interpretations that is worth noting is that no declarations have been made on the jurisdiction over marine scientific research, a matter that is complex in itself, and that there are only two declarations of a general type in the field of marine pollution.

In terms of dispute settlement, on the other hand, various declarations of interest have been made regarding the exclusive economic zone, which must be understood within the context of the problems about these procedures and their relationship with the substantive aspects of that zone's régime.

Although many of the declarations of States have a casuistical nature, or refer to the protection of given interests, they help to identify the practice and the interpretation of the Convention. In same cases, the interpretations will have a general scope, while in others they will help toward an understanding of the position of a State individually considered. In yet other cases the declarations have important legal effects, as occurs with the optional exceptions of art. 298. It is due to the influence of this practice that in some matters the declarations have met with objections, which fulfill a rôle similar to that of protest, although such objections have not referred to the exclusive economic zone.

5. Evaluation of the Exclusive Economic Zone in the Light of National Legislation and Practice

Some of the developments that have been discussed above have prompted the concern about whether the Exclusive Economic Zone could be turned into some form of territorialized jurisdictional zone of the coastal State.[21] It should be noted, however, that since the Convention was signed national legislation and practice has reflected a greater degree of harmonization with it, a process that everything indicates will continue, without prejudice to the interpretations or national positions that will attempt to protect given interests. It can be observed that there is already a basic understanding about the exclusive economic zone concept and the principles that characterize its régime. The principal discrepancies remain at the level of specific régimes that are applied to certain categories of matters within the exclusive economic zone, but sometimes those discrepancies are not so much a result of an intention to contradict the Convention's provisions as of the fact that there are opposing interpretations about its extent. In this sense, there is more of a struggle among diverse interpretations than between the conventional régime and the legislations mentioned.

This trend is reaffirmed by the fact that there have been very few protests about the implications of the exclusive economic zone for freedom of navigation and communications, which would be the first affected by any trend towards territorialization. For example, the United States government has issued only four such protests referring to issues such as Burma's claim to restrict overflight over the exclusive economic zone, Haiti's restrictions to the passage of vessels carrying hazardous waste, or the Maldives' use of baselines which are not in accordance with the requirements of international law. Cuba, Libya, Nicaragua and Greece have also received protests about flight restrictions of different kinds,[22] being the issue of overflying one that has been considered at the International Civil Aviation Organization.

In any case, nothing would support the idea that the exclusive economic zone could be fundamentally distorted as a consequence of national legislation and practice. There will always be problems of adjustment, where diplomatic and dispute settlement procedures will always have an important correctional rôle to play. But these problems do not contradict the concept indicated and its legal nature, which, on the contrary, is reaffirmed within the context of this national legislation and practice.

II. Issues and Trends Relating to the Continental Shelf Régime

The legislation relating specifically to the Continental Shelf is notoriously less numerous than that concerning the exclusive economic zone in the period intervening after the signature of the Law of the Sea Convention. In point of fact only 23 States among the 142 included in the 1986 United Nations compilation of maritime zones have made use of the new criteria contained in the said

---

21 *René-Jean Dupuy*, La mer sous compétence nationale, in: *René Jean Dupuy/Daniel Vignes* (eds.), Traité du nouveau droit de la mer, Paris 1985, 219-273 (256).

22 *Roach* (note 3), 11-12.

Convention in this field. Thereafter these figures have not changed significantly.[23] At first sight, this phenomenom would appear as rather surprising, but in closer examination it can be seen that it responds to a logical development.

1. The Integration of the Continental Shelf and Exclusive Economic Zone Régimes

One of the salient characteristics of contemporary law of the sea has been the process of integration between the continental shelf and the exclusive economic zone régimes within the 200 mile area. This process will not be explained here since it has been examined at length by various authors.[24] It should be noted, nevertheless, that this process has had a profound influence on the criteria concerning the delimitation of maritime offshore areas as effected by the decisions of the International Court of Justice and other tribunals.

The essential point to retain is that while there is an integration between the two régimes there has been no merger or subordination between these concepts, each keeping with its own legal characteristics and autonomy. In view of this situation, as explained by *Churchill* and *Lowe*, there are now two legal bases for the coastal State's rights in relation to the sea-bed: one is the continental shelf doctrine and the other the exclusive economic zone concept in so far as it also covers the sea-bed and subsoil within the 200 mile distance.[25] Although separate, these bases coexist in the same geographical area.

This particular legal development explains to a large extent why the legislation on the continental shelf has been so limited to date. Most coastal States have in fact relied on the exclusive economic zone legislation to ensure their rights to the sea-bed and subsoil of the 200 mile area. On the other hand, since the basic provisions of the continental shelf régime have been firmly rooted in customary international law there has been no great need to enact specific legislation in order to safeguard those rights. It follows that within the 200 mile area the continental shelf rights cannot any longer be examined separately from the exclusive economic zone claims.

2. The Outer Limit of the Continental Shelf

Because of the reasons explained above a large number of States has kept with the criteria established in the 1958 Convention on the Continental Shelf as to the determination of the outer limit of this area. Fifty States still rely in their legislation on the 200 meters depth plus exploitability, while three claim only 200 meters depth and one only exploitability. In addition, the very impressive

23 Law of the Sea Bulletin (note 2).

24 *See in particular Kwiatkowska* (note 13, 1989), 6-19.

25 *Robin R. Churchill/Alan V. Lowe*, The Law of the Sea, Manchester 1985, 111.

number of 77 States have indicated no criteria at all on this point; in most of these cases, however, the 200 mile exclusive economic zone approach will prevail for the sea-bed and subsoil.

Among those States that have incorporated the criteria of the 1982 Law of the Sea Convention, 17 claim the outer edge of the continental margin or the alternative 200 mile distance, while one has referred only to the continental margin and three other only to the 200 mile breadth. Two countries have claimed the 200 mile distance and the criteria of 100 miles from the 2,500 metre isobath. Still one other has claimed the 200-350 mile criteria as will be commented below.[26]

From the conceptual point of view none of these legislations depart from the Law of the Sea Convention, or in certain respects from customary international law, but there are in some cases difficult technical problems arising from the obscure drafting of art. 76 of that Convention. Some of these technicalities might in due course be clarified by the Commission on the Limits of the Continental Shelf.

Two separate issues can be identified in the implementation of art. 76 in so far as these technicalities are concerned. The first is whether a State can apply different criteria for different areas of its continental shelf, following the most convenient alternative in each case; for example, to apply the 350 mile rule in one area and the 100 mile from the 2,500 metre isobath rule in the next area. Nothing seems to prevent this interpretation in the actual drafting of the Convention.

The second issue relates to the implementation of art. 76, para. 6 of the Convention in relation to islands located on submarine ridges. Chile and Ecuador have relied on this provision, although with a very different extent, while Iceland and Madagascar have also been reported as relying on these technical criteria for establishing the outer limit of the continental shelf.[27]

On 12 September 1985 the Chilean government issued a proclamation claiming 350 mile continental shelf sovereignty for Easter Island and the neighboring island of Sala y Gomez, based on art. 76, para. 6 of the Convention.[28] Chile has not yet ratified the Convention, but is a signatory to it. This situation does not involve an argument in favour of the application of customary law on the matter, but should only be regarded as an application of conventional law in an anticipated

---

26 Law of the Sea Bulletin, No. 11, July 1988, 54-56.

27 Ecuador and Madagascar apply the 200 nautical miles or 100 nautical miles from the 2,500 metre isobath criteria, *see* Law of the Sea Bulletin, No. 11, July 1988, 54.

28 For the discussion of this proclamation *see generally Francisco Orrego Vicuña*, International Ocean Developments in the South East Pacific: the Case of Chile, in: Law of the Sea Institute Proceedings 21 (1989), 217-229 (221-223), the commentary by *Kilaparti Ramakrishna* at 263-265, and the discussion by *Oxman, Orrego, Djalal* and *Koh* at 270-278.

manner in the sense of art. 18 of the Vienna Convention on the Law of Treaties. In fact, the Chilean proclamation is specifically grounded on the text of the Convention.

A protest of the US government delivered in similar terms to both Chile and Ecuador is based on "customary international law on delimitation of the continental shelf as reflected in art. 76 of the Law of the Sea Convention." While it is understandable that not being a signatory to the Convention, the United States has relied on customary law to base its protest, this reference leads to a problem of substance, namely whether in fact art. 76 can be regarded as part of customary law. There is no doubt that some clauses, like that of para. 1, for example, can be regarded as customary law in view of the extent and uniformity of national practice on the matter, but the same cannot be said of other provisions, such as those of paras. 4 to 6. It should therefore appear that the US government has made its arguments based on conventional law to which it does not intend to become a party for the time being.

A more important problem is that related to the interpretation of paras. 4 to 6 of art. 76. In the US view "Article 76 (6) may, however, only be invoked if the conditions precedent in Article 76 (4) ... are fulfilled," what in fact amounts to require the application of the continental margin methodology to situations which have been treated separately because, precisely, of their different legal and technical nature.

The very complex drafting history of this article is clear on one point: the continental shelf of submarine ridges was treated as a special case because the general continental margin-deep ocean floor approach did not cover well this very peculiar situation of islands and other configurations. Because of this, art. 76, para. 3 contains a reservation to the extent that the deep ocean floor and oceanic ridges are not included in the concept of the continental margin or submerged prolongation of the land mass, just as art. 76, para. 6 makes a reservation to the effect that it shall not apply to submarine elevations that are natural components of the continental margin.

Easter Island and Sala y Gomez Island are quite clearly separate and different from any prolongation of the land mass; neither have they, nor most oceanic islands, a geomorphological configuration that could be compared to a continental margin. On the other hand, they are typically islands located on a submarine ridge, which is the situation specifically taken into account in art. 76, para. 6. So why then require the application of the criteria of art. 76, para. 4, which is not at all related to this case? It has been concluded that such requirement is inappropriately invoked.[29] The conclusion of the United States protest that "that part of Chile's continental shelf claim falling beyond a 200 nautical mile limit

[29] *Kilaparti Ramakrishna/Robert E. Bowen/Jack H. Archer*, Outer Limits of Continental Shelf: a Legal Analysis of Chilean and Ecuadorian Island Claims and U. S. Response, in: Marine Policy 11 (1987), 58-68 (66).

is without legal foundation" is therefore unwarranted and based on a feeble argument. The claim has a clear foundation in the Convention.

The fact of having a legal foundation in the Convention does not mean, however, that the claim is entirely free from another kind of problems, mostly related to technical aspects of the matter which have, of course, an influence on the legal construction of the proclamation and the Convention itself. It has been rightly commented that while the axis and length of the East Pacific Rise can be measured easily, its breadth and the pertinent criteria for its determination cannot be well established.[30] It follows that a 350 mile delimitation can be justified and measured in some parts of the submarine ridge, following generally a north-south direction in the case of Easter Island and an east-west direction in the case of Sala y Gomez Island; but the same cannot be said of those other parts related to the breadth of the ridge, where a 350 mile limit could be partly covering the deep ocean floor beyond the ridge.

The intention of the proclamation in this regard is not entirely clear. By referring to this shelf as a whole and to the applicable baselines it would assume that the 350 mile criterion was intended to apply all around the islands. However, it should be noted that no map or illustration has been issued in this case, nor any official explanation given; furthermore, a televided press conference where the proclamation was to be explained was cancelled. This could be taken to mean that the precise implementation of the proclamation is still pending. It is suggested that such implementation be undertaken only after extended legal and technical consultations.

It is possible to conclude that the proclamation is well founded on conventional law,[31] but that in turn its precise area of application should be further refined in order to deal both with the complex legal and technical issues included. One other aspect of the implementation which is pending is the determination of the straight lines fixing the outer limit of the shelf in accordance with art. 76, para. 7.

From the point of view of international law this claim evidences once again the complex implementation of highly technical conventional provisions and how very difficult it is to argue that such provisions might have become a part of customary international law.

The Ecuadorian proclamation was issued on 19 September 1985 and claims the entire continental shelf extending from the South American continent to the Galapagos Islands.[32] This proclamation involves, on the one hand, the 200 mile

30 *Op. cit.*, 65.

31 For an opinion to the contrary *see Rüdiger Wolfrum*, The Emerging Customary Law of Marine Zones: State Practice and the Convention on the Law of the Sea, in: NYIL 18 (1987), 121-144 (142-143).

32 *Teodoro Bustamente*, Ocean Law Developments in Ecuador, in: Law of the Sea Institute Proceedings 21 (1989), 230-235 (233-235).

distance measured from the continent, and, on the other hand, the 100 mile measured from the 2,500 metre isobath rule in the Galapagos Islands, with the combined effect of claiming the Carnegie Ridge and linking it up with the continental shelf attached to the continent. In part the proclamation relies on the technical criteria of art. 76 with regard to ocean islands and submarine ridges, but in a much more complex interpretation and historial context than the earlier Chilean claim. The Ecuadorian proclamation has also been the matter of a US protest.

3. Specialized Legislation on the Continental Shelf

In spite of the fact that legislation claiming continental shelf rights is relatively scarce, there is a wealth of legislation throughout the world relating specifically to the exploration and development of oil, gas and other natural resources of the continental shelf.[33] On many occasions this type of legislation contains references to the rights of the State under international law to such areas or refers to the claims made or the rights arising under given treaties and conventions. Since it is up to the State to define the conditions of such activity, this body of legislation is in harmony with the applicable rules of customary or conventional international law.

There are, however, some aspects of particular interest for international law in these legislations and related agreements. Firstly, there is the question of delimitation and boundary arrangements concerning the continental shelf between adjacent and opposite countries. This aspect will not be examined on this occasion, but it should be borne in mind that it is heavily influenced by the issue of the access to natural resources, including the establishment of joint development areas among the countries concerned.

A second aspect of special interest relates to the technological changes characterizing the offshore oil and gas industry and its ability to extend operations into increasingly difficult environments,[34] including both the Arctic and the Antarctic. The environmental concern emerging from continental shelf development has prompted new bilateral and multilateral arrangements in order to prevent transboundary environmental harm, including new approaches to the question of liability and the posting of bonds and other forms of remedial action. The specific issue of Antarctic mineral development, including the application of the continental shelf concepts and outer limits to the Antarctic offshore areas, is dealt with under the Convention on the Regulation of Antarctic Mineral Resource Activities of 1988.

The third issue that ought to be mentioned is that related to shipwrecks lying on the continental shelf, which is gaining prominence every passing day. Two

---

33 *Churchill/Lowe* (note 25), 119-121.

34 *R. A. W. Hoos*, Political and Technological Changes Affecting Oil and Gas Development in the Canadian Arctic, in: Law of the Sea Institute Proceedings 22 (1989), 61-70.

basic approaches illustrate the matter. The first argues that not being shipwrecks a natural resource of the continental shelf they do not fall under the functional jurisdiction of the coastal State; a refined interpretation of art. 303 of the Convention has been made in support of this view.[35] The second approach is of the view that wrecks do appertain to the coastal State's continental shelf jurisdiction in view of them being a resource, an approach that is reflected in at least one national legislation[36] and eventually in a number of domestic laws on maritime matters.[37]

4. Evaluation of Continental Shelf Trends

It follows from the above discussion that, like in the case of the exclusive economic zone, there are no important conceptual differences between national legislation and practice on the continental shelf and the rules of the 1982 Convention or customary law, which in this particular matter has a greater rôle to play.

There are, however, differences as to the specific régime applicable in this area, particularly with regard to the criteria for determining the outer limit of the continental shelf beyond the 200 mile distance where applicable. Only the basic provisions of the Convention on the Law of the Sea, unlike its very detailed technical rules, can be regarded as having been incorporated into customary international law.

While in general the functional nature of the coastal State rights over the continental shelf, limited to the exploration and exploitation of natural resources, is reflected in national legislation, the latter tends to be more comprehensive on this point. In fact, the laws and regulations on oil and gas exploration and development tend to treat the continental shelf more as an integral part of the national territory than as a functional zone under international law. This limited form of "territorialization" has been generally accepted since most countries share the same interest in the matter. This trend may lead to a further expansion of coastal State rights over the shelf, as for example to include jurisdiction over shipwrecks. Marine scientific research, control of pollution, and offshore installations, among other matters, might equally be affected by this particular trend to the extent that they involve the continental shelf. Although not being this a dramatic form of consented affirmation of coastal State rights, there is here an important difference with the case of the exclusive economic zone.

---

35 *Brian J. Hoyle*, Historical and Archaeological Treasures, in: Law of the Sea Institute Proceedings 22 (1989), 84-88.

36 Australia, Historic Shipwrecks Act 1976, US Department of State (note 1), 12.

37 *See* the discussion by *Gold* and *Hoyle*, in: Law of the Sea Institute Proceedings 22 (1989), 89-92.

III. Straits Used for International Navigation: the Continuing Uncertainty

National legislation and State practice concerning straits used for international navigation is more difficult to assess in view of the ongoing debate about whether the provisions of the 1982 Convention on the Law of the Sea have resulted or not in the development of customary law. As a matter of fact, this debate is more doctrinal than practical, and hence little attention has been paid to practice as such and much to the process of formation of customary rules.

In any event, there are two aspects of the practice that are interesting to retain. The first relates to the question of innocent passage and the second to the efforts done by major powers to interpret practice in support of the argument favouring customary law in the field.

1. Divergent Practice as to Innocent Passage in General

Because of the complexity of the régime on straits contained in the 1982 Convention, besides transit passage there are three cases in which innocent passage applies, namely that of art. 36 — which is the normal innocent passage — and those of arts. 38, para. 1 and 45, where innocent passage is non-suspendable. There is thus a connection between these cases and the practice applying to innocent passage in general, which presumably will also apply to such straits.

The major issue in the matter of innocent passage has been and continues to be the requirement by a number of coastal States of advance notification or authorization for the passage of warships. 36 States have made explicit claims in this regard[38] and a good number of other have kept a discreet silent in their legislation or practice. Three States have changed their policy on this requirement, namely Bulgaria, Turkey and the USSR.[39] Protests have been issued to those 36 States by the United States government, but this, of course, does not change the fact that international law has not yet settled the question.

A related issue is the passage of nuclear-powered ships or ships carrying nuclear weapons or similar cargoes. Three States have required permission for this passage — Egypt, Oman and Yemen AR — while three other require prior notification — Djibouti, Pakistan and People's Democratic Republic of Yemen.[40] This very issue has been discussed also in the context of the South Pacific Nuclear Weapon Free Zone Treaty as well as under the Latin American Treaty of Tlatelolco.

---

[38] *Roach* (note 3), 9.

[39] *Op. cit.*, 9.

[40] *Op. cit.*, 8-9.

The United States/USSR Joint Statement of 23 September 1989 on the Uniform Interpretation of the Rules of International Law Governing Innocent Passage[41] is a major diplomatic effort directed towards the affirmation of one particular interpretation of the matter, putting forward the view that the provisions of the 1982 Convention on traditional uses of the oceans "generally constitute international law and practice," while also encouraging States to "harmonize their internal laws, regulations and practice with those provisions." This last element involves of course the recognition that practice is to some extent at variance with this interpretation of such provisions.

Other types of efforts have also been made by major powers in this context, involving the actual operational enforcement of given interpretations of the law. The United States freedom of navigation program has during over a decade exercised operational assertions against more than 75 objectionable claims of 47 countries, including the Black Sea assertion of 1986 and 1988, the Gulf of Sidra in 1981 and 1986, and the use of the Northwest Passage.[42] Similarly, the USSR has made assertions in the Bosphorus and Dardanelles by means of the passage of ships which is not entirely in agreement with the terms of the Montreux Convention of 1936.[43] Some of these assertions involve, of course, straits used for international navigation. But neither this policy alters the state of international law on the matters concerned, although it certainly contributes to orientate State practice in a given direction.

2. The Practice Relating to Transit Passage and Freedom of Navigation

It is not the case to recapitulate here the strong discussions that took place on the régime of straits during the negotiations leading to the 1982 Law of the Sea Convention. They clearly revealed that there were fundamental differences in national policies, legislation and practice. The relevant discussion today is whether this situation has changed and if so to what extent.

Recent surveys of the state of national legislation and practice on this matter show that there has indeed been a change. Firstly, there is the case of straits governed by longstanding historical conventions which remain unaltered and which generally refer to freedom of navigation through straits. At least one of these conventions — the 1881 Treaty between Argentina and Chile governing the Strait of Magellan — has been further reinforced by the Treaty of Peace and Friendship of 1984, particularly insofar free and unimpeded navigation in the eastern access to the Strait is explicitly established.[44] Next, there is the case of

41 For the text of the Joint Statement *see* ILM 28 (1989), 1444.

42 *Roach* (note 3), 12-13.

43 *Churchill/Lowe* (note 25), 87.

44 *Hugo Caminos*, The Legal Regime of Straits in the 1982 United Nations Convention on the Law of the Sea, in: Recueil des Cours 205 (1987-V), 9-245 (221-222).

States that have established freedom of navigation and occasionally of overflight in relation to straits by means of their national legislation or practice, such being for example the situation of Sao Tomé and Principe and People's Democratic Republic of Yemen.[45]

Thirdly, one finds the legislation, practice and policy of major maritime nations, which tend to reaffirm either the régime of transit passage or the concept of free passage or other similar expressions. This is of course the case of the United States and the USSR,[46] Great Britain and France.[47] A similar approach has been followed by the 1978 Torres Strait Treaty between Australia and Papua-New Guinea, the basic standard of which is the régime of transit passage.[48]

A fourth and different category is that of States which have left a high seas corridor or other similar arrangement in straits under their potential jurisdiction, restricting the breadth of their territorial waters to this effect. This is the case of the former German Democratic Republic, Japan, South Korea,[49] Sweden and Denmark.[50] It is interesting to note, however, that some of this practice can also be read in a different way, that is, it may indicate the policy of avoiding the régime of transit passage in order to prevent its transformation into customary law.[51]

Fifthly, there is the case of States that have accepted in some way the new régime or given expressions of it, but with evident reluctance or reservation of rights. This group includes important States bordering straits, notably Spain, Canada, Oman, Malaysia, Indonesia and Singapore,[52] the latter three having entered into very specific understandings with major maritime powers as to the status of the Malacca and Singapore Straits in relation to transit passage. This means, of course, that there is here a highly qualified acceptance of the meaning and extent of the conventional provisions which really casts an important doubt about their relationship to customary law.

Sixthly, a number of other States have kept a very discreet silence on the whole issue, included among which is the important case of Morocco. The signature of the Convention by the latter without accompanying declaration has

---

45 *Op. cit.*, 220, 223-224.

46 *Op. cit.*, 206-209.

47 *Op. cit.*, 209-212. *See also Jean-Pierre Queneudec*, Chronique du droit de la mer, in: AFDI 33 (1987), 639-646 (641-644).

48 *Tullio Treves*, Notes on Transit Passage through Straits and Customary Law, in: *Adriaan Bos/Hugo Siblesz* (eds.), Realism in Law-Making. Essays on international law in honour of *Willem Riphagen*, Dordrecht/Boston/Lancaster 1986, 247-259 (254-255).

49 For these cases *see Caminos* (note 44), 216-218.

50 For the situation of Sweden and Denmark *see Said Mahmoudi*, Customary International Law and Transit Passage, in: ODILA 20 (1989), 157-174 (172-173, note 64 thereof).

51 *Op. cit.*, 172-173, note 64.

52 *Caminos* (note 44), 213-216, 218-220, 224-226, 228-231.

been interpreted as an acceptance of the régime of transit passage. The situation of Greece is similar.[53]

A last group is that of States that have purported to restrict transit passage through straits, this being for example the case of Iran in relation to the Strait of Hormuz. Six States have been grouped in this category, all of which have received protests from the United States government.[54] Archipelagic transit passage has also raised the issue of straits in this other context, but this aspect is beyond the scope of this work.

These differing national policies are related in part to issues of security and defense, but also in part to the concern about environmental matters and the control of pollution. To some extent this concern is reflected in the very régime of transit passage, but it has been clearly raised in more specific contexts, such as the arrangements referred to above for the Malacca and Singapore Straits, the Strait of Gibraltar in connection with the issue of nuclear weapons, and the 1990 Protocol concerning specially protected areas and wildlife of the Wider Caribbean Region as organized under the 1983 Cartagena Convention. This last Protocol refers to the adverse environmental effects of passage of ships in protected areas "without prejudice to the rights of innocent passage, transit passage, archipelagic sea lanes passage and freedom of navigation, in accordance with international law."[55] All of these special arrangements suggest that coastal State rights for the regulation of marine pollution under the régime of transit passage are not generally regarded as quite sufficient, thus requiring additional measures.

The survey of national legislation on the issue of transit passage quite clearly shows that there has been a change since the negotiations of the Third United Nations Conference on the Law of the Sea, and quite a dramatic one since the earlier 1958 arrangements. This change, however, does not seem to support in an unqualified manner the argument favouring the development of a rule of customary law in the matter. In point of fact, while it would appear that the concept of free and unimpeded passage has gained ground, either in terms of the transit passage itself or in some other form, the specific characteristics of the régime applicable to such passage are still very much open to discussion.

The works of *Treves*[56] and *Caminos*[57] on the issue of straits in customary law conclude that while this process might be well advanced it has by no means come to an end, and that different conclusions might be extracted from the examination of State practice by those who support one thesis or the other. Another interesting study by *Mahmoudi* discusses the possibility that transit

---

53 For these cases *see Treves* (note 48), 254.

54 *Roach* (note 3), 9.

55 *Op. cit.*, 16-20.

56 *Treves* (note 48), 258-259.

57 *Caminos* (note 44), 231-232.

passage might have become a part of customary law not by means of its own weight but because of its link with the 12 mile limit of the territorial sea, the latter having clearly evolved into customary law.[58] This amounts to a new dimension of the package deal approach, in which the whole package is transformed into customary law, while at the same time evidencing that transit passage in itself has not enough support in State practice as to become customary law in its own merit.

The conclusion that seems to emerge from all of the foregoing is that, as it has happened with the exclusive economic zone and the continental shelf, one can recognize that the basic concept of transit passage might have become or is becoming a part of customary law but not so the specific conventional régime embodied in the 1982 Convention.

58 *Mahmoudi* (note 50), 165-168.

Marine Scientific Research: State Practice versus Law of the Sea?

Wolf Plesmann and Volker Röben*

I. Introduction

The scientific investigation of the ocean has only relatively recently become a matter of concern to the international law of the sea. As the exploitation of living and non-living resources of the sea and the sea-bed has become of economic interest, more and more coastal States claim larger areas to be under their national jurisdiction. Consequently, the freedom of marine scientific research (MSR) which was virtually unencumbered three decades ago, is nowadays restrained by numerous regulations and by discretion of States. It is in their interest of protecting their resources and also the environment that influences States' reactions to the ever-increasing number of MSR projects.[1]

Accordingly, an international legal framework concerning MSR has come into existence.[2] Basically, there are two sources of the international legal régime of MSR, i. e. a conventional and a customary one.[3] As to the first, the relevant

---

* *Wolf Plesmann* and *Volker Röben*, Student Assistants, Institute of International Law, University of Kiel. For fruitful discussions during the symposium the authors wish to express their gratitude towards Mr *Tullio Treves*.

1 For a more complete analysis *see Alfred Soons*, Marine Scientific Research and the Law of the Sea, Deventer 1982, 1-8.

2 There is a considerable amount of writing on this topic, *see*, e. g., *David Attard*, The Eclusive Economic Zone in International Law, Oxford 1987, 106-123; *Axel Borrmann/Hermann Weber*, Meeresforschung und Meeresfreiheit, Hamburg 1983; *Robin R. Churchill/Alan Vaughan Lowe*, The Law of the Sea, new rev. ed., Manchester 1988, 288-306; *William Burke*, National Legislation on Ocean Authority Zones and the Contemporary Law of the Sea, in: ODILA 9 (1981), 289-322; *Jon L. Jacobsen*, Marine Scientific Research under Emerging Ocean Law, in: ODILA 9 (1981), 187-199; *Annick de Marffy*, La recherche scientifique marine, in: *René-Jean Dupuy/Daniel Vignes* (eds.), Traité du nouveau droit de la mer, Paris 1985, 957-974; *Tullio Treves*, Principe du consentement et nouveau régime juridique de la recherche scientifique marine, in: *Daniel Bardonnet/Michel Virally* (eds.), Le nouveau droit de la mer, Paris 1983, 268-285; *Rüdiger Wolfrum*, Der Schutz der Meeresforschung im Völkerrecht, in: GYIL 19 (1976), 99-127. An exhaustive bibliography can be found at *Soons* (note 1). For a listing of the available records of the Proceedings of the Third United Nations Conference on the Law of the Sea *see Churchill/Lowe, op. cit.*, 21.

3 *See generally* on the sources of the modern law of the sea *Churchill/Lowe* (note 2), 4 *et seq.*

provisions of the Geneva Conventions of 1958[4] remain binding on at least the States Parties. The 1982 Convention on the Law of the Sea,[5] although not yet having entered into force, is of legal relevance insofar as it not only may point the way to emerging international law but may also contain *already* binding customary international law.[6] It is generally agreed upon that different legal régimes apply to MSR according to, firstly, where it takes place, i. e. in the territorial seas, the exclusive economic zone (EEZ) or on the continental shelf and, secondly, what kind of research is concerned.[7]

In fact there is a distinction made between so-called "fundamental" ("pure"/ "basic") and "applied" scientific research. The former refers to scientific research intended to increase human knowledge about the world, whereas the latter refers to research undertaken primarily for specific practical purposes. The notion of MSR in principle covers both kinds. However, all projects for the purpose of locating natural resources are not being considered as MSR but are regarded as resource exploration.[8]

MSR is not a self-contained system. It is intimately linked to other fields of the international law of the sea. Suffice it to mention the fields regarding the protection of the environment, the régime of closed and semi-enclosed seas, international liability, co-operation etc.[9]

The purpose of this study is first to present State practice in the field of MSR against the background of the MSR régime of the Convention.[10] Subsequently

---

4 *Cf.* art. 2 and 5 of the Convention on the Continental Shelf, UNTS, Vol. 499, No. 7302; art. 2 of the Convention on the High Seas, UNTS, Vol. 450, No. 6465, does not list MSR among the expressly guaranteed freedoms of the high seas. The freedom to conduct MSR, however, is mentioned in the commentary of the International Law Commission to art. 27, in: Yearbook of the ILC 1956, Vol. II, 278. *See*, for further discussion, *Wolfrum* (note 2), 101 *et seq.*

5 Text: UN doc. A/Conf. 62/122 with Corr. (hereinafter: the Convention). The Convention has been ratified up to December 1989 by 42 States: according to art. 28, para. 1 sixty ratifications are needed for the Convention to enter into force.

6 *Cf. Rüdiger Wolfrum*, The Emerging Customary Law of Marine Zones: State Practice and the Convention on the Law of the Sea, in: NYIL 18 (1987), 121-144; *Churchill/ Lowe* (note 2), 18 *et seq.*; *Hugo Caminos/Michael R. Molitor*, Progressive Development of International Law and the Package Deal, in: AJIL 79 (1985), 871-890. For MSR this will be dealt with specifically *infra* 3. a).

7 *Soons* (note 1), 45; *Churchill/Lowe* (note 2), 289 *et seq.*

8 *Soons* (note 1), 7 with further references.

9 For a review *cf. Soons* (note 2), 327 *et seq.*

10 For other studies dealing with State practice in the field of MSR *cf. John Knauss/ Mary Katsouros*, Recent Experience of the United States in Conducting Marine Scientific Research in coastal States' EEZ, in: *Thomas A. Clingan* (ed.), The Law of the Sea: What lies ahead, Honolulu 1986, 297-309; *Warren S. Wooster*, Research in troubled Waters: US Research Vessel Clearance Experience 1972-1987, in: ODILA 9 (1981), 219-239; *Alfred Soons*, The Developing Régime of Marine Scientific Research: Recent European Experience and State Practice, in: *Lewis M. Alexander/Scott Allen/Lynne Carter Hanson* (eds.), New Developments in Marine Science and Technology: Economic, Legal and Political Aspects of Change, Honolulu 1988; *E. Hey/Albert W. Koers* (eds.),

an analysis will be done from a legal and a practical point of view. The results of such an analysis will therefore be twofold. It will first indicate whether the provisions of the Convention on MSR have succeeded in striking an acceptable balance between the interests of coastal States and researching States and, by virtue of this, whether they have become customary international law or are in the process of becoming it.[11] Secondly, the analysis will help identify the most frequent practical problems which have to be overcome in order to render MSR more effective and fruitful.[12]

For this, the authors will rely on the practical experience gathered by the German research vessels *Meteor*, *Poseidon* and *Sonne* during different cruises. The study will focus on MSR in the territorial seas, the EEZ and on the continental shelf of coastal States.[13]

II. Provisions of the Convention

MSR is dealt with in Part XIII of the Convention.[14] Thus the general provisions of Section I apply to MSR in the waters of coastal States as well. Its specific régime, however, is found in Section II, art. 245 *et seq.*[15] Article 245 recognizes the coastal State's full sovereignty with respect to MSR.[16] Consequently, there are no limits to the coastal State's discretion when granting consent for MSR to be conducted in its territorial waters. Article 248 *et seq.* are concerned with MSR in the EEZ and on the continental shelf. Basically, three questions of eminent practical importance are dealt with in these provisions.

Concerning the coastal State's consent, a distinction is made between fundamental MSR, on the one hand, and applied, on the other. Whereas the former has to be granted in normal circumstances, the latter is subject to the coastal State's full discretion.[17] A genuine feature of the Convention is that the consent is implied if there is no reply to a request for consent within six months.

The International Law of the Sea, Issues of Implementation in Indonesia, Rijskwijk 1983, 156-168.

[11] *Cf.* Art. 13, para. 1 (a) UN Charter according to which the General Assembly is to promote and encourage the progressive development of international law as a means of maintaining international peace and security.

[12] According to art. 246, para. 3, MSR has to be undertaken for the benefit of all mankind.

[13] The State practice is taken from documents and files provided by the *Leitstellen* of *Meteor*, *Poseidon* and *Sonne*. The authors wish to state that the present study would not have been possible without the generous help of, especially, captain *Heino Schmickler*, *Meteor-Leitstelle* Hamburg, and Dr. *Karl-Friedrich Nagel*, Ministry for Science and Technology, Bonn.

[14] For a complete review *see Soons* (note 1), 139 *et seq.*; *Churchill/Lowe* (note 2), 292 *et seq.*; *de Marffy* (note 2), 961 *et seq.*

[15] This régime is very similar to that provided for in art. 5, para. 8 of the Geneva Convention on the Continental Shelf (note 4); *cf. Wolfrum* (note 2), 121 *et seq.*

[16] *Cf. Soons*, in: *Hey/Koers* (note 10), 160; *Treves* (note 2), 269 *et seq.*

[17] *Cf.* art. 246, para. 5; *Churchill/Lowe* (note 2), 293.

When requesting consent, the researching State has to provide the coastal State with specified information on the following: the ship and its equipment, the objectives and methods of the research and, finally, the area in which the research is going to take place.

When conducting research, certain duties have to be complied with. They are, in principle, threefold: Participation of the coastal State's personnel, be it scientific or official, has to be permitted; additionally, a whole set of obligations concern the results of the research; the coastal State has to be provided with data and samples, but only if those can be divided. Furthermore, the researching State may have to provide assistance in assessing the results of the cruise. Yet, it has to be stressed that the coastal State's prior consent to publishing the said results is required only in the case of applied research.

III. State Practice

1. Preparation of a Research Cruise

The preparation of a research cruise generally begins eight to twelve months before the actual departure of the research vessel (RV). Having arranged the cruise, the first step for the planning authority is to obtain information about the extent of the maritime zones claimed to be under national jurisdiction. This is to determine to which States a request for consent has to be submitted.

At this stage, problems might occur concerning the delimitation of the claimed zones between two States and the seaward extension.[18] Very often the general statement of a EEZ of 200 nm without giving information about the baseline is not sufficient to determine its exact extent.

The next point is to know, whether the coastal State requires a request for consent for MSR activities in the specific zones. If there is no information available, German organizations normally apply for consent.

At this stage of the preparation, the first diplomatic steps are put forward to determine the probability of acquiring consent for the project. At the same time, the scientists involved contact their colleagues in the coastal State.

German organizations in general use the ICES form[19] in applying for consent. The so-called ICES application form was introduced to ICES in 1984 by the

---

[18] The Intergovernmental Oceanographic Commission (IOC), Working Group on Legal Questions Related to Scientific Investigation of the Ocean, 1st meeting (1968), Doc. Sc/IOC-IV/ 15, 4, states that this is one of the major problems for MSR.

[19] Text in: Conditions and Clearance Procedures for the Conduct of Scientific Research in Waters under National Jurisdiction in ICES Member Countries, 1990, available at the International Council for the Exploration of the Sea (ICES), Palaegade 2-4, DK-1261 Copenhagen K.

Foreign and Commonwealth Office of the United Kingdom and was updated in 1988. This form assembles all points of interest for the coastal State and had been in use in the UK and in the FRG five years before its introduction to ICES. It is now used between several ICES members, however German practice is to use it for nearly all applications. Only the USSR and Ireland demand a different application form, also available in the ICES publications. All in all, the ICES form addresses nearly all points raised by arts. 246 and 248 of the Convention.

2. *RV Meteor*

The 1987 cruise led the *Meteor* to three different seas, i. e. the Mediterranean, the Red Sea and the Indian Ocean. While conducting different kinds of MSR, all were classified as fundamental MSR. Scientists from more than 20 countries participated in different aspects of the MSR projects.

The ship began its mission in the Mediterranean Sea. Coastal States' consent had to be requested from Greece and Egypt. Israel was satisfied with a mere notification that *Meteor* was conducting research in its waters including its territorial seas. It has not enacted any specific legislation in the field of MSR.

The Greek harbour Heraklion was the first port *Meteor* called on. Greece[20] requires request for its consent with regard to MSR irrespective of whether the research is to take place in its territorial seas or EEZ (as stipulated in a diplomatic note of 31 January 1978[21]). The delay is a two month period. Apart from providing the usual information, the researching State has to allow a Greek scientist to participate in the research. Furthermore the results, which are to be communicated to the Greek authorities, must be published.

In conformity with the diplomatic note, the consent was granted without further conditions. The uncertainty about the exact delimitation of the Greek and Egyptian EEZs, however, was considered a practical problem by *Meteor*.

Obtaining the Egyptian consent should not have caused any problems either. In fact, Egypt has ratified the Convention[22] and has declared, in a declaration upon ratification,[23] that it will exercise its sovereign rights over its EEZ, *inter alia*, according to Part XIII of the Convention. Because of this, Egypt forms

[20] Greece has signed the Convention on 10 December 1982.

[21] Diplomatic Note, No. 6257.1/207/AS 90, 31 January 1978, from the Ministry of Foreign Affairs. The texts of the respective national legislation are provided in: The Law of the Sea, National Legislations, Regulations and Supplementary Documents on Marine Scientific Research in Areas under National Jurisdiction (a report by the Office of the Special Representative of the Secretary-General on the Law of the Sea, New York 1989) and *R. W. Smith* (ed.), Exclusive Economic Zones Claims: An Analysis and Primary Documents, Dordrecht 1986; unless otherwise stated all legislation referred to in this study may be found in these publicatons.

[22] Egypt has ratified the Convention on 26 August 1983.

[23] Declarations of 26 August 1983 upon Ratification of the United Nations Convention on the Law of the Sea.

part of the few States which make reference to international law in their internal legislation concerning MSR.

In practice, however, things did not evolve that way despite diplomatic missions by the German embassy and the scientific leader of the expedition. Negotiations eventually failed as Egypt's very restrictive conditions for granting consent, as they are laid down in the Egyptian rules concerning foreign maritime research in maritime zones under Egyptian legislation,[24] were simply regarded as unacceptable. Egypt demanded the following:

— the handing over of all samples of soil and minerals taken from the soil and subsoil, intact and prior to laboratory analysis. Furthermore, it demanded a share of all samples of other kinds;[25]

— the provision of the original computed tapes on the research results to Egypt;[26]

— the request for prior Egyptian consent to any publication of the research results.[27]

On its way back, *Meteor* tried again to obtain consent for conducting research in Egyptian waters. The Egyptian denial was all the more astonishing when one considers a change in Egyptian legislation prior to the request by which Egypt replaced its formerly declared EEZ with a mere contiguous zone. The lack of Egyptian consent had a very detrimental effect on the overall scientific value of the cruise as well as on Egyptian knowledge in this field, since no scientist from this country was able to participate in the cruise. Port Said, however, was called upon by *Meteor*.

The next stage of its cruise-agenda led *Meteor* to the Red Sea where research was carried out in the waters of Sudan, People's Democratic Republic (PDR) Yemen and Djibouti.

Sudan has no pertinent legislation on MSR. Consent, however, was granted without further conditions. This may be stressed as the scientific programme concerned geological research as well.

On the way out, *Meteor* was allowed to conduct research in Yemenian[28] waters, within a project by UNESCO, with a Yemenian research officer participating. The situation had entirely changed when *Meteor* was heading back and asked for consent again. Although PDR Yemen has not communicated any legislation concerning MSR to the United Nations, it mentioned a decree according to which consent had to be granted by the president and raised the following conditions

---

24 These rules were provided to the authors by the Embassy of the Arabic Republic of Egypt in Bonn, unfortunately without the date of entry into force.

25 *Cf.* No. 4 of the rules (*loc. cit.*).

26 *Cf.* No. 10, 14 of the rules (*loc. cit.*).

27 *Cf.* No. 7 of the rules (*loc. cit.*).

28 PDR Yemen signed the Convention on 10 December 1982.

for the consent to be granted: Yemen would decide the area within which research might be conducted; furthermore a copy of the results of the research was to be communicated before publication. More conventional were the conditions with regard to Yemenian scientists participating in the cruise and that *Meteor* not infringe upon the activities of oil companies in Yemenian waters.

Finally, *Meteor* arrived in Djibouti. This State[29] in its Act on territorial seas, EEZ and continental shelf[30] claims exclusive sovereign rights to regulate MSR in its EEZ. Accordingly, permission was given for *Meteor* to conduct research and to dock in the Djibouti harbour.

Unlike the above-mentioned States, no consent could be obtained from Saudi Arabia, Somalia, Ethiopia and PDR Yemen.

The case of Saudi Arabia,[31] in which consent was requested two times, may shed some light on the detrimental effects of the uncertainty of domestic law. Indeed, the first Saudi denial was based on the grounds, that the domestic legislation on MSR still hat to be adopted. Furthermore, the denial was extended to the Saudi EEZ even though Saudi Arabia had not declared an EEZ at that time.

The close relationship between MSR and other domains of the law of the sea is highlighted by the Saudi Arabian authorities denying *Meteor* entrance into a harbour when there was a person on board in need of medical treatment. These events impeded the fruitful scientific co-operation between the researching and the coastal State which began one year before.

No consent could be obtained from Ethiopia[32] either. Ethiopia has not enacted any specific legislation on MSR. This fact may explain why it did not become clear which Ethiopian authority was competent to decide upon *Meteor*'s request. As there was no answer to the said request, Ethopia's silence was regarded as a polite way of saying "no".

Consent was also requested of Somalia,[33] a State that claims 200 nm of territorial seas. *Meteor*'s request was entirely rejected on the grounds that there was no bilateral agreement between the researching and the coastal State on MSR.

Finally, *Meteor* was not successful when requesting consent from the PDR Yemen.[34] In its legislation this State has established its jurisdiction over MSR in its EEZ.[35] PDR Yemen's demand for additional information and the acceptance

[29] Having signed the Convention on 10 December 1982.

[30] Law No. 52/AN/78 concerning the Territorial Sea, the Exclusive Economic Zone, the Maritime Frontiers and Fishing.

[31] Saudi Arabia signed the Convention on 7 December 1984.

[32] Ethopia signed the Convention on 10 December 1982.

[33] Somalia ratified the Convention on 24 Juli 1989.

[34] PDR Yemen ratified the Convention on 21 July 1987.

[35] Act No. 45 of 17 December 1977 concerning the Territorial Sea, Exclusive Economic Zone, Continental Shelf and other Marine Areas.

of Yemenian scientists on board were considered to be acceptable. On the contrary, the demands of the conclusion of a bilateral agreement, the handing over of the research results and necessary prior Yemenian consent to any publication of the results of the research were not accepted by *Meteor*, who, accordingly, did not conduct any research in waters under Yemenian jurisdiction.

During the next phase of the cruise, *Meteor* was scheduled to enter the waters of Oman, India and Pakistan.

Oman[36] issues a form concerning MSR which requires the researching State to furnish information equivalent to that requested by the ICES-form.[37] Furthermore, Oman asked for, and received, supplementary information about the ship. The conditions under which Oman granted its consent were, in particular, that Omanian scientists participate in the research and that a copy of the results be submitted to the Omanian authorities, all of which were agreed upon.

Given the length of its coast, India's[38] consent for MSR to be conducted in its waters was of some scientific interest. On the legislative side, the relevant Indian Act[39] claims that its exclusive jurisdiction over the EEZ and the continental shelf — both of which extend to 200 nautical miles — covers MSR as well.[40] Conducting MSR presupposes a licence or a letter of authority.[41] The power to determine the conditions under which this licence will be granted is conferred to the central government.

Actually, *Meteor* was unable to obtain the required Indian consent. The negotiations failed as the coastal State's conditions for granting consent were regarded as unacceptable. The Indian conditions referred to a government proforma dated 29 November 1984, adherence to which was, however, demanded for the first time in 1987. The conditions were basically twofold. The first set centers on information to be furnished with regard to, in particular, the precise planned and effective route of the ship, the exact "bio-data" of the participating scientists. Accordingly *Meteor* gave "supplementary information" including the names of all the scientists although this was regarded as already going beyond international law. Moreover, the Indian conditions covered points such as providing the research data, samples,[42] the requirement of a consent for publication and special control by an Indian official on board *Meteor*.[43]

---

36 Oman ratified the Convention on 17 August 1989.

37 Request for Foreign/Regional Vessel Operation in Omani Waters to Conduct: Survey/Research/Fishing.

38 India signed the Convention on 10 December 1982.

39 The Territorial Waters, Continental Shelf, Economic Exclusive Zone and Other Marine Zones Act No. 80 of 28 May 1976.

40 Section 7, para. 4 c of the 1976 Act (*loc. cit.*).

41 Section 7, para. 5 of the 1976 Act (*loc. cit.*).

42 No. 11 (a) of the proforma.

43 No. 11 (b) of the proforma.

The Pakistani[44] legislation[45] on MSR is strikingly similar to that of its Indian neighbour. As in India, it is up to the Pakistani Government to elaborate the conditions for granting consent. In practice, however, the only Pakistani condition ensured that a Pakistani scientist participated in the research. *Meteor* docked in Karachi.

The third main part of its cruise led *Meteor* along the east coast of Africa. Madagascar,[46] with its harbour Nosy Be, and Kenya, with its harbour Mombasa, welcomed *Meteor*.

Madagascar in its legislation[47] claims sovereign rights over MSR in its EEZ without further specification. In practice, however, the only problem encountered was the lack of clearly delimited territorial seas which was not covered by the consent granted.

Kenya[48] focusses in its legislation on MSR related to fisheries. The Presidential Act[49] authorizes regulations that may deal with the taking of samples, reporting of scientific data and training personnel. Even though this was somewhat unclear, consent to the research was promptly granted.

Tanzania[50] has included its entire legislation on MSR in the Act concerning its EEZ,[51] where it is stated that consent is needed when conducting MSR and that the Tanzanian Government is empowered to enact specific regulations.

The Tanzanian side, however, accepted — in the course of the negotiations — that under international law different legal régimes apply to MSR in territorial seas and to MSR in the EEZ. It remains unclear why this State eventually denied its consent for MSR.

On its way back to Hamburg, *Meteor* touched upon the waters of Italy,[52] Spain[53] and Portugal.[54] These countries granted consent without further conditions.

Upon examining the legislation of these States concerning MSR,[55] it may be stated that, firstly, all of them have submitted MSR to a specific régime. Further-

44 Pakistan signed the Convention on 10 December 1982.

45 Territorial Waters and Maritime Zones Act of 22 December 1976.

46 Madagascar signed the Convention on 25 February 1983.

47 Ordinance No. 85-013 of 16 September 1985 establishing the Boundaries of the Maritime Zones.

48 Kenya ratified the Convention on 2 March 1989 (Signature on 10 December 1982).

49 Presidential Proclamation of 28 February 1979.

50 Tanzania ratified the Convention on 30 September 1985.

51 Territorial Sea and Exclusive Economic Zone Act of 1989.

52 Italy signed the Convention on 7 December 1984.

53 Spain signed the Convention on 4 December 1984.

54 Portugal signed the Convention on 10 December 1982.

55 Italy: Note of 9 July 1984 by the Ministry of Foreign Affairs on Regulation of Scientific Research by Foreign Vessels in Areas under Italian Jurisdiction; Spain: Royal

more, they distinguish according to whether the MSR is to be conducted in the territorial seas or in the EEZ. The legislation concentrates on consent (Spain and Portugal admitting tacit consent), the information to be provided and the duties to be fulfilled when carrying out the research. In all respects, the national legislation closely follows the equivalent provisions of the Convention. It is important to note that these conditions can apply to the same extent to research conducted in the territorial seas as in the EEZ. Thereby these States differ from the approach adopted by the Convention.

Some specific points in the legislation of the said States may be worth mentioning.

Italy, for instance, imposes upon the researching State an obligation to seek prior approval for the dissemination of the results of the research when directly related to exploration and exploitation of resources under Italian jurisdiction.

Strangely enough, Spain expects research ships to undergo a special consent procedure when calling on Spanish ports independently of whether the ship has carried out any research in Spanish waters.

Portugal is the only State examined in this cruise, that names the competent authority for granting consent in its Act. On the other hand, a single approach to both the territorial seas and the EEZ entails risks as Portugal raises conditions regarding MSR,[56] which, for the EEZ, cannot be based on art. 246.

The last State to be examined in this cruise is Morocco.[57] Morocco states in its Act on the EEZ that it has exclusive sovereign rights over MSR in this area and that a prior permit for conducting MSR is needed.[58] Moroccan authorities referred expressly to international practice as codified in the Convention in establishing the condition that data concerning the living and non-living resources in Moroccan waters may not be published without prior Moroccan consent.

3. RV Meteor/Brazil

Having examined a whole research cruise of *Meteor* another example shall be provided with regard to experiences in Brazil[59] during 1989. *Meteor* sailed at the end of October 1989 southbound along the Brazilian coast.

Decree No. 799/1981 of 27 February 1981 concerning Regulations Applicable to Marine Scientific Research Activities in Areas under Spanish Jurisdiction; Portugal: Act No. 37/77 of 17 December 1977 regarding the Juridical Status of the Portuguese Territorial Sea and The Exclusive Economic Zone, Decree-Law No. 119/78 of 1 June 1978, Decree-Law No. 52/85 of 1 March 1985.

56 Article 19 Decree-Law No. 119/78 of 1 June 1978.

57 Morocco signed the Convention on 10 December 1982.

58 Act No. 1-81 of 18 December 1980, promulgated by Dahir, No. 1-81-179 of 8 April 1981, establishing a 200 nm Exclusive Economic Zone off the Moroccan Coast.

59 Brazil ratified the Convention on 22 December 1988.

Brazil's regulations on MSR are very detailed and have been codified in the Decree No. 96.000 of 2 May 1988. The subject of the decree is the procedure of consent to MSR projects in the Brazilian territorial seas of 200 nm and the Brazilian continental shelf. Generally, it may be said that Brazil with respect to MSR treats its territorial seas nearly the same way the Convention treats the EEZ. In the following only the differences shall be considered.

Article 2 of the Brazilian decree requires that all MSR to be authorized has to contribute to Brazil's scientific and technological development. This precondition clearly does not correspond to the provisions of the Convention, according to which consent shall be granted if MSR is conducted in order to increase scientific knowledge of the marine environment for the benefit of all mankind. This provision has not been interpreted narrowly and consent has been refused because of it. Another precondition is included in art. 5 of the Brazilian decree, as consent shall only be granted when the requesting organization has at least attempted seriously to enter into a research agreement with Brazilian entities. In *Meteor*'s case such an agreement was concluded, but *Meteor* notified the Brazilian authorities quite late as to its existence. Consent was then granted by decree on 3 October, but could only be officially notified to the crew one day prior to departure from Ponta Delgada (23 October 1989). This may indicate, that Brazil in practice demands such an arrangement. It surely is very helpful to obtain consent for a MSR project.

As to the information to be provided before the cruise, it may be mentioned that nearly all information required by the Brazilian Government is mentioned in art. 248 of the Convention. Not only the scientist in charge has to be named, but also all other scientists on board along with the respective *curricula vitae*.

Another detail to be mentioned is the fact that in art. 6 IV of the Brazilian decree, a complete report is required by the Brazilian authorities not more than 12 months after the completion of the cruise. Thus far this requirement has not created any difficulties.

Brazilian legislation ensures the differentiation between fundamental MSR and exploration and exploitation of living and non-living resources in its art. 18. All exploration and exploitation is placed under a special régime and consent may be refused if safety interests etc. are not observed.

In fact, *Meteor* did not meet any substantial difficulties in Brazil. As the cruise was made in German/South-American co-operation, there were 16 German and 14 South-American scientists on board. The organizing authorities faced the problem that the application had to be made in the Portuguese language, and that many *curricula vitae* had to be furnished. This took considerable time and therefore the preparation period before the official application was prolonged. Consent was nevertheless granted before supplementary information about the crew members reached Brazilian authorities. The German authorities did not, as provided for in art. 254 of the Convention, inform Bolivia, a land-locked State, about the MSR project.

4. RV Poseidon

Poseidon normally cruises in the Northern Atlantic and in the Baltic Sea. Thus, it has gathered experience in the Icelandic waters.

Iceland[60] requires a request for consent in the territorial seas, the EEZ and the continental shelf. Article 9 of the Icelandic legislation[61] provides that consent for research projects in the EEZ and on the continental shelf shall be granted if the project is carried out for peaceful purposes and in order to increase knowledge about the marine environment. Consent may be withheld as provided for in art. 246, para. 5 of the Convention. Information to be provided according to art. 10 of the Icelandic law is the same as foreseen in art. 248 of the Convention. Article 10 of the law provides for a tacit consent as given in art. 252 Law of the Sea Convention. The ICES was informed about several further conditions posed by the Icelandic authorities.[62] Icelandic authorities reserve the right to have a scientist or an official observer aboard the research ship; actually the Icelandic Government never took advantage of this provision when *Poseidon* performed research in Icelandic waters. Six months after the completion of the cruise, a cruise report and preliminary results are to be given to the Icelandic authorities. A final point is that Iceland demands the use of the ICES form for all applications. To date, *Poseidon* has never had any problems with Iceland's MSR régime.

5. RV Sonne

The area covered by research cruises of RV *Sonne* is particularly widespread. In the following, experiences with the Philippines[63] and Indonesia[64] will be examined.

Philippine regulations on MSR activities are included in the Presidential Decree No. 1599 of 11 June 1978 establishing an EEZ and for other purposes and in the Presidential Decree No. 1015 of 22 September 1976. The only relevant point for MSR is that either a licence has to be demanded or an agreement has to be entered into with the Philippine authorities before research may be conducted. In 1987, *Sonne* obtained consent from the Philippines without problems, even for geoscientific investigations within three nm off the coast.

---

60 Iceland ratified the Convention on 21 June 1985.

61 Law No. 41 of 1 June 1979 concerning territorial sea, EEZ and the continental shelf.

62 *Cf.* Conditions and Clearance Procedures for the Conduct of Scientific Research in Waters under National Jurisdiction in ICES Member Countries (note 19), 10.

63 The Philippines ratified the Convention on 8 May 1984.

64 Indonesia ratified the Convention on 3 February 1986.

Indonesian legal regulations on MSR are included in the "Act No. 5 of 18 October 1983 on the Indonesian EEZ." In art. 7 of the annex it is stated, that all MSR in the Indonesian EEZ requires prior consent of the Indonesian Government. No limits to the discretion of the Government are elaborated here, nor are there any requirements to be fulfilled by the researching State mentioned. Nevertheless, the principle of tacit consent is laid down in this very article. The preparation of the 1986 research cruise was somewhat difficult, as the Indonesian Authorities advanced numerous conditions, some of them of military importance. Indonesia wanted to obtain ownership of all scientific results, leaving mere copies to German scientists, and even wanted to prohibit publication of the results. An implementing arrangement with an Indonesian entity was entered into, which was also difficult to negotiate. In the end, nevertheless, conditions were minimized, and the research cruise within the territorial seas and the EEZ was successfully concluded.

IV. Analysis

1. Legal Analysis

The legal analysis of the State practice presented above may start with a closer look at States' domestic legislative situation given its tangible and durable character. Three different types of legislation can be distinguished:[65]

Some States simply determine that they have sovereignty to regulate MSR in areas under their jurisdiction.[66] Other States spell out that consent will be required for conducting MSR in any of their waters.[67] Both types of legislation hardly devote any explicit distinction with regard to whether the MSR project takes place in the territorial seas, the EEZ or on the continental shelf. This, however, may partly be due to the mere convenience of regulating MSR only once in a legal document, whether it is concerned with the EEZ or the territorial seas.

Finally, some States do specify the conditions to be fulfilled, the information to be provided and the procedures to be observed when applying for consent.[68] When doing so, States tend to follow the régime of the Law of the Sea Convention closely, sometimes to the point of taking the same systematic approach as the Convention. On this level, however, there is an important distinctive feature of State practice. These States extend their regulations to MSR in their territorial seas as well,[69] whilst the Convention refrains from setting up any regulations for this area.

65 *Cf. Attard* (note 2), 119 *et seq.*; *Curchill/Lowe* (note 2), 294 *et seq.*

66 *Cf.* State practice: Egypt, Djibouti, PDR Yemen, Madagascar.

67 *Cf.* State practice: India, Pakistan, Tanzania, Morocco, Philippines, Indonesia.

68 *Cf.* State practice: Greece, Oman, Italy, Spain, Portugal, Brazil, Iceland.

69 *Cf.* State practice: Spain, Portugal, Greece.

Whether a request for consent will be successful depends, however, upon the actual State practice. Interestingly enough, practical discussions arise with regard to the same questions as dealt with in the Convention with respect to granting consent. Therefore, three major points must be examined more closely.

Firstly, the Convention and State practice are in complete harmony with respect to requiring the State conducting research to request the coastal State's prior consent for carrying out research.[70] Furthermore, requesting consent six months prior to the planned research seems to be generally agreed upon.[71] Much less clear, however, is whether the elaborate distinction by the Convention between MSR concerning territorial seas, EEZ and continental shelf is reflected in State practice. With due prudence, one could say that the basic idea is accepted as evidenced from the fact that, in practice, this distinction is retained at least as a valuable argument.[72] On another point, the régime of the Convention and State practice seem not to coincide. Indeed, *Meteor* did not rely on the concept of tacit coastal State consent, although there were two cases where the coastal State did not respond at all to its request.[73]

The second field is that of the necessary information to be provided to the coastal State. When looking at State practice one may say that the kind of information mentioned in art. 248 and that requested in practice are nearly identical. If a coastal State requires further information, it will generally be furnished within reasonable limits.[74] These rare cases, however, cannot tilt the balance found in art. 248.

In this respect, one has to have a closer look at the ICES form. In furnishing detailed information, it parallels most of the points mentioned in art. 248. The question arises as to how to ascertain the legal relevance of this form. Obviously, it cannot reveal any binding character as it manifestly lacks any norm-creating character. Yet there is no denying the fact that, on the one hand, researching States use this form as a matter of routine and that, on the other hand, coastal States very rarely request supplementary information. It may therefore be considered whether the use of this form does not, already *de lege lata*, entail a shift of the burden of proof from the researching to the coastal State with regard to the "completeness" of the information provided.[75]

The third question to be dealt with is the conditions that the researching State has to fulfill when conducting research. As we have seen, State practice in this

70 Only Israel was satisfied with a mere notification.

71 For an exception *cf.* Greece (note 21).

72 E. g., when negotiating with Tanzania.

73 Saudi Arabia and Ethiopia.

74 As in the case of India and Oman.

75 For the international relevance of such rules *see Corfu Channel Case*, in: ICJ Reports 1949, 18; furthermore Preliminary Objections in the *Case concerning Right of Passage over Indian Territory*, in: ICJ Reports 1957, 141 *et seq.*; *Durward Sandifer*, Evidence before International Tribunals, Charlottesville 1975.

field concentrates on the same points as the Convention. The obvious conclusion to be drawn is that the régime of the Convention suits the needs of States. It also seems to be in tune with what coastal States regard as appropriate conditions to be imposed upon researching States. This is valid, firstly, with regard to the participation of coastal States' scientific and official personnel. This is less obvious concerning samples and research data. While most States follow the guidance of the Convention and some do not demand anything, some States go far beyond what is provided for in art. 249.[76] In the latter case, however, the researching State generally renounces conducting the research at all. At this crucial point the law is still uncertain.

What has been said above applies to the publication and dissemination of the research as well. The distinction made by the Convention between publishing the results of fundamental research and that of research which is of direct significance for the exploration and exploitation of natural resources is retained in practice.[77]

The above analysis draws one into an attempt to ascertain the present legal relevance of the Convention's régime in the field of MSR. The International Court of Justice has stated that a codification may, alternatively, crystallize, restate or be the point of departure for customary international law.[78] It is rather the latter category which fits with art. 245 *et seq.* Indeed, the present study shows that there exists a remarkably coherent State practice with regard to the concepts as codified in art. 245 *et seq.*[79] But it displays at the same time considerable State practice that does not "fit" with the said concepts; furthermore, the latter States do not feel the need to justify their practice with respect to art. 245 *et seq.*[80] And there does not seem to be sufficient evidence that States consider themselves to be legally bound by the said concepts even when acting correspondingly.[81] In the view of the authors the régime of the Convention, therefore, does lead the way to the "up-and-coming" law, but does not yet constitute customary international law. That is not to say, however, that art. 245 *et seq.* are not already of legal relevance. What can be said is that the régime of the Convention shapes and reflects State practice concerning MSR decisively; there is no difference between States having ratified the Convention and those that have not. Therefore, researching States can for the most part place a degree of confidence in the fact that a coastal State will adopt an attitude more or less corresponding to the

[76] *Cf.* State practice: Egypt, India, PDR Yemen.

[77] State practice Morocco, Greece.

[78] *Cf.*, especially, *North Sea Continental Shelf Cases*, in: ICJ Reports 1969, 23 *et seq.*

[79] It is generally agreed upon that international customary law presupposes coherent State practice, including the most interested States and corresponding *opinio iuris*.

[80] With the remarkable exception of Indonesia; it has, however, to be kept in mind that this State has ratified the Convention.

[81] Only Morocco and Egypt state their being legally bound; again the latter State has ratified the Convention.

concepts of art. 245 *et seq.*, if that State has not declared otherwise.[82] Regarding legitimate confidence international law provides the concept of estoppel.[83] A coastal State would then be estopped to invoke that it does not consider art. 245 *et seq.* to balance interests in an acceptable way. Included within the estoppel concept is passive conduct,[84] which is, however, only relevant if there is a duty to act.[85] Such a duty can be derived from State practice including "general toleration of the international community"[86] of a certain practice.[87] Though a cautious approach is called for, a coastal State may be bound to act given the characteristics of fundamental MSR: the researching State does not foster its own national interests but that of mankind;[88] MSR cannot be conducted at all without the coastal States' consent; finally MSR is costly and requires lengthy preparation in advance. An obvious conclusion would be that, in the absence of a pertinent domestic regulation, the provisions of the Law of the Sea Convention may have to be applied as evidence of the internationally agreed upon régime of MSR. Obviously it would have to be decided for each single provision whether it can be applied this way.[89] The provision in question would have to be self-executing.[90] The very detailed character of art. 245 *et seq.* ensures that this will very often be the case.

---

82 An appropriate means would be legislation.

83 *See generally* Separate Opinions of Judges *Alfaro* and *Sir Gerald Fitzmaurice* in the *Case concerning the Temple of Preah Vihear*, in: ICJ Reports 1962, 39-51; and of Judge *Bustamente y Rivera* in the *North Sea Continental Shelf Cases*, in: ICJ Reports 1969, 61-65; *Derek William Bowett*, Estoppel before International Tribunals and its Relation to Acquiescence, in: BYIL 33 (1957), 176-202; Commentary of the International Law Commission to Draft Article 4 Law of Treaties, in: Yearbook of the ILC 1963, Vol. II, 39 *et seq.*

84 For the relevance of passive conduct (e. g. silence or the absence of protest) *see* ICJ Reports 1960, 192, 231; 1962, 6, 32 furthermore Judge *Alfaro* (note 69), 41 *et seq.* with exhaustive references to international case law; *Ian Brownlie*, Principles of Public International Law, 4th ed., Oxford 1990, 641 *et seq.*; *Alfred Verdross/Bruno Simma*, Universelles Völkerrecht, 3rd ed., Berlin 1984, 393, para. 615. This is somewhat difficult to distinguish from the concept of acquiescence, *see* ICJ Reports 1984, 392, 411-413 (§§ 43-47) and Judge *Fitzmaurice* (note 69).

85 *Bowett* (note 83), 197 *et seq.*; *Antoine Martin*, L'estoppel en droit international public, Paris 1979, 275 with further references; *Philippe Cahier*, Le comportement des Etats comme source des droits et d'obligations, in: Institut Universitaire de Hautes Etudes Internationales (ed.), en Hommage à *Paul Guggenheim*, Geneva 1968, 237-265, 250-260.

86 *Fisheries Case*, in: ICJ Reports 1951, 130; *Bowett* (note 83), 199.

87 *See* Judge *Alfaro* (note 83), 45 *et seq.*; *Hersch Lauterpacht*, The Development of International Law by the International Court, London 1958, 168-170.

88 Art. 246, para. 3; *cf.*, with regard to this point, *Wolfrum* (note 2), 123.

89 *Wolfrum* (note 6), 144.

90 For the self-executing character of customary international law *see Gennady Danilenko*, Application of Customary International Law to Municipal Law, in: *Grigory Tunkin/Rüdiger Wolfrum* (eds.), International Law and Municipal Law, Berlin 1988, 13-23; *Walter Rudolf*, Incorporation of Customary International Law into Municipal Law, in: *op. cit.*, 24-40.

2. *Factual Analysis and Proposals*

What strikes one most in analyzing State practice are the detrimental effects that legal uncertainty may have on MSR.

This may be illustrated by comparing the policies of Egypt and Brazil. Both, being parties to the Convention, go beyond its provisions, yet to a different degree.[91] As Brazilian conditions are laid down in the national legislation, it was, however, possible to adopt proper measures; that was not the case with Egypt.

Indeed, legal certainty would have two major advantages. Firstly, in enacting legislation States would be forced to reconsider whether their policy with respect to MSR is compatible with the international law of the sea. Secondly, researching States would have a basis on which to foresee which conditions the coastal State may raise for granting consent.

It is therefore suggested that the international community insists that coastal States establish clear legislation in the field of MSR. This may be done in referring to the sophisticated system of the Convention, which is at least partly self-executing.[92]

On the coastal States' side, several points have to be considered. Firstly, a competent authority for granting consent should be named. Secondly, the different maritime zones should be delimited, especially the baseline should be established in detail.[93] Coastal States should decide to generally accept the use of single form by the researching States.[94] This would be an important contribution to legal certainty.

Further factual problems arise in connection with the régime of the Convention itself. In this respect, one has to distinguish two cases.

Firstly, there is State practice that is clearly contradictionary to the régime of the Convention. It is difficult to discover a remedy for this predicament. However, we may hope that the persuasive effect of the Convention will ameliorate the situation.

Secondly, practical problems occur frequently when it comes to properly applying the fundamental concepts of art. 245 *et seq*. These are the differentiation between "fundamental" and "applied" MSR, on the one hand, and between the legal régime of EEZ and continental shelf and that of the territorial seas, on the other hand. It is therefore paramount that these differences, which are clear-cut on the theoretical level, become easily manageable on the practical level as well.

---

[91] *Cf. supra* III. 2, 3.

[92] *Supra* II.

[93] Research teams sometimes have to make the considerable effort themselves, as they have to know which State has to be asked for consent; *cf.* Cruise Report of *Meteor* Cruise 5/2 by Prof. Dr. *Hjalmar Thiel.*

[94] Appropriate forms would be, e. g., the ICES-Form, or the Form elaborated on the expert conference in New York, September 1989.

As far as "fundamental" and "applied" MSR are concerned, several attempts to distinguish them abstractly on the legal level have already been undertaken.[95] In the view of the authors, this approach does not seem to be appropriate. Definition should rather be made from a scientific point of view; furthermore it should start by saying what is "of direct significance for the exploration of ... resources," thus defining any other MSR activity as "fundamental."[96]

Inasmuch as EEZ and territorial seas are concerned, the practice of those States which apply their EEZ régime to the territorial seas should be followed, as discretion of the governments is thereby limited. On the other hand, it has to be seen that the ratio of the EEZ concept is to confer powers to the coastal State for economic purposes; fundamental MSR is in no way covered by this ratio.[97] In order to use their EEZ properly, coastal States are to be reminded by the international community of their limited discretion in this zone. Pointing this out is all the more legitimate as the conceptual difference between territorial seas and the EEZ is generally accepted in State practice;[98] the particular field of MSR cannot be excluded from this.

Some further points should be mentioned. Firstly, a clear difference has to be made between a ships' function within a MSR's specific régime and its remaining quality as a ship as such. Research ships therefore have "classical rights," which this quality entails, *inter alia*, the right to call upon a port in case of distress. This must be accepted independently of whether the research vessel is classified as a merchant or a State ship. Secondly, delays play an important rôle in the preparation of MSR cruises. In order to shorten these delays, which hinder *ad hoc* actions, two different approaches may be considered. On the one hand, the amount of information to be provided to the coastal State could be limited considering what is needed to enable the coastal State to participate effectively; general use of a single language is called for; furthermore everything that contributes to legal certainty would be helpful in this respect, e. g. naming the competent authorities. On the other hand, coastal States' authorities should decide upon the application in proper time; four months as foreseen by the Convention should at least be respected. Finally, it may be stressed that a coastal State demanding a bilateral agreement on MSR has no foundation in international law.

V. Conclusion

The present study sheds some light on the legal and factual situation of MSR within the framework of the law of the sea.

---

95 *Soons* (note 2), 118 *et seq.*

96 *Cf.*, with respect to this question, *Wolfrum* (note 2), 119 *et seq.*

97 *Wolfrum* (note 2), 123 *et seq.*

98 For an analysis of State practice *see Wolfrum* (note 6), 132 *et seq.*

From the legal point of view, as holds true for the Law of the Sea Convention in general, the MSR's legal régime is still developing. Two aspects, however, arise within the microcosm of MSR as compared to the general law of the sea. That is, firstly, that although art. 245 *et seq.* have to deal with highly technical matters, these provisions have succeeded in concentrating on those points that State practice is concerned with as well. These fields are: the granting of consent, the information to be provided to the coastal State on the MSR project and the conditions to be respected by the researching State when conducting the consented MSR. It may be said that art. 245 *et seq.*, which strike a balance between the interests of the researching State, and the coastal State, are reflected in State practice, even with regard to detail. On the other hand, however, generally accepted principles of the new law of the sea do not at least entirely reflect the field of MSR. That can be said of applying different régimes to MSR in the territorial seas as opposed to in the EEZ. Article 245 *et seq.*, therefore, have shaped State practice in the field of MSR decisively.

Summing up, therefore, it is justified to think that in many respects the provisions of art. 245 *et seq.* point the way at least to the future customary international law of MSR. Yet, a crucially weak point of art. 245 *et seq.* cannot be ignored on the way: the question of whether the coastal State has improperly withheld its consent to a particular MSR project is not subject to compulsory third party settlement.[99] Consequently, it is only their intrinsical value that could make binding law out of the said provisions. *De lege lata* the authors suggest that a coastal State may be estopped from invoking that it cannot accept the concepts of art. 245 *et seq.* unless otherwise made clear.

From a factual point of view, the study distinguishes three major groups of practical problems arising. That is, firstly, legal uncertainty, secondly, applying the different fundamental concepts of the MSR régime of the Convention and, thirdly, miscellaneous problems, occurred in the reported cruises.

Legal uncertainty on conditions for consent to a MSR project represents a major problem for the scientists and the organizing entities. In order to remedy the situation, the authors put forward different proposals. We, firstly, suggest that coastal States enact legislation concerning MSR by using the self-executing provisions of art. 245 *et seq.* Secondly, a single form should be generally agreed upon by the international community. It is worth considering whether the use of the form generally agreed upon does not oblige the coastal State to prove that the information provided by the researching State is not sufficient.

The application of MSR's fundamental concepts, on the other hand, is primarily a matter of international concern. Two proposals are to be made with respect to this point. Firstly, a scientific definition of "applied" MSR would make it possible

---

99 *Churchill/Lowe* (note 2), 293; *Wolfrum* (note 6), 144. Except for procedure foreseen in Annex V; for details *see Churchill/Lowe, op. cit.*, 330 *et seq.*

to define "fundamental" MSR negatively, such a definition being easier to handle in practice. Secondly, it is submitted that the conceptual differentiation between territorial seas and EEZ, being internationally accepted, is valid in the particular field of MSR as well. The international community should place emphasis upon this point and, at least in the long run, would be successful in doing so.

Having elaborated on State practice, the authors have a final thought with regard to the juridical interpretation of the Law of the Sea Convention. In fact, a certain interpretation of the concept of consent as provided for in art. 246 may be called for. That is because the Convention presupposes the freedom of marine scientific research beyond the territorial seas[100] and extends this notion to the EEZ as well. That is derived from the wording "consent shall, in normal circumstances, be granted";[101] and that, furthermore, this consent may even be implied.[102] Thus, the Convention expresses that coastal States' consent is not necessarily of material importance. With a view to achieving freedom in MSR this approach by the Convention is simply consequent. Indeed, limiting freedom by preventive measures (i. e. consent) would be a more restrictive approach than providing coastal States with repressive means; consequently the latter are foreseen in art. 253. In the authors' view, therefore, "consent" may be read as "notification."[103]

100 Article 87, para. 1 (f); this is customary international law, *see Wolfrum* (note 2), 102; *Jonathan Moore*, The Future of Scientific Research in Contiguous Resource Zones: Legal Aspects, in: The International Lawyer 8 (1974), 242-261 (245). The situation is less clear with regard to the Area, *cf.* art. 143, para. 1.

101 Article 246, para. 3.

102 Articles 247 and 252.

103 *Cf.* the proposals put forward by Austria and other States during UNCLOS III (UN doc. A/Conf. 62/L. 19); *see Wolfrum* (note 2), 117 *et seq*. This is the actual practice of few States as the United States of America (Note to the United Nations of 13 October 1988 on United States Practice Relating to Marine Scientific Research), the Federal Republic of Germany (Note to the United Nations of 25 July 1988, especially para. 3) and, apparently, Israel.

Discussion

Picht:

I have a question with respect to Mr *Treves'* presentation. I am surprised, or puzzled even, that there have been so few applications with respect to the pioneer investor status along the provisions of the Convention, and the limited number of others coming from outside, in particular, since these applicants have waived a large part of the obligation, for example, the payment of fees. My sense is that there could have been many more applicants under these conditions. I am wondering why there have not been more than just the few you mentioned. Do you have an explanation?

Further, you referred to the relative ease with which the problems of overlapping claims have been solved so far. Is it not just an indication of the relatively low value of the stakes that are involved? Stated otherwise, suppose the prices for the relevant metals go up substantially, something you never know in advance, I anticipate that the fight over claims and over overlapping claims would be much harder. My conclusion is that you cannot infer from the relative ease of settlement in the past to how tough the struggle will be in the future.

Treves:

First you asked why there are so few applications for pioneer investor status. Well, out of eight possible applications there are four, this is fifty per cent. Perhaps that is not so little. As there is no prospect for sea-bed mining now even the applications that are there are — I would say — more of a symbolic than of real nature. As to the second question, the process of eliminating overlaps was not easy at all. It lasted various years, and was a very complex and energy-consuming process. Maybe it was made less difficult because there is no immediate urgency to go to sea. You asked me whether it would be easier or more difficult for us if there were more interest. I do not know. It might be easier because people would see an immediate result and this could facilitate a compromise. It might be more difficult because the stakes would be higher, but this has to be seen in practice.

Kwiatkowska:

I would like to ask three questions concerning the matters presented by *Francisco Orrego*, but in view of equal experience in those matters of *Tullio Treves*, in a case, *Tullio*, where your opinion differs, I would very much like to hear it as well. The questions are all raised by the recent practice of States and they are as follows: The first relates to the Netherlands' practice which has recently been under consideration and it involves the issue of parallelism, or, as *Francisco* said, integration between the exclusive economic zone and the continental shelf. For States which did not establish exclusive economic zones, what is in your opinion the scope of rights as regards the continental shelf, with respect to artificial islands? My understanding is that art. 60, which applies *mutatis mutandis* to the continental shelf, implies that coastal States have the right with regard to all artificial islands on the continental shelf and not only those related to mineral resources exploration/exploitation. I include sedentary species but it is not relevant to my problem. Therefore, if you have exclusive jurisdiction in art. 60, para. 2 and you are a State which does not have an exclusive economic zone, I assume that you have the exclusive jurisdiction with regard to whatever matters will arise in connection with the installations and not only those strictly related to oil exploration. I base this on the general application of art. 60 to the continental shelf in cases where you do not have economic zones.

The second issue is raised by the practice of Malaysia. You mentioned, *Francisco*, that art. 73 forbids imprisonment. Nevertheless, several States provide for it. That is one thing, the other thing is: several States like Malaysia do not impose imprisonment but impose excessive fines which are really impossible to pay. And therefore, on this basis, Malaysia puts an innumerable amount of Thai and other fishermen into prison. Formally, they say, they observe the Convention because they do not impose imprisonment. Now, do you find the imposition of a fine which is impossible to pay as contrary to art. 300 on good faith, or would you say that the issue is irrelevant and that Malaysia conforms to international law because it does not impose any imprisonment?

The third issue relates to what we perceive as *l'enfant terrible* of ocean boundary making, and that is the rocks "which cannot sustain human habitation or economic life of their own." Do you think the norm of art. 121, para. 3 passed already into customary law, do you think these so-called "rocks" are permitted under general international law, to generate their own continental shelf and economic zone? *Dolliver Nelson* advocates at some point with extensive argumentation that it could already be regarded as customary law. My feeling would be the opposite, I suppose perhaps it is the norm which is even not "generalizable" into general international law. What would be your opinion, because I think this will remain a very controversial issue?

Treves:

I think *Barbara* has posed a very interesting question, namely what happens to the right on installations for a State that, not having proclaimed an economic zone, has just a continental shelf. All States have a continental shelf whether they proclaim it or not. Her view is that the rights on installations on the continental shelf would not be touched by the limitations, that are in the Convention in art. 60 for the installations within the EEZ. I beg to differ for two reasons: one is that art. 80, which concerns the shelf, makes a reference to art. 60. This would admittedly not be so relevant while the Convention is not in force. The second reason, which I think more relevant, is that the rights for any State on a continental shelf are rights for the purposes of the exploration and exploitation of resources. This conditions the whole régime including the installations. Thus, the exception is the rule of the Convention on artificial islands. This is the aspect where we should study whether the Convention corresponds to customary law or not.

Orrego Vicuña:

A short comment on the first question. I think that the question is really that the régime of artificial islands was devised as a régime on its own, more associated with the continental shelf than with the exclusive economic zone. To the extent that the régime of art. 60 contains some limitations, those would be equally applicable to the continental shelf. The problem is, which are the real limitations contained in art. 60, particularly in terms of the extent of the jurisdiction of the coastal State? I would separate the case of artificial islands which anyhow falls within the jurisdiction of a coastal State without restrictions. But in relation to installations and structures, whether only some categories of installations and structures fall under the jurisdiction of the coastal State is where I think the problem lies.

The second question is related to the problem of imprisonment and excessive fines. In my view the Convention should be read rather restrictively in this regard, from the point of view that what is actually prohibited is imprisonment for fishing violations. If a State imposes fines, even if they are high, to the effect of discouraging illegal fishing it is entitled to do so. I would add that a State has the right to apply penalties of imprisonment for other kinds of violations which are not related to fishing. For example in Chile, there is at present a case including Norway and Denmark against Chile, concerning two officers of a merchant ship which collided and caused the death of Chilean fishermen, who have been held as a preventive measure, not because of a fishery violation but because of a violation of the normal criminal laws, which is in itself a ground for such measures.

Finally, in relation to the problem of rocks and boundaries, whether they have been integrated into customary law or not, I would say no. In my view, the problem is that State practice as regards this question is still very scant. There is nothing that one could see to develop a general trend. It is likely that in the future the trend may be favourable to coastal State jurisdiction, because it is the kind of issue which all coastal States probably would be interested in developing some way or the other. But so far, I do not see that the practice is enough to justify a customary law status.

Kiderlen:

Thank you very much. I am most grateful for the statement of Dr. *Orrego Vicuña*, particularly as he stated — and the statement was accompanied by all kinds of reflections and examples — that what we used to call creeping jurisdiction of the coastal States, is in his view no longer a current trend in the practice of the law of the sea. The Law of the Sea Convention, even though it has not yet come into force, apparently proves to be a success already now in limiting to some extent and in channelling the interests of coastal States. But I have a few questions relating to some issues you mentioned. With respect to the continental shelf and the application of art. 76 in particular, the paragraphs dealing with the limitation of the continental shelf, other than para. 1, I would like to mention the opinion which is also officially largely held, at least in the Federal Republic of Germany. The possibility of extending the continental shelf beyond 200 miles is to a large extent linked to the installation of the Commission on the Limits of the Continental Shelf, which has to be set up after the entering into force of the Convention. So I would underline what Dr. *Orrego Vicuña* said, that these paragraphs cannot so easily be regarded as already now being part of international law. I would like to stress this argument also by saying that there is a link established in art. 76 between the installation and the operation of that commission and the possibility to make use of the paragraphs other than para. 1 of art. 76. I would like to mention for instance that not only the United States, but as far as I remember also the Federal Republic of Germany protested against the extension of the continental shelf beyond 200 miles by the Republic of Chile and by Ecuador in its time.

The second remark concerns the Arctic. If I understood correctly, Dr. *Orrego Vicuña* said that the Arctic issue, the issue of maritime zones of national legislation in the Arctic, is not affected by the régime as set forth in the Convention. I would like to put a question mark behind such a view. I think the Arctic is one of the neuralgic areas where I could foresee problems arising between the régime set forth in the Convention as to national maritime zones, and national aspirations of coastal States to go beyond this régime. The Arctic is, contrary to the Antarctic, mainly covered by water, which is part of the high seas. Before this background I think legal measures taken by Arctic coastal States may sometimes appear questionable. One cannot discard some of the concerns.

Third question: I would like to come to perhaps a minor note regarding developments in Chile. Recently an idea has been promoted to declare or to consider something like a "mare presential," apparently as a new instrument of international law. Quite frankly this sounds a little awkward, but perhaps Dr.

Orrego Vicuña could give some explanation as to the concept behind this, and with respect to its relation to the legal régime of the Law of the Sea Convention.

One last remark concerning transit passage: in this area as well we have quite an established official opinion in the Federal Republic of Germany, which has already been mentioned by Dr. *Orrego Vicuña* at the end of his speech. Indeed, the introduction of the instrument of transit passage is to be seen as the counterpart of the extension of the territorial sea from three to twelve miles. Out of this extension of the territorial sea originated many dozens of new straits. As part of a specific "package deal" the Law of the Sea Conference wanted to counterbalance this increase of straits through the régime of transit passage for international straits. If countries, as Dr. *Orrego Vicuña* rightly noted, make use quite freely of the 12 mile limit of the territorial sea and are in the same time reluctant to acknowledge transit passage, this is contrary to the link accepted by the Law of the Sea Conference. In our view both institutes together have become part of customary international law.

Orrego Vicuña:

Thank you very much for those interesting questions. First, in relation to art. 76, indeed, it has some operational link with the Commission on the Limits of the Continental Shelf. But I would see this link not as paralyzing the implementation of art. 76 necessarily as from now, but only leading towards the submission of disputes about the technicalities of implementation to that commission. For example, a country could eventually anticipate the implementation of measures under art. 76, in spite of the Convention not being in force, and if there is a technicality about the implementation that arises it can be submitted to the Commission once it is established. It is not a case of applying the Convention as customary law, but rather of an anticipatory application of a conventional text and what could be regarded as an application of the general clauses of the Vienna Convention of the Law of Treaties.

On the question of the Arctic, I really did not intend to say that there was no problem in relation to the Convention. What I said was that the new technological developments leading into areas like the Arctic and the Antarctic were as such posing new issues and elements, but in that technological development there was nothing contrary to the Convention but merely new elements coming out.

The third question relates to the idea developed by the Commander in Chief of the Chilean navy, regarding the existence of what has been termed "presence at sea," an area of the sea where the national presence would be felt. It really has no legal implications, the legal side of it being very much within the framework of the exclusive economic zone and continental shelf claims, including eventually the 350 mile claim around Easter Island, high seas fisheries in the area and a number of other elements. The only element where there is a legal implication is the one related to straddling stocks. Chile like a few other countries is facing an increasing problem in terms of stocks being exploited beyond the 200 mile area, with very negative implications within the 200 mile area and there has been an effort devoted to try to come to terms with that, either through negotiations or by some other means. In his statement there was a specific reference to the need to come up with solutions in that particular area, not mentioning what the solutions were, but the implication is that there is a need to search for that as is also the case with Canada and the US in the North Pacific and a few other countries.

In regard to the final issue of the transit passage and the 12 mile territorial sea, that is quite clear in the terms of the package. So the question is really again whether transit passage as a conceptual element became a part of customary law or the whole régime with all its specifics did so.

Lagoni:

Instead of a question I would like to add three small points to Dr. *Orrego*'s excellent presentation on the exclusive economic zone. It seems to me that for a State such as the Federal Republic of Germany, with hardly any non-living resources in its continental shelf and limited living resources off its coasts in the North Sea and the Baltic Sea, the principal importance of an exclusive economic zone (which Germany surprisingly does not yet have) would be the extended jurisdiction for the protection and preservation of the marine environment. I can imagine that the environmental protection could generally gain importance for establishing such a zone. Secondly, Dr. *Orrego* rightly pointed out that States tend toward anticipatory application of the Law of the Sea Convention. One could add, however, that some of them forget an anticipatory application of the safeguards for international shipping, which are also provided in Part XII of the Convention. Anticipatory application, no doubt, has to include the obligations to respect the safeguards, as well. These safeguards create certain problems one of which has already been mentioned. Article 320 of the Convention permits only monetary penalties for marine pollution. In Germany, monetary penalties are imposed on the basis of the salary of the offender. If he has a low income calculated in Deutschmark, his fine for illegal pollution of the sea may be considerably below the costs for discharging the slop or waste at a reception facility in a port. In this situation, it may be more economical for the shipping company to reimburse the offender for the fine, than to use the reception facilities. Realizing this, the competent criminal court started to detain offenders before their trial and tended to sentence them for imprisonment. Because it is much more expensive for the shipping company concerned to leave the ship waiting in a port until the captain or the chief engineer, who is responsible for the pollution, has been replaced. This very effective threat of pre-trial detention or imprisonment will be lost, when art. 320 enters into force.

Rebagliati:

A few comments on those very substantive and important presentations that we have heard today and some subsequent comments. In relation to the very first presentation made by Prof. *Treves*, I would like to pick up the two possibilities he suggested at the very end in relation to the clear picture that he gave us regarding pioneer investments, namely the need for tackling the problems he so ably described, for either looking to the PrepCom for adjustments, in particular to resolution II and possibly to the Convention, or to what he called a dialogue, though he refrained from further elaboration on that, probably waiting until the "round table." I will just confine my comments at this point to these remarks.

I think a word of caution should be placed in relation to the first suggestion. For both, political and legal reasons, trying to make an effort though of course honest and well intended within the PrepCom to amend a resolution passed by the Conference, and even to imply a modification to the Convention (I would not say amend because that would be legally impossible to do as he knows), I assume he is probably thinking about ways and means to interpret the Convention, or to trigger some kind of machinery for amending it formally. In any case, trying to have the Preparatory Commission endeavouring to undertake such a job would be legally objectionable. Politically, which is probably just as important, it would probably be fruitless like some of the efforts already made within the Commission to have universal acceptance. I say this because if all the main actors, both members and non-members of the Commission, do not participate and earnestly devote themselves to this adjustment, that is badly needed, such an effort is not likely to succeed, or at least to succeed within a short period of time. That is why I would strongly suggest to concentrate all possible attention on all the ways and means available to obtain a solution for this crucial problem relating to Part XI.

On the very important presentation made by Prof. *Orrego Vicuña*, I do not know if I can share his moderate content about the possibility of having national legislations growing and developing as they are, with some kind of discrepancy or variance in relation to the Convention, but in any case letting us leave it without having the Convention coming into force. I see this situation (he probably sees it in the same way, but tried to put it more optimistically) as a potential crisis situation, not necessarily a world-wide crisis but a potential crisis for bilateral, regional and even some global conflicts, which may arise from different applications of a convention which has not yet come into force. Therefore countries, even signatories or parties, without the Convention coming into force, will more freely interpret what the Convention provides and will follow whatever will be more in conformity with their national interests. Until all major groups of countries are parties to the Convention, they would probably behave in such a manner which would not totally be incompatible with the Convention, though would be much more in conformity with individual countries' interests and historical perception of their international law relating to national maritime spaces. And that is true for the three maritime spaces he described, and it is also true for those like archipelagic waters as we learned the other day from Dr. *Kwiatkowska*'s presention, and comments relating to some discrepancies about those interpretations by her and other attendees of this symposium. And again the possibility of conflicting interpretation in crucial matters, such as the one relating to the outer limit of the continental shelf, mentioned by Counsellor *Kiderlen* and clarified by Prof. *Orrego Vicuña* is another example of these potential conflicts that we may easily face on a national/international level. I would have to subscribe to the explanation given by Prof. *Orrego Vicuña* in respect of the outer limit of the continental shelf and the continental margin beyond 200 miles. That is something very well-known to all participants and scholars, and it is taken not only from the doctrine but precisely from the famous *North Sea Continental Shelf Cases*, in which the Federal Republic of Germany was the successful plaintiff. That is why I do not see any difficulty in admitting the concept of the continental margin as appertaining to the coastal State wherever it lies, provided that they meet the criteria of being an integral part of the continent. Though the precise delimitation, or the outer limit precisely defined, is subject to criteria which are not at this moment part of customary international law, and nothing is against of anticipating to the direction international law may point, something has to be done to specify the limits of the outer continental margin.

Finally, I would like to attempt to summarize these remarks by saying what we are purely experiencing as countries both within the PrepCom and outside the PrepCom, within the Convention (to cover those who signed or ratified) and outside the Convention, playing different rôles and attitudes in different scenarios. Countries which have not signed or did not take part in the Convention and which at this moment are outside of the Convention are trying to consolidate provisions of the Convention, provisions other than those relating to Part XI, in particular, provisions relating to the freedom of navigation and some precise limits to coastal State jurisdiction. Countries which are within the Convention or within the PrepCom sometimes try to make an effort (though honest) contrary to the Convention and its resolutions, for the sake of universality. Countries within the Convention or within the PrepCom, and which generally behave in accordance with it, will, however, in their national legislation (when it comes to the continental shelf, straits of other maritime spaces under that jurisdiction) not necessarily follow the Convention, despite the fact that they are active participants in the PrepCom and are willing to have a universally accepted convention. And that is because, at present, they do not feel that the Convention is alive. For the time being, it seems suitable to further protect particular national interests until the picture becomes clearer.

Another scenario is that relating to bilateral regional arrangements, which are also taking place, some of them are in accordance with the sense of the Convention, and some others are contrary to the intention of the drafters of the Convention. Whether this is legal or illegal depends on the perspective. We can analyze it and of course we cannot say that it is illegal to contravene a Convention which is not yet law so far, unless some parts of it are part of customary international law. So it is not very clear. What I am saying probably is not very clear, though I am trying to do my best, but the picture itself is not clear and is becoming more and more unclear. That is the last point I want to make, to focus on the second possibility that Prof. *Treves* mentioned in his presentation, which he called the "dialogue" and which would have to involve all representatives and international officers concerned, in order to tackle this lack of clarity with the view to avoiding precisely the type of conflicts, which I am afraid will arise, with a frequency that we are not probably assessing in a due manner at this moment.

Wolfrum:

I would like to start with the remark just made by Mr *Kiderlen*. He pointed out that the phenomen of "creeping jurisdiction" has been put aside by the Law of the Sea Convention, although this Convention has not yet entered into force. Although I tend to agree with him in general, I am not entirely sure about the specifics. I do agree — and this has very well been presented by Prof. *Orrego Vicuña* — that States tend to accept the exclusive economic zone concept and the continental shelf concept and apply it. However, he pointed out a reference has not always been made to the exercise of coastal State jurisdiction limitations or the safeguard of the rights of other States. This problem has already been touched upon the first day by Mr *Bouch*. He argued that if no mention was made of the freedom of navigation in the coastal sea this does not mean that the very littoral State objects to the innocent passage or objects to transit passage. Hence, it is very difficult to properly evaluate the lack of mentioning certain limitations.

I am inclined to agree with Prof. *Orrego Vicuña* who advocates a limited interpretation of art. 230 LOS Convention. The example pending before the Chilean Courts he referred to seems to be similar to the *Lotus* Case and just as the judgment rendered by the lower court. Finally, I would like to endorse his view that innocent passage or transit passage is connected with the extension of the coastal sea to 12 miles. If we accept the 12 mile limit as becoming or having already become customary international law the same would apply to innocent passage and transit passage and the inherent limitations to coastal States.

May I pose a question to Prof. *Treves*. As I read para. 7 (b) of resolution II it seems to be quite evident that the annual fixed fee of $US 1 million has to be paid by every registered pioneer investor from the date of the allocation of the pioneer area. There seems to be little room to invoke the *rebus sic stantibus* clause. Has it been taken into account that the moratorium on such payments weakens the financial resources of the Preparatory Commission and thus increases the burden for the UN budget? One should not overlook the fact that the funding of the Preparatory Commission from the UN budget has been questioned by at least one State.

Finally, I would like to direct a question to Mr *Röben* or Mr *Plesmann* whoever prefers to answer it. As far as I can recall, there are several littoral States limiting the access of research ships to their harbours. Where is the respective basis in the Law of the Sea Convention, if any?

Craven:

We had two excellent textbook papers on States practice as it appears to be evolving into customary law, and as it appears to be evolving from customary law into the words of UNCLOS III. Hearing these presentations one feels very, very comfortable to realize that except for straddling stocks, except for rocks and islands, except for scientific research and a very few other things that we probably have a régime in place. I was particularly interested by Dr. *Orrego*'s feeling as I was of some of the previous commentators that creeping jurisdiction has been stopped in its tracks. As I heard the examples given were not examples of challenges to limited sovereignty régimes through the mechanism "creeping jurisdiction" but were cases in which you could say "creeping jurisdiction" had not taken place because an overt expansion jurisdiction has already been granted by the terms of the régime of the EEZ. I would like to then focus a question with respect to some installations that I think are going to appear in the very near future which will really raise this question as to whether or not the EEZ is a jurisdiction which has fundamentally high seas freedoms or whether it is a jurisdiction which is basically territorial. These are as follows: in the United States' Magnussen Act on fishing, the act defines a fishing vessel as a vessel which pertains in some remote way to fishing. Therefore, a floating sales room for fishery products falls within the jurisdiction of the Magnussen Act as a fishing vessel and is therefore capable being boarded by the United States Coast Guard in "any place at any time." But we have other functional examples developing which are usually associated with fixed installations. Of course, we see that the fixed installation does come under the exclusive economic zone. But how about the following: What is the jurisdictional régime for floating military bases — extremely large complexes of an entire military base — which float and are slowly mobile? How about floating foreign trade zones in which the commodities to be traded do not relate the resources of the EEZ? How about floating factories which do not use the resources of the EEZ? How about floating cities, how about the floating convention centers and other large items which are just not navigating through the EEZ? And the question I really have is that how do I advise my entrepreneurs who are proposing to build and deploy these things? Will they be able to deploy them successfully in the EEZ of a hostile coastal State?

Lilje-Jensen:

Prof. *Orrego* referred to the recent incident or collision off the coast of Chile — it was in April, I think — involving allegedly a Chilean fishing boat and a Danish-owned ship flying the Norwegian flag. The two Danish officers were detained. I am afraid I do not quite agree with Prof. *Orrego* in saying that this is a case falling within Chilean jurisdiction, as the collision took place 40 nautical miles off the coast. We certainly do think that this will be a case for Norwegian or Danish jurisdiction. Accordingly, a formal demarche was made in Santiago. I just wanted to put things straight making this observation.

My second point refers to the paper on the State practice concerning marine scientific research. You state here and that is in your conclusion that there is legal uncertainty and it appears very well from your paper. I think that it is an extremely important paper in giving the facts from real life, from experience on a research vessel that is different than something you can look up in a book. I am just afraid your conclusion is discouraging to a certain extent. In fact, there should be no conflict of interest in many respects, as also the coastal State in many ways should be able to profit from the results. I see here that some States made certain demands beyond any reason and so, in fact, you have to give up the research from which that State, mankind, or a lot of scientists and other people would have been able to benefit. You suggest that States enact legislation concerning MSR by using the provisions of art. 245 *et seq.*. I think this whole thing asks very much for some kind of harmonization. I have no solution, of course, I am sorry. But I would like to hear your opinion how such a harmonization might be obtained. Which type of forum could be envisaged? Would it be practical to start on a regional basis or could you imagine some kind of international forum to bring about harmonization of the rules and regulations applying to research vessels?

Jesus:

My first comment with respect to what I think is a pertinent remark made by Mr *Kiderlen* on the question of the extension by national legislation of the continental shelf to the outer limits of at least beyond 200 miles, 350 or less but beyond 200 miles. I believe that if you read the series of provisions of the Convention dealing with the question of the continental shelf including Annex II that established the Commission on the Limitation of the Continental Shelf, you come to the conclusion more or less along the lines of what has been mentioned by Mr *Kiderlen* that, while States could establish the 200 mile zone for the continental shelf, the extension of the continental shelf beyond that seems to be subject to the prior submission of the necessary data to the Commission on the Continental Shelf. That means that until the Commission is established in accordance with Annex II to the Convention (18 months) and after the entry into force of the Convention, it could be perhaps in contravention with the provisions of the Convention to establish a larger continental shelf, larger than 200 miles. And that is so, especially if you read the provisions in the light of what is established in art. 4 of the Annex II that established the Commission on the Limitation of the Continental Shelf which, in fact, says that where a coastal State intends to establish a continental shelf beyond 200 miles, it shall submit particulars of such limits to the Commission. That means that any continental shelf beyond 200 miles could not legally be established unilaterally without the prior submission of the data to the Commission on the Limitation of Maritime Boundaries. In that respect, I believe that Mr *Kiderlen* might have a strong point and certainly might have a lot of support especially from the majority of countries that are parties to the Convention which can only establish a 200 mile continental shelf limit.

Now, I would like to make two small comments, too, on the pioneer investors. One is to dispel the impression that seems to creep in our discussion that the pioneer investors (the registered pioneer investors) are not going to comply with certain of their obligations. I must say that they themselves in the last position document, that they have submitted, have made it clear that they would comply with all their pioneer obligations. Now, the problem that is to be discussed is the question of the obligation of one million dollars. If you see the history of negotiations of that clause you come to the conclusion that the *ratio legis* of para. 7 (b) of resolution II which sets the obligation of one million dollars was essentially a safeguard clause to guarantee to the Preparatory Commission, and therefore to the Authority, that upon and after the registration of a given pioneer investor he would not sit on the site and cease to invest in developing that site to the extent that it was in the interest of the Authority to have that site developed. So it was a clause that was created to force him to do something in his own pioneer area. It is because of that ratio legis that the provision of para. 7 (b) itself established that the one million dollars, to be paid by the pioneer investor, had to be taken into consideration by the Authority, in this instant case by the Council, in the financial terms of the contract applied for by that pioneer investor. In other words, it is a kind of advanced payment, if I can put it that way. The one million dollars is a kind of advanced payment. We came to the conclusion that that kind of obligation would not last more than three or four years in accordance with the intention of the legislative history of that clause because the Convention was supposed, more or less, to come into force in 1985, and therefore they would have to pay perhaps two or three million dollars since the registration was not supposed to take place before 1983, which was a target date for the overlapping claims to have been solved. And these overlapping clauses were only solved after the end of 1986. All things considered, it is obvious that if we can (through this agreement that we are trying to shape up and hopefully we might be able to adopt a consensus of agreement on that basis next meeting of the PrepCom), if we can engage the registered pioneer investors in the system through this agreement that we are working out to achieve through a difficult arrangement or mechanism, then the finality of that provision of para. 7 (b) (that is to say to make sure that they will develop the sight in due time) will have been achieved and the practical problem that the pioneers have would have also been solved. I believe that it is in this context that we can say that the obligation of one million dollars is not being paid but we have to take into consideration that that is not a payment as a compensation or payment due on account of operations. Paragraph 7 (b) was an expediency that was found to oblige them to engage into the system. If we can circumvent the problems that they have by engaging them in another way, then we are in keeping with the spirit at least if not with the letter of that provision of para. 7 (b) of resolution II.

My last comment is with respect to the need for the so-called potential applicants to apply for registration. I believe that it would be, that is my opinion, in the interest of the potential applicants — and here we have two groups of potential applicants, those that normally are known as potential applicants mentioned in resolution II by name, and those that are developing nations — it would be in the interest of these two groups to apply for registration because as we all know the pioneer system consist essentially of two rights. Two priorities are granted to the registered pioneer investor, one is the priority to obtain a contract, a priority over any other applicant other than the Enterpise and a priority in obtaining a production authorization also over any other contractor other than the Enterprise. The earlier you apply for the pioneer status the better is your position as against any other applicant for a plan of work. That is why I think that in the perspective of the solution of issues of Part XI we might think that there would be an interest of all potential applicants of the two groups to apply to be registered. I am glad to note that at least one or two of the potential applicants, not perhaps in the first category, are already prepared to apply to be registered before the entry into force of the Convention which is a good sign in the sense of strengthening the sea-bed system.

Lee:

I would just like to make a brief comment. I believe there are good reasons that one should apply a stringent test to whether or not certain rules have come into customary international law. I am grateful to the main speakers, Professors *Orrego Vicuña* and *Treves*, who have taken a very cautious position on this question in their presentation and also in their answering of questions whether certain rules have become customary international law. I think, apart from the fact that there have been inherent difficulties in ascertaining whether a rule has become international law or not, there are also good policy reasons that at this stage we have to be more cautious. First, up to now jurists still could not agree how long and how to assess *opinio iuris*. Second, we are facing a crossroad, as Prof. *Wolfrum* has rightly chosen as the theme of this symposium. The crossroad that I see is the universally accepted treaty régime on the one hand versus the reliance on inconsistent national legislation on the other. If we apply a loose standard to what may constitute customary international law we are reducing the value and the goal we are trying to achieve for a universally accepted treaty. If one applies a loose standard, anything can easily be referred to as customary international law. Then, why a universally accepted treaty? I think we will have to be very cautious.

Nagel:

I work for the Federal Ministry for Research and Technology in Bonn. This ministry handles most of our outgoing requests for consent to conduct marine scientific research in waters under foreign jurisdiction. When discussing individual applications for the consent with other States we have had the experience that the provisions of Part XIII of the Law of the Sea Convention are practically always taken as the basis for arguments in those cases. This is probably simply due to the absence of any traditional legal régime on marine scientific research. There are, of course, often different opinions on the interpretation of certain clauses of Part XIII. But I am not aware of any controversy about accepting these provisions as the basis for discussion.

It is my impression that during the last years both sides — coastal States and researching States — have gone through a certain learning process. They have learned how to handle requests, they have learned to better understand each other's needs and the balance those needs have found in Part XIII. This learning process has, however, brought about one learning effect which I consider very dangerous and which has already been mentioned today by Mr *Lilje-Jensen* and yesterday at the luncheon by the acting director of the Institute of Marine Sciences. I am talking of the fact that scientists in some cases or in certain areas tend to restrict their research or not to do any research at all rather than going through the cumbersome procedure of applying for consent to the coastal State. Such a prohibitive effect on marine scientific research cannot be in the interest of any State, be it a coastal or researching State, given the importance of research — especially fundamental or environmental research — also for the coastal or other States. So, I think what we all have to strive for and to work on is to avoid any unnecessary bureaucracy in handling those requests. During the years to come we will have to work on simplifying, shortening and accelerating the procedures for granting consent for marine scientific research. This could be done, for example, by designating shorter lead times for the submission of requests (shorter than six months) and by limiting the amount of information to be provided to the coastal State by the researching State. Such simplified procedures should preferably be agreed upon on a regional basis. In my view it is absolutely necessary that we make some progress in that area.

Ballah:

First, I want to raise a question on creeping jurisdiction. But I think Prof. *Wolfrum* has dealt with it. There is only one point of concern particularly for countries that are geographically disadvantaged and developing countries. Such countries are finding it difficult to gain access to the surplus in neighbouring exclusive economic zones. We have always had difficulties with that during the Conference. There is a further difficulty now where coastal States see the need for managing straddling stocks. This is likely to lead to a further creep in the jurisdiction and the prevention of some of our States even taking stocks beyond 200 miles. Now the other point I wanted to direct to Dr. *Orrego* a point for more information and clarification, but Mr *Lilje-Jensen* has raised it. I wanted to find out from him whether Chilean jurisdiction since the 1982 Convention is different in that the new land calls for a 12 mile territorial sea, an exclusive economic zone of 200 miles and a continental shelf so-called which may run to 350 miles. If that is so and the incident, I think, is an important incident, I think it is a new *Lotus* type of incident. I think Prof. *Lilje-Jensen* has said that the accident took place about 40 nautical miles from the Chilean coast. So, I want to know under what rules is Chile exercising a criminal jurisdiction? I think it is going to be an important case for our books.

Kapumpa:

First of all, I wish to comment on what Prof. *Wolfrum* said a few minutes ago with regard to his reading of the clarity with which the various obligations that are contained in resolution II have been made. I only wish that Prof. *Wolfrum* was with us at the Preparatory Commission. His perception and clarity of understanding would have assisted us to resolve some of our issues. The question I have for my good friend Prof. *Treves* is as follows: Does he see the implementation of some of the obligations, such as the one million dollars, as an unrealistic burden imposed on the registered pioneer investors or as the rightful expectations of those organizations which have been accorded, upon registration, the exclusive rights to carry out pioneer activities in the pioneer areas allocated to them?

Orrego Vicuña:

I will reply very briefly to various of the most interesting comments raised. First, in relation to what Mr *Rebagliati* has mentioned I think that the problem is really that States generally, with a few exceptions, are behaving today without the Convention in force in a manner similar to what they would behave with the Convention in force. That is, in their legislation they do not have a contradiction with the Convention except to the extent that there are differing interpretations of the Convention. Those would appear anyhow even if the Convention would be in force. So really the question is whether this behaviour is likely to change, and my view is that it is not likely to happen because it is already part of a trend. In this same regard I think that I can mention what Prof. *Wolfrum* referred to as those cases where there is no reference to given rights, for example, with regard to freedom of navigation. Whether that can be understood as complying with the freedom of navigation or as opposing freedom of navigation, I think that throughout the examination of national legislation one finds a very great number of cases in which certain rights of third parties are not mentioned, in spite of that they were not subject to any form of trespassing or violation. That means again that the simple omission is not tantamount to a violation or an attitude opposing that obligation or that particular type of right under the Convention.

Next, I would like to refer to *John Craven*'s review of the problem surrounding new uses of the sea, where he is absolutely correct as he has been in the past in pointing to potential uses of the sea. I think that this will come. Now, whether it is a part of national jurisdiction under the EEZ, or a part of freedom of navigation or communication depends very much on the nature of the installation or floating platform, or on the nature of the use. And for that matter I think that the test will be particularly one for art. 59 of the Convention, whether under that article coastal States may claim jurisdiction if the activity taking place is somehow associated with the use of its resources or with the use of its economic zone from the point of view of the purposes for which it was established. For example, if there is a floating factory on the economic zone I think that there would be a case for an argument in favour of jurisdiction of the coastal State, or if there is a free trade zone established on the floating platform. But that is something that will have to be probably adjudicated on a case-by-case basis.

One last element of substance is related to the interpretation that has been mentioned by Mr *Kiderlen* and Ambassador *Jesus* regarding the problem of the situation of continental shelf claims beyond 200 miles. Here we have two different situations. First we have the general situation of continental margin claims under para. 1 of art. 76. I have no doubt whatsoever that that is part of customary law as it existed long before the Convention was ever signed. In that respect one could not subject the rule of customary law in force to the establishing of a given institution like the Commission on the continental shelf limits. Another case is, for example, that of claims beyond 200 miles which apply other clauses of the same art. 76, like that which I mentioned of Chile and Ecuador. There you could not argue really in terms of a customary law for these other situations, because they were not a part of customary law before the Convention was signed. But it is a case, as we discussed earlier, of an anticipatory application of the Convention in which there is no need to wait for the establishment of the continental shelf Commission. It can be implemented immediately, provided that in the event of a future dispute or technical difficulties in the implementation this might be submitted to the Commission and eventually corrected. But it does not actually stop States from pursuing that claim.

And finally in relation to what Mr *Lilje-Jensen* mentioned with regard to the new *Lotus* case arising in Chile. The basic point is that although the Danish, and I understand the Norwegian Government, have argued that this event occured 40 nautical miles from the coast that fact was yet unclear. According to the families of the fishermen that were killed the incident took place much closer to the coast. That would provide perhaps an important key to the jurisdictional question. In that light I can answer Prof. *Ballah* on two grounds. Firstly, that if it is within territorial jurisdiction, within the 12 mile territorial sea, the jurisdiction would be exercised on the general jurisdiction for criminal offences under the criminal code. If it is beyond the 12 miles it would be an identical case to that of the *Lotus* case, in which the title would be under the provision of the criminal code calling for the exercise of jurisdiction in the case of offences that have affected the interests of Chileans beyond territorial jurisdiction. So either way you would arrive at a similar manifestation of jurisdiction. But the first point is that the facts are disputed and to that extent the judge began by trying to establish what happened and where in order to deal with the case from that point on.

Treves:

I think the main points addressed to me concern the obligations of pioneer investors. I would say 99% of what I wanted to say has already been said by Ambassador *Jesus* and I subscribe to at least 98% of what he said. Just two small remarks. The first is in reply to a specific point raised by Prof. *Wolfrum* about whether the non-payment of the 1 million dollar fee has been seen in the light of reduced resources for the PrepCom and its consequences for the UN budget. I think that it has not been seen in this light and that there is also perhaps good reason for this. At least according to the resolution, the million is not to be paid but is to be due. The problem is from what point in time you owe the million. The negotiations have changed to some extent the terms of the question but not that much. As far as the point just raised by Ambassador *Kapumpa,* I think there we have a contrast between the very strong legal case presented by those who say that the obligation is written in para. 7 (b) and therefore has to be paid, and the very strong political argument presented by those who say they cannot pay and will not pay and that, if the other States do not like it, the whole construction collapses because without pioneer investors there is no activity, no Authority, nothing.

Röben:

I want to start with the point raised by Prof. *Wolfrum*. Indeed we had a case of a ship, the *Meteor*, being denied entrance to a harbour in the Red Sea when it had a sick person on board the ship who was in need of medical treatment. This is clearly illegal both under international customary law and under international conventional law. But we do not think that this was really due to any kind of opposition to, but perhaps due to a misconception or misunderstanding of what is the specific régime of marine scientific research. So, I mean one could say that in this case the harbour authority did not distinguish between the quality of the ship as such and its quality as a research ship. This therefore may serve as an example of what has been said by Prof. *Orrego Vicuña*. He said that the basic ideas of the exclusive economic zone are accepted under international law, but that sometimes actually in specific fields they are not completely applied. The explanation he advanced was that this is perhaps due to different interpretations. I think practice in the field of marine scientific research confirms this view, because very often the very elaborate distinction between the régimes applicable to the EEZ and the territorial seas are retained when advanced as an argument, even if not retained in the legislation of the States.

The second point I will comment on only very briefly in order to give *Wolf Plesmann* time to answer. This point was raised by Mr *Lilje-Jensen* and I fully agree with him when he says that harmonization is called for. It is very important to try to foster the legal certainty. On the other hand, I think that when studying or when analyzing State practice, one can see that the present régime as laid down in art. 245 is generally accepted. It is a very sophisticated, generally acceptable régime. Perhaps it is more important to insure that this régime is generally acknowledged as striking the acceptable balance between the interests of coastal States and researching States and start from this perspective in order to harmonize domestic legislation.

Plesmann:

I have to make two remarks. I want to say that we are glad that Mr *Nagel* from the Ministry for Research and Technology arrived at the same results from our study as we did. In my next point I would like to refer to Mr *Lilje-Jensen*. He asked if we would prefer a regional or a universal forum to fight against the legal uncertainty in the field of maritime scientific research. Personally, I would propose a universal forum. There are at the moment two organizations which deal with the problems of maritime scientific research: the International Council for the Exploration of the Seas, which is a forum for the researching States, and a mediterranean organization, which considers regional problems of MSR. As these organizations have not helped too much in arriving at legal certainty all over the world, a universal level is now needed. In our paper we focussed a little bit on whether changes in the Law of the Sea Convention could help to "fight" against the legal uncertainty. Since there are many diplomats present I will finish with the following statement: It is necessary that the States codify regulations on maritime scientific research in zones under their jurisduction. It is not appropriate just to proclaim to have jurisdiction, as many States do, as the researching States really cannot know how to apply for consent. For the development of knowledge about the oceans it is very important for the researching States to know if and how they have to apply for consent to their projects of maritime scientific research in maritime zones under foreign jurisdiction.

Straddling Stocks, Protection of the Environment and Drug Control: Unsolved Problems of Coastal States' Powers and Obligations

Olivier Jalbert*

I. Introduction

High seas activities giving rise to concern in the international community today are a reflection of global trends. They deal mainly with the exploitation of resources, the environment and specific problems such as drug-trafficking. Not surprisingly, the international community in general, and coastal States in particular, turn to the high seas, an area where international law does not always offer an effective enforcement framework to address these problems.

Several activities taking place on the high seas are increasingly recognized as injurious to the global community. Coastal States are legitimately at the forefront of such concerns, because what happens on the high seas can have a direct and detrimental effect on waters under their jurisdiction and, ultimately, on their territory.

This topic is of immediate concern to my government. Without minimizing the importance of environmental protection or the challenge posed by drug-trafficking, I would place particular emphasis here on "straddling stocks" or fisheries conservation generally.

In this regard, it is paradoxical that at a time when certain provisions of the United Nations Convention on the Law of the Sea are still being debated, other provisions have been applied *de facto* for many years and, with the experience, we are now in a position to assess their merits or shortcomings.

II. Straddling Stocks

As you all know, the so-called "straddling stocks" are fish stocks which occur in the exclusive economic zones (EEZ) of two or more coastal States, or between the EEZ of a coastal State and the high seas adjacent to it. The former occurrence

* *Olivier Jalbert*, Deputy Director of the Legal Operations Division, Department of External Affairs, Ottawa, Canada.

involves the exercise of jurisdiction by two or more States in their respective EEZ and is not likely to give rise to particular problems. I will focus on the latter situation, which is significantly more difficult. The problem with "straddling stocks" stems from the application of two distinct legal régimes to a single stock — that of the coastal State in its EEZ, and the high seas régime beyond the EEZ. This, to say the least, is a less than ideal situation since, in order to be effective, a single management régime must apply to a stock as a whole, not to a portion of a stock.

While "straddling stocks" are found in various parts of the world such as off the coasts of Argentina, Chile, Peru, New Zealand, the USA and USSR, it is on the eastern coast of Canada that this problem has taken on the greatest magnitude in terms of its impact on the fishing industry and on the livelihood of thousands of fishermen and their families. For Newfoundland fishermen, straddling stocks are not a theoretical problem. It is *very* real: Entire communities are now unemployed as a result of the closure of fish processing plants caused by reduced quotas. Several fish stocks — crucial to the fishing industry of Atlantic Canada — straddle the boundary between the Canadian zone and the high seas. While Canada has sovereign rights over the fish within its zone, fleets from distant fishing States are able to fish — and in many cases, over-fish — the stocks outside the Canadian zone thus undermining the conservation régime of the coastal State.

III. Applicable International Law

The *United Nations Convention on the Law of the Sea*, which in our view is reflective of customary international law in this field, contains several provisions on straddling stocks. Broadly speaking, it attempts to establish a balance between the interests of the coastal State and the principle of freedom of the high seas. However, the results of this effort at compromise is a régime which is not stated in as clear and unambiguous a way as would have been desirable and, as shown by experience, is proving largely ineffective.

Article 63 provides that coastal and distant fishing States shall "seek to agree" on the measures necessary for the conservation of straddling stocks, either directly or through regional organizations. However, no specific course of action is provided in the absence of agreement on such measures. It should be noted that this problem had been foreseen by coastal States during the negotiations leading to the conclusion of the Law of the Sea Convention. Canada co-sponsored a resolution providing for third party settlement when the coastal State and States fishing for the same stock in the high seas adjacent to the EEZ were unable to agree on appropriate conservation measures. Unfortunately, this proposed amendment met with resistance from several distant water fishing nations, and had to be withdrawn in the closing stages of the conference.

In our view, art. 63 must be interpreted by reference to other provisions of the LOS Convention applicable to rights and obligations of the coastal State in the EEZ and the régime applicable to the high seas. Article 116 of the LOS Convention provides that the right to fish on the high seas is subject to the rights, duties and interests of coastal States. These include *inter alia* the duty of the coastal State to ensure that "the maintenance of the living resources in the EEZ is not endangered by over-exploitation" pursuant to art. 61, para. 2. Thus, a strong argument can be made that, in case of disagreement, the management régime of the coastal State in its EEZ for a straddling stock should be applied to the high seas portion of that stock.

This argument is further reinforced by other provisions applicable to fishing on the high seas. Article 117 sets out the obligation of States to take, or to co-operate with other States in taking, such measures as may be necessary for the conservation of the living resources of the high seas; art. 118 requires States to co-operate in the conservation and management of living resources and, to this end, to co-operate in the establishment of subregional or regional fisheries organizations; and finally, art. 119 provides that in determining the allowable catch and establishing other conservation measures, States shall take measures which are designed to maintain or restore populations of harvested species at levels which can produce the maximum sustainable yield.

These provisions establish that the right to fish on the high seas is not unrestricted. The rights of fishing States are subject to the interests of coastal States, and particularly the obligation to take appropriate conservation measures. If the Convention requires coastal States to take appropriate conservation measures, it follows that there is a concomitant duty on fishing States to allow coastal States to fulfil these obligations. In other words, high seas fishing States must not engage in fishing practices which undermine the conservation practices of coastal States.

IV. Regional Organizations: NAFO

To put it bluntly, our experience so far with the Northwest Atlantic Fisheries Organization (NAFO), has been that regional organizations are unable to resolve the straddling stocks problem as well as other related problems. NAFO was founded in 1978 — after States such as Canada had extended their fisheries jurisdiction to 200 miles — to promote the optimum utilization, rational management and conservation of fish stocks in the Northwest Atlantic.[1] Its membership includes Canada, the European Community, Japan, and the Soviet Union. The main purpose of NAFO is to ensure the adoption of appropriate conservation measures for the Northwest Atlantic fisheries, including several straddling stocks.

[1] Convention on Future Multilateral Cooperation in the Northwest Atlantic Fisheries of 24 October 1978, published in: Official Journal of the EEC 1978, L 378.

In recent years, NAFO has proved unable to cope with serious problems that have put in question its ability to fulfil its object and purpose. By making abusive use of the so-called "objection procedure", one of its important members has disregarded the quotas set by NAFO on the basis of scientific advice, and has unilaterally declared much higher quotas for itself thereby contributing to the depletion of stocks, reducing the relative shares of other NAFO members and causing serious harm to the fishing industry of Atlantic Canada.

This serious problem has been compounded by two forms of unregulated fishing, which have an impact not only on straddling stocks but on the Northwest Atlantic fishery as a whole. The first is that nationals of member States have had increasing resort to registration of vessels in non-member countries, thus escaping quotas and creating a new dimension to the problem of flags of convenience. The second is increasing activities of vessels from non-member countries which have not had a historic presence in the area. There is, thus, an uncontrolled and unrestricted fishery in the Northwest Atlantic, carried out in parallel to the fishery conducted under the auspices of NAFO, and for which no reliable data is available.

These activities, together with the over-fishing activities mentioned above, threaten the fish stocks. Quite simply, no management régime can achieve its objectives if it is undermined by unregulated activities. This situation serves to emphasize the shortcomings of the LOS Convention with respect to straddling stocks and high seas conservation in general.

These apparent gaps or deficiencies in the applicable rules of international law have led us to seek solutions, consistent with the LOS Convention. I would like to share with you some of the rules or principles which we believe are implicit in the LOS Convention and, in light of the experience in the Northwest Atlantic, should be made more explicit to ensure appropriate management of straddling stocks and high seas fisheries. Our purpose is further to elaborate on rules embodied in the LOS Convention. These rules can be summarized as follows:

1. States have an *obligation* to establish regional organizations in areas of the high seas where their nationals have traditionally fished with a view to adopting effective and enforceable management régimes to regulate fishing in such areas;

2. when a competent regional organization is in place, high seas fishing may be undertaken only in accordance with quotas and other rules adopted by that organization, i. e. only under the framework of such an organization;

3. States have a duty to ensure that their nationals refrain from engaging in fishing activities outside of the framework of regional organizations;

4. States whose nationals fish on the high seas, must ensure that such activities do not impact adversely on the resources under the jurisdiction of the coastal State and, with respect to straddling stocks, the management régime applied to

the high seas portion of the stock must be consistent with the relevant laws and regulations of the coastal State.

V. International Co-operation on Enforcement

International practice demonstrates that, in order to be effective, conservation measures require international co-operation beyond zones of national jurisdiction to ensure effective enforcement, which in turn is essential to any conservation régime. Two examples come to mind. First, the NAFO Convention makes provision for a scheme of joint international enforcement in the NAFO regulatory area. The scheme allows for boarding and inspection of vessels on the high seas by the contracting parties, acting as inspectors for NAFO, in order to monitor compliance with NAFO quotas and other rules. Violations are reported to the flag State, which is required to consider and act on these reports.

A second example of high seas enforcement co-operation is the 1988 USA-USSR Agreement on Mutual Fisheries Relations.[2] Under this agreement, each country agreed that its nationals and vessels would be subject to the fisheries resource management laws of the other country when these vessels were fishing outside their EEZs for "living resources of the continental shelf appertaining to the other party or for anadromous resources that originate in the waters of the other party." Each country also consents to boardings of its vessels by the other country to verify compliance.

These two cases provide promising examples of enforcement beyond national jurisdiction. The USSR/USA agreement is the most innovative. Its use could be expanded upon to address enforcement problems on the high seas and, in particular, straddling stocks, where the coastal State has a particular interest.

VI. Protection of the Environment

While protection of the marine environment has been traditionally understood as pollution prevention, it has acquired a new broader meaning in recent years: It is now applied, quite rightly, to certain fishing practices such as driftnet fishing and should encompass any form of fishing, for there is an important environmental dimension to depletion of fish stocks.

With respect to driftnetting, significant advances have been made globally in efforts to stop this practice. The most important is the UN General Assembly resolution calling for a moratorium on high seas driftnetting by 1992 unless

---

[2] Agreement between the Government of the United States of America and the Government of the Soviet Socialist Republics on Mutual Fisheries Relations of 31 May 1988, reprinted in: House Document 100-207, 100th Cong., 2d sess., 1988.

effective conservation and management measures are taken to prevent unacceptable impacts of these fishing practices, and cessation of such activities in the South Pacific by 1991.[3] However, much remains to be done and greater consensus will have to be developed internationally on the degree of acceptability of this fishing practice.

Regional efforts include the Wellington Convention,[4] the signatories of which have pledged to prohibit their nationals and vessels from using driftnets in the South Pacific. From the coastal State vantage point, the agreement between Canada, the United States and Japan to establish an observer programme for the Japanese squid fishery in the North Pacific is significant. This programme, whose goal is to monitor Japanese driftnet fishing practices in the North Pacific, provides for the placing of Canadian and US observers on board Japanese squid vessels. It demonstrates that effective conservation action on the high seas requires close international co-operation.

Turning now to the protection and preservation of the *marine environment* in this more traditional acception, it is fair to say that with very few exceptions, enforcement of existing rules on the high seas remains in the hands of the flag State. While Part XII of the Law of the Sea Convention (which in our view reflects customary international law) lays down a comprehensive enforcement régime for port and coastal States over vessels found in their ports, territorial seas and exclusive economic zones, it remains virtually silent as to high seas enforcement. For this we must look to art. 92, which, for environmental purposes, virtually assures the flag State exclusive jurisdiction over a vessel on the high seas.

VII. The Intervention Convention

This reflects an overriding attitude in the international community, which continued to prevail during UNCLOS, that the freedom of the high seas should be interfered with as little as possible. Exceptions could be made, however, for those acts which the entire world abhorred, such as slave trade; or which posed a direct threat to shipping and commerce, such as piracy. Another exception to this rule to come about before UNCLOS was the *International Convention Relating to Intervention on the High Seas in Cases of Oil Pollution Casualties*,[5] otherwise known as the Intervention Convention. This convention allows States Parties to take such measures on the high seas as may be necessary to "prevent, mitigate or eliminate grave and imminent danger to their coastline or related interests from pollution, or the threat of pollution of the sea by oil following on

3 GA res. 44/225 of 22 December 1989.
4 *See* UN Doc. A/44/807.
5 Reprinted in: ILM 9 (1970), 25-44.

a marine casualty." A 1973 protocol[6] extended coastal States' powers of intervention to some harmful substances other than oil.

UNCLOS recognized this exception by giving coastal States some environmental jurisdiction. Article 221 of the Convention, while not directly giving coastal States the right to take action against pollution casualties, does provide that the Convention is not prejudicial to the rights that coastal States already enjoy pursuant to international customary or conventional law to intervene "beyond the territorial sea."

It is interesting to note the reference to customary international law. It has been argued, though not conclusively, that apart from the intervention convention, there may be a customary rule of international law which allows coastal States to take action to protect themselves from harmful activities outside their jurisdiction. The careful wording of art. 221 is evidence of this, and could reflect a well founded attitude that high seas freedoms have to be subject to the needs of the international community, and the legitimate interests of coastal States.

VIII. Dumping

This same attitude is also evidenced elsewhere in the Law of the Sea Convention, and stems from the provisions of the *London Dumping Convention* (LDC).[7] The LDC grew out of the 1972 Stockholm Conference on the Human Environment and entered into force in 1975, remaining an effective multilateral forum for the prevention and control of marine pollution by the deliberate disposal of wastes.

The Law of the Sea Convention, in extending jurisdiction to coastal States over dumping activities, makes specific reference to the continental shelf. As you are all aware, the definition of continental shelf in art. 76 includes its full physical seaward extension, and therefore can include some of the sea-bed and subsoil lying under the high seas.

Article 210, para. 5 requires the express prior approval of coastal States for any dumping activity on the continental shelf, by giving them the right to permit, regulate and control dumping in this area. Moreover, as the matter has to be considered with other States that may be adversely affected by such activity, it also recognizes that States other than the coastal State directly involved may have legitimate interests in areas beyond their national jurisdiction. This further reinforces the view that the international community is willing to develop international law in a direction that gives States directly affected by activities on the high seas some control over these activities.

---

6 BGBl. 1985 II, 596.

7 Reprinted in: ILM 11 (1972), 1291-1314.

IX. Basel Convention

A recent example of this is the *Basel Convention on the Control of Transboundary Movement of Hazardous Wastes*,[8] concluded in 1989. It contains a resolution which invites *inter alia* the executive-director of UNEP and the Secretary-General of IMO, to review existing regulations and practices with respect to the transport of hazardous wastes by sea. They can recommend measures additional to those in the Basel Convention which could assist flag, coastal and port States in fulfilling their responsibilities with respect to the protection of the marine environment. With the structure thus in place, it is possible that such recommendations in the future could involve measures which affect the movement of hazardous wastes on the high seas.

X. Drug Control

Efforts to control and eradicate illicit traffic in narcotic drugs is yet another example of activities taking place in part on the high seas and widely recognized as harmful to the international community. Thus, it is not surprising that a provision on illicit traffic by sea was included in the recently concluded *United Nations Convention against Illicit Traffic in Narcotic Drugs and Psychotropic Substances.*[9] Paragraph 3 of art. 17 of this Convention provides that a party which has reasonable grounds to suspect that a vessel "exercising freedom of navigation in accordance with international law" and flying the flag of another party is engaged in illicit traffic may notify the flag State and request authorization from the latter to take appropriate measures such as boarding, search and, ultimately, detention.

While this provision is innovative, its effectiveness remains to be seen. Negotiations leading to the conclusion of the Convention revealed important differences of views regarding the scope of art. 17. Several States argued that this provision would not apply to vessels in the EEZ, as these would be subject to the jurisdiction of the coastal State or the flag State. Others argued that, since the rights of coastal States in the EEZ are restricted to economic and environmental rights, the provisions of the Convention should apply to vessels beyond the territorial sea. This difference of interpretation of applicable international law was avoided by the use of the words "exercising freedom of navigation in accordance with international law." Although recourse to constructive ambiguity permitted the conference to reach consensus, legal problems remain and the potential for conflict in the future is obvious.

---

[8] Reprinted in: ILM 28 (1989), 649-686.

[9] Reprinted in: ILM 28 (1989), 493-526.

The effectiveness of this provision will depend also on the degree of support for the Convention, since the rights granted are applicable only as between parties to the Convention. Less than broad support would enable traffickers to register their vessels in States that are not a party to the convention or States which are a party to the Convention but, as a practice, do not grant permission to board vessels flying their flag. Nothing in art. 17 obligates parties to grant permission to board when presented with reasonable proof that a vessel is engaged in illicit traffic. In short, art. 17 is a timid departure from the principle of flag State jurisdiction, the effectiveness of which will depend ultimately on the political will of the parties and on additional arrangements between them. It is however a realistic step forward in an effort to tackle a very serious problem of enforcement, which represents a challenge to the international community.

XI. Conclusion

Activities on the high seas affect mankind, just like activities anywhere else in the world. When these activities become recognized by the international community as being sufficiently injurious, adverse, or otherwise repugnant to man or his environment, they are regulated. The traditional freedom of the high seas has meant that the enforcement of these regulations has fallen to the flag State. There have been a number of activities, however, where the international community, faced with a need for more effective enforcement, has seen fit to permit States other than the flag State to enforce its dictates.

There is increasing recognition by the international community that several activities which give rise for concern within areas of national jurisdiction, such as the management of living resources, the environment and drug trafficking, also require regulation outside national control. It is not surprising that this increased awareness is often led by coastal States, which are most affected by unregulated activities on the high seas.

The key to this concern to develop further rules to regulate these high seas activities is effective enforcement. As the world grows increasingly aware of the dangers posed to its resources, environment and illicit activities, the need to strengthen enforcement on the high seas is becoming apparent. The most obvious emerging solutions, for the most pressing problems, require a departure from a purely flag State enforcement system.

Discussion

Rebagliati:

Let me congratulate Dr. *Jalbert* for his presentation which, as he said, was far more complete than the title of it suggested, and well illustrated with analogies which enlightened the details of these issues. It is clear that this subject not only concerns the high seas. It is an issue which concerns other maritime spaces, particularly adjacent to the high seas, and normally that includes the exclusive economic zone. It is also partially new. The problem is in fact regretfully quite old. Early before the Law of the Sea Convention was adopted, it already existed, though, of course, within a different framework. This problem arises where two different countries fish in adjacent areas, one closer to the coast of one of them being at that time territorial sea, or an area of the exclusive economic zone or fishing zone for a time, and the adjacent area which was high seas. Now, with a broader limit for the exclusive economic zone and the necessarily adjacent high seas regularly, the problem is more conspicuous. But the problem, in fact, is old enough and draws different solutions, however, not satisfactory at the very present. There is a vacuum here which the Law of the Sea Convention or other multilateral conventions have been trying to fill, but still there is an uncertainty, and kind of eagerness, particularly on the part of coastal States, for the lack of full regulation of this problem, and by full regulation I do not mean unilateral regulations only, but regulations which would be the result of co-operation between the coastal States concerned and other countries fishing in areas adjacent to the exclusive economic zone.

I also share the view that the long-distance fishing countries, particularly after the Law of the Sea Convention was adopted, felt a little more reluctant to co-operate in this particular issue, although co-operation is clearly needed. We sincerely hope that this attitude is temporary, because the preservation of straddling stocks is something which affects, of course, the coastal States, but it also affects the long-distance fishing countries which are as much as the coastal States interested in keeping the substantial yield of those stocks. It is even possible that the coastal States will overfish and this could also lead to depletion or put into risk the level of sustainable yield of straddling stocks; though this is not the most common case. In fact, it is in the potential interest of long-distance fishing countries, which honestly embark in this co-operation in a form that may be equitably arranged between them and the relevant coastal State.

Summarizing what I could suggest, as a general remark, is, that there is a need for these regulations by some regional organization, some global organization and by some bilateral agreements, and that there is a feeling, particularly by coastal States, that this matter is not fully regulated, that the preservation of straddling stocks is at danger, and that earnest efforts should be made by all parties concerned in order to fill this vacuum which the Law of the Sea Convention was unable to complete. That would not only be a benefit for the respective States concerned. Of course, they will benefit from the stocks, but much more the co-operation will result in avoiding future disputes. Because even if this is a kind of loose obligation upon States according to the LOS Convention and in accordance to other norms of international law relating to the preservation of the environment, it still is a legal obligation and States in this regard are under an obligation that may lead to a legal dispute, if not political, which of course, is subject to the settlement of disputes procedures which may be applicable.

Jalbert:

At some time during the Conference on the Law of the Sea, UNCLOS III, it was felt that the establishment of the 200 mile zone would resolve the fishing problems in the world. We find that it has not, and why has it not solved the problems? It is quite simply that this line was drawn without reference to the actual extension of the continental shelf and, thus, the location of fish stocks, and it just happened that in many places in the world the 200 mile limit cuts across fish stocks, which makes management extremely difficult. I would like to emphasize one point you mentioned and that is that the Law of the Sea Convention provides merely a framework of very broad obligations, which will require to be developed further. The framework applicable to high seas fisheries needs to be further developed. We believe that the time has passed where freedom of fishing could be exercised by anyone, anywhere, and at any time. Clearly the capacity to fish in the world now much exceeds the resources available. Measures must be taken to ensure that high seas fishing is carried out on the basis of sound management practices, and we believe that the current legal framework must be fully implemented.

Treves:

I want to make two quick observations. The first about the 1988 convention on drugs. I think you were very accurate in saying that the Convention makes a timid departure from tradition. Perhaps, there is in art. 17 one, not very big, but real element of obligation for States. It is true, the article does not oblige States to give authorization to board ships or to take other coercive measures. However, it obliges them to answer quickly to the request for flag verification and also to requests for authorization to board. They can say yes or no, but they have to answer quickly. And this puts them under a certain pressure. So, it is timid, but it is a departure. As to the four points on straddling stocks, I would just remark that what is controversial is the last half of the last one, namely that the regulations to be adopted by the competent organization have to be consistent with the rules on management adopted by coastal States. We are grateful, however, for this well-reasoned statement of the coastal States' position. It is evident that the distant waters fishing States will have different opinions.

Jalbert:

As to the first point, I fully share your view. I would say that it is as far as it was possible to go at this time, and we should not minimize the importance of this step. I think it is a very significant one. With regard to the second point, there is a very controversial issue. First of all, I referred only to the adoption of conservation measures, i. e. the determination of the total allowable catch. I am not suggesting that the coastal States should enjoy exclusive access to the stock. The total allowable catch should be shared in proportion to the percentage of the stock inside the EEZ and by distant-fishing States in the proportion which is outside. The whole issue is to agree on what the conservation measures should be, what the level of fishing should be. In practice, it is a very difficult issue and, as we know, States often disagree as to what the level of fishing should be. This has been our experience in the North-West Atlantic, and we have had the feeling in Canada in recent years that the positions of some members of the NAFO organizations have not been based on scientific data available, but merely on short-term needs of their fishing industry. We believe that this is a very short-sighted approach and a very dangerous one, and we do not like it, because we pay the price. Canadian fishermen have to stay home, because quotas in our EEZ have been reduced and they see that the foreign fishermen are fishing just outside the 200 miles zone as much fish as they are able to catch, based on unilateral quotas. This is extremely frustating, both for our fishermen and for the Canadian Government.

Wolfrum:

I have only three remarks. When the Law of the Sea Convention decided upon the establishment of the exclusive economic zone, everybody within the law of the sea community believed that the problems related to fishing were solved, as the coastal States gained respective jurisdiction or property rights — to use an economic term; it was expected that the management of the fishery resources would be administered by the coastal State concerned. This resulted in the dissolution or modification of certain fishery organizations such as the North-West Atlantic Fisheries Organization (NAFO). It seems that it was premature to deprive the fishery organizations of their prior functions. The fishery organizations, however, will now serve a quite different purpose. Formerly, fishery organizations were distributing fish resources. In the case you presented, they will primarily have the task of concentrating on conservation and only when the conservation purposes have been sufficiently achieved, can they provide for distribution. Apart from the functions the fishery organizations are meant to serve, they still face a problem which they have been facing for ages. All rules and regulations issued by fishery organizations are binding only upon the member States, whereas the problem of how to bind non-members has not yet been solved. Thus, fishing vessels may escape the jurisdiction of international fishery organizations by "flagging out," a problem common in respect of shipping which makes the enforcement of the rules on the protection of the marine environment rather problematic. This problem can be solved either by making the flagging out impossible or by vesting fishery organizations with the power to bind non-member States or by further extending the jurisdiction of the coastal States.

In respect to your last point, Mr *Jalbert*, I fully share your view that the principle of freedom of navigation needs to be reconsidered — so far it concentrates upon the freedom of movement. This no longer meets the present concerns. One should rather ask to what extent the freedom of movement may be detrimental, either to the coastal States or the world community. It is necessary to submit this freedom to certain limitations such as those necessary to provide for the safety of shipping or the protection of the marine environment. Here again, the problem of "flagging out" and of the binding of non-member States by instruments serving common interests, e. g. the protection of the marine environment, still exists. In both respects the Law of the Sea Convention does not offer much help.

Jalbert:

A few words to address one point you raised, e. g. fishing by non-members of regional organizations. While at the present time, major problems are the establishment of conservation measures and agreement on conservation measures among members of regional organizations, I believe that the most important problem we will be facing in the coming years is the presence of vessels of countries that are not members of a regional organization. It is a growing problem, and I did propose solutions in my statement to address it, because I believe that it is going to become a very important one. Let me refer to figures applicable to the NAFO regulatory area. From 1984 to 1988, in accordance with our sightings the presence of foreign vessels — non-member vessels — in the area increased from 11 to 48, and it was estimated from the number of days of presence in the area and the number of vessels that in 1988, 20 per cent of catches were made by non-member vessels. This is in addition to the quotas that are established and fully taken by the members of the organization. So, clearly, there is overfishing in the NAFO area and the problem is increasing. It is increasing also because nationals of some of the NAFO member countries change the registration of their vessels from their own country of origin to new member countries where they can easily reflag their vessels. They can fish without respecting the quotas of the organization and, thus, increase their catches. So, my own personal view is that this is going to become the most important problem in the near future.

Murray:

It was a very interesting and very thorough presentation, through which we got perhaps a little bit of a gleam of self-interest with the question of unemployment in Newfoundland, about which obviously we are all very sorry. The point to be made is, I think, that if you export that unemployment to a distant deep sea-fishing State instead, then that unemployment does not become any less pernicious, because it is not any longer in Canada.

I am not arguing against firm conservation measures, because I think it is very necessary and the existence of operating regional co-operation bodies is extremely important; but these operate on a basis of enlightened self-interest, a realization by the countries fishing that if you fish out the stocks, in the long term it is going to be to nobody's benefit. I do not think it is possible from the existence of the practices of certain organizations to adduce any system of law at present, which would enable you to say that membership of such an existing organization is compulsory. On your question that these organizations must adopt the conservation regulations of a coastal State (one obvious point is, the high seas do not have any coastal States, you cannot be a coastal State to the high seas, or they would not be the high seas): It would obviously be very helpful if regional fishery organizations can agree to common conservation regulations, and if those States which consider themselves to be coastal in this context or have considerable straddling stocks in question within their exclusive economic zone were able to adapt the regulations to those agreed. The idea that a State should be able, unilaterally to attempt to enforce those regulations, is, I think, quite out of question.

Now I have two questions: I have seen reports, I think early this year, of a Canadian Government Committee of some kind, a technical committee, which presented a report on precisely this problem which made, I think, recommendations which seemed to go beyond what is permitted under the Law of the Sea Convention. I would like to know if you know the report I am speaking of, I am afraid I cannot give you much detail and what its status was and what is going to happen to it. And secondly, could you give me some information of the progress of the Canadian Maritime Jurisdiction Bill C 39, at what stage it is now, and particularly whether some of these ideas you have mentioned are liable to or could find their way into that bill?

Nelson:

It can be argued that one of the factors which hastened the reception of the concept of the exclusive economic zone was a failure of regional fishery organizations to conserve fishing stocks. Is it possible to argue now, and I would like to get your impression on this, that a failure of regional fishery organizations to deal with the straddling stock issue can possibly lead to further extension of coastal States' jurisdiction?

Lee:

I had intended to ask a question related to your first point and to what Mr *Murray* has said. Mr *Jalbert* referred to four principles, which he called the Canadian principles or rules. I am quite interested in that. They seem to go further than the LOS Convention. It would seem that — maybe I am wrong to have understood it in this way — that if you make obligatory participation in regional organization as a principle, then you would be in direct conflict with the freedom of the high seas on the one hand and conservation on the other. I was wondering to what extent these "Canadian principles" enjoy general support.

Jalbert:

First, since Mr *Murray* made a direct reference or comment on the export of unemployment, I feel compelled to take up this issue, because I think that the exact opposite happened. It is quite interesting to note that the period when the EEC began objecting to NAFO quotas and fishing well above these quotas, coincides with the entry of Spain and Portugal into the EEC, two very important distant fishing States. And one is tempted to conclude that since the EEC has a sound conservation management régime in its own waters, that there was no room for the Portuguese and Spanish fleets. It was tempting to let these fleets find more fish in areas of the North West Atlantic, at the expense of Newfoundland fishermen.

That being said, I will take up your two questions. You referred to a Government Committee and a report that was published in recent months. I assume you are referring to the *Harris* report. It is a non-governmental committee of experts, which was established by the Canadian Government to examine the problem of a major stock in the Canadian zone, the northern cod stock. This is the most important fish stock in the Northwest Atlantic. It is almost exclusively found in the Canadian EEZ and it is in a very bad condition, arguably because of overfishing outside Canada's zone. It happens that a very small portion, about 5 per cent of the stock, is at any time beyond Canada's EEZ, and foreign vessels fish the stock in the area where the stock is found outside the Canadian zone. Thus, the conservation régime adopted within the Canadian zone is undermined by fishing immediately beyond our zone. The Canadian Government established this committee to examine ways, first of all, to try to assess the state of the stock, and second, to propose measures to restore the stock. This committee made recommendations to the Canadian Government with respect to how to deal *inter alia* with the foreign fishing problem. It also recommended much lower quotas in the Canadian zone, which the Canadian Government agreed to in part, and the quotas have been considerably reduced in 1990 as compared to previous years. With respect to international co-operation, the Committee recommended that Canada negotiate agreements with States fishing that stock and, if that were not possible, that Canada contemplate extending its jurisdiction beyond 200 miles to cover the stock in its entirety. The answer to your question is that Canadian Government did not take up that option.

You also referred to a new law that is before the Parliament, Bill C 39. This legislation does not extend jurisdiction beyond 200 miles except for sedentary species and, in my view, it is fully consistent with the Law of the Sea Convention. Its effect with respect to maritime areas is merely to extend application of certain laws on the continental shelf or with respect to fishing activities, but it does not depart in any way from the provisions of the Law of the Sea Convention.

I now turn to Mr *Nelson*'s question which, I believe, I just answered. No extention of jurisdiction is being contemplated at this time. We are looking for, as I mentioned and proposed, certain measures, which would be agreed internationally, to address problems relating to fishing on the high seas. Other options, I assume, would be contemplated if we find that there is absolutely no other solution, but extention of jurisdiction, and I believe that the Canadian Government is on the record in this respect, is not an option.

With regard to Mr *Lee*'s comments on whether there is conflict between freedom of navigation and the principles I proposed, I do not belive so. I think that the principles I proposed deal strictly with fishing activities. To that extent it means lesser freedom, if freedom is understood in a traditional sense, that fishermen are free to go out and fish as much as they want and where they want. We think that these days are over and that fishing in the high seas should be regulated by regional organizations just as much as it is regulated in the 200 miles zone of the coastal States. Otherwise, the stocks will be depleted.

Picht:

I assume we all agree that there is a need to establish some special jurisdiction that matches the straddling fishing. The answer of an economist is clear: establish exclusive property rights and privatize the property rights. I am not going into any details in this proposal; it is well established. Note, however, that we have an analytically equivalent case in the Alpine region in Switzerland. In the high regions of Switzerland, pasture fields were common property for ages. Gradually some of them turned into private property régimes, while in some other areas we still have common property. My prediction is that we ultimately end up with private property rights régimes everywhere in the high Swiss Alps. The same might come true for straddling fish some time.

It seems to me that there is another issue here as well. We might consider paying off those fishermen who are currently fishing in these areas for *not* fishing. For example, your government could make some payments to prevent them from fishing and thus, in a way, establish property rights. This costs money, alright, but on the other hand, your fishermen are apparently so productive in catching fish that if they are better than anybody else, they might make enough money to pay others off. *Vice versa*, if the others are better, they should pay you off for not fishing, and have a surplus left for themselves.

Jesus:

My country happened to be one of the co-sponsors along with Canada and other countries during the Conference of a proposal, to introduce a clarification to art. 63, para. 2, to take care of the needs for co-operation between the two categories of States in the conservation of species and straddling stocks. I believe that the freedoms of the high seas, as contained in the Convention, have to be respected. After all, we all benefitted from those freedoms, but we also believe that the concept itself of freedom has some qualifications in whatever field of human endeavours. I think that those qualifications, as contained in the Convention, of the freedoms of the high seas are more or less three, not only applicable to the high seas, but also, I would say, to the whole new law of the sea. One is the protection of the marine environment; I do not think that anyone will disagree that in the exercise of the freedoms of the high seas, any nation has the legal duty, as contained in the Convention, to respect the rules for the protection of the marine environment. We have also another principle, that is the qualification for the exercise of freedoms in the context of the principle of the peaceful uses of the oceans. And another one is the conservation of the species in general which is somewhat a corollary of another one which is today a timely problem, the protection of the environment in general, to the extent that they are interrelated. So, we have to see on the one hand, the right or the freedom of any nation to fish in the high seas, but at the same time, co-operation must exist amongst all nations to take care of the conservation principle, that is the qualification to the exercise of these freedoms. Whenever those freedoms tend to jeopardize legitimate rights especially contained in the Convention, because of disregard or lack of co-operation to take care of the principle of conservation, then there is a problem, there is a conflict that should be regulated.

Now, we all know that there is a celebrated phrase of a jurist that says that anyone has the freedom, the right to go to hell with the cloths that he brings on, provided that, on passing, he does not touch on the rights of other people. This is precisely the idea. Anyone has the right to fish in the high seas, provided that he does not touch upon the rights of other people. And it is a fact, that this is a problem that is increasing. Today, Canada must be the country with the most visible costs caused by this problems, but all coastal States, developing coastal States, are potential victims in the future, and as the needs grow, it is most probably that this problem will grow also in proportion. Now, I believe that nothing would be against the Convention, because, as Mr *Jalbert* said, the Convention tries to lay down the basic principles on the question of conservation, and asks States to co-operate and even to establish international organizations. Most probably, this issue, as it becomes more problematic, will require a new convention regulating the fishing in the high seas.

Perhaps the time has not arrived, but I believe that in the future, as this problem gains momentum, the only way to solve this conflict which is a real conflict, will be through a set of international regulations, that has to be respected by everybody, essentially to overcome the problem of the regional organizations that are not respected by the people fishing outside the jurisdiction of these organizations, or that are not members of the organizations. If I may sum up, my point is that, yes, freedom should be recognized, however, there is an underlying principle of conservation of species that, I think we all agree, we have to take care of. Through co-operation we have to find a solution that will satisfy the two groups of States, coastal States and the States fishing in the high seas.

Mathanjuki:

I find the tip by Mr *Jalbert* a very useful one, as some of the speakers have indicated, it highlights some of the problems of a number of smaller countries, because these problems will have to be faced. I am aware, currently within the Indian Ocean zone we have a major problem of fishing as relates to the use of the equipment which has already been banned in the South Pacific, the drift-net, which is a net that extends sometimes up to 60 kilometres. Here you find a vessel only needs to come just adjacent to the EEZ and, of course, do as much private fishing as possible using this kind of net. Sometimes even taking some of the mammals which are not necessarily required for purposes of economic use. So I do see that actually there is an urgent need for the regulation of the fishing industry in the high seas, to prevent overfishing, which later spills to the EEZ. And where necessary, I suppose the UN has a major rôle to play, particularly in the development of harmonious conservation measures amongst coastal States. This also calls for an agreement amongst coastal states, whereby they would be required to use standardized methods of fishing, so that some of the stocks will not completely disappear. And at the same time for the developed countries, so that some of this equipment which is not used in some areas, can be restricted world-wide, not every country is aware of the kind of equipment which is in use at its waters, even though it has licenced fishing. So, I do also see a need for this type of regulation urgently in the future.

Jalbert:

With respect to drift-net fishing, I share the views just expressed, and here we are facing a different problem. It is not a problem of fishing effort, but of fishing method. And it shows that we must take a good look also at the methods, not only at the quotas. I can fully endorse the comments made by Ambassador *Jesus* who, I believe, exposed the problem very well. He referred quite rightly to the existence of a conflict. It is a very difficult conflict, because it deals with livelihoods of people, and this is a very serious matter.

Wolfrum:

Be careful on that latter point, although I quite see it. It would perhaps contradict your opening remarks a bit.

Deep Sea-Bed Mining and the Protection of the Environment: Developments in Pollution Control, Responsibility and Liability

J. Enno Harders*

In the focus of deep sea-bed activities is the mining of polymetallic nodules. All its basic methods have the potential for harming the environment. The techniques include (1) airlift pumping, (2) hydraulic or hydrolift dredging, and (3) continuous bucket dredging. In addition to obvious marine effects caused by prospecting, exploration, and mining; the loading of the resources for transshipment and the land-based processing of the resources present potential environmental problems due to trace metals and very harmful processing chemicals.[1]

Aside from the Law of the Sea Convention[2] (LOS Convention), which is not in force yet, little international law is applicable to deep sea-bed mining. The 1973/78 MARPOL Convention[3] and the 1972 London Dumping Convention[4] would to some extent apply. The MARPOL covers pollution other than the release from operational activities from ships and similar devices, including fixed and floating platforms. MARPOL will be primarily applicable to the noted transshipment and processing stages of the deep sea-bed mining.[5] The London Convention applies to vessels, aircraft, and fixed and floating platforms and to the deliberate disposal of waste into the sea ("dumping"). As the London Dumping Convention excludes the case of matter placed in the sea for a purpose other than disposal, its application to deep sea-bed activities is very unlikely. The LOS Convention, therefore, will be the major international instrument which provides

---

* *J. Enno Harders*, LL.M. (Brit. Col.), Research Assistant, Institute of International Law, University of Kiel.

[1] *See*, among others, *Hjalmar Thiel*'s presentation in this Vol.

[2] United Nations Convention on the Law of the Sea, Montego Bay, Jamaica, 10 December 1982, UN doc. A/Conf. 62/122 of 7 October 1982 with Corr.

[3] International Convention for the Prevention of Pollution from Ships — MARPOL, 2 November 1973, in: ILM 12 (1973), 1319-1444, and Protocol of 1978 Relating to the International Convention for the Prevention of Pollution from Ships, 1 June 1978, in: ILM 17 (1978), 546-578; *D. P. O'Connell/I. A. Shearer*, The International Law of the Sea, Vol. 2, Oxford 1984, 1003-1006.

[4] Convention on the Prevention of Marine Pollution by Dumping of Wastes and Other Matter, 29 December 1972, as amended, in: ILM 11 (1972), 1294-1314; *R. R. Churchill/A. V. Lowe*, The Law of the Sea, 2nd ed., Manchester 1988, 276, 268-270.

[5] MARPOL (note 3), art. 2, para. 3 (b) (ii); Annexes IV and V are to regulate the discharge of sewage and garbage.

for environmental protection against damage from deep sea-bed activities.[6] This conventional framework will be outlined first, before the drafted Deep Sea-Bed Mining Code and the novel provisions on State responsibility and liability are analyzed.

I. Law of the Sea Convention

The corollary to art. 136 LOS Convention asserting that "the Area and its resources are the common heritage of mankind" is the protection of the marine environment against impediments resulting from deep sea-bed uses.[7] In fact, it has been claimed that the protection of the marine environment in the Area is the *conditio sine qua non* for deep sea-bed activities.[8]

1. The Substantive Law of the Convention

Central to the protection of the environment in the Area is art. 145.[9] Against "harmful effects" from sea-bed activities, the necessary measures must be taken by the International Sea-Bed Authority ("Authority") to effectively protect the environment. Further, art. 145 (a) identifies "harmful effects" to the marine environment: "pollution and other hazards to the marine environment, including the coastline" which are to be prevented, reduced and controlled. Even further, there must be no "interference with the ecological balance of the marine environment." Hazardous activities receiving special attention are "drilling, excavation, disposal of waste, construction and operation or maintenance of installations, pipelines and other devices related to such activities." In general, provision is made for "the prevention of damage to the flora and fauna of the marine environment."[10] It so appears that practically all aspects of marine pollution from deep sea-bed activities are covered. But the LOS Convention carries the *caveat* that harmful effects not closely linked with deep sea-bed mining are excluded from the scope of art. 145. This follows from the very definition of "activities in the

---

6 For early accounts *see Richard Frank*, Environmental Consequences of Deep Sea-Bed Mining, in: Proceedings of the Law of the Sea Institute 10 (1976), 319-325; *James N. Barnes*, Pollution from Deep Ocean Mining, in: *Douglas M. Johnston* (ed.), The Environmental Law of the Sea, Berlin 1981, 259-284; *E. D. Brown*, Pollution from Sea-Bed Mining: Legal Safeguards, in: Environmental Policy and Law 10 (1983), 122-134.

7 *Rüdiger Wolfrum*, Die Internationalisierung staatsfreier Räume, Berlin *et al.* 1984, 510, 511.

8 *John Warren Kindt*, Marine Pollution and the Law of the Sea, Buffalo, N. Y. 1986, 1017.

9 *See* No. 11 of the Declaration of Principles Governing the Sea-Bed and the Ocean Floor, and the Subsoil Thereof beyond the Limits of National Jurisdiction of 17 December 1970 (GA res. 2749 (XXV) of 17 December 1970, reprinted in: ILM 10 (1971), 220-223 (222)).

10 Article 145 (b) LOS Convention.

Area" of art. 145 which is defined in art. 1, para. 1 (3) as all exploration and exploitation activities of the resources in the Area.

The Authority is the addressee of the provision regarding necessary measures for the protection of the environment (art. 145), but States have an important rôle to play here as well (art. 209).[11] Articles 192 and 194 accordingly, States are to protect the marine environment from activities under their jurisdiction which includes any activities sponsored by them.[12] Furthermore, arts. 192 and 194 are directed not just towards States Parties but any States.[13] These more general rules are supplemented by art. 195 and 197 in that States are under the duty not to transfer damage or hazards or transform the type of pollution into another type of pollution. In the case of imminent danger of the environment, other States notified assist in combating the accident; States develop contingency plans to this end which, as such, is a means of enforcement.[14]

2. *Enforcement of the Convention's Provisions*

As with regard to enforcement, art. 145 provides that necessary measures shall be taken in a manner not inconsistent with the regular marine pollution provisions of Part XII. Further, art. 145 prescribes that the Authority is to adopt such rules to prevent pollution from deep sea-bed mining which may fall within the scope of Annex III, Basic Conditions of Prospecting, Exploration and Exploitation. In its art. 17, the category of "rules, regulations and procedures of the Authority" includes the protection of the marine environment, but is limited to exploration and exploitation activities as well as operational pollution and on site processing. All pollution arising from transshipment is thus excluded from the Authority's competence and underlies the régime of MARPOL. Any dumping may consequently fall into a lacuna, for the London Dumping Convention is not applicable as shown *supra*.[15]

States are required by art. 209 to adopt national legislation which is no less effective than the international rules, regulations and procedures established in accordance with Part XI for the protection of the marine environment from activities in the Area. These standards are presumably the regulations established by the Authority under art. 145.[16] The rules are to prevent, reduce and control marine pollution from deep sea-bed activities and are re-examined if necessary.[17] States then adopt the relevant laws and regulations for their vessels, installations,

[11] *Wolfrum* (note 7), 510.

[12] Articles 192, 194 LOS Convention.

[13] *Wolfrum* (note 7), 511.

[14] Articles 198, 199 LOS Convention.

[15] Article 17, para. 2 (f) of Annex III; on enforcement *see Churchill/Lowe* (note 4), 276, 277; *Kindt* (note 8), 1017-1020.

[16] Article 209, para. 2 LOS Convention.

[17] *Loc. cit.*, para. 1.

and structures and other devices under their flag, of their registry or operating under their authority. For enforcement of the international pollution regulations, art. 215 states that enforcement with respect to pollution from activities in the Area shall be governed by the provisions of Part XI: all relevant enforcement powers rest with the Authority and States Parties.

States Parties, moreover, assist the Authority and take all the measures necessary to ensure compliance as provided by art. 139, they bear this responsibility and liability for damage.[18] A State Party, however, is exempted from that liability if it has taken all measures necessary to ensure compliance (art. 139, para. 2). Every applicant for deep sea-bed mining undertakes to accept such control by the Authority.[19] Furthermore, under art. 162, para. 2, the executive organ of the Authority, the Council, can issue emergency orders and orders for the suspension or adjustment of operations, to prevent serious harm to the marine environment arising out of activities in the Area. The Council disapproves areas for exploitation by contractors or the Enterprise in cases where substantial evidence indicates the risk of serious harm to the environment. Here, the Council shall step in if there is risk of serious harm, but only at the stage of exploitation, not at the stage of exploration. Finally, the Council establishes the appropriate mechanisms for inspection of the activities in the Area (art. 162, para. 2 (x), (z)). In addition, the Legal and Technical Commission, at the request of the Council, supervises activities in the Area and reports to the Council.[20]

Annex III will also ensure compliance with the Authority's pollution regulations. Prospecting may commence only after the Authority received assurance that the proposed prospector will comply with the Authority's pollution regulations and will accept verification by the Authority of compliance.[21] Exploration and exploitation take place according to a contract between the operator and the Authority. Part of the conditions of the contract is that the Authority's regulations on pollution prevention are strictly observed.[22] Failure to do so resulting in "serious, persistent and wilful violations" of the basic terms of the contract, Part XI, and of the stipulations of the Authority will lead to the contract being suspended or terminated, and monetary penalties being imposed on the contractor.[23]

The task of giving more flesh to this framework was delegated to the Preparatory Commission for the International Sea-Bed Authority and for the International

18 Article 153, para. 2 LOS Convention; on the developments of these concepts *see M. W. C. Pinto*, Reflections on International Liability for Injurious Consequences Arising out of Acts not Prohibited by International Law, in: Netherlands Yearbook of International Law 16 (1985), 17-48 (28).

19 Article 4, para. 6 (b) of Annex III.

20 Article 165, para. 2 (c) LOS Convention.

21 Article 2, para. 1 (b) of Annex III.

22 Articles 3, 4 of Annex III.

23 Article 18, paras. 1, 2 of Annex III.

Tribunal for the Law of the Sea (PrepCom).[24] The Mining Code drafted so far by Special Commission 3[25] will also include provisions for the protection of the environment in the Area.

II. Deep Sea-Bed Mining Code

The Code will deal with all aspects of prospecting, exploration, and exploitation in the Area.[26] Since 7 September 1983, the UN Secretariat (Office for Ocean Affairs and the Law of the Sea) prepared several working papers on each part of the future Mining Code. Its Draft Part VIII is entirely concerned with the protection of the environment. The 25 arts. together with the other Parts of the Draft will form one comprehensive Mining Code which can be read independently of the LOS Convention or its Annexes. Following two readings of each Part in the respective Commissions of PrepCom, the Mining Code will be eventually adopted by the Council and the Assembly of the International Sea-Bed Authority.[27]

A first working paper of the Office for Ocean Affairs and the Law of the Sea was submitted on 15 November 1989. The Draft Regulations' Part VIII, Protection and Preservation of the Marine Environnment from Activities in the Area, is the working paper of 8 February 1990[28] which was submitted by the UN Secretariat for first comment to the eighth session of Commission 3.[29] Aside of more technical provisions which contain procedural requirements, it is provided for such as environmental reference zones, environmental impact statements, and contingency plans. The compliance of these rules is controlled and enforced through a reporting system, inspection rights, emergency powers and penalties, as well as through a liability scheme for pollution damage. Additional provision is made for dispute resolution concerning the application of these regulations. Insofar, the Draft and its relevant provisions on the environment resemble procedural and substantive provisions from offshore legislation elsewhere. In this context one may point out that for the United Kingdom and specifically for

24 The mandate for the drafting of the sea-bed mining code is based on resolution I of the Third United Nations Conference on the Law of the Sea which provides for the establishment of the PrepCom and gives some details of its work.

25 PrepCom established Special Commission 3 in 1983, although it is not mentioned by paras. 8, 9 of resolution I. *J. A. Walkate*, Developments in Special Commission 3 for the International Sea-Bed Authority and for the International Tribunal for the Law of the Sea: Drafting the Future Deep Sea-Bed Mining Code, in: Netherland International Law Review 36 (1989), 152-178 (152, 153).

26 *Id.*, 153, 154.

27 Articles 160, para. 2 (f) (ii), 162 para. 2 (o) (ii) LOS Convention.

28 UN doc. LOS/PCN/SCN. 3/WP. 6/Add. 5 of 8 February 1990.

29 Preparatory Commission for the International Sea-Bed Authority and the International Tribunal for the Law of the Sea, Eighth Session, Kingston, Jamaica, 5-30 March 1990, *see* UN doc. LOS/PCN/L. 79 of 28 March 1990.

Norway solid offshore régimes have been developed over the years which could be of much guidance for further elaboration of the Draft's stipulations.[30] The other prime source the Draft drew upon is the Convention on the Regulation of Antarctic Mineral Resource Activities (CRAMRA).[31]

1. Scope of Application

The scope of the Regulations is the protection of the marine environment against "harmful effects which may arise from activities in the Area," including the activities of the Enterprise (art. 1). Harmful effects will most probably not only be felt in the marine spaces "beyond the limits of national jurisdiction," the Area, so that ecosystems distant to the Area are also protected. All harmful effects from activities in the Area arising in other parts of the oceans fall under the Regulations which in turn cover over a large portion of the earth's surface.

a) Definition of Pollution

As any other catalogue on environmental protection, the Draft regulations set out with a definition of marine pollution (art. 2) which forms the basis of Part VIII on marine protection. The preliminary Draft was based on a very broad definition of marine pollution. It referred to introduction of substances and energy into the marine environment which result or are likely to result in deleterious effects.[32] This definition was proposed in 1969 by the Joint Group of Experts on the Scientific Aspects of Marine Pollution (GESAMP)[33] and gave an impetus to the 1972 United Nations Conference on the Human Environment.[34] The GESAMP definition, amended though, through its acceptance by other international agreements, found its way into the LOS Convention.[35] The definition of the LOS Convention was not carried forward to the Draft. The reason may lie in the fact that the commonly used GESAMP definition faced wide opposition during the deliberations of CRAMRA,[36] which is the latest international instru-

---

30 *See Federico Foders/Rüdiger Wolfrum et al.*, Meereswirtschaft in Europa: Rechtliche und ökonomische Rahmenbedingungen für deutsche Unternehmen, Tübingen 1989, 171-208. Similary, the US Deep Seabed Hard Mineral Resources Act (note 50) is serving as a model for the Draft.

31 Reprinted in: ILM 27 (1988), 868-900; not in force.

32 Article 103, para. 1 working paper of 15 November 1989.

33 GESAMP, Report of the First Session, London, 17-21 March 1969, UN Doc. GESAMP I/11 (1969), 5 para. 12; *M. Tomczak, jr.*, Defining Marine Pollution: A Comparison Used by International Conventions, in: Marine Policy 8 (1984), 311-322 (317, 318).

34 Declaration of the UN Conference on the Human Environment Action Plan, Recommendation 92, Annex III (General Principles for Assessment and Control of Marine Pollution) UN doc. A/CONF. 48/8 of 16 June .1972 and Corr. 1, para. 197.

35 *See Tomczak* (note 33), 321.

36 *Henry C. Burmester*, Liability for Damage From Antarctic Mineral Resource Avtivities, in: Virginia Journal of International Law 29 (1989), 621-657 (636).

ment of relevance here, so that respective efforts may not have been seen very promising for acceptance in the Draft.

The present definition of damage to the marine environment consists of two components: the one is that of "marine environment," the other "serious harm to the marine environment." Pursuantly, it is prescribed that

> (1) "marine pollution" means the physical, atmospheric and biological components, conditions and factors which interact and determine the productivity, state, condition and quality of the marine ecosystem, including the coastline, the waters of the sea and oceans and the airspace above those waters, as well as the sea-bed and ocean floor and subsoil thereof;
>
> (2) "serious harm to the marine environment" means any effect from activities in the Area on the living and non-living components of the marine environment and associated ecosystems beyond that which is negligible or which has been assessed and judged to be acceptable by the Authority pursuant to these regulations and the relevant rules and regulations adopted by the Authority and which represent:
>
> (a) significant adverse changes in the living and non-living components of the marine and atmospheric environment;
>
> (b) significant adverse changes in the ecosystem diversity, productivity and stability of the biological communities within the environment; or
>
> (c) loss of scientific or economic values which is unreasonable in relation to the benefit derived from the activity in question; ....

Articles 2, para. 2, and 105, para. 1, therefore expressly exclude any mineral activity from the Area which is unacceptable or causes "serious harm to the environment." The Draft makes clear that from the outset any activity in the Area causing serious harm may not take place and is prohibited.[37] Unless it is proven that the activities will not cause serious effects to the marine environment and associated ecosystems of the Area, mining undertakings will not commence. It follows that in the absence of effects causing serious harm, a particular activity cannot be labeled pollution. This exactly is the approach taken by CRAMRA.[38]

It must further be emphasized that the definition expressly comprises both direct and indirect introduction of substances and pollutants into the environment. For example, substances employed not for marine purposes, but in such as transshipment of the natural resources and ultimately entering the sea through air or otherwise, are readily embraced by the Draft's formula referring to "any effect from activites in the Area beyond that which is negligible."[39] Operational pollution and so-called development damages[40] are prohibited, for the harm

---

[37] Article 105, para. 2 of the Draft.

[38] *Rüdiger Wolfrum*, The Unfinished Task: CRAMRA and the Question of Liability, in: International Challenges 10 (1990), 27-32 (27); *Burmester* (note 36), 637; the relevant process is prescribed by arts. 2 para. 2, 108-111 of the Draft.

[39] Article 2, para. 2 of the Draft.

[40] *Martine Remond-Gouilloud*, Insurance, Liability and Compensation, in: Marine Policy 15 (1990), 236-242 (241).

caused will most probably amount to more than just negligible damage. This definition includes activities not normally dangerous — i. e. effects from operational activities — but that could cause unusual damage.[41]

Under any circumstance, it must be noted that the Authority would have at its conceptional basis a different definition of pollution as is applied by the LOS Convention and ultimately by the States Parties to it.[42] In fact, the assessment of the proposed activity is the key to environmental protection and the definition of pollution in the Draft.

b) Material Scope of the Definition of Pollution

First, it must be noted that the definition appears to refer only to such environmental effects as are of serious nature. Polluting substances are therefore banned if "serious harm" is caused, although it may be difficult to assess in the particular case whether the substance is of such nature or not. Most conventions on the environment rather apply and annex a list of substances deemed to be harmful[43] than to leave determination of the substances to the international organizations established. In the end, much discretion and flexibility is retained by the Draft for the Legal and Technical Commission to do so.

There is consequently the question of the exact nature of harmful effects. In other words: what is the threshold level so that serious harm amounts to "significant changes" in the marine environment and thus damage? No minimum threshold for pollution is established but even a minor harm would seem to have relevance for the definition purposes.[44] The Draft now identifies, like CRAMRA, damage as being the effect[45] upon the environment and its ecosystems beyond that which is negligible or assessed acceptable at the time of authorization. Damage is not being explicitly defined, but any effect *per se* results to serious harm in the meaning of the Draft (1) if not assessed and judged acceptable by the Authority and (2) if it represents significant adverse changes to the environment. Although the contractor has done its environmental assessment already, any impact which was not assessed in the authorization procedure and not judged acceptable, for whatever reason, or assessed and not judged acceptable, constitutes a damage.[46] In the end, the Draft's definition of pollution is more than a definition

---

41 *Burmester* (note 36), 636, 637.

42 *Cf.* on such pragmatic approach *A. L. Springer*, Towards a Meaningful Concept of Pollution in International Law, in: International and Comparative Law Quarterly 26 (1977), 531-557.

43 E. g. Convention for the Prevention of Marine Pollution by Dumping from Ships and Aircraft, Oslo, 15 February 1972, in: ILM 11 (1972), 262-266; Convention for the Prevention of Marine Pollution from Land-based Sources, 4 June 1974, in: ILM 13 (1974), 352-376; *see Churchill/Lowe* (note 4), 278, 279.

44 For CRAMRA *see Burmester* (note 36), 636, 637.

45 CRAMRA's (note 31) term "impact", Art. 1, para. 15, was chosen because "effect" would have been inconsistent; *Burmester* (note 36), 636 and note 91.

as it effectively provides for environmental impact assessment of the effects caused by the proposed activity.

More precision is given at this point to the definition of marine pollution through para. 2 of art. 2 on the Draft Regulations' use of terms. This provision defines "significant adverse changes"[47] in the marine environment and the ecosystem. It is based on the US Regulations for Commercial Recovery and Revision of Regulations for Exploration Supplemental Proposed Rule (1987).[48] The "significant adverse environmental effect"-clause was introduced by the US National Oceanic and Atmospheric Administration in 1987. Because of lack of scientific data, ten environmental factors were promulgated in 1987 in order to determine such significant adverse effect. Relevant factors are, among others, quantities of pollutants discharged, threats to species according to the US *Endangered Species Act*, and marine water quality criteria of the US *Clean Water Act*. These standards are to apply to the assessment and granting of permits and to the monitoring of the relevant project.[49] The Draft appears to follow this approach in as it delegates to the Council for further elaboration of the significant adverse changes-standards contained in art. 2, para. 2 (art. 105, para. 3).

2. *Environmental Reference Zones*

A provision long asked for by the then International Union for the Conservation of Nature (IUCN) was the requirement of environmental reference zones for deep sea-bed mining during the Third Conference of the Law of the Sea. This concept was not retained in Part XI of the LOS Convention but is incorporated into the Draft (art. 107). Experience can be drawn here from US legislation, that is, the *Deep Seabed Hard Mineral Resources Act of 1980*.[50] The Draft makes provision for two kinds of such zones: impact reference zones in the mining site, where each contractor's activities are assessed against the environmental effects. This zone serves for assessing possible changes in the "flora and fauna" of the marine environment.[51] There are preservation reference zones where no mining is allowed in order to maintain "representative and stable biota of the

[46] *Wolfrum* (note 38).

[47] Article 2, paras. a-c of the Draft.

[48] Section 971, 101, Regulations for Commercial Recovery and Revision of Regulations for Exploration, Supplemental Proposed Rule (1987), 52 Federal Register 34, 748, 34, 749 (1987).

[49] *Loc. cit.*; *John Warren Kindt*, Dispute Settlement in International Environmental Issues: The Model Provided by the 1982 Convention on the Law of the Sea, in: Vanderbilt Journal of International Law 22 (1989), 1097-1118 (1110 note 54).

[50] *See* US Deep Sea-Bed Hart Mineral Resources Act, Section 109 (f), 30 USC § 1401-1473 (1982 & Supp. V 1987); Regulations (note 48), Section 971, 603. *See Brown* (note 6), 129-133; *Richard J. Greenwald*, Deep Sea-Bed Mining. Environmental Monitoring Site Proposals: Implementation of the Stable Reference Area Concept, in: Law of the Sea Institute Proceedings 22 (1988), 466-479.

[51] Articles 107, para. 1, 2 para. 3 of the Draft.

sea-bed."[52] The former zone equals the "impact reference areas" and the latter the "preservational reference areas" of the US deep sea-bed statute. As with this legislation, no mining may commence in the Area before the environmental reference zones are designated and mining contracts are issued. The contractor himself declares the zones in a part of the proposed site. Article 107 again requires more elaboration unless it is intended to give the Authority much discretion with respect to these environmental reference zones. The following provisions (arts. 108-112) prescribe for the assessment of marine environmental impact in the application process.

3. Marine Pollution Control Measures Taken by the Operator

There will be two different catalogues which must provide all relevant information before approval of a working plan for exploration is given by the Legal and Technical Commission. The one is the environmental impact report, the other the environmental impact statement (art. 108). The environmental report is meant to provide the relevant data collected during prospecting.[53] For the stage for which it is impossible to provide exact data or to foresee all possible effects, namely, exploitation, a working plan must include an environmental impact statement that draws on the experience gained during the previous exploration.[54] More specific on the contents of an environmental impact statement is art. 109. Here, data in order to assess likely effects, descriptions of the material used, and an assessment of the effects on the marine environment must be given. It may be recalled in this context that serious harm to the marine environment representing significant adverse changes is referred to by the Draft as including the ecosystems and unreasonable loss of values.[55] This proviso will lead the applicant to extensively research all possible pollution arising and all damages to the ecosystems as well as impacts such as loss of values. Article 110 on the procedure regarding the approval of environmental reports or environmental impact statements prescribes that the Legal and Technical Commission examines the elaborations and determines whether the particular stage of activity "can reasonably be expected to result in serious harm" (art. 110, para. 2). Only where substantial evidence is received, proposed areas for exploitation shall be disapproved.

The terms and conditions regarding the protection of the environment to be included in the contract of work are further outlined. A plan to monitor all effects of the activities are accompanied by specific requirements: (1) The contractor must avoid and minimize the risk of serious harm "to the fullest possible extent"; (2) by so doing he applies "where practicable the best available technology"; and (3) each contract carries a contingency plan with respect to "incidents which

---

52 *Loc. cit.*, para. 2.

53 Article 108, para. 1 of the Draft.

54 *Loc. cit.*, para. 2.

55 Article 2, para. 2 of the Draft.

are *likely* to cause serious harm" (art. 111, para. 1). The minimization requirement stipulated reflects art. 194, para. 3 of Part XII LOS Convention. The technology requirement moreover is common to US environmental legislation and has been also adopted here from the US *Deep Seabed Hard Mineral Resources Act.*[56] With regard to best available technology where practicable, it is doubtful whether the contractor applies the most economic or the most efficient technology. The preliminary version of the Draft required "significant pollution"[57] to be responded to, only, so that the requirements on operational pollution are effectively strengthened. In combination the stipulations will cause the contractor to heavily invest in environmental technology as well as in know-how and personnel. This approach has long proven successful in the legislation of the US with regard to municipal pollution control.

Provision is made for contingency plans in the contract itself where incidents "are likely to cause serious harm."[58] The double standard of the LOS Convention referring to respective response capabilities of States[59] is not reflected in these provisions. The Draft therefore requires all States, regardless of their economic and technical capabilities, to maintain the highest level of contingency standard possible. But, of course, under the Draft the Authority is still vested with discretion and it may stipulate in accordance with the letter of art. 199 LOS Convention, which privileges the developing States.

In more detail, contingency plans are prepared prior to actual activities and include measures to warn, to exchange information as well as measures for the removal, reduction and prevention of serious harm (art. 112). Also provided for is relevant co-operation among the contractors in case of contingency. The Draft could be more precise in explicitly requiring all contractors to continuously conduct emergency exercises and to jointly provide all necessary technology personnel and equipment in case of risk to the environment. Respective experience has been gained from offshore activities in the North Sea and such measures could be made compulsory by the Draft and enforced by the Authority.

4. *Enforcement of the Draft Provisions*

a) Enforcement by the Authority

Annually, reports must be promulgated concerning the effects of the activities on the marine environment,[60] and incidents which are "*likely* to cause serious harm" (art. 113), including the measures taken, are reported promptly to the

56 *Supra* (note 50); Article 111 (c) of the Draft.

57 Article 111 (e) of the Draft.

58 *Loc. cit.*; *cf.* art. 199 LOS Convention.

59 Article 199 LOS Convention.

60 Art. 113, paras. 1, 2 of the Draft.

Secretary-General as well (art. 114).[61] Provision should be made so that the assessment of the damage is not just left to the Authority but considered already by the contractor itself and also enclosed in these reports. The duty to immediately report all "likely" effects on the environment will cause that the Secretariat is informed at all times about the environmental situation in the mine site. The annual reports as well as the environmental impact statements are made publicly available which together will provide considerable information about the likely environmental effects of the activity.

The Secretariat was careful enough to make detailed provision on the rights and duties of inspectors aboard vessels and installations of the contractor (art. 115). So empowered by art. 153, para. 5 LOS Convention, inspectors monitor the contractor's activities. They are to have furthermore reasonable access to records, logs and documents there. Nevertheless, the inspector shall not unduly interfere with the operations but may ask for the necessary assistance by the contractor and his employees. Before an inspector is stationed aboard, relevant information are given to the contractor. It is of interest that no internal inspection system of the contractor is established as is provided for offshore activities in Norway.[62] However, para. 5 of art. 115 makes reference to compatible inspections by the Authority, the sponsoring State, or States which may reinforce each other.

In an attempt to make its regulations air-tight, the Secretariat provided for a certificate of compliance issued by the contractor which affirms that all measures with regard to the environment as well as to avoid serious harm from the environment and the coasts are in line with the contract.[63] The contractor moreover certifies that he applies all minimization efforts to the fullest extent possible. It thus accepts another major obligation for the protection of the environment.[64] This certificate is not meant a superfluous instrument but a re-enforcement of the contractor's responsibilities.

Emergency powers are vested in the Council for the purpose of preventing "serious harm" to the marine environment (art. 119). The Secretary-General promptly reports any such incident to the Council and the Legal and Technical Commission, the latter of which in turn makes recommendations to the Council accordingly. Where respective action is pending, the Secretary-General may immediately suspend or adjust activities of the contractor.[65] The LOS Convention provides for no other instruments than recommendations to be made by the

---

61 Article 114, para. 2 of the Draft; the major details of the incident are included in the report, such as the co-ordinates of the area affected, the likely effects on flora and fauna, a description of the action taken, and of the monitoring.

62 Regulations concerning the Licensee's Internal Control in Petroleum Activities on the Norwegian Continental Shelf by Royal Decree of 28 June 1985 pursuant to Act of 22 March 1985 No. 11 pertaining to Petroleum Activities (The Petroleum Act).

63 Article 116 of the Draft.

64 *Loc. cit.*, para. 2.

65 Article 119, paras. 1, 2, 4, 5 of the Draft.

Commission to the Coucil,[66] but interim emergency powers of the Secretary-General[67] may be based upon the general clause of art. 145 LOS Convention. These emergency orders are appropriately supplemented by an additional power of the Authority (art. 120). In case that the contractor does not take the action required or does not comply with an emergency order, the Council may step in and take the necessary measures to prevent or minimize "serious harm."[68]

The legitimate interests of coastal States against pollution, which are maintained by art. 142 LOS Convention, are carried forward by art. 118 of the Draft. Whereas the LOS Convention says that due regard must be paid to such interests, it is on the one hand the contractor who is responsible to avoid serious harm to the marine environment.[69] On the other hand, the Secretary-General may be requested to take the necessary action where a coastal State believes that sea-bed activities are likely to cause serious harm to its marine areas or its coastline and land territory.[70] The type of pollution covered here is not damage, but any activity which is likely to cause damage or threat of damage so that powers are delegated to act not just against damage but against effects which may cause pollution. The response action of the coastal State *via* the Secretary-General does not derogate the coastal States' rights to take itself all necessary action under Part XII LOS Convention or other international agreements.[71] Measures contemplated for a coastal State are not given, but it will most probably rely on art. 194 LOS Convention. First, however, the Secretary-General must be notified in order to inform the sponsoring State of the intended action.[72]

Further enforcement is provided by penalties and monitoring by the Authority. Article 123 on penalties is equivalent to art. 18 of Annex III of the LOS Convention. In case of serious, persistent and wilful violation of the basic contract terms or in case of the contractor's failure to comply with a decision of the dispute settlement body, the rights of the contractor may be suspended or terminated.[73] Any other contract violations not so covered, may result in proportionate monetary penalties levied by the Authority. Before, however, the contractor must have had a reasonable opportunity to exhaust its judicial remedies.[74]

The Legal and Technical Commission is required to prepare a monitoring programme for the assessment of "risks or effects of pollution" for the marine environment (art. 124).[75] The programme is approved by the Council and imple-

66 Article 165, para. 2 (k) LOS Convention.

67 Article 119, para. 5 of the Draft.

68 Article 120 of the Draft.

69 Article 118, para. 1 of the Draft.

70 *Ibid.*

71 *Loc. cit.*, para. 3; Art. 142, para. 3 LOS Convention, *see,* e. g., Art. 194 LOS Convention.

72 *Loc. cit.*, para. 2.

73 Article 123, para. 1 of the Draft.

74 *Loc. cit.*, para. 2.

mented by the Commission.[76] The rules and procedures of the Authority are then re-examined by the Commission from time to time (art. 127).[77] In case of dispute the Sea-Bed Disputes Chamber of the International Tribunal for the Law of the Sea, or the special arbitration tribunal established, Annex VII of the LOS Convention accordingly, are competent to interpret or apply the regulations.[78]

b) Enforcement by the States

At the preliminary stage of the Draft it was the contractor who was encouraged to prevent pollution to the marine environment and to prevent damage to its flora and fauna as well as to give effective protection against "harmful effects directly resulting" from sea-bed activities.[79] Now, the general obligation of art. 194 of the LOS Convention is included in the Draft (art. 104) which serves to emphasize the States' responsibility with respect to environmental protection from activities in the Area.[80] The obligations of the sponsoring State, in addition, are enforced by the duty to regularly inspect the activities of its contractor, to ensure compliance with the mining contract as well as with the measures stipulated by the Authority, and to transmit the reports of its inspectors to the Council (art. 117).[81]

States must even intervene in case the contractor does not comply with the terms of the contract and its obligations under the LOS Convention concerning the protection of the environment (art. 121, Draft). In other words: the States execute national enforcement powers in the Area *vis-á-vis* the contractor under its flag.[82] It has been noted that a member State of the Authority who is in gross and persistent violation of the enforcing of the LOS Convention's provisions against a contractor under its flag may be suspended from its seat in the Council.[83] Such practice could function as a bar against "flag of convenience"-practices in deep sea-bed mining.

For an effective protection of the environment parallel with the system of primary rules and the rules on enforcement there must be always a system of rules providing for responsibility and liability in the case of violation of the substantive set of rules. The rules on responsibility and liability are final to the system which is designed to protect and preserve the "marine environment from serious harm to the marine environment in the Area."[84]

---

75 Article 124, para. 1 of the Draft; *see* art. 165, para. 2 (h) LOS Convention.

76 Article 124, paras. 2, 3 of the Draft; *see* art. 165, para. 2 (h) LOS Convention.

77 *See* art. 209, para. 1 LOS Convention.

78 Article 124 of the Draft.

79 Article 104 working paper of 15 November 1989.

80 Article 104 of the Draft.

81 Article 117, para. 1 of the Draft.

82 *Kari Hakapää*, Marine Pollution in International Law, Helsinki 1981, 285.

83 *Op. cit.*, 284.

84 Article 1 of the Draft.

5. *Liability Provisions of the Draft*

The liability régime (art. 122) establishes not only the liability of the contractor or the Enterprise for third party damage,[85] but for that regarding preventive measures and for the repair of serious harm to the marine environment, too.[86] A sponsoring State responsibility and liability for breaches of its international obligations[87] is established aside of the contractor's liability.[88] There is thus a liability system where two régimes co-exist: one mainly for the sponsoring State, through public international law, and the other for private entitites, such as contractors.

a) Responsibility and Liability of the Contractor

The general clause on contract obligations compels the contractor to take all necessary measures for marine protection (art. 116). Next, the contract requires the minimization to "the fullest possible extent"[89] of, and the responding by contingency plans to, such effects which would cause and are likely to cause serious harm, respectively, to the marine environment.[90] This duty is re-inforced by the duty to take timely action for containment and abatement action where serious damage occurs or threatens to occur.[91] Therefore, art. 122 on liability must be read with the general clause of art. 116, which obliges the contractor to prevent, reduce, and control pollution.[92]

Stipulation is thus made that

> 1. [t]he contractor carrying out activites in the Area shall respond with necessary and timely action, including measures to prevent and contain, minimize and repair, if such activities result in or threaten to result in serious harm to the marine environment[.][93]

and that the contractor is liable for

> (a) serious harm to the marine environment arising from its activities in the Area, including payment to the Authority in the event that the contractor has not taken adequate action to contain, minimize and repair the serious harm.[94]

---

85 Article 122, para. 2 (b) of the Draft.

86 *Loc. cit.*, paras. 1, 2; *see* art. 22 of Annex III of the LOS Convention.

87 *Loc. cit.*, para. 4 of the Draft.

88 On the economics of liability in pollution control *see Kathleen Segerson*, Risk Sharing and Liability of Stochastic Externalities, in: Marine Resource Economics 4 (1987), 175-192; *James P. Opaluch*, Marine Pollution and Environmental Damage Assessment: Introduction, in: Marine Resource Economics 4 (1987), 151-154 (152). Economists argue that liability incentives are potentially more cost-effective for pollution control than are traditional command-control regulations; *ibid.*

89 Article 111 (b) of the Draft.

90 *Loc. cit.*, (e), art. 112, para. 1 of the Draft.

91 Article 122 para. 1 of the Draft.

92 Article 116 of the Draft.

93 Article 122, para. 1 of the Draft.

The liability clause states that the contractor is liable where "serious harm" occurred and payment must be made to the Authority if the contractor was unable to contain, minimize and repair such harm.[95] To that extent, third party damage as envisaged by the Draft is hinged upon serious damage.[96] Not clearly covered, therefore, is the case where the party was prevented from taking profit it would have made, had the incident not occurred. The same applies to costs incurred to a third party resulting from response actions such as co-operative response actions stipulated.[97] The liability frameworks of national laws are left intact by the Draft so that the damaged party may seek redress there.[98] Not included in this part of the Draft is contributory action to the environmental damage by the third party or another contractor. The liablility in offshore activities generally is jointly and severally,[99] a concept which also should be incorporated here.

Even where no such third party damage occurs but "only" serious harm to the marine environment, the contractor will have to provide respective payments. Through this proviso the notion of "ecological damage" requiring compensation for such irreparable damage is implemented. The basic principle of this regulation is that an offender causing irreparable damage to the environment should not be in a better position over a contractor liable for damage to property.[100] Although compensation for ecological damage is paid, it is asssumed that nature's self-restoration powers recover the injuries inflicted by man. Otherwise there would be no response to deterioration of nature at all.

The liability for restoration of the ènvironment is the one component of environmental damage. The other is generally the liability to make re-imbursement for the reasonable costs of necessary response actions incurred to any other party. This approach was taken by CRAMRA.[101] Therefore, liability for environmental damage in the form of payment for restoration seems to be inclosed but the Draft does not clearly say so. The Draft is less clear than the liablity provisions of the previous working paper and still seems to stipulate the responsibility of the contractor to fully restore the environment to the state it was before the damage.[102] This was very explicit in that the contractor was strictly liable for "restoration to the *status quo ante*."[103] Now it is not clear what activity the contractor is to do in order to restore the environment. It is only provided that he has to take response actions and that the strict liability results from ineffective

94 Article 122, para. 2 (e) of the Draft.

95 Article 122, para. 2 (a) of the Draft.

96 *Loc. cit.*, (b).

97 *See* art. 112, para. 2 (g) of the Draft.

98 Article 122, para. 5 of the Draft.

99 E. g. sections 9, para. 1, 39, para. 2, and 43 of the Petroleum Act (note 62).

100 *Wolfrum* (note 38).

101 Article 8, para. 2 (d) CRAMRA (note 31).

102 Article 119, para. 1 working paper of 15 November 1989.

103 *Ibid.*

response measures causing "serious harm to the environment including payment to the Authority."[104] Therefore, it should be made more clear whether such payment is for the restitution in kind or monetary compensation.

Rather the Draft prefers to introduce a definition of damage, serious harm, which incorporates significant adverse *changes* to the environment. Here it appears that the definition taken for pollution of the marine environment[105] is one of liability, for the changes in the environment may result in liability for restoration.[106]

Aside of this question, the other is concerning payment in the event that the re-establishment of the marine environment to the *status quo ante* was not possible. The Draft provides that it is the Council which brings the claim for improper restoration of the environment as well as for its re-imbursement of reasonable abatement costs.[107] The question of who will pay for the restoration has been answered by the Draft in part. Pursuant to art. 122, para. 2, it is the contractor. But no guidance is given how to calculate the amount of compensation required. Little precedent exists and, for instance, the *SS Zoe Colocotroni*[108] may be of limited help here. Nevertheless, provision is made that in case of dispute the amount of compensation is decided upon by the Sea-Bed Disputes Chamber of the International Tribunal for the Law of the Sea or an arbitration tribunal in accordance with Annex VII of the LOS Convention. The final decisions are enforceable in each States Parties' territory.[109] From other liablity régimes one may derive the following to be included in such payment: (1) all costs incurred by the Authority for response actions, (2) payments to a fund for the enhancement of response actions or for some joint co-operation with respect to the environment, and (3) some sort of punitive damage. The Draft should be more clear in this respect and should include the three-tiered system mentioned.

The contractor cannot invoke any limitation but the defenses of *force majeure*, armed conflict or act of terrorism for all instances provided for in para. 2 of art. 122. However, the defenses are further narrowed in that they are not available if the natural disaster was reasonably foreseeable or if "reasonable precautionary measures" could have been effective.[110] The defenses, furthermore, do not privilege a contractor against the liability as far as its obligation to take response actions is concerned.[111] An important element in this system is the responsibility and liability of the contractor's sponsoring State.

---

104 Article 122, paras. 1, 2 (a) of the Draft.

105 *See* art. 2, para. 2 of the Draft.

106 Article 122, para. 1 (a) of the Draft.

107 Article 122, para. 2 (a), (c) of the Draft.

108 *Commonwealth of Puerto Rico* v. *M/V Colocotroni*, in: 628 F2d 652 (1st Cir. 1980).

109 Article 122, paras. 9, 10 of the Draft; *see* art. 21, para. 2 of Annex III of the LOS Convention.

110 Article 122, para. 3 of the Draft.

111 *Loc. cit.*, para. 2.

b) Responsibility and Liability of the Sponsoring State

Pre-conditional for sponsoring State liability is that the State failed to enforce its obligations under the LOS Convention or the Draft against the contractor (art. 121). This liability serves one major purpose: to enforce the obligations of the sponsoring State. The previous version carried a second purpose: to provide for payment in case that the operator is unable to satisfy its liability.[112] This supplementary liability of the sponsoring State is not part of the Draft though.

The responsibility of the sponsoring State under art. 139 LOS Convention is re-emphasized by the Draft's art. 121. The sponsoring State is obligated to ensure that the contractor is carrying out all activities in conformity with the LOS Convention and the contract. This must be ensured by the State's legal order.[113] But the sponsoring State is exonerated from its reponsibility and liability for any damage if it established reasonable appropriate measures for compliance of the contractor.[114] This liability of the sponsoring State for breach of Draft obligations functions as in the following:

(1) the sponsoring State is generally not liable for damage;

(2) but is liable for damage if it caused the damage by any failure of a contractor sponsored by it to comply with its obligations if that State party has adopted laws and regulations and taken administrative measures which are, within the framework of its legal system, reasonably appropriate for securing compliance by persons under its jurisdiction,[115] and, moreover,

(3) the rules of general international law on liability may apply to a specific case of damage.[116]

Therefore, this provision acknowledges the principle that a State is responsible for its international unlawful acts, which is here the failure to secure compliance by its contractor through laws and regulations and appropriate administrative measures.[117] There is a burden of proof on the Authority to show unreasonable measures on the part of the State.[118]

The State liability under general international law[119] is different from the one regarding the specific liability of the State to ensure compliance by its contrac-

112 Article 119, para. 2 working paper of 15 November 1989.

113 Article 121 of the Draft; *see* art. 4, para. 4 of Annex III of the LOS Convention.

114 Articles 121, 122, para. 4 of the Draft; art. 4, para. 4 of Annex III; art. 139 of the LOS Convention.

115 Article 122, para. 4 of the Draft.

116 *Loc. cit.*, para. 7 (a).

117 *Chorzów Factory* Case, PCIJ Series A, No. 17 (1928), 28; *see Eibe Riedel*, Damages, in: *Rudolf Bernhardt* (ed.), Encyclopedia of Public International Law (EPIL), Instalment 10, Amsterdam *et al.* 1987, 68-75 (69).

118 On non-fault state responsibility in CRAMRA *see Burmester* (note 36), 649.

119 Article 122, para. 7 (a) of the Draft; *Barbara Kwiatkowska-Czechowska*, States' Responsibility for Pollution Damage Resulting from Exploration for and Exploitation

tor.[120] Generally, responsibility and liability for environmental damage result from the principle *sic utere tuo ut alienum non laedas*, the principle which is incorporated in Principle 21 of the Stockholm Declaration,[121] and which developed from the *Trail Smelter*[122] and the *Corfu Channel*[123] cases.[124] The general obligation of the Draft compels the States to protect and preserve the environment.[125] The sponsoring State is thus under the major obligation to regularly inspect the contractor's activities and to "reasonably" ensure compliance with all measures of the Authority and the terms of the contract.[126] This is the due diligence-standard with respect to the sponsoring State's responsibility.[127] However, a resulting veil may be pierced with the international liability clause of the Draft which provides for the application of existing international law of liability (art. 122, para. 7 (a)).

c) Unlimited Liability without Fund for Compensation

Apart from not providing limits on liability, or for its further elaboration by an additional protocol, the establishment of a fund for pollution damage is not envisaged.[128] This is in consequence of the fact, that the liability of the Draft is unlimited. But international precedence exists for the difficulty of obtaining insurance for such unlimited liability.[129] Although insurance seems to be the adequate supplement to liability, there is not necessarily such linkage. Strict liability specifically is independent of coverage offered by the market and it is not up to liability law to follow the insurance market. Once insurance is available at the market, it will be provided with restricted coverage anyway.[130] Therefore,

of Seabed Mineral Resources, in: Polish Yearbook of International Law 10 (1980), 157-176 (164, 165).

120 Article 122, para. 4 of the Draft.

121 Declaration of the United Nations Conference on the Human Environment, UN doc. A/CONF. 48/14 of 16 June 1972 and Corr. 1, reprinted in: ILM 11 (1972), 1416-1429.

122 *US* v. *Canada*, in: Reports of International Arbitral Awards, Vol. III, 1938-1981 (1965).

123 *UK* v. *Albania*, ICJ Reports 1949, 4 (22).

124 *See Burmester* (note 36), 652, 653.

125 Article 104, para. 1 of the Draft.

126 Article 117, para. 1 of the Draft.

127 *Alabama Award* (1872), in: *Herbert W. Briggs*, The Law of Nations, 2nd ed., London 1953, 1026 (1027, 1028); *Rylands* v. *Fletcher* (1868), L. R. 3 H. L. 330.

128 However, indication is made that a fund may be established for cases where liabilities are not met by the contractor; *see Burmester* (note 36), 641, 642.

129 E. g., the 1970 *Arctic Waters Pollution Prevention Act* of Canada, Revised Statutes of Canada 1970, c. 2 (1st Suppl.) as amended by P. C. No. 1985-1597, 9 May 1985; because insurance companies were unable to provide unlimited coverage for arctic shipping, the Statute became operative in 1972 when limits were introduced by the subsequent Arctic Waters Pollution Prevention Regulations, Consolidated Regulations of Canada 1978, c. 354, as amended by Statutory Regulations and Orders 1981, 447.

130 *Remond-Gouilloud* (note 40), 240.

national and international instruments of environmental law introduce the principle that where the prescribed liability ends, the fund's liability begins.[131] Effectively, any residual liability for environmental damage not compensated is then absorbed by a fund. The 1971 Convention on the Establishment of an International Fund for Oil Pollution Damage[132] supplements, and provides for additional compensation under, the 1969 International Convention on Civil Liability for Oil Pollution Damage.[133] However, a sponsoring State liability is instituted and not a fund if, first, the States Parties' measures, legislative and administrative measures alike, did not reasonably ensure compliance, and, second, its contractor failed to abide by its obligations.[134] There is no limit established to such liability for breach of obligation, as it is the principle of international law that a State is fully responsible for its internationally unlawful acts.

The primary responsibility for environmental damage and liability for subsequent damages is placed upon the contractor.[135] Unless a protocol will specify liability ceilings or establish a fund for compensation of damages not covered by the contractor, the defenses to the contractor's liablity[136] may result in cases where damage is not compensated at all. When it is impossible to show that the sponsoring State failed to establish reasonable securing compliance, residual liablity may go uncompensated. A first measure should be to establish a fund for cases where the sponsoring State enforced all obligations and damage occured regardless of all precautionary measures. However, the Draft as it stands goes far in (1) that it did not establish liability ceilings for the contractor and (2) in that the sponsoring State's liability will cover any damage not absorbed by the contractor, because it will be very difficult to show that its measures for compliance of the contractor together with its inspection duties *vis-á-vis* the contractor were of reasonable nature to prevent damage. It will be therefore most probably the case that its liability covers all damage not compensated by the contractor. If one looks at CRAMRA, the Draft may well develop over the time so that the States may require provisions for a fund, and on some residual liability for sponsoring States. It may be successful to strengthen State liability and to provide for full compensation for environmental damage.

131 *Wolfrum* (note 38), referring to the International Convention on the Establishment of an International Fund for Compensation for Oil Pollution Damage, 18 December 1971, in: ILM 11 (1972), 284-302, and Protocol, 19 November 1976, in: ILM 16 (1977), 621-630.

132 Reprinted in: ILM 11 (1972), 284-302.

133 Reprinted in: ILM 9 (1970), 45-67, and 1984 Protocols, in: ILM 23 (1984), 177-195.

134 Article 122, para. 4 of the Draft; *see* art. 4, para. 4 of Annex IV of the LOS Convention.

135 *See* on the trend in the conference on the LOS Convention to move obligations from the state towards the contractor *Pinto* (note 18), 28, 29.

136 Article 122, para. 3 of the Draft.

A more difficult question of liability refers to the cases where neither the contractor nor the sponsoring State breached any obligations but the activity nevertheless resulted in pollution. This is where para. 7 (a) of art. 122 of the Draft comes to work and requires the "application of existing rules on liability and the development in acordance with international law of further such rules."[137] Aside of the fact that the ILC at present is dealing with "international liability for injurious consequences arising out of acts not prohibited by international law", international law is unclear yet as how far the liablity of the State goes. The one view follows the due diligence-standard as applied by the Draft: a State is only liable for such damage if it did not duly control the respective activity. The opposite view establishes the principle of such liability, according to which a State is automatically liable for damage caused outside its territory by a lawful activity under its jurisdiction or control.[138]

Overall, the Draft follows the trend in CRAMRA concerning the protection of the environment and State responsibility. Precedents already exist as far as strict liability for contractors is concerned. Such conventions as the 1962 Convention on Liability of Operators of Nuclear Ships,[139] the 1963 Convention on Civil Liability for Nuclear Damage,[140] and the 1969 Liability Convention[141] as well as the 1972 Convention on International Liability for Damage Caused by Space Objects[142] provide for strict liability of the operator. The Draft differs from these treaties as it apparently embraces damage to the environment and loss of or damage to property of a third party or loss of life or personal injury of a third party.

These conventions do not provide for the compensation of environmental damages *per se*, but rather damage caused to property. International agreements so far have an indirect effect only upon the protection of the environment. Their main concern is not of the environment, but of human beings. Where restoration costs are part of the liability scheme, conventions are truly oriented to the environment. The Draft even seems to go a step further by providing for payment in the event that restoration was not achieved and so encompasses an additional element with a view to further the protection of the environment.[143] The reason

137 Article 122, para. 7 (a) of the Draft; *see Mohammed Bedjaoui*, Responsibility of States: Fault and Strict Liablity, in: EPIL 10 (note 117), 358-362 (360).

138 *Burmester* (note 36), 652.

139 AJIL 57 (1963) 768; *see Constance O' Keefe*, Transboundary Pollution and the Strict Liability Issue: The Work of the International Law Commission on the Topic of International Liability for Injurious Consequences Arising out of Acts not Prohibited by International Law, in: Denver Journal of International Law 18 (1990), 145-208 (170-174).

140 UNTS, Vol. 1063, No. 16197.

141 UNTS, Vol. 973, No. 14097.

142 UNTS, Vol. 961, No. 13810.

143 *See SS-Zoe Colocotroni* Case (note 108); the concept developed in this case is entrenched in the 1984 London Protocol of the 1969 Liability Convention (note 133); *Remond-Gouilloud* (note 40), 242. The difficulty of integrating economic concepts of

why damage to the environment has not yet been accepted in international treaty law, let alone international customary law, is that the pricing of damage to environmental resources is not only difficult. It is equally difficult to decide which intensity of serious harm materializes a damage to the environment. Both questions are to be elaborated in the Draft or an additional Protocol.

III. Conclusion

As the reports on the effects of deep sea-bed mining prove, the development of the deep ocean resources require specific environmental protection.[144] In protecting the marine environment against harmful effects resulting from activities in the Area, a type of pollution is addressed which clearly falls between the class of potential serious pollution such as from nuclear power accidents and the class of risks arising from normal daily activities such as driving cars in Europe. Deep sea-bed mining is part of discrete serious environmental risks and amenable to management through technological standards.[145] The central issue cannot longer be whether to act on an assumed environmental threat or to wait for further scientific proof when the threat may have become reversible only over several generations.

But the Draft's contract for deep sea-bed activities will be submitted to a carefully designed approval process which will ensure that all technical measures regarding prevention, containment, minimization, and repair of damage are implemented. The Draft endeavours to hereby establish basic rules for the prevention of damage to the marine environment resulting from deep sea-bed activities.

This rudimentary framework is modelled along the lines of the LOS Convention, CRAMRA, and offshore legislation[146] and is summarized as follows: first, activities in the Area are prohibited unless permitted by the Authority (art. 105, para. 1); second, the permission for such undertaking depends upon the positive decision that such activities can be savely pursued (arts. 2, para. 2, 105, para. 2); and third, the activities must be in accordance with the rules set out by the Draft (art. 116, para. 1). The crux of such environmental protection is, however, that the Authority and the Commission at the same time are to facilitate deep sea-bed activities as well as to protect the environment against resulting effects.

---

natural resource value into the legal order must be solved, it is said, by a number of legal actions. *Roger C. Dower/Paul F. Scodari*, Compensation for Natural Resource Injury: An Emerging Federal Framework, in: Marine Resource Economics 4 (1987), 155-174 (166, 171).

144 *See Thiel* (note 1).

145 *Sanford E. Gaines*, International Principles for Transnational Environmental Liability: Can Developments in Municipal Law Help Break the Impasse?, in: Harvard International Law Review 30 (1989), 311-349 (348).

146 *See Foders/Wolfrum* (note 30), 171-179 (United Kingdom), 192-196 (Norway).

In practice, one and the same organ may find it difficult to act according to the opposite goals of resource development *vis-á-vis* environmental protection.[147] International non-governmental organizations moreover could have some degree of involvement in procedural questions here.[148]

Aside of enforcement measures by the Authority and the contractor's sponsoring State's, liability provisions are in the focus of the Draft. The contractor is held strictly liable when it fails to comply with the obligations. Failure to comply means that the contractor has not taken the necessary response actions it was required to take, or it has taken these measures and damage occurred in spite of the preventive measures. Thereafter, the environment was not properly repaired.[149] These provisions go well beyond that what is stipulated by the 1969 International Convention on Civil Liability for Oil Pollution Damage.[150] The Draft cautiously follows the path of CRAMRA's liability régime insofar as it makes no specific mention of limits to the sponsoring State's liability with respect to prospecting, exploration, or exploitation. It is the sponsoring State's due diligence responsibility to ensure such proper activities of the operator. Before any State liability is applicable though, it must be proven (1) that the contractor did not take all appropriate measures and (2) that the damage arising from activities in the Area would not have occurred or continued if the sponsoring State had carried out its obligations.[151]

The Draft finally provides that the further development of the international law on liability may very well apply to individual cases of damage under the Draft. Another element in which the liability rules of the Draft attempt to develop international law lies in the fact that the notion of damage appears to cover more than the negative effect on rights or interests attributable to a single State or a third party. Liability for restoration of the environment to the *status quo ante* seems to be imposed upon the contractor and should be more clearly entrenched in the liability scheme.[152]

The Draft incorporates the universally accepted "polluter pays"-principle which involves in turn the pricing of environmental resources and the reducing of profits and places the burden of environmental protection in its appropriate place — on

147 *Kindt* (note 8), 1011, observes that the LOS Convention itself is lacking a balance between development and environmental protection.

148 *Cf. Philippe Sands*, The Environment, Community and International Law, in: Harvard International Law Review 30 (1989), 393-420 (394, 412-417).

149 Article 119, para. 1 (a) of the Draft.

150 *See Burmester* (note 36), 643.

151 *See* art. 119, para. 2 of the Draft; art. 8, para. 3 (a) CRAMRA (note 31), and also *Wolfrum* (note 38).

152 *See* proposed Council Directive of the EEC, 15 September 1989, Art. 2, para. 1: injury to environment is defined "an important and persistent interference in the environment caused by a modification of the physical, chemical or biological conditions of water, soil and/or air, insofar as these are not considered do be damages"; *cited* by *Remond-Gouilloud* (note 30), 242.

the developing enterprise.[153] The costs of deep sea-bed development are internalized, whereby the developer bears the costs of environmental protection as part of the costs of resource development. The Draft, in its providing for specific obligations for the contractor, a detailed control mechanism, and strict, unlimited liability, may therefore act as an incentive[154] to both the contractor and the sponsoring State for effective prevention of environmental damage in the Area. In addition, Special Commission 3 is furthermore to elaborate the system for deterrence and compensation in order to guarantee a stable but environmentally sound legal order for activities in the Area.

---

153 *Kindt* (note 8), 1020.
154 *Segerson* (note 133).

Research Perspectives on Protecting the Marine Environment during Deep-Sea Mining

Initiative for research developed by the TUSCH Research Group, Germany*

I. Introduction and Objectives

During the decade of the 1960s, predictions for the demand of metallic resources resulted in the incorporation of marine reserves, including those of the deep sea, along with terrestrial reserves. In the years thereafter, German firms initiated prospecting activities followed by exploration of deep-sea ore deposits. The polymetallic nodules of the Pacific Ocean and the metalliferous muds of the Red Sea were of primary economic interest. Today, the metalliferous crusts on Pacific seamounts, the massive sulfide deposits in oceanic spreading regions, and the phosphorite occurrences on shelf areas and on seamounts are also included. While various international consortia, including German concerns, concentrated upon exploration for polymetallic nodules, *Preussag AG* extended its research to include the production of metalliferous muds in the Red Sea on an industrial scale. Ocean mining tests were carried out on the Blake Plateau in 1970, in the central tropical North Pacific in 1978-79, and in the Red Sea in 1979. They have demonstrated the technical feasibility of harvesting manganese nodules, as well as metalliferous muds, in economically significant quantities.

The marine environment would be significantly influenced if mining of these deposits were carried out without prior consideration of the environmental impact. Protection of the deep-sea environment is thus of the highest social and scientific priority, has far-reaching socio-economic consequences, and entails political implications. Deep-sea environmental protection is particularly complex, since the consequences affect the global ocean, since it is relevant to national and international interests and territories, and since an international legal and regula-

* Member institutions of TUSCH are listed under section IV. 1.; the authorship of this article is as follows: TUSCH Research Group: *Helmut Beiersdorf, Klaus Figge, Peter Halbach, Hermann Rudolf Kudrass, Eckehard Mittelstaedt, Claus Dieter Sattler, Jan Scholten, Gerd Schriever, Erwin Suess, Hjalmar Thiel, Horst Weikert.* This text is condensed from a document entitled: "Forschungsperspektiven zum Schutze der marinen Umwelt bei der Erzgewinnung aus der Tiefsee", prepared for the *Bundesministerium für Forschung und Technologie*, Bonn; the text was translated into English by *Eric James Foell*, IHF, University of Hamburg, and presented during this symposium by *Erwin Suess*, GEOMAR, Kiel.

tory framework for the planned activities — the law of the sea — exists to an as yet insufficient extent. Furthermore, deep-sea mining and environmental protection present science and technology with new, large-scale and still unsolved basic problems. At the present time, a Commission of the United Nations (the Preparatory Commission for the Sea-Bed Authority) is concerned with the development of regulations and the solving of legal questions associated with mining the deep-sea. The work of this Commission has resulted in the creation of a draft of the Mining Code which is heavily based on an existing American version. Deep-sea environmental protection is referred to in the document, although marginally because:

— the required basic knowledge of deep-sea ecosystems is lacking,

— the effects of deep sea-bed mining on the environment extend completely beyond any existing experience both on spatial and temporal scales.

Therefore, it is necessary to improve the state of knowledge on the deep sea in general, and especially within the regions of economically significant ore deposits. The primary assignment of TUSCH scientists cannot be to develop the Mining Code, but their research should be so designed that the results ultimately will be relevant to help define legalities. Within this framework, the TUSCH Research Group has designed an inter-disciplinary and inter-institutional research program in which environmentally relevant research efforts would be carried out, whose general objectives are to:

— increase basic knowledge of the deep-sea ecosystem, chemical, geological and physical environment, and meso-scale distribution processes;

— publish results in the refereed scientific and technical literature;

— influence strategies and technical developments for deep-sea mining; and

— support, advise and monitor, on an independent basis, development of the Mining Code and national laws for deep-sea mining activities.

The current document defines research activities aimed at understanding the present oceanographic systems in potential mining areas and initially concentrates on environmentally relevant information in connection with the mining of ferromanganese nodules. It is clear that in a revision and future versions the focus would shift towards polymetallic sulfides, crusts and perhaps ore deposits on the continental shelves. It is the philosophy of the TUSCH scientists that, based on detailed knowledge of the natural state and distributions of substances, mass fluxes and conversions, benthic and pelagic populations, and meso- and large-scale currents, the impact of deep sea-bed mining upon the ecological system may be predicted and measures suggested to carry out mining in an environmentally acceptable manner.

II. Deep-Sea Mining

Existing concepts on the methods of harvesting metalliferous muds and ferromanganese nodules allow deduction of certain impacts that will accompany mining operations. During the collection of ferromanganese nodules, the upper surface of the sediment will be removed. As a result, its structure will be changed and organisms, from bacteria to fishes, will be disturbed, displaced or killed. The sediment resuspended during the harvesting operation are expelled by the mining system, will form a near-bottom plume which will be dispersed by the current régime and will affect both near and distant components of the deep-sea ecosystem. The collection of metalliferous muds will, in general, have the same effect. Mining of massive sulfides will likely distribute fewer fine-grained sediments than nodule mining, although a greater remobilization flux of dissolved chemical species is expected. This will particularly be the case during mining of hydrothermal sites on active spreading ridges.

Corresponding to these problems, the research topics and their inter-relationship are schematically represented in Figure 1. The regions of the ocean most severely affected are the seafloor, the sediment-water interface, the bottom water, and the mid and upper water column. Material reservoirs which are affected by deep-sea mining are shown as boxes and the important processes between them as arrows. Research topics of particular importance are numbered from 1 to 7 and, for better illustration, are enclosed by ellipsoidal shapes. Research on these topics is outlined in the main body of this document. The overlap of the ellipsoidal shapes signifies the degree of inter-disciplinary research effort which is anticipated.

Industrial mining of deep-sea deposits has to be carried out at extensive scales in order to be economical. This involves the transport of considerable quantities of ore materials. The concentration of resource metals in the ore determines both the useable and the unusable portion which will have to be disposed of, i. e. returned to the ocean, during various phases of the mining process. Environmental problems for deep-sea mining are related to this mass transport and hence at least the orders of magnitude of the anticipated mass transport scales associated with the collection of ferromanganese nodules and metalliferous muds must be known. Several scenarios for mining ferromanganese nodules and metalliferous muds are available, but no such economics-of-scale calculations exist for mining manganese crusts, massive sulfides, and phosphorites.

1. Manganese Nodules

a) General Aspects

Ferromanganese nodules are depositional products which form through continuous or episodic growth of concentric layers around a central nucleus. In

Inititiative TUSCH Research Group

Research topics and objectives

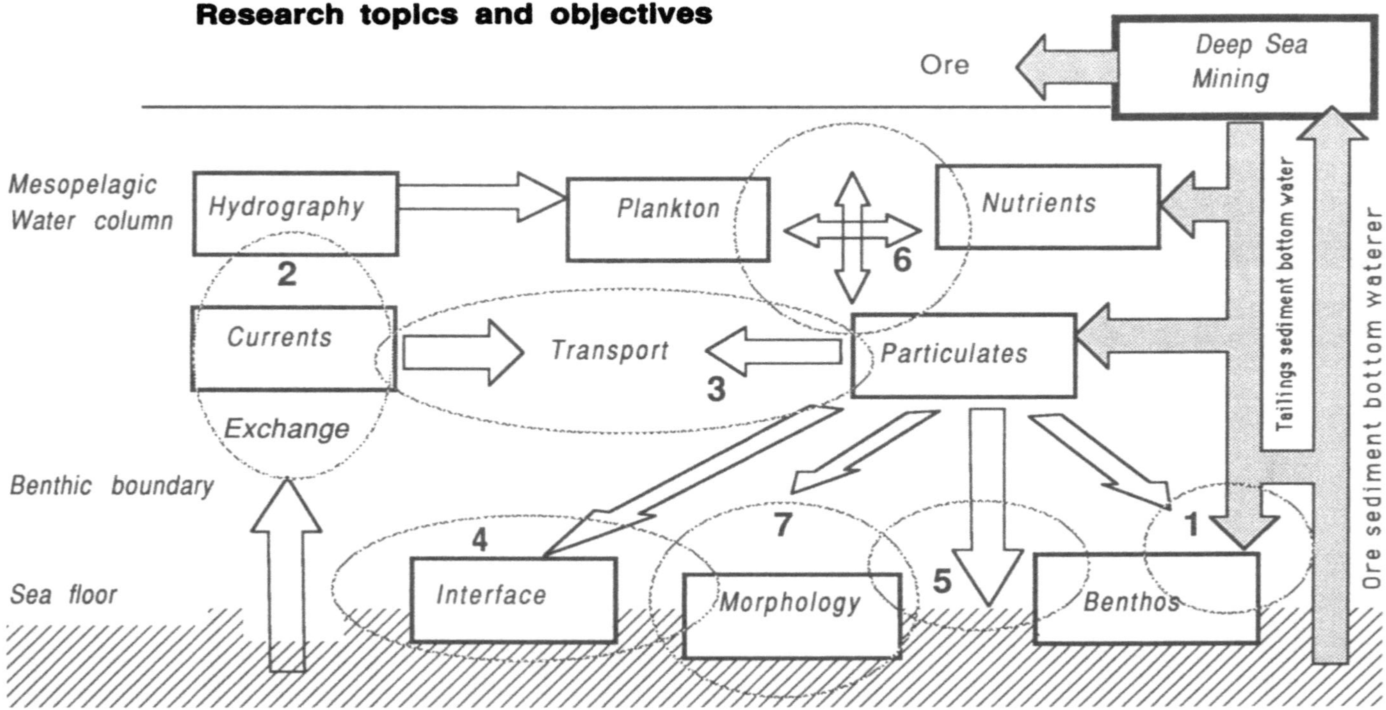

1 Recolonization
2 Currents in the far field
3 Currents in the near field and material dispersal
4 Material exchange and chemical environment
5 Particulates and sedimentation
6 Effect on plankton
7 Geologic base line and micro-morphology

Figure 1

general, two modes of genesis are distinguished in this process: a hydrogenetic and early diagenetic growth. During hydrogenetic growth, nodules are formed primarily from hydrolysed colloidal manganese and iron oxides as well as detrital alumino-silicates incorporated from the near-bottom waters.

Early diagenetic nodules, in contrast, form in the upper, water-rich layers of the sediments. As a result of degradation of organic substances in the sediment, oxygen is utilized which lowers the redox potential enough to mobilize manganese. The property of manganese to dissolve preferentially to iron under these conditions results in a fractionation of the two metals. The mobilized Mn-ions migrate, together with other cations such as copper and nickel, upward and enter the more oxidizing diagenetic zone of the sediment/seawater interface where they precipitate as crystallized solids (10 Å manganates) around nuclei. This process occurs over several millions of years and results in the finely layered concentric structure of nodules.

The most commonly occurring nodule type in the deep sea is a mixed form resulting from both of the described growth processes: the lower half is embedded in the sediment and grows through early diagenesis, while the upper half extends into the bottom water and grows hydrogenetically. The morphology of the mixed nodule type is largely ellipsoidal.

Since the transfer rate of elements in the sediments is most often higher than that in seawater, the early diagenetic nodules grow more rapidly (few millimeters to centimeters per million years) than the hydrogenetic nodules (one to several millimeters per million years). As a consequence the hydrogenetic nodule material contains less manganese and also less copper and nickel than the early diagenetic material does; in contrast, the slower growth rate supports the enrichment of cobalt.

Important to the formation of nodule deposits is, next to a slow sedimentation rate and influx of organic substance, the availability of material for nucleation. Starting material for nuclei can be basalt fragments, fish bone remnants, or broken pieces of old nodules. The latter very often provide nuclear material, especially for mixed-type nodules.

b) Ferromanganese Nodule Mining and Environmental Impact

Nodules lie on the surface of the seafloor with about one third of their volume extending above the sediments. Coverage at some localities reaches 80% of the seafloor. For commercial harvesting, several methods have been suggested and tested. One of the methods employs a towed or self-propelled collector system which removes the nodule layer with its surrounding sediments from the seafloor. Most of the sediment is to be separated from the nodules near the bottom, and the nodules are then either pumped or moved upward by air-lift through a pipestring to the mining ship. On the mining vessel, the nodules will probably be ground up and transferred to an ore carrier in slurry form.

The impact upon the ecosystem resulting from harvesting ferromanganese nodules will occur at three levels:

— on the seafloor;

— in the near-bottom water layer;

— in an as yet undetermined depth where waste material is discharged.

The collector system, consisting of a mining vehicle and a collector, sinks into the bottom, pushes the sediment aside, compresses the strata, and destroys the organisms across the full width of its track (15-20 meters). In some designs the collector itself will have little contact with the seafloor. Nodule collection can take place under a variety of mechanisms in which the surface sediments will be removed to a greater or lesser degree. As far as possible, these sediments are not to be brought to the ocean surface, but are already to be separated out near the seafloor. As a result, a sediment plume will be formed in the near-bottom water layer which will spread, resediment, and damage organisms living on the seafloor to an as yet undetermined extent in nearby and more distant areas. Besides these impacts, the removal of the hard substrate represented by nodules will preclude recolonization by sessile organisms. In this sense, the mining of nodules will result in a permanent change to the deep-sea ecosystem. An as yet unknown portion of sediments will be raised to the surface along with the nodules. To this is added material abraded from the nodule surface during lifting. Finely particulate material will also be generated during mechanical treatment of nodules aboard the mining ship. These sediments, and the particulate matter mixed in with them, are to be discharged into the ocean. They will influence the ecosystem at and below the discharge depth.

Along the path of the turbid sediment plume, geochemical and biochemical alterations will increasingly take place. Additional nutrients, mobilization or adsorption of metals and trace elements, as well as a stronger biological oxygen demand will be the most obvious impacts. Effects upon the plankton and nekton are also likely.

Quantitative information is especially needed for impact estimation related to ferromanganese nodule mining. Economic calculations are mostly based on a mining volume of 10,000 tons of raw material per day and mining ship at an average abundance of 10 kg/m^2. This corresponds to an area of 2 square kilometers per day that will be affected by the collector system. The additional area that will be influenced through resedimentation can not be estimated without experimentation. Since the area already mined will primarily lie down current of the mining operation so as not to cover future mining areas with a sediment layer, the sediment clouds whirled up during mining will, after some time, predominantly affect the previously mined regions and such interspersed zones not accessible to the collector system.

The extent of environmental effects is difficult to estimate and depends upon the penetration depth of the collector system, the separation of sediments above the seafloor, the nodule abundance density, and, with respect to abrasion, the nodule type. In order to estimate their order of magnitude, we make the following assumptions: abundance of 10 kg/m^2; 10,000 tons mined per day; depth of nodules in the sediment of 2.5 cm; sediment volume mobilized by one mining unit of 45,000 m^3/day.

When considering the entire spectrum of ferromanganese nodule mining, further environmental effects can be identified which, in our opinion, can be avoided through appropriate regulatory measures. They include impacts through:

— organic and inorganic wastes and waste waters from the mining ship and ore transport vessels;

— processing waste waters from the transport vessels in the mining area and along the transport lanes;

— introduction of processing wastes (tailings) into the ocean in connection with processing operations on land; and

— socio-economic effects which can differ according to the processing regions and also according to the metals obtained.

Even though at present there are no reliable quantitative data available from which the environmental impacts in the oceans can be derived, it can be stated unequivocally that impacts will occur in the various zones. These must be precisely identified, quantified, extrapolated to industrial mining levels, and evaluated for their effects upon the oceanic environment through further research.

2. *Metalliferous Muds*

a) General Aspects

Commercially interesting occurrences of metalliferous muds are currently known only from the deep Red Sea. At various locations within the central valley of this young rifting ocean, hydrothermal solutions enriched with metal compounds emerge from the basal rock. These solutions are highly saline since the hot waters also dissolve rock salts from the underlying strata. Due to the chemical conditions in the solutions, metallic components precipitate and concentrate in multiple layers in the soft muds at the valley floors. Various isolated basins exist in the Red Sea with quite differing oceanographic conditions. The qualitative and quantitative structure of the muds in these deeps also show considerable variability.

The largest of these deeps, the Atlantis II Deep, was extensively examined by *Preussag AG* from 1977 to 1981. It covers an area of 60 square kilometers and its metalliferous mud deposits are on average 10 meters thick.

b) Mining of Metalliferous Muds and Environmental Impact

In 1979, a pre-pilot mining test (PPMT) was carried out by *Preussag AG* under contract with the *Saudi-Sudanese Red Sea Joint Commission.* This demonstrated the technical feasibility of mud mining using a vibrating hydraulic suction head designed to bring the more compacted deposits in deeper layers into a suspension which then was sucked into the pipestring. Aboard the mining vessel, the recovered material was separated into two phases using a floatation process during which it was simultaneously diluted with seawater and treated with chemicals. The desired phase constituted a residue of about 2% of the total volume mined and contained the floating metal components. About 98% of the original mud volume, diluted by a four-fold increase of water and addition of chemicals, had to be pumped back into the ocean. During commercial mining of about 100,000 tons of mud per day, about 98,000 tons of mud in its original consistency, but diluted by a four-fold amount of water, would be re-introduced into the Red Sea.

During the 10 to 15 years of mine life, the mud deposits of the Atlantis II Deep would be largely removed. Since these sediments are anoxic, biota would not be affected except for bacteria whose living space, however, would remain intact, at least in the remaining undisturbed sediments.

The mud suspension and hydraulic removal processes would introduce muddy sediments into the near-bottom water layer. Since this layer is separated from the Red Sea deep water by a sharp salinity gradient, its effects will similarly be confined to the deeper layer of the Atlantis II Deep. This portion of particulate sediments would resettle in the vicinity from where it was removed, but by drifting into regions outside of the Atlantis II Deep below the salinity stratification yet above the sill depth, this material would join tailings being returned to the sea.

The mining process includes the re-introduction of rejected tailings into the sea which constitute about 98% of the volume of mud mined. The anoxic muds will, however, be altered during the mining and floatation processes mainly through oxygenation. New chemical bonds and solution equilibria will be introduced and at the same time, the oxygen concentration of the waters will be reduced. Furthermore, xantates added as floatation enhancing substances can only be partially reclaimed and recycled. The models on the disposition of tailings do not yet predict whether the material will to a large extent sink vertically to the ocean floor or if a permanent or transient sediment plume would result. During the pre-pilot mining test, the fate of this particulate matter could not be determined to a sufficient degree and questions on where the particles actually settle and on which portions drift over great distances must remain open.

3. Manganese Crusts

a) General Aspects

The existence of large areas of cobalt-rich and platinum containing manganese crusts was demonstrated by the German MIDPAC project in 1981. The largest and qualitatively best occurrences are located in the submarine ridges and plateaus surrounding the Central Pacific Basin, above all within the exclusive economic zones of Johnston Island and Hawaii (both USA). Manganese crusts were also found in the Line Islands, Marshall Islands, near Marcus Island (Japan), and south of the equator in the area of the Phoenix Islands and Tuvalu. The genesis and growth processes having been understood, research efforts are currently concentrated on the qualitative and quantitative analysis of ore content of these raw materials as well as on a characterization of the topographic relationships in the ore crust fields. Attempts to mine manganese crusts from the deep seafloor have not yet taken place. With reference to the environmental problems that would be associated with such mining, data on the local distributions of unconsolidated sediment and on the biological activity in the affected deep-sea ranges are presently being collected.

b) Mining of Manganese Crusts and Environmental Impact

Unlike manganese nodules, manganese crusts grow solidly attached to the seafloor. For commercial mining purposes, it is therefore necessary to separate them from their substrate by some suitable means before collector systems can be employed. In this regard, two methods are under discussion which both ultimately involve pumping of material to the mining ship. One method, in the sense of classical mining, involves a purely mechanical collector system which, with help of a preceding hammering, cutting or scraping mining head, would separate the ore from the substrate and simultaneously break it up before being removed by a "vacuum sweeper" system. The other method would make use of the varying petro-physical characteristics of the ores and underlying substrate in that appropriate shock and ultrasound waves would be used to separate the ore from the rocky substrate. The pieces of crust would then have to be taken up by a collector system and further reduced in size.

Impacts upon the oceanic ecosystem can be expected to occur at three levels: at the seafloor on the flanks of seamounts, in the corresponding near bottom water layers, and in the water column. During the separation of metalliferous crusts, sessile and vagile organisms would be killed, or massively disturbed and driven away. Sediments would be resuspended, similar to the situation in manganese nodule mining, and would form a near-bottom plume at the depth where mining takes place. Due to the carbonate-based constituents of the loose deposits found in the lesser water depths where submarine ore crusts occur, the resuspended material would clearly be more coarse-grained so that large portions of the sediment cloud would settle sooner than in the case of mining manganese nodule deposits. During the mining of ore crusts, a certain amount of sediments will also be retrieved to the surface and some abrasion of ores will take place. These components will, moreover, be supplemented by waste waters derived during cleaning of the mined ores aboard the mining vessel. Hence tailings are expected to be discharged into the ocean at the mine site, whereby an additional sediment cloud will be introduced. In the event that fine-grained ores accumulate for some time in the region of the oxygen minimum zone, heavy metals would be released and would influence the ecosystem.

4. Massive Sulfides

a) General Aspects

The first massive sulfide deposits were discovered in 1976 by the American submersible "Alvin" in the Galapagos Rift spreading center. It was a milestone in the study of marine minerals research and provided a unique opportunity to experience "live" and *in situ* how sulfide deposits are formed. Several deposits that represent geologic predecessors of massive marine sulfides are currently being mined on land.

Active oceanic spreading centers within the global plate tectonic framework are the areas for hydrothermal activity which leads to the formation of massive sulfide ore bodies. As a consequence of seafloor spreading and continental drift, seawater penetrates into the deeper layers of the oceanic crusts where it is heated and returned to the seafloor by convection. Through loss of seawater magnesium within the hydrothermal system, the pH of the circulating water decreases and seawater sulfate is reduced to hydrogen sulfide. Metals such as iron, manganese, zinc and copper are dissolved from the oceanic basalts by the reducing, acidic, hot and sulfate-free waters. Through ascent and with the colder seawater, sulfides form near the outflow areas and in the hydrothermal fields whereas chimney-like structures of metallic mineral phases eventually also containing oxides are formed at the vents.

In association with hydrothermal vents, a specialized faunal community has developed. In addition to high dissolved hydrogene sulfide, manganese and methane concentrations and the turbidity of the seawater, as well as high heat fluxes in the sediment, the fauna is a good indicator for the presence of recent hydrothermal activity and hence massive sulfide ore formation.

b) Mining of Massive Sulfides and Environmental Impact

Massive sulfides usually are large, three-dimensional ore bodies characterized by considerable structural and material hardness. The technical mining process can thus not be, as in the case of ferromanganese nodules and crusts, based on a planar process, but must take a three-dimensional approach requiring the excavation of large volumes. As to how far the aggressive hydrothermal solutions will hinder mining technology or can themselves be mined as concentrated metal-rich solutions is presently not known. Under consideration for potential mining of massive sulfides are above all those layered deposits which are no longer active, but are of young enough age to be free of a sediment cover.

In addition to the primary metals such as Fe, Mn, Zn, Cu, Pb, and Ag, these deposits also contain highly toxic trace metals (As, Hg, Sb). During mining, release of these elements may occur. Additionally, it can be expected that the unique hydrothermal vent communities which are based on sulfur oxidizing bacteria would be destroyed.

5. *Phosphorites*

a) General Aspects

The most important non-metallic raw materials in the marine environment are the phosphorites, primarily flourocarbonate apatite and hydroxyl apatite, whose phosphate (P_2O_5) content is of particular interest to fertilizer production. Two types of phosphorites are distinguishable: shelf phosphorites as well as phosphorites on seamounts (seamount phosphorites). Shelf phosphorites are often associated with zones of high biological productivity generated by upwelling of cold, nutrient-rich deep waters on continental slopes such as those along the coasts of Ecuador/Peru, Namibia and South Africa. In the surface waters of these zones, the phosphate incorporated by the fauna and flora is constantly replaced by upwelling so that a particularly high population density can develop. On the other hand, phosphate reaches the sediments through production of fecal pellets as well as through dead organic detritus where it is released through biochemical processes and concentrates in the pore waters. Once certain phosphate solubility limits in the pore waters of shelf sediments are exceeded, water-rich phosphate flakes are precipitated which with time and through loss of water crystallize and thereby build small nodules or crusts. Due to sea level fluctuations or seasonal current pattern changes, these deposits are periodically eroded and winnowed whereby the phosphate nodules are selectively enriched so that eventually a phosphate-rich lag deposit remains.

The formation of phosphorites on seamounts can be traced to a replacement process in which the carbonate ions of carbonate sediments is substituted by phosphate ions.

b) Mining of Phosphorites and Environmental Impact

Phosphorite deposits often occur on seamounts in conjunction with manganese crusts. Therefore, the same mining systems as discussed above come under consideration. Systems similar to those used for manganese nodule mining may possibly be considered for pelletal phosphorites occurring in shelf areas.

The same impact levels and effects discussed for manganese crusts are applicable to seamount phosphorites. During mining of shelf phosphorites, the sediments will be, as in the case of ferromanganese nodule mining, resuspended to some extent. A significant disturbance and destruction of the abundant faunal community living in the shallow shelf area is to be expected.

III. Research Topics

1. Seafloor Boundary Layer

During deep-sea mining, considerable amounts of seafloor will be removed or mobilized. The removal and redeposition of the material would lead to changes in the original structure of the sediments, the turbidity and chemical composition of the near bottom water layer, and would alter the fine-scale morphology of the seafloor. This would affect the marine environment, both nearby and at greater distances. In order to evaluate these changes, the geological and morphological baseline conditions in the mining area and in the affected more distant areas must be investigated in addition to the biological, chemical and oceanographic conditions.

Research perspectives: Baseline study

Existing geological and mining deposit data must be reviewed. This would be followed by field studies to clarify the geological-sedimentological history and genesis of manganese nodules. Thereby, a broad-based sedimentation model would be developed. At the same time, the base parameters for later mining would become better understood, such as, for example, the soil mechanical properties of the seafloor, the ore concentrations, and the micro-morphology.

From an analysis of baseline conditions, mining related changes in the mining areas themselves, but also in neighboring regions, may be predicted. The following questions must be answered:

— What can be expected to be mobilized?

— When and where will it be redeposited?

The damaging effects of the mobilized material must be analyzed such as, for example, the metal or nutrient exchange between suspension and seawater. Experiments that examine sediment dispersion on artificial sediment surfaces must also be carried out.

Since the micro-morphology of the seafloor would be altered during mining, the near-bottom current conditions will also be changed. Thus it is necessary to determine the morphology in its original condition and to model the mining-related morphological changes. From this, current and transport models for the mining period and the degree of mining activity can be calculated.

From the baseline data and preliminary experiments, a sedimentation model will be constructed that also incorporates the paleo-oceanographic conditions of the regions in which mining and presumably the damaging effects will take place. The paleo-oceanographic data can be used for an evaluation of the transport mechanisms for the suspended material.

2. Chemical Environment of the Seawater/Sediment Interface

The chemical environment of the sediment/water interface in the deep ocean is primarily controlled through the accumulation of metabolizable organic material from the pelagic zone. This accumulation rate, which in the form of particle flux measurements is a central research subject for marine science, determines the oxygen and nutrient balance of the deeper waters, the distribution of benthic assemblages, and the mobilization or deposition of metals and trace elements. This rate is closely tied to the formation of ferromanganese nodules and ores. Seasonal, climatic or anthropogenic changes in particle production within the surface waters of the oceans result in a rapid coupling with the chemical environment of the seawater/sediment interface through this mechanism. Any impact, such as expected in deep-sea mining, would ultimately influence the chemical environment through this coupling mechanism. The effects of this impact must be addressed by research topics.

At the deep-sea floor, the chemical environment of the seawater/sediment interface is characterized by the processes of "oxidative and sub-oxic diagenesis" and thereby constitutes a portion of the entire early diagenetic process spectrum. The oxidative/sub-oxic "window" during early diagenesis in the boundary layer is typified by oxygen consumption and nitrate reduction reactions. The sub-oxic environment is characterized by reduction of manganese and iron oxides. In oxidative and sub-oxic diagenesis, free oxygen reduction encompasses a large, undifferentiated range in redox potential, while the remaining reactions are more limited and thereby represent a better-understood segment of the diagenetic spectrum. Since formation and occurrence of ferromanganese nodules largely takes place in areas characterized by oxygen and nitrate reduction, a more detailed subdivision of the oxidative environment than previously achieved is required to understand its present condition and its sensitivity to change. It can be assumed that ferromanganese nodules, crusts and metal-enriched horizons within the sediments contain a highly-resolvable representation of these "windows" on oxidative diagenesis. It is thus possible, for example, that the various iron and manganese phases that are often interpreted as concentric growth rings in ferromanganese nodules can be attributed to certain redox conditions in the seawater/sediment interface and thereby represent a record of environmental conditions.

Research perspectives: Redox potential

Deep-sea mining may have the following consequences:

— nutrient and metal release from the interstitial water or sediments through deeply penetrating destruction of the surface;

— increased oxygen depletion in the waters above the mining site as a result of resuspension of oxidizable particles (see Table 1);

— increased oxygen depletion due to a newly formed, resedimented seawater/sediment interface;

— change in the depth of the redox boundary in the sediment brought about by changed particle flux;

— increased bioproductivity in the pelagic zone as a result of fertilization with iron.

Table 1

Impact on Oxygen consumption

Ferro-manganese ore mining: 10.000 tonnes/day

Suspended sediment: 1000 times more

Total suspended particles: 10^{13} grams/day
Containing: 1 wt-% organic carbon
of which only 1 wt-% is readily oxidized

Total suspended oxidizable carbon: 10^{9} grams/day

One gram of carbon uses up 1.2 litres of oxygen

Total oxygen consumption: 1.2 10^{9} litres/day

Deep oceanic oxygen consumption: 44 µl litre^{-1} year^{-1}
or 1.2 10^{-1} µl/litre of ocean water per day

How many litres of ocean water have their oxygen extracted by the suspended sediments from mining ?
1.2 10^{9} x10^{6} microlitres per day /
1.2 10^{-1} microlitres oxygen/litre of ocean water per day
Answer = 10^{16} **litres**

How much ocean volume, at 5000 m depth, is represented by 10^{16} litres ?
Answer = **45 km x 45 km x 5 km**

Is this a significant impact on the oceanic environment ?
Answer **YES**

As with the other investigations, a way to quantify these consequences is based upon knowledge and understanding of the actual conditions in the potential mining area which then leads to the capability of predicting conditions under varying impacts. The research objective is the chemical environment of the seawater/sediment interface and of the bottom water body, and their reaction to changes in material flows in the surface waters, within the water column and to the seafloor. The determination and understanding of current conditions require knowledge of the sediment facies and depositional environment as characterized by distribution of:

- oxygen, nitrate and metal fluxes into and out of the sediment;
- position of the redox boundary in the sediment;
- particle fluxes in relation to bioproductivity, water depth and current conditions;
- solid phases of iron-manganese compounds as controlled by redox conditions.

3. Benthic Communities

The living communities on the seafloor will be disturbed in two ways during deep sea-bed mining. The collectors will take up sediment and animals within the collector tracks. As a result, the animals will be killed, damaged or may be discharged with the sediments and might survive. In any case, the take-up of mineral resources from the seafloor will involve stirring up sediments which will drift to more or less distant areas and be resedimented. In an as yet undetermined nearby area, the resedimented layer can become so dense that the organisms may no longer be able to burrow through the additional sediment layers and will die. This is certainly the case for the sessile epifauna which can not avoid being covered by sediment.

The planned research activities must therefore clarify what impacts the benthos can adjust to and how rapidly the living community on the seafloor can be regenerated.

Research perspectives: Recolonization

Answers to the questions regarding recolonization are expected as a result of the DISCOL research project which has been supported since 1988 by the Federal Ministry for Research and Technology. After an investigation of baseline conditions, a large area was disturbed in 1989. Even though this disturbance does not fully correspond to commercial mining, the process and sequence of recolonization can be determined. For this, a very slow fluctuating process can be anticipated, similar to what is known for shallower waters. A duration of one or even two decades is anticipated before no further differences can be detected from the prior state of colonization of the sediments. The living space and community will in any case be altered for the long term through the removal of nodules as a hard substrate. For purposes of further planning, the entire question on recolonization of disturbed deep sea areas requires some results from the currently active experiment.

In the future, the reaction of organisms on and in the seafloor to being covered with sediments must be examined by means of additional experimentation. Occasional large-scale events that lead to the burial of bottom animals occur naturally as a result of sediment slides on continental slopes. These are, however, so rare that we can not wait for such a "natural experiment". On a smaller scale, burials occur regularly through burrowing activities. The fauna in areas near to sediment discharge associated with digging of holes or burrows or with the search for food is certainly to some limited extent adapted to burial. The effects of large-scaled and thick burial by sediment must, however, be investigated.

4. Suspended Particulates and Currents

Particulate matter occurs in the open oceans in various forms, among which the remains of dead organisms (biogenic) and minerogenic particles can be distinguished. In general, their size is so small that the material can be kept in suspension in moving waters and can drift away with the currents over large distances. The natural distribution of suspended particulates is not uniform. One can observe regionally horizontal as well as vertical distribution patterns.

In general, the largest suspended material concentrations are found in nearshore areas where the minerogenic components dominate, while at greater distances from shore the suspended particulate loads are lower, although the percentage of biogenic components is very high. An occasional lateral input of predominantly minerogenic material in the near bottom layer originates from periodically occurring turbidity currents which can drift over very long distances.

In terms of vertical distribution, low concentrations of suspended particulates, often of less than 20 micrograms per liter, occur between 500 meters of water depth and 500 meters above the seafloor. An increase in the form of a turbidity zone (nepheloid layer) of varying thickness is found near the bottom. Vertical transport of suspended particulates occurs to a large degree by way of biological processes. The sinking rate of particles is distinctly raised through formation of aggregates (fecal pellets, mucus formation). This effect should, however, be less effective in the deep sea due to its lower biological activity. Upward directed hydrodynamic transport can result from turbulence or, in the case of steep submarine features, through internal pressure waves. On the seafloor, resuspension of deposited suspended particulates can result from organism activities and currents.

The concentrations of suspended materials relate to:

— the light penetration;

— the distribution of dissolved and particulate substances;

— the determination of sedimentation rate, and

— constitute a potential nutrient source for animals.

A change in the natural distribution pattern, especially the massive distribution associated with mining activities, will have considerable effects upon the marine environment, especially upon the animal world adapted to the current conditions. This is true for both the region near a mining area due to the anticipated high sedimentation rate of resuspended sediments, but also for regions farther away which will be influenced by the fraction that remains in suspension longer and by the material discharged from the mining vessel. Knowledge of currents in nearby and distant areas is required in order to make definitive statements about distribution, transport and concentration.

Research perspectives: Dispersal processes

As a result of deep-sea mining, significant quantities of particulate materials will be introduced into the near bottom and intermediate water layers and will be transported by the currents. Their transport and sinking behavior must be researched in detail in order to recognize their near and distant effects and possibly to make predictions. The required investigations can be outlined as follows:

— current directions and intensities at the depths of sediment introduction and dispersal of the sediment plumes;

— qualitative and quantitative determination of the particulate substances in the sediment plumes;

— modelling of currents and particle transport in the near-field to the mining activities;

— modelling of currents in the far-field.

Whereas the first two problems require collection of samples and measurements of currents at sea, the two following problems involve theoretical development of circulation and dispersion models. For research purposes, distinctions have to be made between the models for the near-field encompassing the expanse of the mining area and the immediately adjoining sea regions (spatial and temporal scales: 10 - 200 km; throughout the entire water column; hours to years), and the models for the far-field encompassing the expanse of an ocean basin or an entire ocean (spatial and temporal scales: 200 - 6000 km; throughout the entire water column; 1 - 100 years).

How much of a cleansing effect can be expected in the water through the formation of aggregates with help of biogenic slimes remains an unanswered question. The formation of aggregates and their rapid sinking are known, but the large mass of particles resulting from the discharge of mined sediments will not be able to be bound together. The effect of aggregate formation must be considered in the investigations.

5. Relationship of Chemical Elements in the Water Column and the Bottom Boundary Layer

In order to judge the environmental suitability of deep-sea mining, it is of significance to investigate the changes in the water chemistry of the oceans resulting from such activity. For this it is necessary to quantify the natural chemical reactions in the water column, as well as those caused by these anthropogenic changes.

The chemistry of the oceans is essentially determined by biological productivity, ocean circulation, as well as the input of materials by rivers, atmosphere and hydrothermal activity. The behavior of the dissolved inputs is dependent upon their chemical and biological reactivity. Three classes of elements can be distinguished based on their chemical behavior:

— conservative elements (e. g. Li, Na, Mg, Ca, U); these are characterized by low interactions with biogenic and lithogenic particles. They have very long residence times in the ocean of > 10^5 years.

— biolimiting or recycled elements (e. g. Si, P, N, Ca, Fe, Ni, Zn, Cu, Cd). they are taken up by organisms as nutrients or micronutrients. Due to biogenic cycling, these elements are enriched in the surface waters, but are returned in stages to the ocean water with increasing depth and decay of the organisms. Regeneration even takes place in the sediments. The residence time of biolimiting elements in seawater lies between 10^3 and 10^5 years.

— particle reactive elements or scavenged elements (e. g. Al, Fe, Pb, Th); they interact with other particles and hence their distribution in the ocean is determined by these reactions. They are fixed through oxidative or hydrolytic processes on to sedimenting particles and continually accumulate in the sediments. Their residence time is < 10^3 years.

With respect to their behavior in the water column, the biolimiting and particle reactive elements are of special significance for judging the environmental suitability of deep-sea mining. They are included in biological cycles and can become toxic (e. g. Al, Cd) at elevated concentrations.

Research perspectives: Remobilization and scavenging

It is necessary to make a preliminary investigation of the natural baseline conditions in the ocean areas being considered for deep sea-bed mining. Specifically, the concentrations and gradients of biolimiting and particle reactive elements in the deep waters as well as the interactions of dissolved elements with sediment particles, i. e. scavenging rates of individual material categories and residence times of particle reactive elements, must be modelled. The interactions between resuspended or natural nepheloid layer and the dissolved substances should also be included in these studies. From these investigations, the "background" of natural exchange processes in the water column and in the boundary layer may be derived.

Through mining of mineral ores, the water chemistry should be influenced in a variety of ways. 1. Resuspension of sediments and the admixture of pore waters should result in a significant loss of biolimiting and particle reactive elements in the water column. 2. Dissolved components exchange with the suspension, are partly absorbed and carried off with the suspension cloud.

The scope of these processes is element and particle specific. Furthermore, it depends upon the residence time of the suspension cloud, the elements in seawater, as well as the composition of the suspension.

The effects of mining activities on chemical processes in the ocean can be ascertained from a comparison of the chemical interactions released by deep-sea mining with the natural "background". Such comparisons will have to be repeated in a time-series analysis format in order to document the changes in the systems.

6. Plankton

The understanding of biological systems in the pelagic realm and the evaluation of effects of deep-sea mining upon plankton and nekton populations require broadly based ecological investigations. Marine as well as terrestrial research over the past 20 years have shown that we are not in a position to be able to investigate and understand ecosystems in their entire complexity. Therefore, we must more specifically ask where massive disturbances will be created and what effects these will have. The pelagic zone will be strongly altered by the sediment masses resulting from deep sea-bed mining, both directly over the seafloor and at meso-pelagic depths. It is in these zones that the plankton and nekton investigations, including population composition analyses and experimental research, must be concentrated. In this we assume discharge of sediments lifted through the pipestring at meso-pelagic depth (e. g. 1,000 meters). In the case of discharge at the sea surface or at 200 meter depth below the euphotic zone, the plankton and nekton at these depths must also be investigated.

At first glance, the organism communities of the deep sea pelagic zone appear to be less affected by deep-sea mining than those of the benthos, since its members are mobile (zooplankton) to highly mobile (nekton) and can thus avoid disturbances as long as these do not affect unusually large portions of their living space. This reality makes it more difficult to detect and follow direct and indirect effects and changes in the pelagic fauna which, in comparison to the seafloor and to the terrestrial situation, occur additionally in a three dimensional space. Based on very recent investigations, we can not exclude that the concentration of pelagic organisms rises significantly within about 100 meters of the deep seafloor. Undoubtedly, special and largely unknown animal communities live there, occasionally supplemented by free-swimming larvae of bottom animals. Various species carry out migrations from the sediment into the near-bottom water layer. These near-bottom living bentho-pelagic fauna interact intensively with the bottom dwelling benthos and also draws a major portion of its nourishment from the bottom. These close relationships indicate that the effects upon the seafloor and benthos will also carry over to the plankton and nekton of the bentho-pelagic zone.

A second zone of animal abundance is found in the meso-pelagic upper regions of the deep sea (up to 1,000 meters). The presence of this organism assemblage, consisting mostly of animals of only a few centimeters in size, is partly recognizable on acoustic records as the deep scattering layer (DSL). It moves at dusk to the upper 100-200 meters of the ocean and migrates before dawn back down to its habitual residence depth between 500 and 1,000 meters. Migrations of organisms to even greater depths are insufficiently researched and have only occasionally been shown to occur to a maximum of 1,500 meter depth.

The two cited faunal assemblages should be viewed as critical elements of the entire deep sea pelagic zone. By means of their biomass, these animals transport organic material from deeper regions of the sea into the near-surface zones and back again. This constitutes a biological transport system by which potentially damaging materials can be rapidly distributed to the surface through portions of the water column and can enter the production processes that sustain the marine system. The effects of deep sea-bed mining can thus not be seen to be confined only to the plankton and nekton, but must also be recognized for their ecosystem-related, more distant effects. Our understanding of interrelations are, however, meager since there hardly exists any good quantitative data on the composition, numbers, and biomass of organism populations at greater depths.

Research perspectives: Deep-sea ecosystem analysis

The risk evaluations for deep seabed mining require analyses and total perspectives of regional systems that are not at all understood, and of large spatial systems that are only beginning to be understood. Biological investigations of the deep sea at various spatial and temporal scales must therefore be supplemented by investigations of the non-living environment in order to be capable of ecological evaluation and further use. The characterization of water masses, light and particulate conditions, horizontal and vertical currents, and water chemistry required for meaningful results in the plankton and nekton investigations falls primarily upon the appropriate non-biological disciplines. The biological work itself entails collecting/analysis and experimental components. It must, since it is long-term, begin distinctly before the disturbances resulting from commercial mining in order to document the biological structures and processes in their natural state. In addition to a population analysis, the basic biological processes and rates must be determined which in all probability contribute to structuring the entire deep sea system.

Basic to the pelagic investigations is the determination of vertical distributions of organisms and their living communities within the water column. Through this, we receive information on where and how the biological relationships change with increasing depth. Counts of individuals and biomass values are required to determine animal assemblages, associations, and population sizes, as well as to ascertain their temporal and spatial fluctuations. In this connection are mentioned above all the diurnal and ontogenetic vertical migrations carried out especially by the organisms of the deep scattering layer for feeding and reproduction in the surface layers, but also those that were observed for near-bottom living animals.

The population analyses must be supplemented by laboratory work on species-specific determinations of physiological and biological processes such as feeding rates, respiration rates, digestion rates, reproductive and mortality rates, as well as of physical condition (biochemical structure). The totality of these quantitative data is a precondition for descriptions of the biological material flows through the water column and their changes by means of mathematical models.

Finally, corresponding comparative investigations are to be undertaken on organism communities and species *in situ* in the disturbed environment or under controlled laboratory conditions. Indirect, long-term effects, which in part consist of sublethal manifestations, can only be recognized through experiments using indicator species. This includes the physical particle loads on gelatinous or mucus-producing organisms which limits their drifting or swimming abilities and reduces their narrow energy reserves, especially when the animals take up unusable particles during feeding. Toxicological effects of released metal compounds upon organisms can again be revealed only through use of indicator species in appropriate experiments. Pressure and temperature appear to be the essential critical parameters for the experimental work.

A condition for answering all questions posed is a definitive identification of species. This requirement is extremely difficult and time consuming since especially the bentho-pelagic fauna contains numerous, still unknown species upon which relatively scattered work has been done worldwide. This assignment also requires close co-operation with scientists at other institutions.

IV. The TUSCH (Tiefsee-Umweltschutz) Research Group

1. National Aspects

The work of the Research Group is to be carried out primarily in the South Pacific (Peru-Bauer Basin) in the region of a German mining claim. In this way the activity will not only serve the purposes of environmental research, but will also provide environmental data for industry. The TUSCH Research Group which includes, in addition to participating scientists from the institutions listed below, representatives from the federal government, from agencies and from commercial organizations. Through this membership, there is a coupling with economic and political developments. This is of particular significance with the present Research Group since meaningful evaluations for deep seabed mining can only be undertaken when mining technology and potential impact levels are known and can be addressed by appropriate research activities.

Scientists from the following institutions are currently associated with the TUSCH Research Group:

Institute for Biochemistry and Marine Chemistry of the University of Hamburg (IFB);

Institute for Marine Science of the University of Hamburg (IFM);

Institute for Hydrobiology and Fishery Science of the University of Hamburg (IHF);

Federal Hydrographic Office, Hamburg (BSH);

Geological-Paleontological Institute of the University of Kiel (GPI);

Institute for Applied Physics of the University of Kiel, Department of Marine Technology (IAP);

Research Center for Marine Geosciences of the University of Kiel (GEOMAR);

Federal Agency for Geology and Raw Materials, Hannover (BGR);

Institute for Fluid Mechanics of the University of Hannover (IFS);

Center for Marine Raw Materials of the Technical University of Clausthal (ZRM);

Institute for Mineralogy and Mining, University of Aachen (IML).

2. International Aspects

The development of research on deep-sea environmental protection in the Federal Republic of Germany is summarized in this document. In Great Britain, the Natural Environmental Research Council is financing a project which is attached to DISCOL. France, India and the Soviet Union have begun to assemble basic data on their mining claims, and Japan plans, possibly jointly with the USA, to follow the impacts of a mining test (PPMT). In the USA, experimental research has been discussed and related pilot experiments have been carried out.

While past and present research plans involve small individual projects which can be carried out on a national basis, scientists from the TUSCH Research Group consider international cooperation to be very important in order to secure efficient work in this broad field. It also considers it to be extremely important that large-scale test mining be accompanied by extensive monitoring for evaluation of impacts of deep sea-bed mining. A pre-condition for this is that such tests should far exceed the magnitude of the PPMTs carried out in 1978/79, so that the results can be extrapolated to commercial mining. This implies that considerable effort must be carried out with optimal international co-ordination.

Discussion

Jenisch:

First, I see a problem regarding the unlimited liability as foreseen in the draft environmental protection regulations which have been highlighted by Mr *Harders*. As industries usually take out insurance policies for their activities, an unlimited liability might not be insurable.

Second, the impressive list of obligations imposed on deep sea-bed miners is perhaps a disincentive for the mining industry, pioneer investors or other potential miners to undertake any activities and invest in deep sea-bed mining. My question to Mr *Harders* is, therefore, whether you have been in contact with representatives of the mining industry to receive their reactions to the draft mining code regulations — and if not, what would be their foreseeable reactions?

Harders:

As a newcomer to this field I have had indeed little contact with the mining industry so far. But the consortia are fairly cautious at the moment to go further into deep sea-bed mining and it seems that they have taken the approach of awaiting the developments which are coming in the future. The second question, as far as liability is concerned, is, of course, a major issue in this draft. We know from State practice that this liability issue carries the question of where to obtain insurance in order to cover this liability. Second, we are only able to insure the activities under the draft if the insurance business is capable of providing proper insurance. I may cite here the instance of Canada where we have the example of the Arctic Waters Pollution Prevention Act. This Act became operative two years after it was actually tabled in and brought through Parliament. This was simply because of the fact that no insurance for the strict liability provision of the Arctic statute was available. The question of liability in this case was a bar to having any operation under the Act. I do not know how the insurance business is responding to this draft, but I would think that we will have here a similar case.

Thiel:

I would like to add that we do have contacts with the industry, and the industry more and more takes care of the environment or considers that they have to take care. In most instances they realize that caring for the environment is not very expensive, it is a minor part of the total investment. And, I think, in this way they are still happy with the advice they get from the ecologists.

Koch:

Just one remark with regard to the question of Mr *Jenisch*. The industry interested in deep sea-bed mining obtained the draft on the protection of the environment, but so far, there has been no reaction from that side on the provisions of that draft. I do not know whether this is a good sign or a bad sign, we will have to wait and see.

Morrison:

To what extent do the licencing proposals or the mining code proposals concern the issue of limitation of liability and inadequate capitalization of the companies? Any insurance scheme, I know of, has a limitation of liability in it, which means that if the liabilities go over it, you go back to the resources of the company. Any mining operation, I know of, always tries to limit its liability in that way by keeping the operating company in a limited liability situation, and insolating the parent company from responsibility. Is there any control on that in the mining code?

Harders:

The draft does not have any ceilings regarding the limitation of liability at all, and I can say that the draft, at this stage, does not provide any ceilings for the liability of the contractor.

Kimball:

I would like to make three comments and ask one question of Mr *Harders*. One of the things that is very interesting about these draft regulations of the PrepCom is that they have gone further than some existing international law in some areas. In other areas they have gone back to some concepts that have evolved further since the LOS Convention itself was first adopted, for instance in the area of liability. Strict liability is now a concept that is promoted more, whereas liability is tied to wrongful acts in the LOS Convention.

One of the complications that you get into, in some of the details that are in the present draft regulations, is that, while no one would deny that at some point in time when mining activities may take place, a lot of detail will be required, a lot more specificity, at this point in time we do not know enough to be able to provide that detail. Yet these drafts in some cases are quite detailed. It might be useful to think about a general framework at the present time based on what we know, setting general standards that should govern sea-bed mining, leaving the details for a time when we have more information, for instance in relation to the question of limits to liability. There is no way, anybody can address limits to liability or the details of a liability régime at this time for deep sea-bed mining.

Just one comment on the industry viewpoint. There are a number of countries that have national laws regarding deep sea-bed mining, the US being one of them. The US law and regulations probably have more detail in relation to the environmental aspects of deep sea-bed mining than most of the others. While industry has not particularly favoured this, it is a part of doing business today, and a cost that industry has been willing to assume in the little bit of work they have already done on deep sea-bed mining.

The question I wanted to ask Mr *Harders*, is one he alluded to briefly in his presentation, in relation to the vessels engaged in deep sea-bed mining, whether in relation to prospecting, mineral recovery, processing or transport. It is clear that the LOS Convention does provide for measures to control pollution from vessels. What organ, do you think, should elaborate those rules in relation to vessels, because, certainly, if any processing takes place on vessels, it is not presently covered by the scope or mandate of the Sea-Bed Authority. Today there is some question about this, given the way the Convention is drafted, but basically processing was not meant to be covered by what the Sea-Bed Authority would regulate. I therefore wonder whether those rules should be developed through IMO, or, on the basis of national legislation, re-packaged and issued by the Sea-Bed Authority. How do you see those more detailed rules being written?

Harders:

As you pointed out, between the first working paper and the draft there seems to be a sort of development in steps. It is not a smooth development, some parts of the working paper have been kept in the draft and some good parts have been deleted. Now we are at a stage, where the draft still has to be developed. But as far as we do not have proper data to estimate what the harmful activities will actually be in the future, we can think about whether discretion should be the key for the Authority to manage these effects. But as I wanted to point out in my presentation, we have some experience so far from offshore régimes. These régimes approach the problem as to environmental pollution by discretionary powers granted to administrative bodies and through a framework of legislative instruments. Sure, one could take the same approach with regard to deep sea-bed mining, but it should be somehow balanced between the uncontrolled discretion of the Authority and having certain standards set by the draft, as long as the States Parties have an impact on the drafting of the rules. As to your question of whether the vessels engaged in the deep sea-bed activities and in having the material transported to the coast should fall under the scope of the draft: we have seen from the presentations by Prof. *Suess* and by Prof. *Thiel*, that there is considerable impact. At this stage, these activities are covered by either the MARPOL or the London Conventions but only to a limited extent in so far, as the operational activities are not covered but disposals only. It seems to me the better solution to have IMO working on the vessel source pollution, although the draft and the Convention address the serious pollution which is felt not just in the Area, but in distant ecosystems as well. I would like to have IMO retain the power to control the vessels engaged in deep sea-bed activities.

Picht:

Mr *Suess*, I assume we all like real numbers. Yet we need to interpret them and we need to know how you derived the numbers. With respect to your interpretation, maybe I have missed it, but I thought your presentation fell short of a conclusion with respect to the significance of the impact of oxidization on the ocean. Further, with respect to your assumptions, am I correct in having heard that for each ton of metal harvested there is the equivalent of 1,000 tons of material that is moved around and finally relocated again in the sea? Could you please explain how this comes about? I am not sure whether a factor of 1,000 is correct having listened to Mr *Thiel*'s presentation earlier. It appears to me that the numbers heavily depend on how we dispose the material stirred up. And if this is so, then your cube of 45 x 45 x 5 km might shrink to much smaller proportions.

Wolfrum:

My question follows the same line, Mr *Suess*. If I understood you correctly, the deep sea-bed serves, I say it in general terms and you may at once correct me, as a kind of buffer for oxygen. If your argument is that this buffer function cannot be preserved or upheld when deep sea-bed mining takes place, then it may undermine all attempts undertaken to protect the ozone layer.

As far as I remember, two different approaches to deep sea-bed mining were discussed in the industry circles, namely the so-called three metal and the four metal approach. If my recollection is correct, the three metal approach was favoured by many envisaging the abandonment of maganese at sea. Would that have additional negative effects?

Suess:

Let me begin with a brief clarification: I presented an example, using oxygen consumption to illustrate the kind of research one should be doing in order to get eventual answers. Obviously I do not have an answer yet, and therefore, arriving at a sweeping conclusion, as Mr *Picht* would like me to do, is quite premature. On the other hand, the question of whether or not such a box of ocean of 45 x 45 x 5 km being depleted of oxygen is significant or not, was actually intended for the audience to think about. Personally I think yes, it is extremely significant.

Your second point concerning the assumptions about the material that was being resuspended during the mining operation, being higher by a factor of 1,000.

I suppose that is a high estimate; but on the other hand, only 0.1 % of organic matter is assumed to be oxidized, which is a very conservative assumption. In summary my answer to your question is, yes, the factor 1,000 is on the high side, but the additional assumption of only 0.1 % of oxidizable carbon is definitely on the low side. Overall, the total estimate therefore should probably be quite reasonable.

The other two questions concerning the buffer capacity of the ocean in regard to oxygen: If such an anthropogenic activity, as deep sea-bed mining, causes an oxygen depletion comparable to that which takes place in the natural environment unaffected by mining, that illustrates the limit of this buffer capacity. Your second question about the disposition of the excess manganese, I can only surmise that it would probably not be pure manganese which is being added back to the ocean, but rather that this excess contains a considerable amount of other metals which could have harmful effects.

Thiede:

I would like to address also the topic *Erwin Suess* has spoken about. He described a project which consists of a very complex network of organizations of industries and academia and also government. I think, this is typical for the German set of boundary conditions to be able to carry out such a project. They are going to conduct a very complex investigation, they are going to collect a very complex and expensive set of data, maybe from one or two areas. As far as I can see, the personnel capacity of the German institutions will not last longer than to cover more than one or two areas. So, my question to the audience is, how do we go about getting other comparable data, what incentives are there for other nations, what kind of international steering is there from international organizations to carry out such studies of the deep sea environment?

The other point I want to make is that this type of investigation requires a type of a scientist which actually does not exist at the moment. Most of our marine scientists come from the classical disciplines like biology, chemistry or geology and so on, but this type of environmental topic requires individuals trained in interdisciplinary work. I cannot see the organizations which are able to carry out the massive training effort which is needed to make it feasible over a decade. Therefore, I would request from the national organizations a lot of incentive in steering to make it possible to train the people we need to carry out these investigations.

Koch:

I would like to come back to the discussion started by *Lee Kimball* and Mr *Harders* on the question of discretionary power of the Authority in interpreting the standards which should be contained in the rules on the protection of the environment. As we, at the moment, do not have enough knowledge to draw up concrete standards, we have to rely on criteria which are open to interpretation. They have to be elaborated more carefully at a later stage and supplemented and concretized in order to give the deep sea-bed mining enterprises in advance an exact picture of the concrete requirements for the protection of the environment. The draft foresees that. It provides in art. 105, para. 3 that these criteria, which are at the moment phrased in a very general way and are open to wide interpretation, that they should be elaborated at a later stage when sufficient knowledge is available. I think, this is a very important feature of the draft submitted by the Secretariat because it does not try to solve the problem now, at a time, when we lack the necessary knowledge, but leaves the way open for further elaboration. This approach has to be kept in any case. There was a debate in the Preparatory Commission whether the Authority is the right institution to further elaborate these criteria. Some doubt was voiced whether the Authority should be entrusted with this task, because the Authority has the Enterprise and may be more interested in deep sea-bed mining than in the protection of the marine environment. The fear is that the criteria, which will be elaborated further at a later stage, might not be sufficiently tough because of this conflict of interests. I do not see how we can avoid this, because in any case the States will be involved in the elaboration of the concrete standards. As members of the Authority and of other relevant organizations, they will be always in this conflict of interests.

Thiel:

I have two comments and one question. My first comment will address the question Prof. *Thiede* raised: Yes, there are not enough scientists to cover all the projects which should be done, but we are in contact with colleagues from other countries and we try to stimulate research in this direction internationally.

The next comment is on the mining code, and I would like to say that we all should very much appreciate that the environment is mentioned and included in the mining code. This is a very rare situation that in industrial developments the environment is considered early enough, that regulations can be developed in due time. In the mining code we find quite a number of expressions which were mentioned as well in the paper by Mr *Harders*, such as: harmful effects, adverse effects, damage etc. All these expressions are very nice to read, and we have to consider them, but all of these, of course, are not quantified. We need to quantify these terms also under oceanographic aspects. We are aiming at quantifications as well as this is done within other research groups. After some years we should be able to come up with proposals, how to define a harmful effect under these conditions of mining. And I think that we are proceeding in the right direction.

My question: we heard about the contractor and the duties of the contractor to conduct scientific work, as it is expressed in the mining code. Does this mean that the contractor has to do this work himself or does the contractor hire subcontractors? Who will be doing that part which is meant to be research? I think that the contractor cannot do it himself, so he does need the help of scientists. I think Mr *Harders* may be able to answer this.

Dicke:

I would like to make one short remark and ask a question for Mr *Harders*. The remark: scientists sometimes ask whether the notions they use are or are not true, and in this sense I would like to challenge the notion of an "anthropocentric approach" of environmental law. It is true, in international law that the overwhelming approach to protect the environment was concerned with interests of States and their citizens to use available resources. But is that an "anthropocentric approach"? In my view, this conclusion would reduce human beings to basically egoistic beings which have or have not interests. It would neglect that human beings are capable of taking responsibility. And it is this latter aspect which we have to take into account when it comes to the question of how legal norms can be founded. Legal norms cannot be founded upon self-interested, egoistic beings; on the other hand, every single legal norm must be founded upon the responsible freedom of human beings. Because the notion of an "anthropocentric approach" hides this important distinction, I would be very grateful if you could add a "so-called" before the term "anthropocentric".

Now my question: When you mentioned the enforcement of the draft, you elaborated on the liability rules, but you made mention of the reporting system, too. Could you, please, give some additional information with regard to this reporting system and, in particular, on the question of how the reports are to be evaluated?

Lee:

I would like to ask Prof. *Suess* to clarify one point. In his proposal, the maritime prospectus — does he intend to study the impact from the displacement of mining, does it include the placing back of materials, and whether they are of the same kind of impact? I noticed that Prof. *Wolfrum* has raised a similar question, which, a few days ago, I also asked Prof. *Thiel*. In Prof. *Thiel*'s presentation, he recommended that the waste or material should not go back to the marine environment. In that case that would raise, I think, difficulties in terms of investments. But it might be more economical if you can dispose of the 97 per cent of the three million tons of trail materials back to the marine environment. In your prospectus would this have any effect and should this be taken into account?

Harders:

I would like to address the question raised by Mr *Koch*, as his question touches upon further elaboration of the draft. We are in the critical situation that deep sea-bed mining seems to be visible, although we do not know when and under what terms. At the same time the scientists are still working on proper environmental protection and they have lined out of what has to be done. This problem would be either addressed by giving more discretion to the competent organ, the other way would be to have the most stringent requirements possible implemented. What experience do we have so far? The US have been in a position to come up with certain criteria of their deep sea-bed regulations. Although considerable discretion is retained, there are standards set up which limit this discretion. If discretion shall be retained in the draft, the next question would refer to the standard term of pollution we are using in the draft. "Serious harm" is the key-term of the draft which addresses the protection of the environment. This term will be further elaborated on by the Legal and Technical Commission. But the application of proper terms for pollution control is not just the answer to the question. The second part of the answer is that a liability system re-inforces the protection of the environment. These two components have to properly address the protection of the environment in the Area. In my opinion, it would not be the right approach to leave as much discretion as possible to the Authority and, as soon as we actually have deep sea-bed mining, to see then how it works and to come up with new standards. A middle way has to be found, and I think this draft will be not the last one.

I may now come to the question by Prof. *Thiel*. The quantifiable definitions of harm to the environment have to be further elaborated on by the Legal and Technical Commission in the future. But it is difficult to implement such a standard in the draft. Of course, we will have independent consultants advising the Legal and Technical Commission in addition to the scientists and experts represented in the Commission. At any time the Commission itself is in a position to call upon independent consultants in order to ask for specialist assessment. As to the question regarding the contractor himself: as I see the draft, there is an obligation that the contractor himself has to have scientists available to him, who may be either directly employed or may be consultants working for him. These scientists are coming up with the assessment of the data collected during the activities. With this I may link my answer to Dr. *Dicke*'s question as that over the years, and the draft says "from time to time as necessary," the standards will be updated and reviewed by the Legal and Technical Commission. That means that the Commission will either raise the standards or lower the standards, so there is considerable flexibility in that.

Suess:

I would like to address Mr *Lee*'s questions first. My estimate did not differentiate between the displaced material and the returned material nor the tailings. However, it is very important to differentiate between the three, because the displaced material near the bottom behaves differently in regard of the consumption of oxygen than the returned sediment or the tailings. Probably the effects of the returned material would be higher than that of the displaced material because this is where the efficiency of the oxygen consumption comes in. In that regard my estimate was conservative. The last comment I would like to reserve to *Jörn Thiede*'s remark, which he addressed to the group here as a whole: How do we foresee this kind of research as being really globally applicable. *Hjalmar Thiel* has addressed this question already by saying presently we are limited by the number of scientists and expertise to do a proper job. I would imagine that the TUSCH initiative which originated from the Bundesministerium für Forschung und Technologie (Federal Ministry for Research and Technology) is an exemplary one in that it leaves planning and implementation up to the scientists as well as to the politicians. We think it is a good start to look at one or two areas and to then try working these out as examples for what could happen globally.

Round Table: Modifications to the Law of the Sea Convention: The Choice of the Right Format

Wolfrum:

To get the discussion started, I would like to pose to you a few questions. Before doing so, however, let me explain the assumptions upon which — I think — we all work.

I do believe that we all strive for a universally acceptable régime on the law of the sea, and that, given the new developments on the scientific, technological, and economical levels, the acceptability of the régime for the deep sea-bed needs to be enhanced. The second assumption is the following: we agree that deep sea-bed mining will not take place in the near future and that economic, technological, and scientific conditions and knowledge will have to increase before deep sea-bed mining may take place. Finally, I am sure that there is a widespread assumption that any deep sea-bed mining activity — should it ever take place — will have to take place under the *common heritage* principle. However, one should discuss what that exactly means.

These are my three assumptions. Let me on this very basis pose my questions which are designed to structure this discussion a little bit, although from experience I know that any attempt to structure a discussion is destined to fail.

Firstly, are there any questions which are cause for concern by some States at the moment and which need to be regulated or solved? If the answer is affirmative, which I assume, have these problems to be solved right now, or is there any possibility of postponing the solutions to certain problems? Secondly, if there are certain questions still to be solved, what is the appropriate forum? Thirdly, if such negotiations are successful, what is the best format to implement them, legally speaking? Let me again emphasize that these questions are simply a loose guideline for the discussion.

Ballah:

I want to start by responding to one of the assumptions, and as we do in the Prepcom and in the Special Commission, too, we have created a group, an expert group which is dealing with assumptions that would advise eventually as to what is the best operational option, or a range of options on which the PrepCom can decide. Now, assuming that commercially viable sea-bed mining is not likely to take place for another 20 to 30 years, is there any need then at this point in time to seek to modify any provisions of the Convention in Part XI because any modification or amendment that you make today might really in the light of the developing technology not be quite relevant at that point of time in the future? Is it not possible then for all States to accept the Convention as it is, because Part XI, which will not become applicable or at least not before 25 or 30 years, is really in a Convention a non-implementable part of it, which would be virtually in a state of animated suspension? Now, some of us have felt that as a result it is neither necessary, nor desirable, nor practicable to make any modifications to the Convention at this time. It is not necessary, maybe, because the Convention already represents a balance of those competing and conflicting interests, and that balance is delicate and sensitive. And, therefore, Part XI is part of that whole process, particularly since it is a non-implementable part in the short or medium term. It can therefore be ignored. Can we arrive at a position whereby we all can agree, if Part XI needs to be modified or amended, that only that part of it will be amended? I have my doubts. I doubt that we can isolate just that part of it. And if the parties agree to any modifications of the Convention as such, whether those parties who are not quite satisfied with some of the other provisions would agree. Take, for example, Trinidad and Tobago as a small, geographically disadvantaged State, a small distant water "fisher" in the Caribbean which it has been traditionally and habitually for a number of years. We are quite dissatisfied with the provisions on the access to the surplus in the EEZ. And, therefore — that is important for us — maybe, the deep sea-bed provisions are not as important for us. We may therefore seek to open up certain issues on which accomodations have been reached. Take for example: you give up something in order to get the major maritime powers to come aboard the Convention. You give transit passage, you give archipelagic sea lane passage, and you give that in exchange, hopefully for the major maritime powers, to be more generous in their approach of Part XI, so that they would agree to the *common heritage* principle. And, therefore, in that regard, is it not important to protect the navigational interests of the whole international community as against a resource interest of some coastal States? Some of us fear that if we go back into reopening some issues, the territorialists (there used to be a group like that) will now want that total and complete bundle of rights in their territorial seas. Are these not greater dangers than a danger of a Part XI, which may not come into play for another thirty years? And these are some of the questions which, I think, need to be answered. It is not desirable in all parts and I think, Prof. *Edward Miles*, my good friend and compatriot, has said that not only is it not useful to try to modify it at this point of time, but it is downright dangerous to do so. I think what he did say was that it is dangerous, because there are significant points of instability on the line of the rest of the treaty, I think he also went on to say that (well he did not quite say it like that, he is far too gentle) it is an international legal absurdity basically for people to believe that the rest of the treaty with all its delicate instability really constitutes something called customary international law.

Rebagliati:

I would like to make the point. In fact, Mr *Ballah* provoked me, because I share many of the ideas he put forward, but I do not necessarily share his conclusions. I would like to dispute these arguments, although I fully share many of his fears.

When we recall the situation in which the international community was in the late '60s, it was potentially dangerous speaking about the law of the sea, and the conclusion finally was that the *common heritage of mankind* was a concept to be shared. Within this concept and the package deal envisaged at that time, the Law of the Sea Conference was convened in 1970 by resolutions 2749 and 2750 of the General Assembly. At that time we all remember the national legislations' mosaic and also the regional approaches to the law of the sea. They were not necessarily concurrent and compatible and the whole international community was, both on the academic level and on the State level — the government level — deeply worried about the possibilities of conflicts, conflicts in relation to navigation or overflight, fishing, etc. We can all remember that it was true for all regions, not only for developing countries' regions, but equally and also included was the North Sea region. Of course, I am referring to fisheries conflicts that arose here with even potential use of force, though fortunately without any dramatic consequences.

I like to mention these elements because the aim of a general codification or progressive development of international law in the field of the law of the sea was felt at that time and was completed after many, many efforts in 1982 with the view of superseding that kind of very unsatisfactory and potentially explosive situation in the field of the law of the sea and peaceful relations, both from the economic point of view, from a point of view with respect to the exercise of rights and freedoms and, of course, regarding the benefit of countries which do need the natural resources of the seas, particularly adjacent to their coasts, for their own development. So, it looked like we nearly achieved this general package in a very difficult but orderly manner after many efforts in almost 10 years, a little less for the Conference, but a little more if we take into account the whole exercise.

Now, I was saying that I share his assumptions and amongst them is that the need for a universal acceptance of this law of the sea, either of this particular Convention or any other adjusted convention, is felt. It is appropriate to think about what would happen if the Convention does not achieve this universality we are willing to have but that we do not have at this moment. One of the possibilities is that of going back or even worse, to a situation similar to the late

'60s, and with examples put forward by Mr *Ballah*, and with interpretations which will vary with the Convention. The Convention does not embody customary international law in its totality. It, of course, incorporates several norms of customary law and it would not be necessarily illegal to proceed at variant with the Convention, either for Part XI or for the rest of the Convention. So, the explosive situation will easily arise from a legal and from a political point of view. The economic prejudices will be felt for all, but especially for the developing countries which need the resources of the sea in areas beyond national jurisdiction, and which really need capital for purely utilizing the resources in their own maritime jurisdiction, and will need the transfer of technology for their own scientific research in the oceans. The anarchic situation, though, may benefit some approach like the territorialist approach or some other opinion from a nationalistic point of view approach. It will hinder at the end the rights and interests of poor countries. Maritime powers will also face difficulties in trying to demonstrate that freedom of transit through straits and other elements of the package deal are customary law, although they cannot be qualified as such. There are many arguments which can be cited in any particular case because all the straits used for international navigation differ from each other. This is particularly one of the conflict areas with great potential.

That may be the situation as things go, if universality is not achieved and we again arrive at the assumption that for the time being the exploitation and exploration of the sea-bed is not urgent. I could take this point by Mr *Ballah* as something very relevant, that it is a potential area for conflicts, not necessarily at this moment, but it is latent. It may develop into conflicts if countries continue to behave in a manner which is without due regard to the Convention, because it is not in force. As the exploitation of the sea-bed will not take place in the immediate future, it would be an advantage to explore the possibilities of achieving that universality which we all share and to face a problem that we all recognize. The potential conflicts may arise in a moment in which vested interests in relation to the deep sea-bed are not clear. They are, of course, present, but they are not in immediate pursuit of the exploitation either through the régime or other unilateral or small groups of countries' arrangements, that, we all know, are prepared and were prepared and were ready to develop at the time it was felt that the exploitation could take place. So, I think, it could be opportune, to explore these possibilities in a timely fashion in order to achieve that universality which is needed for reasons I tried to summarize before.

Now, this adjustment, is it an adjustment concerning all aspects of the Law of the Sea Convention? I think, that all countries gave way somewhat in that Convention, and there is no single country that I can imagine that could have got all its positions fully reflected in the Convention, either in fishing or in navigation or in other forms and modalities of the uses of the seas. Of course, that was also true for Part XI. That was particularly one of the features of the package deal and global arrangement in which so many States are or were involved during the negotiations. So, there is such a possibility of a broad reopening, but the possibility of a success in that reopening for adjustments here and there, it is — I could say — completely marginal. The source for looking into a possible adjustment should be the main or key element that may be before us. And I identify it with a lack of universality, and that in turn leads us to the régime relating to the international sea-bed area. And for that reason I could foresee the possibility of the exploration of adjustments to the Convention and its related instruments, only, I would stress the feasibility not only in relation to Part XI — not because States are fully satisfied with all the other parts, but because it is an impossible task to adjust everything, and because particularly the reason for the lack of universality resides in this part.

I think, the present organ which is the Prepcom, would not be the place to explore these possibilities, because of legal and political implications. As for the legal implications, of course, we can always look for a legal argument and look for a reason. But in this very harmonious atmosphere, I could say, there is not a clear mandate for this commission to embark on this because it has a different responsibility and a mandate to fulfil. And also for political reasons, it is a matter of principle. It is not for an organ which is in line with the Convention, which is a consequence of the Conference, whose members are either parties or likely to become parties to the Convention, to embark in an exercise to amend it. The Commission represents an environment in which all members are likely to come to a general agreement. Precisely, those who are in disagreement are not members of the Commission, but the universality has to be sought with them. So, politically, it would be a kind of weird, little exercise that the Commission would embark on a possible negotiation in which one of the main parties is not legally present. And, again, it would be favouring the adjustment or amendment of the Convention in respect of which members of the Commission by themselves are in agreement. So, how can they favour an amendment without having an appropriate stand by the parties which are really looking for such an amendment?

And this is the last point. If we all share the view that universality is sought and there are parties that may be in a position to honestly embark themselves in looking for that universality, ways and means other than through the organs of the Convention or of the UN should be explored, at least at the earliest stages, and all, all parties concerned should participate in such an exercise. Otherwise it will just be a very futile effort towards a very, very unmeaningful result. So, I would suggest as a very first step the exploration of this issue in a very informal way (and the Conference on the Law of the Sea resorted to that procedure constituting several groups, one of those, which is well known, contributed very much to the success of the Conference, and that was the *Evensen* group which was referred to this morning). There are many of such experiences which States or delegates can benefit from. A last clarification is that in performing such an exercise, though the PrepCom may not be involved officially, members of it, I will not say "may," but I will say "should" be involved, and its authorities should also be involved. A very informal private and unofficial link between parties to this exercise and the PrepCom should be established, though that link will not have any meaning with respect to the lawful work that the PrepCom is performing.

Platzöder:

The question of modification of the deep sea-bed régime and the adoption of an appropriate legal instrument to give effect to such modifications, has in my mind three aspects: a historical, a political, and a legal aspect.

The deep sea-bed régime as contained in the Convention was more or less already adopted at Geneva in 1980. If my memories are correct, at that time there was a general feeling that the results of the negotiations were not satisfactory at all, neither to the industrialized nor to the developing countries. But it was also generally felt that the Conference was not in a position to do any better. It was very clear that much more work would have to be done and much of it would have to be left to other fora than the Conference. Consequently, Conference resolutions I and II were negotiated and relevant final clauses were incorporated into the final text. This approach, that the deep sea-bed régime would have to be further developed and later adjusted or modified, was common knowledge in 1980. One might even say that such an assessment of the situation was based on a consensus. In 1981, the United States changed its attitude and its delegation, and finally left the negotiations in 1982. I think that if the United States would have stayed with us, then we would not have to discuss the question of the format of modifications, because we would have altogether explored and exploited the Convention and would have developed the régime as contained in the Convention. This is the historical aspect.

The political aspect, I think, is the following: It is no secret that the work of the Preparatory Commission is overshadowed by the fact that the United States has not returned. And it is not known whether the US Government will continue its policy of the empty chair forever. It is, however, known that the US Government has different problems with the Convention, as other industrialized countries with interests in deep sea-bed mining. I think, as long as this uncertainty of whether the US comes back or not prevails, it is difficult to achieve results in improving or adjusting the Convention. It has been suggested that a protocol might help out during this impasse.

Speaking as a lawyer now, I think, I can agree with our Chairman, Mr *Jesus*, that we should first discuss substance, and second the question of format. But we also have experienced that in international politics, problems of substance can sometimes be overcome by formal or procedural devices, and for these reasons, I would like to see the question of the format also as a means to pave the way for a comeback of the United States. I think, we should at least see if and whether a proper format, even if it is only a specific term, would facilitate the United States in rejoining the negotiations. A protocol, legally speaking, might raise some difficult problems, because the Convention contains specific amendment procedures and also a provision in art. 311 concerning the relation between the Convention and other agreements. I think, we would have to be very careful that the protocol fits into the amendment procedures and in art. 311. Lawyers have to be very innovative and inventive sometimes, and I am sure that these difficulties could be overcome.

Maybe, I can make a very preliminary proposal. The Conference started with a gentleman's agreement, and why should not the long process be concluded with a gentleman's agreement? We could elaborate provisions which would enable the Convention to be ratified by many States, if we could waive or suspend certain provisions which are not relevant today, because deep sea-bed mining might not take place for a long time.

Zegers Santa Cruz:

We are speaking of a quest for universality here, and we have a Convention which is signed by practically the whole world except around ten countries, among which the most notable are the United States, the Federal Republic of Germany, and the United Kingdom, and those countries have objections to Part XI, that is to the sea-bed provisions. Taking note of this, the Group of 77, or its chairman, made an important statement last year, saying that the group was prepared to hold — I do not remember what the word was — conversations or dialogue or negotiations, including people who are not necessarily participating in the work of the Preparatory Committee, for the object of achieving universality. After that, the General Assembly discussed a resolution on the Law of the Sea, and in that resolution, the idea of the Chairman of the Group of 77 was incorporated. It was discussed at the time of the resolution, whether some other issues could be discussed in these negotiations and they were excluded: it was limited to aspects of Part XI, not defined. I think we are there, from the moment that everybody is a signatory of the Conference except a few countries. Those who are not prepared to sign at the moment mainly object to parts of the sea-bed régime. There lies our discussion and that — I think — is the thrust of what the Group of 77 and the General Assembly said. I heard the eloquent, clever, and well-presented point of Ambassador *Ballah* that was brilliant, but I believe that, at the moment, we are there.

Now, if this is the case, I would try to give a reply to your three questions. Can some questions or issues be postponed? Ambassador *Jesus* made a proposal. He made a division of issues, he said that some issues have to be solved before the entry into force of the Convention, but others could be left for a review after the entry into force of the Convention. I would add to that, it was discussed this morning, the possibility of using art. 154 of the Convention, the periodical review.

To make a review, imagine, we have two sets of problems: one set would be resolved before the entry into force, and the second after the entry into force. There could be a kind of review which is not the review of the following article, it would be a review in which probably the work would be conducted by consensus, and in which pending matters or the matters we have decided to review could be examined. I think, Ambassador *Jesus* suggested a list of questions which would have to be resolved now.

He mentioned amendments to the review clause as relates to amendments to Part XI, the legal problem of having an amendment to Part XI approved by three-quarters of the members without going to Parliament. He said that it was a non-issue, because everybody was in agreement to settle it. Then he mentioned one problem in decision-making, which was the insured seat for the United States. Again, he said, it was a non-issue, because everybody would agree to that. He mentioned a third thing, which was the cost and size of institutions, and he gave the reasons why those could easily be settled in the first stage.

Then he mentioned, if I am not wrong, the problems of the transfer of technology, economic policy on the sea-bed and other issues for a second stage. The issues could probably be divided into two parts and one could use the periodic review of the five years.

I have the idea that we should be flexible. We have here discussions, consultations, negotiations; all this is a process, and for that we need a lot of flexibility and perhaps a lot of fora. They can be academic fora, they can be informal gatherings, they can be informal groups, but, of course, a rôle must be played by the Preparatory Commission. That rôle is to be determined by the results of consultations, dialogues, academic exercises, etc. It would be desirable that they go through the Preparatory Commission in a given mode.

As to how all these things could be done legally, I believe, it is more important first to have a substantive agreement. I am told that in the recent conference on the ozone layer, countries agreed to in fact amend the Montreal Protocol without the requisites of the Montreal Protocol, in order to get into effect the prohibition of fluorocarbons before time. With an unanimous agreement it will be done, because there was a political will to do it. The rules of the Vienna Convention were in a way not needed and maybe it can be done again. If it could be done, it would be much better to have authoritative consensus decisions by the Preparatory Commission, for instance. If not, we would probably need a protocol which would form an integral part of the Convention, at least for the amendment part. But if it were a protocol, one would have to be very careful, because one would have to end with a protocol if one had exhausted everything else and not begun with that decision. If we began with a protocol, people will want everything within the protocol, it would be the negotiation of a new conference on the law of the sea. So, I think, the legal form is the very last part of it. These are my reflections.

Jesus:

I believe that I have tried to address in my statement two of those issues, that is to say, the need to address the problems, the question of the forum in a very detailed manner, and I purposely left out my ideas on the question of format, or form of any kind of recommendation to be made to the issues of Part XI. Let me add something that I have said in respect to the two issues, that I have spoken about extensively in my statement, and like some of the comments or views expressed here today. On the first issue we have addressed the problems now. I believe that I have made more or less known my views on this issue by devising a dichotomy in accordance with which certain of the issues would have to be necessarily dealt with now before the entry into force of the Convention, as the prerequisite to rally the support of those that have problems with Part XI, so that by having achieved satisfaction on those points, they could become parties to the Convention, and a second element of that dichotomy is to leave the substantial issues for later negotiations dependent on two conditions, rather conditions on two events to be produced in the passage of time. One is the happenings that have to take place from now up to the creation of conditions for operation in sea-bed mining, which — as some people say — might not take place in 20, 30 years from now. That condition makes it impossible for us even if there was the political will to address all of the problems, to realistically address the issues, because we might be reaching consensus or compromising on issues that we do not know about, due to the fact that they depend on factual circumstances, that we will know in the future.

So, from the pragmatic point of view, it is important that even when we are politically in agreement to address those issues, that we leave them for a later consideration, at which time we will be in a better position to know the grounds that we are stepping on. The other condition was by delaying the consideration of those issues to a later stage, those issues that I tried more or less in general terms to indicate, we would be facilitating the political compromise that we could reach at this stage before the entry into force of the Convention, precisely to rally the support of those countries that have had difficulties to join the Convention. Now, it is a fact that some have said that without the United States in the PrepCom it will be difficult for us even to reach compromise on those issues that I said — in accordance with my view — could be solved before the entry into force of the Convention.

Let me make a factual statement here in this regard. The United States has, in accordance with the rules of procedure of the Preparatory Commission, the right and the prerogative to fully participate in the deliberations of the Preparatory Commission, as the United Kingdom and FRG have been doing. These two delegations are observers to the Preparatory Commission, but they have the same rights in the Preparatory Commission as any full member of the PrepCom, because we made this decision in the beginning. They can fully participate in the work of the Preparatory Commission, in fact they have been more active than many member delegations, as we all know. They can make proposals as any other delegation, can argue contrary to any other proposal that might have been made. So they are full participants, and in fact our rules and procedures maintain that they have the right to fully participate in the deliberations of the Preparatory Commission, the only thing that they do not have, and that makes them different from the full members, is the right to vote. But we do not negotiate in the PrepCom and take decisions by voting. So, therefore, in practical terms, there is no difference whatsoever. Had the United States decided in the context of this kind of compromise to come to the Preparatory Commission, to try to bring its views to the solution of those issues that can be solved, we would be closer to compromises.

Now, I believe that on the question of format of the amendments we should pursue this from the perspective of what has to be done. I have always avoided the term "amendment," as I did in my statement or in any conservation that they have, to avoid this legal complication that would arise if you were to think about amendments even before the entry into force of the Convention. To me, there is no need in fact for us to come up with a protocol, a formal legal document, to introduce formal amendments to the Convention before the entry into force of the Convention. If we are in fact taking into account that any accommodation to be made was to be made upon the strategy that I tried to apply, in other words the granting of a seat to the United States in the Legal and Technical Commission and in the Council, to address the problem of decision-making, to take care of the problems that sometimes emerge with decision-making in the Council and the Assembly and the financial aspect of these institutional arrangements, to take away the fear that many, if not all delegations have, arising out of financial concerns, if we were to address those things, in my view, we would not need a formal document to amend the Convention. And why? First, because we will get rid of the legal difficulty and probably a political difficulty to do so before the entry into force of the Convention. Second, because we would be totally within the current mandate, in my mind, of the PrepCom to address the problem. The strategy that I have been following is to address the difficulty of decision-making procedure in the Council and the Assembly, as I have tried to explain in my statement, through the mechanisms of the Legal and Technical Commission and through the mechanisms of the Financial Committee. And there we have ample mandate to deal with it, whatever the people participating in the work of the PrepCom decide as to the decision-making in those organs is totally within the mandate of the PrepCom, because the Convention does not indicate what kind of procedures should be adopted by these two bodies in the decision-making. So, we would have full mandate to address these problems, if this problem of decision-making was to be addressed in the framework of the strategy that I have devised.

Now, on the question of financial institutions it is obvious that even there we do not have any problems because it seems to me that everybody agrees on the reduction of costs to the maximum. On the question of a seat for the United States, I do not think, that it would be out of our mandate to make a recommendation as a matter of a gentlemen's agreement to the Authority that whenever those organs were to function, the United States would be given a seat in its capacity as a major producer, as one of the largest investors and so on. So, those are the issues that, I think, we can address totally within our mandate and not involve formal amendments.

Now, the problem that might require some formality is the agreement in accordance of which Part XI will not be implemented, that is to say, the rules and provisions of the Convention as well as regulations, that we might have prepared in the PrepCom dealing with the exploration and the exploitation of resources, will not be implemented, until the Authority itself through the mechanisms that they will choose at that time, and in confrontation with events that meanwhile will happen, will take a look at the whole set of the problem of the mining operation of the Enterprise, in the light of the environmental studies that meanwhile have to be undertaken, in the light of the market conditions of that time that might dictate different approaches to production ceiling, in the light of the evolution of the technology and the property rights that meanwhile might happen to influence a kind of solution for the difficulty we face with compulsory transfer of technology. In the light of these happenings, then the Authority, through the mechanisms it would choose, could address the problems. I do not want to use the word amendment and I am not going to use it because it might cast a negative impact upon the strategy.

Between the position of those that would like to get rid of the international sea-bed régime and of those that have substantial difficulties with the régime and would like to see it modified, there lies a possibility of a compromise based on a kind of a moratorium in the implementation. But knowing that, the régime would at a later stage be taken up again for adjustments thus salvaging Part XI. That is my idea. If that was to be such a compromise on the second element of my approach, then the question that might be posed, as I said, is, which format should have such a compromise? A protocol, a gentlemen's agreement, as has been suggested here, an understanding as we have been doing in the practice of the Preparatory Commission? I believe that a gentlemen's agreement adopted by the Preparatory Commission, an understanding, an agreement of understanding as we have been doing in the PrepCom on various issues, would take care entirely of the concern of those that would like to have a kind of formal document, embodying any kind of agreement, but I do understand the problems that some countries might have with respect to the "visibility," as Prof. *Treves* put it the other day, when he mentioned that such a document should have a form so as to influence the parliaments of those that have to ratify or accede to the Convention. But, in doing so, we might be aware of legal problems that might arise. I tried the other day to answer the question posed by Prof. *Treves*, to explain one of those problems. And that was, if we were to require a formal document, protocol or other embodying such an agreement to be part and parcel of the ratification or accession process, then we would have to think that such a protocol would also have to be ratified by those 43 countries that have ratified the Convention, and that might pose a lot of difficulties and even bring problems into the process of entry into force of the Convention itself. So, that is one of the problems that might arise.

Another problem, and this seems to be more substantial, a legal one, that might arise with such a protocol being part and parcel of the Convention, and having to be adopted formally, signed and ratified, is the fact that the Convention seems to imply that no other documents, no other legal document adopted, legally speaking, would change any provision of the Convention, to the extent that even, if you agree to that document, the argument can be made, that the document cannot supersede the Convention. If you go to the final clauses, you will find substantial argument for this position. Now, if you were to agree to give satisfaction to all those through a gentlemen's agreement, to an understanding of the task of the PrepCom to embody such an agreement, to delay the consideration of the substantial part of the mining code for a later stage, then the amendments to be made to the system itself would have to be made in the context of the review conference, in which case it totally fall within the philosophy of the Convention for changes to be made to it. In other words, you will have to guarantee that changes can be made at a later stage, at which time the mechanisms for amendments to the Convention can be easier introduced to the Convention than now, at least in legal terms. One could thus anticipate the application of the letter and spirit of art. 155 related to the Review Conference in respect to the Convention. The only change that one would introduce is the change of the time period in which to implement that article and not its substance.

I think, that is a reasonable thing to do, especially in the view that the anticipation of the application of art. 155, para. 2 was dictated by changing circumstances. If we were to reach agreements to do so, I do not think, it would create major legal difficulties. Those are my views on the question of format. To me the format cannot be seen irrespective of the substance. If you are going to solve the substantial issues, then perhaps you would need a formal document, but I believe that it is difficult to convince the majority of us here that we could solve all the problems now, for the two reasons that I have tried to outline. What we should do at this stage, is to rally the support of those that have problems with the Convention. In my view, as I previously stated, we address their concerns by giving them some satisfaction and delaying a solution for a later stage, a delaying in such a way as to give them the assurance that the pending issues will be addressed in due time in the future, and that is the only way that we can salvage Part XI and the related annexes. The other radical way is to just forget the system. Politically, it seems difficult to have the support of the overwhelming majority of countries just to accept such a radical solution and legally it might jeopardize the whole Convention.

Valle:

Being a diplomat, I cannot totally dissociate my thoughts from those of my government. I must say, at the outset, that the final answer of Brazil to the text of the Convention will be coming in the next few months. The Executive will be submitting a draft law to Congress in order that national legislation be adjusted to the Convention provisions as a whole, mainly the question of the territorial sea, the EEZ, the continental shelf etc. In my personal capacity I could disagree with that decision, but I do not. It would be quite paradoxical for me to do so. Therefore my views on the Convention should be clear. On the other hand, I am, of course, realistic, and in being so, I have advocated as others, as all of us probably, the need for universalization, and as previous speakers have said, we must devise a strategy in order to reach universalization and to make the Convention acceptable to those parties, that — I do not want to single out countries — have not gone beyond signing the Final Act. But there are questions that may allow us to further reflect on how to reach a compromise. One of them is the conclusion that we have come to through a group of experts that deep sea-bed mining will take 20 to 25 years. So, why concentrate immediately on questions pertaining to deep sea-bed mining. Therefore, timing is on our side in this case. This allows us room for reflection and reinterpretation of certain provisions of the Convention. I would not favour a revision of the text at this time. I do not think that its effectiveness has been tested as it has not come into force. However, we still have not exhausted consultations. We have held consultations within the PrepCom, outside the PrepCom, bilaterally, in small groups, in several formats. We have not institutionalized anything other than the PrepCom, but I would not discard any possibilities in terms of consultations. The rôle of the PrepCom is crucial, but it is limited because many countries, or several countries, do not attend the PrepCom. The rôle of the Chairman in his personal capacity is crucial and has been during the past few years, and the rôle of the UN Secretariat should be essential as a neutral body, which can come up with possible grounds for compromise.

Allow me now to say a few words on the Group of 77. The Group of 77 are placed in a singular situation within the framework of negotiations. Why? Because they — the 77 — are practically the equivalent of those who have ratified the Convention. There are two groups: One is the group of countries that have ratified the Convention, the other is a political, informal group established to negotiate on behalf of developing countries. In this case there is a coincidence in that almost all of the ratifying States are members of the G-77. Therefore, the burden on the so-called "77" is much larger, or it can be seen as much larger, since we are the core of the ratifying States. The Group of 77 has played a very important rôle in the past few years, especially if we consider one particular issue which is the implementation of the pioneer investors obligations. We have shown extreme flexibility. There was a minor break-through, if I might call it that in the session of Jamaica, where we came to agree on an approach to the implementation of these negotations. We are also a realistic group. We are loyal to our principles, but for the sake of getting the PrepCom out of the situation in which it was, we aim to find common ground which may, as Mr *Jesus* said in the morning, lead us to a satisfactory conclusion in August, through an agreement which is implementable, and resume at a later stage questions that still cannot be settled. So, in summary, by all means let us strive for universalization; but in my view we should still try to protect one of the major legal documents produced by the United Nations in its history, without premature amendments. As I said, there is room for reinterpretation; there is room for deferral, but I do not think that right now there is room for rewriting.

Kiderlen:

I can directly relate to what Mr *Valle* has just said: I think there is a unanimous opinion shared by all of us, that we need the Convention, and we need it in a universal way, because the Convention without universality will not serve its purpose. I think, there is a conviction, a very broad one, to that extent from America to India, from Germany to New Zealand.

The stumbling stone on the way to universality, of course, is Part XI, the deep sea-bed mining régime being tied into the package of this Convention, which in fact forms two Conventions in one. Well, the question of how to deal with Part XI gave birth to all kinds of ideas and combinations. One of them was to make use of the possibility of an advanced application of the rest of the Convention, other than Part XI. This probably gets close to the limits of the Vienna Convention and also may not be completely appropriate in the situation in which we find ourselves. Indeed, to some extent we also need Part XI now: Although the exploitation of the sea-bed is not at hands, we need regulations for the interim phase of deep sea-bed mining, that is for the phase before exploitation takes place. This phase may include exploration, training, research, in particular environmental research, and also other business.

So, the thesis has been forwarded, and I do support it, that we should deal with what is necessary for this interim phase, now, and postpone the discussion of the rest of Part XI. That is, we should not aim at perfect solutions now, of what we might think would fit Part XI, but just think of those things which are within our grasp and which we need to deal with in the framework of that interim régime. In this respect it also seems legitimate to single out Part XI, and insofar, I think, the position is legitimate not to open the Pandora's box of changes of the whole of the Convention, but to limit ourselves to Part XI. Of course, Part XI is part of the overall package of the Convention, but it also is a special part, a package deal in itself, and the rest of the Convention also forms in itself a package deal. The second argument would be that, at least in the perspective of an interim régime, we would not try to change the balance between these two sub-package deals, but rather adapt the one area, the area of Part XI, to the changing reality under a very practical and pragmatic view. This adaptation would not be a change in relation to the other parts of the Convention. So I think, there is a strong argument to limit ourselves in our endeavours to Part XI.

But here we arrive at another crucial question: What is it that has to be done at this time? I think we are faced with a broad preparedness to come to pragmatic solutions, and, I think, that is really what unites us and will bring us forward. On the other hand, we have to be aware of the necessity that all our parliaments will have to ratify the Convention as it stands, with all the details of Part XI which have been discussed and negotiated more than ten years ago. I think, the original sin, so to speak, has been committed at the time when all these tiny and detailed regulations came into the Convention, which we do not partly like anymore for very pragmatic reasons. Partly, perhaps, we do not like them because of fundamental and more ideological concerns. So, the limited, pragmatic approach which we may envisage to deal with Part XI gets into a kind of dilemma, when we have to present the whole of the Convention to parliament. At the end of our pragmatic approach, therefore, we must have a solution which to some extent addresses also those issues which we do not have, and do not want to have on our table now, because we have to tell parliament how it should look at those regulations concerning the Review Conference, production limitation, technology transfer, all these things that might not be of great importance now, but which are in the Convention. In order not to return to a kind of comprehensive approach, which we all do not like, we must try to address these problems in an appropriate way, we must at least include in our pragmatic approach some clear guarantees, on the one hand guarantees, of course, that the sea-bed mining régime, which might be applied in 20, 30, or 35 years, will not be a régime completely different from what is in the Convention, on the other hand, some guarantees for possibilities of reviewing these provisions which have not been tackled now in the framework of an interim régime, when the time comes, so that no automaticity is envisaged or included in our solutions as to what may happen 20 or 30 years from now. So, we are facing the challenge not just to install a kind of interim régime. It might, indeed, not be so difficult to combine an interim régime with a qualified moratorium of deep sea-bed mining and I think, solutions are more or less at hands. But also, and that is the second part of our endeavour, we have to lay the grounds for a perspective of a fair deal for those other matters which we might like to reconsider before deep sea-bed mining really becomes operational. Altogether, when we limit our task to what is necessary now, we still have to open up a perspective, already now, for that later stage of consideration of Part XI which for the moment we do not want to address.

Kapumpa:

Mr *Wolfrum*, I shall confine myself, as much as possible, to some of the very good introductory questions you raised and by agreeing that I hope to be able to come out with my personal point of view of this very important issue. The three assumptions you gave are agreeable to me. The first one being that we are all anxious to find a universally acceptable Convention and that there are certainly some difficulties to achieve such universality. Deep sea-bed mining is not likely to take place in the next few years. Eight years ago it was thought to be just around the corner. Finally, and much more important, are the difficulties inherent in the assertion that whatever deep sea-bed mining will be done, it will be done under the overall umbrella of the *common heritage of mankind*.

Now, Mr *Wolfrum*, you posed three questions, the first one being that whether or not there are some issues, some questions which concern some States, and if these can be resolved now or later. The answer, I think, is obvious. The answer to these issues that some countries have is that even my own country does have some problems with the Convention, but fortunately, there are no problems which have precluded us from signing the Convention in 1982 and ratifying it the following year. I am aware that some countries do have problems that are much more difficult to resolve than in my country. How do you discuss such issues in an appropriate forum? I think we have to go back slightly, and more or less what most people have said, that if the United States had remained within the forum of the Preparatory Commission after Montego Bay, (well, they did not come to Montego Bay but I am assuming had they come to Montego Bay) and remained with us, I think, today, what we are discussing would be a non-issue, and I sincerely believe that if they had signed the Final Act, and, thereafter, continued to participate as observers, they would have discovered that some of the concerns in fact could be resolved very easily. The problem we had is the United States not participating in our discussion groups, and even their friends — FRG, Britain or such countries — would not speak on behalf of the United States. Therefore, it also means that even the concerns they would have wanted to raise, they were not able to raise them. Unfortunately this means that the longer we stay away from each other, the more we misunderstand each other's intentions and views. We all know this from a very simple analogical human level: If you quarrel with your wife, or your girlfriend, or whomever, and you decide not to talk to each other for two hours, and if you come back two hours later you may find that you had nothing to quarrel about. But if you decide that because you have quarrelled, you will not speak to each other for the next six months, you may get a divorce, unless, of course, you had the intention to get a divorce, then that is a different matter!

So, Mr *Wolfrum*, I have a feeling that if the United States would have remained with us and we had continued to talk to each other, we could have discovered that their concerns were and are really not difficult to resolve. Hence last year,

I was privileged to serve as the Chairman of the Group of 77, and I issued that statement not only as Chairman of the Group of 77, but I believe in that statement as well. In that statement, it was said that we are ready to talk to the United States or any other country about their concerns, and that we would not set any preconditions to such a discussion, and that was, I think, a very bold statement in the sense that we did not want to say: First of all, come to the Preparatory Commission and then we will talk to you! Or first of all, sign the Final Act and then we can talk to you! We simply said, we can sit down and talk. The hope of that statement is that we can now begin, first of all, to understand what these concerns of the United States are, particularly in relation to Part XI. And now, as this particular, very timely symposium is indicating, we are all agreed that we have become cleverer than we were in 1982, and we have now concluded that sea-bed mining is not around the corner. Therefore, the issue of Part XI is not at present difficult to take care of, in the sense that the diplomatic style of putting aside issues which need not immediately be resolved can be applicable in this particular case. That is number one.

Number two: We have discovered that in the Preparatory Commission we have been able to resolve some problems which looked like they could not be resolved then by virtue of creative interpretation of rules and regulations, and arising out of that we formulate understandings: the New York Understanding and Declaration on the question of resolution II and the time table therein to implement it, to overcome the overlaps on the applications by pioneer investors. This is quite a clear example. What we are doing now in determining the issue of implementing the obligations of the registered pioneer investors, is another example of the style, the methodology, we can apply, without the necessity of amending the Convention, to resolve the problems that the United States and any other country may have.

That even brings me to the third point, Mr Chairman, that is the question that if there are those problems, what is the best format in which it could be done, and what is the forum in which this could be done. First of all, as somebody, who is a full member of the Preparatory Commission, my answer would be that the Preparatory Commission would be the best forum, but I am also a realist, a pragmatist and I do not pretend. I am aware that some people feel uncomfortable with the Preparatory Commission, because they have not been within the Preparatory Commission since its inception, and it would probably be too much to expect the United States to come in and want to join us right now. So, as such, I am ready to sit down in any forum, whether it will be under the auspices of the Institute of International Law in Kiel or whether it will be under the Law of the Sea Institute in Hawaii, or whether it will be under any other forum. I am prepared to go there, talk, and discuss. But what I am not prepared to do is to go there and talk to myself. And that is extremely critical. I am not prepared to come to Kiel, I am not prepared to go to Hawaii, I am not prepared to go to

Tokyo, I am not prepared to go anywhere in the world if I am talking to myself or even to *Jesus* of Cape Verde and *Ballah* of Trinidad and Tobago, because I know their viewpoints and I agree with them. What I want to do is to go there and listen to the United States. Then I know we have made some progress. And therefore, Mr *Wolfrum*, I am prepared (and I am very sure that most of my colleagues who have signed and ratified the Convention, or have signed the Final Act are prepared) to sit down with anybody, including the United States, anywhere in the world, to commence discussions, but the United States must begin to talk to us. Now, to be fair, and I try to be fair, I am aware that the United States, having listened to the Group of 77 last year, has embarked on a very honourable routine, to begin initially on a bilateral basis, to very preliminary consultations and discussions on their concerns. But I have said what I have just said publicly so that we push them a little bit. We do not want to wait five years just to find out how to begin talking. I think, time (well, we have plenty of time since sea-bed mining is not just around the corner) is not with us, for I think we cannot wait too long to begin talking to the United States. I think, it is time now that the United States realize that it is a very genuine will, a very genuine desire on the part of those who are in the Convention to talk to them genuinely.

I think this forum has given us the opportunity to show that people are aware that Part XI (while it is sacred, it is not a sacred cow from India) can still be pushed here and there. Yesterday, I did mention that I do concede that the formula in Part XI is a formula that I have difficulties with. My colleague in the Zambian delegation, who is an engineer, has said that he is not sure whether that formula will really assist Zambia as a copper-producing country. Therefore, it is only a formula that is there and can be there forever. In view of the new knowledge that we are acquiring through technology and the various operational methods that are in the field now, it is quite possible that some informal arrangements can be made even to the formula itself. The principle behind why the formula was made is, among other things, to help and to assist my country. If such help can be found elsewhere there is no need for me to use the formula. If other issues relating to compensation, relating to economic adjustment can be looked at and perfected, I am quite happy with that. I cannot see why we should use such a formula, if I see and prove that the formula will not help my country at all. So, I think, we can only come to all these things, if we will begin talking to each other.

Finally, I would not myself be very keen to talk in terms of amendments to the Convention. I think there is a specific problem within at least the Group of 77 on that. And therefore — whatever we will try to do —, let us not talk in terms of amending the Convention, even if it relates to Part XI. But let us talk, first of all, in terms of understanding what these problems are, and let us try to see how to resolve them by creative interpretation and understandings and declarations, and then arising out of that when the Convention comes into force, then there is a legal institution which will be empowered, in accordance with the provisions of the Convention, to amend the Convention in whatever format we may want to amend it.

Treves:

I have the impression that we are all adding bricks to a common wall. Even though, sometimes, we add bricks from different sides, it is always the same wall. I would think that we agree that Part XI and, indeed, any régime on seabed mining, will start being applied only when certain events which do not depend on the will of the States happen. A group of States thinks that, if these events happened today, they would be happy with Part XI as it is. Another group thinks that even if these events were to happen today, they would not be happy. But the fact is that we all agree that these events have not happened and that they are not bound to happen for a while. So, we have time to think and negotiate on how we would like a régime to be for a time relatively far away. The problem is that we also want to have the Convention in force because we are convinced that the Convention is very important, mostly for the other 17 parts of it.

How can we overcome this dilemma? I very much agree to many of the things that Ambassador *Jesus* has said. We need to concentrate first on procedures and later on substance. We should agree about the triggering mechanism to put in motion the procedure for changing or for creating a different régime, and the mechanism for applying such régime when certain events happen. At the same time we have to take into account certain legal and political realities. And legal and political realities can be seen if we answer to your first question, Prof. *Wolfrum*. From the view point of those who are not satisfied with Part XI as it is now, what we need is to be sure in legal terms that Part XI, once we ratify the Convention, will not be applied against us, provided that we do not agree to apply it. And this requires some legal mechanism. I fully understand that it is a bit odd to talk about amendments to a convention that is not in force. From a legal view point, of course, the parties to a treaty, be it in force or not, can do whatever they want if they all agree to do something. A recourse to a protocol, even if perhaps the word is not very agreeable to hear, is a technique that has been used in a smaller law of the sea framework, namely that of the so-called MARPOL Convention. States agreed in 1973 on a Convention on Pollution from Ships, and they realized later that certain changes had to be made, because nobody wanted to ratify the Convention. They made the changes and then they ratified both the Convention and the changes, and now we have the MARPOL Convention of 1973/78 in force. So, the technique is clear. The problem is the will to resort to it. I agree that, if we could do without this technique, it would be better.

This morning I indicated that the process through the PrepCom can still yield certain results. I am afraid it cannot yield the result of giving an insurance that Part XI, as it is, will never be invoked against parties to the Convention, if, for instance, the process for revision or for interpretation were to be unsuccessful. So, there has to be something that a government like mine, the Italian government, can tell the Parliament when they submit the texts for ratification. We need to be in a position to tell parliament that, although the Convention contains Part XI, there is an equally binding agreement according to which Part XI will not be used unless we agree to use it, and we will agree to use it if it is changed in a way that is satisfactory for us. I agree fully that, fortunately, we have more time than anticipated because deep sea-bed mining is far away in time. We should reflect on whether entry into force of the Convention before these arrangements are agreed upon will not be a time bomb disrupting the process. Ambassador *Kapumpa* has said that it might even be a positive element because, once the Convention is in force, there are mechanisms which may be resorted to for changing it. However, seen from the view point of those who do not like Part XI as it is now, these mechanisms would be completely out of their control. So they are, in political terms, counterproductive. I think we have to work on the triggering mechanism and on the proceedings to produce something visible which could permit ratification.

Kimball:

I am going to take the approach that I heard Ambassador *Jesus* take this morning, when he discussed the issue of the one million dollar fee due from the registered pioneer investors. I found it was very useful when he went back and reviewed the purpose or rationale behind this provision in the Convention, and then interpreted that or used that rationale as a basis to modify the application of the provision at the point in time in which it will be applied.

May I first restate the obvious in relation to the question you have asked: What issues need to be resolved and, if so, which at this point in time and which at some later point? It might be useful to restate, and this goes to the point Ambassador *Ballah* raised when he spoke initially in this group, that it is clear that nobody is talking about reinterpreting or rewriting what the *common heritage of mankind* in the general principles as stated in the Convention is, or was meant to be. Those principles presumably would be preserved in a way everybody in this seminar has been addressing. I do not think there are many difficulties in restating or reassuring that that is the case. That being the case, Part XI was set up for the purpose of meeting different States' interests in looking at resource development in the deep sea-bed area. Since a lot of details of how mineral resources may be developed, and the means to do it, are affected by when they may be developed — by the market — which is at some point in the future, we cannot really address the details today because of changing economics and changing technology. What we need is a framework. Ambassador *Jesus* in his presentation when this seminar commenced laid out some aspects of decision-making organs, their composition, the way they take decisions, that were useful.

They are also a prerequisite to addressing all other basic issues — the means for taking decisions later on. These decision-making issues would be one of the primary things to be dealt with in the near term, as opposed to economic and technological details to be addressed later on. Another aspect is the cost and size of the institutions. It is relatively obvious that there would have to be some solution in the near term on those issues.

Turning to the details themselves, I think, Mr *Kiderlen* and *Tullio Treves* and others have mentioned that one of the problems is that there are some details that, we always knew, would have to be written later, and PrepCom has started to address a number of those. It is just barely starting to address some, and there are yet many that it has not even begun to address. On the other hand, some of the detailed provisions are actually written into the Convention. So one could take the details presently in the Convention and what was always assumed would be developed in detail later on, and put these as a complex of issues to be dealt with in the future. A critical question then becomes this issue of the trigger: Does the complex of issues put aside then remain to be agreed once "unfrozen" or do the details remain in force until they are changed. All of these "details" questions probably have to be addressed in a single manner, as something to freeze for now and come back to in an agreed manner at a future point in time.

On your questions two and three: the forum and the manner in which whatever results from the process are translated into reality. On the third point, I am a great believer in "form follows substance." The form is not the first thing that needs to be addressed. There are a number of concerns on both points from all sides. As the outlines of the substantive results of how to deal with these issues are further addressed in a variety of consultations of this kind (informal), the forum and "form" questions will follow relatively easily. I do admit the point that the "form" the substantive results take must be addressed before a number of countries will ratify the Convention.

Murray:

I do speak with some small hesitation. I have calculated quickly on the back of a piece of paper that, around this table, you have probably over three hundred years total of service to the law of the sea — an awful lot of dedication and effort to solve this problem. I have a rather unique perspective, that only some six months ago, I had never heard of the United Nations Convention on the Law of the Sea. So I can only claim, I think, to have 0.15 per cent of the expertise of this table, I shall hope to make my contribution correspondingly brief. But sometimes it is helpful not to be saddled with the weight of history, not to be concerned about what happened at a meeting 15 years ago, when you got into what is regarded a very difficult position, to be able without knowing all the history, to look at it and not say: "How did we get here, whose fault is it?" but rather: "How do we get out?"

I have the strong feeling that people have started to shift to that attitude and the more it can be adopted, the better. I came to this six months ago, as I said, never having heard of it, so I am able to speak to only a limited extent. Like my colleague from Brazil I am not able to speak on a personal basis, because I am a diplomat. Nevertheless, I can put things in a much more personal way, than if I were making a formal government statement. The views, I express will not differ radically from those of my government.

I came to this subject, I read the Convention through from cover to cover in a long sitting. My training is that of a historian, and as a historian, one of the skills you acquire is you can usually date a document by its contents, without knowing in advance when it was written. The thing that immediately came to my mind, particularly on Part XI, is that this is a document of its time. The ideas could only have been conceived in the early '70s because that was when they were briefly fashionable. It has now been overtaken. To someone coming new to it, there is no doubt at all that the adoption of such a document could not now, if we started with a blank sheet of paper, be seriously considered. I am sure that is true. That is a fundamental point. Some few countries may still hold the same views but the weight against it would now be so overwhelming, it would never be seriously tabled.

World-wide there has been an acceptance, spectacularly, over the last twelve months that everywhere (maybe I exempt Albania) the idea that the best way to run any economic system is by control, by production limitation, by fixing prices, is not the way to go. It fails to deliver anything to the consumer. It fails to maximize wealth. Such ideas are being dropped. We have seen it in Eastern Europe, we have seen it in the changing orientation of countries in Western Europe, including my own, in the way they conduct their affairs. We have seen it in Africa. I accept entirely the points made by Ambassador *Kapumpa* about the short-term pains, and a short-term can be several years, of structural adjustment programmes — I lived four years in Africa — and there is no doubt that the long-term benefit can be upset to some extent by substantial difficulties in the short term. But in Africa, as well, policies are becoming more market-orientated and the problem of Part XI is that it is not market-orientated at all.

I apologize for speaking on such fundamental level, but that is the problem. The ideas of *Adam Smith* have world-wide gained ascendancy over the ideas of *John Maynard Keynes* or *Karl Marx*. I am very pleased about that, because Mr *Smith* was a Scotsman, *Keynes* English, and *Marx* was German. After the last World Cup I need to be assured that Scotland is better than England and Germany in something, and economics seems the best thing for Scotsmen like me to take pride in. So, some things in Part XI have to go, I do not like to dispute with the potential consensus which is based on ideas of procedure, but I would not like it to be based on a failure to realize the very fundamental difficulties which countries like my own have with the ideology and the economic incorrectness of Part XI.

Production limitation, transfer of technology, arts. 144 and 151 have to be *excised*, it is not a matter of a few changes to make it acceptable. I agree absolutely with the proposition made most notably by Chairman *Jesus* that now is not necessarily the time we have to go into the detail of exactly how this is to be done. But I would not like to stop the debate on substance completely, because it has reached an interesting stage and we saw some very good ideas, e. g. on joint ventures, which in principle could solve a lot of the problems and will give an alternative route on the transfer of technology. I also commend the idea that once the production limitation problem is solved, there should be firm anti-subsidy divisions, which deserves to be followed up. These questions can be looked at. But we do not need now to have a detailed replacement to Part XI.

On the other hand, it is fundamental that we cannot have a moratorium which leaves Part XI hanging over us; on this I agree with my friend Dr. *Treves*. The idea that Part XI would be left like a sword hanging above us, with a very thick rope through which a candle burns and in 25 years time it will drop in our stomach; I do not like this idea at all. I maybe have a personal slant on it when others around this table do not. In the year 2015, I shall not have had the good fortune to have retired. I will still be working, and possibly will have to solve the trouble. So, the idea of leaving Part XI in its entirety for someone else somewhere in the future to solve does not appeal to me.

If I may use a short analogy if we are going to put some sort of moratorium into play, it has to be like a caterpillar going into the chrysalis, it has to be a chrysalis moratorium, where what comes out has undergone a metamorphosis, and become a butterfly. With a chrysalis, two things can happen. We can have a butterfly at the end, or if things go badly wrong, we will get nothing. The one thing which will never happen is that the caterpillar comes crawling out again. That is the sort of situation we have to have with Part XI, if we are going for the moratorium.

This has to be formal; I would never have a chance of convincing my government that they wish to accede, if there is not a formal guarantee that this is the case. There has to be some kind of protocol of understanding. I am not a lawyer, I would not pretend to be able to discuss this in this distinguished company, but it has to be in a legally guaranteed form. I do accept that this is going to bring about difficulties for the countries who have already ratified. Fortunately, in this respect, many of them have not taken enormous steps to bring all their national legislation in line with the Convention, and I particularly expect that not many have legislation on sea-bed mining which they would need to change. They would need to go back and ratify the protocol as well. I do see the legal problems which can come there.

I have spoken on a more basic level, but I hope this helps to contribute to the debate.

Sherman:

I like to start my own observation with an anecdote about Ambassador *Mumba Kapumpa*. He is the only one that I know who would not want to talk to *Jesus*. Having said that I would like to find out what are the issues other than Part XI of the Convention, that make it difficult for a number of countries not to accept the Convention as it is, because we are looking for ways in which, I believe, we can make the Convention acceptable to a larger majority of States including the industrialized States. I think we should identify the problem areas, and proceed on to finding ways on how best we can resolve these issues to make the Convention more universally acceptable. The question is then, what forum should be used, because we see that legally it is impossible to use the Preparatory Commission to make the changes, because as far as we know, the Preparatory Commission is only to give effect to the provisions of the Convention and not to change them. Not being a lawyer and not being one who attends the General Assembly, I would like to find out from the Preparatory Commission chairman here, if a political resolution that is adopted by the General Assembly could be an appropriate umbrella under which these negotiations can take place, would that be adequate? I would appreciate if our PrepCom chairman *Jesus* could respond to that; for I believe, if we take a political decision in the General Assembly, the United States as well as every other State that is likely to be party to the Convention, is a member of the General Assembly and could participate in this particular decision.

Jesus:

The question posed to me was to what extent a General Assembly resolution passed by a probable unanimity or consensus would satisfy that legal requirement as to the satisfaction to be reached, so that the countries that have to ratify or accede to the Convention would be sure that the compromise is going to be respectable because it has legal validity. My answer is a negative one and strongly so, because the resolution, unless it is approving a legal text, has no legal binding effect, even when adopted by unanimity. It can indicate the political position on that issue obviously, if it is embodying some principles of law, some rules of law or a declaration on matters related to law. If adopted by unanimity and respected in a course of years by all countries, it can be a conventional source of customary international law. And many examples have been given by scholars in this respect. But, *per se*, it would not be a legal document, it could be a political document because of its acceptance and acceptability after its adoption by everybody, a conventional source of customary international law, if it embodies a declaration of rules of law. So, I think that possibility would perhaps be the worst. If I were representing my country as a legal expert in this matter, I do not think that if my country had a problem with Part XI, that I would advise it to accept this resolution approach as a method of reaching the legal certainty that is sought for the ratification and accession to the Convention. Let me add, however, there are a lot of ways that we can explore to provide the legal certainty to those that have to go to the parliaments and show them that the document has legal validity, so that they can ratify the Convention, without interfering with a formal amendment to the Convention.

Karev:

My task is facilitated by the previous speakers. I have a feeling that persons sitting at this table are more or less of the same view on the present situation of the Law of the Sea Convention, and are aware of the necessity to have a universally accepted Convention. In order to reach this goal it is essential to make some changes in Part XI. Ambassador *Kapumpa* said that it took us seven years to come to that understanding. And I ask myself how many years it will take us to go from this understanding of necessity to have some changes in Part XI to real changes in Part XI, especially taking into account the fact that time, I think everybody agrees, is not pressing, we have at least 20 or 25 years before deep sea-bed mining can begin. At the same time we have now 43 ratifications of the Convention. For its entry into force less than 20 ratifications are necessary. I think that if we continue with preliminary talks before beginning any official negotiations in order to bring changes to Part XI, we can already on this preliminary stage have a situation where the Convention entered into force.

Politically and legally the situation will become more complicated, from my point of view. That is why I agree with those here who said that maybe the best way of doing is not to elaborate understandings or some new rules of procedure, which, as Mr *Treves* said, would not be sufficient for everybody. I am almost sure that it would not be completely sufficient. Maybe the best way is to reach an agreement that Part XI will not be used or applicable without agreed changes. From my point of view, a protocol or some other document stipulating only these provisions will not be enough. We need something more, some provisional rules for the transitional period. Mr *Kiderlen* said that we will need in the future provisions for such activities as exploration, research programmes and training. That is why some additions to the document will be necessary, provisions which will guide our activities during this transitional period from non-use of Part XI to its entry into force. As to a forum for the elaboration of such document, I do not think that there will be great difficulties in the choice. PrepCom or some other forum, this is really not so important. I think, we can be more or less flexible in this question. The substance of negotiations is more important for all of us.

Craven:

Until Ambassador *Murray* made his intervention, I just was going to pass, but he reinforced a little history that I would like to impart to this group. Allow me this history in a form which is not exactly how it took place, but in the form of a parable or analogy or perhaps a metaphor.

In 1974, the sovereign state of Hawaii decided that it would start its own deep sea-bed mining efforts. And so, the state of Hawaii organized its own enterprise. The resource we were going to mine from the ocean was not the manganese nodules, but we were going to mine the deep ocean water. We intended to mine the deep ocean water, because we were sure that this would produce ocean thermal energy, that would be economically viable and make a great profit not only for Hawaii but for the entire Pacific. And so, in 1974, we built a laboratory, but it was not until 1982 that we finally completed the pipeline that brought that deep ocean resource to the surface. Now, as has been proposed for the enterprise, the state of Hawaii decided that the only way that it could get its resource developed was by the technique of joint venture. So, we invited large numbers of pioneer investors to come and exploit the resource. Our first pioneer investor, a young student from the university, said, "I am going to invest in your resource," and we said "Wonderful, provided that you are going to develop ocean thermal energy," and he said, "No, no, no! Ocean thermal energy will not be developed for at least 20 or 30 years," he said, "but this resource that you have, this deep ocean water is, I think, an ideal medium for growing nori (the seaweed that the Japanese use as the edible wrapper for sushi). And he said, "There is a great big nori market, and I think, this resource will grow nori." That young man now has seven acres in production and he has fifteen seaweeds which he now calls "sea vegetables," and the most successful one, which he is going to get endorsed by the White House, is called "sea broccoli," and he is making a large amount of profit.

So, we went and we sought another investor. And another investor came, and we said to him, "Will you develop ocean thermal energy?" And he said "No, no, no! Ocean thermal energy is 20 or 30 years away, everyone knows that it will not be profitable until then," and we said "Well, what do you want to do?" He said, "I want to grow Californian kelp, and I want to cut the kelp down, and I want to seed abalone, and I want to seed sea urchins, and I want to grow these products and make a lot of profit." And so he started and discovered that he can grow not only abalone and kelp and sea urchins, but that he could grow oysters and salmon; and he now has sixteen acres of salmon farm, he is producing 1,500 pounds of salmon per day, he has asked for seventy acres. And very shortly Hawaii will be the largest producer of salmon in the world.

So, we tried other people, and we got somebody came who is now doing fifteen acres of algae. And then we invited somebody to come and we asked him all the same question, "Will you work on OTEC (Ocean Thermal Energy Conversion)," and he said "OTEC is 15 to 20 years away." Similarly the next entrepreneur came and is now building 20 acres to grow lobsters. So we went abroad and called the Japanese and said, "Gentlemen of Japan, you certainly are going to develop this resource in the way that we want it developed." And they came in and they looked at it and said, "Yes, it is very interesting, but OTEC is 20 to 30 years away," and so they have two efforts going, one is the farm to grow pearls, and the other one is a farm to grow a flat fish called "Hirame" — I do not know how to pronounce this right —, and they know that this is a prime delicacy. Well, this experience repeats and repeats so that now we have a farm that grows strawberries and lettuce with the condensate of deep ocean water, we now have a distillery. Our most recent entrepreneur appeared and we, "What do you want to do?" He said, "Well, you have a tremendous number of visitors, this is becoming a visitors laboratory, so, I am going to build with my own money a visitors center and make a profit out of this. We now have a proposal for a restaurant and a hotel."

Finally, the Canadians and the British arrived and once more we asked, "Well, are you going to develop OTEC?" We thought they would say, "OTEC is 20 years away," and they said, "OTEC would have been 20 years away, but now you have all these industries that are bringing the cold water up to surface. And if we do not have to pay the costs to pump cold water to surface, then we are going to design an OTEC plant, which will be profitable now." So they are now building an OTEC plant, of a very small size, about 160 kilowatts, it will be installed in one year, but the chief thing about it is, it is not designed as a demonstration model, it is designed to make profit, a return on investment. And as soon as that happens, why then, the smart people here in Germany and other nations will come rushing in now to get their pioneer investor status, and the University of Kiel is going to show up and they are going to take electrical energy from OTEC and they are going to make hydrogen with it, and we will have transportable fuels. And so on and so on until we have self-sufficient ocean societies.

What is the lesson that we have learned? We learned several lessons. The first lesson we learned is that everything that was successful was done as a joint venture. We did everything as a joint venture. We learned that the State is unable to carry out enterprise by itself, for as soon as the bureaucrats of a State get involved they engage in a bureaucratic process which we call "solution avoidance." They work on a problem and they see all the difficulties involved and they do not want to resolve it. But by bringing in a joint venturer and telling the joint venturer that it is putting all his money in, and that the only return he is going to get from it is profit, all of a sudden, you start to see solutions developing.

The next thing that we learned, which I think is a lesson that we have just started to learn about the manganese nodules, is that we were completely wrong as to the value of this resource, and what the resource is about. We thought we knew exactly what we are going to do as far as ocean technology is concerned. We are absolutely and completely wrong. If anyone had said to us that the most important profitable products were going to be pearls or oysters or strawberries or that kind, we would have said, they are out of their minds.

Now, what does this mean as far as the deep sea-bed is concerned? What it means is that there probably is a resource out there. The only thing you can be absolutely sure of is — excepting to be sold as souvenirs or monuments to sit outside this hotel — manganese nodules are not the resource, and the one thing that we can be absolutely sure of is that the mining formulas which appear in the Treaty have nothing to do with reality. And so, we need to resolve this issue and we need to get moving, for we are caught in a terrible bind of the fact that we have gone through all these years of negotiations and we have been negotiating about things which are really meaningless. There is no question about that. And so, we are meeting here today and listen to a lot of solutions, and the one solution which sounds best to me is a solution which will open up an avenue for doing something akin to what we have done in Hawaii and, at the same time, not changing a word of the text, not changing anything at all. Now, what is the magic word in the text that makes a solution possible? The magic word is "joint venture." Nothing I have heard here on tells me that there is anything at all which requires any changes of the law of the sea for the PrepCom to recommend or suggest that the Enterprise will not engage in any enterprise of any sort, unless they engaged in some form of joint venture. I think that such a condition can be an administrative detail within the umbrella of the law as it exists right now. And, I think, this could be an avenue that the PrepCom could pursue.

There is one other condition that I believe to be absolutely vital, and that is to reinforce what Ambassador *Kapumpa* said, and that is that we cannot do this unless we bring the United States to the conference table. It was suggested that it might be done in Hawaii, and I am now inviting you all to come to a workshop, a workshop that the board has not authorized yet and some board members are here, and I am sure that they will authorize it. Come to a workshop in Hawaii, and you will have an opportunity at that time to visit the first successful site of all the things mined in deep-ocean water, and you will have the opportunity to participate in a workshop which will help us to establish machinery for resolving that which we already know how to resolve. If we held this workshop in December, when it is cold in our nation's capitol, I can guarantee that the public servants from Washington, D. C. will be there.

Scully:

There is probably only one issue, that I could raise, which would be of interest to anyone else in the room, which is the question I think, Ambassador *Kapumpa* posed, among others. That is when or if the United States is going to return to the process and engage in the dialogue and negotiations. On that point, let me say, that I do not have the faintest idea. In the discussions here, we have heard a lot of interesting thoughts, which may have a favourable impact. I think both

John Craven and Ambassador *Jesus* have made some very interesting points which are worth pursuing. My points can largely be made by referring to the comments of others. There are many things I think I would have said, but that have already been said by others, and there are those who would like to bring this to a reasonably rapid conclusion.

I would like to make a point about universality, since that is a point that have been discussed in some considerable detail. Everybody in this room has supported the concept of a universal convention. The term universality is used a lot but not necessarily well defined. In my view, we have concentrated on one aspect of the two important aspects of universality. We have concentrated upon the question of participation, the numbers of nations that may be parties at some time in the future to the Law of the Sea Convention. Even if there were no difficulties, even if we had universal signature of the LOS Convention, it seems to me that we are still a long way from universality in terms of ratifications. At best, I think, that process would take decades, even if we were able to resolve the outstanding issues that raise questions about whether some States will ratify at all. One of the issues that has come up throughout our discussions is the package deal — the balance of interests — that is reflected in the Convention. We have concentrated upon sea-bed mining, which is decades away at a minimum, and perhaps, as *John Craven* suggested, manganese nodules will never be mined. But it seems to me that the other issue of universality faces us right now, the issue of the uniform interpretation of provisions that were carefully and arduously negotiated as compromises in the LOS Treaty, that are now being acted upon. These include the extensions of jurisdiction, and other features of the Convention on whose basis States are acting. An important aspect of universality is the process in finding universal interpretations, agreed interpretations and practice with regard to those parts of the LOS Convention which are being implemented, whether it is on the basis of customary law, or, as I heard the phrase, anticipatory implementation of the Convention. In the long run, that is the real test of achieving a universally acceptable convention, a universal convention, and a universal practice with regard to what is going on right now.

With respect to the sea-bed, the question of Part XI, I wish to make a couple of points. I think, and I agree very much with Dr. *Treves*, who indicated that, if one is looking to solutions, one has to deal with the reality which is that because of Part XI the Convention, as it now stands, is not going to be ratified by a significant number of States. There are lots of possible ways of fixing Part XI, by including forum and format issues, once the will to find the solution is there. But if there is to be a LOS Convention which includes Part XI and is ratifiable on a universal basis, it seems to me that the question of the trigger has to be addressed, the question of providing assurances, if not a guarantee, that specific solutions will be found, at least a guarantee that the existing provisions would not be imposed upon States against their will. Otherwise, I do not think the Convention is going to be ratified by a significant number of States. In looking at the question there may be promise in the approach mentioned by Ambassador *Jesus*. One aspect which seems to me would be very essential in his question of the trigger. What would be the trigger for dealing with those issues recognizing — and this may be in fact part of the solution as well as part of the problem — that we are not in a position to anticipate what might be the situation, in what in fact might be the promise, if any, that the deep sea-bed may offer in the future.

Zegers Santa Cruz:

I am agreed on all these procedural points: to deal with Part XI; to have negotiations or conversations; to have several fora etc.; and to the idea of Ambassador *Jesus* to postpone some matters. But on this question of postponement a new idea has come; it is called "moratorium" and otherwise. At the beginning, Ambassador *Jesus* suggested to suspend the application of norms of exploration and exploitation. That seems, more or less, interesting. But then, Counsellor *Kiderlen* spoke of a moratorium of Part XI and he spoke of two Conventions. And then, Prof. *Treves* went further and asked for a binding instrument not to apply Part XI unless something has happened.

I would like to caution against something. To divide the Convention will be completely unacceptable, because in fact it may kill Part XI. If you suspend Part XI by a binding instrument, unless you agree on something further, you have separated the Convention. You have segregated Part XI. I would like to emphasize what *Lee Kimball* said very wisely, that in any postponement some essential matters have to be retained. Of course, if we are going to postpone rules of exploration and exploitation, we have a *common heritage*, we have all the principles, we have a number of policies and things. And yet we have a Part XI. And we have a unified Convention on the Law of the Sea. If we want to apply what Prof. *Treves* proposed which, I think, he has not thought through, we kill Part XI and we divide the Convention. That division of the Convention is against the Convention itself. Because the Conference was asked by the General Assembly to deal with a unitary law of the sea (i. e. the sea-bed and a number of other matters as a unit). Then we approved the Convention also as a unit. Then, on signature, the Chairman told us, that it was a package, an indivisible package, and so we signed it. Now is not the moment to divide it. That is clearly unpromising. I do not want to throw cold water on a promising aspect. Postponement is all right, suspension of rules of exploration and exploitation can be considered, but Part XI cannot be segregated or killed if we want a Convention. That is my first remark.

A second one, which I would like to make, is to correspond to everything, that Mr *Craven* said, and to applaud. When he spoke of joint ventures, I have not mentioned this in the beginning, but I would like to come back to what we discussed here for half a day, to joint ventures as an option. The parable which

Mr *Craven* presented, is a very interesting one. If you have an optional procedure on joint ventures, perhaps you do not need to fall into all these problems of postponement, binding instruments and so on, I think, but that is something to be explored.

When you think of a *common heritage*, and this is my final comment, I would like to refer to market economy and to what Mr *Murray* said. My country has applied for fifteen years consistently a market economy, and successfully. But I do not see any contradiction really, when we are speaking of a *common heritage* or a common patrimony. That is, when you have the mankind as the owner of a resource. An international authority on its behalf has the best entitlement to act like a State would. I see no problem in applying certain things like a policy of exploitation, I do not see that it can be incompatible with the market. If the sea-bed would be what is legally called a common, there could be ground for objections, but, of course, we all agreed that it was not, it was something else, a common patrimony, and then the matter is different. I finally would make the reflection, going back to market economy, that what Dr. *Craven* said about the joint venture system, it may provide a market solution which should be studied when we deal with all these negotiations.

Roffe:

I have noticed in this discussion what I would qualify as broad general understandings. The first, the need for universality. The second, a broad understanding concerning flexibility, shown especially by the Group of 77, that today is the main actor in the process of the law of the sea. The third general broad understanding relates to the difficulties in Part XI of the Convention, and on the need recognized by all parties to have some type of adjustment. And the fourth, is this broad recognition, by everybody, of the changing economic, technological and political realities that necessarily demand a review of a number of assumptions.

In the light of this broad consensus, that I perceive, I have some questions. And basically, a major one. If we have this broad consensus, what are then the difficulties we are facing in the process of the entering into force of the Convention? As an outsider, I believe that there is a need to clarify at least two broad issues. The first one is that besides what I perceived the natural desire of all negotiators in a very long process of making operational the instrument, there is a need to assert more clearly what are the actual needs, what are the real interests for the entering into force of the Convention. We need to separate these two questions, the interest of the negotiators of reaching the final goal from the real interests and needs of having the Convention entering into force. The second, probably the most important issue that needs to be clarified is that given all the concessions that apparently the Group of 77 is ready to make, what about the attitude of important and key players like the United States? Do those countries have a real interest in joining the Convention? What is to be gained by those countries in joining the Treaty? My last remark is that if the answer to this very last question was positive and, bearing in mind the prevailing flexibility of all groups, to move towards a solution of the existing technical questions should not be a difficult task.

Sherman:

I would like to hear from Mr *Scully*, who is a United States civil servant from Washington, D. C., his views on the possibility of a dialogue with the US to join the UN Convention. In light of the fact that the Group of 77 at the Preparatory Commission had indicated its willingness to enter into a dialogue with interested parties and in view of the discussions here, there seems to be the need to have the United States, *per se*, to join in these negotiations. I think if the United States joins, it will prompt other countries, especially the industrialized ones, to want to join the Convention. The Group of 77 statement was made last September in New York, and almost a year has now passed. However, I have heard of late that there are some movements now in Washington. In view of our willingness to enter into a dialogue, is there any suggestion that the United States is prepared now to move in that direction? If so, would the United States be prepared to go to Kingston or to New York as an observer so that the Preparatory Commission can have discussions on its concerns? I have raised this particular question because we are interested in trying to find ways in which we can hopefully get the United States to become party to the Convention.

Scully:

I have to respond to that, although I doubt very much that the United States will come to Kingston. I would note the United States is in New York 12 months of the year.

Sherman:

Our concern is that the United States is an important member of the United Nations in New York and has not participated in previous discussions. Such a posture does not help us to resolve the problems. The issue now is to get the United States to participate in the work of the Preparatory Commission so that it can indicate its concerns on which we then could have a dialogue and see how we can best accommodate those concerns.

Scully:

It is not likely that the United States is going to participate in the PrepCom. Now, in less of a predictive capability, I simply know that it is not the only form of dialogue.

Discussion

Morrison:

A lot of you have been talking about getting the United States back to the table. But one of the things that I as a teacher of constitutional law in the United States must emphasize: the getting the United States back to the table or getting the United States' signature on the document does not mean having the United States ratify the document. In the light of the controversy which is going on for nearly a decade, that would be a very difficult task. And to have the United States as a full participant in this, seems to me to be perhaps further away than even those who would like to have us participating in the process. Let me emphasize that I am speaking entirely privately.

My second proposition is, as I have been listening to modalities here, one potential modality that has completely been omitted is the one that may in fact be most analogous. There is one other international organization which never came into being as a legal entity, but which has been very successful in fact. That is the International Trade Organization and the General Agreement on Tariffs and Trade. One of the possible modalities is a protocol of provisional application. I am not particularly endorsing that, but I must say that I was surprised not to have heard that put on the table as an option. Perhaps one of the reasons I have not heard put on the table as an option, is that in part I see the law of the sea delegations sitting at the table, and that may be the solution that is furthest from your hopes or desires or wishes, but it may be the solution that is most promising in order to bring the Convention into force to some degree. Such a solution might not be completely without Part XI but rather include the principles of Part XI and the text of the rest. I simply offer that as an alternative that might be thought about.

Hafner:

I have only one short comment and one question. The comment relates to the form in which an additional instrument should be adopted. I share the view of those, who propose or who state that there must be a formal document, a legal document, since any other solution would not give an asssurance to the States that the other States would also be forced to apply these particular provisions. On the other hand, only a resolution or something like a resolution would give the States the right to use some sort of "pick and choose" principle to pick up what they want and apply only the provisions in this respect. In this respect I am of the opinion that any such protocol would certainly not be subject to art.

311 of the Convention, since it would be taken prior to the entry into force of the Convention. But on the other hand, such protocol could be subject to another effect, and another legal provision of international law and which has not been discussed here: this is art. 18 of the Vienna Convention on the Law of Treaties, which obliges the States not to defeat the object and purpose of a treaty, if they have signed the Convention. To more than 150 States that have signed the Convention, art. 18 of the Vienna Convention on the Law of Treaties already applies. Hence, I would like to raise the question of whether this art. 18 would also have to be and will be taken into account in the course of negotiations which could go on concerning such a protocol.

Lagoni:

The question has been asked: What is the interest of having the LOS Convention entering into force? It seems to me that there is a clear interest, which, however, is not related to its Part XI, because deep sea-bed mining will not start in any foreseeable time — and when it comes, it will take place in economically and technically different circumstances than we have today. Therefore, the interest to have the Convention entering into force stems from other Parts which played only a marginal rôle in our discussion during the last days. I would particularly mention the parts on straits used for international navigation, on exclusive economic zone, on environmental protection, and on safeguards for shipping. Except for Part XI, the Convention is a well balanced legal instrument, and a very modern, too. There are three reasons to have the Convention entering into force. The first one is simply to avoid legal uncertainty. Everybody — or at least every lawyer — knows that customary international law is often disturbingly uncertain, and sometimes States tend to read into customary law exactly what they want to read out of it. The second reason is to avoid creeping jurisdiction. I fear that without the LOS Convention coastal States will extend their continental shelf beyond 350 nautical miles. Who will prevent them from doing so, if the Convention fails? I fear that there will be enough reasons to argue that the 350 miles or the 200 miles of the EEZ is only an artificial limit having been adopted at a certain time and under certain circumstances which will have changed then. Besides that, creeping jurisdiction may even easier occur within the existing zones. The third reason is simply to avoid conflicts. And conflicts can most effectively be avoided by binding third party settlement. But also for another reason Part XV on dispute settlement could turn out to be the most important part of the whole UN Convention on the Law of the Sea. The outstanding importance of certain courts or tribunals for the development of the law is well known. Americans know it from their Supreme Court. The European Communities would look differently without the European Court, and the legal system of the Federal Republic of Germany owes a lot to its Supreme Constitutional Court. Considering the gaps and loopholes of the law of the sea, it is, no doubt, very important to have an effective LOS Tribunal in Hamburg as soon as possible.

Koch:

Fernando Zegers cautioned against dividing the Law of the Sea Convention. I do not think that it is necessary to take Part XI totally away, and agree on a moratorium. I think it would be sufficient to agree that negotiations on those provisions should be postponed which deal with the substantial questions of deep sea-bed mining and which are controversial and on which it will not be possible in the near future to reach an agreement because we do not know the circumstances under which they will be applied and under which circumstances deep sea-bed mining becomes economically viable. Then I think, it is not possible to talk of separating Part XI from the rest of the Law of the Sea Convention. It would be only a wise proceeding to put aside those parts which are controversial and on which we cannot reach agreement at the moment, and agree that we will negotiate later.

Maquieira:

I listened very carefully to what has been said this afternoon and during the whole day, particularly with regard to this morning's statements. Concerning other parts of the Convention it seems that countries are behaving in a way as if they would have behaved if the Convention were enforced. This leads me to the question of sea-bed mining. I have been following very closely the work of the Preparatory Commission. The current work of the Preparatory Commission in the area of the mining code with its Special Commission 3, which is related to Annex III and the system of exploration and exploitation contained in the Convention, shows extreme difficulties in finding consensus on some of the basic issues, it is regretful to say, but we have a repetitive summary of the debates we had in 1981 and in 1982 regarding issues like the financial terms of contract, issues like the production policy, issues like transfer of technology. It becomes in that context increasingly necessary to look for viable possibilities of finding some type of consensus which would lead us to some progress on this. Now, as I mentioned yesterday, there is an area in the Convention, Annex III, with little work be done, and I think, it would be necessary to take it up in a consistent way. We have one attempt and it was floored, and we did not get anywhere in this discussion and that is the issue of joint ventures. That is one area. And this is very important, that is one area of the mining code. There is no detailed provision regarding that institution, so it would seem to me in the light of what is going on in PrepCom, in the light of an evolution of the thought process within PrepCom and outside PrepCom, that we might have to look to a two pronged, or two track approach by which e. g. the Preparatory Commission in the area regarding the system of exploration and exploitation, i. e. the mining code, would concentrate on a joint venture scheme, and parallel to that, consultations could be held outside of the Preparatory Commission to look into the questions of we have been discussing here today. I frankly do not see, I do not think that you can either use a Preparatory Commission by itself for this purpose or leave the Preparatory Commission completely devoid of activity until these issues are solved. In my view we have to look at this two track approach, to take up the joint venture scheme in the Preparatory Commission and to look to other issues, even the issue, Ambassador *Jesus* proposed, of postponing certain of the issues for later consideration outside of the Preparatory Commission, given that there are certain realities which govern the decision, there are some parties who will not participate in the Preparatory Commission for reasons best known to themselves who need to have a possibility to exchange views with the developing countries, if we are really considering a balanced quest towards universality.

Kapumpa:

Part XI is not just sea-bed production. So, those who talk about postponing or putting in the freezer or moratorium of Part XI, should remember that Part XI is not just sea-bed mining, but Part XI includes also the establishment of the Authority itself. So, I want to refer to that point that when we talk about any postponement of anything we are really referring to those parts of Part XI which relate to sea-bed production, because, in fact, it is under Part XI where we have the establishment of the Authority, the Assembly, the Council, the Secretariat, the settlement of disputes, of advisory opinions, and so on.

Treves:

I want to answer some questions by Ambassador *Zegers*. I get very worried when I am — albeit jokingly — accused of being the Convention killer, or Part XI killer. I am far from this. I only tried to give a more legal and political form to things that were in the air in the speeches of many of us. I would not want to revive Part XI. But we might have it "born again." Then, a small remark on the last intervention by my good friend, Ambassador *Kapumpa*: If there is no sea-bed mining, what is the purpose of the Authority?

Kapumpa:

(laughing) . . . living in the Convention!

Jesus:

I share the view of Ambassador *Zegers*, that we should be very careful about developing the idea of separating Part XI from the Convention, because politically such an idea might create more problems for us; and probably that would be the worse idea to be followed to address the problems that we all realize exist. My second comment is to Prof. *Morrison*. He said that he was somewhat puzzled by the idea that we have not explored many devices and that we have not explored the device that it is very common in situations like this, to adopt a protocol for provisional implementation. I would say that in fact the whole strategy we have been trying to discuss is precisely to follow his device that he mentioned. But in a different way, we say we are exploring the possibilities of a protocol the goal of which would not be to provisionally implement, but, provisionally, not to implement, so the device has in fact been discussed. My third short comment is in respect to what should be negotiated and what should be left out? In my previous statement I said that the issues to be reported to the next 25, 30 years would be based upon a compromise to be worked out prior to the entry into force of the Convention, which would lay down ground rules and what I called guidelines, that would take into account the triggering factor obviously. So, in fact, something has to be implemented, and if something has to be implemented, it should represent a minimum of the structure of the Authority. That is why it is important at this stage to discuss the question of financing and decision-making. Otherwise it does not make sense. So, it is important to be aware that for a complete compromise to be reached, then, at least an illusion of the implementation of Part XI has to be accepted. That illusion can be achieved through this minimal structure, to monitor the activities of the registered pioneer investors, the development of technology and so on and so on.

Wolfrum:

Let me try to briefly summarize some of the ideas which have been exchanged, although I am fully aware of the fact that it is absolutely impossible to summarize three hours of discussion.

It has become evident from the discussion that we all are trying to assemble bricks to build a house, certainly a house according to the same characteristics. There is a common understanding that the use of the sea needs to be regulated internationally, such regulations cannot be left for national legislation or national administration. This leads to the further conclusion that any international legal régime for the governing of the use of the sea has to be truly universal. There is no need to explain at great length why such a régime on the use of the sea is necessitated. The strong interrelationship of the various forms of uses and the intensity of uses of the sea have rendered the present anarchical system as inappropriate in which each State regulates its activities or the activities of its citizens as its responsibility. Furthermore, it has been pointed out that, e. g., dispute settlement procedures can never be established only by customary international law, to that extent an international agreement is mandatory. It has been pointed out in this context that dispute settlement procedures have not only a value of their own, but alter the total system of a régime.

In dealing with those issues of Part XI which require some modification, the discussion has touched upon three different aspects: which are those issues, which need modification now and which can be left for a later stage. Let me try to tackle the problem from a different point of view, namely the possible ways and means how changes or rather modifications — I want to avoid the word amendment — could possibly be made. One way would be the re-interpretation of certain rules of Part XI, including Annex III and IV, which can be done by the rules and regulations currently under discussion in the Preparatory Commission. Such rules and regulations are anyhow — technically speaking — nothing else but an authoritative interpretation of the Law of the Sea Convention. Some of the rules of Part XI under discussion are flexible enough to be considered for such a re-interpretation, e. g. the rules on the transfer of technology, production policy, fees and even the composition of the Council and the Commissions thereto. Since the rules and regulations can be changed later by only a relatively high majority such an approach offers sufficient security to every member.

Nevertheless, some of the rules of Part XI objected to cannot be dealt with so easily. This is, for example, true with respect to art. 155 LOS Convention. In this respect it seems to be the only option to alter or postpone art. 155 LOS Convention by agreeing upon a specific protocol or understanding. There are, however, certain further issues, which cannot easily be postponed or altered. In this respect it may be perhaps advisable to take recourse to the "package deal" approach and to form a new package. Along this line I refer to the ideas introduced by Prof. *John Craven*. He mentioned that one could envision an enlargement of the functions of the Sea-Bed Authority and the Enterprise since other uses of the sea and the ocean floor have become technically feasible and may be more attractive than mere deep sea-bed mining. Thus, one may think of — as a matter of compensation — empowering the Enterprise by the means of joint ventures to engage in activities such as OTEC.

Apart from that, one might bring into force the general ideas of Part XI and postpone the rest, since there will be no deep sea-bed mining for the next 25-30 years to come.

I have not forgotten, however, the remark of Ambassador *Kapumpa* arguing that Part XI does not only regulate deep sea-bed mining, but also the establishment of the Authority. This raises the question about the functions of the Deep Sea-Bed Authority until the time is "ripe" for commercial activities. Mr *Ballah* could give us an answer to that, for his subcommittee has been working to spell out functions such as training programmes or the co-ordination of scientific research in the respect of deep sea-bed mining, etc. These would be viable functions for a small authority which at least preserves the underlying philosophy of Part XI, namely that the deep sea-bed must be internationally administered.

Let me come to the last issue, regarding the forum where the negotiations envisaged should take place. It is not going to be PrepCom alone nor should PrepCom be put aside completely. There are certain flexible means between these two extremes. Account has to be taken of the fact that the format of the outcome influences the determination of the forum. Rules and regulations can only be decided upon in PrepCom, they may, however, be prepared outside of it. To negotiate a Protocol, however, would not be within the mandate of PrepCom. There is a relationship between the forum and the format. This should be taken into consideration.

Closing Remarks

Sherman:

I have been requested to give thanks to the Institute of International Law at the University of Kiel on behalf of the distinguished participants here. I consider this privilege as a singular honour. As I indicated at the reception on the first night of the Symposium, I believe it was the Institute's own guiding principle of international solidarity that prompted it to invite such an array of eminent scholars and public servants here to Kiel, to address a number of significant issues concerning the Law of the Sea Convention and to see how these issues can be modified to make the Convention more universally acceptable. In that regard, eighteen excellent papers were presented during the course of the last three days which threw light on some of the difficulties that are likely to present problems for a number of States, especially key industrial countries, to accept the Convention. We would like to take the opportunity now, after the fine exchanges that have transpired in the last three days, to extend our special thanks and appreciation to the Institute, particularly to Prof. *Rüdiger Wolfrum* and his fine staff who have been very kind and instrumental in organizing this very important symposium. We think really the Law of the Sea Convention is at a crossroads. I hope that the suggestions that have come out of our deliberations here will go a long way in providing an opportunity for additional exchanges so as to make the Convention more universally acceptable. We wish further to extend our appreciations to the Government officials here, the staff of the Conti Hansa hotel and to all of those generous contributors who made this important Symposium possible. We want to thank all of you, and again, on behalf of these distinguished participants we want to say a very big "thank you" for the privilege to participate in such an important and timely Symposium on the Law of the Sea Convention.

Morrison:

My word is only to second the gracious statement that was made on behalf of the Advisory Board to say that it makes us proud and we thank very much the Director and the staff of this Institute.

Wolfrum:

Therefore I may declare the symposium closed.

ANNEX

GEOMAR — A New Scientific Concept, a New Road to the Transfer of Technology

Jörn Thiede and Harald Bäcker*

The properties, structures and formation processes of the global seafloor make an exciting research perspective for the modern marine geosciences. The investigation of the global seafloor attracts many scientists because of its global perspective, the multitude of unsolved scientific problems, the importance of the seafloor for understanding the modern environment, the richness of its known and unknown mineral resources and the numerous possibilities for the use of the seafloor by mankind.

Over the past 20-30 years, the geosciences have developed from a rather descriptive to a modern, quantitative discipline of the natural sciences which uses its own methodology and which has led to many high tech developments. Inspiration from the marine geosciences has contributed to this development because they have produced the hypothesis of plate tectonics, which helps us to understand the short and long-term history of the variability of our earth. The most recent discoveries of dynamics and processes along plate boundaries pose dramatic questions to the scientific community.

Marine geosciences have achieved unexpected rapid and successful scientific progress over the past years; therefore, they face a continuously growing number of research incentives. Large areas, such as in the polar oceans, in many parts of the global deep-sea basins, along extended stretches of the coastal areas comprise seafloor areas whose geological properties are poorly known or completely unknown. Geologic processes and anthropogenic influences result in rapidly varying seafloor properties which must be continuously investigated.

The methodology of modern marine geosciences is comprised of a multitude of physical, chemical, biological and specifically geoscientific tools and techniques. They are the subject of continuous change, of enlargement and further development depending on changing scientific and technical targets and requirements. Today, the marine geosciences are dependent upon expensive instrumentation and modern technology.

---

* Prof. Dr. *Jörn Thiede*, GEOMAR Research Center for Marine Geosciences; Dr. *Harald Bäcker*, Geomar Technologie GmbH, D-2300 Kiel 14.

Research in the marine geosciences is carried out at many research institutions in Germany, but in many instances these institutions have not been able to cope with this new scientific progress. The future tasks, namely the protection of the natural properties of seafloors and the exploration of the seafloor for its non-living resources, demand the establishment and enlargement of scientific capacities with the capability:

— to support first-rate research in the field of the marine geosciences;

— to address technically and financially demanding research objectives in disciplines which are presently not covered in Germany;

— to develop, organize and carry out large scientific projects in close co-operation with private industry; and

— to support the transfer of science and technology to developing countries.

The scientific perspectives for the marine geosciences as well as the existing deficits in Germany were recognized almost 10 years ago by various organizations such as the German Research Foundation (DFG), the Federal Ministry for Research and Technology (BMFT) and the research institutions which are involved in this field. A means for solving some of these problems was included in an extensive memorandum by the DFG *Geokommission.* A central part of this DFG study was the proposal to establish a new Research Center for Marine Geosciences to be called "GEOMAR". All of the German coastal states competed for this institution, but only the state government of Schleswig-Holstein proposed the foundation of a new GEOMAR Center to be located in its capital, Kiel, with the aim of strengthening existing capacities and its marine geoscientific research capability in Germany.

GEOMAR — The Kiel Perspective

The plan for GEOMAR in Kiel was developed by the Christian Albrechts University and its marine research groups in close co-operation with other public and private institutions. Innovative ideas led to proposals for the establishment of a public foundation which co-operates closely with a privately organized and financed company. Both GEOMAR and this branch of private industry have developed their activities in the port city of Kiel with its environment of scientific, industrial and political contacts.

GEOMAR was planned as the nucleus for an industrial and technological research park and it is hoped that it will promote marine geoscientific and marine technology activities in Kiel. GEOMAR will be integrated into the scientific disciplines of pertinent institutions in Germany and in neighbouring foreign countries. However, GEOMAR will also be different because of its qualities and size, because of the specialization of its scientific departments, its organizational possibilities and because of the close integration of basic and applied research. GEOMAR will seek co-operation with industry and will attempt to build up a new scientific organization comparable to similar marine geoscientific research organizations in France, the United Kingdom, Canada, the United States, the Soviet Union and Japan.

According to the ideas of the founders, GEOMAR will be comprised of the following four units: GEOMAR Foundation with its Research Center for Marine Geosciences, the private GEOMAR Technologie GmbH (see Figure), as well as a technological research park and a study center. Numbers one and two of these four units have already been established.

Foundation for Marine Geosciences GEOMAR

During the summer of 1987, the state government of Schleswig-Holstein established the GEOMAR foundation (by public law) with the aim of developing activities within the field of marine geoscientific research. In order to pursue this task, the foundation supports a research institution, hereinafter called the GEOMAR Research Center for Marine Geosciences of the Christian Albrechts University, and its four scientific departments. The Research Center carries out integrated and interdisciplinary scientific studies in the field of marine geosciences, as well as in a number of joint central facilities.

The scientific departments of the GEOMAR Research Center address central themes of the marine geosciences which carry specific scientific promise in the future. The central scientific themes and departments of GEOMAR are presently comprised of 1. marine environmental geology, 2. paleoceanology, 3. marine geophysics and 4. petrology of the oceanic crust.

The scientific departments are headed by professors at Kiel University. They are supported in their scientific work by scientists in tenured and non-tenured positions. The state government of Schleswig-Holstein contributes to GEOMAR by financing tenured positions (at present, 60 positions are financed by the state government). The research perspectives of these departments are clearly within the field of basic research but they provide for many contacts to applied research as well. In particular, the tasks within research and development comprise:

- basic research in central fields of the marine geosciences;
- co-operation with other marine geoscientists and related disciplines inside and outside Germany;
- initiation and co-ordination of major research programs;
- participation in educational activities in the field of marine geosciences;
- the establishment and management of a GEOMAR Study Center;

— conceptional development of innovative research methodology and technology in the field of marine geosciences.

The foundation also hopes to function as a point of contact for industry by:

— furthering co-operation between science and the marine technology industry;

— pursuing the economic and political aspects of aid to developing countries in the field of maritime activities;

— attracting and evaluating foreign requests for co-operation for their economic technical perspectives.

The GEOMAR Technologie GmbH (GTG) supports the foundation and its institutions as a partner and co-ordinator for the technological aspects of its activities.

The Technical Component of GEOMAR

The working group of the *Geokommission* of the German Research Foundation (DFG) established the idea of a new research center within the marine geosciences. Various discussions in Kiel which contributed to the idea of GEOMAR have added the component of a subdivision into two parts, one part devoted to basic sciences supported by a publicly financed research institution and the other part as a company which provides technical service support and development.

This model, which was developed by the state government of Schleswig-Holstein, Kiel University and the Chamber of Industry and Commerce, was hoped to supplement the research groups within the field of the marine sciences in Kiel. But it was also hoped that this model would establish contacts and co-operation with the offshore industry in a much better and more efficient way than is conventionally possible. The Kiel region has a long tradition of supporting offshore and marine science techniques in industry. For example, the echosounder was invented here, and Kiel houses at least four companies which produce CTD probes for research.

The organization of the GEOMAR Technologie GmbH (GTG), which was founded in March of 1988, provides the incentive for many companies to participate in this venture. Presently, shares are held by seven large industrial conglomerates and a commercial society (wirtschaftlicher Verein), the "GEOMAR Unternehmensgemeinschaft (GUG)", which is open for new members and which is composed of 25 - 30 small and medium-sized industrial enterprises with maritime interests.

The Tasks of the GTG

The focus of activities of the GTG comprises a professional technical service for the GEOMAR Research Center, development of instrumental systems and activities within technology transfer.

The services provide technical assistance which cannot be carried out by scientists at the research center. They cover the maintenance and servicing of scientific instruments, repairs as well as user-oriented adaptations and new developments in research instrumentation. In addition, assistance is offered to all marine institutes in preparing, organizing and carrying out expeditions at sea. The GTG can cover all logistic tasks and organize as well as maintain programs for collecting a diverse set of marine data and samples.

GEOMAR related service activities available to other customers are supplemented by more general activities within the development of technology and its transfer, as well as by the promotion of industry activities.

The mandate of technology transfer in the area of seafloor research is supported by close regional interlacing of scientific and industrial components within the GEOMAR complex. This close proximity supports fruitful co-operation and frequent daily contacts.

An institution devoted to basic research within the field of geosciences is not an unlimited pool of ideas for futuristic technologies such as a technical university, which can foster completely new industries. The classical situation of technology transfer, namely attempts by an institute to exploit the results of its own research in companies in order to market them, is not typical for an institution like the GEOMAR Research Center. Challenges and opportunities awaiting GEOMAR involve the completion of scientific projects with the help of the professional application of conventional technologies and of the development of innovative methodologies. Increasingly quantitative, problem-oriented research activities requiring measurements to be taken at water depths of up to several kilometres demand methodologies and technical efforts which go beyond the means of small conventional geoscientific working groups. The administrative co-ordination of the technology needed at a public research institution frequently has disadvantages which can only be overcome with the aid of private industry. The efficient personnel policy of a private industrial enterprise makes it possible to reduce the technical support staff necessary for a public institution by half.

Peak work loads and extreme specialization can be managed through the attraction of external specialists which allow additional new contacts. Technical resources are held in reserve not only to cover the needs of the own institutions but they can also be used for third parties. This allows in particular small research teams of universities to pursue, under their own responsibility, attractive, innovative and demanding marine research.

The GEOMAR Equipment Pool

A central equipment pool for scientific work at sea and on land is one of the main advantages of GEOMAR. The GEOMAR equipment pool is organized and managed by the GTG, but instruments are provided and used not only by the GTG but by the GEOMAR Research Center and other scientific institutions in and around Kiel as well. This pool was established in 1989, is being continuously enlarged and the GTG furnishes the necessary service capacities, workshops, and a duty-free depository for instruments, transportation, etc.

The main advantages of an instrument pool which is centralized and managed by private industry are the following:

— Servicing of the instruments by qualified and specialized technicians. This guarantees the continuous availability of the instruments and a reduction in the rate of loss of instruments as well as in downtime because of instrument failure;

— access for small research establishments to modern and complex research instrumentation within the field of marine sciences;

— economic investment of research funds on the basis of frequent deployment as well as avoidance of duplication of instrumentation;

— improvement in the rate of innovation of the instrument pool due to frequent replacement;

— improvement of technology transfer on the basis of interdisciplinary deployment and in the application of instrumentation in projects organized jointly by academia and industry, including the development of prototypes;

— a point of contact for international co-operation and projects which offer assistence to developing countries;

— provision of partial funding to cover expenses for the instrument pool the exploit the aggressive rental activities in the market-oriented organizing company.

GEOMAR has established the "Containerized Marine Service System" (COMASS) as one of the central components of the instrument pool. Standardized containerized units will comprise facilities which are otherwise typical for a research vessel, such as laboratories, tool shops, winches etc. COMASS will make it possible to use non-specialized, rather primitive ships as platforms for goal and task-oriented global activity within the field of marine sciences ("ships of opportunity").

Technical Developments

The most important motivation for the participation of small industrial enterprises in the foundation of GEOMAR were prospects for potential participation in the development of the technology which is needed to support the scientific activities of a large research center aiming at some of the most extreme global environments. It is particularly important for small and medium-sized companies to gain better access to international research activities. Restricted national markets, in particular in Europe, in most cases do not justify the effort for new developments in research instrumentation. This cannot even be balanced out by financial support incentives from the government which are particularly aimed at small and medium-sized industries.

The GTG concentrates and integrates its technical development, if at all possible, in large international co-operative projects. These projects are comprised of a technological component, a research program and the deployment of technological developments.

An example of this is the project MIPAMEHR (Modular Instrument Package and its Application in Mediterranean Hydrothermal Research), which is supported by the European Community. It is based on the OFOS (Ocean Floor Observation System), which has been developed by PREUSSAG AG with support from the BMFT and has been used with great success in numerous campaigns. A new complex deep-tow system will be developed which makes it possible to monitor properties of the seafloor and of bottom-water masses by means of physical and chemical sensors. Partners in this project are, in addition to GTG, the Department of Geology and Paleontology of the University of Kiel, the Chemical Institute of the University of Newcastle and the Greek Center for Marine Sciences in Athens.

The GEOMAR Technology and Research Park

Analogous to large marine research institutions in the US, GEOMAR offers a location in close physical neighbourhood to the research center (on the Fishmarket locality) to small companies with very special service and development capabilities. A direct contact between companies, the research center and the GTG is particularly advantageous. Similar to technology centers at other places, such companies can obtain logistic support through the GTG and government agencies.

The GEOMAR Study Center

The GEOMAR Research Center and the GTG will found the GEOMAR Study Center in the near future. The Study Center will offer various types of educational programs within the field of the marine geosciences, marine technology and marine sciences. Some components of the program at the study center, in particular educational programs for graduates, will be part of the academic program of the Faculty of Mathematics and Natural Sciences of the Christian Albrechts University. The study center will be supported and organized, managed and financed as well as used by GEOMAR in close collaboration with other partners such as the Kiel University. It will contain two components which, however, can be extended as needed, for example:

(1) Continued education for graduate scientists;

— graduate school for marine geosciences;

— education of geoscientists from developing countries;

— continued education of "continental" geoscientists and marine scientists;

— efforts to provide information and continued education in interdisciplinary projects within the marine geosciences;

(2) educational program for marine geotechnicians.

Location and Regional Advantages for GEOMAR

Kiel as the location for a geo-marine research center has a number of advantages as compared to other potential locations:

— The city is located on the shores of a relatively open bay of the western Baltic Sea at the entrance to the Kiel Canal. Despite intensive industrialization of the coastal zone around the inner fjord, the waters are still relatively clean.

— Institutions of the University with relevance for GEOMAR and the Department of Oceanography (IfM) are the most attractive co-operative partners for GEOMAR, but the region is also characterized by a broad concentration of maritime research institutions, actually the largest one in all of Europe. These institutions form the necessary academic environment as a base for the location and the potential of GEOMAR to achieve results at an early stage.

The compound of an old fishmarket in Kiel-Wellingdorf on the eastern shore of Kiel Fjord at the mouth of the Schwentine river is an ideal location for GEOMAR because it offers great spatial potential for the development of new buildings and it has a long deep-water quay which allows most research vessels to dock directly in front of the laboratories.

For the construction phase of GEOMAR the government has approved of step-by-step expansion. The area of the fishmarket can be made available piece by piece for the use of GEOMAR to keep pace with the needs of the growing research population of GEOMAR. Preparations for the new building will start in 1991 based on a competetive selection of proposals prepared by over 30 northwest European architects. In the meantime, the first scientific working groups at GEOMAR and the GTG are housed in old, but renovated buildings. Here space has also been found for the establishment of some of the central facilities of GEOMAR (core lab = Lithothek, instrumentation pool, data center, library, etc.). The new building will be ready for occupancy in the years 1993-1995.

The existing old buildings on the fishmarket premises are not suited for the installation of complicated and demanding natural science laboratories. As a preliminary transitional measure, lab facilities have been established in mobile containers. They are an important first step for later use in the mobile containerized system for expeditions which can be structured according to the tasks and be sent mission-oriented to the farthest areas of this world (COMASS, see above).

Experience and Perspectives

The planning, foundation and establishment of GEOMAR has been supported enthusiastically by many institutions. The *Geokommission* of the German Research Foundation (DFG) and its working groups produced an exciting idea. Here in Kiel, a new and partially functioning research center has been established in less than three years in a defunct industrial area. This founding period has been supported tremendously by the state government, which found that the potential for this new research center was promising.

The foundation of such a research center has met with many obstacles. The original plan was to establish GEOMAR as an institution jointly financed by federal and local governments. It was impossible to reach this goal at the very beginning, but it is still a long-term perspective for GEOMAR. The availability of federal funding for scientific research within the fields of marine sciences and marine technology is insufficient and is a great obstacle to the further development of GEOMAR. This is particularly astounding in comparison to the ample funds available for aerospace research, which, however, should be of lesser importance for mankind than a detailed knowledge of the properties and history of the hydrosphere.

An increase in and strengthened support for marine activities in Kiel, Hamburg, Wilhelmshaven and Clausthal, activities which were supported by the *Wissenschaftsrat* at its last evaluation, are accompanied by virtually no increase in federal funding. This has resulted in increased competition and a decrease in the possibilities for carrying out co-operative research between the various institutions. It cannot be the task of the state government to finance large scientific projects which will be carried out in the global ocean in the future. For example, there is no federal support for the mid and long-term curation of seafloor samples which have been collected with great efforts on the part of scientists, in ship time and in finances, and which will be a basis for the work of future generations.

However, difficulties in achieving sufficient funding are only a portion of the problems which GEOMAR has encountered during the phase of its foundation and the early years of its activities. Many of the obstacles faced by the GEOMAR model are based on traditional and conservative ways of doing research, on the difficulties in combining basic scientific work and industrial as well as economic management. Competences for steering and directing the marine sciences are not very clearly divided between the federal government, state government and the city of Kiel. They result in increasing difficulty in reaching quick decisions.

Basic marine sciences in Germany are carried out by traditional research institutions which are entirely supported by public funds. The GEOMAR model of Kiel is trying to involve private companies in the day to day running of affairs by managing lab facilities and by supporting the activities of scientists by highly specialized and well-qualified technicians. This model requires the transfer of funds which have previously been used to cover the salaries of government-employed technicians to a post within funding schemes which make it possible to buy the services of third parties. However, we consider this to be a mere formality and we think that this will force scientists to account for needed technician time in a much more realistic way than has be done in the past.

Another area which requires new thinking involves the investment in ships and instruments for research. Up to now and with very few exceptions, it has been the rule that research vessels are made available on a national base. They are equipped by the scientists using the research vessel. An institution with global activities needs to choose the instrumentation both in terms of instrument carriers and of instruments which fit the envisaged tasks and which represent the most economical solution. In addition, it is irresponsible on the part of the Federal Republic of Germany that important future technologies for marine sciences (for example scientific drill ships, manned submersibles, unmanned remote operated deep-sea verhicles, towed acoustic systems) are not available in the country and that their development potential is not made available to the research community.

Foreign countries and research institutions have shown great interest in the establishment of GEOMAR, since it offers important perspectives for marine scientific and technical co-operation across borders. This can be documented by many invitations and visitors, by research vessels using the dock facilities at GEOMAR, by the applications from and successfull recruiting of foreign scientists to GEOMAR and by a number of co-operative agreements with leading foreign research institutions. GEOMAR will continue to grow because the marine geoscientists offer an important future contribution to managing and understanding our environment.

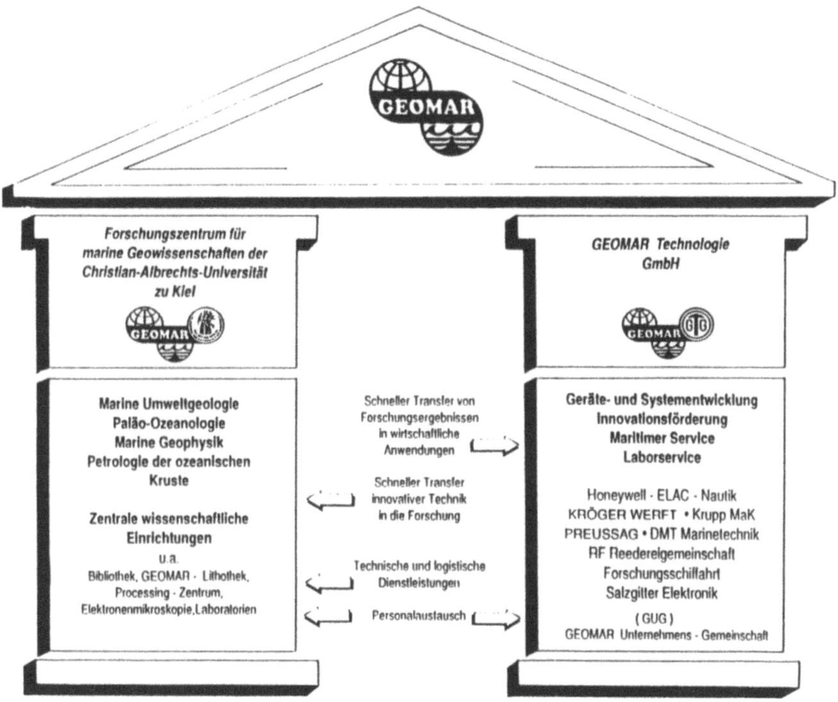
GEOMAR
Forschungszentrum für marine Geowissenschaften der Christian-Albrechts-Universität zu Kiel
GEOMAR
Marine Umweltgeologie
Paläo-Ozeanologie
Marine Geophysik
Petrologie der ozeanischen Kruste
Zentrale wissenschaftliche Einrichtungen
u.a.
Bibliothek, GEOMAR - Lithothek, Processing - Zentrum, Elektronenmikroskopie, Laboratorien
Schneller Transfer von Forschungsergebnissen in wirtschaftliche Anwendungen
Schneller Transfer innovativer Technik in die Forschung
Technische und logistische Dienstleistungen
Personalaustausch
GEOMAR Technologie GmbH
GEOMAR
GTG
Geräte- und Systementwicklung
Innovationsförderung
Maritimer Service
Laborservice
Honeywell - ELAC - Nautik
KRÖGER WERFT • Krupp MaK
PREUSSAG • DMT Marinetechnik
RF Reedereigemeinschaft Forschungsschiffahrt
Salzgitter Elektronik
(GUG)
GEOMAR Unternehmens - Gemeinschaft

List of Participants

Agoes, Dr. Etty A., Indonesian Center for the Law of the Sea, University of Padjadjaran, Bandung, Indonesia

Bäcker, Dr. Harald, GEOMAR-Technology GmbH, Kiel, Germany

Ballah, Lennox F., Institute of Marine Affairs, Cavenage, Trinidad & Tobago

Balz, Dr. Manfred, Federal Ministry of Justice, Bonn, Germany

Bernhardt, Prof. Dr. Rudolf, Max Planck Institute for Comparative Public Law and International Law, Heidelberg, Germany

Bianchi, Dr. Andrea, Institute of Public and International Law, University of Siena, Italy

Bizzarro, Denise A., Esq., Institute of International Law, University of Kiel, Germany

Bouch, Derek, Department of Trade and Industry, London, England

Brockhoff, Prof. Dr. Klaus, Institute for Research in Innovation Management, University of Kiel, Germany

Brown, Prof. E. D. (B. L., LL. M., Ph. D.), Cardiff Law School, University of Wales, Great Britain

Craven, Prof. John P., Law of the Sea Institute, University of Hawaii, USA

Dannelke, Sabine, Federal Office for Shipping and Hydrography, Hamburg, Germany

Dicke, Dr. Klaus, Institute of International Law, University of Kiel, Germany

Fitzmaurice, Dr. Malgosia, Institute of Interntional Law, University of Amsterdam, The Netherlands

da Fonseca-Wollheim, Hermann, Commission of the European Communities, Brussels, Belgium

Görner, Dr. Gunter, formerly of the Ministry of Foreign Affairs, Berlin, GDR

Golitsyn, Vladimir, Office of Legal Affairs, United Nations, New York, USA

Grunenberg, Horst, Member of Parliament of the FRG, Bonn, Germany

Hafner, Dr. Gerhard, Institute of International Law and International Relations, University of Vienna, Austria

Harders, J. Enno (LL. M.), Institute of International Law, University of Kiel, Germany

Heinz, Dr. Ursula E., Institute of International Law, University of Kiel, Germany

Hillo, Pia, Ministry of Foreign Affairs, Helsinki, Finland

Imnadze, Dr. Levan B., Institute of World Economy and International Relations, Moscow, USSR

Jacobsson, Marie, Ministry of Foreign Affairs, Stockholm, Sweden

Jaenicke, Prof. Dr. Günther, Leimen, Germany

Jalbert, Olivier, Department of External Affairs, Ottawa, Canada

Jenisch, Dr. Uwe, Ministry for Economics, Technology and Traffic of the Land Schleswig-Holstein, Kiel, Germany

Jesus, José Luis, Ambassador, Permanent Mission of the Republic of Cape Verde to the United Nations, New York, USA

Kapumpa, Mumba S., Ministry of Finance, Lusaka, Republic of Zambia

Karev, Serguei, Ministry for Foreign Affairs, Moscow, USSR

Kateka, James L., Ambassador of the United Republic of Tanzania to the Federal Republic of Germany, Bonn, Germany

Kiderlen, Hans-Joachim (M. A.), Foreign Office, Bonn, Germany

Kimball, Lee A., World Resources Institute, Washington D. C., USA

Koch, Joachim, Federal Ministry of Economics, Bonn, Germany

Kollwentz, Dr. Walter, Metallgesellschaft AG, Frankfurt am Main, Germany

Kortum, Dr. Gerhard, Institute of Marine Sciences, University of Kiel, Germany

Koschorreck, Wilfried, Federal Ministry of Finance, Bonn, Germany

Koske, Prof. Dr. Peter, Institute for Applied Physics, University of Kiel, Germany

Kwiatkowska, Prof. Dr. Barbara, Netherlands Institute for the Law of the Sea, University of Utrecht, The Netherlands

Lagoni, Prof. Dr. Rainer, Institute for the Law of the Sea and Maritime Law, University of Hamburg, Germany

Lee, Roy S., Office of Legal Affairs, United Nations, New York, USA

Lilje-Jensen, J. R., Ministry of Foreign Affairs, Copenhagen, Denmark

Linton, Hans, Ambassador, Ministry for Foreign Affairs, Stockholm, Sweden

Mahmoudi, Said, University of Stockholm, Sweden

Mansi, Ariel Ricardo, University of Mar del Plata, Argentina

Maquieira, Cristian, Foreign Ministry, Santiago de Chile, Republic of Chile

Mathanjuki, Peter K., Ambassador of the Republic of Kenya to Rwanda, Kigali, Rwanda

Morrison, Prof. Fred L., Law School, University of Minnesota, Minneapolis, USA

Murray, C. J., Foreign and Commonwealth Office, London, England

Nagel, Dr. Karl-Friedrich, Federal Ministry for Research and Technology, Bonn, Germany

Nelson, Dr. L. Dolliver M., Office for Ocean Affairs and the Law of the Sea, United Nations, New York, USA

Orrego Vicuña, Prof. Dr. Francisco, Institute of International Studies, University of Chile, Santiago de Chile, Republic of Chile

Pavlovsky, Vyacheslav A., Ministry of Foreign Affairs, Moscow, USSR

Philipp, Dr. Christiane, Institute of International Law, University of Kiel, Germany

Picht, Prof. Dr. Hartmut, School of Business, Indiana University, Bloomington, USA

Platzöder, Dr. Renate, Stiftung Wissenschaft und Politik, Ebenhausen, Germany

Plesmann, Wolf, Institute of International Law, University of Kiel, Germany

Rao, Bhimsen, Department of Ocean Development, New Delhi, India

Rebagliati, Orlando R., Consul General of the Republic of Argentina, Miami, USA

Röben, Volker, Institute of International Law, University of Kiel, Germany

Roffe, Pedro, UNCTAD Secretariat, United Nations, New York, USA

Saiga, Fukimo, Ministry of Foreign Affairs, Tokyo, Japan

Scholz, Wesley S., Department of State, Washington D. C., USA

Scully, Tucker R., Department of State, Washington D. C., USA

Sherman, Thomas W., Deputy Minister of Lands, Mines and Energy, Monrovia, Liberia

Skinner, Geraldine, Department of Foreign Affairs, Dublin, Ireland

Steinkamp, Dr., Preussag AG, Hannover, Germany

Stoll, P. Tobias, Institute of International Law, University of Kiel, Germany

Suess, Prof. Dr. Erwin (Ph. D.), Research Center for Marine Geosciences (GEOMAR), University of Kiel, Germany

Thiede, Prof. Dr. Jörn, Research Center for Marine Geosciences (GEOMAR), University of Kiel, Germany

Thiel, Prof. Dr. Hjalmar, Institute for Hydrobiology and Fishery Science, University of Hamburg, Germany

Thomas, Uwe, Ministry of Economics, Technology and Traffic of the Land Schleswig-Holstein, Kiel, Germany

Treves, Prof. Tullio, Permanent Mission of Italy to the United Nations, New York, USA

Tytgat, Denis, Commission of the European Communities, Brussels, Belgium

Valle, Henrique R., Ambassador, Ministry of External Relations, Brasilia, Brazil

Vidas, Davor (LL. M.), Institute of International Law and International Relations, University of Zagreb, Yugoslavia

Vignes, Prof. Daniel, Brussels, Belgium

Wolfrum, Prof. Dr. Rüdiger, Institute of International Law, University of Kiel, Germany

Zegers Santa Cruz, Fernando A., Consul General of Chile, London, England

Zima, Dr. Lucy, Wintershall Nederland B. V., Den Haag, The Netherlands

MIX
Papier aus verantwortungsvollen Quellen
Paper from responsible sources
FSC® C105338

Printed by Libri Plureos GmbH
in Hamburg, Germany